JOHN M. PRITCHARD
Formerly Education Officer, Department of Education, Kenya

Africa

A STUDY GEOGRAPHY FOR ADVANCED STUDENTS

Revised Metric Edition

Longman

Acknowledgements

The author wishes to thank very sincerely the following people and organisations for their considerable help in preparing the material for this book:

S. D. Asimeng of the Ghana High Commission; D. G. Mackenzie of East Africa Industries; the Information Division of Unilever Limited; the Chief Inspector of Mines, Mines Division of the Ministry of Lands, Mines and Labour, Sierra Leone; W. D. Anderson of Esso Standard Libya Inc.; the Town Clerk, Lagos City Council, Lagos, Nigeria; the Nigerian Federal Ministry of Information, Lagos, Nigeria; E. Hainsworth, Director of the Tea Research Institute of East Africa, Kericho, Kenya; E. D. Gleason of the Anglo-American Corporation (Central Africa) Limited, Kitwe, Zambia; W. W. Nelson of the Transvaal and Orange Free State Chamber of Mines, Johannesburg, South Africa; J. H. Bevier of the Firestone Plantations Company, Harbel, Liberia; R. Lukman of the Ministry of Mines and Power, Lagos, Nigeria; E. Hawei of the United Arab Republic Embassy; W. Stuart of the Coast Province Cotton Committee, Malindi, Kenya; the Public Relations Office of the Department of Information, Dar es Salaam, Tanzania; E. Mungai, Settlement Officer, Kikuyu Estates, Kenya; T. Agar, Limuru, Kenya; D. G. Hunt, Mwea Irrigation Scheme, Kerugoya, Kenya; E. Potts, Morogoro Sisal Estate, Tanzania; the Press and Information Office of the Federal Government of West Germany; I. Izat, Sassa Coffee Estate, Kenya; Y. F. O. Masakhalia, Ministry of Economic Planning and Development, Nairobi, Kenya; the Chief Research Officer, High Level Sisal Research Centre, Thika, Kenya; G. S. Dugdale, Librarian, the Royal Geographical Society; Miss G. D. Callard, Associate Editor's Secretary, The Geographical Magazine; the Hon. Secretary, the Geographical Association.

We are grateful to the following for permission to reproduce copyright material:

Author and the London weekly journal *East Africa and Rhodesia* for extracts from 'Farming in the Rhodesias' by Rt. Hon. Lord Hastings; The Proprietors of *The Geographical Magazine, London* for an extract from 'The Bamenda Highlands' by Michael Thomas from issue dated August 1966; The Ministry of Agriculture for an abridged account from *Rhodesia Agricultural Journal.* Oxford University Press for an extract from 'African Agrarian Systems'. Barrie and Rockliffe Ltd. and Coward-McCann Inc. for abridged extracts from 'Sahara' by George Gerster. The Proprietors of the *New Scientist* for an extract from 'Sudan Challenges the Sand-Dragon' by J. Tinkler from issue dated 24 February 1977.

The publishers are grateful to the following for permission to reproduce photographs in the text:

Paul Almasy for pages 29, 98, 146, 186, and 212; East African Railways for page 215; Food and Agriculture Organisation for page 249; Ghana Information Services for page 164; Hoa-Qui for pages 15 top, 15 bottom, 31, 33, 76, 146, 204, 209, 228, 253, and 256; Alan Hutchison Library for pages 37, 115, 116, 134, 225, 244, and 245; Kenya Information Services for page 11; Picturepoint for page 192; Paul Spearman for page 32; Tanzania Information Services for page 223; Zambia Information Services for page 31.

The cover photograph was kindly supplied by Bruce Coleman Ltd.

LONGMAN GROUP LIMITED
Longman House,
Burnt Mill, Harlow, Essex CM20 2JE, England

First published 1969
Metric edition 1973
Revised metric edition 1979
Fourth impression 1982
ISBN 0 582 64636 7

Printed in Hong Kong by
Wilture Enterprises (International) Ltd.

About This Book

This book has been written primarily for those students who are beginning to study the geography of Africa at an advanced level. It attempts to present a clear and up-to-date picture of the geography of a continent which has been the focus of attention over the last score of years for an ever increasing number of research workers. There is a tremendous volume of material now available of a geographic or economic nature, but much of it is not always readily available to the student and much of it is of a very high academic standard unsuited to his needs.

I have attempted to bridge this gap by presenting geographic material in a way which breaks away from the more formal approach. Instead of the more usual method of description on a political and regional basis the book selects those aspects of Africa's geography which are most important and, especially in the economic sections, which reflect modern trends and conditions. The method is thus, after preliminary discussion where necessary, to sample in depth rather than give broad general pictures.

By virtue of its very technique the book does not claim to cover every aspect of a rapidly developing continent but as wide a selection of sample studies as possible has been chosen, although greater attention has been given to regions lying south of the Sahara in view of examination tendencies.

At the end of each chapter, where appropriate, the work for the student is divided into several sections – general questions based partly on the text and partly to guide research work; a selection of topics which have been designed for group discussion, followed by suggestions for practical work in the field. In the statistical sections (Appendix 2) the opportunity is given for practice in transforming up-to-date statistics into pictorial graphs and charts.

Great reliance has been placed on statistics and tables, especially in the economic sections, and every effort has been made to obtain the latest facts available. I have attempted to draw the maps and diagrams as clearly as possible, omitting those which the student can find readily in any atlas and concentrating on illustrating specific themes in the text.

In conclusion, it is hoped that this new approach to the study of the geography of Africa will prove refreshing and stimulating to both teacher and student.

J.M.P.
December, 1968

The 1979 metric edition of Africa: A Study Geography for Advanced Students has been completely revised with reference to the many changes that have taken place in Africa during the 1970s. All statistics have been brought as up to date as possible and numerous statistical tables have been included in a new appendix, instead of at the end of each chapter. Because of its vital importance to economic development in general, the chapter on population has been largely re-written while readers will find two additional chapters, one dealing with problems and their solutions in agriculture, and one with the use and abuse of Africa's natural resources. The themes of these three new chapters sound a warning note to students about the increasing exploitation of Africa's resources.

J.M.P.
March, 1979

Contents

CHAPTER ONE

The physical background

The land

The origins of Africa

The Theory of Continental Drift – the movement of the lighter continents on the heavier, softer rocks of the earth's crust – is popularly associated with the name of A. Wegener who expounded his ideas in 1912 and 1924, but the concept had been stated earlier in 1910 by F. B. Taylor and in 1911 by H. B. Baker.

It was suggested that Africa had been part of one huge continent, Gondwanaland, and attention was drawn to the similar rock structures along the coasts of western Africa and eastern South America, and the jig-saw fit of the southern continents. Again it was found that there was an almost identical geological sequence of strata in the Karroo of South Africa, the Deccan Plateau of India, and the plateaux of South America and Antarctica; several small folded ranges in Argentina and the Falkland Islands are similar in structure and age to the folded Cape Ranges of South Africa; glacial striations on rock surfaces in South Africa suggested to the geologists that ice movement was not from the Antarctic region, but from some large landmass which once existed to the north-east in what is now the Indian Ocean (see page 17). Rocks formed during the Permo-Carboniferous period in South Africa and Australia show striking similarities which suggest they were formed under identical climatic conditions, possibly as one continuous belt. Recent research into the remnant magnetic properties of rocks in relation to the earth's polar axis seems to support the theory and to suggest that Africa had become almost stationary, by the end of the Mesozoic era, about 70 million years ago.

The acceptance of the Continental Drift Theory would explain several features of Africa's structure and relief: the folded Atlas ranges would have originated when sedimentary rocks were squeezed between northward drifting Africa and rigid Eurasia (Fig. 1.17); the warping and faulting of Africa's

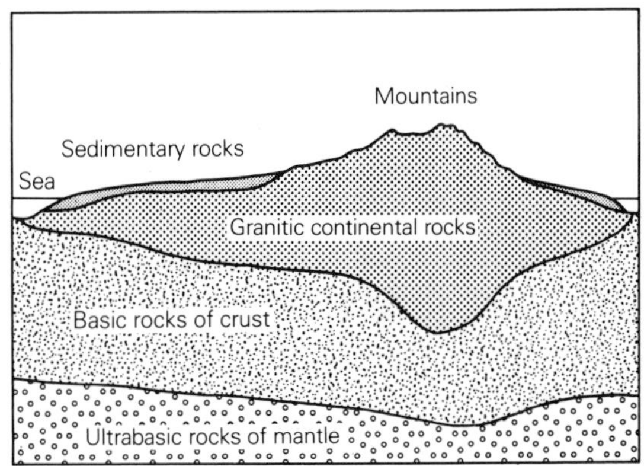

Fig. 1.1 Relationship of continental landmass to basic rocks

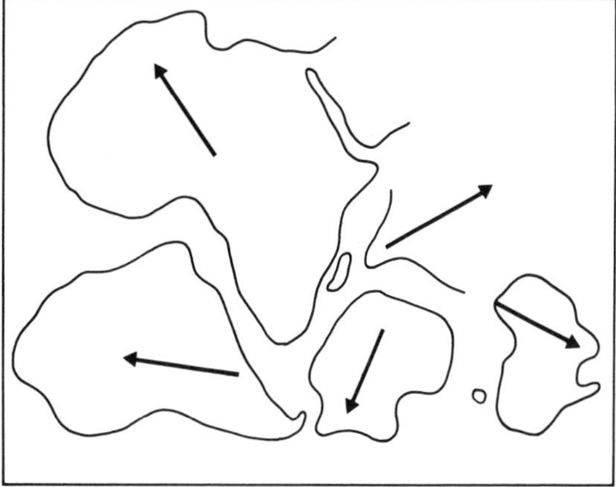

Fig. 1.2 The break-up of Gondwanaland

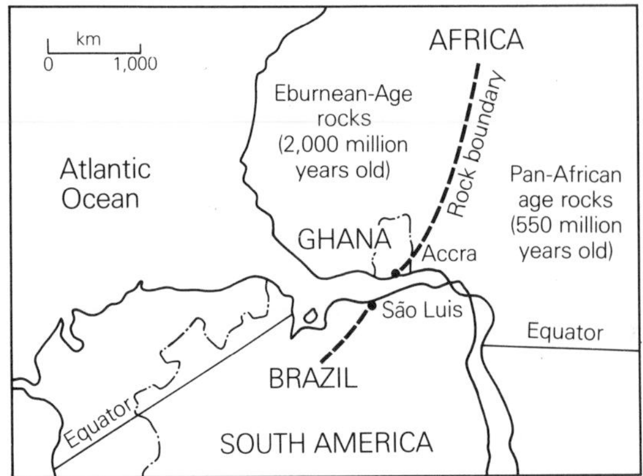

Fig. 1.3 Recent evidence of the drift of the continents: Radioactive dating of Africa's rocks reveals that the continent is divided into two distinct geological regions – the eastern Pan-African region some 550 million years old and the western Eburnean region 2 000 million years old. A computer study of the shorelines of the two continents by Bullard revealed that the rocks would match perfectly down to a depth of 900 m if the continents were joined. Further work by Hurley and others shows that the boundary between the two geological regions in Africa is continued in northeast Brazil exactly where it was predicted.

Another modern geological technique, that of studying the changing patterns of the earth's magnetic field, indicates that the ocean floor between Africa and South America is widening at the rate of two centimetres a year and this rate exactly accounts for the present distance apart of the two continents if drift began 200 million years ago – the estimated time at which the continents are believed to have begun drifting apart.

Other evidence supporting drift includes:

a Bore-hole drillings in eastern Brazil and Cameroon show the same rock sequences of Lower Cretaceous age when the continents were joined, followed by salt deposits in the early Upper Cretaceous suggesting an inflow of sea water when the continents were disrupted. After this the rocks have different sequences suggesting they were formed independently, i.e. after the breakup.

b Continental crust discovered in 1974 on the ocean bed off Natal may be a lost section which lay between Antarctica and the south-eastern coast of Africa.

c When the southern continents are pieced together as Gondwanaland, certain geological features occupy matching positions across coastal joints, e.g. doleritic lavas of Mesozoic age extend through southern Africa, Antarctica and into Tasmania; a vast depression or geosyncline of Precambrian age is indicated in Argentina, the Cape region, through Antarctica and in eastern Australia.

plateau surface might have been caused by the sundering of Gondwanaland's several parts from the keystone of Africa; the numerous basin-like depressions of Africa's surface may have been internal drainage basins for the original rivers of Gondwanaland.

The map (Fig. 1.3) shows some of the evidence which supports the idea of continental drift. It is based on the work by the English geophysicist Sir Edward Bullard and American geologist Prof. Patrick Hurley. (Further evidence of earth movements is discussed in the section on the Great Rift Valley, page 7).

Size, shape and position

Compared with other continents Africa possesses at once similarities and contrasts. Its huge area of 30 300 000 km² (nearly 20 per cent of the earth's land surface) is remarkably compact with none of the penetrations of ocean common to Europe, North America or Asia. Thus, although Africa is the second largest continent after Asia (44M km²), three times the size of Europe (10M km²), and bigger than North America (20M km²), it has a much shorter coastline. Africa has similar plateau surfaces to those of Australia, South America and India, but no vast mountain barrier to create sudden climatic and vegetational contrasts.

Africa's position is unique for it fairly straddles the equator, stretching 4 000 km to north and south; 77 per cent of its area lies within the tropics and over 25

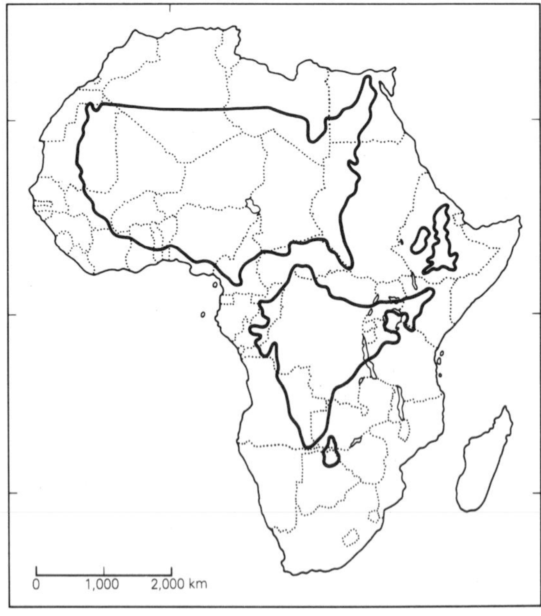

Fig. 1.4 The size of Africa

per cent is covered by the great wastes of the Sahara.

Africa is huge, sprawling over 72 degrees of latitude from 37°51′N (just west of Cape Blanc) in Tunisia to Cape Aghulas at latitude 34°51′S, a distance of 8 000 km, or equal to a journey between New York and Hawaii, London and Tibet, or Tokyo and Brisbane. The greatest length east-west, approximately 7 200 km, lies between Ras Hafun (51°50′E) and Cape Verde (17°32′W). The continent is virtually an island connected to the Sinai Peninsula by a narrow isthmus cut by the Suez Canal and separated from Spain by the 14-km-wide Straits of Gibraltar. The Straits of Bab el Mandeb separate Africa from Arabia by only 32 km of water.

Africa's position has clearly affected its historical and political development. Its huge bulk jutting out into the southern oceans presented a troublesome obstacle to be rounded as swiftly as possible by sailing vessels plying to and from the East. As an appendage to politically-minded Europe of the late nineteenth century it was laid open to nearly eighty years of colonial rule, a period of transition unparalleled in any other continent. Africa's position in relation to the industrial regions of Europe and North America created for the continent a role of raw materials supplier, a period from which it is now beginning to emerge.

Fig. 1.5 Approximately one-third of Africa can be termed low-lying. Certain of the structural basins (Fig. 1.6) lie at considerable altitudes.

The relief and structure of Africa

Africa consists of a series of plateaux, higher in the east but gradually declining towards the west, the general altitude relieved by great shallow basins and their river systems, by the deep incision of the Rift Valley, and by the often magnificient volcanoes, fault blocks and inselbergs.

The basis of this simple relief is a stable block of ancient crystalline rocks of Precambrian origin, rocks which sometimes rise to the surface in parts of the continent but are often masked by later sedimentaries and volcanic outpourings. This rigid block has withstood the tremendous forces which elsewhere have formed the Alps of Europe and the Himalayas of India, and fold ranges of this age are confined to the edges of the block in the Atlas and the Cape regions. But the plateau crust has not entirely escaped the effects of earth movements, for vast warpings have formed huge shallow basins and great horizontal movements have cracked the surface into giant fault lines.

Nigeria: Plain and inselberg landscape, near Zaria. The granitic dwala (right) is capped by a castle koppie formed by weathering along pressure release joints.

The plateaux

Although the volcanoes and rift valleys are spectacular the most lasting impression of Africa's relief is one of monotonous level plateau surfaces varying between 600 and 2 600 m, the latter in the Maluti mountains in Lesotho, surfaces often so flat that they are called plains. They result from long periods of erosion which removed vast quantities of weathered rock and soil from the continental surface to the sea beds off-shore. In order to adjust itself to the redistribution of these eroded sediments from higher to lower altitudes, the continent has risen slowly over thousands of years, a process termed *isostatic readjustment*. The rise was greatest in the east and south of Africa where the Drakensberg and Maluti mountains average between 1 500 and 2 100 m, rising to over 3 280 m in the Mont aux Sources. The uplift did not take place all at once but in stages, each stage separated by long periods when the forces of erosion had more time to smooth down the surfaces. The

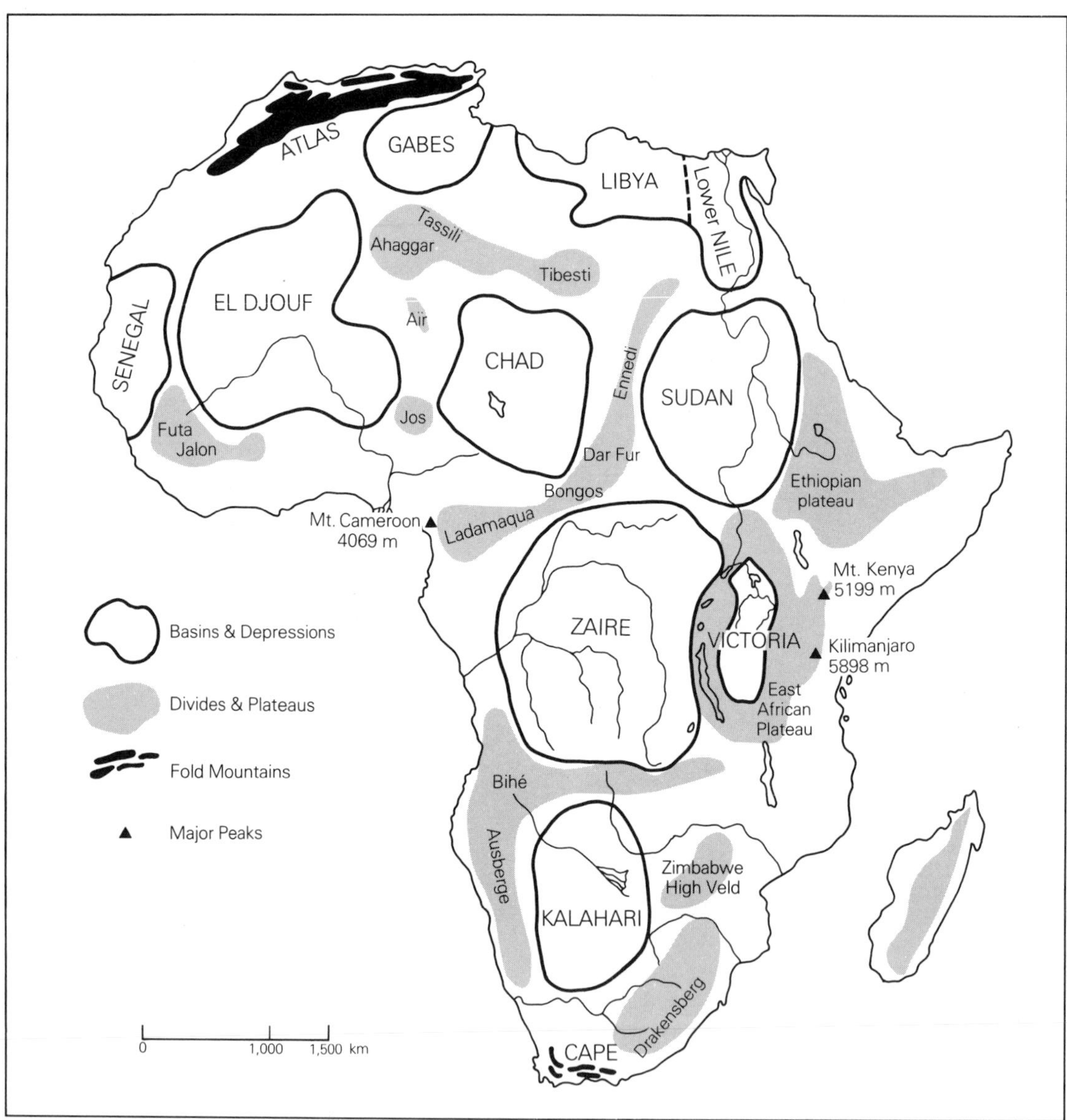

Fig. 1.6 The relief of Africa – structural basins and their divides

most important of these erosion levels or *pediplains* are often separated by steep, low escarpments, the lowest of which usually form an abrupt drop to the narrow coastal plains; at this junction point rivers usually form rapids and waterfalls.

Remnants of old land surfaces sometimes jut up from these plateau surfaces; these are inselbergs (island mountains, monadnocks, kopjes, bornhardts are other names), the 'left-overs' from former landscapes which remain as resistant mounds. Usually of hard, crystalline rocks, they occur in northern Nigeria, Tanzania, Kenya and South Africa (see the photograph on page 3 of an example from the north of Nigeria).

The distribution of the higher surfaces is seen in Fig. 1.6. Practically all eastern and central Africa lies over 900 m while the plateau surface falls to 300 m and less in the Sahara and West Africa where the general altitude is increased by overlying sedimentaries and rock wastes.

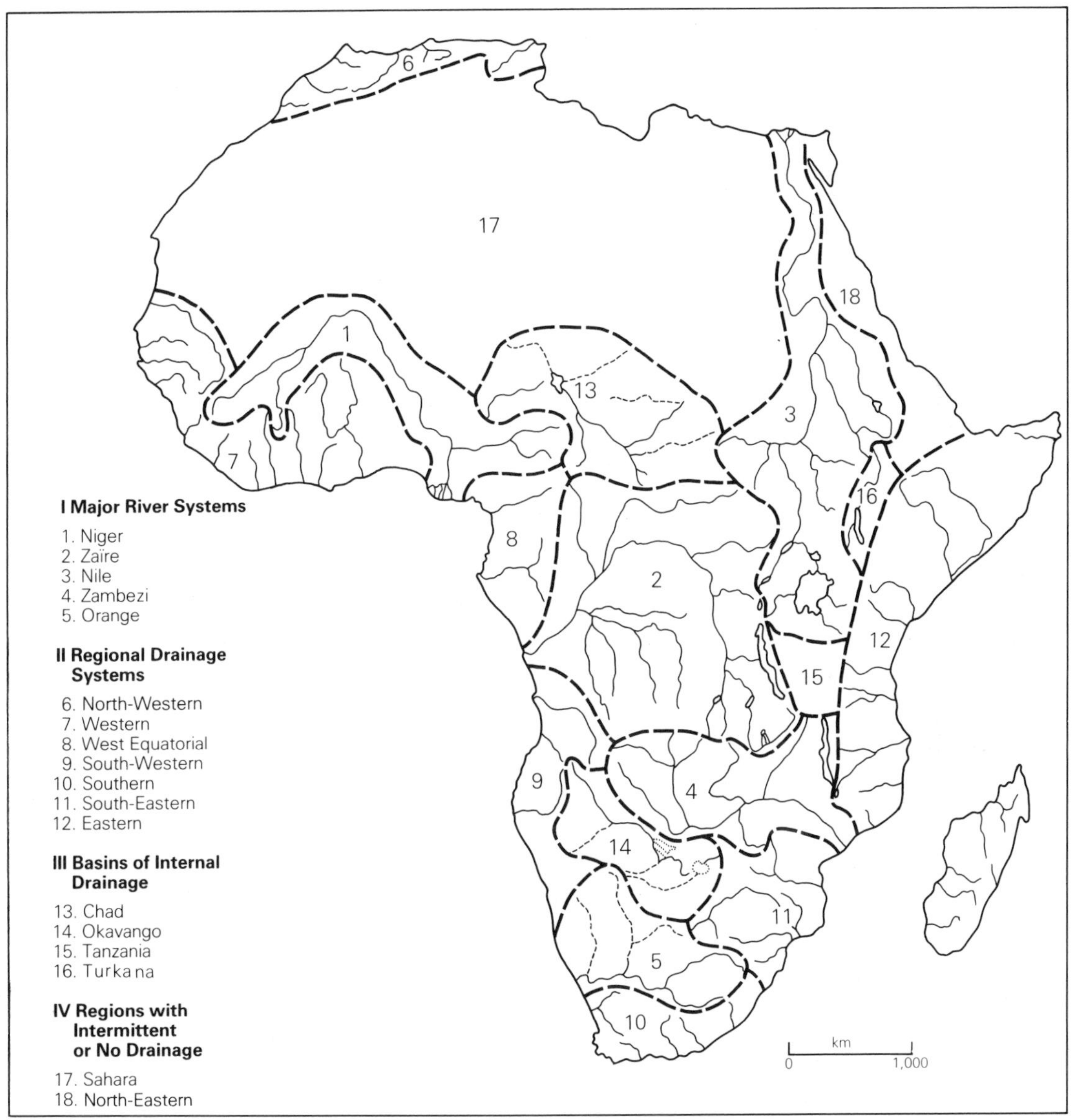

Fig. 1.7 Africa – the pattern of drainage

The basins and divides

A striking feature of Africa's relief is the number of broad, shallow, saucer-like basins separated by plateaux, fault blocks and mountain ranges. These basins have been the deposition areas for the rock waste eroded from the plateau surface and they have gradually subsided leaving between them mountainous divides. The most prominent basins are the Congo (covering over 4,1M km², equal to slightly over half the area of Australia), Chad, El Djouf, Sudan and Kalahari, and smaller ones, e.g. Lake Victoria-Kyoga. Mostly between 300 and 900 m, these basins were initially formed by massive forces (probably originating in the semi-molten rocks below the earth's crust) which have downwarped parts of the plateau. These shallow basins were then invaded by the sea or rivers, the weight of lacustrine and marine deposits causing further depression. Some basins may once have extended beyond the

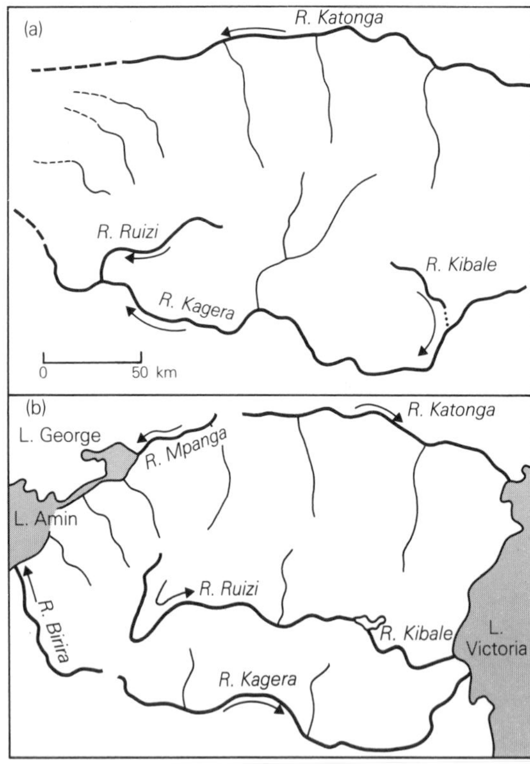

Fig. 1.8 Uganda – reversal of drainage patterns due to back tilting of plateau surface. (*Simplified after J. C. Doornkamp and P. H. Temple*)

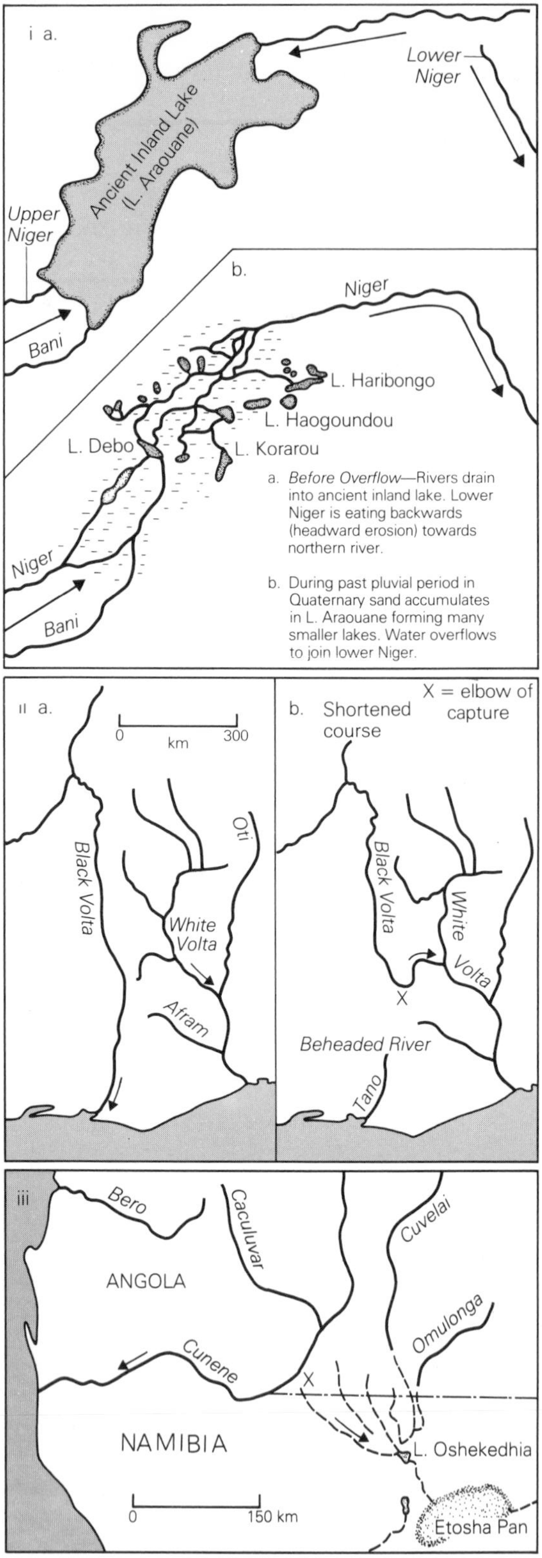

a. *Before Overflow*—Rivers drain into ancient inland lake. Lower Niger is eating backwards (headward erosion) towards northern river.

b. During past pluvial period in Quaternary sand accumulates in L. Araouane forming many smaller lakes. Water overflows to join lower Niger.

Fig. 1.9 Alteration of drainage patterns by overflow and capture

present coasts as the drainage systems indicate, particularly in southern Africa. Here, the Orange flows westwards following the general gradient of the land, but the Limpopo and the Zambezi flow to the east. It is possible to explain these flow directions by accepting that Africa was once a vast area of internal drainage with no coasts (the keystone of Gondwanaland) and the rivers poured their sediments and waters into depressions to form gigantic lakes. When Gondwanaland foundered, the lakes drained away and the original rivers found outlets to the sea across the basins or, like the Chad basin, persisted as regions of internal drainage. The effect of local back-tilting of areas of the plateau surface is seen in many parts of Uganda where the reduction of gradients has caused rivers to form irregular marshy lakes such as Lake Kyoga and profoundly altered the flow patterns of many rivers.

Bordering the basins are sharp divides which in the case of the Ruwenzoris rise to nearly 5 200 m. These dividing rims may consist of higher parts of the plateau, e.g. the Jos and Futa Jalon regions and other crystalline and volcanic massifs such as the Ahaggar and Tibesti plateaux. Volcanic cones and the tilt of fault blocks often add to their heights. Other important divides are the Drakensberg and Maluti Mountains between the Kalahari and the east coast plain, the Ennedi, Dar Fur and Bongos between the Chad, Sudan and Zaïre basins, and the Bihé between the Zaïre and the Kalahari.

The Great Rift Valley

The great Rift Valley is probably the most spectacular of all Africa's surface features. Approximately 7 200 km long with 5 600 km within Africa, it

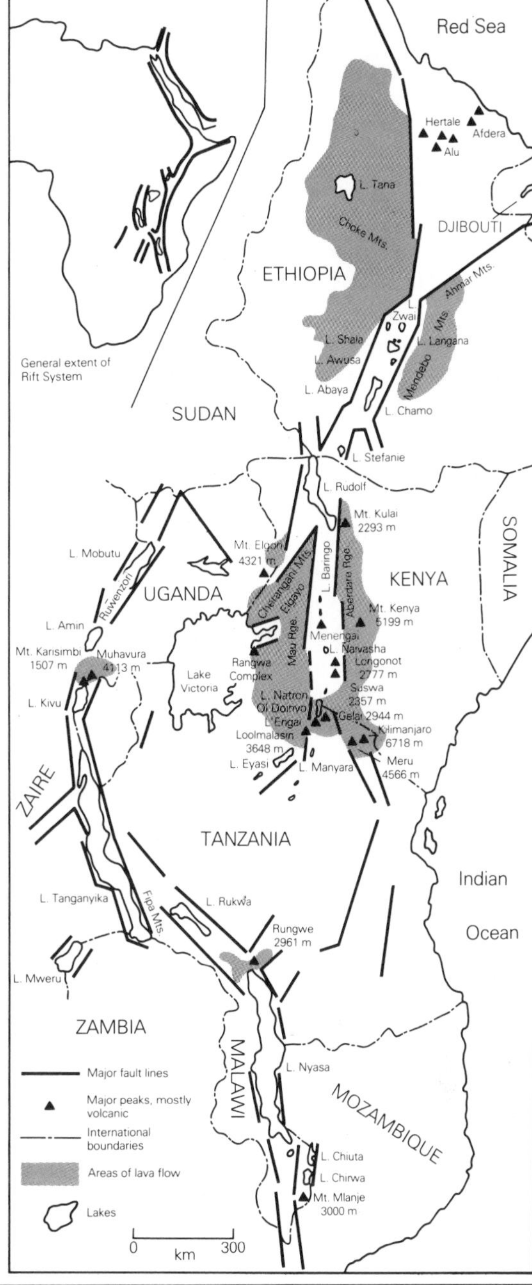

Fig. 1.10 The Great Rift Valley. The diagram below is a cross-section of the valley at Latitude 1°45′S. (*Simplified from Report No. 42, Geol. Survey of Kenya*, 1958.) Right: Extent of Rift Valley in eastern Africa.

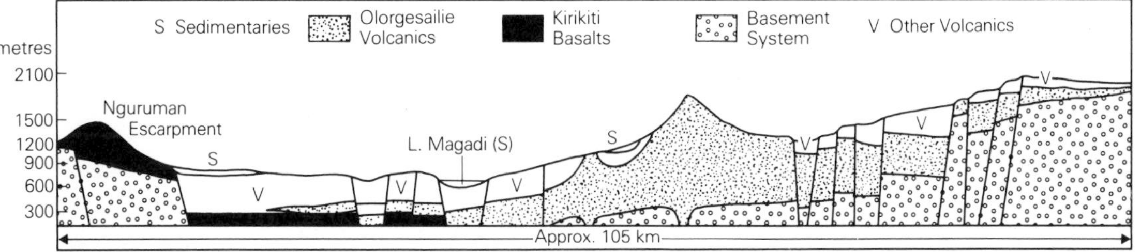

begins near Beira and extends northwards to Lake Malaŵi. Here it divides into a western arm through Lakes Tanganyika, Kivu, Amin and Mobutu, fading out gradually about 250 km north of Lake Mobutu, and an eastern arm marked by low (150–300 m) escarpments in Tanzania. The latter is clearly marked in Kenya by several small lakes occupying fault basins and depressions – Lakes Magadi, Naivasha, Elementeita, Nakuru, Hannington, Baringo and Turkana. Here the valley sides fall steeply from the plateau surface at about 2 100 to 1 500 m on the valley floor, with the Mau and Aberdare fault blocks towering to over 3 000 m above sea level.

In Ethiopia several small lakes mark the valley's course – Stefanie, Chamo, Abaya, Langana and Zwai. The valley follows the Awash river course then spreads over a wide area in the Danakil region; here it divides into the Gulf of Aden and the Red Sea, the latter 2 000 km long and 340 km broad and forking at its north-western end into the Gulf of Suez and the Gulf of Aqaba, which leads northwards into the Jordan Valley.

The Rift Valley thus forms a long scar on the surface of Africa equal in length to one-fifth of the earth's longitudinal circumference. Its floor width varies from 30 to 100 km with valley sides sometimes rising one or two thousand metres above the graben floor, the heights often accentuated by the upthrown and tilted horst blocks flanking the valley – Mitumba Mountains, the Aberdares, the Cheranganis, the Mau Ranges. The height of the floor also varies considerably from 650 m below sea level in Lake Tanganyika's bed and 90 m below sea level in Lake Malaŵi, to 1 500 m above sea level in the Lake Kivu region.

Such a tremendous feature could only have been formed by colossal forces causing pressure and tensions within the plateau crust of Africa.

During the 1920s and 1930s, geomorphologists and geologists such as Gregory and Wayland attempted to explain the formation of the Rift Valley by stating two differing theories:

a that forces of tension have caused a lengthening of the upwarped crust, this being relieved by normal faults;

b that forces of compression have caused the shortening of the arched crust by means of thrust or arched reversed faults, older rocks being forced to override younger rocks on both flanks of the valley.

The tension theory suggests that the African plateau in the Rift region was first upwarped and that the central part of this upwarped arch – 'the keystone' – dropped. Step-faulting occurred on both sides of the valley. Many of the faults slopes in Kenya and Tanzania, especially those in offshoot rifts such as the Rukwa depression, have been shown to be normal or tensional faults, and most geologists believe the eastern arm of the valley was formed by tensional faults.

Upwarping of the crust is also suggested in the compression theory, but in this case the crest of the arch is thrust downwards by the weight of the flanking blocks pushing over it in reversed faults. Certain sections of the Western Rift in the Ruwenzori region and along the eastern shores of Lake Mobutu show evidence of reversed faulting.

In both theories it will be seen that step-faulting can occur, and this often masks the true nature of the major faults in many areas. Certainly there is evi-

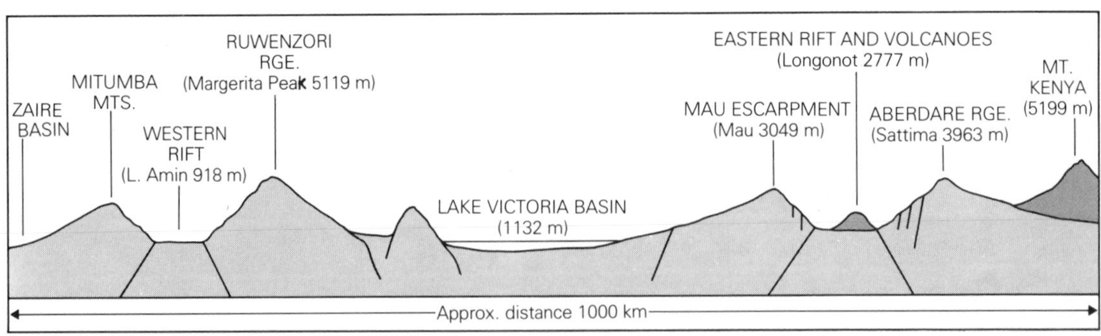

Fig. 1.11 Diagrammatic cross-section from eastern Zaïre to western Kenya

dence for both theories, compressionists stating that it would take considerable horizontal pressure to raise the valley floors to the heights they attain in the Lake Kivu, Ruwenzori and Kenya regions while tensionists cite the great depths of the floor in Malaŵi and Tanzania as evidence of tremendous forces of tension.

These theories are now generally regarded as being inadequate to explain the immense scale of the Rift Valley faulting. Instead many geophysicists link the Rift Valley's formation to the theories of plate tectonics and sea-floor spreading. These theories were first given substance by H. Hess of Princeton University. Convectional currents caused by radioactivity and primitive heat in the softer plastic rocks beneath the earth's crust cause lateral movements in the lithosphere. Where the lateral forces are pulling away from each other on the ocean beds, tension, faulting, earthquakes and volcanic activity occur, e.g. in the mid-Atlantic and off the eastern coast of Africa. These linear zones of seismic disturbance are the boundaries of vast sections of the earth's crust which Hess calls 'plates'. Africa forms part of one of these plates as does Australia, Antarctica, South America and the other continents. Thus, in some cases, the plates are slowly drifting away from each other, the rate of drift between the African and South American plates being about 2 cm a year. As the plates move away from each other, magma wells up between the plates, cools, solidifies and attaches itself to the rear end of the plates.

The Great Rift Valley probably lies in a region of the earth's crust beneath which lateral movements in opposite directions are producing tension. The Valley may thus be the division line between crust slowly moving eastward and the rest of Africa. Certainly, the Arabian Plate is slowly moving away from the African Plate causing seismic disturbances, fracturing and faulting along the bed of the Red Sea.

In West Africa, a study of aerial photographs of Nigeria has shown a series of parallel linear fractures in the earth's crust, called lineaments by geologists, which are lines marking vertical faults. They are uniformly straight and regularly spaced (Fig. 1.12), and are crossed by two other less continuous sets of fault lineaments at an angle of 45°. These latter fault lines show evidence of horizontal shearing, and displace the north-south faults by several kilometres in places.

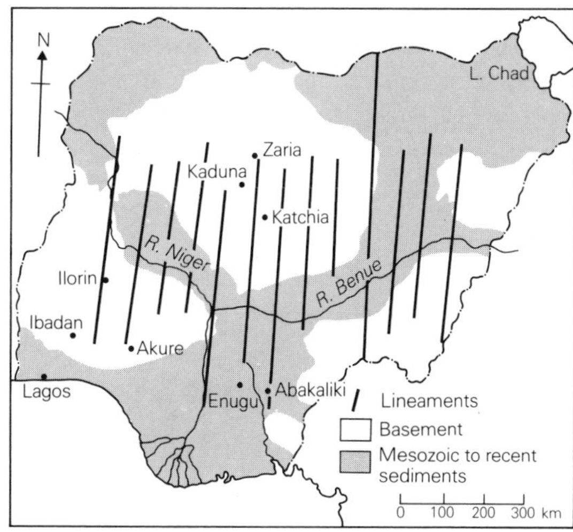

Fig. 1.12 Nigeria: map based on aerial photographs showing lineaments or meridional fault lines and sedimentary basins

The pattern of these fault lines appears to be the result of horizontal compressive forces in the earth's crust. It is thought that the fault lines may have been formed deep in the earth's crust in the basement rocks; their pattern was maintained in the sediments which later partially covered the basement system by seismic shocks along the fault lines. These linear

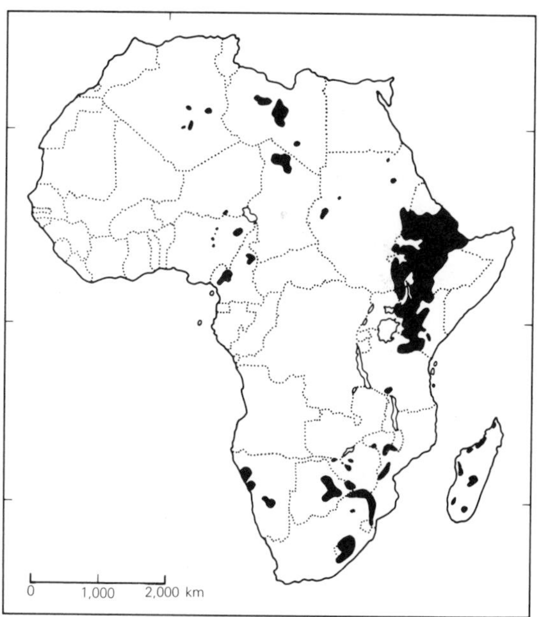

Fig. 1.13 The extent of Cretaceous, Tertiary and Quaternary lavas in Africa. Cretaceous lavas are almost entirely located in southern Africa and Malagasy

fractures, or failure zones, have provided easy paths of penetration for the upward movement of molten igneous rock, and the lineaments now appear as lines of solidified intruded granite, associated with base metal and tin deposits such as those around Jos and Abakaliki.

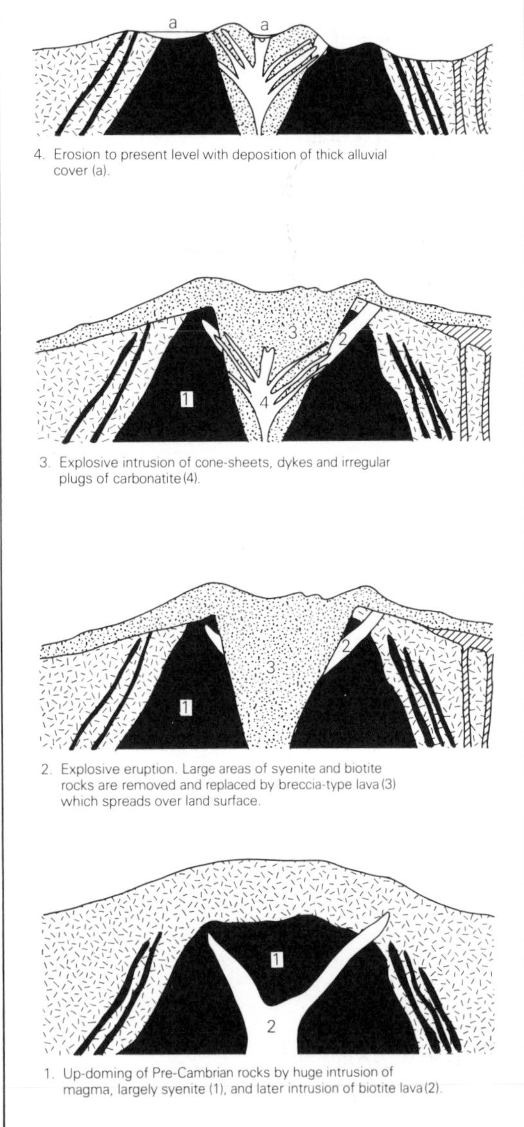

Fig. 1.14 Kenya – the evolution of the Rangwa complex and the Kisingiri volcano, Nyanza, Western Kenya. (*After G. J. H. McCall*)

Volcanic activity

The colossal pressures responsible for the Rift Valley were also the initial cause of the volcanic activity associated with the Rift region and on the adjacent plateaux during the Tertiary and Quarternary periods. Deep caps of lava and numerous magnificent volcanoes were formed – Kilimanjaro, Africa's highest peak (5 894 m), Mount Kenya (5 199 m), Mount Elgon (4 322 m), the eroded plug of Tororo rock, Uganda, Mount Meru (4 566 m), Jaeger Summit (3 220 m) and Loolmalasin (3 648 m); these are all associated with the eastern arm of the Rift. In the west lie the Mufumbiros where the extinct volcano Muhavura (4 113 m) marks the borders between Uganda, Zaïre and Rwanda. More localised faulting in East Africa caused many minor volcanoes to form, such as those of the Gwasi area south of the Kavirondo Gulf in Kenya (Fig. 1.14). Volcanoes such as Longonot (2 777 m) on the floor of the Rift Valley 56 km north-west of Nairobi show evidence of comparatively recent activity; Longonot is an explosive type which has developed a huge crater. Steam jets and hot springs are common in this region.

In West Africa evidence of volcanic activity is associated with the Jos and Aïr plateaux, the Cameroon and Bamenda Highlands and the islands of Fernando Po, São Thomé, Principe and Annobon. Just south of Kumasi is the volcanic caldera some 10 km in diameter, now filled with water, called Lake Bosumtwi, while near Dakar there are extensive lava flows. Further north in the Sahara, the Ahaggar and Tibesti Plateaux form weird regions of sculptured volcanic pillars and plugs. Evidence of intrusive granite deposits in the linear fault zones in Nigeria have already been mentioned.

Southern Africa was also subject to igneous activity, but this occurred at a much earlier time, during

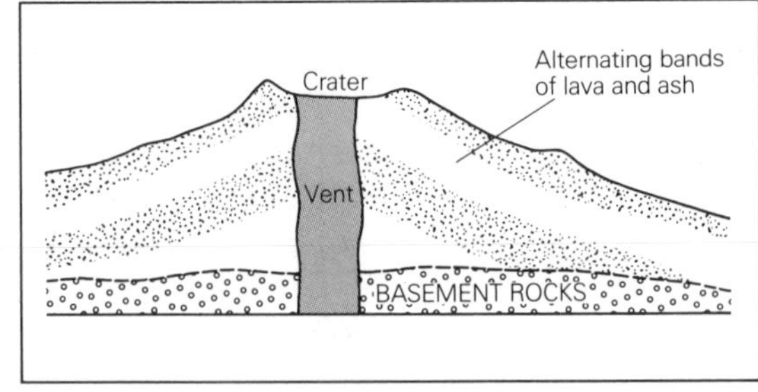

Fig. 1.15 A cross-section across Mount Elgon, Uganda

Kenya: The glaciated volcanic plug of Mt. Kenya from the south. Arêtes, glaciers, U-shaped valleys, scree and nevé are clearly seen.

the Mesozoic period, and did not produce volcanoes. For example in the Transvaal masses of lava intruded into overlying rocks, piercing the surface and spreading over the plateau for some 480 km, their great weight causing the downward sinking of the underlying rocks; in some places these lava cappings are nearly 10 km thick. Many of the volcanic necks and pipes have been plugged by solidified lava and contain numerous diamonds as well as other minerals – tin, chromite and platinum. The 560-km long lopolith (the Great Dyke) of central Zimbabwe contains rich bands of chromite.

Folded mountains

The folded mountain ranges of the Atlas and Cape regions at the northern and southern extremities of Africa form entirely different landscapes from those already discussed. Structurally the Atlas Mountains of the Maghreb are similar to the great alpine system of southern and central Europe and were formed at about the same geological period. They consist of folded layers of sedimentary rocks, mainly limestone, formed in some vast sea which lay between Africa and Europe, while some deeper crystalline rocks have also been thrust upwards testifying to the power of the

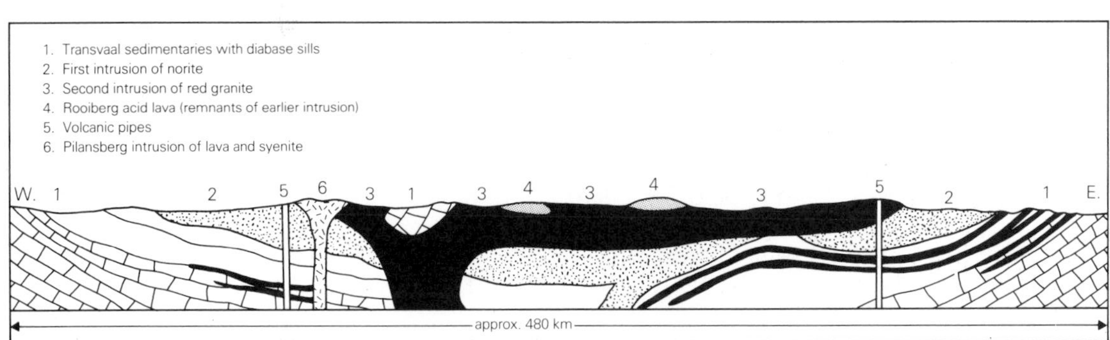

Fig. 1.16 South Africa – diagrammatic section across the bushveld volcanic complex. (*After A. L. du Toit*)

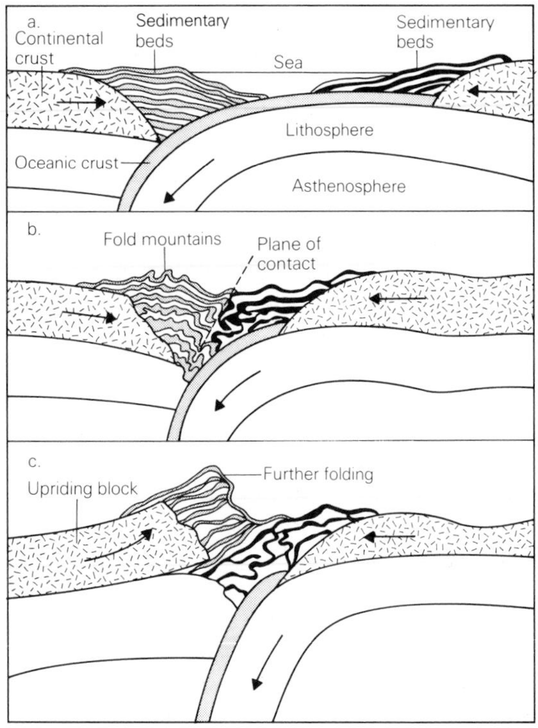

Fig. 1.17 The formation of fold mountains by earth plate movement: a) Lithosphere plate moves due to convectional currents caused by heating in earth's mantle; continental crustal blocks move towards each other. b) Sedimentary material pushed in front of each crustal block now collides and folds. c) Further folding caused by upriding of left hand block.

folding processes. Several steep-sided distinct ranges have been eroded into rugged and wild landscapes unlike anything else in Africa.

The coastal ranges rise in the western Rif to over 2 150 m and continue westwards into the Tell region in a separate more broken range between 900 and 1 800 km, highest in the Great and Little Kablye Mountains; they end as high cliffs at Cape Blanc in eastern Tunisia.

A central chain is formed by the High and Sahara Atlas. The High Atlas (4 000 m) extends from Agadir on the Moroccan coast north-eastwards for some 800 km. High peaks of basic crystalline rock – Jebel Toubkal (4 194 m), Irhil M'Goun (4 071 m) and Volcan du Siroua (3 306 m) – illustrate the tremendous nature of the folding. In the lower north-east the crystalline ranges sink below limestone rocks.

To the east of the High Atlas and parallel to it lies the Saharan Atlas, a series of sandstone and limestone ridges and plateaux – the Monts des Ksour, the Djebel Amour and the Monts des Ouled Naïl – which continue into the Aures Mountains. In Tunisia the Aures (1 200–1 800 m) turn north-eastwards towards the Tell Atlas and end at Cape Bon. The Middle Atlas is shorter than the other ranges but is still a formidable barrier rising to 3 340 m above the River Moulouya.

Between the Tellian and High Atlas lies the Plateau of Shotts (a shott is a shallow salty lake)

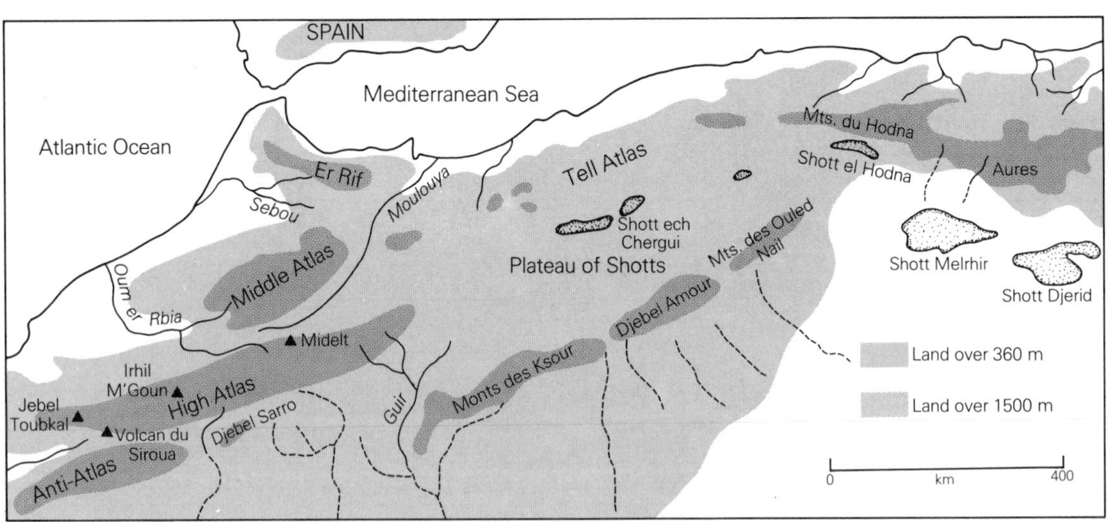

Fig. 1.18 The Atlas Region

which stretches for about 800 km from east to west but narrows in the east between the Tell and Atlas ranges. The Plateau stands at about 900 to 1 200 m, is very monotonous and is lowest in the east. Its many lakes dwindle with the dry season but are fed by small rivers during the winter rains.

To the west lies the Moroccan Mesita or table land, an ancient plateau which formed a resistant boss against which parts of the ranges were folded. Subject to tremendous pressures the plateau mass wilted and subsided, especially in the south.

In the extreme south of Africa lie the folded mountains of the Cape region. These were formed at a much earlier period than the Atlas ranges and were possibly connected with the Sierra Ranges near Buenos Aires, Argentina, and the mountains of the Falkland Islands. The Cape ranges have been worn down and then uplifted to form a complex system. The Oliphants and Cedarberg mountains trend north-north-west then give way to the east-west trending Langeberg and Groote Swarteberg ranges. A series of ranges then continues for 320 km to the eastern coast, averaging between 1 370 and 2 150 m in altitude – the Kougaberge, the Groot-Swartbergreeks, the Kammanassiesberge, the Outeniquaberge, and the Groot-Winterhoekberge. The ranges are separated by flat, fertile valleys in the west which become increasingly drier towards the east.

The Atlas and Cape regions are not the only areas to have suffered intense folding in Africa. In fact, the continent has experienced seven mountain-building events or periods of *orogenesis*, the earliest occurring 3 000 million years ago. These ancient mountain ranges have long since been eroded although some remnants still survive, e.g. in the Akwapim-Togo-Atakora ranges in West Africa, and in the Kariba region and Eastern Highlands of Zimbabwe. Geomorphologists refer to those parts of Africa which have been stable for over 1 500 million years as *cratons*, while those regions which have been deformed more recently are termed *orogens*.

Desert landscapes

So far we have been concerned with the effects of structure on the surface features of Africa. But landscapes change with time and the steady work of erosive forces. Nowhere is this more evident than in the Sahara which extends 4 800 km from the Atlantic shores to the Red Sea coast with a maximum width of 1 900 km, and covers one quarter of Africa's surface. Such a desert is equal to the whole of Europe between the Mediterranean and the Baltic shores and from Ireland to the Urals. Within its confines there is a considerable diversity of landscape.

These landscapes are the result of powerful erosive forces. The changes between the hot furnace of the day and the freezing conditions at night expand and contract rock surfaces and undoubtedly weaken the rock structure. Sudden cooling by occasional rain showers may cause thin flakes to break off (*exfolia-*

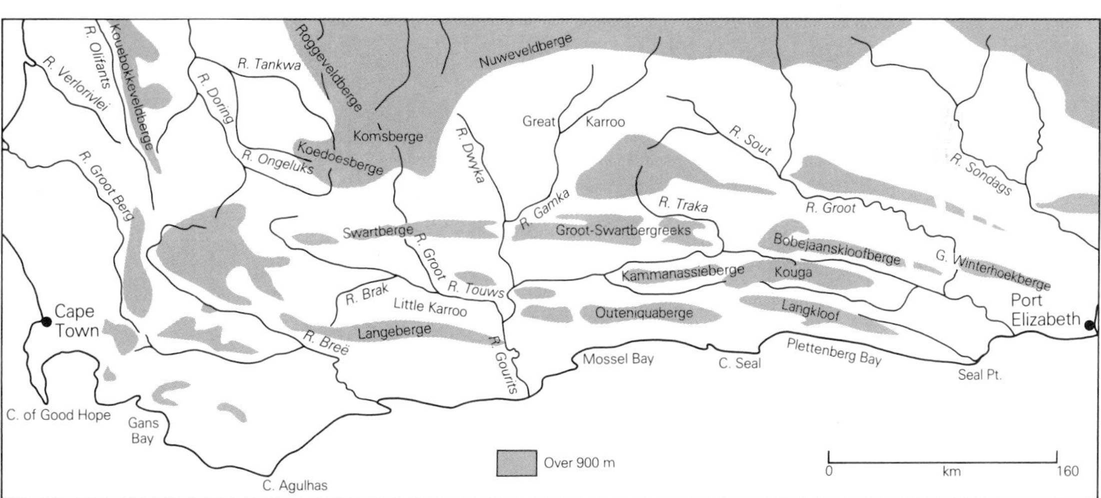

Fig. 1.19 The Cape Ranges and drainage patterns. The diagram illustrates how the major rivers such as the Gourits and Groot cut sharply through the east–west trending ranges. This is an example of superimposed drainage.

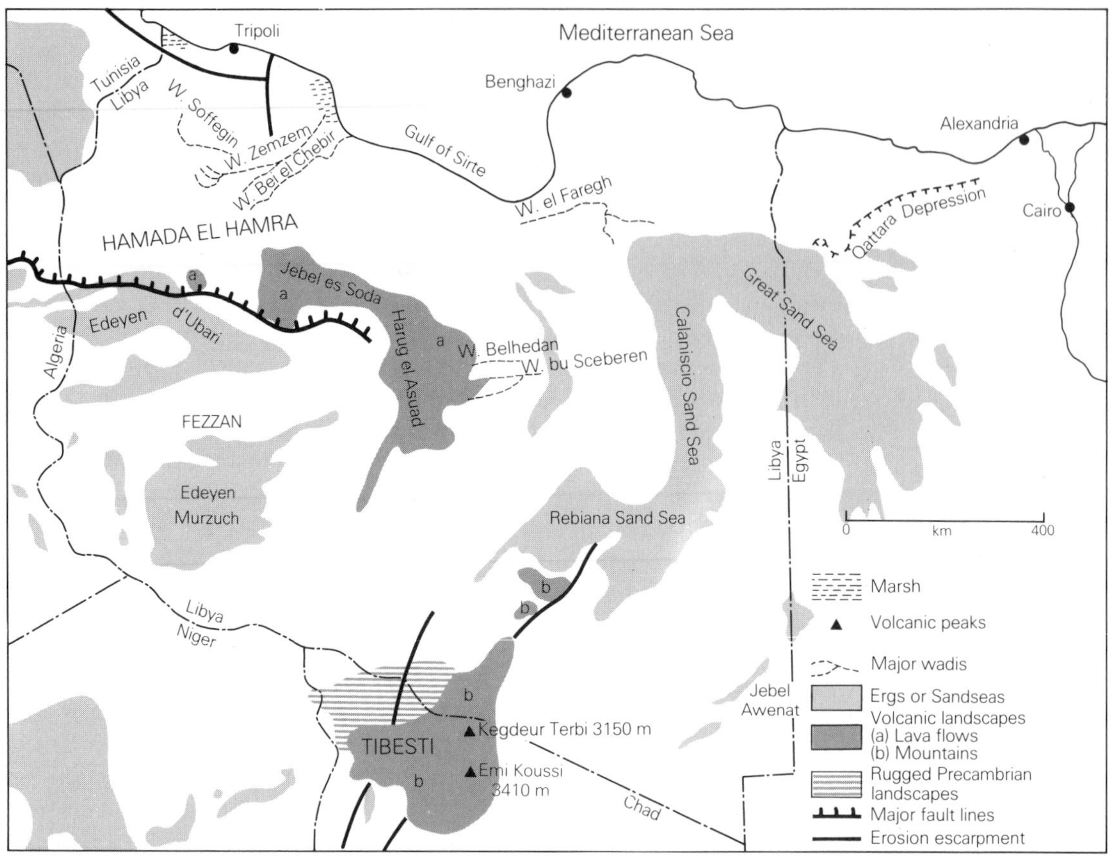

Fig. 1.20 Libya – showing distribution of desert landscapes

tion), which are further broken down, and their minerals with their different rates of expansion are prised loose. The desert sands are the result.

Winds sculpture the exposed rocks. Sand particles are rubbed smooth by jostling one against the other, during storms particles are flung at rocks and, since sand (as opposed to dust) never rises more than a metre or so from the ground, it is the bases of the rocks which become undercut. Wind and its agents, sand grains, reduce the surfaces of the deserts by removing all loose particles (*deflation*), smooth and polish bare rocks surfaces (*abrasion*), and wear down the eroded particles one against the other (*attrition*).

Rain, despite its scarcity, is also an effective erosive agent. Sudden freak rainstorms are very destructive since there is little vegetation to protect the desert surface. *Wadis* become raging torrents for a few brief minutes and huge amounts of loose sand and stones are moved. Chemical weathering also occurs on the shaded undersides of rocks where dampness is caused by moisture moving to the desert surface from below by capillary action.

Desert landscapes may thus vary with the dominant erosive agent and the particular rock of a region (sedimentary, volcanic or basement). *Hamada* is a flat, rocky desert which has been swept clear of sand particles and any dust by the action of the wind. The Hamada, el-Hamra or Red Desert, lying between Tripolitania and the Fezzan (Fig. 1.20) is such a pebble-strewn desert extending for nearly 320 km. It rises gradually to the 1 200 m peak of Jebel-Es-Soda, the Black Mountain, where dark basalt lavas form an extensive cover.

Resistant rocky massifs form a different class of desert landscape. In the Fezzan of Libya the scenery is wild and rugged and fades south-eastwards into the Acacus, an area of sharp limestone cliffs falling steeply towards the west and criss-crossed and gashed

by narrow gorges. Here Jebel Awenat is a vast crystalline mountainous massif cut by a series of steep valleys of alpine nature and rising from a table-land 1700 m high. To the south, granite rocks form an uneven surface 600 m above the desert levels; here enormous blocks have been cut by deep fissures and tortuous defiles, the broken rocks lying in irregular heaps called *gargaf.* There is no doubt that many of these features could not have resulted from the present scant rainfalls of these desert areas, but that they are more the relics of features produced by running water during past pluvial periods.

More volcanic and crystalline massifs are seen in the Aïr, Tibesti and Ahaggar plateaux. These massifs, subject to thousands of years of desert erosion, have been transformed into a weird lunar landscape of towering pinnacles, volcanic plugs and cones.

Ergs or sand seas (Libyan – *Ramla*, Tuareg – *Edeyen* or *Idehan*) are found over much of eastern Libya and

Mauritania: The Amadjar Pass in the Adrar massif. This is an extensive wadi. The courses of the main channel and tributary channels are marked by vegetation. The resistant surface rock layers have been breached and the slopes will gradually retreat.

Algeria: The Ahaggar massif. Remnant volcanic plugs overlook the dissected lava surface.

in the Murzuk and Ubari regions of the Fezzan where, just south of the Hamla region, lies a vast area of shifting sand dunes and jagged rocks. The colours vary from the dazzling white of limestone through the red and grey of argillaceous deposits, to the black of basalt lava sands. But ergs are seen at their best in the western Sahara where they occupy about 15 per cent of the surface area. The sand seas have different landscapes; some consist of rank after rank of *barchan dunes* (Fig. 1.21), huge crescent-shaped hills of sand trending north-east to south-west in response to the prevailing winds. The dunes travel slowly across the landscape by the removal of sand from rear to front until they become 'fossilised', that is, too ponderous at their centres, and remain fixed, a stage usually reached when the barchan is about 880 m wide and 35 m high.

In other ergs the *seif dune* may dominate the scene. Seif dunes occur in large groups or in ridges up to 80 km long and 90 m high. They are elongated in the direction of the winds and are found in regions where winds are apt to change course, giving rise to a fairly strong secondary wind. Thus a barchan may form first during strong north-easterly winds, but has one of its horns elongated by a change to a more easterly wind.

Many geomorphologists are now of the opinion that water plays a greater role in sculpting desert landforms than does insolation and wind. About one million years ago, during the Pleistocene period, long wet periods (called *pluvial periods*) sometimes lasting over 20 000 years, alternated with long dry periods (*interpluvial periods*). Woodland and savanna flourished in parts of the Sahara, there were many more lakes and oases than now, and the present desert regions were then populated with many species of animals now only associated with the present savanna. The pollen deposits, now fossilised, of oak, pine and cypress trees have been found in ancient mud deposits in the Sahara. Thus many of the present landforms of the deserts of Africa are explicable in terms of the action of running water.

The mountainous regions of the Fezzan have already been described as due to water action. The parallel retreat of slopes and the formation of extensive pediplains in the arid and semi-arid regions can only have been caused by extensive river networks and, indeed, aerial photographs show the pattern of such networks, the rivers being now non-existent. The large *alluvial fans* which are typical landforms at the base of escarpments in arid regions are formed by running water resulting from freak storms and the pluvial periods of the past.

In the Sahara there are no perennial water courses but the large number of *wadis* testify to the erosive

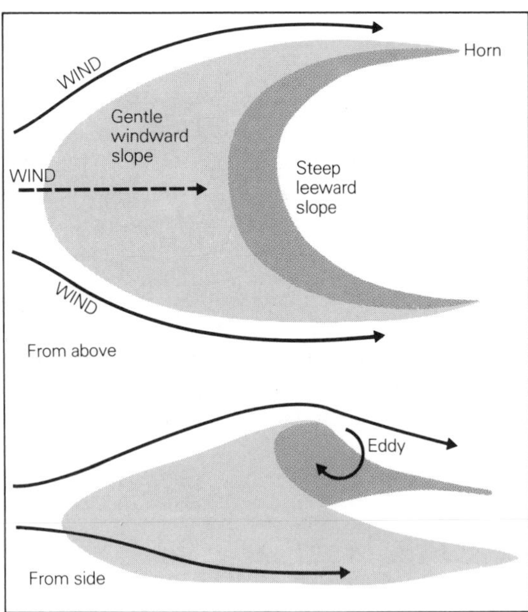

Fig. 1.21 A barchan dune

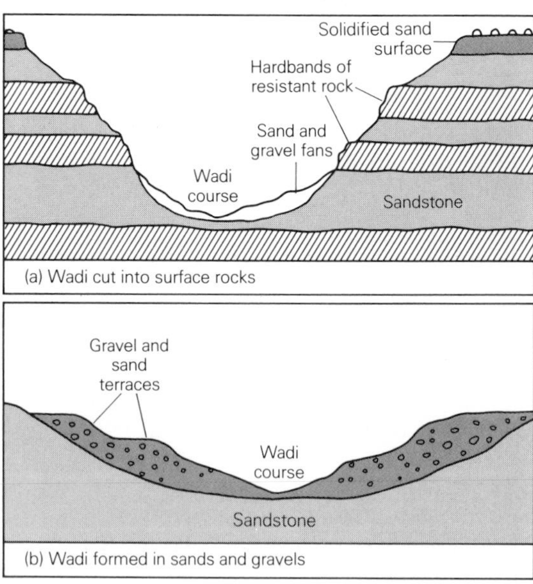

Fig. 1.22 Cross-sections across two types of wadi

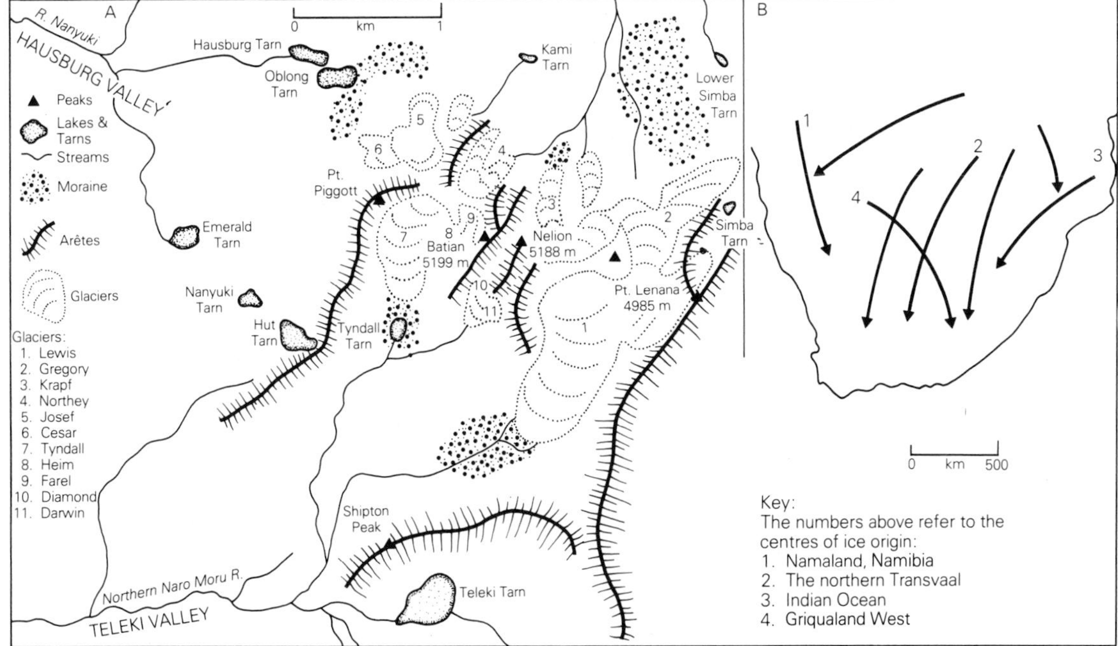

Fig. 1.23 Glaciated regions in Africa. Existing glaciers in Africa are limited to the higher parts of the Ruwenzori Range and to Mount Kenya (*Diagram A*), a volcanic peak now greatly eroded. Mount Kenya once probably reached to over 6 100 m and the original plug, made of resistant nepheline syenite, is now exposed and forms several jagged peaks the highest of which are Batian and Nelion. Point Piggott and Lenana are also remnants of the old plug. Glaciated valleys extend down to 3 000 m but the eleven remaining glaciers are retreating fairly rapidly and none is below about 4 500 m today. The greatest ice erosion probably occurred at about the same time as the Great Ice Age of Europe.

Diagram B shows the main direction of the Dwyka Ice sheets over southern Africa. This glaciation occurred towards the end of the Palaeozoic and left behind it large areas of tills which have since compacted into tillites; some of these tillites have been found as far north as the Zaïre Basin. The main movement of the ice sheets is from north-east to south-west, and this is also put forward as evidence of the theory of continental drift, for it suggests that when the southern continents were joined together they were covered by a single vast ice sheet.

effect of water produced by infrequent storms. The Wadi Zemzem in Libya is about 160 km long and flows, when filled, into the Tauorga marshes. It has a straight course and, like its tributaries to the south, carries their combined waters in times of flood to the Gulf of Sirte, after crossing wide stretches of desert and steppe. The Wadi Bey el Kebir and the Wadi Tamet el Mgenes are its two most important tributaries. The more impressive wadis with steep, rocky walls have been proved to be the result of powerful water action when the climate of the region was wetter.

The coasts of Africa

Africa's coastline has few deep gulfs and penetrating estuaries, and no extensive deep fiords such as those found in Europe or North America. The old sailing ships found few good harbours which offered natural protection; instead there were river mouths blocked by sand bars, hazardous coral reefs, shallow lagoons and beyond, the desert, rain forest or mountain ranges. The map (Fig. 1.24) shows the major types of coastline along Africa's shores; of these the most prominent are:

Sand Bar and Lagoon Coasts – these stretch 900 km along the West African coast from Cape St Ann to a point just east of Lagos. The shallow waters just off-shore break the rotational motion of approaching waves which deposit long lines of sand a short distance from the coast, to form bars backed by shallow lagoons. While these lagoons form a natural inland waterway for light craft they are too shallow for ocean-going vessels which have to anchor in the deeper open sea. Entrance channels to ports have to be constantly dredged and artificial harbours have been built at Sekondi-Takoradi, Tema, Abidjan and

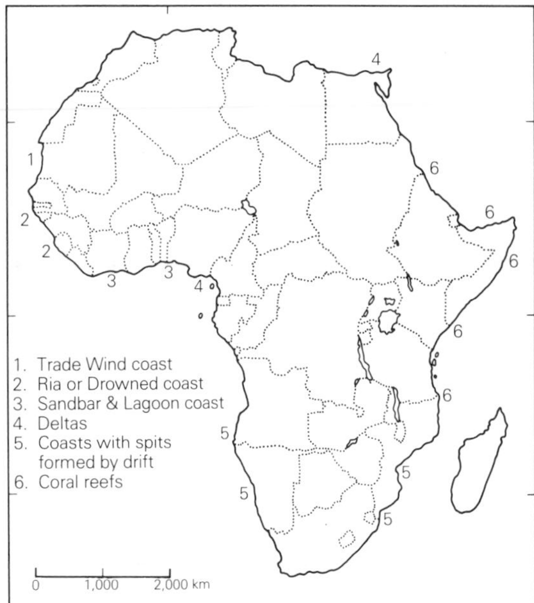

Fig. 1.24 Africa – types of coastline. At 1 the prevailing trade winds have caused sand to drift southwards, filling the bays and smoothing the coastline.

Lagos. Behind the off-shore bars the lagoons may be split into a complicated network of sandy islands and water channels. The water drains away through narrow gaps in the outer bars, which are often made very shallow by a submerged bar.

Many of the lagoons are being gradually filled with river silt and will eventually become marshy strips. Occasionally the line of sandspits and bars is broken by prominent rocky headlands chosen as sites for early trading posts and forts. These then are coasts of aggradation – they are being continuously added to and built up with sediments.

Ria Coasts extend in a 1 000-km long strip from Dakar to Sherbro Island, including the coasts of Sierra Leone, Guinea and Guinea Bissau. Lowland and river valleys have been submerged by a rise in sea-level to produce a jigsaw pattern of deep inlets and small islands. The Sierra Leone estuary is a superb example of a ria with mountains on the south rising sheer out of the sea to nearly 900 m, and is one of the finest natural inlets to be found on the West African coast. Numerous rias also occur along Lake Victoria's shores.

Coral reef and lagoon coasts occur along the shores of the Red Sea, Somalia, Kenya, Tanzania and Mozambique. Here natural conditions are ideal for the growth of polyps, the minute sea creatures which live in colonies, forming their hard skeletons from calcium carbonate extracted from the sea water. It is the skeleton which remains after the polyps' death to pile up and form off-shore reefs and extensive lagoon floors. Polyps will only live, however, in shallow, clear, warm water (20°C) and thus do not flourish along the cooler Atlantic shores of Africa. The reefs, lying between one to two kilometres out to sea according to water depth, enclose calm stretches of

Fig. 1.25 Block diagram illustrating a sandbar and lagoon coast
1 Rotary motion of waves is broken in shallow water
2 Sand particles accumulate to form bar
3 Silt brought down by rivers accumulates in lagoon

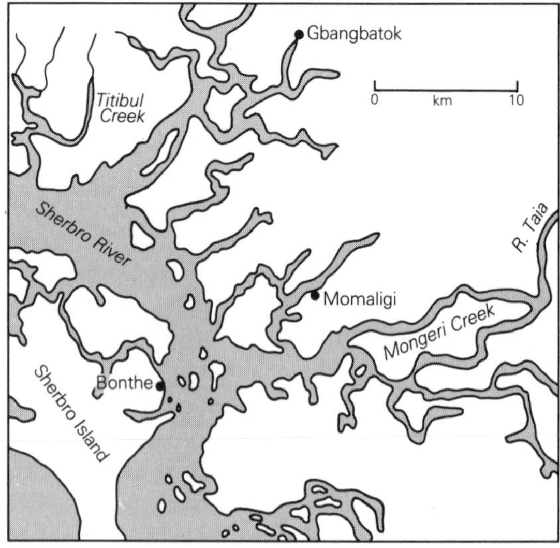

Fig. 1.26 Sierra Leone – ria coastline

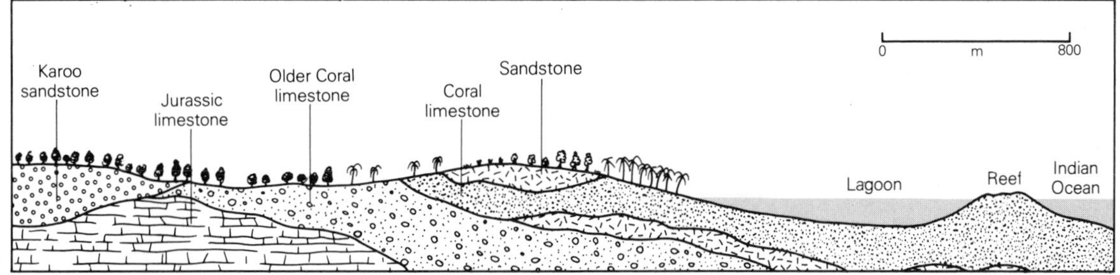

Fig. 1.27 Kenya – cross-section of coral reef coast north of Mombasa

shallow water in the lagoons, which are fringed on the landward side by dazzling white beaches of eroded coral grains. Large islands of coral, formed when the land was more submerged than at present, lie off-shore, their bases undercut by wave action; inland, raised beaches of coral are common. Where muddy streams enter the sea the polyps cannot exist and there are breaks in the reef. Such coasts provide few good harbours, except where there has been local sinking of the land as at Mombasa's Kilindini Harbour (the Place of the Deep Waters).

Raised beaches, similar to those of the Pleistocene coral raised beaches of the East African coast, are found elsewhere in Africa. Such beaches are due to isostatic uplift of the continent. Much of the Sierra Leone peninsula shows evidence of uplift in the raised beaches at approximately 45 m and again at 12 m above sea-level. The broad coastal plains of Mozambique, Liberia, the Ivory Coast and Ghana are due to uplift, and Ghana has many examples of raised cliffs and beaches in the Sekondi area. Along the Namib coast further south, raised terraces are sometimes 100 m above present sea-levels and just north of the Orange River mouth are raised beaches which stand 25 m above their former level. Along the southern Cape coast in South Africa raised beaches and exposed wave-cut platforms are evident, e.g. at Hermanus.

Other coastal features

One of the contributory factors to the smoothness of Africa's coastline is the rarity of river *estuaries*. Only the River Gambia has an estuary of a length comparable with those found in Europe or North America; it extends some 150 km upstream of Elephant Island and was formed by an increase of sea level. It is approximately 10 km wide near the sea but narrows to between 2 and 3 km wide further upstream and is lined with level banks of silt called the *bantos faros*.

But *deltas* are the usual natural feature of Africa's river mouths, and the Niger and the Nile form oustanding examples. The Niger delta is a cuspate or arcuate type, its curved shores extending 480 km from near the Benin River to Opobo, 80 km west of the Cross River outlet. The Niger outlet marks the extreme point of the arc at the Nun entrance west of Palm Point. Numerous other rivers, some distributaries, others separate from the Niger, form a broad fan. Called the 'Oil Rivers', due to the large quantities of palm oil produced in this region, many are navigable by ocean-going vessels for short distances while others, particularly those on the west

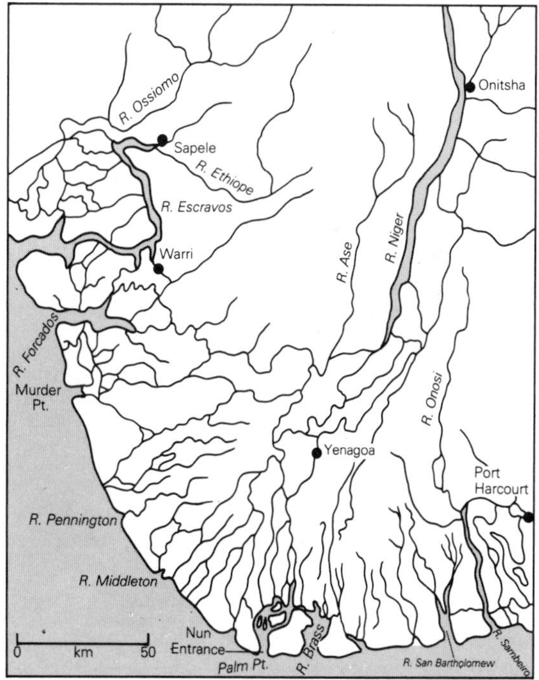

Fig. 1.28 Nigeria – the Niger delta

coast, have had their entrances blocked by drifting sands caused by long-shore drift. Entrances to ports such as Sapele and Warri along the Escravos and Forcados rivers must be kept dredged and protected from drift by breakwaters. Transport overland in the delta is made difficult by the wide areas of mangrove swamps and population densities are comparatively low.

The Nile delta, on the other hand, is densely populated over about 70 per cent of its area and, while being smaller than the Niger delta, is nevertheless a magnificent example. Its coastal arc is some 240 km long and its greatest extent inland at the delta apex is about 180 km. The numerous distributaries are banked by levees and in the case of the two main arms these levees have been built out into the Mediterranean at the Masabb Rashid (Rosetta Mouth) and the Masabb Dumyat (Damietta Mouth). Light currents along the coast have formed long sandpits enclosing large lagoons – the Bahra Maryut, the Bahra el Idku, the Bahra el Burullus (60 km long by 15 km wide), and the Bahra el Manzala (48 km long by 18 km wide). Surrounding these lagoons are broad areas of marsh too salty to reclaim.

Longshore drift occurs along various stretches of the African coast where there are strong currents and wind. Sand accumulation in bays and the development of sandspits are the result. Bathurst stands on a hooked sandspit which ends at Banyan Point and is backed by low, swampy St. Mary's Island. Sand eroded from sandstone rocks and silt from the interior brought by the Gambia River have collected at a point where the river current slackens in deeper water and meets drift caused by the south-west

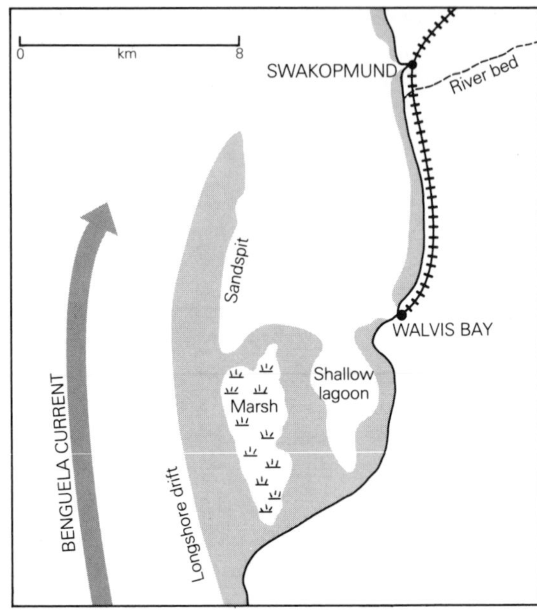

Fig. 1.30 Namibia – sandspit formation near Swakopmund

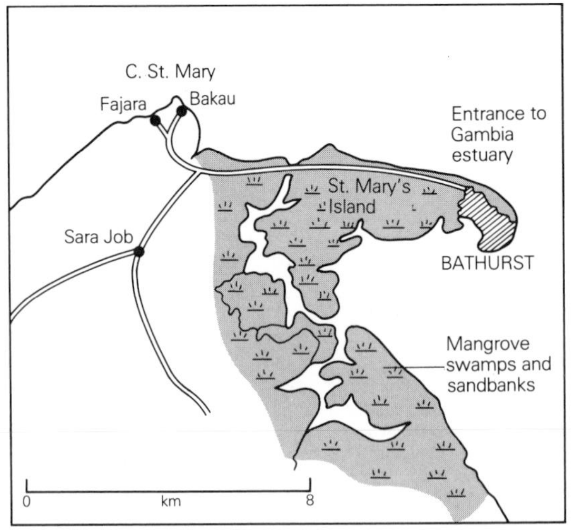

Fig. 1.29 The Gambia – a hooked spit

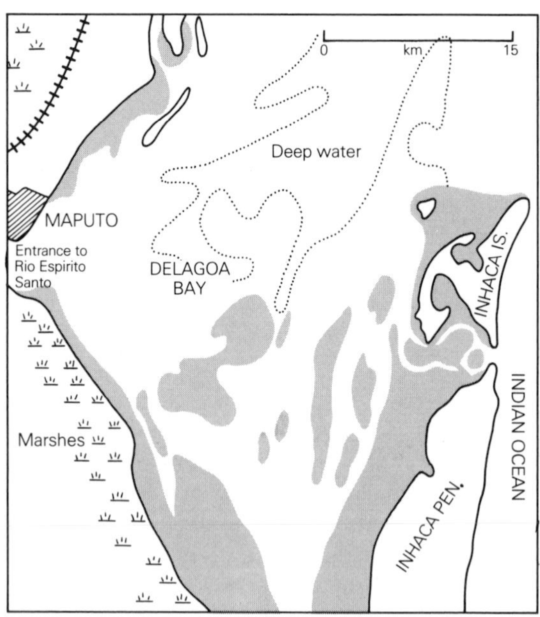

Fig. 1.31 Mozambique – silt accumulation in Delagoa Bay

winds. At Walvis Bay in Namibia the northward drift of sediments carried by the Benguela Current has formed a 15-km long spit backed by salt marshes and a shallow lagoon. The opposite effect is seen on the east coast in Mozambique where the Inhaca Peninsula acts as a gathering arm for drifting silt brought down into Delagoa Bay by the southward flowing Mozambique Current; added to this are the sediments of the Tembe and Esperito Santo rivers. Constant dredging of Maputo harbour is necessary.

The climate

With over three quarters of its surface within the tropics Africa does not experience the great temperature contrasts of Europe, Asia and North America. While in those continents much of the climate can be explained by the effect of air masses of greatly differing temperatures, the explanation of Africa's climate is more of a problem. The isolation of vast regions and the large expanses of desert and rain forest have made the collection of reliable data difficult. However, many of Africa's climatic characteristics can be explained by the movement of air masses which differ from one another in their amount of moisture and their relative stability rather than in their temperatures. These air masses come into contact along a broad ill-defined convergence zone which moves across the continent in response to temperature and wind changes – the Inter Tropical Convergence Zone or ITCZ – to which many meteorologists have given the characteristics of a frontal zone similar to those of Europe and North America. The conditions which give rise to the movement of air masses and produce this frontal zone may be described as follows:

Climatic conditions – the southern hemisphere's summer

Temperatures

By January the sun produces intense heating in Botswana, Zambia and Zimbabwe, and most of the southern half of Africa has temperatures between 21 and 26,5°C with extremes of 32°C and over in Bushmanland. In contrast, the northern part of the continent is relatively cool with mean temperatures of 10°C in the Atlas region and 15,5°C in the northern Sahara.

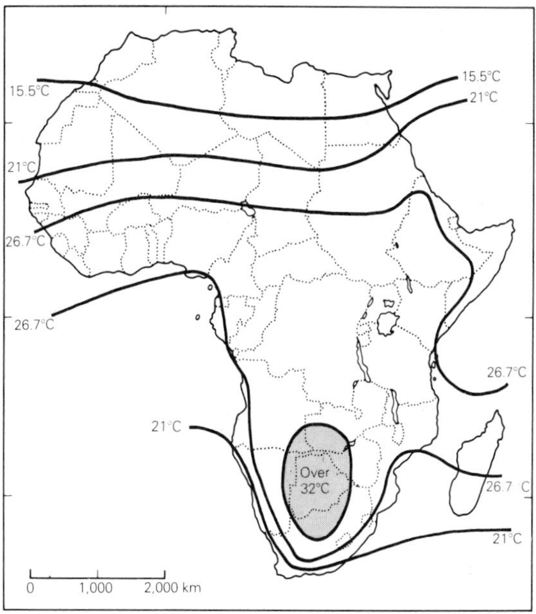

Fig. 1.32 January – actual surface temperatures

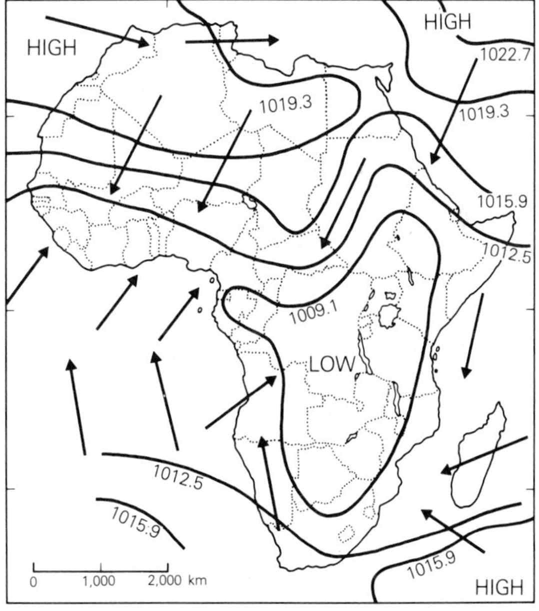

Fig. 1.33 Pressure and winds – general conditions from November to April (figures in millibars)

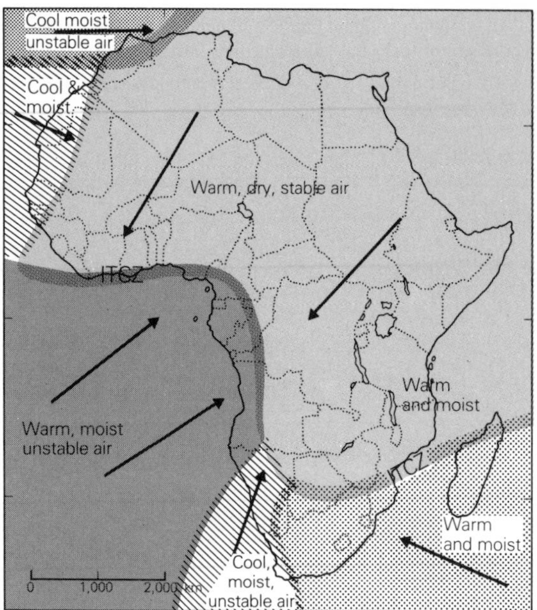

Fig. 1.34 January – diagrammatic representation of airmass movement and position of airmass fronts

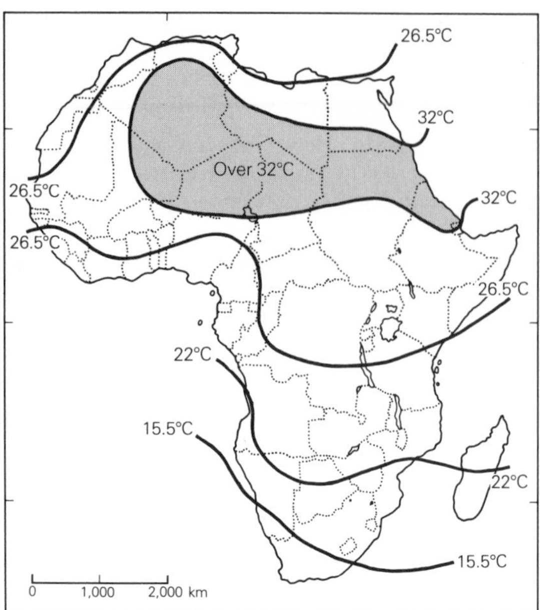

Fig. 1.35 July – actual surface temperatures

Pressures

The intensity of insolation over southern Africa from November to April causes low pressure conditions in this region, while relatively high pressures develop over the cooler south Atlantic and Indian oceans. Over cooler north Africa, high pressure develops, separated from that of continental Europe by a low pressure system over the relatively warm surface of the Mediterranean Sea.

Winds

Winds from the northern high pressure zone penetrate southwards through the interior of the continent towards the low pressure zone of the south. These north-easterly *harmattan* winds from the Sahara bring the hazy dust laden atmosphere experienced in West Africa during the early part of the year. Relatively high pressure over the south Atlantic and the south-westerly monsoons oppose their progress in the west. Along the eastern coast the North-East Trades and Asiatic monsoonal winds also penetrate southwards to converge with easterly trade winds and Atlantic south-westerlies onto the low pressure system of the south.

The ITCZ

This follows the West African coast, bends southwards through the Cameroons and Zaïre, then eastwards through Botswana and the Mozambique coast.

Air masses

Virtually the whole of the Sahara, West Africa and the northern Congo are influenced by dry, stable air. The eastern half of Africa receives similar dry air from Arabia borne by the north-east trades. Towards the south-east this air mass has picked up moisture over the Indian Ocean and becomes warm and moist. Easterly trade winds bring similar air to Malagasy, the Natal coast and the eastern veld. Warm, moist, generally unstable air affects most of the western coast south of the Equator. In the Maghreb region of the north-west cool, moist, unstable air masses are brought by westerly air streams.

Climatic conditions – the northern hemisphere's summer

Temperatures

Over the broad land mass of northern Africa the sun, now overhead between the equator and the Tropic of

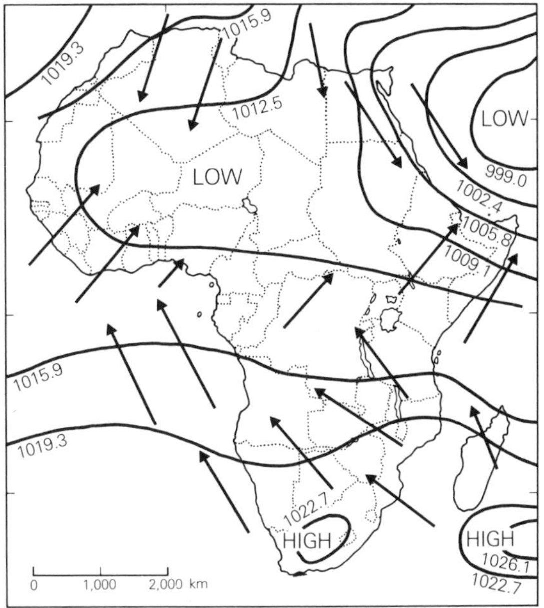

Fig. 1.36 Pressure and winds – general conditions from May to October

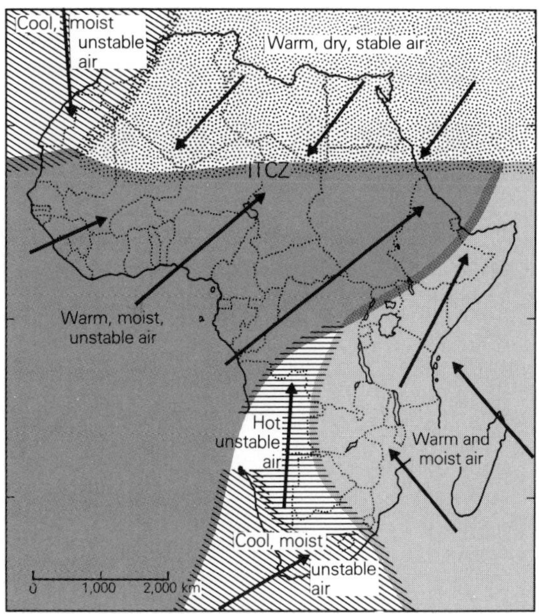

Fig. 1.37 July – diagrammatic representation of airmass movement and position of airmass fronts

Cancer, creates temperatures rising to over 38°C in the shade in the Sahara. The whole of western and central Africa has mean actual temperatures between 15° and 25°C while the south is quite cool with actual temperatures below 15°C.

Pressures

A broad zone of low pressure exists from the west coast to as far north as the southern Sahara and across into Arabia broken only by occasional small zones of high pressure on the cool Ethiopian Highlands. A high pressure concentration lies over South Africa south of Capricorn. Low pressure systems move eastwards sometimes affecting the southern tip of the Cape.

Winds

The south-east Trade winds of the South Atlantic move across the equator and are drawn in across the coast of West Africa by the low pressure zone of the Sahara to become powerful south-west monsoonal winds heavily laden with moisture. The north-east trades retreat to become a weak zone of winds affecting Africa north of Cancer. Most of eastern and central Africa is affected by easterly Trade winds from the Indian Ocean while variable winds, associated with the anti-clockwise movement around the South African high and with the low pressure systems off the southern coast, affect Africa south of Capricorn.

The ITCZ

This lies between the weak north-east winds and the strong south-west monsoonal region. It extends in an almost straight line east-west from the coast of Mauritania to the Red Sea shores of the Sudan.

Air masses

While Africa north of the ITCZ is under the influence of warm, dry air masses, warm, moist air brought by the south-west monsoons pours over the whole of West Africa, penetrating as far as the Ethiopian Highlands to the east and bringing warm, moist, unstable conditions very favourable to turbulent convectional thunderstorms and heavy rainfall. Warm, moist air also approaches from the south-east moving in over the Mozambique and East African coasts. The southern tip of Africa is affected by cool, moist, unstable air brought by depressions.

The conditions described above are the two extremes when the sun is at its extremities in the northern and southern hemispheres. Throughout the

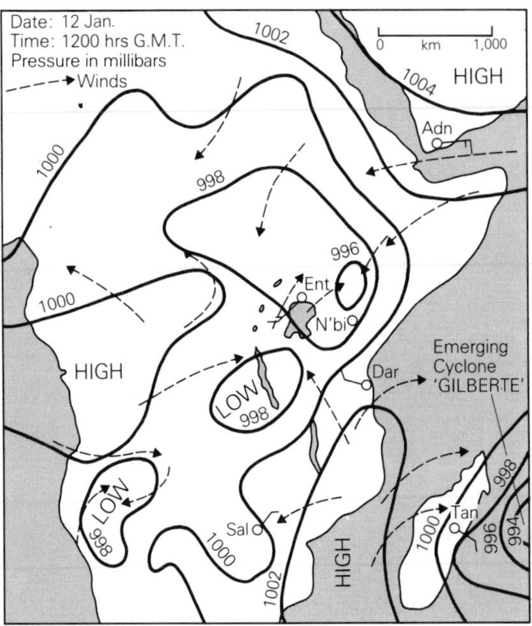

Fig. 1.38 Meteorological conditions over central and southern Africa for a January day. A belt of low pressure extends throughout central and east Africa from the Angolan coast in the south-west to the Kenya Highlands in the north-east. Relatively high pressure zones are centred over the Zaïre Basin, the southern Arabian peninsula and over the Mozambique Channel. The birth of a tropical cyclone at about latitude 12°S to the east of Malagasy seems to be hastening the collapse of the south-easterly high-pressure belt. The northern part of the region shown experienced generally dry weather but rain fell over much of Tanzania, northern Angola and the western coast of Malagasy. Dry, stable air masses over Kenya and Somalia prevented any large-scale convective rainfall, but later in the week a relatively cold air mass, the remnants of an extra-tropical cold front from northern Africa, caused cloud and scattered thunderstorms in the lake region of western Uganda. *(See also page 42 for exercises on meterological maps of Africa)*

year as the sun and its heat move over the continent between the tropics, the pressure belts respond and the wind systems weaken or increase in strength bringing with them associated air masses. This idealised picture is thus never stable but constantly changing. Figure 1.38 shows actual climatic conditions for one day in January (see also Figs. 1.64, 1.65 and 1.66 on page 42).

The effects of the ITCZ

The effects of the ITCZ may only be felt temporarily in any one region as it moves in response to waxing

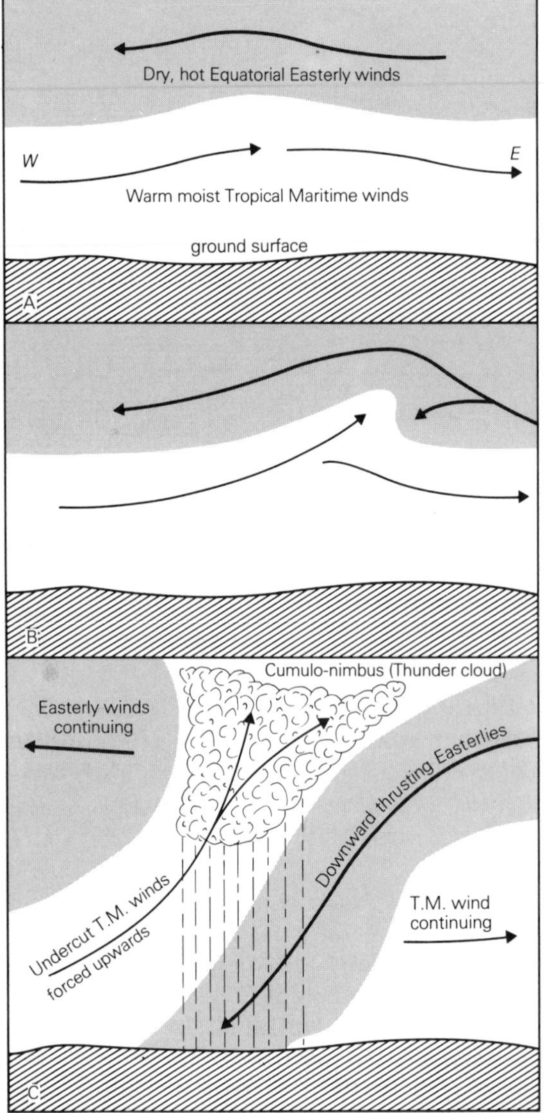

Fig. 1.39 West Africa – causes of turbulence along the squall line

and waning air masses. But its effects may not be seen clearly due to other climatic influences; in East Africa it is not known how much the weather is affected by the ITCZ for variations in altitude, the effects of large water expanses in the lakes, and convectional air currents mask its influence. It is clearly seen in West Africa, however, where its passage over the land is marked by a line of squalls and turbulent, changeable weather (Figs. 1.39 and 1.40). From March onwards the warm, moist air

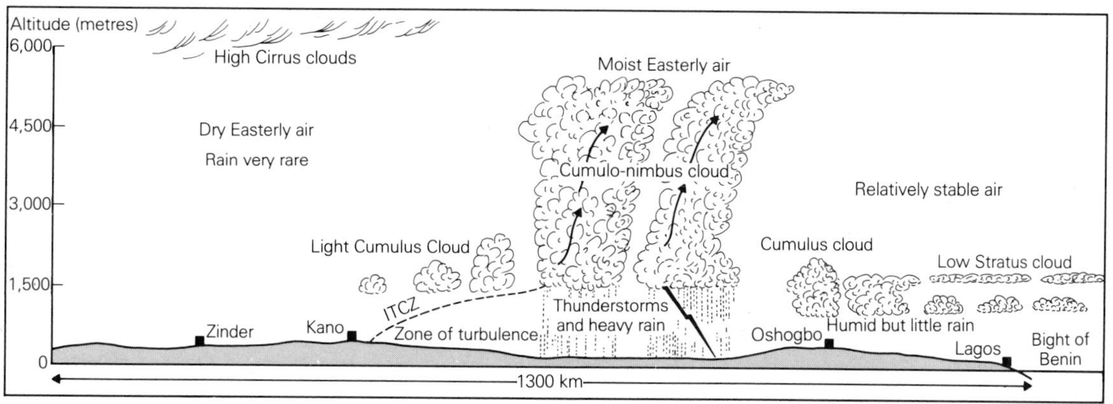

Fig. 1.40 Nigeria – weather zones associated with the movement of the ITCZ

brought by the south-west monsoonal wind sweeps in from the Gulf of Guinea. Like a broad wedge the air mass slices in under the drier, hotter air lying over the continent and forces it to rise. The stronger monsoons make gradual headway against the weakening Harmattan and their convergence zone, the ITCZ, moves slowly northwards. The weather, which up to April or May consisted of dry, dusty days which parch the soil and make nose and eyes smart, begins to change as the south-west winds increase their influence. The once cloudless skies are now fluffed with small white cumulus clouds, temperatures are a little lower, and a warm moistness replaces the harsh dryness. Winds veer from north-east to south-west and blustery weather brings rain showers; these conditions gradually give way to skies heavy with black cumulo-nimbus accompanied by lightning, thunder and heavy rain. As the ITCZ pushed northwards the steady rains of the rainy season proper begin, to last until September or October according to location (Fig. 1.40).

Rainfall belts

In Africa rainfall is thus associated with the passage of the ITCZ, the convectional nature of hot tropical air, and the movement of moist air masses over higher ground (orographical or relief rain). As these influences pass over Africa the associated rainbelt moves with them. From November to April the whole of southern Africa is receiving some rain (Fig. 1.41); the north coast receives rain from the Atlantic, while the rest of north Africa comes under the influence of the hot, dry Saharan air mass which extends itself into West Africa by the Harmattan. The Harmattan rarely reaches the West African coast, which receives some rain from the weak south-westerly monsoon. Rainfall in the southern part of the continent is brought by the south-east trades from the Indian Ocean and from westerly air streams from the South Atlantic, both of which meet at the ITCZ and produce frontal rainfall. Intense heating produces many convectional rain storms. In the deserts of Namibia little rain falls. This is due to the lack of any major relief feature which would trigger off relief rain and to the presence of cool, stable air over an ocean cooled by the Benguela Current. Moreover, the southern Atlantic air stream meets no opposing air mass to cause frontal rain in this region.

Gradually the rain belts and air masses move northwards following the apparent movement of the sun and the northward moving pressure belts. Between May and October a huge belt of rainfall extends from the equator northwards to 15° north latitude and from the coasts of Sierra Leone to the western borders of Somalia (Fig. 1.42). Strong south-westerly air streams blow directly on-shore bringing heavy rainfall in regions of sharp relief – the Peninsula Mountains (Freetown receives 940 mm in July), the Futa Jalon, the Jos Plateau, and the Cameroon (Debundja has 150 mm in July) and Bamenda Highlands. The Ethiopian Highlands experience heavy rain brought by easterly trade winds. Except for the rain introduced by the westerly

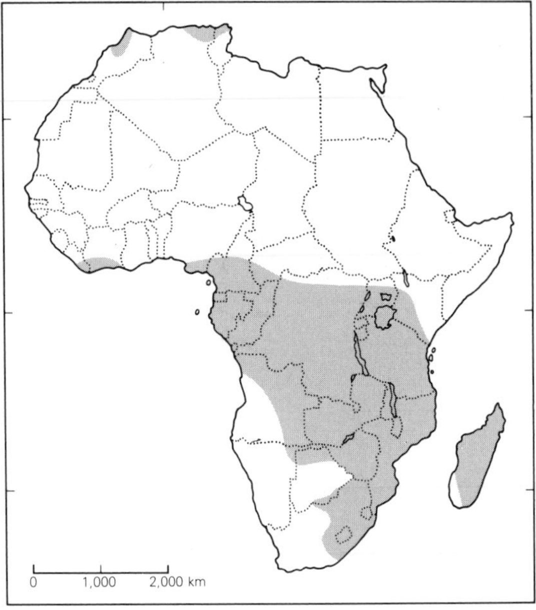

Fig. 1.41 Africa – areas receiving more than 500 mm of rain between 1 November and 30 April

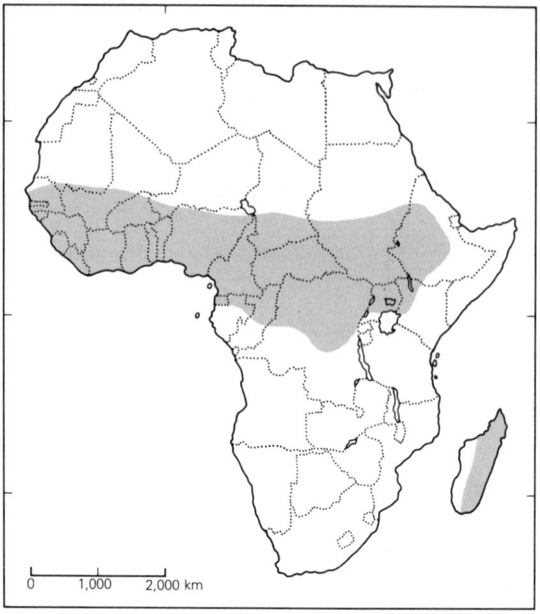

Fig. 1.42 Africa – areas receiving more than 500 mm of rain between 1 May and 31 October

air currents in the south-west Cape region, the rest of Africa receives less than 20 mm of rainfall in July in most areas.

The effect of the movement of rainfall zones across Africa is to produce varying patterns of rainfall throughout the year in different parts of the continent. Flanking the equator are regions which receive rainfall all the year round, since they lie where the extreme southern and northern parts of the seasonal rainbelts overlap. To the north-east and south of this core region lie areas which receive rainfall when the rainbelt (equatorial trough) passes over them, the season varying from three to six months according to position, and a long period of drought when the rainbelt is in the opposite hemisphere. In the Mediterranean coastal fringe rain occurs when the westerly air streams migrate south from Europe, while a three- to four-month drought period is experienced when the region comes under the influence of the dry Saharan air mass. A similar climate with the seasons occurring at opposite times of the year (winter from May to July and summer drought from November to January) occurs in the south-west Cape region, when westerly air streams migrate north or south.

Factors affecting climatic characteristics

While Africa's climatic regions fall into a relatively

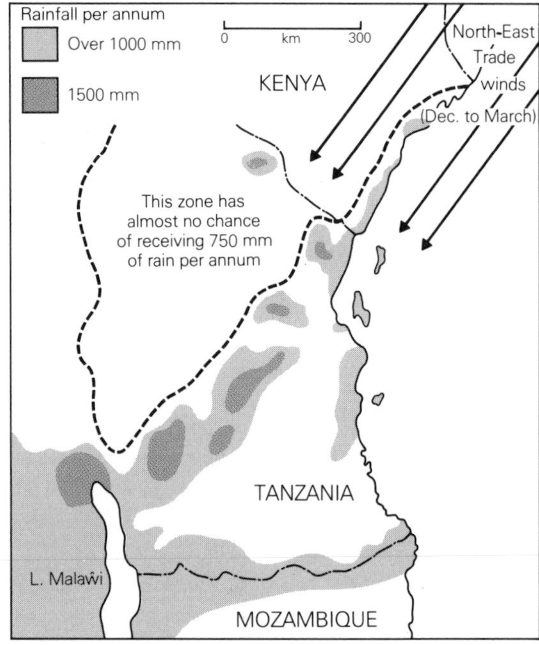

Fig. 1.43 East Africa – the effect of altitude and coast alignment on annual rainfall totals

simple pattern, variations in climatic types are caused by several natural influences:

Altitude

Altitude results in the limitation of true Equatorial Climate largely to the Zaïre Basin. East Africa and Ethiopia do not experience the enervating moistness and stuffiness of Zaïre, while Ethiopia also escapes the great blanket of heat which lies over the Sahara in the northern summer months. Altitudes of between 1 500 and 2 700 m reduce temperatures by between 8 and 14°C giving pleasant annual averages around 18° and 24°C. Such climates are of a cooler tropical nature than those normally associated with equatorial regions.

Relief

Relief can create very great local differences in climate. We have seen the effects in West Africa. In East Africa the Kilimanjaro region of Tanzania is very well watered on its south-eastern side (up to 1 500 mm annually), while a few kilometres to the north-east in the Nyika, rain totals fall as low as 250 mm a year. Relief rain is experienced all along the eastward-facing slopes of the Drakensberg Mountains (Pietermaritzburg's annual total is 900 mm), while to the west the High Veld becomes progressively drier.

Coastal Alignment

The alignment of coastlines may have an effect on rainfall amount received. On the Kenya coast rainfall is not high for an equatorial region (Mombasa 1 210 mm) and totals decrease northwards (Lamu 930 mm). This may be attributed partly to the north-east alignment of the coast, for the north-east trades flow parallel to it for several months instead of blowing directly inland. A similar occurrence is found in Ghana east of Cape Three Points, where annual rainfall totals fall well below 760 mm in a region which should experience between 1 780 and 2 030 mm. This is partly due to the sharp bend of the coast from a north-westerly alignment (at right angles to the south-westerly monsoon) to a north-easterly one (parallel to the monsoon), and to an upwelling of cold waters near the coast. Thus Axim receives over 2 000 mm a year while Accra gets only 700 mm.

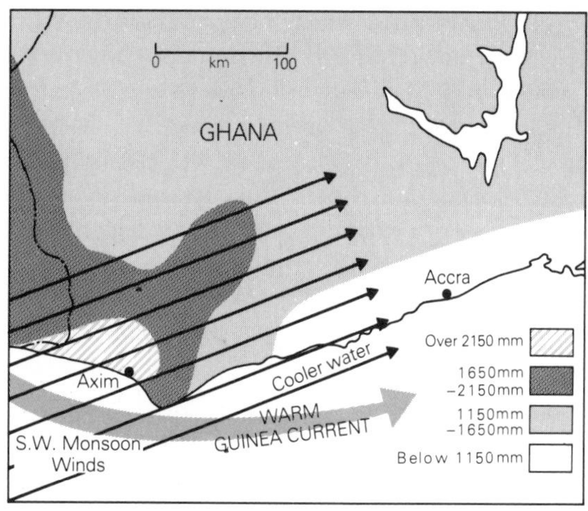

Fig. 1.44 Ghana – the effect of ocean currents and coast alignment on annual rainfall totals

Ocean currents

Ocean currents also affect climate. The cool Benguela Current, flowing northwards along the coast of Namibia, produces a considerable drop in temperatures for stations along the coast (compare Walvis Bay's annual average temperature of 17°C with that of Windhoek's 19°C), and also cools air masses passing over it, so that when they cross the heated land surface they release little or no moisture; this accounts for the narrow strip of pure desert – the Namib – along this coast. The cool Canaries current, flowing southward along the Moroccan coast, often produces cool, cloudy days and frequent fogs. Casablanca has a July average of 22°C, which is 4,4°C lower than Tripoli on the same latitude.

In contrast temperatures are raised slightly on the Mozambique and Natal coasts by the southward flowing warm Mozambique Current. Thus Durban's July temperature of 18°C is 4,3°C higher than Swakopmund's 13,5°C, while Durban has a January temperature of 25°C and Swakopmund 17°C. The warm Mozambique current has a direct economic effect since it allows sugar cane to be grown at a much lower latitude than normal (30°S).

Natural regions – their climate, vegetation and economic use

The correlation between climate and vegetation is

easily seen in Africa where, despite rapid removal of plant life by animal and man, extensive vegetation zones exist. The climate and its associated vegetation affects the patterns of life which man can choose to lead and has a direct bearing on the economic development of a region. Climatic and vegetation regions will be considered as natural regions, and their economic use briefly discussed.

Equatorial regions

Climate

Equatorial climates are limited to areas within 10° of the equator. They are characterised by high daily temperatures of around 26°C a small annual range of from 2° to 3°C and a small diurnal range of 1° to 8°C. Rainfall is heavy throughout the year, often exceeding 2 000 mm. While no month is really dry, there may be two rainfall maxima with the passage of the 'thermal equator', and much rain is largely convectional, often falling in continual sheets for hours. Days and nights are of approximately the same length, the sun rising between 6 and 6.30 a.m. and setting between 6 and 6.30 p.m.

Morning weather is often quite sunny and clear, but the heat builds up during the day until by about 2 p.m. cumulus clouds develop, growing into towering cumulo-nimbus, which give heavy rainfall accompanied by thunder and lightning. As temperatures cool during the evening, the clouds thin or disappear, and nights may be moonlit and starry.

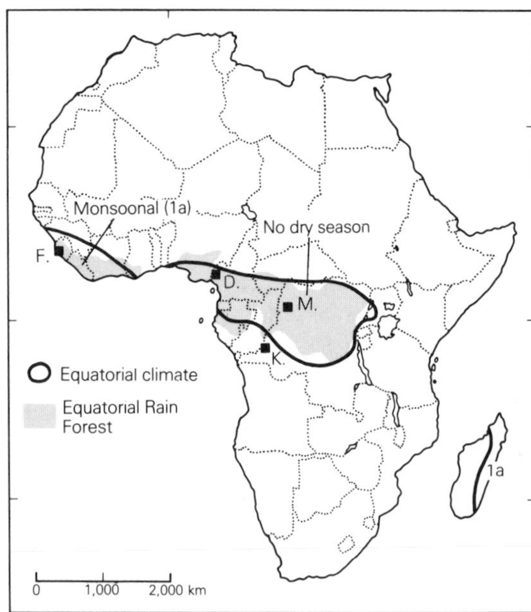

Fig. 1.45 Africa – the equatorial regions. Letters refer to climatic stations

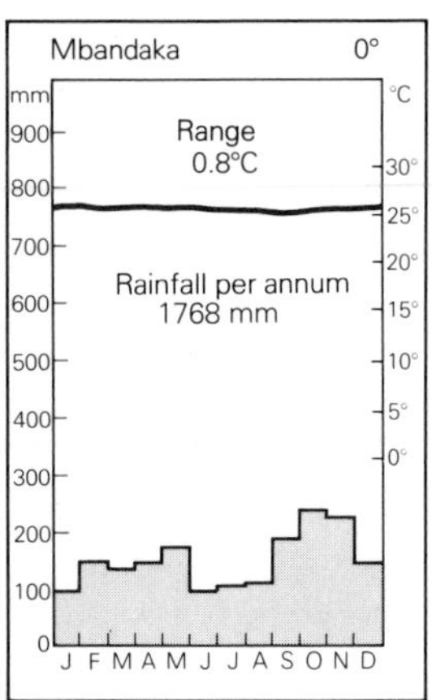

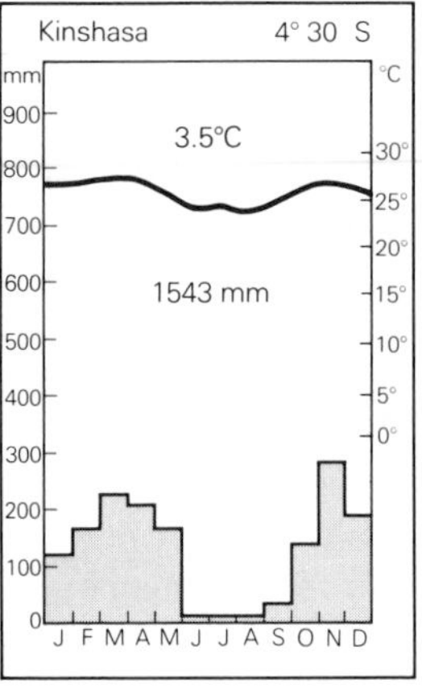

Fig. 1.46 Two types of equatorial climate from the Zaïre Basin. Mbandaka is almost exactly on the Equator, while Kinshasa lies nearly 5°S and displays a short dry season.

Some of the rain may be due to frontal conditions. Warm, moist, unstable air from the South Atlantic meets more stable drier air from the north-east. There is also the possibility that air streams from the Indian Ocean may penetrate far enough to bring rain to eastern Zaïre.

Along the West African coast the Monsoonal Equatorial Climate (see area marked 1a on Fig. 1.45) differs from that of Zaïre by having a definite, though short, dry period. Much of the rain is orographical and totals are high, usually between 2 540 and 4 320 mm a year; Debundja in the Cameroons is the extreme, with an annual average rainfall of 9 500 mm, of which nearly 1 520 mm falls in July and only 190 mm in January.

Vegetation

The hot, rainy, humid conditions give rise to dense tropical rain forests which stretch in a broken 960-km wide zone for 2 250 km from the eastern Zaïre boundary to the Gabon and Cameroon coasts; they are continued along the West African coast (in a strip 240 to 320 km wide in places) from the Niger Delta to the Sierra Leone coast and in narrow ribbons along the lower reaches of tropical rivers. Tropical rain forest covers 2 280 000 km^2, or about eight per cent of Africa's surface.

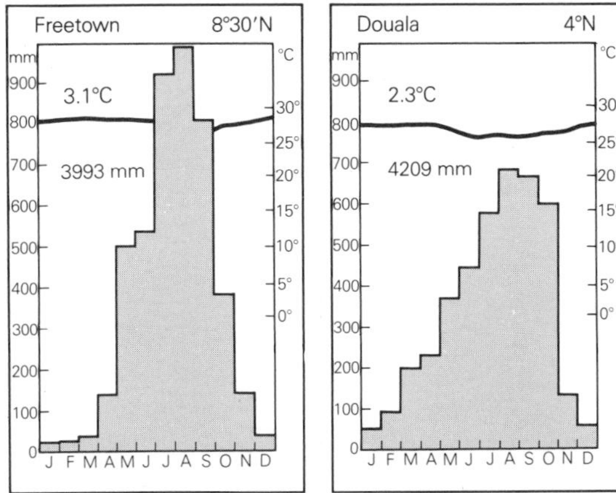

Fig. 1.47 Equatorial climate – the effects of relief

Nigeria: Rain forest. Note the dense bush, tall smooth tree trunks, feathery crowns of the trees and parasitic plants (left).

The rain forest consists of a wide variety of trees, the tallest reaching up to 40 m, their smooth, straight trunks crowned with feathery leaves and branches. Younger and smaller species form a secondary 'canopy' between 15 and 20 m. Between the trees straggle parasitic lianas while the floor is thickly covered with herbs, ground creepers and low bushes. Many trees develop buttressed trunks and, near river banks, stilt roots. Trees overhang rivers to form tunnels or galleries (gallerial forest). There are no 'pure stands' of trees as in temperate coniferous forests; balsa, rubber, mahogany, sapele and ebony grow close together, a hundred varieties often being found in a square kilometre. The rate of plant growth is very rapid and secondary growth soon springs up in cleared patches.

Economic uses of the environment

The tropical rain forests contain many useful plants and trees. Durable and expensive woods are selected and floated down to saw mills, large plantations grow oil palm, rubber, cacao, citrus fruits, bananas and coffee. A wide variety of vegetables and fruits is also grown for subsistence – bananas, pineapples, mangoes, rice, yams, sweet potatoes, sugar cane, ginger, groundnuts, tobacco and cotton, the last three crops being grown on the drier fringes of the region. Oil for cooking, for lamp fuel, for soap and for sale to plantations is provided by the oil palm; the kola nut is grown as a stimulant; and the raffia palm supplies fibre for baskets, nets, ropes and mats. The wild life of the forests is hunted by small isolated groups of people with bows and arrows, snares, nets, pits and traps, and yields a wide range of meats. At one time large areas of these forests remained virtually untouched by man, but they are now being extensively cleared for cultivation and for the extraction of minerals.

Tropical regions

Climate

Tropical climates and their associated savanna vegetation lie in a broad zone fringing the Equatorial Region and forming a transition zone towards the true desert. Hot season temperatures are higher, cool season lower, and diurnal (14° to 17°C) and annual

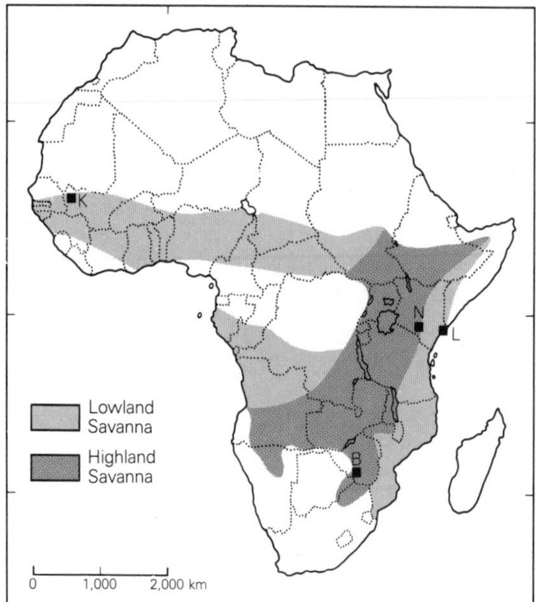

Fig. 1.48 Africa – two tropical savanna regions

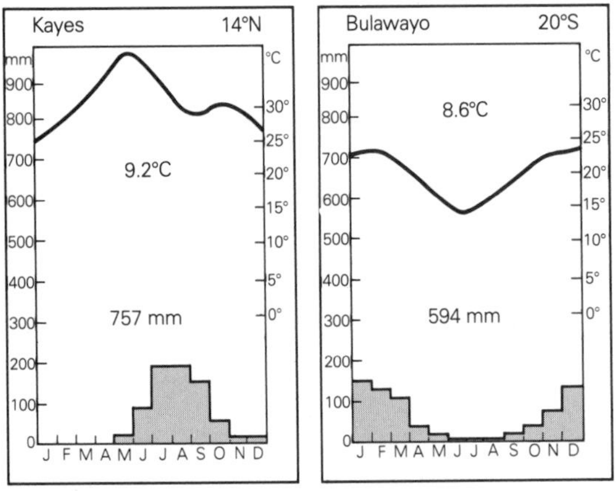

Fig. 1.49 Africa – two examples of tropical climate

ranges (up to 8°C) are greater. They differ most in the annual distribution and amount of rainfall varying from 2 030 mm on equatorial margins to 380 mm towards semi-deserts. The characteristic wet and dry seasons are caused by the north-south shifts of the rain belts over Africa. In West Africa a dry season dominated by the Harmattan (November-March) is followed by a generally cooler, rainy period brought by the south-west monsoons.[1] In East Africa

[1] Nearer the equator the hottest months occur in March or April and September or October as the sun apparently crosses the equator.

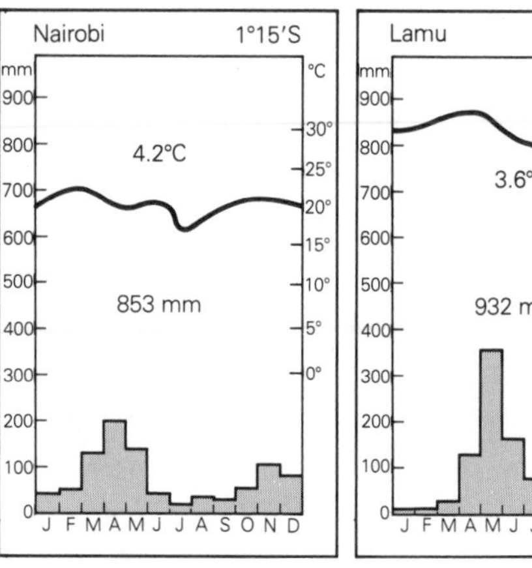

Fig. 1.50 Two examples of modified tropical climate. Nairobi's temperatures are reduced by approximately 10°C since it stands at 1 670 m, and its double rainfall maxima is caused by the North-East and South-East Trades; Lamu has an exaggerated 'Long Rains' due to on-shore South-East Trades (see Fig. 1.43).

double rainfall maxima occur (March–April, September–October) brought by the north-east and south-east trade winds. Tropical climates thus display both dry, semi-desert conditions and rainy periods of almost equatorial intensity.

Modification due to altitude occurs on highland regions throughout East and Central Africa and in West Africa. Temperatures are lowered by 8° to 11°C to annual averages of between 18° and 21°C although annual and diurnal ranges remain the same. Nights can be decidedly chilly and in certain months of the year, e.g. in June and July in the Kenya Highlands, comparatively cold weather occurs with layers of grey cloud and early morning mists. Variations in rainfall may occur within small areas due to the rain shadow effect of high mountains. Thus Nanyuki, Nyeri and Meru all lie within a 50 km radius of Mount Kenya but Nanyuki (710 mm) and Nyeri (760 mm) lie in the rain shadow, while Meru (1 330 mm) stands on exposed eastern slopes.

Vegetation

Savanna is the usual vegetation of tropical climates but there is a great difference between that of the equatorial fringes and that of the semi-desert margins. Three types of savanna are illustrated. Considerable areas of savannah are 'derived' from denser natural vegetation thinned by bush fires and clearing by man.

In the cooler, wetter climates of tropical high-

Kenya: Savanna plains of tall grass, thorn bush and euphorbia.

Zambia: Woody savanna.

Tanzania: Flat topped acacia savanna in the Serengetti National Park.

lands, dense forests of very tall trees (cedar, podo, camphor, yellowwood) with yellowish-white trunks and feathery crowns of branches and leaves are the natural vegetation. The trees rise to 50 m and the undergrowth is dense with creepers, bushes, shrubs, sedges, flowering plants, giant ferns and lianas. Dense leaf canopies restrict light penetration and the trees grow very close together. Fewer species grow in these altitudes but tree growth is very rapid, some camphor trees adding 2 m a year in their younger stages. These forests lie between 2 100 and 2 400 m, and give way to bamboo and grasslands at higher levels.

Economic uses of the environment

The savanna lands were once the roving grounds of vast herds of wild animals but today such herds are relatively few, due to the ravages of poachers and hunters. To see game in its natural state one must go to the big game parks and reserves such as Ngorongoro Crater in Tanzania, Tsavo Park in Kenya, and Kruger National Park, South Africa.

The wetter zones provide numerous useful trees, such as the oil palm, shea butter tree and kola nut tree. Here intensive farming is possible where drier bush is cleared and burnt to plant crops during the rains. In some areas small plantations of coffee, sisal, rubber and cotton have been established.

The acacia savanna provides extensive grazing land for nomadic tribes, but the longer drought season limits the range of crops to grains (millet, sorghum, maize) and groundnuts, beans and sweet potatoes. Cash crops, e.g. tobacco and cotton, can be grown with irrigation. The better-watered areas are suitable for low-density cattle rearing. In the desert grass areas serious overgrazing may occur; here some poor grains may be grown and cattle are often moved to wetter uplands in the dry season.

The montane forest zones once extended down to about 1 500 m, but they have been greatly cleared for cultivation. These tsetse-free areas provide some of the finest grazing and agricultural land in Africa, highly suitable for dairy and beef cattle, sheep and plantation crops. Settlement is dense and crops are grown for subsistence and cash. In the East African highlands, cultivation is extended above 2 400 m and even some exotic forest areas are being cleared.

Semi-arid and desert regions

Climate

These are regions of low rainfall and high evaporation. Semi-desert regions receive between 380 and 500 mm of rain a year, but the air is usually very dry and sultry. True deserts display climatic extremes of

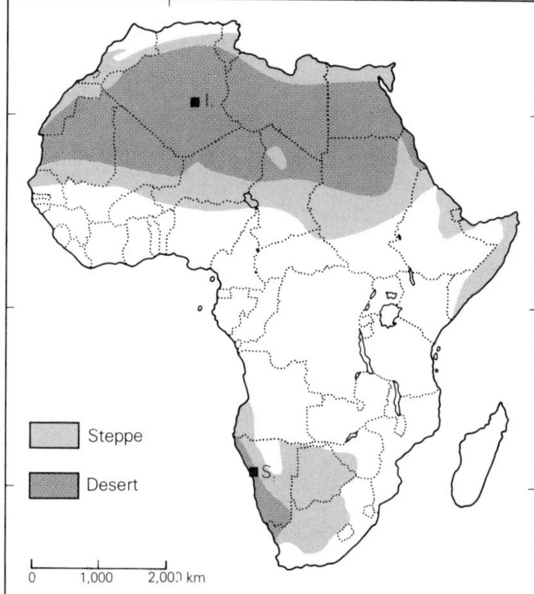

Fig. 1.51 Africa – the semi-arid and desert regions

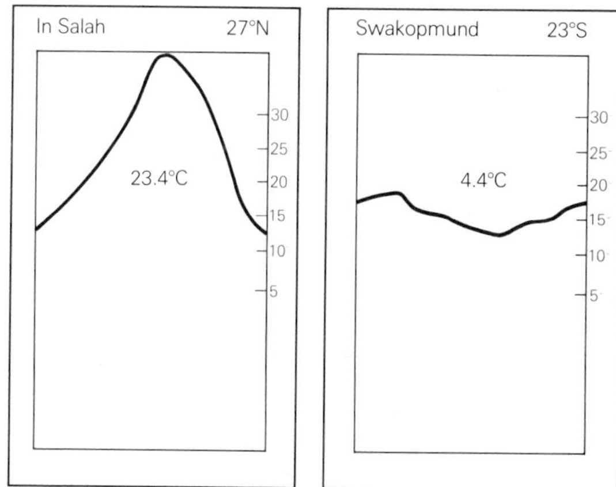

Fig. 1.52 Two examples of desert climate

Upper Volta: Sahel savanna.

58°C in the shade during the daytime in the hot season, falling to 4°C at night, while mean annual temperatures vary between 10° and 35°C. Skies are cloudless and burning hot days give way to clear, sparkling cold nights, when rapid radiation often produces frost. The irregular rainfall is usually below 250 mm a year, and evaporation rates are so high that falling rain may never reach the ground.

Vegetation

In semi-arid regions cacti, bunch grass, small woody plants and patches of dry, short grass occur, with an outburst of flowering plants during brief rain storms. Flowers derived from wind-borne seeds may appear briefly in true desert areas.

Economic uses of the environment

The semi-deserts may be used briefly by herders in a particular rainy season. In the deserts cultivation is non-existent except at oases. The Sahara, however, is the centre of intense economic interest in view of the many mineral reserves it contains (see Chapter Nine).

Mediterranean regions

Climate

The Mediterranean climate displays part desert and part cool temperate influences. Hot, dry summers about three months long give way to the light showers and cooler temperatures of autumn, winter and spring. Great variation is caused by altitude; in the Atlas ranges 150 mm of rain may fall annually with snow in winter, while coastal zones receive less than 500 mm in dry years. Summers are hot (24°C August) and sunny, but winters are cool (13°C January) with many clouds, damp air and rain. In the Plateau of Shotts the altitude creates cold winters with frost, bitter winds and snow storms; the summers are desert-like, with cool nights and hot days with clear, cloudless skies.

In the southern Cape the hottest, cloudless period is in January and February with temperatures in the 22°–26°C range; these drop to 13°C during the cool season (June–August) when skies are overcast and blustery rainstorms are brought by westerly air streams.

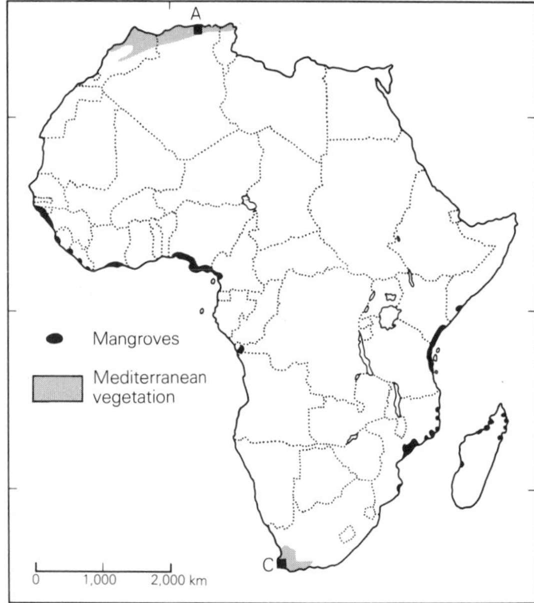

Fig. 1.53 The regions of Mediterranean vegetation and mangroves – both are a response to a limited climatic environment

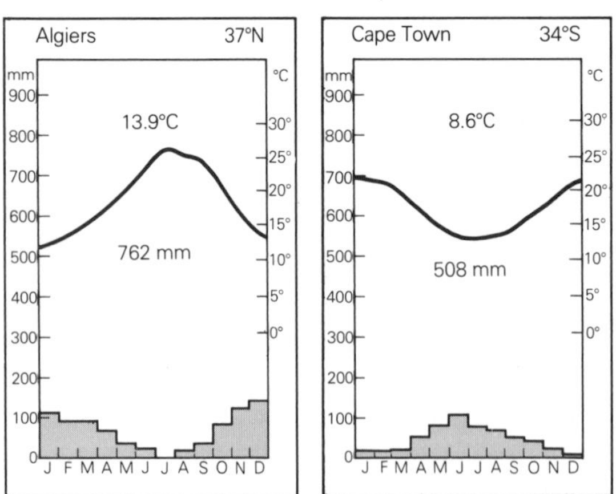

Fig. 1.54 Two examples of Mediterranean climate

Vegetation

This varies with altitude, rainfall amount and the length of the dry season. The higher Atlas are clothed with open forests of medium-sized cork oak, cedar, ordinary oak, Spanish Chestnut, pine and fir trees, and short grass slopes. In the lower valleys and hills small trees and bushes, such as brambles, myrtle, clematis and wild rose, often form impenetrable thickets. This type of vegetation is referred to as *maquis*.

Economic uses of the environment

The Atlas forests produce cork, timber and esparto grass. Here cereals and potatoes are grown and sheep, goats and cattle grazed. The lowlands produce wheat, citrus fruit, olives, grapes and vegetables, as well as supporting livestock. Parts of these regions were settled by European farmers (see Chapter Five).

The high veld grasslands

Climate

This is a temperate interior or continental climate with low temperatures for Africa, ranging between 10° and 18°C with a frost risk during cool season nights (late May to mid-August). Rainfall ranges from about 760 mm in the east to 400 mm further west, with a fairly dry period during the cool months. The moisture is brought by westerly air streams from the Indian Ocean.

Vegetation

Trees are rare at these low rainfall levels. The southern Transvaal and Orange Free States are pure grassland areas with an unbroken grass cover about a metre high, which withers to a drab yellow-brown in the dry season. Trees may grow along river valleys, in the wetter east, or in high water table areas. Similar grassland is found on the Kenya, Tanzania and West African plateau surfaces.

Economic uses of the environment
This is good grazing land and can support large herds of cattle, sheep and goats with good management, but the dry season is always a problem. The main crops include maize, potatoes, citrus fruits and deciduous fruits grown with irrigation.

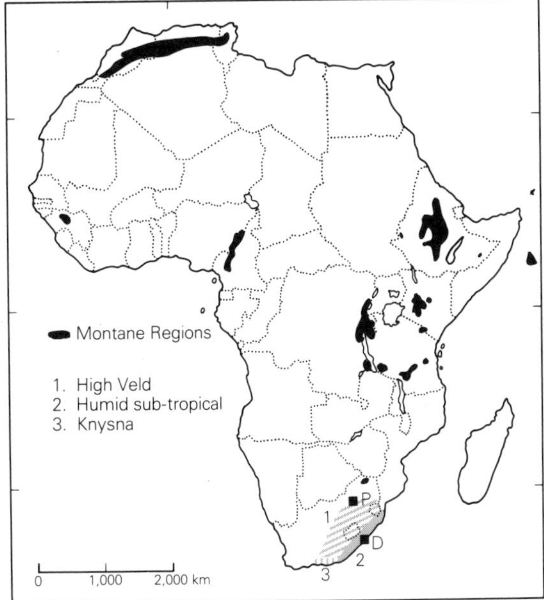

Fig. 1.55 Africa – the high veld, humid sub-tropical, Knysna and montane regions

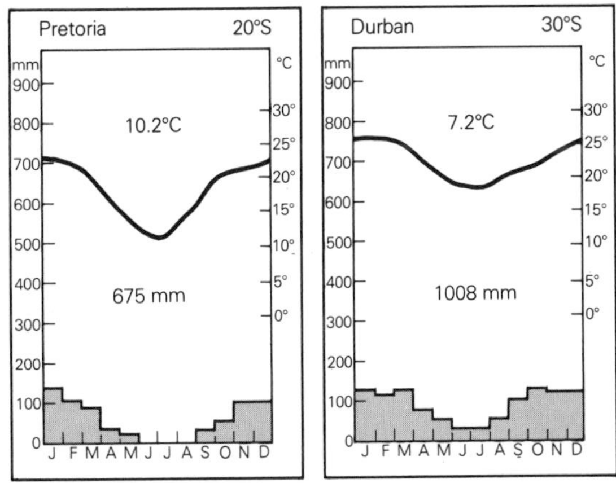

Fig. 1.56 High veld and humid sub-tropical climatic types

The humid sub-tropical region

Climate
This region is limited by the sudden rise of the plateau to the west. It extends along the Mozambique, Natal and eastern Cape Province coastal zones. Here the rainfall is between 890 and 1 140 mm, with most falling during the summer (November–April). Temperatures decrease towards the interior and frost is a great risk in cooler months. Relief and summer convectional rain occurs throughout the region.

Vegetation
A narrow strip of palm trees grows along the warm, moist coast, while inland much of the former acacia and savanna bushland has been cleared for settlement and cultivation. On the cooler, wetter slopes to the west temperate rain forest appears.

Economic uses of the environment
The warm, moist coastal belt is ideal for sugar cane growth. Citrus fruits, bananas, some rice, pineapples and some cotton under irrigation are grown, with dairying and market gardening near the bigger centres. Cattle are reared in Zululand. Inland, wattle tree plantations and small farms concentrating on dairying and the growing of maize, citrus fruits, potatoes, cotton and tung oil are important.

The warm temperate coastal region (Knysna region)

This is a small region extending for about 320 km from west to east between Mossel and Algoa bays. It is a transition zone between the Mediterranean zone of the south-west and the humid subtropical zone of the eastern coast. It receives rainfall all the year round, in winter from the cyclonic storms of the westerly wind belt, and in summer from easterly winds. Port Elizabeth on Algoa Bay receives 570 mm annually and C. St. Francis 680 mm, although in some areas the annual rainfall may exceed 1 270 mm.

This climate gives rise to a dense temperate

evergreen forest with some tall trees rising up to 50 m, but with an average canopy height of 10 to 20 m. The trees include yellowwoods, stinkwood, black ironwood, Cape Beech and white ironwood, although there are many other varieties. The undergrowth is often very dense with thick fern growth. Much of the forest has been cleared, but that which remains is state protected.

Alpine regions

On the highlands of Ethiopia, Kenya, western Uganda, Rwanda, Burundi and Malaŵi, above about 2 500 m the bamboo forests give way to alpine meadows of tussocky grasses, lichens and mosses, which in turn fade into windswept rocky slopes and ice fields. Even on the higher slopes weird plants such as giant lobelia and groundsel exist. These areas are too cold and inaccessible to be economically useful. The effect of altitude on vegetation is seen in Fig. 1.57.

Coastal vegetation

Along salty or brackish water courses in tropical Africa – coastal creeks, lake shores and river mouths – one usually encounters mangrove swamps. They occur in the Niger delta, along most of the West Africa coast and from Somalia to Natal. These forests grow along the water line between high and low water marks where there is rich, silty soil. The trees may reach 23 m, but are usually around 10 m. They form dense bushy stands with tangles of stilt-like roots exposed at low tide. The East African mangroves are similar to those found along East Asian coasts. Freshwater mangroves develop around lake shores.

The mangrove does have some economic uses. Its leaves serve as fodder for camels in East Africa, the light wood is used in carpentry or for fish net supports, the bark has a high tannin content and the wood makes excellent fuel. In East Africa there is a considerable trade with Arabia which uses the rot-resisting poles (*boriti*) for house construction.

The soils of Africa

Soil formation

Soils are the result of the interaction of the factors so far discussed – rocks, climate and vegetation. Soil is a tangible element which can be seen, felt, modified, improved and also ruined by bad farming methods. Soil is the material in which all plant life grows; it is the loose substance which rests on the upper part of the rock surface and is formed by bacteria and other agents breaking down organic substances and mingling them with minute minerals derived from the underlying rocks. Soil thus contains minerals, humus (decayed vegetative matter) and, in its pores, water and air. Without soil all life would cease to exist.

Climate, living organisms, the parent rock, the relief, and time all play an important part in soil formation.

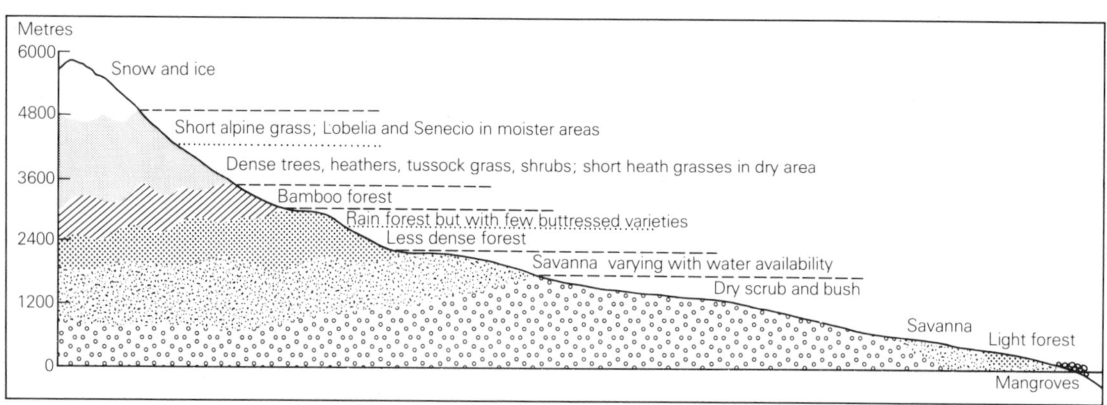

Fig. 1.57 The effect of altitude on vegetation

Nigeria: Mangrove swamp in the Niger delta.

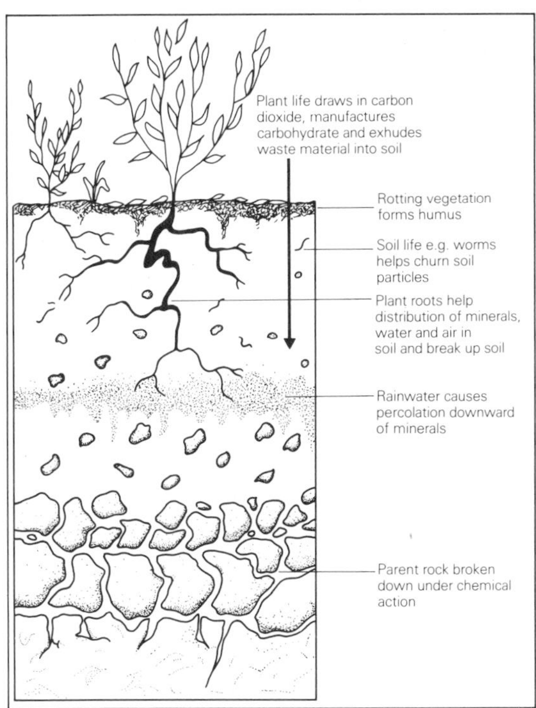

Fig. 1.58 Elements of soil formation

Climate

Weak carbonic acids in rain water, alternate wetting and drying in tropical regions, expansion and contraction caused by heating and cooling in deserts, and deflation by winds, gradually break down rocks to minute particles. The heavier the rainfall and the higher the temperatures, the greater the degree of weathering of parent rock, and the deeper the soil formation. Once formed, however, the soil may be leached of its surface minerals by heavy downpours. But in Africa the deepest soils are not always formed in the regions of heaviest rainfall and highest temperatures, for here hard lateritic layers form and prevent deep soil formation.

Living organisms

Man and domesticated animals alter the soil by adding fertiliser, overgrazing the land and cultivating certain crops. Vegetation protects soil from the rain's leaching effects, extracts carbon, oxygen or nitrogen from the atmosphere, and passes it through the soil, and the plant enriches the soil when it decays. Rock may be shattered by root growth and acids exuded by roots. Bacteria and small organisms are very active in hot, wet tropical climates, decomposing dead vegetation and releasing nutrients. Termites churn up the surface soils, changing the local soil type and the resultant vegetation.

The parent rock

African soils are formed from volcanic, granitic or sedimentary rocks with smaller zones of aeolian, lacustrine or alluvial sediments. Volcanic soils are often clayey with a low quartz content; sandstone and granitic soils are high in quartz and looser in structure. This looseness assists the downward leaching process of rain water.

Relief

In steep mountainous areas soils are thin because of powerful erosion and thinner vegetation cover at high altitudes. In flat or undulating country soils have more time to develop and erosion is less, and it is there that more mature soil profiles are formed.

Time

Soil passes through periods of youth when it is thin and not properly formed, maturity when it is deep and fertile, and senility when the soil has been leached or mined of its minerals by bad farming.

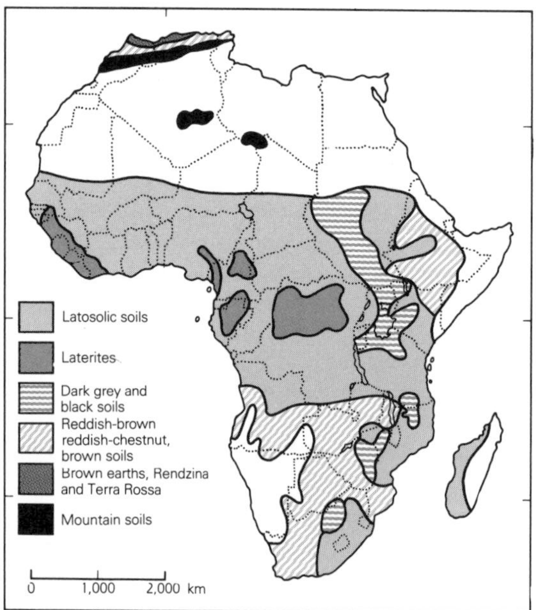

Fig. 1.59 Africa – simplified map of soil types

Deep soils retain more water and help plants and man to survive longer periods of drought.

The distribution of the major soil types of Africa is shown on the map (Fig. 1.59).

Four major soil types of Africa

Latosolic soils

Chiefly in equatorial and savanna regions. Heavily leached of salts and silica; upper layer contains much aluminium and iron oxides, has reddish colour. Soft soil when first exposed but sets brickhard in hot sun. Forms above water table where constant alternate wetting and drying penetrates. Aluminium minerals may dominate surface minerals to form bauxite. A poor soil, acid and lacking mineral nutrients.

Laterites are harder than latosols, often forming a rock-like layer composed mainly of iron (Fe) and aluminium (Al). They are really fossil soils, the remnants of soil forming processes which occurred thousands of years ago.

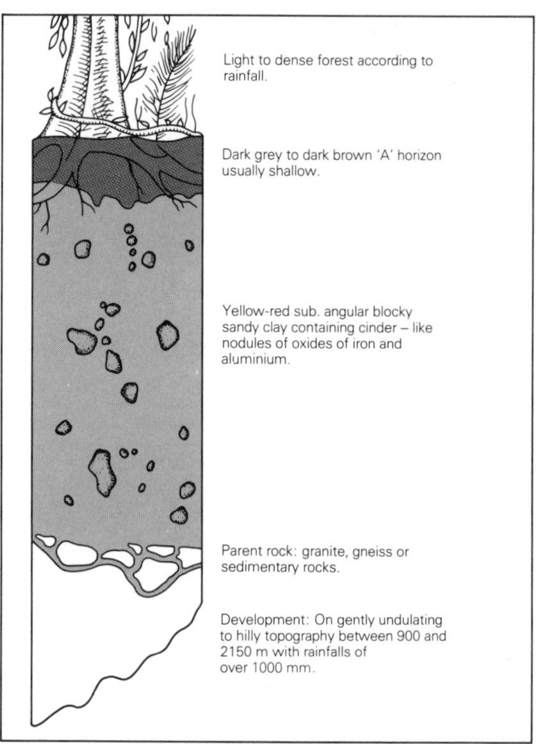

Fig. 1.60 A latosolic soil: sandy clay loam

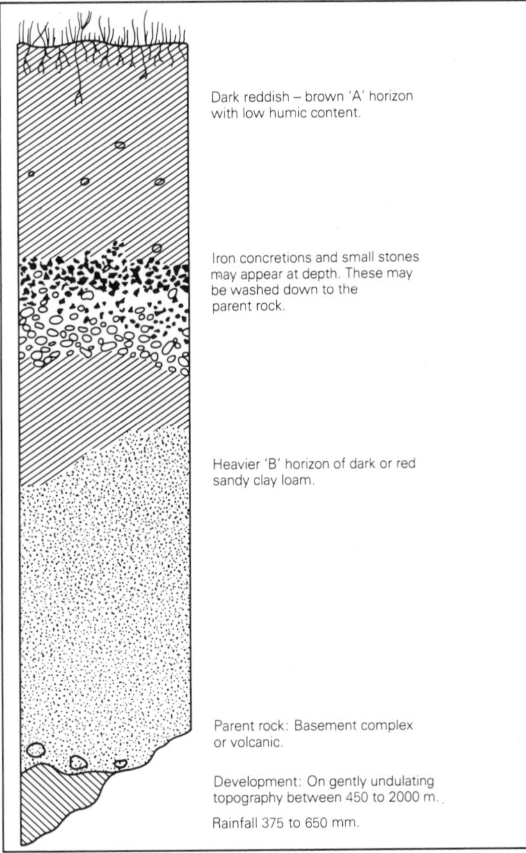

Fig. 1.61 A dark red soil

Red loams

Another tropical soil. Well developed on rolling or dissected land with rainfalls exceeding 1 000 mm and high temperatures. Parent rock – granite, schist or sandstone. Mainly found in wetter savanna regions and not too heavily leached. Long dry seasons check effectiveness of bacteria, but there is often good humus development. Colour – dark red to brown. These soils are fairly fertile; they are deficient in alumina but fairly rich in ferrous oxides and silica.

Dark grey and black soils

Usually developed on flat level plains. Grey and black soils in the tropics are not necessarily associated with dark rocks as they may be found in association with anything from crystalline limestones to granites. Colour – dark grey to black. Heavy textured with high lime content in upper layers and with varying proportions of phosphorous and nitrogen. Physically bad for cultivation – dried and cracked during dry seasons, sticky and heavy in rains; the best crops are pineapples and rice. Occur in areas with between 500 and 760 mm of rain. Sometimes called *Black Cotton* but they are not to be confused with the rich chernozems of America and Russia.

Desert soils

Shallow profiles due to absence of leaching by rainfall. Thin, stony or sandy. Colour: yellowish grey to reddish brown with no humus. High lime content. Many of these soils are aeolian in origin and thus bear little relation to the rock over which they rest. Some are very alkaline where water has evaporated in pans leaving thick accumulations of minerals.

Other soil types occur in smaller areas in Africa. The *Brown Earths* are dark brown, loamy to sandy, are generally leached of potash and nitrogen and are only moderately fertile. The *Rendzinas* are dark brown to grey, loamy, are associated with limestone regions, and thus have a high lime content.

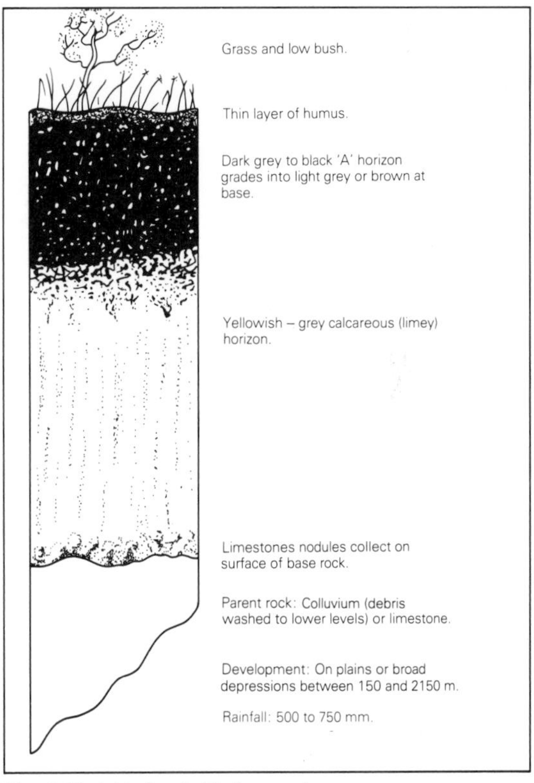

Fig. 1.62 A black soil (black cotton)

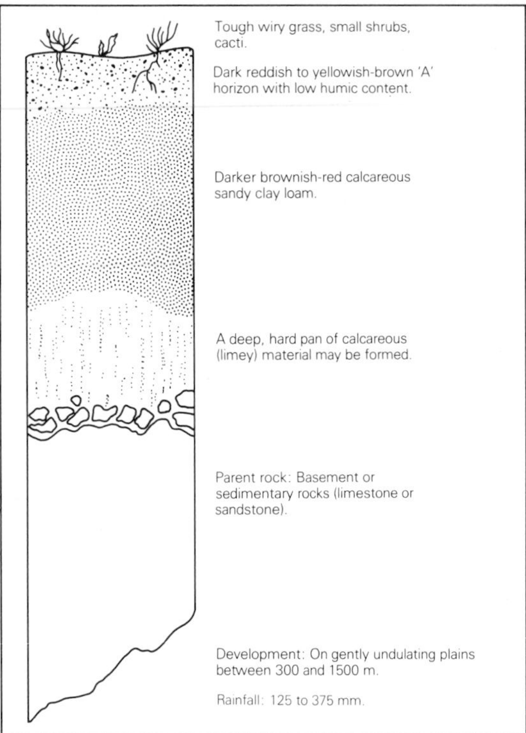

Fig. 1.63 A red desert soil

The erosion of the soil

The soils of Africa are not particularly rich. If food production is to be maintained, this rather poor asset must be carefully protected against the action of natural forces – winds, rain and gulleying – and of man and his animals.

The removal of forest cover

Vegetation removal leaves the soil unprotected. In Liberia, until recently, some 280 000 ha of forest were burnt each year for crop clearings, while in Ghana 1 800 km^2 were cleared annually; already two-thirds of Ghana's forests have been removed. The effect of a sudden tropical downpour on such unprotected surfaces is extremely destructive. A 25 mm fall in one square kilometre would release 23 200 t of water on the soil per hour. Such heavy torrents occur in semi-desert areas on rare occasions and here, where there is little protective vegetation, the whole top soil may be washed away along gulleys, dongas and wadis. In the semi-desert regions of Kenya and northern Tanzania, unusual heavy November rains often create havoc with soils. The heavy falls are often fifteen times greater than the normal averages.

Overgrazing

Overgrazing by domesticated animals on the fringes of savanna and semi-arid areas helps soil erosion. In the Masai region of southern Kenya where cattle need as much as two hectares each to live comfortably, only one hectare is available for each head of Masai stock and the herds of goats and sheep. The grass is first nibbled to the roots and the exposed dusty top soil is removed by wind. In Swaziland there are nearly 600 000 cattle, nearly a quarter of a million goats and 50 000 sheep living on a land area which can only support about 450 000 cattle alone; soil erosion in this small country is an ever-present menace.

Over-cultivation

Over-cultivation will exhaust soils. In Senegambia moderately good soils have been turned into semi-desert wastes by over-cropping with groundnuts and millet. In view of declining soil fertility, the Igbo-speaking farmer of southern Nigeria must reduce the number of years of fallow and give up crops which take too great a toll of soil minerals. In Eastern Nigeria small gulleys, initiated by the removal of a patch of forest for cultivation, have developed into huge scars over 150 m deep, now impossible to check. The constant growing of the same crop year after year removes the vital minerals which cannot be replaced, due to the high cost of imported artificial fertiliser. In West Africa groundnuts extract much of the phosphorus and nitrogen from the soil. Some 41 000 t of phosphate are lost from Nigeria's northern soils annually due to exports of groundnuts. The soils of Lesotho, already naturally poor due to unreliable rainfall, steep slopes and sparse vegetation cover, are being gradually destroyed by overgrazing and unchecked gulleying. In nearby Swaziland 30-m deep gulleys have been eroded by heavy rainstorms. Danger areas in South Africa lie in the summer rainfall zone of Natal on the eastern slopes and in the Karoo, where surface vegetation is often killed by drought, leaving the surface soil unprotected against sudden thunder showers; gulleying and sheet erosion result. (See Chapter Thirteen for further discussion on land deterioration.)

Soil conservation

Soil erosion can be checked by several methods. Among the most important are afforestation, controlled grazing, irrigation, soil stabilisation, contour ploughing, planned crop rotation, herd reduction and the reduction of pastoral farming areas in semi-arid regions.

Forests planted in highland regions prevent rapid run-off, increase the amount of moisture in the atmosphere and provide a source of national wealth. Trees grow quickly in tropical regions; tall cypresses and pines grown in the Kenya and Tanzania highlands can be felled after 35 years but would take 100 years to mature in Scandinavia. On average the yield per annum of tropical pine is about six times that of the temperate regions, due to more rapid growth. In Kenya 6 000 ha of exotic pine are planted each year and there are now a million hectares of plantations producing valuable soft woods. In Swaziland plantations of pine (73 000 ha) and eucalyptus in the Pigg's Peak and Mankaiana Districts provide soil protection and a variety of wood products.

In timber-rich Nigeria careful conservation is necessary, selected trees being immediately replaced with new saplings, while in Ghana, the forest area of 240 000 km^2 is only just sufficient to retain rainfall and prevent rapid runoff. At one time dense forests covered most of Sierra Leone, but less than five per cent of this land is forested, although forest management was introduced as early as 1911. Now trees are replaced as soon as they are cut, an essential action on the steep slopes of this country.

In Lesotho a soil conservation programme has been in operation since 1936. Even so, soil erosion and expanding cultivation have reduced the available arable land to about one-eighth of the country's area. Graded terraces, dams, water disposal spillways, and contour buffer grass strips in mountain areas are all in use. More than 200 000 ha have been terraced, nearly 300 000 ha given buffer strips, nearly 700 dams constructed, and nearly three million trees planted, while livestock is controlled in communal grazing areas.

Even so much more could be done. Many Governments have inaugurated agricultural schools and financed travelling experts to teach lessons of soil conservation to African farmers, for it is the farmer himself who is, in the end, responsible for the use or mis-use of the soil of Africa.

(See also Chapter Thirteen for further discussion.)

Questions

1 With the aid of a sketch-map, describe the main structural divisions of Africa.

2 What is meant by continental drift? What are the various proofs cited to explain this movement? Answer these questions with specific reference to the continent of Africa.

3 Outline the major relief features of one of the following regions of Africa, and indicate briefly their effects on the climate of the area you have chosen:
East Africa, West Africa, North Africa or
Africa south of the Zambesi.

4 Show, by means of annotated sketch-maps and diagrams only, the physical features of *three* of the following: (i) a lagoon coastline; (ii) a ria coastline; (iii) a coral reef coastline; (iv) a coast with sandspit development; (v) a delta coastline. All your examples should be in Africa.

5 Outline two major theories which would explain the formation of the inselberg and plain landscape.

6 With the aid of sketch-maps and diagrams describe the extent of the Rift Valley of Africa and discuss the theories regarding its origin. Reference should be made to the theory of plate tectonics.

7 With special reference to Africa, describe the land forms most commonly associated with volcanic activity.

8 Write an essay entitled 'Desert Landscapes in Africa'.

9 Water is the most important landscape forming agent in deserts. Discuss with reference to the deserts of Africa.

10 Comment on the character and distribution of forest in Africa.

11 Draw a large clear sketch-map to show the

divisions of Africa into major climatic regions, and justify your divisions.

12 On a blank map of Africa draw the main regions of vegetation, give a brief description of the vegetation of each region and relate these to the climatic conditions.

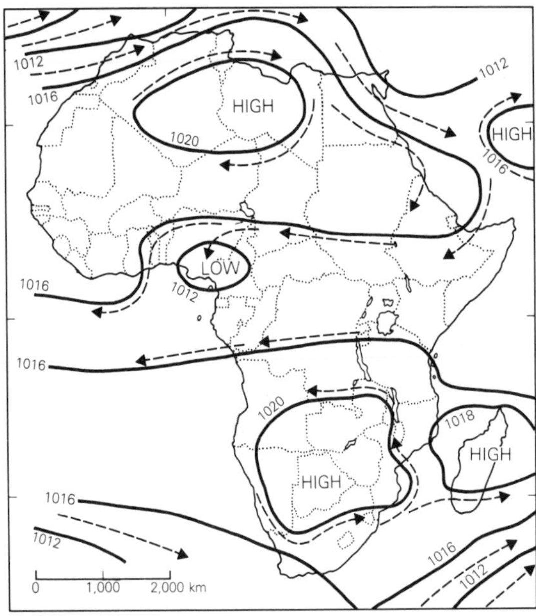

Fig. 1.64 Climatic exercise: Map 1

13 What is meant by the soil profile? To what extent may variations in the soil profile be related to differences in climatic regime? Specific reference should be made to climate and soil zones in Africa.

14 Discuss the main factors, both natural and human, which lead to erosion of soil in Africa. With reference to specific work being carried on in Africa, show in what ways soil erosion is being combated.

15 Figures 1.64, 1.65 and 1.66 show climatic developments over Africa on three separate days in one year. For each, write a description of the climatic conditions similar to that for Fig. 1.38.

Discussion topics

The following is a list of topics which would provide the basis for group discussion, essays or additional notes:

1 The structure of the southern continents and their apparent relationship to one another.

2 Local weather conditions and their relationship to general climatic controls, and to influences affecting the climate of the country as a whole.

3 Which is most important in soil development – parent rock, climate or vegetation?

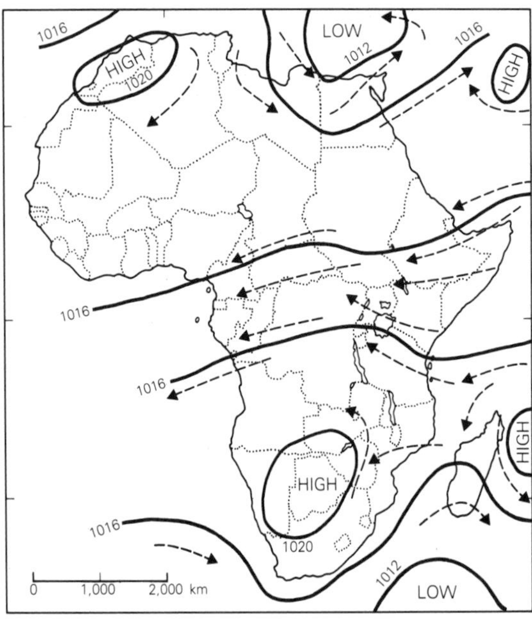

Fig. 1.65 Climatic exercise: Map 2

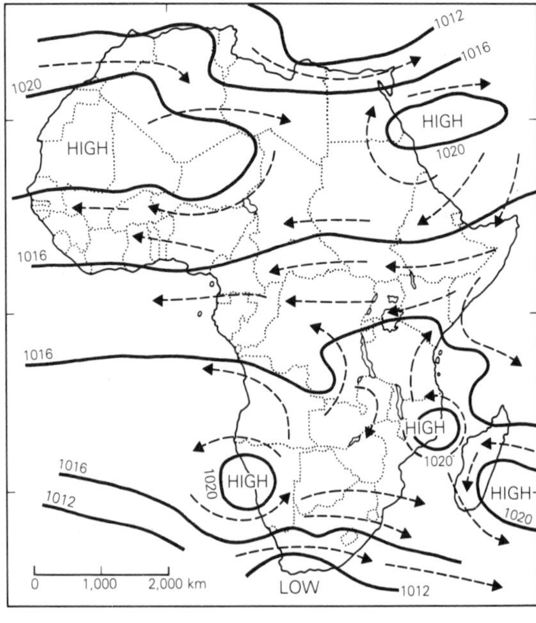

Fig. 1.66 Climatic exercise: Map 3

Practical work

Examining bodies are tending to attach increasing importance to questions which demand evidence of a student's fieldwork and first-hand knowledge of a subject. Typical questions on physical geography might be:

1 Discuss the soil type and vegetation of two contrasted areas with which you are familiar *in the field.*

2 Describe a soil survey which *you have personally carried out.* A large clear map is essential.

3 Describe the physical features, climate and vegetation cover and soils of any area *with which you are familiar.* Sketch-maps and diagrams are essential.

The following topics are suggested as vacation work:

1 The study of local relief features – hills, rivers and coastlines. If possible the student should obtain the local geological publications for the area for an explanation of the landforms.

2 The study of local climatic factors and the collection of climatic data. This entails the use of simple meteorological instruments.

3 The digging of a section through the soil to give a soil profile. This might be done in several areas of the student's home district where the soil varies noticeably. Relate the soil profile to rainfall amount, vegetation cover and parent rock. Areas of soil erosion and conservation methods could be located and described.

CHAPTER TWO

A brief historical geography of Africa

The attraction of history for the geographer is that it enables him to visualise the life of man in relation to his environment at past stages of his evolution, and gives important clues to the present pattern of settlement and economic development. In this chapter we shall be concerned with the geographical aspects of man's record on the African continent – the migrations of peoples from the earliest times, their adaptation to their environments, the economic growth of powerful states, the development of trade and the growth of urban centres. Such investigation depends on the written evidence of early travellers and, because of the paucity of written records beyond the tenth century A.D., on the evidence produced by archaeologists working in Africa.

Early man in Africa

Although still a controversial topic, it appears likely that it was in Africa that man began to develop as a separate being, distinct from the animal primates by his ability to walk erect and to fashion simple tools for his own use. Discoveries on Rusinga Island in Lake Victoria by the late Dr Leakey have suggested that a creature called Proconsul Man dwelt there 25 million years before the present, and that nearly two million years ago Zinjanthropus was fashioning crude stone tools in the Olduvai Gorge, Tanzania. Homohabilis (1,8 million years ago) evolved before Zinjanthropus (1,75 million years ago) and was a later discovery of Dr Leakey's at Olduvai Gorge. He survived alongside Zinjanthropus down to about 800 000 B.C. before becoming extinct. He was more agile and intelligent than Zinjanthropus and is widely regarded as the true ancestor of modern man. In southern Africa another tool fashioner named Australopithecus is known to have existed, and there is evidence from Morocco of a more advanced being called Pithecanthropus. The Lothagon jaw, discovered by B. Patterson at Lothagon near the southern end of Lake Turkana, is of a man-like creature who existed 5,5 million years ago.

A great deal of material has been discovered in East Africa where pre-historians believe that Homo Sapiens first appeared. Here, beginning about half a million years ago, archaeologists have distinguished four distinct pluvial or rainy periods roughly coinciding with the Ice Age periods of Europe. It was in the last of these periods, some 12 000 to 14 000 years ago, that Homo Sapiens was well established in Africa as a hunter and gatherer, familiar with the use of fire and dwelling largely in caves. In the denser forests to the west early man was using grubbing sticks to gather roots and perhaps a few simple tools to cultivate plants.

At this point in time we observe the emergence of different physical types among Homo Sapiens. These included an ancestral type of Bushman who occupied parts of the Sahara, the plateaux of the north-east, and much of southern Africa; a distinct negroid type beginning to move outwards from the forested regions; the forefathers of the Pygmy peoples whose origin may have been part negroid and part Bushman since they bore similarities to both human stocks; and a Caucasian group which some anthropologists have termed Hamitic, and who may have migrated from regions outside Africa and into the north-east.

The economy of these different human groups was at first based on hunting and fishing, the latter occupation particularly practised by the negroid peoples who seem to have been the only ones with a semblance of a settled way of life. But about 7 000 years ago a new phase of life began, involving the cultivation of plants and the domestication of wild animals. In lower Egypt the change was relatively sudden and based on the fertile inundations of the Nile, but elsewhere the change was gradual, hunting and fishing among the negroid peoples being combined with the cultivation of a few small patches. By 4 000 B.C. a relatively densely settled area had begun to emerge in the lower Nile valley, its peoples depending on the cultivation of wheat, barley, flax and vegetables on the higher land away from the marshes, and on the tending of herds of sheep, goats, pigs and cattle. There is evidence here of activities such as pottery making and linen weaving.

In the lighter woodlands of the savanna regions in central and west Africa, negroid groups were beginning to cultivate poorer cereals such as millet and rice, and at Nok in the Jos Plateau region stone tools, pottery and iron jewellery working were known at least by 1 000 B.C. Basing evidence on modern language distribution, archaeologists have suggested the gradual movement outwards of Bantu-speaking peoples from a source region believed to be near the Cameroon Mountains onto the surrounding plateaux, absorbing all but the remotest of the negroid and bushman stocks. These Bantu-speakers practised dry pastoralism and cultivation in wetter areas.

Ancient African kingdoms

There is some evidence to suggest that there was a movement of negroid peoples towards Egypt, and one school of thought believes that these migrants had some influence on the development of culture and civilisation in ancient Egypt. Certainly by 4 000 B.C. the beginnings of an organised kingdom first appeared on the African continent in the lower Nile, and this was to have a profound effect on the development of later African kingdoms. For several thousands of years the dynastic kingdom of Egypt was the centre of culture, trade, religion and political power, its ships sailing round the north-eastern coast of Africa in the quest for gold, ivory and slaves, its expeditions penetrating deeply along the Nile valley.

The influence of Egypt spread southwards along the corridor of the Nile valley to its vassal states of Nubia and Kush. The latter's power grew, especially from the third century B.C. when its capital moved southwards from Napata to Meroë. Here it lay at the centre of trading routes for ivory, ebony, gold, slaves and ostrich feathers along the Nile valley and the Sudan region to the west, and here there were large deposits of iron ore and the wood fuel to develop the iron industry. Cloth weaving and irrigation were well-known arts.

But by the middle of the first century A.D., Kush began to decline and gave way to the growth of another kingdom – Axum (Aksum), noted for its huge ivory market, its splendid stone buildings and monuments, its pottery manufacture, and its trade in gold, silver, camels and slaves. By the middle of the fourth century A.D., Axum's armies caused the final break-up of Kush to the north, and some historians believe that many Kushites fled to the west where they influenced the development of the great Sudanic kingdoms.

Before we discuss the Sudanic kingdoms let us consider developments in northern Africa. Carthage, founded by the Phoenicians and therefore non-African in origin, developed an oriental culture and acquired a semitic language which owed much to the Egyptians. Its power lay in its merchant fleets which sailed to northern Europe, the Middle East and present-day Turkey and Greece, and to the shores of West Africa, carrying cargoes of dyed cloths, skins, hides, ostrich feathers, precious metals and stones, copper and bronze.

Eventually the Phoenicians were absorbed by the Berbers – the inhabitants of the Maghreb or Western Lands. The name Berber is of Latin origin but the original language of the Berbers has affinities with that of the present-day Tuaregs of the Sahara. The Berbers were hunters, cultivators and nomadic pastoralists. Very few pure Berbers can be found today, due to centuries of inter-marriage with the Arabs, but many people of Berber origin still live in the higher mountainous regions of the Maghreb and in the Sahara.

Egypt and the Berber lands succumbed to the might of the Romans, who built towns and strategic routeways, ports and aqueducts, bridges and archways throughout the northern coastlands of Africa. Christianity followed them, but the whole region was later overrun by the Arabic invasions from the east, first of Egypt in the seventh century A.D., and

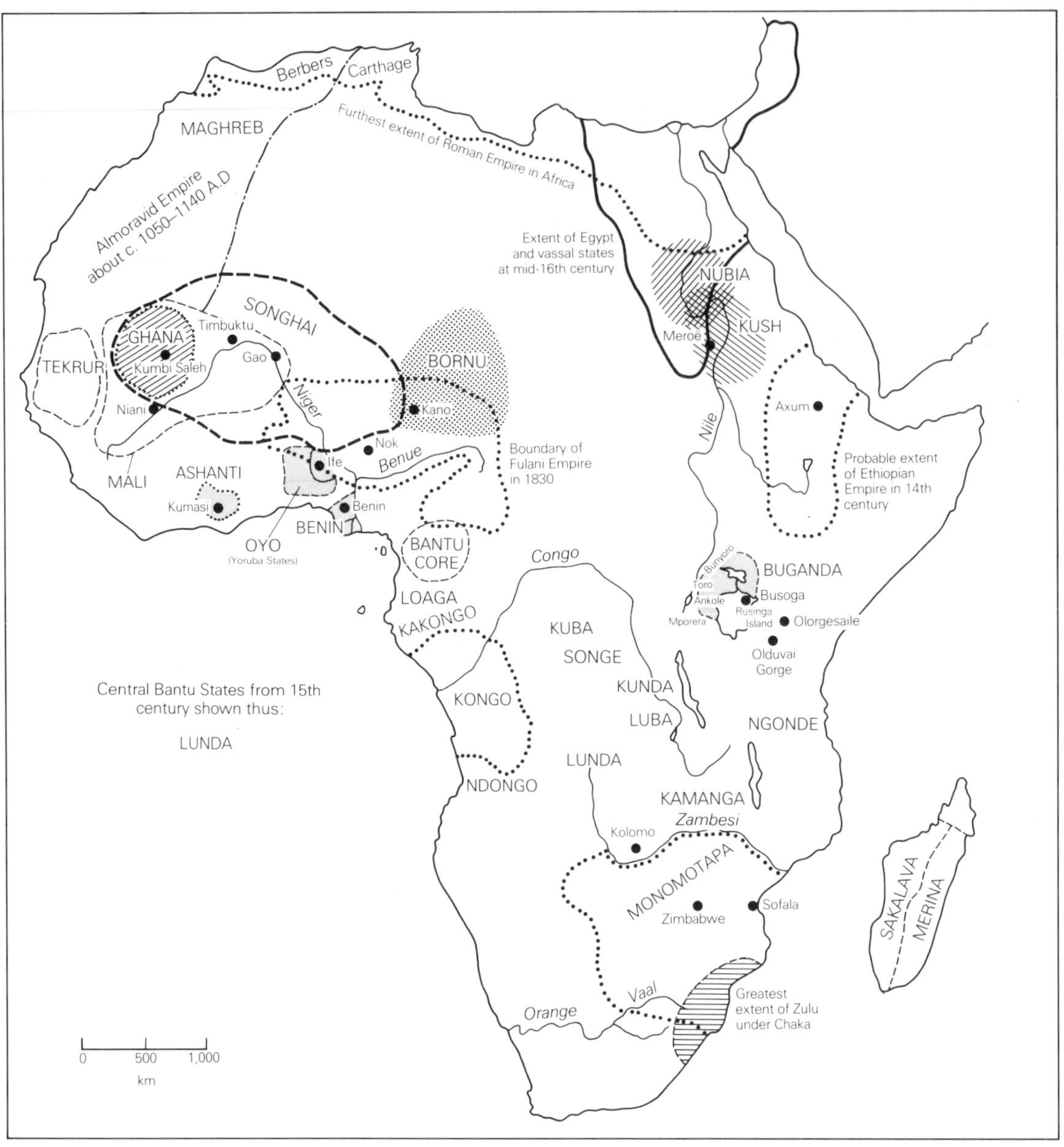

Fig. 2.1 Africa – some archaeological sites, ancient kingdoms and empires

then the whole of North Africa in the eighth. The influence of these peoples was thus superimposed on the earlier cultures and within Africa itself an Arabic culture developed, more associated with the mixture of peoples in North Africa and with Spanish influence, than a pure product of the east. Even today there remain fundamental differences between the Arabs of the Maghreb and those of Egypt.

Between approximately the fifth century and the sixteenth century several organised kingdoms waxed and waned in the Sudanic regions of West Africa. These kingdoms were often quite large, sometimes containing over a million people of different origins and speaking different tongues, but generally ruled by one strong group who controlled the central core of the empire and held sway by military superiority

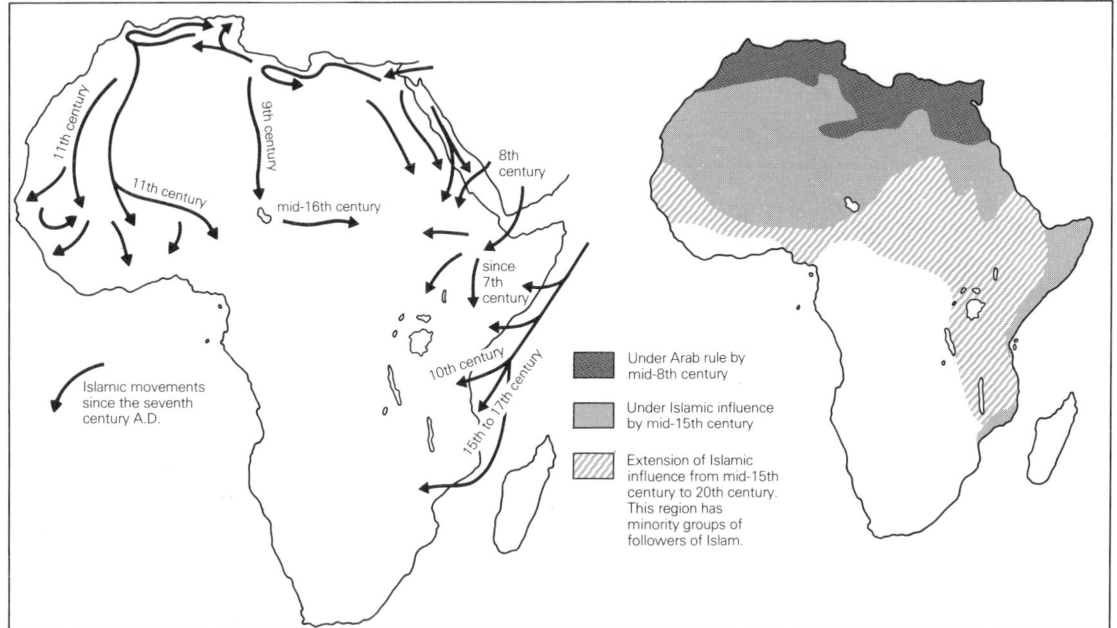

Fig. 2.2 Africa – Arab movements and the spread of Islamic influence

over a vast outlying area of subjugated peoples, for their external boundaries were often ill-defined.

Ancient Ghana, whose last capital was centred on Kumbi Saleh, was the first powerful state to make its appearance in West Africa. There is much evidence to show that this kingdom's cultural and political history extended back to the fourth or fifth century A.D., although the first written record occurs in the work of an eighth-century Arab author. At first Ghana developed as a loose confederacy of states lying between the Senegal and the upper Niger, its ill-defined boundaries expanding and contracting in response to its changing fortunes. Certainly by the eighth century, and probably before, Ghana had become an important commercial centre, peopled by traders and sedentary cultivators. Through trade Ghana acquired tremendous wealth, which made possible the formation of large well-equipped armies to further extend its empire. For hundreds of years its stable government was based on the profits of the trade with nations to the north in gold, precious stones, kola and slaves and with those to the south in salt, and also in other commodities such as copper and iron. A system of taxation operated for goods leaving and entering the country, and Ghana's commercial interests spread as far as Morocco.

The contacts with North Africa helped the spread of Islam throughout Ghana in the tenth century, until, weakened by internal struggles over the division of spoils and revenues, and hard hit by the disruption of trade with the north, the capital city eventually fell to the invading Muslims (the Almoravid Berbers) in 1076. A series of droughts weakened the resistance of the fast-decaying empire, and it had virtually ceased to exist by the twelfth century. There was to be a long period of confusion before the foundation of Mali brought more stable conditions.

The decline of the Ghana empire was accompanied by the increase in power of the Mali or Manding kingdom, whose first ruler came from the small. state of Kangaba, near the head waters of the River Niger. By the mid-thirteenth century Mali's power was at its zenith; its capital lay at Niani on the left bank of the Niger which had been the capital of Kangaba. Under Mansa Musa, Sundiata's even more illustrious successor, the Mali empire grew to enclose Jenne, Timbuktu and Gao, and its power and influence was widespread. Trading caravans came from as far as the Maghreb, Ethiopia, Libya and Egypt, and Timbuktu and Jenne became great centres of Muslim scholarship. But those who followed Mansa Musa were unable to harness the power of the empire he had built, and control the rivalries among the member states that had been absorbed into it. In the fifteenth century Mali began to decline and eventually succumbed to the power of the Songhai or Gao empire with its capital at Gao. By the early sixteenth century Songhai extended over the former area of Ghana and into parts of the Hausa territories of present-day northern Nigeria. Organised armies, extensive trade and progressive agriculture brought great stability to Gao. By the time that Columbus reached America in 1492 Songhai was established as the dominant West African power.

Songhai flourished for about 200 years, before the Moroccan invaders, equipped for the first time on a large scale with firearms, and aided by internal dissensions in the Sudan kingdoms, swept through Timbuktu and Gao at the end of the sixteenth century. Isolated resistance continued throughout the former empire, contributing to the disruption of organised government for many years. There is also little doubt that the encroachment of the slave traders in the south about this time also played a part in Songhai's downfall and the subsequent confusion. By the end of the sixteenth century the last of the great mediaeval empires in the savanna zone had disappeared, to be replaced by several minor states of the Hausa, Kanuri (from Bornu), the Mossi and Bambara. These states had already been significant before the fall of Songhai, and many of them later came under the control of the Fulani.

From the tenth century onwards centres of strong government developed in the dense forest zone of West Africa. Here the forces of Islam feared to penetrate an environment unsuited to methods of warfare which had evolved in the open savanna. They had come to rely on the superiority of cavalry over infantry, but in the forested areas, not only was the movement of horsemen restricted, but it was difficult to obtain fodder for the horses, who quickly fell prey to the sleeping sickness carried by the tsetse fly. This was an important factor in limiting the extent of the various Sudanic empires to the savanna regions. In the forests, kingdoms based on urban organisation in large heavily defended cities and towns developed – Oyo which flourished from the tenth century onwards and reached the height of its powers in the seventeenth and early eighteenth centuries, and Benin, which reached its zenith in the sixteenth and seventeenth centuries and whose king was reputed to be able to raise an army of at least 100 000 men. The economy of Benin rested on its exports of cloth, beads and various luxuries, as well as the trade in slaves, although the latter did not develop until the sixteenth century.

Another great independent kingdom which developed during the late eighteenth and early nineteenth centuries was Ashanti with its capital of Kumasi. Its power was based on its huge trade in gold, slaves and kola and its well-organised army. The collapse of Ashanti in the nineteenth century was due partly to the inherent weaknesses of the provincial system of administration, which had never fully incorporated vassal states into the empire and given them a sense of allegiance to it: More important still was the intervention of the British, which resulted in the destruction of the empire's military strength.

South of the equator our information regarding the ancient African kingdoms is less complete. The Kongo Kingdom was the most important of several states in the Zaïre Basin and was well known to the Portuguese. The date of the Kongo's foundation is not certain, possibly some time in the thirteenth century, but it is known that the state was well-organised and sent ambassadors to Europe. It possessed a small well-trained army, a system of taxation collection and several industries – iron and copper smelting, palm oil extraction, boat building, pottery making and weaving. The fostering of the slave trade, intrigues and internal wars among its peoples by the Portuguese greatly contributed to the decline of the Kingdom of Kongo.

In the present-day area of Zimbabwe it is known that another great nation existed, probably centred on Zimbabwe itself. The nation was a confederacy of small 'states' – the Makalanga Empire, or the empire of Monomotapa as the Portuguese named it on their maps. In the early sixteenth century the empire entered into trade with the Portuguese, who took over trading interests from the Arabs through Swahili 'middlemen' who brought gold, ivory and slaves down to the port of Sofala in exchange for cotton textiles and beads. This trade was, however, interrupted by the constant clashes between Bantu tribes in the interior. At its zenith the Makalanga Kingdom is believed to have extended from the coast as far inland as the Okavango Basin, and as far south as the Orange and Vaal Rivers.

In this southern lobe of Africa, records are obscured by the waves of Bantu invasions which swept southwards from the central regions of Africa. These movements began about the beginning of the Christian era and, by about the eleventh century, loosely organised tribal confederations were developing, their economy based largely on pastoral farming. By the end of the seventeenth century the pastoral Bantu were firmly settled on the high veld and the loose tribal associations had been welded into small but powerful nations. But under the incursions of the Europeans, the Zulu and the Matabele, the nations of the veld Bantu began to disintegrate. From the ensuing chaos at least one national identity was preserved – that of the Basuto peoples whose leader Moshesh gathered his followers together in the Basuto Highlands and accepted British protection for the small state, now called Lesotho, before his death in 1870.

Other great kingdoms of the interior include the well-organised Kingdom of Buganda, discovered by the early explorers as the seat of power in Uganda and surrounded by several smaller states – Toro, Bunyoro, Ankole and Busoga – which had experienced similar power in previous years.

Some great cities of the past

Before we discuss the external influences on Africa's more recent history we should, as geographers, take note of some of the great urban centres which flourished in Africa. Meroë, for example, the capital of Kush, was a flourishing city some two thousand years ago. It grew in importance as a political centre when the capital was moved from Napata, and it was a noted iron mining and smelting centre. Meroë also lay close to the caravan routes along the Atbara corridor, from the north to Ethiopia and to the ports along the Indian Ocean. Meroë's iron products were exchanged for silks and bronzes from China, for cotton goods from India, and for the products of Arabia. By the first century B.C. Meroë was a city with thick-walled palaces and pyramids decorated with mural paintings.

In the ancient Sudanese kingdoms in West Africa the towns and cities grew as centres for trading, administration and defence. Audaghost, now long vanished, lay at the southern terminal of trans-Saharan caravan routes. When discovered by the Arabs it was a very large city with fine public buildings, several markets, and was surrounded by date palm groves. In 1076 the Almoravids took Kumbi Saleh, the capital of Ghana. From their reports it appears that Kumbi consisted of two towns some distance apart but connected by housing which had spread between them. One citadel was the royal seat of the king enclosed by a defensive wall, while the other was the commercial sector containing the Muslim market and warehouses. The city covered approximately three square kilometres and had a population of about 30 000 – a very large city in those days. It was an entrepôt for the salt and copper from the north and the gold from the headwaters of the Senegal. Glass, Mediterranean pottery, agricultural tools, iron spears, nails, knives and lances found at the site indicate the nature of trade. Taxes were levied on all goods leaving and entering the city walls.

Although Timbuktu never became the centre of an important state or empire because it was too vulnerable to the attacks of Saharan raiders, by the twelfth century it had become a trading centre of great importance, and it lasted much longer than other cities founded at approximately the same time in the west. Salt, gold, copper and slaves were again the basis of commerce, and the city had many court buildings and numerous commercial warehouses. Silk cloth, refined weapons, horses and camels were brought here from the Mediterranean and deserts to the north, and kola nuts from the forest zones of the south. By the fifteenth century it was also renowned as a centre of learning and scholarship. Today the city that was once one of the key points of the ancient Mali empire is part of the modern Republic of Mali.

Kano was another great trading centre at the terminus of trans-Saharan routes. It has been well described as it was in the mid-nineteenth century, that is, before the coming of the colonisers, by Heinrich Barth, the German explorer. He estimated the population to be about 30 000 in 1855 and noted that the wall enclosed a very large area, probably to give refuge to people from without in times of trouble. Between January and April, the busiest time of the year, the population swelled to 60 000. The cotton and cloth woven and dyed in Kano was carried by camel to Timbuktu (Barth estimated this trade as 300 camel loads annually), to Ghat, Ghadames and Tuat. Shoes, leather sandals and twisted leather straps made in Kano were exported across the Sahara to North Africa, while tanned hides and dyed sheepskins were sent to Tripoli. The kola nut was imported from the south in large quantities – five hundred ass-loads a year – and natron (sodium carbonate) and salt were important commodities which provided employment for many people.

Descriptions of the forest cities to the south are few. Benin, according to one description, was the largest city in the southern regions of Nigeria in the late seventeenth century. The palace quarter was separated from the main town but the whole was enclosed by a three metres high wall of stakes with several gates. The city is said to have had a perimeter of eight leagues or about 40 km. There were thirty main streets with many intersecting alleys, the buildings being one-storied structures of wood. Benin was centrally situated for the administration of the Benin state and was close enough to the distributaries of the Niger to control much of the trade with European merchants through its outport at Gotton. Cotton cloth manufactured in the city, together with coral, slaves, jasper stones, leopard skins and pepper were exchanged for velvet, brass bracelets, beads, mirrors, iron bars, printed cloths, crystal beads and citrus fruits.

Much conjecture surrounds the origins of Zimbabwe, the mediaeval city of Monomotapa, but the evidence sifted so far seems to suggest that this was a great Bantu capital which was first developed in the eleventh century A.D. (although iron working people had probably lived there since the seventh century), and which later became the greatest of a string of settlements from central to southern Africa. It may have been the centre of a vast mineral empire of gold, copper, tin and iron workings which spread in their thousands from present-day Shaba to Botswana and Natal. Its trade dealt in these minerals and also in slaves, salt, cloth, ivory and other luxury goods from China and India, and articles of trade brought by the Portuguese to the port of Sofala.

These are but a few of the great urban developments of Old Africa which flourished in the distant past. Many other examples are to be found throughout northern Africa and along the eastern coasts.

Obstacles to foreign penetration

The existence of such well-organised kingdoms in Africa did much to prevent penetration of the interior by European and Arab traders and travellers. Although the coasts were well charted by the early eighteenth century, much of the interior was practically unknown to outsiders. It is not hard to find reasons for this lack of knowledge. The coasts were bordered by harsh deserts, swamps and dense forests, and there was little to attract the fleeting voyager who stopped only to take on water and fresh fruit or to make minor repairs. Moreover, the coastline had few deep inlets to allow vessels to penetrate far inland without risk of attack. There were few harbours and many hazardous sand-bars, coral reefs and off-shore winds. The major rivers were often impassable for large vessels, due to falls and rapids.

But the main obstacle to inland penetration was provided by the people of Africa themselves. The coastal Africans were usually hostile, associating the explorer with the slave trader. Wherever slave trading flourished, as along the coasts of East Africa, the trader (usually an Arab) discouraged any settlement which might reduce his influence. Certainly in West Africa it was the unshakable determination of the well-organised and powerful African states to allow no interference in their internal affairs which prevented inland penetration by foreigners for so long.

Early traders

It is well known that long before the Portuguese set foot on the African continent, organised trade was flourishing along the coasts. There were contacts with the Middle East, India, Indonesia and even mainland China soon after the dawn of the Christian era. In fact the first known reference to the slave trade appears in the *Periplus of the Erythrean Sea*, a Greek chronicle of the eastern seas, in 60 B.C., which states that slaves were the most important commercial article of the coasts of eastern Africa.

The Arabs themselves had begun settling along the

East African coast as early as the first century A.D. and under them the slave trade flourished. Slave routes ran into the highlands and to the borders of Zaïre, and large slave markets were established at Bagamoyo, Kilwa, Mombasa, Malindi, Mogadishu and Mozambique. The true power of the Arabs did not extend very far inland but lay in the small kingdoms and principalities along the coast, each with its fortified town. Industry was encouraged – the minting of coins, weaving, pottery making, wood and ivory carving, and leather working; trade grew in gold, slaves, skins, rhinoceros horn, ivory and ebony; and agriculture was fostered – sheep and cattle rearing and the cultivation of tropical fruits. But these activities were largely confined to the coasts.

The Portuguese were also content to set up their trading posts and forts along the coasts and nowhere did their control extend more than a few kilometres inland, except in Mashonaland where, in the seventeenth century, their traders safely traversed the lands of Monomotapa in their quest for gold and slaves. But north of Cape Delgado on the eastern coast the Portuguese had only a tenuous hold, and here their interests met with the opposition of the Arabs. Their most northerly stronghold of power lay at Fort Jesus, Mombasa, which succumbed to the forces of Oman in 1698.

European travellers

The Portuguese, however, made a decided contribution to western Europe's knowledge of the geography of the African continent, particularly its coasts. They occupied Septa (now Ceuta) in 1413, discovered the Madeira Islands in 1418 and the Azores in 1432, and rounded Cape Bojador in 1435. In 1488 Bartholomew Dias sailed past the mouths of the Niger and landed at Mossel Bay, having reached the southernmost tip of Africa. Vasco da Gama, seeking a direct trade route from Europe to the Far East, landed at St. Helena Bay in 1497 and sailed on to Mossel Bay. From there he skirted the eastern coasts, anchoring first in Mozambique Harbour and then at Mombasa in 1498, where he clashed with the Arabs. He visited Malindi and proceeded to Calicut on the south-west coast of India, which was his main objective.

The Dutch, too, were early travellers in Africa, their first settlement being made at the Cape by Jan

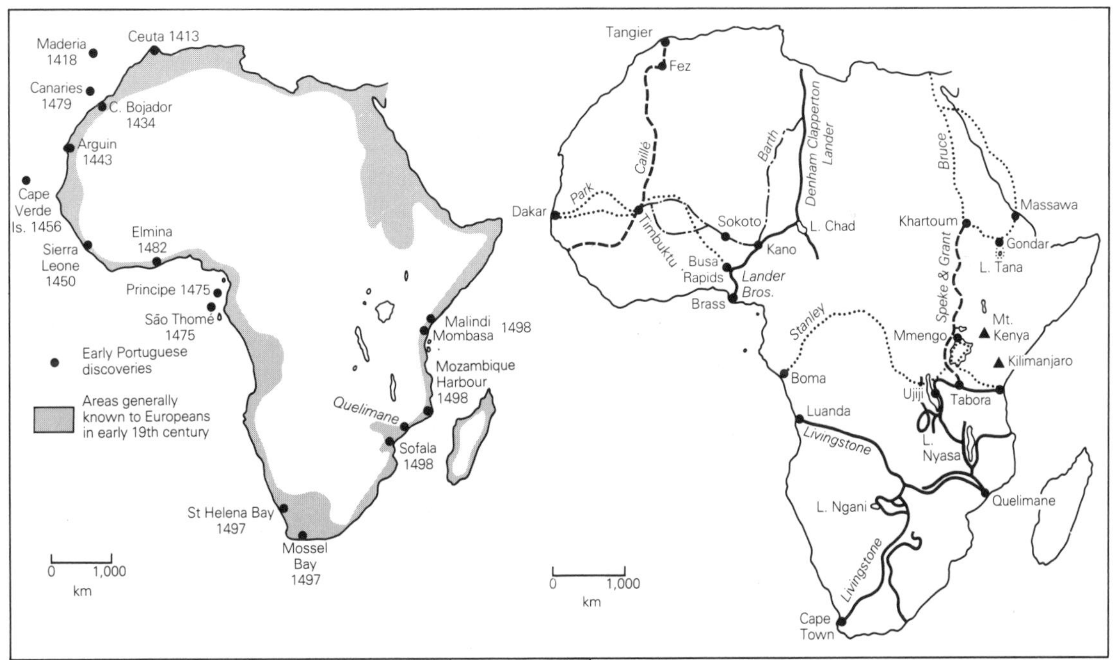

Fig. 2.3 Africa – European penetration

van Riebeeck in 1652. More settlers arrived in 1684 and began to move outwards from the Cape. In 1685 an expedition under Simon van der Stel discovered the Copper Mountains, but it was not until the Great Trek of 1835 that considerable exploration and settlement of the interior began.

The late eighteenth and the nineteenth centuries saw increasing European penetration into the interior of Africa. It is impossible here to give a detailed account of the journeys of individual travellers, but the main routes covered are shown on the map (Fig. 2.3).

European colonisation

These journeys heightened Europe's interest in the African continent and within the space of the next thirty years Africa came swiftly under the political and economic control of the western European nations. The reasons for this rapid intervention at such a comparatively late date are numerous and intricate. Among the more important of them are:

1 *A desire for economic expansion.* Europe needed overseas resources and markets for her growing industries, and each country was spurred on by the competition with its rivals and the fear of being left out of a settlement allocating territory.

2 *Political expansion* overseas and the extension of European culture were considered by some states, particularly France, to be essential to the full development of nationhood.

3 *The influence of missionaries* and reformers who desired to urge government intervention to suppress the slave trade, to spread ideas of Christianity, and to influence economic development for the benefit of both European settlers and Africans.

4 *The protection of nationals.* European governments considered they needed to 'protect' their nationals in Africa at mission stations and mineral workings, safeguard their trading interests, and protect vital communications.

5 *The greater knowledge of the geography* of Africa provided by the travellers, and the greater accessibility of the continent with the opening of the Suez Canal in 1869 and the increased speed of the new ships.

By 1879 European politics were spreading into

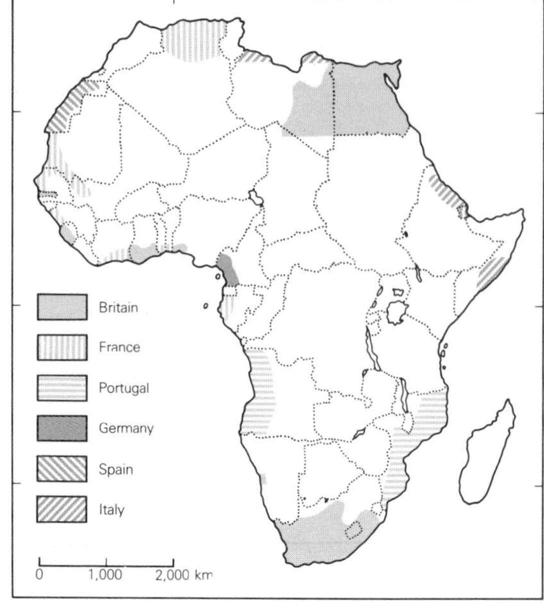

Fig. 2.4 European spheres of influence in Africa prior to the Berlin Conference of 1884

Africa. The interest of Belgium and Germany in acquiring territory in Africa caused a feverish scramble for land by Britain, France, Italy, Spain and Portugal. At the Berlin Conference of 1884 the spheres of interests of these countries were agreed on, but it was not until 1891 that they were finally settled and even then many clashes still occurred. Britain and France nearly went to war over the Sudan and Cecil Rhodes encountered opposition from the Matabele and the Portuguese. Rhodes' ambition was to see Britain as the leading colonial power in a broad region from the Cape to Egypt, and for this reason he took control of Bechuanaland to counter German moves in South West Africa. He also attempted to gain control of the mineral wealth of the Boer Republic in the Transvaal, an act which was eventually to lead to the outbreak of the Boer War in 1899. The occupation of Morocco by the French and of Libya by the Italians in 1911 ended the carving up of Africa between the European powers. Only Ethiopia and Liberia remained as independent nations.

The African colonies became competitive symbols of European power. The Europeans soon came to the conclusion that, to maintain effective control, permanent administration based on a good communications network was essential. For this money was

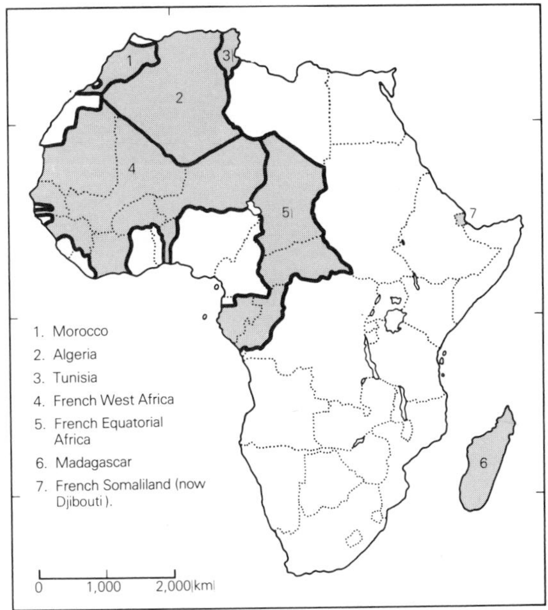

Fig. 2.5 Africa – territory under French rule in 1914

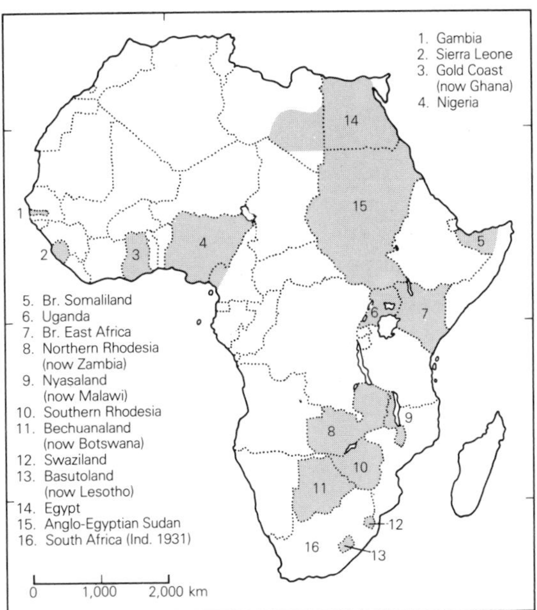

Fig. 2.6 Africa – territory under British rule in 1914

needed, and to obtain revenue for development they introduced new crops, stimulated European settlement, obtained the sale of mineral and land rights to individuals and big companies, often in direct contravention of the land tenure system known to Africans, and improved communications. The railways became the key to effective administration, at least in easily accessible areas, and to the successful economic development and the ease of military operations in times of local resistance.

By 1914 the pattern of colonial government was already hardening. Policies differed, however, from one territory to another; the British favoured governing through chiefs while the French and Belgians largely replaced the traditional leaders with men of their own choosing. Portuguese, French and Italian possessions were considered as parts of the ruling country and, in theory, their inhabitants could claim to be citizens of Portugal, France or Italy, although in practice full citizenship rights were only granted to a selected few. In the British-ruled territories of East, Central and South Africa, settlement by Britons was encouraged, the settlers being expected to play an active part in the economic and political development of the country. This policy worked in South Africa and Rhodesia, where the European element built up tremendous power and dominated both the political and economic spheres of the country. In Kenya the European (mainly British) farming community, although much smaller in numbers than in Rhodesia, also had an effective voice in the government, but its policies often clashed with those of the official colonial administration. Eventu-

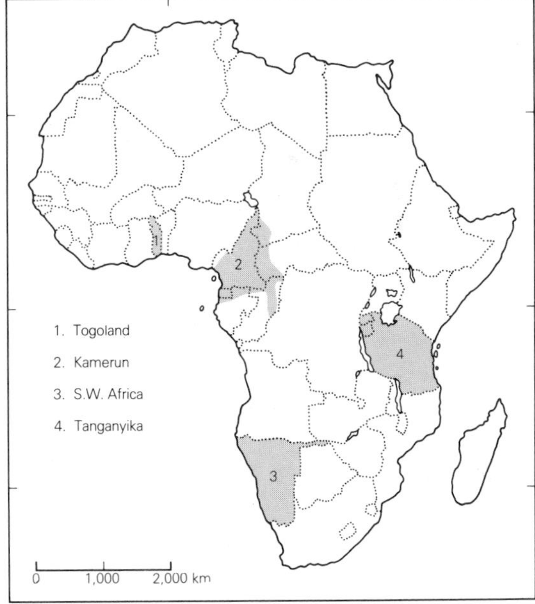

Fig. 2.7 Africa – territory under German rule in 1914

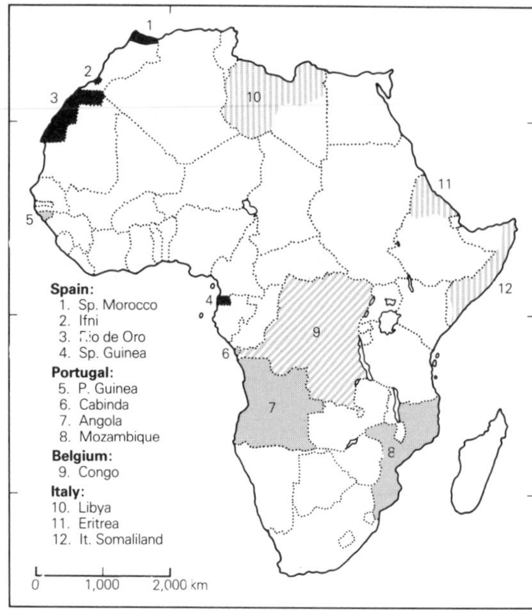

Fig. 2.8 Africa – territory under Spanish, Portuguese, Belgian and Italian rule in 1914

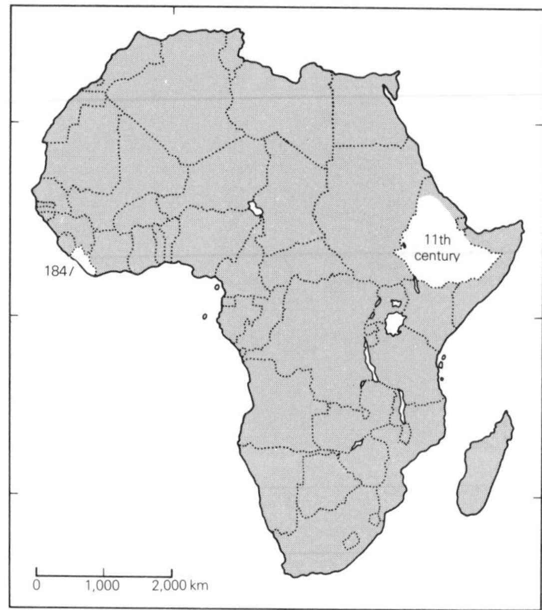

Fig. 2.9 Africa – Liberia and Ethiopia, the territories free of external political rule in 1914

ally this European minority was too small to have a significant effect upon official policy and the move to independence under African rule, but for two decades it posed a serious problem for the colonial government.

In contrast the European has come to dominate the economic and political life of South Africa where, since the seventeenth century, Europeans of Dutch and British ancestry have settled in large numbers. Since the end of the nineteenth century they have organised the African labour and natural resources of the region to found a powerful nation. The Afrikaners are a people who have forgotten much of their Dutch ancestry and do not regard themselves as having any ties with Europe.

The 1914–18 War produced several changes to the political map of Africa. Germany's ideas on running a colony were never allowed to develop, for by the Treaty of Versailles she was shorn of her African possessions by the victorious European powers, her rivals in Africa. Germany was thus the first major power to be forced out of Africa. South West Africa became a mandated territory under South Africa, Togoland and the Cameroons were divided between the British and the French, and German East Africa was partitioned, Tanganyika and Ruwanda-Urundi becoming mandated territories under Britain and Belgium respectively.

Economic trends

The inter-war period saw increasing activity by the European powers in the exploitation of Africa's resources, particularly her minerals. European farmers had introduced new methods, railways and roads were extended into remote areas to open them up for production and trade, and great investments were made in the extractive industries. The greatest economic development was in the south, where roads were planned to form a network to serve the mineral workings of the Rand, Shaba and the Rhodesias. These mining areas became magnets for the emerging force of African industrial workers. But the pace of secondary industrial development in the colonies, as we shall see later, failed to keep up with that of the extractive industries. By the 1930s the African territories were still largely suppliers of raw materials or processed raw materials to the industrial nations of the world.

The Second World War (1939–45) resulted in the exclusion of Italy from Ethiopia (1941) and later her withdrawal from Libya (1951) and Eritrea, although she was allowed as a mandatory power in Somaliland for a further ten years. The war stimulated production in the mining, secondary industrial and agricultural spheres. The mining industries of the Congo and what is now Zambia were expanded, the latter country leaping to importance with its vast resources of copper. This boom extended itself into the post-war years, especially in southern Africa, and the trend has been to invest more capital into the development of secondary industries (see Chapter Ten). The trend in agriculture is to diversify and avoid too great a dependence on single crops such as coffee and cocoa which are frequently subject to the vicissitudes of the world market.

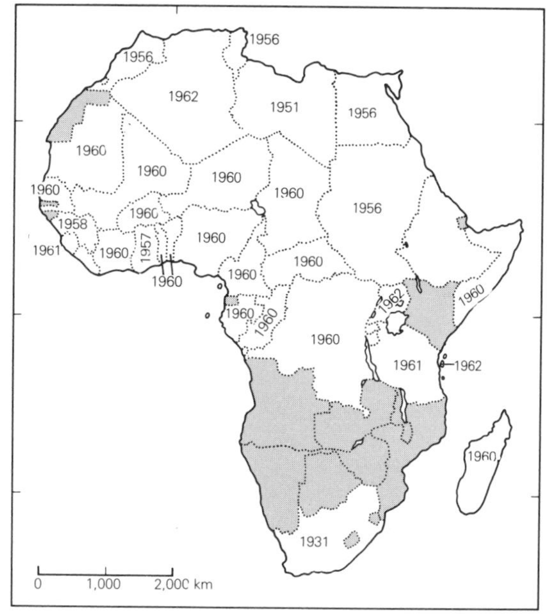

Fig. 2.10 Africa – territories free of external political rule in 1962

Recent trends

The 1950s saw the development of several political trends in Africa. First, many of the former colonial territories achieved their independence; secondly, there was the emergence of the Arab-speaking North African bloc; thirdly, there was a deeper entrenchment of European power south of the Zambezi in former Rhodesia, the Portuguese territories and South Africa, where any move to majority rule was vigorously resisted.

During the 1960s no less than 28 countries in Africa achieved their independence from colonial rule while Rhodesia declared unilateral independence (UDI) in 1965. Events in the 1970s, however, have brought to a head existing problems and have created new ones. In 1975, after 500 years of Portuguese rule in Mozambique, political power passed into African hands. Mozambique, however, has strong economic ties with South Africa built up during Portuguese rule, e.g. the port of Maputo depends for a large part of its revenue on the handling of the exports and imports of the Rand (p. 139); 115 000 Mozambicans work in the Republic's mines and they are paid partly in gold sent direct to Mozambique (about US$16 million a year); South Africa is the only large potential customer for the power generated by the Cabora Bassa scheme.

The position in Angola, which gained its independence in November, 1975 from Portuguese rule, has been aggravated by civil war between major tribal and political groups and by the interference of outside power blocs. To the south, South West Africa, now called Namibia by the United Nations Organisation and declared a direct responsibility of that body, is still under the control of South Africa under a mandate granted by the old League of Nations, a defunct body. The South African policy is to grant independence in terms of the Turnhalle Conference held in Windhoek.

In central Africa political considerations continue to hamper economic development. The closure of the Rhodesia–Zambia border deprived Zambia of a natural outlet for her copper and resulted in a considerable loss of revenue to Zimbabwe's transport concerns. Zambia's alternative outlets (see p. 187) are at best unreliable due to port congestion and civil war. Rhodesia lost the use of Mozambique's ports since that country became independent and closed its borders and had to build an alternative rail route to South Africa (p. 105).

Further north, the rival claims of Morocco and Algeria to Spanish Sahara, which possesses some of the world's richest deposits of phosphates, have been resolved in 1975 by Spain's transfer of the territory to Moroccan and Mauritanian rule. On the Red Sea coast the granting of independence by France to the

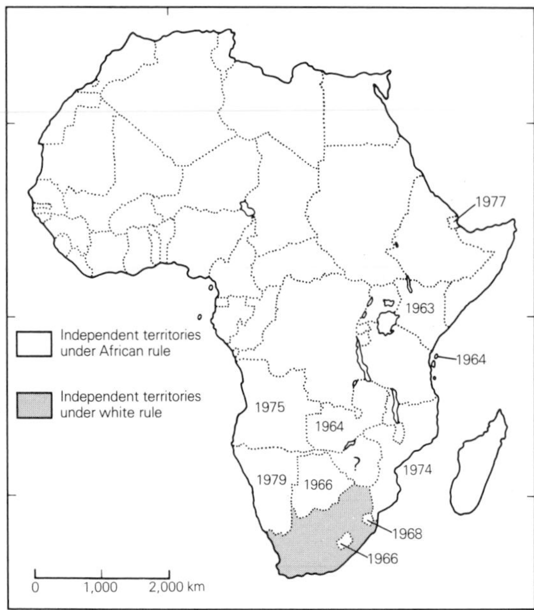

Fig. 2.11 Africa – the political picture in 1979

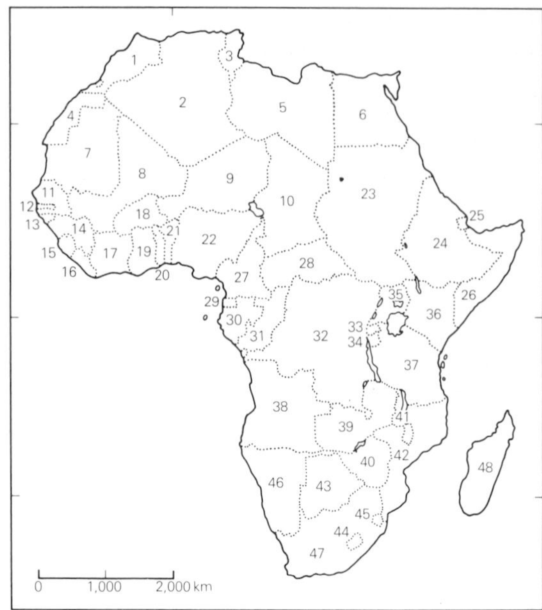

Fig. 2.12 Africa – the 48 states in 1979[1]

1 Morocco
2 Algeria
3 Tunisia
4 Former Spanish Sahara[2]
5 Libya
6 Egypt
7 Mauritania
8 Mali
9 Niger
10 Chad
11 Senegal
12 Gambia
13 Guinea Bissau
14 Guinea
15 Sierra Leone
16 Liberia
17 Ivory Coast
18 Upper Volta
19 Ghana
20 Togo
21 Benin
22 Nigeria
23 Sudan
24 Ethiopia
25 Djibouti
26 Somalia
27 Cameroon
28 Central African Republic
29 Equatorial Guinea
30 Gabon
31 Peoples' Republic of the Congo
32 Zaïre
33 Rwanda
34 Burundi
35 Uganda
36 Kenya
37 Tanzania
38 Angola
39 Zambia
40 Zimbabwe
41 Malaŵi
42 Mozambique
43 Botswana
44 Lesotho
45 Swaziland
46 South West Africa (Namibia)
47 South Africa
48 Malagasy Republic

[1]The Transkei was granted full independence by the South African Government in 1976, but this is not recognised by the United Nations.

[2]Under Moroccan and Mauritanian administration.

State of Afars and Issas was accomplished in 1977, although there appears less likelihood of Ethiopia granting a separate existence to her Eritrean province where there is a strong separatist movement. The opening of the Suez Canal and the return of the Sinai oilfields to Egypt by Israel may promote a measure of peaceful co-existence in that region. Other zones of friction which have erupted in the 1970s have been along the borders of Angola and Shaba Province in Zaïre, in the Western Sahara along the borders of Algeria and the former Spanish Sahara, along the Sudan–Ethiopia–Somalia borders, and in the frontier zone between Namibia and Angola.

Conclusion

The last 25 years have seen the emergence of over forty new nations in Africa. It is as yet too early to predict whether these nations will continue in their present form. Africa is a continent which has been subject to outside pressures and influences since the earliest times of the Arab influx, and more so during this present century. Will these new nations succumb to new forms of exploitation or become spheres of interest and influence for external forces? These questions can only be answered by the geographers and historians of the future. Many African nations are rightly suspicious of any offers of aid from external sources and fear a more subtle form of exploitation, a fear which has led to a general policy of non-alignment.

This does not necessarily mean, however, that the nations of Europe should play a decreasing role in the economic development of Africa. On the contrary, the two continents have many incentives to encourage mutual co-operation in seeking solutions to their respective economic problems. Of all the world's continents they are the two which have had the greatest contact with one another down the ages, geographically they lie close to each other, while over seventy years of colonial rule have left their imprint on the laws, administration, culture and language of the new African states, and on the pattern of development of their social services. Moreover, 60 per cent of Africa's trade is with Europe.

Yet the closer association between these two continents should not be between individual nations, but should take place within the framework of regional organisations (see Chapter Twelve) so that no one country can dominate another. This aid on a regional basis has been advocated by the Council of Europe as long ago as 1957, but its inception presupposes closer co-operation between the nations of Europe themselves.

CHAPTER THREE

Population – Growth, distribution, structure and problems

Population growth: estimates and censuses

A United Nations estimate made in 1976 stated the population of Africa to be 413 million. With an average annual increase of 2,6 per cent the figure for 1978 stands at 440 million or slightly over 10 per cent of the world's total population. At this growth rate Africa's population will have doubled within 27 years and by the year 2000 there will be 815 million people living on the continent. Africa's birth rate of 45 per thousand is the highest of all the continents (compare Latin America's 36 per thousand, Asia's 32, North America and Europe's 15) and is far above the world average of 30 per thousand. The annual growth rate of 2,6 per cent, however, is slightly less than the highest world rate displayed by Latin America (2,7 per cent) because of Africa's high death rate of 19 per thousand compared with Latin America's 9. Africa's infant mortality rate of 154 per thousand is far above the world average of 103, and well above the second highest rate of Asia (116 per thousand). The rate of growth of Africa's population is likely to increase as a steady improvement in medical facilities reduces the infant mortality rate and extends average life expectancy beyond the present 45 years. Indeed, recent population studies have revealed that, while the annual growth rate of all other continents is levelling out and in some cases decreasing, Africa's rate shows the opposite trend.

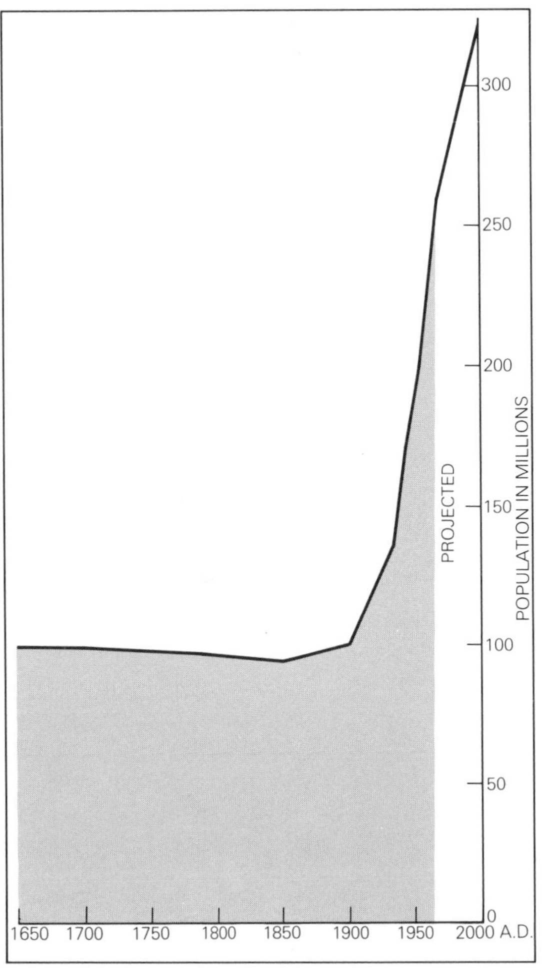

Fig. 3.1 The growth of Africa's population (1960 estimate)

Moreover, estimates of Africa's population have generally been on the low side (see, for example, Fig. 3.1), so that there may be even more people than the estimates indicate. For example, Uganda's census of 1931, which formed the basis for later estimates, proved to be very inaccurate; it was a 'census by assembly' in which the people of each district were instructed to assemble at certain places at a given time to be counted. Thus, the estimate for Uganda's population in 1947 was based on the 1931 total and gave the figure of 4 063 000, while the more accurate census of 1948 revealed the figure to be 4 993 965 – nearly a million more! Again, in Kenya, several factors make many of the early censuses useless as growth indicators and as bases for comparison. Four enumerations were made in 1911, 1921, 1926 and 1931, but these only applied to Europeans and Asians, while Africans and Somalis were not included. It was only in 1948 that the first census to include all the people of Kenya was carried out and this revealed a total of 5,4 million. But the 1962 census could not be directly compared with that of 1948 because of several boundary changes, and the population figure of 8 636 263 for 1962 has since been considered to be on the low side in the wake of later censuses. Kenya's population now exceeds 15 million.

Since 1945 attempts have been made in nearly every country in Africa to produce reliable statistics on population since these are vital to economic planning and, in 1975 alone, 21 censuses were being carried out on the continent. Even though the recent censuses are undeniably more accurate, doubt is still cast upon the results, as has happened in Nigeria. In 1963 a census was held in Nigeria which revealed the population to be 55,67 million, while the 1973 census showed an increase to 79,76 million. The Economic Commission for Africa believed that both figures were over-estimates, but UN statisticians thought that the 1963 census figure was too low and that 59,6 million was more correct, while for 1974 the figure should have been 81,8 million. The 1973 census was not accepted by the present government which bases its figure for 1976 of 78,7 million on the 1963 census grossed up at 2,7 per cent per annum. Those who agree with this figure state that statistics applicable to the workforce, numbers in schools, markets for consumer goods, etc. seem to be consistent with 78,7 million and state that the northern parts of Nigeria, which claim a high population, are not as densely populated as the south. Whatever the true figure, and it now exceeds 80 million, no-one can deny that between 1963 and 1973 the population of Nigeria appeared to have risen dramatically by 50 per cent, that one-fifth of Africa's population consists of Nigerians, and that Lagos is the fastest growing city in the world.

This rapid and accelerating growth of Africa's population is essentially a feature of the last 30 or 40 years, as Fig. 3.1 shows. This steep climb in the population growth rate to the nearly vertical is termed *exponential growth* and is very dangerous because it takes place almost unobserved until the problem it creates suddenly appears, often so quickly that it is almost impossible to stop. Thus it appears that in 1650, that is, before the significant immigration of Europeans and Asians, the population of Africa was about 100 million, but 200 years later in 1850 it had dropped to 95 million. Inter-tribal warfare, the slave trade, war against the colonisers and new infectious diseases in addition to old ones, account for this decline. By 1900, estimates of Africa's population varied from 120 million to 141 million and it was probably around the 130 million mark. Since then the rise has first been steady and then has shown a rapid exponential acceleration: UN estimates give figures of 141 million in 1920, 191 million in 1940, 277 million in 1960, and 336 million in 1968. In 1978 the figure was about 440 million. From a base figure of 95 million in 1850, therefore, it took Africa's population 90 years to double itself by 1940, then only 33 years to 1973 to once more double itself to 380 million. The 1978 population of 440 million will take only 25 years to double itself at present growth rates. This rapid rise is due to better conditions of living, higher standards of hygiene and medical care, and improvements in diets and child welfare. While these things are welcome, the increasing population in many countries of Africa is placing a growing strain on the continent's natural resources and creating serious problems for the governments concerned (see Chapter 13, p. 255).

The distribution of the population

Africa's present population of 440 million represents 10,7 per cent of the world's 4 160 million people. Spread over the continent's area of 30,3 million square kilometres (slightly over 22 per cent of the world's total land area) Africa's population shows an average density of nearly 15 people per square kilometre. This is very sparse when compared with the United Kingdom's 225 per square kilometre and is roughly on a par with the Soviet Union and North America. But it is a misleading picture because vast areas of the continent such as the Sahara and Kalahari deserts and the tropical rain forests are almost

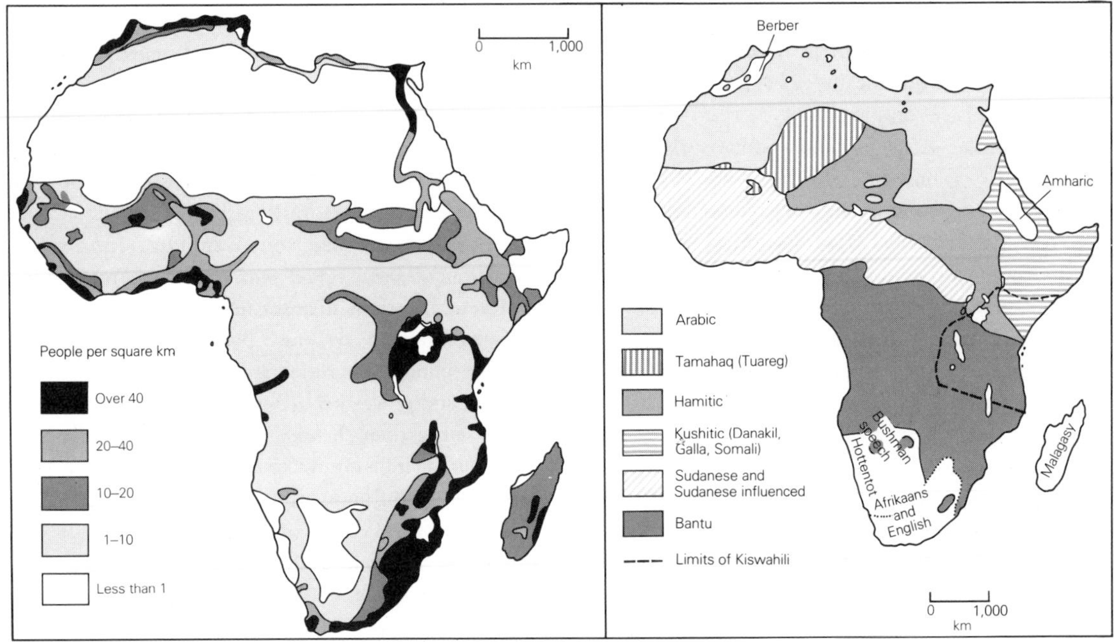

Fig. 3.2 Distribution of population in Africa (*simplified*)

Fig. 3.3 The major language groups in Africa

uninhabited, and about half the area of the continent has densities falling below 17 per square kilometre. Certain areas form pockets of very high population density since these are best in terms of soils, relief, climate, and accessibility – the delta of the Nile, the coastal zone of the Maghreb, the Ethiopian Highlands, the shores of Lake Victoria, the highlands of Rwanda and Burundi, the coastal regions of West Africa, the better favoured areas of northern Nigeria, the Natal coastal zone, and the several islands off the coast. The reader will find more detailed references to the factors which have led to high population densities in some of these regions elsewhere in this book and it is only necessary here to outline the major influences on population distribution.

Physical influences

a *Relief* has three main effects on population density and distribution. In extremely high regions – the Ruwenzoris, the upper slopes of high mountains such as Cameroon, Mount Kenya and Kilimanjaro, slopes are too steep, vegetation and soils almost non-existent and snow and ice prevent any permanent settlement by man. However, in some cases remote areas of relatively high relief may, despite their paucity of natural resources, be chosen as refuges by man. Thus in West Africa areas of the Jos Plateau were chosen by the Birom peoples to avoid the slave trader; the Fulani chose the remote higher plateaux of the Futa Jalon and Bamenda Highlands to avoid the tsetse fly; the Wanderobo existed until recently in the remoter, higher parts of the Aberdares in Kenya; the Lesotho peoples retreated into the Maluti Mountains to avoid the clashes of the Bantu on the plateaux of southern Africa. Such people have had to adapt their way of life to adverse physical conditions. Again, huge physical barriers such as the Atlas Mountains and the Drakensberg Ranges influenced the direction of movement of people, channelling them along the coastal plains and hindering inland penetration. On the other hand, the vast expanses of level plateaux in interior Africa provided few obstacles to the early movements of racial groups (see Chapter Two).

b *Climate* is the biggest single influence on overall patterns of population in Africa. Temperatures have little to do with this, but rainfall amount and reliability exert a tremendous influence. Areas with generally less than 380 mm per annum can support few crops unless the rain is concentrated in a short season, and even rainfalls of 500 mm or more are virtually useless if evaporation rates are high. The vast expanse of the Sahara, the Kalahari desert, the semi-desert regions of Somalia, the Nyika region of central and southern Kenya are naturally regions of low population density. However, people do obtain a meagre existence from these regions – the Bushmen, the Masai, the Turkana and the Bedouin – but their life is a precarious one and death rates are high during lean years. In these regions isolated pockets of dense population exist wherever water is plentiful – the oases of the deserts, now becoming over-populated, and the regions where rainfall is caused by increased elevation – the Tibesti and Ahaggar plateaux of the Sahara, the Kilimanjaro region, the Marsabit region of Kenya, and the Futa Jalon plateau.

c *Soils* may affect settlement over a wide region or may exert purely local influences in small areas. Swamp soils, once drained, are rich and peaty and can support high densities of population, as along the coasts of Sierra Leone, the Gambia, and Liberia. Latosols are difficult to work and deficient in minerals and cannot support dense populations; the low population of the 'Middle Belt' of West Africa and in parts of the Zaïre basin is partly caused by latosols. In small areas man will try to work the better soil areas first and these are the most densely settled. Thus in the Kenya highlands the red volcanics were the first to be chosen by African and European alike, while the Black Cotton soils were neglected until population pressure enforced their gradual use.

d *Vegetation*, the result of climate and soils, can affect settlement in its own right. The dense rain forests of the Zaïre basin and West Africa hindered penetration and the development of communications and, as a result, settlements tended to keep on interfluves fairly close to the rivers. In the extreme southern parts of the Niger delta swamps have also prevented settlement. The thorn scrub and tough grasses of the drier savanna lands are unattractive to most domesticated animals and some vegetation zones, such as the miombo woodlands of Tanzania and dry bush areas, are the home of particular pests which exert a special control on man's settlement pattern.

Human influences

a *Slave trading* is directly responsible for the pattern of settlement in certain regions of Africa. The low density 'Middle Belt' of West Africa, lying approximately between latitudes $7\frac{1}{2}°$ and 10°N, is a poor area in soils and natural resources but it was also a source region for slaves; it was assailed from both the coasts and from the northern interior. The same can be said of the sparsely populated areas of Tanzania's interior Nyika zone.

b *Ancient political kingdoms* (Chapter Two), while no longer existing, can still be said to exert an influence over population distribution. Thus dense populations are found in southern Benin, Buganda, and the area of Yorubaland and Iboland. The zones between these old kingdoms were a kind of nomansland where tribal clashes were of frequent occurrence, and these zones tend to be regions of low population today.

c *The spread of settlement* by the Europeans and the development of resources by them has tended to alter the pattern of human settlement over the last century. In that period large population concentrations have appeared on the Rand, the Shaba–Zambia Copper Belt, and in the mining zones of West Africa (see Chapter Nine). In small remote areas one may suddenly find a concentration of people engaged in mining, as at Kilembe in Western Uganda, the Mwadui diamond settlement in Tanzania, the Magadi Soda settlement in southern Kenya, or the oilfields of the Sahara. Wherever communications have been improved or extended,this has attracted settlement along their routes. Both ancient and new cities have become zones of population concentration and rapid growth (Chapter Seven).

d *Stability of government* in particular regions has attracted population settlement. Thus the Kano region is a zone of dense population because of stability of government brought throughout the centuries by first the Hausas, then the Fulani Emirs, and later the British.

Population migrations

The Arabs

We have seen in Chapter Two that the first large

population migration to affect Africa was that of the Arabs or Semites who flooded northern Africa in the seventh and eighth centuries and penetrated into Spain between the eleventh and fourteenth centuries. They spread their religion and language throughout northern Africa and the Sahara, intermingling with the native Berber tribes of the Maghreb until the two became indistinguishable. People of Arab blood in Africa represent well over a quarter of Africa's total population.

The Slave Trade

At the beginning of the sixteenth century, however, Africa suffered great reductions in its indigenous population due to the slave trade. The trade reached its peak in West Africa in the late eighteenth and early nineteenth centuries. It is estimated that from West Africa alone some 20 000 000 slaves were taken to plantations in Brazil, the Caribbean and southern North America. At its peak the great slave market in Zanzibar handled some 15 000 slaves each year for transhipment to the Middle East and India.

European settlement

The beginnings of true European settlement in Africa were seen in the Dutch settlements of the Cape region from 1652 onwards and these were followed by the British settlers in the late eighteenth century. Between 1836 and 1846 the Boers migrated northwards to escape British rule (the Great Trek). Today, people of European descent in South Africa number 3,8 million, the largest single white group on the continent and immigration into South Africa by Europeans is approximately 40 000 a year.

Settlement in the Cape was later paralleled by French movements into Algeria, especially after 1830. The French government encouraged emigration and by 1848 some 40 000 French had settled in Algeria. This figure had reached nearly two millions by the early 1950s. In Tunisia there were about 200 000 Europeans, mostly French at this period, and in Morocco 325 000.

Europeans spread to East and Central Africa at a later date, from about 1880 onwards, attracted by mineral discoveries and grants of good farming land. By 1960 nearly 300 000 had settled in Rhodesia and Zambia, and nearly 100 000 in East Africa.

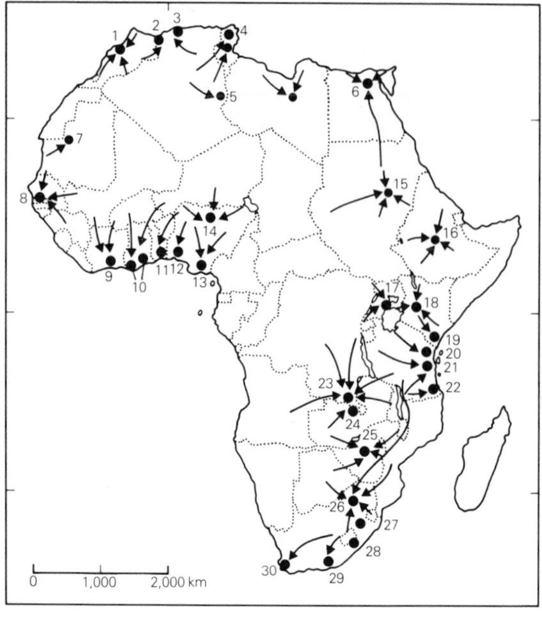

Fig. 3.4 Internal migration of population in Africa (*Partly after Prothero and Dresch with additions*)

North Africa
1 Casablanca
2 Oran
3 Algiers
4 Tunis and olive region
5 Sahara oil wells
6 Cairo

West Africa
7 Iron or mining zone
8 Gambia (groundnuts)
9 Abidjan
10 Sekondi-Takoradi, and Accra-Tema
11 Cotonou
12 Lagos
13 Port Harcourt, oilwells
14 Kano

North East Africa
15 Khartoum
16 Addis Ababa

East Africa
17 Kampala
18 Nairobi
19 Mombasa
20 Tanga
21 Dar es Salaam
22 Lindi-Mtwara

Central Africa
23 Shaba Copper Belt
24 Zambia Copper Belt
25 Salisbury and Mining Belt

South Africa
26 Rand
27 Coal-mining zone
28 Durban
29 East London – Port Elizabeth
30 Cape Town

Asians

The last seventy years have also seen the steady influx of Asians from the Indian sub-continent, although this has been curtailed by law. There are some 300 000 Asians in East Africa and 621 000 in South Africa. The first Asian migrations to Africa began with the need for labour in the sugar plantations of Natal and skilled labour for the construction of railways in East Africa. Later influxes were due to the attraction of better standards of living and the commercial prospects in new markets.

Reversal of immigration trends

Recent years have seen the reversal of immigration trends. With the granting of independence to African states many expatriate Europeans and Asians have returned to their former homelands. In Algeria the European population has dropped to under 170 000, and in Kenya from nearly 66 000 in 1960 to 42 000 today. This is due to the departure of farming communities who have been bought out in land resettlement schemes; in East Africa they are being replaced temporarily by officials, teachers, administrators, and businessmen. In many countries representatives from Russia, USA, Germany and eastern European countries, as well as China and Japan, are now replacing the former expatriate population.

Refugee problem

As we have noted in Chapter Two, the refugee problem is not a new one to Africa. Mass migratory movements were caused in the seventh century by the Arab armies in North Africa while in southern Africa the Swazi, Matabele and Basotho were all originally refugees from the Zulu migrations. In more recent years many people have fled their former homelands to find refuge in neighbouring states, or abroad because of political or religious disagreement and warfare. It is estimated that about 450 000 Portuguese have left Mozambique and Angola since 1975, and about 250 000 Algerian Arabs fled Algeria during the seven-year war against France in the 1960s. About 200 000 of these refugees returned to Algeria when it became independent. The war between the northern and southern provinces of the Sudan caused an exodus of 164 000 refugees to neighbouring Uganda. The sudden influx of such large numbers places a great strain on the host country although some refugees have been successfully settled, e.g. in Botswana 4 000 refugees from Angola were settled in Etsha in 13 villages. Over 2 million refugees live outside their own countries in Africa.

Economic reasons

Considerable movement also takes place within Africa for economic reasons (Fig. 3.4). Many towns in Africa have large populations of African workers who are attracted by the better wages in industry. They try to save enough to buy land and then return to their original rural district. Eventually, however, many decide to stay in the towns. The Rand is a good example of this attraction to industry, for the mines and secondary industries draw Africans from Malaŵi, Zimbabwe, Zambia, Botswana, Lesotho, and Tanzania. In Kenya the main areas of attraction are the central highlands and the coast; in Nigeria the industrially developing coastal regions and, to a lesser extent, the Jos and Bauchi mining areas; in Zambia and Shaba, the Copper Belt; in Ghana the southern industrial towns and the cocoa belt; in Algeria there have been migrations from rural areas to France, and in Libya from oases to oilfields.

The age structure of African populations

African populations are decidedly young when compared with the populations of most other continents. This can be indicated by *the median age* which is the age dividing the population of a country or continent into two equal parts with one half of the people above that age and one half below. If the median age is low, it means that the population is young and is experiencing a high rate of growth; if the median age is high, the population is composed of a large proportion of older people and the rate of growth is low. Britain has a fairly high median age of 34 years and is said to be 'ageing', and the average for Western Europe in general is 32 years. The world average is 23 years but this is higher than Asia (21 years) and Latin America (19 years). But Africa's figure is the lowest of all the continents – 18 years – which means that half the continent's population, some 222,5 million people are 18 years and below.

This indicates that Africa's *dependency ratio* is very high. The dependency ratio is the number of non-working dependents in a population for every 100 workers and is obtained by the following formula:

$$\text{Dependency ratio} = \frac{\text{Number of dependents (under 15 and over 65)}}{\text{Number of adults (15 to 64 inclusive)}} \times 100$$

For example, in Nigeria about 43 per cent of the

total population is under 15 years of age, and roughly two per cent is 65 and over. If we take the 1978 figure for Nigeria's population to be 83 million then the country's dependency ratio would be:

$$\frac{\begin{array}{c}37\,350\,000 \text{ dependents} \\ (\text{under } 15\text{: } 35\,690\,000 + \text{over } 65\text{: } 1\,660\,000)\end{array}}{\begin{array}{c}45\ 650\ 000 \text{ adults} \\ (15 \text{ to } 64 \text{ years})\end{array}} \times 100$$

$= 81{,}8$

This means that for every 100 active people in the population there are nearly 82 people who have to be supported. The dependency ratio for some other countries in Africa is even higher: Botswana 101, Morocco 103, Kenya 104, Algeria 105. These figures are the result of high fertility rates (the number of babies born per female), and the large numbers of children which make up family units. They are far higher than the dependency ratios for industrialised nations, e.g. Japan 48, USSR 54, USA 55, West Germany 56, Australia 58, Britain and France 60.

The age structure of any population is best shown, however, by an age–sex graph or population pyramid, which takes into account the differences between male and female growth rates and numbers. Figure 3.5 shows the population pyramids for Nigeria, the United States and Sweden. The Nigerian graph displays the rapid growth pattern typical of developing countries where there is an unusually heavy concentration in the 15 to 30 age group, and a very broad base formed by the 0 to 14 year age sector. As the younger groups move up the graph into the reproductive age, the potential for population growth increases enormously. This graph displays a low median age, a high dependency ratio, and a 'young population'. The United States, on the other hand, shows a slow growth rate pattern where there is a downward trend in the birth rate. Bulges appear in the graph at 45 to 55 and 10 to 30 years due to increased births after the two world wars, and there is a very narrow base as married couples continue to have small families. This graph has a moderately high median age and displays a general ageing of the population. The graph for Sweden shows a low growth rate, a high median age, a low dependency ratio, and a relatively 'old' population caused by low birth and death rates. Rapid growth countries are at a disadvantage because very large amounts of their budgets have to provide for the dependent sectors (see Chapter Thirteen p. 255).

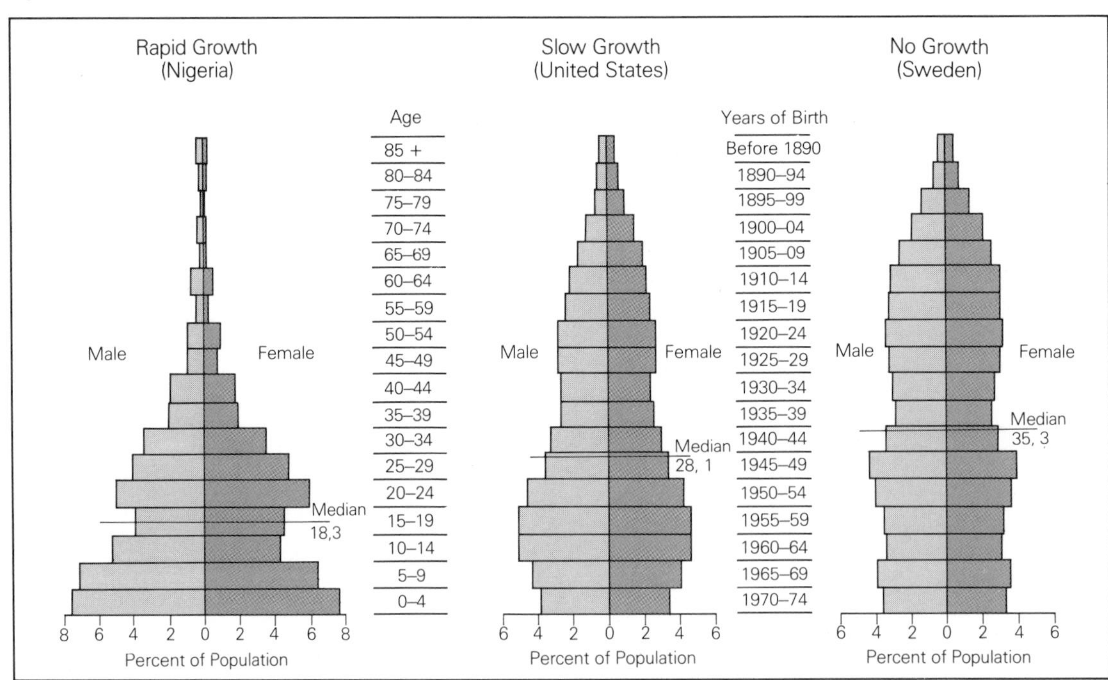

Fig. 3.5 Age–sex graph, or population pyramids, illustrating rapid, slow and no-growth structures

Another aspect of population structure is seen in these graphs – the rapid narrowing of the graph at age 55 and above for Nigeria, compared with the Swedish graph particularly and, to a lesser extent, with the United States' graph. The average life expectancy at birth in Africa is about 45 years, much lower than that of the industrialised world. The graphs (Fig. 3.6) shows that the expectancy in Egypt, Zaïre and Algeria is about 20 years less than that of Sweden, the USA and the UK. This means that the length of productivity of the average worker is shortened and that many within the dependent sector either have a short or even no productive life.

Population problems

The detrimental effect of high dependency ratios and high growth rates to the economy of many developing countries in Africa is obvious. Kenya's annual rate of population growth of 3,4 per cent is producing an increasingly young and dependent sector of the population. Population increase, if not checked, threatens to outpace the rate of economic growth in Kenya, which is at present about 6 per cent per annum. In Zimbabwe the African population represents over 95 per cent of the total, and its natural rate of increase of 3,6 per annum is triple the European rate in that country, and is probably the highest in Africa. The African birth rate is very high at 48 per thousand when compared with the European rate in Zimbabwe of 18 per thousand, and the proportion of young people in the total African population is almost 58 per cent compared with the European 36,5 per cent. The death rate has been considerably reduced in this country because of steadily improving medical and health facilities: since 1900, Zimbabwe's African population has grown from a mere 600 000 to over 6 million today (the 1969 census showed a figure of 4 846 930). By the year 2000, at present rates of increase, the population will be over 15 million, roughly equal to Kenya's population today.

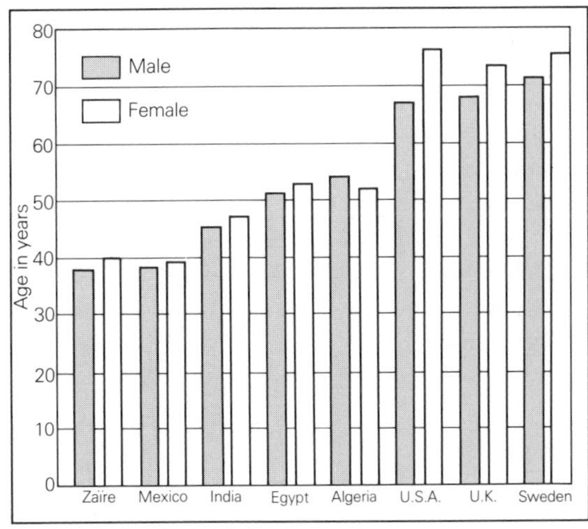

Fig. 3.6 Bar graph of life expectancy in selected countries

Such rapid growth rates place a tremendous strain on natural resources and on social services such as education and health facilities. In the late 1960s Ghana realised that its rapid population growth was draining the national funds so that housing and educational facilities could not be maintained. Over 50 per cent of the population in Ghana is under 18 years and these people are now moving into the reproductive age group, so that Ghana's present high population growth rate of nearly 3 per cent will rise even higher. Moreover, there is still room for Ghana's 1970–5 death rate of 21,9 per thousand people to decline as medical facilities improve. The Ghanaian government's aim is to reduce the annual growth rate of 1,75 per cent by the year 2000, but with a birth rate of 48,8 per thousand there will have to be a limitation on family size to compensate for the planned reduction on the death rate.

The solution to the problem of threatened over-population in relation to resources is a limitation of the family size. Kenya was the first independent African nation to introduce a national family planning programme, and today Nigeria, Ghana, Egypt, Tunisia, Morocco, Mauritius and Swaziland have government-backed schemes, while family planning associations operate in the French-speaking territories. Maternal and child health networks have been set up in 18 African countries and six countries have national population policies. On the other hand, there are 22 countries in Africa with a total population exceeding 65 million which do not have any organised family planning services. Family planning, however, cannot be forced on people. The family unit is an important aspect of African life and a child means extra help with the farming and family work, and a support in old age. Only when families achieve a higher living standard and feel economically secure will the need for extra family members decline.

It is clear that African countries will also have to develop their economies, that is, improve their economic growth rate, by at least 3 per cent per annum, merely to maintain the present standards of living of most of the population. Food supplies must therefore be increased at least at the same rate as the expanding population and at a higher rate if standards of diet and the amount of food available for each individual person are to be improved and increased.

Many people point out that there is still plenty of land left in Africa for cultivation and that only in a few areas such as Kikuyuland, Iboland and the Xhosa region is there considerable over-population. But these areas are usually the best in terms of soil and climate, and any future expansion in cultivation must make use of increasingly poor areas which in many cases are marginal for cultivation. At present the problems of feeding Africa's population are smoothed by loans, imports of foodstuffs and by the increasing productivity of the African farmer as he learns and develops better cultivation techniques. Most African governments give agriculture top priority when spending national funds.

But production of food is not enough. Money must be earned by producing goods which command high prices on world markets rather than by exporting raw materials. Britain, for example, is able to maintain a reasonable standard of living for its population by the export of expensive manufactured articles in return for raw materials and food products. Thus industrialisation is seen as one solution to Africa's population problem, and many nations are vigorously engaged in attracting and establishing new industries. But the pace of industrial growth may be too slow to have a decisive effect; India, for example, suffers from under-industrialisation and over-population. As Fig. 3.1 shows, the next 25 years will be critical ones in Africa's population growth rate.

(For a discussion of population growth in relation to natural resources see Chapter Thirteen, p. 255. See also Appendix 1 for population statistics on each country in Africa.)

Questions

1 Describe and suggest reasons for the population distribution in *either* East Africa (Tanzania, Kenya and Uganda) *or* in Africa south of the Zambesi.
2 What are the major factors influencing the distribution of population in the Republic of South Africa?
3 Relate the distribution of population to geographical conditions in any one country in West Africa.
4 With the aid of sketch-maps, outline the main population migrations to the African continent and within it.
5 Illustrate by means of a sketch-map the distribution of the European peoples in Africa. Attempt to explain this distribution on the grounds of climate, relief, commercial interest and history of settlement.
6 Explain the term 'Age Structure' with reference to the populations of various nations in Africa. Your answer should include explanations of the terms 'median age', 'dependency ratio', and 'age–sex graphs' as means of defining age structure.
7 What are the effects of high dependency ratios and high growth rates on the economies of African states. Compare the ratios and rates with non-African nations.

Discussion topics

1 Discuss the age–sex structure of your own country and explain what effects it might have on present and future economic development.
2 Discuss the importance of regular population enumerations (censuses) to economic planning in Africa.
3 You are to organise a census of your own country. You are asked to plan a census form on which you can ask ten questions. What questions would you ask and why?

Practical work

Typical practical questions on the demographic geography of Africa might be:

1 In connection with any regional survey you have taken part in, (a) outline, by means of a sketch-map, the general distribution of the population; (b) suggest the reasons for this distribution.
2 Discuss and give reasons for the pattern of population in a region familiar to you.
3 Describe and explain the movements of population within your own country or in a district personally known to you.
4 Draw an age–sex graph (population pyramid) for your own country (base it on the last census figures). Then annotate it or write a brief description of the pattern shown.

The following topics are suggested as vacation work:

1 A visit to a local township to study the movement of population to and from the town. This can be done by noting the number of vehicles and pedestrians entering the town on various routes. The exercise should be done on several different occasions to obtain an average, and maps drawn to illustrate the volume of flow.
2 A visit to a local factory might reveal information regarding the movement of people to and from the factory on a daily basis. If possible, the manager should be approached regarding the origins of his employees. Usually factories keep records of an employee's tribal group and place of birth, and maps using the dot method could be plotted to show where the people have come from.
3 The study of local survey maps on a scale of 1:125 000 and less will indicate population patterns and trends of settlement. Simplified dot maps and shading maps could be prepared from the information shown on the survey map.

CHAPTER FOUR

Agriculture 1 – Indigenous farming

The greater part of Africa's population, probably seven out of every ten adults, lives directly off the land either by cultivating the soil or by grazing animals, while some very small groups still live by collecting wild fruits and nuts, and by hunting. Most of the remainder depend indirectly on the land since their occupations involve the processing of primary products, e.g. palm oil extraction, fruit and vegetable canning, the spinning and weaving of cotton, the processing of tea and coffee. Over the last seventy years the European immigrant farmer in eastern, central and southern Africa and in the Maghreb has emphasised the role which agriculture plays in Africa's economy by introducing new techniques, modern machinery, and scientific methods to check disease and soil decline. Irrigation, and road and rail development, have opened up vast new areas to agricultural production, while the industrial demands of Europe and North America have encouraged the spread of plantations throughout tropical Africa.

The pattern of land use

Today Africa displays practically every type of agricultural system, from the shifting agriculture of remote people to the carefully evolved crop rotations of the Igbo farmer, from the experimental state farms in Ghana to the dairy farms and vineyards of the Afrikaner, and from the small Busoga *shamba* to the huge Unilever plantation. Figure 4.1 illustrates the close relationship to the climatic and vegetational zones of the continent. Hunting and gathering and the cultivation of oil palms, cocoa, yams, rubber, bananas and cassava are largely associated with regions of equatorial climate and the rain forests. Tropical agriculture – the growing of grains needing a dry season and crops such as tobacco – is found in those regions of tropical climate with a long dry season, a long wet season and plenty of sunshine. Where rains fall below 650 mm a year cattle ranching becomes more important. In the better favoured parts of Africa – the highlands of East Africa, Zimbabwe and Malaŵi, the fertile lowlands of Natal, and the irrigated Nile valley – commercial crops of cotton, coffee, tea, sugar cane and fruit are grown, sometimes on large plantations. The northern strip of Mediterranean cultivation (vines, citrus, olives) is separated from the tropics by the vast stretch of the Sahara, where cultivation is limited to the meagre fringes of the oases.

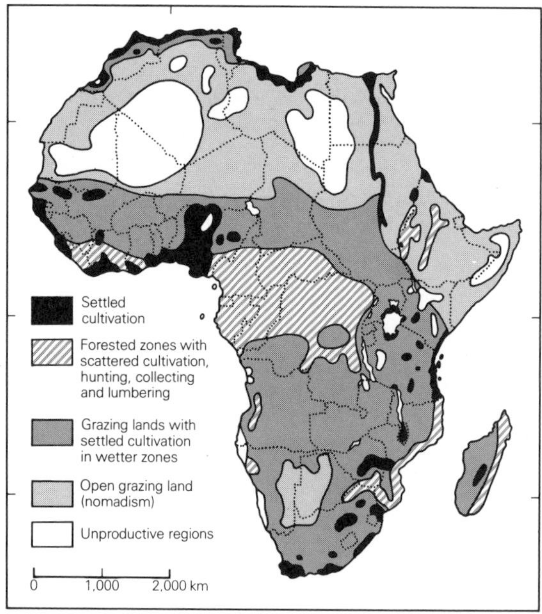

Fig. 4.1 Africa – land use (*simplified*)

Influences on crop distribution and man's use of the land

Rainfall

While temperatures in Africa provide few problems for plant growth, rainfall amount and reliability are of great significance.[1] Some plants are severely limited by rainfall amounts which are more than adequate for others. Ideally, the oil palm needs annual rainfalls above 1 520 mm and temperatures above 20°C; its culture is thus limited to regions flanking the equator. Sisal, however, can tolerate a wide range of rainfall (460 to 1 260 mm a year), and variable soil conditions. But its great need is sunshine and, while it is grown widely in East Africa, it is of little commercial importance in the more cloudy climates of West Africa. Cassava, a basic subsistence crop, is tolerant of wide rainfall variations, variable soils, and can grow in temperatures varying from 10 to 22°C; it is found throughout the tropics and has become a staple food from Mozambique to Gambia. But maize is more limited since, although it grows under a wide range of temperature, 10° to 32°C, and rainfall (250 to 5 080 mm) it requires a better soil and does best in humus-rich, well-drained loams. It is not important in the Zaïre Basin but is popular in the better soils of the Kenya highlands, Uganda, South Africa, southern Ghana and Nigeria.

Economic limits

Besides the natural limit of rainfall and soil fertility there are the economic limits imposed by man himself. A commercial farmer will not cultivate a crop which, after production and transport costs have been taken into account, returns insufficient profit to justify the work and capital he invests. Farmers in central Africa grow tobacco because it brings large profits and commands a high price on world markets; it can withstand the relatively high costs of transport from land-locked countries to the outlets of Durban and Cape Town, and it has helped to finance mixed farming economies (cattle, maize, tobacco).

Pests and diseases

Pests and diseases are other hazards to farming in

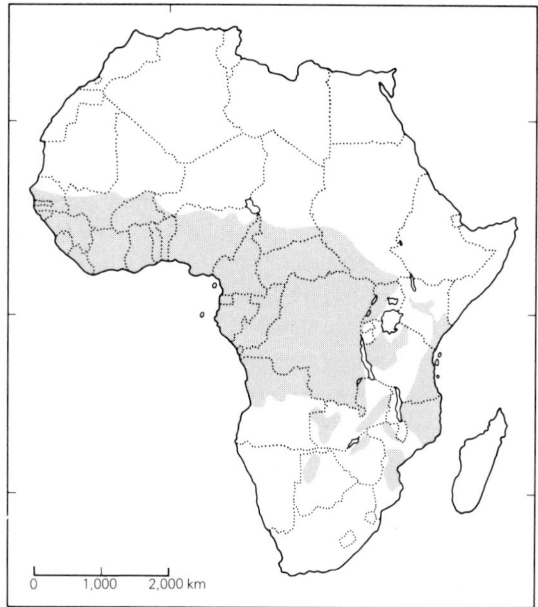

Fig. 4.2 Africa – area affected by tsetse fly

Africa. The tsetse fly brings sleeping sickness to man and the disease *trypanosomiasis* to cattle and, because of its presence, large stretches of land have been neglected and abandoned which might have been farmed successfully. The fly likes bushland and the only permanent solution is to clear the bush and

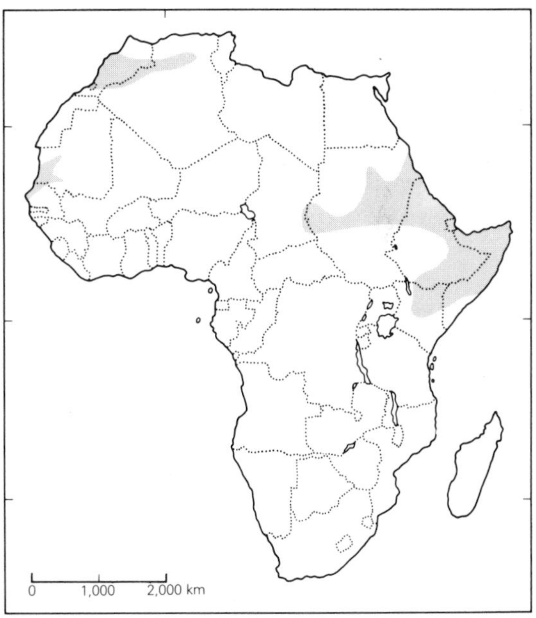

Fig. 4.3 Africa – area affected by migratory locusts

[1] See Appendix 3 for notes on the needs of Africa's main cash and subsistence crops.

encourage soil ploughing. In some parts the fly attacks cattle but not man, so in these areas it is possible to grow crops, but it means excluding meat from an often starchy diet. The fly prevents large areas of Africa from being cultivated and so increases the population of tsetse-free zones.

The locust is another scourge mainly affecting north-eastern Africa (Fig. 4.3). A swarm of locusts may contain as many as 75 000 million insects and weigh approximately 30 000 t. Since a locust eats its own weight in green food daily, such a swarm destroys 30 000 t of vegetation each day. In the 1930s plagues of locusts devastated many areas in West and East Africa. At that time no properly organised method of control existed, and fire, beating, and poison were of little use. Modern methods which are keeping the locusts in check in East Africa include the spraying of swarms with insecticide from vehicles and aircraft.

Another insect which saps man's energies and sometimes causes death is the mosquito which transmits malaria and yellow fever. Malaria is still Africa's gravest health problem: in any average rural community it is estimated that two-thirds of the people will have the infection in their blood at any one time. The Simulium fly spreads River Blindness; ticks carry fevers including leprosy; worms bring bilharzia and hookworm. Other diseases include yaws, kwashiokor, filariasis, tick fever and smallpox. Many of these diseases are being successfully combated by national and international organisations, such as WHO (World Health Organisation), but in many areas they are still a great problem, affecting not only man's health but his ability to make full use of the land.

Sample studies – African land use

Let us now examine some of the methods of land use in Africa. The samples which follow are chosen from as wide and varied a field as possible and, in most cases, are representative of the methods employed over wide regions. In general, although all the samples are based on those existing in Africa today, they have been described in the order in which they probably evolved throughout history (see Chapter Two). Thus man was first a hunter and gatherer and this way of life still exists today (the Bushman and the Pygmy), although very few people now practise it. This is followed by the next stage of evolution – shifting cultivation – as still practised by the Azande in the Zaïre Basin, and it is again emphasised that this occupies a relatively small proportion of the African population. Gradually a more settled form of cultivation developed – bush fallowing – as now seen in the miombo woodlands, and which became more complicated as populations grew. This system is seen in its most advanced form in many areas, especially in Uganda and in southern Nigeria. Variations of this system are seen in the Kikuyu areas of Kenya and in Ghana, where the importance of the cash crop is stressed. We then turn to the less favoured parts of the continent where cultivation is virtually impossible without irrigation, and where man follows a nomadic existence. Following this, some general aspects affecting African cultivation today are discussed, especially the role of cash and subsistence crops in African farming systems. Finally, the importance of the fishing industry is described.

(1) Hunters and collectors

The Bushmen

In the remote unfavourable areas of Africa, indigenous people such as the Bushmen lead lives which have changed little for centuries. The Bushman's way of life, however, is ideally suited to the harsh conditions of the Kalahari Desert, the waterless 'thirstland', which receives only about 250 mm of rain a year; only occasionally do dried up lake beds and clay pans retain some surface water. During the brief rains in September and October and between January and April the grass grows amid the thorny scrub, but is soon burned brown by heat and bush fires.

Here live the Bushmen, a small people of an average height of 1,5 m and with dry, yellowish skins and tightly whorled 'peppercorn' hair. Their ancestors once roamed much of southern Africa and the fringe of the Sahara, but when the white man arrived in the Cape their numbers had been reduced to 10 000, and they were forced to retreat to remoter parts. They are now found in the Kalahari region of

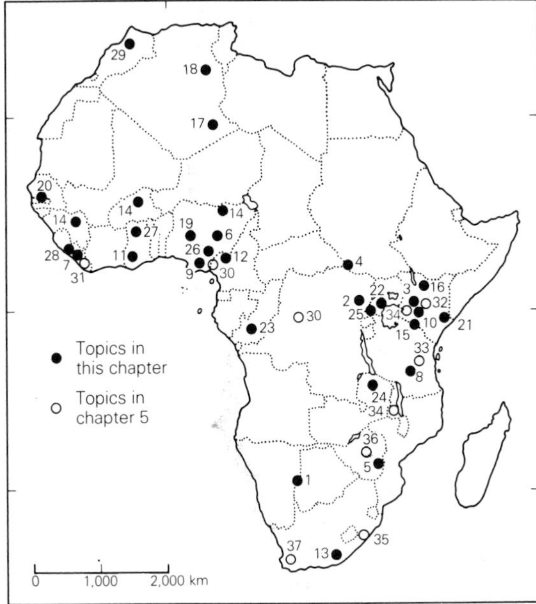

Fig. 4.4 Location of major topics discussed

Hunting and gathering
1 The Bushmen
2 Ituri Forest Pygmies
3 The Wanderobo

Shifting cultivation
4 The Azande
5 The Chipinga
6 The Benue Valley
7 Liberia

Bush fallowing
8 The Miombo Woodlands
9 The Delta and Coastal Regions of Nigeria

Land fragmentation and resettlement
10 The Kikuyu Highlands

Cash cropping
11 Cocoa in Ghana
12 The Cameroon Highlands

Land limitation
13 The Xhosa

Nomadic pastoralism
14 The Fulani
15 The Masai
16 The Turkana
17 The Tuareg

Sedentary cultivation
18 The Souafa

The role of the cash crop
19 Nigeria
20 The Gambia
21 Kenya
22 Uganda

Subsistence crops
23 Congo Republic
24 Zambia

The fishing industry
25 Uganda
26 Nigeria
27 Ghana
28 Liberia
29 Morocco

Plantation and estates
30 Oil Palm estates in Nigeria and Zaïre (Unilever)
31 Rubber in Liberia (Firestone)
32 The Kenya Highlands
33 Sisal in Tanzania (Morogoro Estate)
34 Tea estates (Kenya and Malaŵi)
35 Sugar plantations in Natal
36 Tobacco farming in Zimbabwe
37 Vines, fruit and mixed farming in the South-west Cape

western Botswana and eastern Namibia.

Despite its dry harshness the Kalahari supports a surprising variety of game and edible plants – wild orange, wild fig, berries, nuts, roots, bulbs and tubers – which flourish during the rains. The Bushman's diet also includes frogs, snakes, lizards, ants, scorpions, locusts, bees and their honey. But hunting provides the main food and during the dry season snares are set for the smaller game – anteaters, ostriches and guinea fowl. Duikers are hunted with clubs and poisoned arrows, especially during the dry season when they congregate round water holes. Little is wasted – blood, bones and marrow are eaten; the skins used to make quivers, pouches and blankets; the sinews for thread and bow strings; the bones for whistles, pipes and knives; and the horns for spoons. Flint stones are fashioned into tools, and wood is carved into throwing sticks, fire drills and spear shafts. Hunting is men's work while the women collect berries and roots. Long sticks, bent inwards and tied and thatched with grass, provide temporary shelters. This simple hut is left behind when the group moves on, and new camps are built some distance from the water pans for fear of disturbing the game. Water is stored in empty ostrich eggs plugged with clay, and on the trek a sucking tube is used to draw water from the sub-soil.

The Pygmies

By his skill as a hunter, his trained ability to recognise water sources and his clever use of natural materials, the Bushman is able to use the meagre resources of the Kalahari. He is a nomad like the Pygmies of the Ituri Forest in the eastern Zaïre Basin, who also move around in search of game. Their environment, however, is not as harsh as the Bushman's and unlike the Bushmen the Pygmies have contacts and their life is freely chosen.

The exact number of Pygmy peoples is not known and estimates vary between 100 000 and 200 000 scattered throughout the forests. They have their own tribal groupings and their own regions of influence. The Bambuti Pygmies, for example, occupy the Ituri Forest of north-eastern Zaïre, while the Batwa tribe lives further south in Rwanda and Burundi. Between the Zaïre River and its tributary the Kasai are the Batswa who have intermarried with local Bantu peoples. Another group, the Babinga, lives in the forested basin of the Sangha River, a northern tributary of the Zaïre, and their territory extends through the south-western Central African Republic, Southeast Cameroon, and the north-east of the Congo Republic. Other groups live in Southwest Cameroon and Gabon.

Traditionally the Pygmies are not cultivators but hunters and traders, exchanging game, wild tobacco and grain for iron arrow heads, salt, pottery and matches. Some work part-time for the Bantu by clearing the forest and helping cultivate crops in exchange for food and goods. They are skilled hunters with the net, spear and bow and arrow, and their game includes buffalo, wild pig, antelope, pangolin, okapi and flying squirrel. In the Cameroon region ivory was once an important trade item, but elephants have almost been hunted out of existence. Other sources of food include termites, caterpillars, snakes, wild berries and roots.

The life of the Pygmies is threatened by the exploitation of their forest homelands by timber companies. Some groups have already taken to farming and live in permanent villages.

The Wanderobo

Hunting and collecting must have been very widespread throughout ancient Africa when dense forests covered a wider area. The Wanderobo, now found only in remote spots of the Kenya Highlands and almost extinct, once hunted in the dense forests which formerly clothed the lower slopes of the Aberdares. Their way of life, still carried on on a small scale today, is typical of the forest hunter and collector.

The Wanderobo once inhabited most of the land between the present site of Nairobi and the Chania River, now called the Kiambu District. To the north the Kikuyu practised shifting cultivation, while the Wanderobo were skilled forest hunters and nomads, building temporary huts in the forest depths and keeping to their family groups. They trapped game in pits and collected wild honey, suspending this in skins over pits until needed for beer-making. They traded honey, skins and shields for Masai cattle, Kikuyu goats and sheep, and Kamba arrow poison, while the Kikuyu occasionally hired them to set snares around their cultivated patches. But hunting was their main occupation, each family having a strip of forest covering about 80 ha and bounded by streams and ridge tops. Richer families had two such hunting grounds. Gradually, the Wanderobo were either absorbed by the Kikuyu or their land was bought from them.

African cultivation methods[2]

Early man in Africa lived much as the Bushman in dry regions or as the Pygmies and the original Wanderobo in the forests. But gradually rudimentary systems of cultivation developed, becoming more complicated and efficient as population increased. The various stages of this agricultural evolution can still be seen in many parts of Africa today.

(2) Shifting cultivation

The most basic agricultural system still in use in remote parts of Africa – northern Zaïre, the miombo woodlands of Tanzania, parts of Malaŵi, Zambia, Liberia and Uganda – is termed shifting cultivation. In its original form shifting cultivation can only operate where the population is sparse. It is characterised by the following features:

a The cultivator burns down about half a hectare of forest and sows seeds in the intermixed ash and soil;

b he uses only elementary tools – pangas (machetes), hoes, digging sticks, rough axes;

c little attention is given to the crops until they sprout and ripen;

d when crop yields decline, usually after three years, the patch is abandoned and a fresh area cleared. The cultivator may return to the original patch after many years, but usually he seldom returns.

This system uses much land but there are certain advantages. The constant moves ensure fresh sites and less risk of disease, and the organisation of the work allows time for fishing and hunting. Soil erosion is not serious since only small patches are exposed, and these support many crops so that little

[2] Other accounts of African cultivation, particularly modern schemes, are discussed in Chapters Eight and Thirteen.

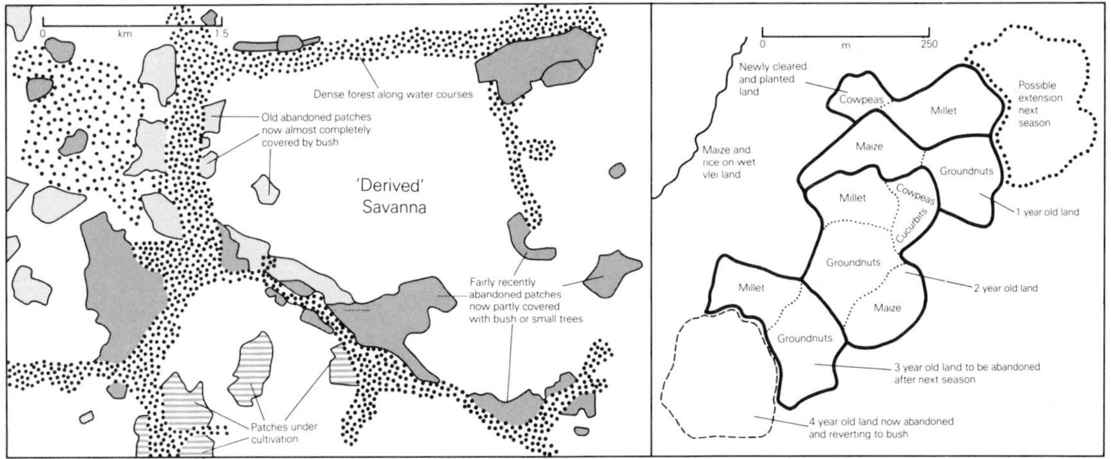

Fig. 4.5 Two examples of shifting agriculture. On the left patches of shifting cultivation at various stages in the Benue Valley region of Nigeria near Makurdi (*based on an aerial photograph*). On the right, the Chipinga system.

bare earth is seen; any soil washed away is trapped at the forest edge or in the dense tangle of crop roots. But there is a very considerable waste of valuable timber which may have taken over a hundred years to grow and is destroyed in a few days. Green manure is ruined and the soil profile profoundly altered by the destruction of bacteria and humus.

The methods used in shifting agriculture vary with the people, their customs, and the variety of their crops. Two variations are seen in the following accounts of the Azande and Chipinga methods.

The Azande

The Azande live to the north of the great bend of the Zaïre River and west of the Nile's headwaters. Their territory of rain forest and open woodland extends 400 km from east to west and 320 km from north to south, where the boundaries of the Sudan, Zaïre and Central African Republics meet. The region has an equatorial climate with a short dry season (November to January) brought by north-easterly winds. There is a wide range of soils and vegetation. Dense gallerial forest and elephant grass border the rivers, springs and swamps, while deciduous woodland grows on valley slopes. On higher, level land lies more open savanna, greatly ravaged by fire, and towards the south-west are the dense forests of the Zaïre. Black soils are common near marshy hollows, with better dark brown and reddish loams in wooded areas.

Here the Azande practise shifting cultivation. They keep few animals, except hunting dogs and chickens, because of the tsetse fly. The men are mainly hunters, the women cultivators. The staple crop is finger millet (eleusine), easy to cultivate since it needs no guarding from wild animals and it can be stored for long periods. Maize is important, especially in the southern moister soils, while other cereals include sorghum, bulrush millet and upland rice. The Azande also grow cowpeas, beans, bambarra nuts, groundnuts and sesame and collect wild palm fruit. Root crops include cassava, sweet potatoes, yams, and cocoyams; in addition fruits – pumpkins, calabashes, bananas, mangoes – and sugar cane, tobacco and chillies are grown. Hemp, cotton and bark are used to make cloth and rope.

Azande tools are elementary – the men possess spears, bows and arrows and throwing knives for hunting, and an iron digging stick for extracting edible roots. In the homestead, agricultural tools include digging sticks, and knives for slashing the bush, house construction, and skinning animals.

Once a site has been chosen where there are few wild animals and a good water supply, the Azande fell the larger trees during the dry season and burn the leaves and twigs against the stumps. Huts for sleeping, cooking and storage are constructed of mud, wood and thatch. Then begins the year of activities shown in Table 1.

Crops are grown until there is a decline in yields, usually after three or four years although good

Table 1 The Azande agricultural year

Month	*Jan.*	*Feb.*	*March*	*April*	*May*	*June*	*July*	*Aug.*	*Sept.*	*Oct.*	*Nov.*	*Dec.*
Rainfall (mm)	0,0	0,0	38,1	76,2	190,5	231,1	193,0	198,1	127,0	114,3	88,9	5,1
Temps. (°C)	25	26,11	25,55	25,55	25,55	25,55	25	24,44	23,33	22,77	23,33	23,88
Activities												
a General	Hunting. Repair of buildings. Termites caught for food.			Guarding of crops against wild animals and birds. Weeding of cultivated patches				Second termite harvest. Repair of huts and tools.		Burning of bush for fresh cultivation. Hunting and fishing by men.		
b Planting of:		Early groundnuts, sweet potatoes, maize and sorghum'			Cassava, rice, yams, groundnuts, okra, maize, sesame, cotton. Finger millet, beans.			Sorghum.				
c Harvesting of:	Old sweet potatoes and finger millet. Some cotton picked.		Mangoes. Sorghum.		Slack period. Harvesting of some unripe groundnuts.			Maize, finger millet, main groundnut harvest. Sweet potatoes, maize and vegetables. Cotton picking.				

harvests may continue for ten years in richer soil areas. The family then moves on to clear another patch.

The Chipinga District of Eastern Zimbabwe

The following account, slightly abridged, illustrates the basic similarities and slight differences between Azande and Chipinga methods. This method is now very limited in the remote regions in the Eastern Highlands of Zimbabwe, but the general method is a common one in Africa.

> While the ground is still workable in April or May, the trees are lopped and the branches piled round the bole. Trees bearing edible fruits are left for food and others for ritual purposes. Only men use the axe, but the women help to pile the wood around the trunk. The land is (then) hoed by the women and the men because it is hard, new ground. The soil is left rough.
>
> Some months later, when the wood is dry, the piles are burnt again and again the land is left alone. After rains have fallen, the seed is sown in December or January and covered by shallow hoeing, which helps to mix the ash with the soil.
>
> A small portion of the land is planted to ground-nuts and another to bambarra nuts. On sandveld soils the greater proportion will be groundnuts. On the larger part of the field a mixture of millet, finger millet, bulrush millet, cucurbits and cowpeas is broadcast and hoed with the soil. Maize is also on the same land mixed with

other crops, but small holes are made with the hoe and several maize seeds planted in each hole. The woman then scuffles soil over the hole with her feet.

One weeding is done in the first season after virgin land is broken up. The work of planting, weeding, reaping, threshing and the making of new land is carried out communally . . .

A new field might be about one hectare. Each year more virgin land is prepared and planted until, after four seasons the whole area is about two hectares. Then a portion of the first prepared land is abandoned and a new piece added each year, so that land is cultivated for four years and then reverts to grass and bush. . . . In addition, vlei land is planted with maize and rice. The same patch is cultivated year after year and shifting tillage is not practised on this wet land.

The cultivator does not recognise any definite period of time for his grass and bush fallow. He judges that the land may be used again when the grass is tall and the bush is high. Alternatively, the whole kraal moves to a new area after four or five years, this being the more usual custom.[3]

Efforts at solution

Such methods are a serious threat to the natural vegetation and to soil fertility. Efforts are being made to convert the Azande to a cash crop system based on cotton but fluctuating prices, a lack of concerted effort between the Sudan, Zaïre and Central African governments, and the remoteness of the area have hampered progress. An experimental station at Yambio, textile mills and strip farming have been introduced in Sudan's Equatoria Province, but yields remain low and the region produces only 0,5 per cent of Sudan's cotton. Coffee and oil palms are also grown but the climate is rather marginal and yields are not high.

In Liberia shifting cultivation had assumed such proportions that 280 000 hectares were being cleared every year for temporary rice plantations. Farmers burned the forest, scattered rice seeds, reaped a harvest for two or three years, then moved on (yields were 560 kg per hectare a year or about 0,2 kg per person per day). Liberia, faced with a rice shortage, was importing over 30 000 t of rice a year. But the potential of the forest lands under organised cultivation is enormous; for example, there are 290 000 ha of freshwater swamps, ideal for rice growing, and each hectare will yield up to 2 700 kg a year – five times that under shifting cultivation. The government is now actively encouraging swamp rice-growing: in 1961 there were 200 ha of swamp rice; by 1973 there were 1 000 ha, which was increased to 2 700 ha in the Foya, Cape Mount and Zleh Town areas by 1974. Rice imports were reduced by 38 per cent and the government aims to make Liberia a rice-exporting country by developing a further 2 000 ha. Experiments with a rotation of dry season crops (cowpeas, sweet potatoes, soya beans, groundnuts, cotton) are being carried out.

(3) Bush fallowing

In the description of shifting cultivation in Zimbabwe it was suggested that the cultivator may return to an abandoned patch once the soil had recuperated. A fallow period is thus introduced which, strictly speaking, modifies the system to bush fallowing. Land is fallow when it is left to recover its fertility so that it can be used after a period of years for more crops. This is the essential difference from shifting cultivation where no long-term organised system of fields is recognised; the family unit occupied in bush fallowing is now fixed in one spot and uses several permanent fields. The length of the fallow period depends on population density, the ideal time being at least ten years, but this is rarely possible in densely peopled areas of Africa.

The miombo woodlands

In central and southern Tanzania many farmers use a simple fallowing system which is probably the first stage of transition from shifting cultivation to bush fallowing. Here lie the *miombo* woodlands, one of the largest uniform vegetation zones in Africa. The monsoonal climate with its alternating wet and dry seasons supports a cover of flat-topped Brachystegia trees and grass.

A month before the rains the trees burst into leaf

[3] From a Rhodesian agricultural pamphlet. Similar methods of cultivation occur in Zambia where it is called 'slash and burn' agriculture, or the 'chitemene system'.

Ivory Coast: Shifting cultivation. The cultivators have cleared a forest area prior to burning. Note the prepared yam mounds.

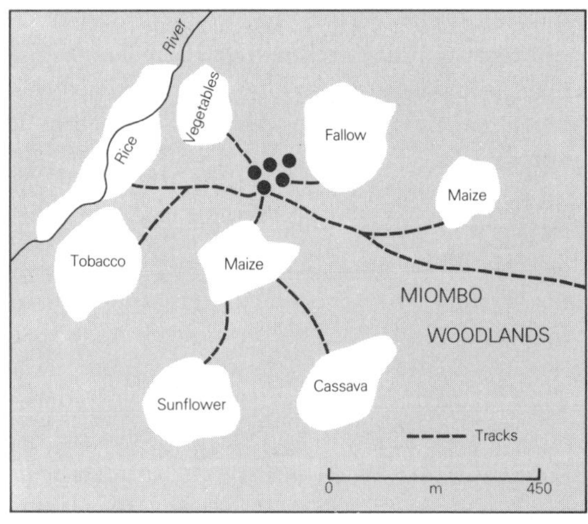

Fig. 4.6 Tanzania – bush fallowing in the miombo woodlands

and in a few days the dry landscape is fresh and green. As the rains die out in May the countryside reverts to its hot, dry monotony and the trees shed their leaves. Man is forced to keep near streams to grow crops continuously and this encourages a fixed field system. The tsetse fly also hinders the spread of settlement, for clearings must be large enough to keep away the bush-loving fly, and the settlements need to be close to water supplies for domestic use and irrigation. A family clears seven or eight fields by chopping and burning, and sows these with maize, cassava and sweet potatoes. The cultivator may plant three crops of maize, two at the beginning and middle of the wet season, and one under irrigation during the dry season. Rice and cash crops – tobacco, sunflowers and sesame – are grown by

Table 2 Climatic statistics for Dodoma, Tanzania (alt. 1100 m)

Month	*Jan.*	*Feb.*	*Mar.*	*April*	*May*	*June*	*July*	*Aug.*	*Sept.*	*Oct.*	*Nov.*	*Dec.*	*Year*
Temps. (°C)	23,88	23,88	23,33	22,77	21,66	20,55	19,44	20,55	21,66	23,33	24,44	24,44	22,77
Rainfall (mm)	154,9	109,2	144,8	43,2	5,1	0,0	0,0	0,0	2,5	5,1	30,5	96,5	591,8

irrigation near the stream. One field is left fallow for four or five years and the others used in rotation.

The Tanzanian Government is taking steps to regulate this haphazard way of growing crops. This large area of territory, with a population of only 2 per square kilometre, has a tremendous potential. Although soils are rather gritty, sandy or clayey loams, they can be very productive with irrigation and scientific farming. Experimental plots are run near Iringa, Urambo, Nachingwea and other spots to teach student farmers how to grow cash crops, especially tobacco. The Kiwere Settlement Scheme 20 km north of Iringa is one of these schemes (Fig. 4.7). By such schemes the government hopes to make a fuller use of the miombo woodlands, to extend areas suitable for settlement by bush clearance, and to provide important export crops.

The coastal lowlands of Nigeria

The miombo woodlands are thinly peopled and bush fallowing there is still in its infancy. Gradually the fields will multiply and a more regulated system, separate from that of one's neighbour, will be adopted. This stage has been reached in the coastal lowlands of south-eastern Nigeria. Here, centuries ago, man practised shifting cultivation, then limited bush fallowing followed as the population increased. Today, the Cross River State supports 3,5 million people.

The coastal lands of the Cross River State are cut

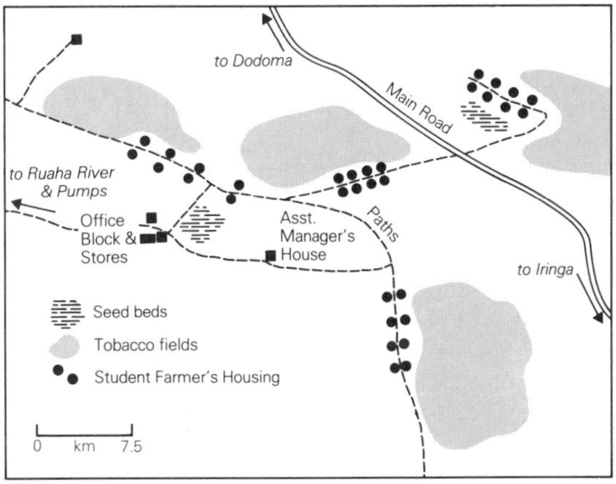

Fig. 4.7 The Kiwere Settlement Scheme in Tanzania. Situated 20 km north of Iringa; altitude 1 200 m; annual rainfall 890–1 140 mm, maximum in December, minimum in November and April. May to September is a very dry period. Temperature 25°–30°C during the day to 18°C at night. Irrigation water from nearby Little Ruaha River. Scheme first opened January 1963 with 30 student farmers, each pupil being given about half a hectare in the first year and over 1 ha in the second – two-thirds for tobacco and one-third for subsistence (maize and potatoes). There are now approximately 150 pupils and the scheme covers 2 800 ha. Tobacco is processed, graded and baled on the spot for shipment to Dar es Salaam.

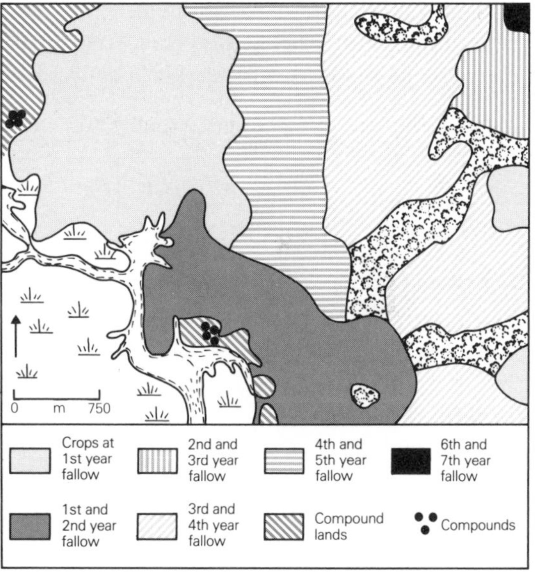

Fig. 4.8 Settlement and land use pattern north of Port Harcourt, Nigeria. In this area the village compounds are well defined and there are no scattered dwellings. The large tracts of cultivated land belong to the village, although individual farmers possess small cultivated plots near to their homes. The land is worked on an 8-year fallow system. (*After W. B. Morgan*)

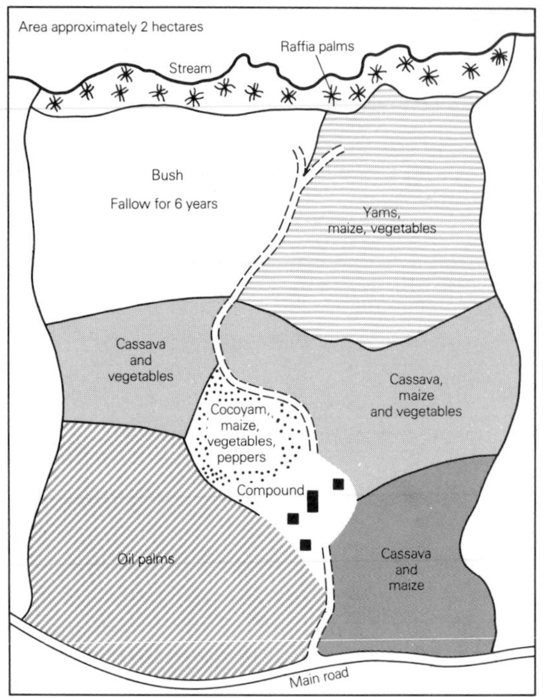

Fig. 4.9 Nigeria – typical farm layout in the coastal lowlands

by numerous small streams, many of them tributaries of the main River Imo which bisects the region; these streams drain southwards from a low hilly region to flat lowlands and coastal swamps. The climate is hot – 26,5°C during the day dropping to 15,5°C at night. Rainfall is heavy (3 050 mm) in the south-east at Calabar to 2 310 mm inland at Aba) with a slackening off between November and March. Soils are generally well drained but heavily leached, are acid, contain few minerals, and are soon exhausted.

Not, then, a very rich area to support the dense population, and the land has been practically cleared of the natural forest. Here the Igbo-, Efik- and Ibibio-speaking peoples are small-scale farmers growing subsistence crops of yams, cassava, bananas, melons, okra, beans, cocoyams, calabashes, rice and vegetables. Most have small permanent vegetable plots near their homes, but the main farm land is cultivated by a fallowing system. A family may have from 2 to 3 ha with 1 ha constantly bearing crops, and in some areas the fallow period has been reduced to three years. Palm groves, some natural, some planted, provide cooking oil and palm wine and the palm provides the farmer with his chief source of income – palm oil. Coconuts are a secondary cash crop nearer the coast.

The men do the harder work such as raking, hoeing, planting and constructing storage shelters and fences, while the women tend the small gardens and help with the harvests. The year's work is shown in Table 3.

Table 3 The Igbo farmer's agricultural Year[1]

Month	*Jan.*	*Feb.*	*Mar.*	*April*	*May*	*June*	*July*	*Aug.*	*Sept.*	*Oct.*	*Nov.*	*Dec.*	*Year*
Temps. (°C)	26,11	27,22	27,22	26,66	26,11	26,11	25,55	25,0	25,0	26,11	26,11	26,11	26,11
Rainfall (mm)	53,3	68,6	162,6	200,7	302,3	398,8	429,3	411,5	414,0	325,1	190,5	53,3	2997,2
Activities *a* General-	Bush clearing	Preparation of yam hills				Weeding					Clearing of bush		
b Planting of:		Yams, pumpkins, melons, maize, calabashes				Beans, cassava, okra, cocoyams Second maize crop							
c Harvesting of:						Early yams First maize General harvesting of other crops			Main yam crop Second maize crop				

[1]Climatic statistics for Calabar, altitude 12 m

All the cultivated land is used and the ground is completely covered by intercropping, for example, beans between maize. One field may yield a harvest for one year using intensive methods while in the following year it will be sown with fewer crops, then it will fall fallow. Thus the Igbo are able to support the dense population by these intensive methods.

(4) Land fragmentation

The farmers of the coastal lowlands of South-eastern Nigeria must supply increasing amounts of food for a growing population from a fixed area of land – the land must produce more. Another serious problem of many farming communities in Africa is land fragmentation – the division of land between members of the landowner's family until the plot size is so small that a severe limit is placed on its productivity. This stage had been reached in many parts of the Kikuyu lands in the Kenya Highlands until recently.

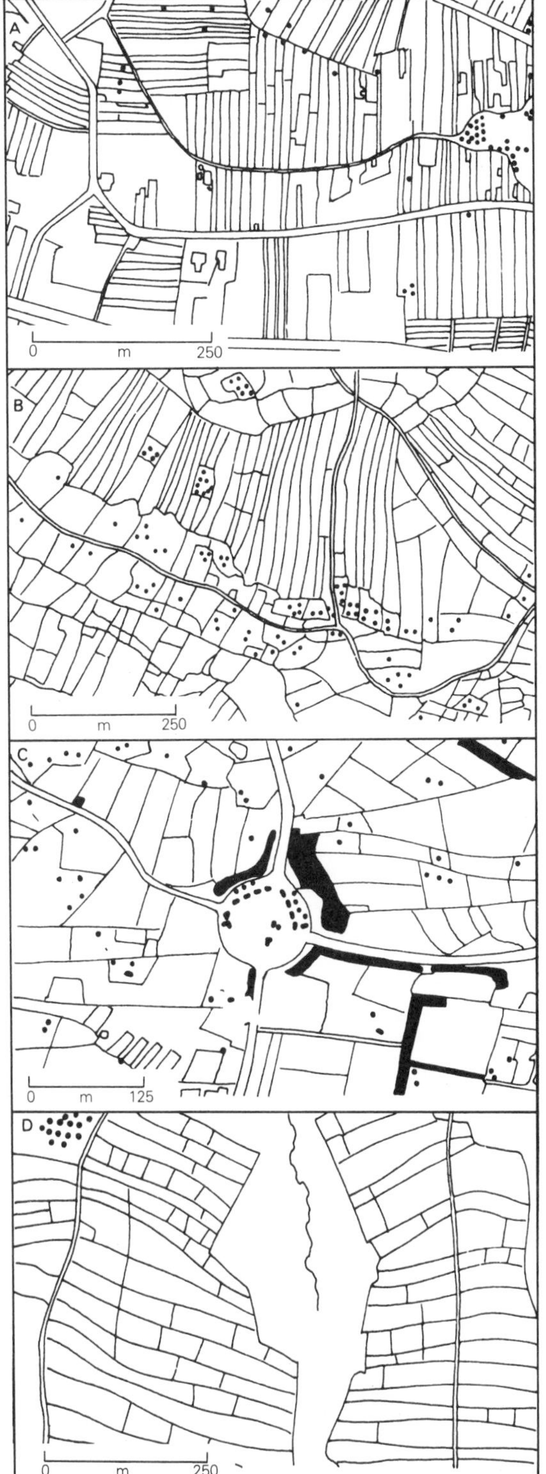

Fig. 4.10 The intensive nature of African cultivation is well shown in these four examples from different parts of the continent. *Diagram A* shows part of the Nile Delta region of Egypt, where irrigation canals form the framework of rectangular field patterns. *Diagram B* shows the strip field pattern associated with villages elongated along road routes in Imo State of Nigeria near Abakaliki.
Diagram C illustrates the field pattern in the Kipsigis peasant farming region near Kericho in western Kenya (the centre circle is a market and the black areas are planted tree wind-breaks).
Diagram D is an example of strip farming from Zezuro peasant farming area, Mashonaland.

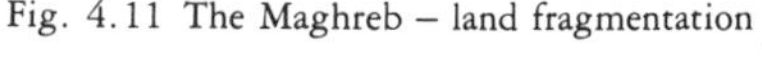

Fig. 4.11 The Maghreb – land fragmentation

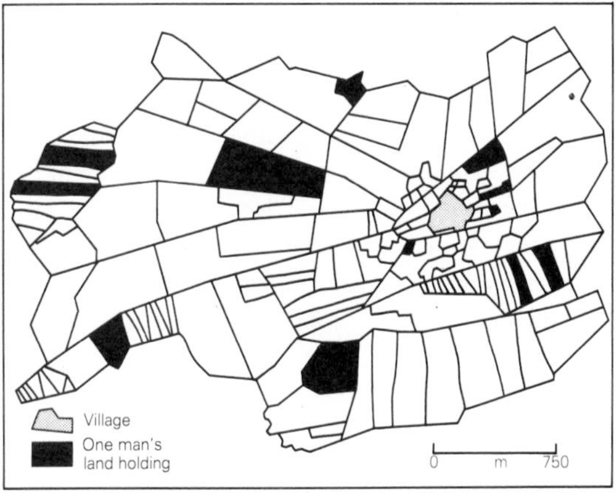

Table 4 Climatic statistics for Nyeri, Kenya Highlands (1 800 m)

Month	*Jan.*	*Feb.*	*Mar.*	*April*	*May*	*June*	*July*	*Aug.*	*Sept.*	*Oct.*	*Nov.*	*Dec.*	*Year*
Temps. (°C)	19,44	20,56	20,56	19,44	18,89	18,33	16,67	17,22	18,33	19,44	19,44	18,89	19,93
Rainfall (mm)	20,3	27,9	53,3	177,9	127,0	30,5	27,9	30,9	22,9	76,2	88,9	76,2	759,4

The Kikuyu

The Kikuyu represent 20 per cent of Kenya's population of nearly 15 million and occupy a particularly fertile region on the lower slopes of the Aberdares between Nairobi and Mount Kenya. Here, between 1 300 and 1 800 m, the soils are fertile, and the rainfall adequate and fairly reliable.

At the beginning of the nineteenth century most of this region was heavily forested; today it is a patchwork of fields, villages and small areas of forest and, before consolidation, it had fallen under the evils of fragmentation. This was a gradual process beginning with land purchases from the Wanderobo. The Kikuyu practised shifting cultivation north of the Chania River but between 1830 and 1890 the pressure of population forced them to buy land from the Wanderobo. Some Kikuyu families formed 'syndicates' to buy large sections of land, and gradually the forests were cleared for cultivation. Wanderobo hunters who did not sell were surrounded by Kikuyu cultivated shambas and found that there was no game left. Thus the basis for fragmentation was set and today many Kikuyu own plots in the old Wanderobo zone (now Kiambu) and in the original Kikuyu zone (Murang'a District).

Other major causes of fragmentation are:

a *Instalment buying of land:* A Kikuyu farmer might have bought one piece of land, then saved up to buy another some distance away.

b *Kikuyu family customs:* A man gave a plot of land to his wife: if he married again he gave another piece to the second wife; a new wife often gave land to other wives; a newly married son was given land by the mother.

c *Tenant lands:* If a man had tenants and was short of land to give as gifts, he would take small pieces from each tenant rather than take one tenant's whole holding.

This complicated system reduced the landscape to a patchwork of queerly-shaped fragments where a man might own a dozen pieces scattered over a wide area. The disadvantages are obvious – time wasted walking between plots, higher fencing costs, inadequate protection against thieves and wild animals, soil decline because of the difficulties of carting manure, and the impossibility of using large-scale machinery on the small fields.

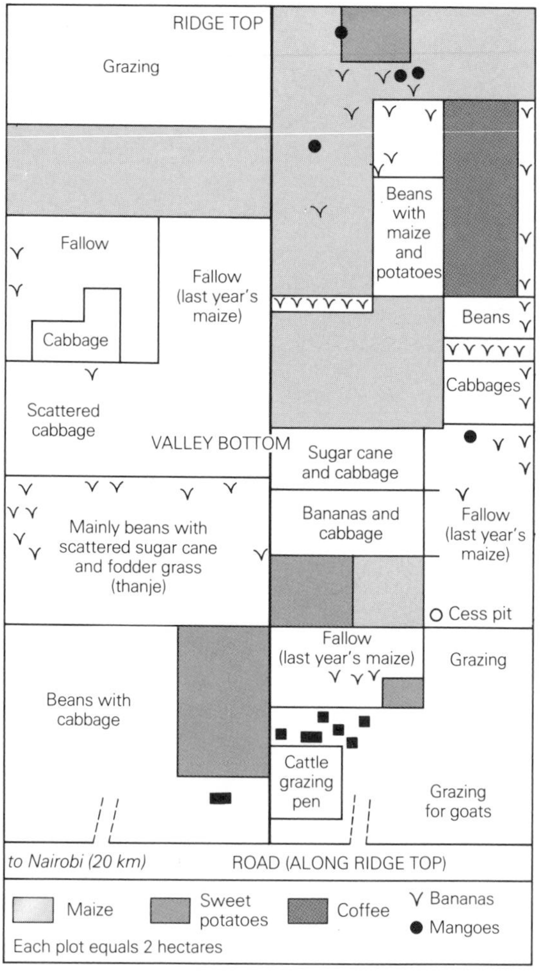

Fig. 4.12 Kenya – land consolidation. Intensive cultivation by the Kikuyu in the Fort Smith district 20 km north-east of Nairobi

(5) Land consolidation

The answer to fragmentation, common to many parts of Africa, is land consolidation. This entails reorganisation of the land into single compact units so that the family has the same hectarage, or land of equal productivity, as before. The new unit is based on the largest holding the man formerly possessed and, if he acquires better soil he must take a slightly smaller land area. The new settlements often lie astride the numerous ridges in Kikuyu areas, with ridge and valley rivers forming boundaries. The slopes are terraced to check soil erosion, and homesteads and villages are set on top of the ridge (Fig. 4.12).

(6) The danger of crop over-concentration

While it is advisable for the African farmer to devote a high proportion of his land to cash crops for export, the dangers of over-concentration on certain cash crops are recognised by African governments. Already world over-production of coffee has resulted in many African farmers being forced to destroy coffee seedlings. Several of West Africa's nations seem particularly vulnerable in this respect.

Ghana

The danger of over-concentration on a particular cash crop is seen in Ghana. The importance of cocoa in Ghana's economy cannot be overstressed and, while other major economic activities are run by large companies, cocoa is almost entirely grown by African farmers on small plots. Nearly 65 per cent of Ghana's foreign revenue comes from the sale of cocoa beans and cocoa butter, and nearly 25 per cent of the central government's revenues come from cocoa. Production has fallen in recent years and this has prompted the government to look seriously at the problems facing the cocoa industry. Ghana's share of world markets has fallen from nearly 37 per cent in the mid-1960s to less than 30 per cent in the mid-1970s.

There are many problems which, combined, account for the decline in cocoa production in Ghana. During the 1960s low prices for cocoa discouraged farmers who could not increase their production because their trees were past their best. As younger people leave the land, the average age of cocoa farmers has risen and is now about 50 years. The effects of swollen shoot disease and damage done by uncontrolled bush fires have taken their toll, and farmers have been reluctant to sustain their investment in the crop. Smuggling of cocoa to neighbour-

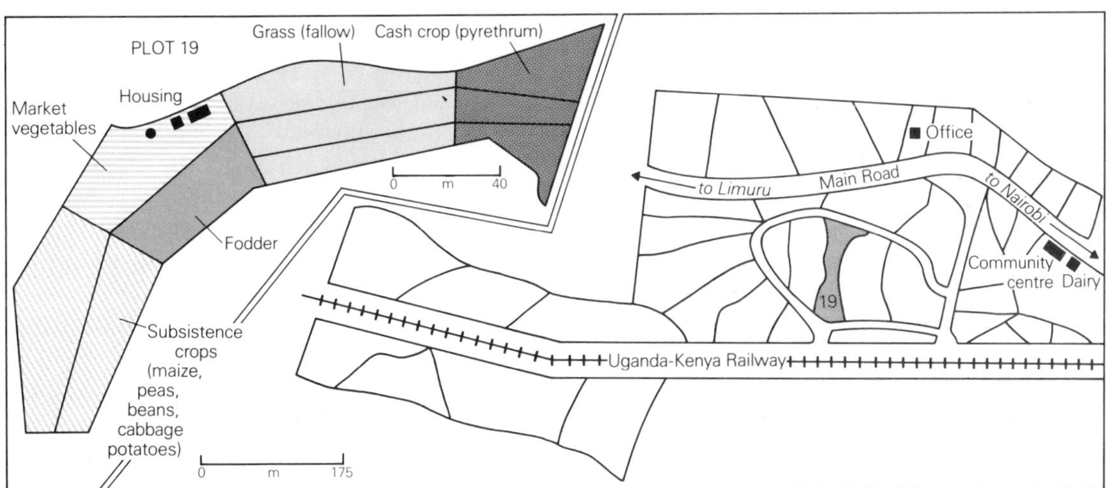

Fig. 4.13 Kenya – land resettlement, showing the Kikuyu use of former European-owned land. The Kikuyu Estates Co-operative (on the right) is made up of two ex-European farms of 250 ha. Altitude 2 100 m; rainfall 760–1 010 mm; water by two bore-holes with reticulation to each plot, the 37 plots averaging 7 ha. Soils are Kikuyu loam – a dark red to red loamy sand.

Former land use: dairying, pyrethrum, wattle. Present land use: dairying, pyrethrum, vegetables, pigs, poultry, subsistence crops. Now supports about 620 people, previously about 50. Detail of one of the plots is shown on the left.

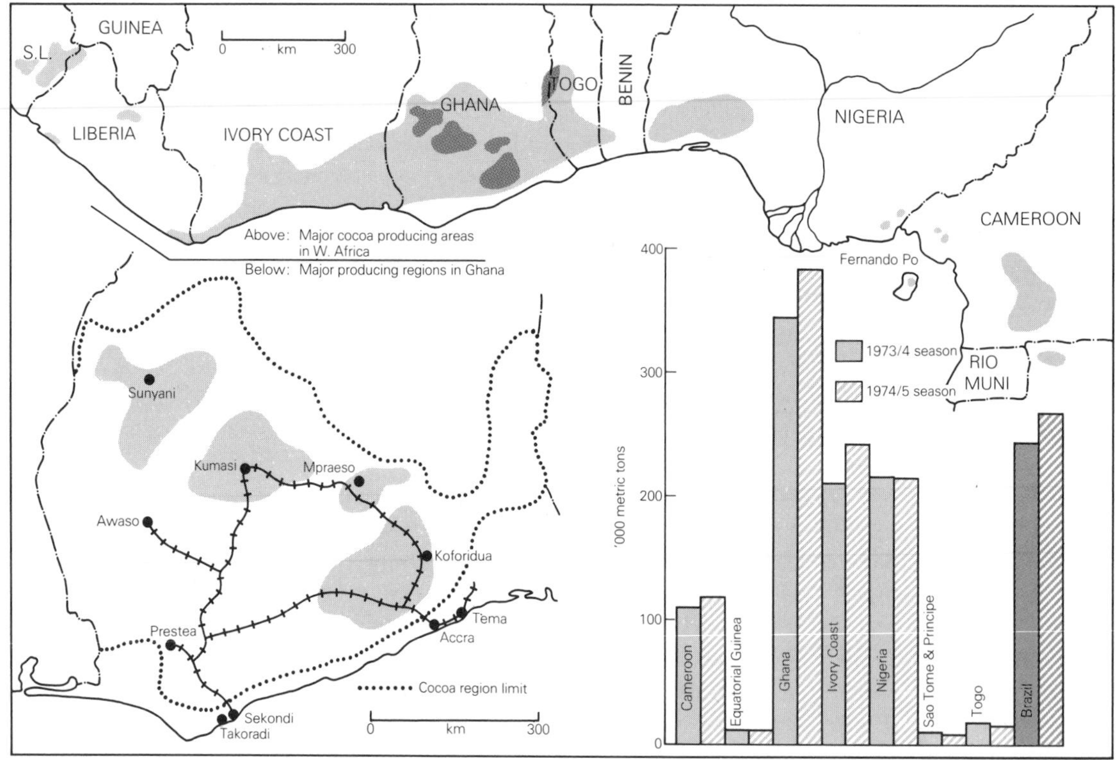

Fig. 4.14 West Africa – cocoa production

ing countries is also a problem, and there is a general lack of good roads in these border areas which would help the farmer to send his crop to markets within Ghana. A brief account of the growth of cocoa farming in Ghana will show how this crop grew to dominate the country's economy.

The export of beans began in 1891 with a shipment weighing only 740 kg, but in 1899 exports reached 330 t. Rubber trees and oil palms were neglected, and the government encouraged small-scale cocoa cultivation by refusing concessions to plantation companies. Cocoa cultivation spread to the empty landscape of the Akwapim area, and by 1914 exports had risen to 50 800 t. The speed of expansion and methods of the early cocoa farmers is described in the following quotation:

> From the early eighteen nineties the migrant cocoa farmers moved westward, on foot, towards the river (Densu), acquiring and planting as they went. In about 1896 the first real 'capitalist-farmers' acquired lands, most of them large ones, on the western bank and soon after 1900 the migration over the river became a mass movement. The women and children joined their menfolk as soon as they were established in the farming area, and in the first decade of the century the towns of the Akwapim ridge lost a great proportion of their population. To many farmers the investment of a large portion of the profits from one land in the acquisition of another land further west became a rapid, compulsive process and many of them soon became travelling managers supervising the work of relatives and paid labourers on their various farms. By about 1905 the most remarkable process of agricultural development ever achieved by unassisted African farmers was in full momentum; by 1911, largely owing to the efforts of these travelling farmers, Ghana became the largest cocoa producer in the world, although twenty years previously she had exported but 740 kg.[4]

[4] Polly Hill.

In 1924 cocoa became the largest single export item, a position maintained to this day. Koforidua was the main area but cocoa planting spread along the communication routes around Kumasi. In 1931 just under 250 000 t were exported; in 1936 310 000 t (40 per cent world production); in 1964 390 000 t were exported (35 per cent of world output). For reasons we have mentioned earlier the production of cocoa has declined in recent years as the following annual production figures show: 1970/1 - 386 000 t; 1971/2 – 457 000 t; 1972/3 – 411 000 t; 1973/4 – 338 000 t; 1975/6 – 385 000 t. Ghana now produces between a quarter and a third of world production. Comparative production in other West Africa countries 1975/6 are: Ivory Coast, 231 000 t; Nigeria, 215 000 t, East Cameroon, 83 000 t.

Cocoa farming has spread from the original south-eastern area inland to Kumasi and westwards to the Ivory Coast border. Rainfalls to the north are insufficient and in the south-west too heavy (1 800 mm). The optimum rainfall for cocoa lies between 1 300 and 1 500 mm a year with a short dry season. The tree likes shade and protection from drying winds and too much moisture encourages fungus growth such as Black Pod, for cocoa is a particularly disease-prone plant. The best soils in the cocoa belt are derived from crystalline rocks such as granite.

Due to disease, the harvests of the original cocoa growing area have declined considerably, from 45 per cent of the total harvest in the 1930s to 15 per cent today. Swollen Shoot appeared in 1931 and by the late 1940s had invaded every cocoa area, reducing production by 60 per cent. No real check other than the cutting out of affected plants has yet been discovered.

Thus two dangers face cocoa growers – the spread of diseases and their (and the country's) dependence on one crop. Should world prices fall[5] Ghana's economy could be seriously affected. The Ghana Government is trying to diversify crop production and introduce more industries, but farmers are reluctant to devote more land on their small one- or two-hectare farms to less profitable crops.

Cocoa farmers do grow other crops – plantains, yams, cocoyams, maize, cassava, kola nuts and oil palms, although cocoa cultivation is the chief occupation. To start a cocoa farm is relatively easy, the undergrowth being burned during dry January and February and seeds planted with other crops during the March rains. Until the plants produce after five years, the farmer subsists on other crops. The trees begin to bear in their sixth year, produce their best harvests in the tenth, and begin to decline after the fifteenth year. The pods develop on the trunks between April and June and the plants must be weeded and brushed until harvesting in September, October and November. A second seed harvest is gathered in April and May.

Once cut, the pods are split open, the beans extracted, piled into heaps, covered with leaves, and allowed to ferment for six days. Then they are spread on mats to dry in the sun and are later sold to the cocoa co-operative.

Cocoa occupies a very important part in the life of the southern Ghanaian farmer and in the life of the country as a whole – some would say too important a part. But no matter what schemes of diversification or industrialisation the government may introduce, cocoa will be important in Ghana's economy for many years to come.

(7) Other problems caused by cash cropping

The Bamenda highlands

The cash crop has been an integral part of the farming system for many years in many parts of West Africa, particularly in the cocoa and oil palm regions. But in some parts of Africa, for example in East Africa, cash crop growing on a commercial scale by Africans was formerly restricted by colonial legislation, and it is only relatively recently that cash crops such as coffee have been introduced into the African cultivation system. Often it has been necessary to clear new land to make room for these new crops and this has brought about problems of soil erosion, land tenure and often ill-feeling between African peoples with different economic interests. Some of these problems have been clearly described in the following passage relating to cultivation in the Bamenda Highlands of the Cameroon Republic:

The basis of permanent settlement here, as in most

[5] On the London market the following prices have been recorded: £554 (1954), £151 (1961), £343 (1969), £320 (1975), over £2 000 (1976).

areas of tropical Africa, is subsistence farming. In addition to maize, other New World crops that have become important here are cassava and, much more recently, the Irish potato, which grows well in the comparatively cool, rainy climate. Some of the most striking changes in the agricultural scene have followed upon the introduction of arabica coffee as a cash crop during the years following the Second World War. Promoted by the Agricultural Department, production has grown from a meagre 15 t in 1947 to well over 2 000 t in recent years. Nearly all of this production has come from peasant farms. A single tea plantation at Ndu is another promising venture in commercial agriculture on the high lava plateau.

The coffee crop has had to be integrated with the peasant's subsistence agriculture in such a way that the farmer and his family can still rely to a high degree on their own farms for their food, while also raising their standard of living by marketing a cash crop. In many places this has been made possible by taking in new farming land on higher and steeper slopes of the farming valleys, risking both enmity with the Fulani, whose grazing land it had traditionally become, and soil erosion on very steep slopes, sometimes exceeding thirty-five degrees. The free-draining, humus-rich soils do not erode easily, and erosion has not yet become a problem on the lava slopes, but many of these changes are quite recent and their full effects are not yet seen. Meanwhile, relations with the Fulani have deteriorated and there exist delicate problems of land tenure and land use which must eventually be decided by legislation.

The coffee bushes are frequently grown on the best soils, forcing women to cultivate the food crops on the steeper and stonier slopes. The men, following advice of the Agricultural Department, employ simple contour ridging and mulching as conservation measures, but the women are either unwilling or unable to do this on the steep slopes, where it is vitally needed.[6]

[6] From an article 'The Bamenda Highlands' by M. F. Thomas.

(8) Land limitation

We have been concerned largely with man's efforts to increase the amount of land available for cultivation in order to keep abreast of population growth. In some parts of Africa the land has reached a point where the cultivable area available is unable to support the population and there is a continuous exodus to the towns. In some cases the land area has been reduced, causing a radical change in the life of the people.

The Xhosa of the Transkei

The Xhosa of the Transkei have had their way of life greatly altered by restrictions on the land available. The climate of the Xhosa reserves (temperatures between 15° and 20°C, annual rainfalls between 380 and 760 mm with 60 per cent falling between October and March, the summer months) is suited to cattle ranching but is rather marginal for crops. The Xhosa once lived in scattered homesteads, tending their increasing herds in a rolling landscape of grassland and scattered trees. Cattle were only killed by disease or for ceremonies. The herds, tended by the men, moved from one pasture to another in a simple rotation. The woman cultivated small patches of millet and sorghum which were abandoned when the family followed the herds to fresh pastures. The Xhosa lived on milk and cereals and crops obtained by exchange for their dairy products.

Over the last hundred years the Xhosa have increased threefold and densities in the region have reached 60 per square kilometre. Xhosa grazing land has decreased due to the encroachment of cultivators and to the Xhosa's practice of growing more and more crops to sell in local markets. The people are now mainly cultivators of maize, wheat and potatoes. Some keep sheep, selling the wool, and there are still herds of cattle, but the pastures are inadequate to support large numbers and many die during droughts. Like the Masai of East Africa, the Xhosa tend to believe that numbers rather than quality are the best indication of a man's wealth. The Xhosa have never grown cash crops such as pineapples and citrus since the white farmer has already captured South African markets. Many men have left the land and today nearly half of the male Xhosa population work outside the region.

Measures are, however, being taken to provide alternative work. The Xhosa Development Corporation has become very active in promoting agricultural and industrial enterprises especially around Umtata. The local farmers are gradually being trained in the fertilisation and irrigation of land, the planning and rotation of crops, and in modern grazing methods.

The Transkei has a cattle population of 1,5 million and the development of the meat processing industry could raise the national income considerably. The Transkei Meat Industry has recently opened a meat-packing factory near Umtata and there is a growing export of meat to the coastal towns of South Africa. Another venture is the expansion of the timber industry; it is planned to plant forest over 4 per cent of the Transkei and to double the numbers employed in forestry.

(9) Nomadic pastoralism

The Xhosa have turned from pastoralism to cultivation from sheer necessity. But large stretches of Africa support true nomadic herdsmen – the drier savanna of West Africa, the Nyika of East Africa, the Kalahari fringes of Botswana, the semi-deserts of Somalia – all are extensive grazing zones where man follows the shifting rainbelts with his herds.

The Fulani of West Africa

The Fulani number over seven million and are spread throughout the Sahel and savanna zones of West Africa from Senegal to Lake Chad (Fig. 4.15). The savanna experiences the long dry season brought by the parching north-easterly Harmattan from October to March, and a wet season from April to September. Rainfalls average between 760 to 890 mm a year. In the southern Sahel rainfall is lower (500 to 760 mm), is less reliable, and lasts only for about four months.

The climate in the savanna zone supports scattered doum palms, baobabs, shea butter trees and shrubs and, during the rains, short grass. In the Sahel the country is more open, trees are smaller and there are more thorn bushes; grass is tussocky and leathery but can still be grazed. The nomadic Fulani also make use of the higher plateaux such as the Futa Jalon and Bamenda Highlands, where much of the former forest has been destroyed by fire and large stretches of secondary tsetse-free grasslands exist.

Like the early Xhosa the nomadic Fulani live almost wholly on the produce of their herds and obtain roots, grains and vegetables by barter from the peoples on whose land they graze. The Fulani move in family groups supported by about a dozen cattle in the savanna zone, while in the drier Sahel there are fewer cattle but more goats and sheep. The main problem of the Fulani is the dry season water shortage which causes the long migrations; the tsetse

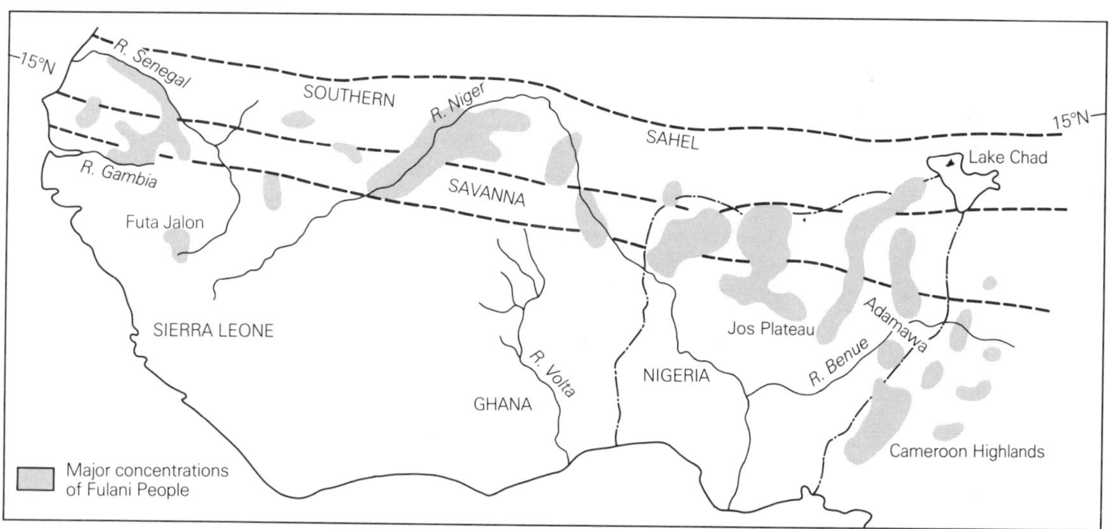

Fig. 4.15 West Africa – distribution of Fulani in relation to the Sahel and Savanna zones

fly is less of a problem although most cattle are only partially immune.

The nomadic Fulani, like the Masai, practise transhumance. During the dry season the grass withers, pools and streams dwindle; the tsetse flies retreat slowly southwards, keeping close to the water courses, then later move north as the rains spread over the land in April and May. As the rains and flies approach, the Fulani move steadily northwards with their herds or seek the tsetse-free uplands of the Bamenda, Futa Jalon, Jos, Bauchi and the Cameroon Republic. As the dry season returns, the Fulani lead their cattle from the highlands and northern areas and move southwards.

The nomadic Fulani's way of life is thus dominated by the wet and dry seasons. During the dry season food is short, some cattle may be sold for food and roots and berries are collected. Wells must be dug and the cattle must be spread out in the search for water. During the rains the cattle thrive on the fresh grass and the Fulani's life is relatively easy.

The Masai of East Africa

The Masai are nomadic pastoralists but, unlike the Fulani, they have complete rights over much of their grazing land. They practise transhumance in a wedge of arid territory known as Masailand, extending from Nairobi southwards into Tanzania between Kilimanjaro and Lake Manyara (Fig. 4.16).

Here again there are long wet and dry seasons with unreliable rains and long droughts. Average rainfalls are between 500 and 640 mm a year, mostly falling between November and April, and temperatures are high, averaging 20°C in the hot, dry seasons. The landscape affects sudden changes with the seasons; during droughts it is dry and dusty, small dust devils whirl across the plains, and steams are dried-up sandy beds. The bark peels off the trees, bushes are coated with yellowish dust and the distant blue highlands shimmer in the heat. When the rains sweep across the land the rolling plains are covered anew with short grass, the winds bring a cool freshness, the streams fill with rushing water, and dirt roads are sticky with reddish-brown mud.

Here the Nilotic Masai graze their cattle. A tall, aristocratic people, many, but by no means all of them, have resisted modern influences and still live simply, scorning the use of modern tools and

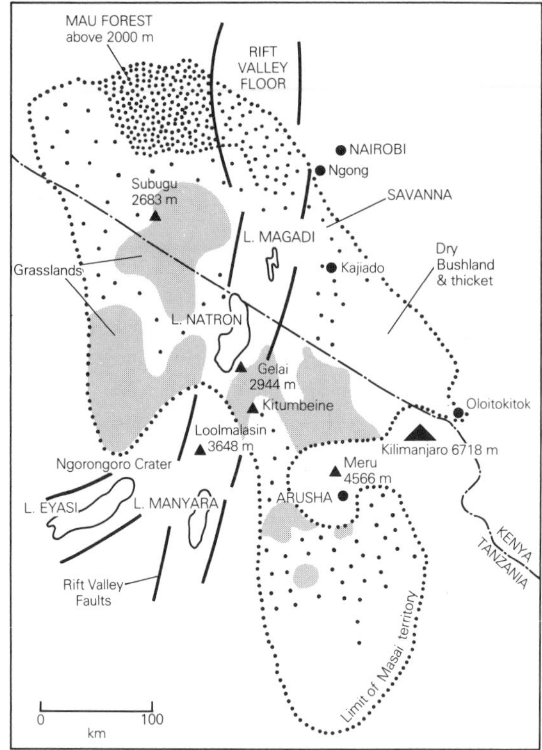

Fig. 4.16 Kenya and Tanzania – the territory of the Masai

weapons. To them cattle, usually the hardy tsetse-resistant Zebu, are a symbol of wealth; but at present Masailand is unable to support vast herds, and overgrazing and resultant wind erosion are serious problems. The cattle die off in hundreds in prolonged droughts as in 1961 and 1974, when piles of dusty cattle corpses littered the plains. The Masai keep donkeys for transport and, to save their precious herds, sheep and goats for meat. Their diet consists of blood taken from a harmless incision in the cow's throat, milk and meat, and a few poor grains.

The Masai have a home area where they live in small *enkangs* (or kraals) and to which they return periodically. Movement from this home area is caused by the alternating wet and dry season of the Nyika. During the dry season the herdsmen move their cattle to the lower fringes of surrounding highlands such as the Mau Forest where, above 2 100 m, it becomes cooler and wetter. This movement occurs with the onset of the two dry periods (December–February, July–September), but when the rains move over the lowland plains in March and again in October the herds are brought down the slopes to graze the fresh grass. Then the Masai women plant maize, millet and sweet potatoes, but tilling the soil is distasteful to the men, who prefer to tend their herds.

Slowly, however, the traditional way of life of the Masai is beginning to change. In certain areas of Masailand, particularly in the Ngong, Loitokitok and Kajiado districts, the government is encouraging agricultural development and many co-operatives have been formed, cattle dips built, loans made to Masai farmers, and land demarcation carried out. In the Kajiado district some land has been consolidated, in the Ngong area near Nairobi some 320 ha of virgin soil have been formed into co-operative land for wheat growing, and kenaf has been introduced to blend with, and act as, a substitute for sisal. Wheat growing and sheep rearing have been combined by Masai living in the Kericho and Nandi districts, and Masai are being instructed in ranching and animal husbandry. There are plans for a new system of land tenure in Masailand which will protect the rights of the Masai in their homeland. These ventures represent the first stages of change in the Masai's traditional way of life but there are many Masai who have not changed and will not give up their nomadic existence for a more settled one.

The Turkana of Northern Kenya

An even more trying region is that of the Turkana of northern Kenya where rainfalls fall below 500 mm a year (see Table 5). This is an inhospitable region of thornbush, dwarf shrubs and sparse grass growth. Depressions or pans sometimes retain a little water and here grasses flourish briefly.

The camel is important here since it is able to eat the thornbush leaves and the leathery tufts of grass; it provides meat, milk and transport. Zebu cattle, goats and donkeys are also kept in this tsetse-free area and Persian black-faced lambs are reared. Some crops such as finger millet are planted where floods occur during occasional rainstorms. Like the Masai, the Turkana live in semi-permanent settlements and mud huts surrounded by thornbush thickets. Famine is a constant threat to the Turkana and each year famine relief measures are put into operation by the Kenya Government.

The Tuareg of the Sahara

The rigorous conditions of environment impose upon the Masai and Turkana a set pattern of life, a pattern which is repeated in the Sahara, and the nomadic tribes must conform to those conditions in order to survive. The Tuareg, like the Fulani, Masai and Turkana, are a nomadic pastoral people who once ranged over the Sahara from the Niger River to Ouargla and Touggourt and as far west as Timbuktu; but now, due to European and Arabic pressures, they are found chiefly in the Air, Tibesti and Ahaggar plateaux and in northern Nigeria. There are approximately 160 000 Tuaregs, of whom 12 000 live in the rugged Ahaggar.

The Ahaggar rises to over 2 700 m and derives a meagre rainfall from south-westerly and westerly air streams. Pastures consist of thin, permanent, wiry grass, scattered shrubs and thornbush concentrated mainly in hollows and along river beds, and the thicker grasses which flourish during brief showers. These are soon eaten by the cattle and the Tuareg are forced to move at least once a month between waterholes and pastures. They must be mobile, carry the minimum of baggage and travel in small family groups. Once a new site has been found the animals are set out to graze and scouts are sent to look for the next fresh pastures.

The Tuareg are also traders, setting out southwards in July, their camels loaded with dates and with salt from the desert pans, and accompanied by herds of donkeys and their special breed of white camels which are exchanged for 'morocco' leather, brass and silver ware, indigo dyed cloth, weapons, tools and pots and pans obtainable at centres such as Kano. The Tuareg return loaded with such goods in January and February. This trade once extended from the Atlas Mountains to the countries of West Africa,

Table 5 Rainfall statistics for Lodwar, Kenya (alt. 500 m)

Month	*Jan.*	*Feb.*	*Mar.*	*April*	*May*	*June*	*July*	*Aug.*	*Sept.*	*Oct.*	*Nov.*	*Dec.*	*Year*
Rainfall (mm)	5,1	7,6	15,2	40,6	22,9	7,6	10,2	7,6	5,1	7,6	7,6	7,6	144,8

but today modern trucking companies have severely limited it. The Tuareg were once masters of all central Saharan trading routes, extracting tolls from merchants in exchange for protection, and plundering caravans. This activity has now ceased and many Tuareg cultivate small gardens and palm groves. The severe droughts of the mid-1970s have caused great hardship among these people.

(10) Sedentary people

The Souafa

In the Sahara proper the desert oases support a truly sedentary population now approaching one million who farm a million cultivated hectares. The reduction of feuds and tribal wars during colonial rule, the more hygienic and sanitary conditions, and the medical care and free food distributed in times of want, have resulted in marked increases in population.

In the Souf area, a north-western extension of the Great Eastern Erg around El Oued, the Souafa people depend on underground water for their palms:

> The eternal glory of the Souf is its palm groves. Flying over the town is like flying over the moon. The Souafa have dug troughs in the dunes and ten, twenty even several hundred palm-trees grow in craters of widely differing sizes. Some of the craters are so deep that the crowns of the palm-trees are below ground-level. In almost all troughs there are draw-wells from which vegetables and tobacco plants are irrigated. They are not used to water palm-trees, for the Souafa have planted the trees so deep that the roots are in subsoil water. The healthy state of the palms shows that there is an underground river, for stagnant water would kill the trees.[7]

The Souf region is rapidly becoming over-populated. At the end of the nineteenth century 160 000 trees supported 21 000 people; by the 1930s there were 65 000 people and about 400 000 palms, while today about 500 000 trees support 100 000 people. The water-table has dropped due to the greater demands on the water supply and the Souafa must dig deeper craters for their palms.

But the Sahara is now being termed 'the Land of the Future' by the Arabs, for besides the great discoveries of minerals over the past ten years, interest is being shown in the agricultural possibilities of the region; for now there is money to invest. In 1955 there were only about a million cultivated hectares of land. The main products were dates from some ten million palm-trees, groundnuts, olives and small amounts of fruit and vegetables. The land supported about 1,5 million sheep and goats and 300 000 camels. Since then over 800 new boreholes and waterholes have been created and new plantations laid out, e.g. at Zelfana, where two million young eucalyptus trees have been planted to anchor the dunes, and new fruit, cotton, vegetables and rice crops are being gathered.

(11) The rôle of the cash crop

The cash crop has been an important part of the cultivation system of the African farmer throughout West Africa, in Egypt and Sudan since the turn of the century and it has become increasingly important in many other countries since the 1930s, largely because of the steady improvement in communications linking with markets. The African farmer has been particularly skilful in adapting the indigenous forest tree into his agrarian system; nowhere is this more evident than in West Africa (cocoa, rubber, oil palm).

Nigeria

In Nigeria approximately half a million hectares are devoted to cocoa, mainly grown on small African farms especially in Oyo and Ondo states, and in a good season the annual crop brings US$500 a tonne to the farmer. In the north the groundnut is also predominantly a peasant crop and there are no large estates. The average groundnut holding throughout northern Nigeria is approximately 0,8 to one hectare and the average yield in groundnuts is nearly 675 kg per hectare. For this crop the farmer will receive prices which have varied from US$200 to $500 per tonne. But the oil palm is Nigeria's chief peasant cash crop and 94 per cent is grown on small farms. The oil palm is indigenous to the southern

[7] George Gerster.

part of Nigeria, south-eastern Nigeria supplying the vast bulk of the oil palm exports. The main area of the native palm oil producing regions lies in the scarplands and plains from Onitsha to Abakaliki. In the oil palm belt successful attempts have been made to improve on the older wasteful methods of oil extraction by introducing hand presses and centralised Pioneer oil mills by the government. In recent years several oil mills have been set up by private enterprise, while the state governments are trying experiments to improve quality and production.

The Nigerian government is anxious to stimulate cash crop output and to this end prices paid for farm produce have been increased in recent years. Although there are a number of plantations in Nigeria, it is the local farmer, who represents about 70 per cent of the working population and accounts for approximately 50 per cent of the GDP of the country, who is the main basis of agriculture. (See Chapter Six.)

The Gambia

Another important cash crop of West Africa, particularly in the drier, sandier northern zones, is the groundnut. In the Gambia the farmers depend for the greater part of their income on groundnuts which are sown in June and July, and harvested in October and November. The crop is entirely raised by peasant farmers. The average annual output is about 80 000 t, or about one tonne per farmer. Some of the crop is grown by the 'strange farmers' who come from Senegal, Mali and Guinea Bissau during the planting season, plant their seeds, reap a harvest, sell it, and return. Many of them now help Gambian farmers with their harvest, are paid for their labour, and also cultivate a small patch of their own.

Kenya

Other examples of important cash crops in the African farming economy include cotton in the Sudan, Egypt, Nigeria and Uganda, rubber in Liberia, tobacco and soil seeds in Tanzania, and cereals and fruit in Algeria. In countries where the growing of cash crops was restricted by colonial legislation, African farmers are now growing increasing amounts of export crops. For example, in 1960 it was true to say that the European farmer of the Kenya Highlands grew nearly 80 per cent of that country's export crops. But now the picture has changed radically as land reorganisation schemes begin to make progress. Consider, for example, the growing importance of African-grown tea to Kenya's economy. In 1965 there were approximately 23 000 African small-scale tea growers and the industry was still monopolised by large expatriate firms and their plantations. The average size of their holdings was just under a quarter of a hectare. By the end of 1976 Kenya had nearly 95 000 growers of tea in all districts, and Kenya was the foremost producer of tea in Africa and third largest exporter after India and Sri Lanka. Kenya's Tea Development Authority aims at having some 40 000 ha under tea and to increase the present 15 processing factories to 25.

Uganda

In neighbouring Uganda nearly all cultivation is in the hands of African smallholders who have a million hectares under cash crops, compared with about 35 000 ha of estate crops of coffee, sugar and tea. Cotton, tea, tobacco, sugar cane and coffee are produced mainly on small farms of about a hectare and a half.

(12) Subsistence crops

But the African farmer must also support his family from the land and, because of this, subsistence crops play a large part in his cultivation system. Thus,

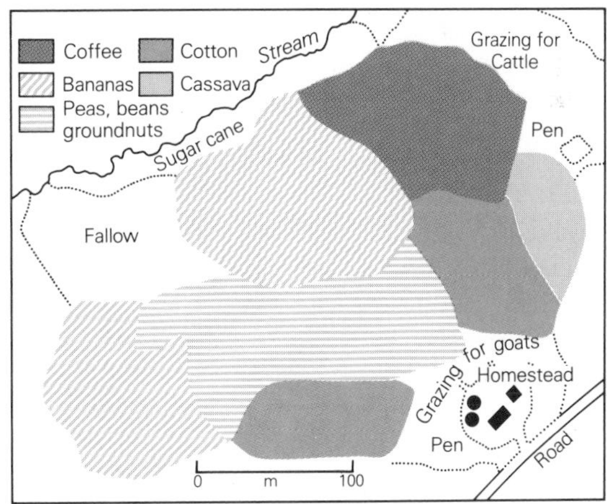

Fig. 4.17 Uganda – cash crop and subsistence cultivation on a Muganda *shamba*

while Ugandan farmers devote a million hectares to cash crops, they also grow over two and a half million hectares of crops for domestic consumption, and it is very rare for more than one-third of the *shamba* to be devoted to cash crops (Fig. 4.17). In Malaŵi cash crops do not form a large part of the cultivable system and the greater part of the farmer's land is used in growing subsistence foods, although any surplus of maize (the staple), sorghums, millet, root crops, fruits, vegetables and pulses are sold in local markets to purchase necessities.

Congo Republic

In the Congo Republic some 60 per cent of the population is engaged in agriculture, mainly for home consumption, and agricultural products represent only 20 per cent of exports (most exports are forestry products). About 75 per cent of all the crops grown are subsistence foods – oil palms, groundnuts, citrus fruits, tobacco, sugar cane, millets, and rice. Small areas of tobacco, cocoa and coffee are grown for sale.

Zambia

In Zambia most of the people are engaged in the cultivation of subsistence crops and it is estimated that about 87 per cent of the total crop production is for home consumption only. Here the principal subsistence crops are maize, millets and cassava, and some livestock is reared for meat and milk. The main commodities marketed are maize, groundnuts, tobacco, cotton and cattle.

Table 6 Africa's annual fish catch 1975

Country	*Catch ('000 t)*
South Africa	1315
Nigeria	507
Senegal	362
Ghana	255
Morocco	211
Angola	184
Tanzania	181
Uganda	170
Zaïre	125
Chad	115
Egypt	107

(13) The fishing industry

Uganda

Many governments in Africa are paying serious attention to increasing the amount of fish caught both in rivers and lakes and off their coasts. Uganda has led the way in the development of fish farms – large rectangular ponds stocked with Nile perch and tilapia – and has introduced additional supplies to many cattle watering points. There are now 8 000 fish farms in Uganda with a potential of about 500 000 kg of fish a year.

Nigeria

In the coastal areas of Nigeria considerable attention is being given to the development of offshore fish resources. The warm shallow waters in the Bight of Benin are one of the richest fishing grounds in the world. To exploit these resources in a region where meat is in short supply, boat construction and the establishment of fish processing plants is encouraged, and fishermen are urged to join local cooperatives. Inland all states in Nigeria operate fish farms and encourage river fishing, and are constructing large fish ponds; Lagos State has set aside nearly 1 000 ha for fish ponds.

Ghana

Fishing is also a major occupation along Ghana's coast and about 25 000 people catch 70 per cent of the fish harvest in this zone. Consumption of fish in Ghana, however, exceeds the supply, and large imports have to be made. Ghanaian fishermen use traditional hollowed out logs some 10 m long as their canoes and there are about 8 000 of these on the country's coastline. While in 1962 about 20 per cent of these vessels were motorised today nearly all have an outboard motor and, as a result, the fish catch has increased fivefold. There is also a small fleet of motorised trawlers whose catch is sold to the 'fish mammies' who sun-dry and smoke the fish for sale.

The main species of fish caught along Ghana's coast during the main season (July to August) is a large sardine, but other fish include tuna, snapper, barracuda and mackerel. A major problem of the fish industry in Ghana is the inefficient processing and marketing by the 'fish mammies'. Fish are dried by laying them on the beaches, thus exposing them to insects and dust. Smoking the catch is done in inefficient clay ovens which use a great deal of fuel. The smoked fish are then sent to market in wicker baskets, sometimes for distances over 750 km, so that they arrive broken and infested with beetles. The government is now experimenting with better ovens, polyethylene packaging of the fish after smoking, and packing in wooden fish crates.

Liberia

Fish is one of the cheapest forms of protein available in Liberia and the most common fish caught off-shore are barracuda, snapper and cavalla, and also shrimps. Fishing is largely in the hands of one company, Mesurado, which markets about 15 000 t a year. Of this, about 3 500 t are produced locally, while the rest is imported from Japanese, Russian and Polish deep-sea trawlers. Mesurado has 12 shrimp trawlers and five fishing trawlers. Some of Liberia's fish needs are provided by the Kru tribe who operate dugout canoes like those in Ghana, but their contribution is small since they have no storage facilities, essential in the tropical heat.

Morocco

One of the best developed fishing industries is that of Morocco. Along Morocco's Atlantic coast, the main fishing grounds for tunny, sardines, mackerel and anchovy, about 90 per cent of the fishing crews are employed, the rest in the Mediterranean. Here over 2 000 trawlers, motorised and sail vessels are used to catch about 250 000 t of fish a year. The largest fishing centres with canning and processing plants are located at Tangier, Casablanca, Rabat, Safi and Agadir.

Other countries, apart from South Africa, which catch significant amounts of fish are:

Kenya: Annual catch, 34 000 t; imports 2 000 t; 30 000 fishermen; 65 per cent of catch from inland waters.

Algeria: Annual catch, 25 000 t; 3 300 fishermen.

Cameroon: Annual catch, 71 000 t; imports 8 000 t; 12 000 employed.

Ivory Coast: Annual catch, 71 000 t; imports 18 000 t; 16 000 employed.

Gabon: Annual catch, 5 000 t; imports 5 000 t; 1 200 employed.

Zaïre: Annual catch, 146 000 t; imports 67 000 t; 63 000 employed.

One of the main problems facing Africa's fishing industry as a whole is the loss of much of the fish catch to non-African nations. Between Tangier and the Zaïre river mouth foreign vessels take two-thirds of the annual fish catch. South of the Zaïre mouth, fish catches by non-African nations have risen from 2 million tonnes in the mid-1960s to nearly 2,5 million tonnes in the mid-1970s. In 1972, for example, South Africa caught 1,1 million tonnes in the South Atlantic and Angola 0,6 million tonnes, while Russia took 0,72 million tonnes, Spain 208 000 t, Cuba 120 000 t, Japan 106 000 t and Bulgaria 28 000 t. The main solution to this problem has been to extend the fishing and other economic rights of African coastal nations to 200 miles offshore – the Exclusive Economic Zone suggested by the Law of the Sea Conference at Caracas in 1974 (see Chapter Thirteen).

A partial solution would be the greater co-operation between the foreign nations and countries of Africa in fishing the continent's waters. Joint fish fleets could be established or foreign nations could base their fleets in African ports. Already agreements have been made between Japan and Kenya and between Russia and Somalia, while Japanese companies have set up a fishing enterprise in Ghana.

The landlocked countries of Africa – Zambia, Mali, Niger, the Central Africa Republic – are at a disadvantage due to high costs of imported protein-rich fish. The quantities obtained from inland fisheries are small compared with those of the coastal nations. Mechanisation of fishing vessels, however, has improved catches as, for example, on Lake Chad, where the catch of 15 000 t in 1958 has been increased to 75 000 t in the 1970s.

(For Questions, Discussion Topics and Practical Work see the end of Chapter Five, page 110.)

CHAPTER FIVE

Agriculture 2 – Introduced cultivation methods

So far the use of Africa's soil by the indigenous African farmer has been discussed and it is now time to assess external influences on farming systems. Apart from the gradual spread of cultivation by the Boer farmer in South Africa from the seventeenth century onwards, real expansion of European cultivation only began towards the end of the nineteenth century. By the 1890s industrial Europe was looking for something more than mere territorial expansion in Africa; vast quantities of raw materials were needed – natural oils to lubricate machines, rubber for wheeled vehicles, and cheap foods requiring vast quantities of edible oils for growing populations. Industrialists saw a rich potential in the African rain forests, where there was scope for the plantation cultivation of oil palms, rubber, cotton, sugar cane, coffee and cocoa.

Major industrial companies in Europe sought concessions in Equatorial Africa from the governments ruling the new territories, and plantations were carved from the forest belt. Elsewhere, individual farmers laid out estates in areas where land seemed unlimited and where climate was suitable for European settlement – the higher plateaux of East Africa and the former Rhodesias.

The advantages of tropical plantations

From the commercial point of view the plantation is much more economical than the purchase of produce direct from local small-scale cultivators. There are several reasons for this:

a The plantation is run by a company with tremendous financial reserves, efficient processing machinery, and control of a vast and efficiently-run marketing network.

b Strict control of plant growth, the breeding of improved varieties, and the use of special fertilisers are easier operations for the large company. Plant products are easier to harvest than under natural conditions.

c The labourers, often transported great distances, are trained in the various aspects of plantation work and acquire specialised skills.

d Harvesting of the produce is carried out quickly, cheaply and efficiently, with economic transport to processing centres.

e Regular supplies of produce are guaranteed by the plantation system; this often justifies the erection of processing factories on the spot, rather than exporting the bulky raw materials over long distances.

f Plantation organisation ensures no wastage; waste is used as fertiliser or as fuel.

The disadvantages of plantations

There are, however, certain disadvantages associated with the plantation and estate system of cultivation. Often the labour, mostly young men, leave their villages and the cultivation of subsistence crops to the women and older folk, although most plantations do provide housing for families. Moreover, large plantations have much capital tied up in labour, machinery and marketing facilities, and they are the first to suffer when prices for their produce fall on world markets. In contrast, the small African farm can weather such economic storms and often produces substantial amounts of export crops when the plantations have reduced their exports, e.g. cotton and coffee production in Uganda. Some types of

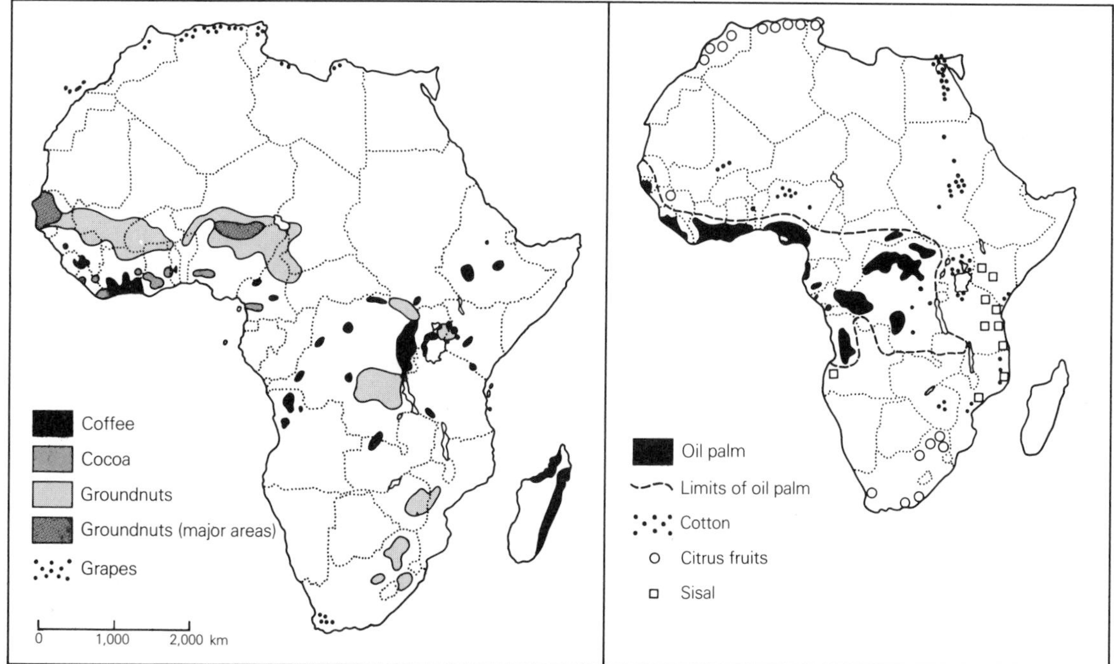

Fig. 5.1a and b: Africa – distribution of some important cash crops

crops are more suited to the small farm, e.g. the rougher types of tobacco grown and cured by traditional methods in Zambia and the south of Tanzania. The small cocoa farms of Ghana need very little capital to begin with, yet they provide 65 per cent of the country's export produce; whether the plantation system would be more successful here is difficult to say.

Plantation organisation

A plantation is extremely large, covering thousands of hectares and run by a huge company, often foreign. Such plantations will have certain things in common. They will be concentrating on cash crops, usually destined for markets outside the country of origin; subsistence crops will be grown only on a small scale to feed the work force, and in some areas labour may have to be brought a considerable distance due to local scarcity, as in parts of the Zaïre rainforests. Many plantations increase their output by buying local produce. The plantation management provides housing, food and medical facilities and sometimes elementary education. Much revenue goes to the government of the host country through the taxation of the workers' wages, export duties on produce, and company land rents. Other benefits often accrue – roads and railways to and from the plantations will speed traffic generally, and enable areas along their lengths to produce crops and market them more efficiently; factories are often set up and provide local employment, and bulk handling facilities at export ports are often financed by plantation companies.

The following examples illustrate the main types of plantation in Africa. The huge Unilever estates are good examples of large-scale organisation and huge capital investment; the Firestone plantations show the great support a country's economy receives from overseas investment, while many of the estates in the Kenya Highlands illustrate the smaller family-owned concern. Large company-owned plantations are seen again in Malaŵi (tea), Tanzania (sisal), and Natal, South Africa (sugar cane). Most of these sample studies lie within the tropical zone of Africa, where plantation methods have flourished over the past eighty years.

Oil palm plantations

From small concessions granted by the Belgians to the Unilever Company of Great Britain in the early nineteenth century, plantations have spread throughout Zaïre into Gabon, Cameroon and, to a lesser extent, Nigeria, producing vast quantities of palm oil, rubber, cocoa, bananas, coffee and smaller amounts of tea. The most important are the palm oil plantations which occupy 61 000 ha or 80 per cent of Unilever's total concession of 77 000 ha in Africa (Fig. 5.2). Unilever was particularly successful in obtaining concessions in the former Congo, where the Belgians made every effort to expand the economy of the country, but in Nigeria plantation establishment had to be far more selective since all land was African-owned or held in trust or, in the most suitable area of south-east Nigeria, very densely settled.

The creation of an oil palm plantation

Site selection and preparation: Climatic conditions are most suitable for the oil palm between 5° north and south of the equator at low elevations; in the Cameroon cultivation has been successful up to 700 m but not above this. Soils are usually poor, but better patches are indicated by richer vegetation, and soil samples are taken and tested for optimum conditions. The oil mills need to be situated close to navigable rivers and on flat land to facilitate road building. Plenty of water is also needed for the various processes and for the workers' use.

Workers' accommodation is built and seed beds laid out in cleared forest patches. Within six months the 150 mm tall seedlings are transplanted in a nursery in rows half a metre apart. After two years they are finally bedded out, and work is begun on the planned plantation layout. Roads are bulldozed on a rectangular pattern and the forest blocks gradually cleared. A cover crop is planted which suppresses secondary forest growth, yields precious nitrogen, scarce in tropical soils, and prevents the earth from being baked hard. The cleared timber is used for house construction or left to rot.

Planting and harvesting: The young trees are taken from the nursery beds and planted in holes 10 m apart in staggered rows. The workers control the growth of cover crops and secondary growth and, as the palm grows, they cut away the drooping fronds to make inspection easier. The African labour force is very skilled, and a cutter must be able to judge when the fruit is ripe enough to yield high quality oil. This is important, since unripe fruit gives a lower yield, and overripe fruit a good yield but of poorer quality, due to fatty acid development. Cutting goes on throughout the year, each tree bearing a fruit head

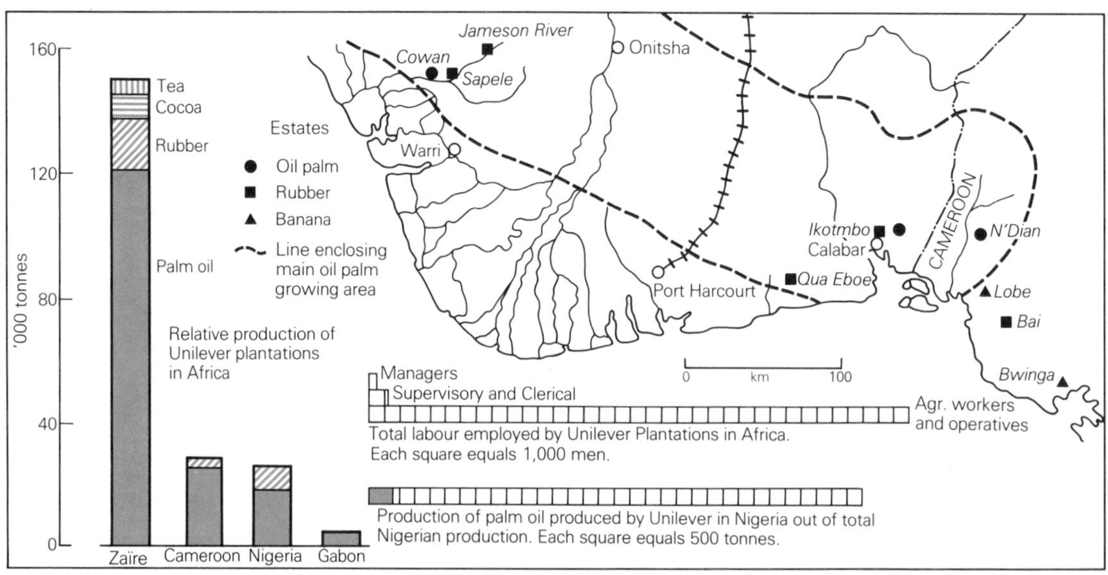

Fig. 5.2 The Unilever Company in Africa (production and employment)

once a week. The cutters use long knives attached to poles or, with taller trees, ladders or waist climbing ropes.

The fruit is often bruised by its fall or by handling, and immediate processing is essential. The fruits are carried in baskets or on poles to lorries or to steriliser cages pulled by a locomotive on a light railway. Lorries are preferred because they reduce carrying and can get closer to the rows of palms. Bulldozed roads are also less expensive to build and can reach all parts of the plantation, whereas railways are often uneconomic if harvests are small.

Processing: At the mill the fruit is weighed, sterilised under steam to arrest acid development, the stalks removed for fuel, and the fruit reduced to a pulp which is passed through oil extracting machines. The oil is stored in settling tanks to separate impurities. The dried shells and fibre are used as fuel, and the cleaned kernels graded and bagged.

Exports: Zaïre produces about 25 per cent of the world's palm oil and large quantities of kernel oil and oil cake; about 80 per cent is plantation produced, the rest comes from wild palms. This contrasts with Nigeria, where 94 per cent is produced on small farms, and only 6 per cent comes from plantations. Figure 5.3 shows the chief export routes. Rail routes run south from Ilebo to Zambia, Zimbabwe and South Africa and bulk oil goes by tank barge to Kinshasa and thence by rail tanker to Matadi where it is transferred to ocean-going oil tankers. There are bulk oil transit stations at Mbandaka, Mosango and Boma. The main countries of destination are the United States, Belgium, Holland, Germany and Italy, with smaller amounts to Britain, Japan, Zambia, Zimbabwe and France. Zaïre now ranks a poor third in world production of palm oil (70 000 t; Malaysia 750 000 t; Indonesia 260 000 t) with the Ivory Coast fourth (40 000 t).

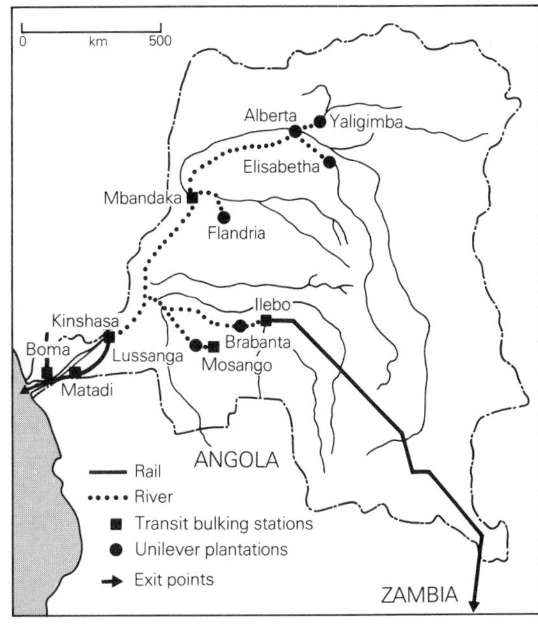

Fig. 5.3 Zaïre – exit routes for Unilever oil palm produce. Border closures at present hinder southern export routes.

Rubber in Liberia

Although palm oil is an important element in Zaïre's economy there is also a wide variety of other plantation crops which helps to broaden the economy, for palm oil represents only 7 per cent of all exports. In contrast, rubber has for years dominated Liberia's economy and in 1945 formed 96,6 per cent of exports. In 1975 rubber represented 12 per cent of exports but this does not represent a drop in output; it is due to the increase in exports of iron ore.

Plantation cultivation has developed in the coastal low-lands of Liberia where rainfalls exceed 2 500 mm a year, the long wet season extending from April to November followed by a moist sticky 'dry' season. Relative humidities rise to 85 per cent, and temperatures (24° to 27°C) are high. Under these conditions cocoa, coffee and citrus are plantation grown north-east of Monrovia, and oil palm and cocoa in the central and southern coastal plains. But the largest plantations are those of the American Firestone Company located north of Harbel and at Cavalla in the south-eastern corner.

The history of rubber in Liberia goes back to 1910 when the British planted 800 ha at Mount Barclay near Monrovia, but abandoned the project ten years later due to falling world prices. In 1924 there were only 400 ha producing half a million pounds worth of rubber. Physical conditions were examined by Firestone, which badly needed plantation concessions in view of Britain's monopoly of Malayan sources. The failure of Henry Ford's rubber plantations at Belterra and Fordlandia in the Amazon Basin in the 1920s due to labour, disease and transport problems, reduced the hopes of the motor industry in the United States of receiving regular rubber supplies from that source. In 1926 the US Firestone Company obtained 99-year leases in Liberia to establish plantations, and rubber has since played a vital role in Liberia's economy. Housing estates, roads and dispensaries were built and by 1928 6 100 ha had been planted, rising to 22 000 ha by 1933. The Second World War stimulated production especially when Malaya was overrun by the Japanese. Today 43 000 workers (including 30 000 skilled tappers) tend 11,5 million trees, which produced most of Liberia's exports of rubber. In recent years, higher prices for rubber have more than doubled the value of rubber exports, although the quantity exported has remained fairly steady: 1972 exports were 83 million kilogrammes valued at US$25 million; 1973 – 86 million kilogrammes at $37 million; 1974 – 86 million kilogrammes at $55 million; 1975 – 83 million kilogrammes at $46 million.

Rubber is still a very large item in exports (12 per cent), but its relative importance has decreased due to growing exports of iron ore. The main plantation is at Harbel on the Farmington River 25 km from the coast, while a second plantation lies 40 km inland on the Cavalla River, which is navigable only for small craft owing to sandbars. Shallow draught barges navigate the bars and the liquid latex is pumped into the holds of tankers. There are storage tanks at Monrovia.

The Harbel Plantation may be approached from the south-east along the Farmington River. The extreme southern section of this 34 000 ha estate is occupied by the processing factory, the clinical research laboratory, a dispensary, transport buildings and administrative offices. The remainder of the plantation is divided into 45 separate sections to facilitate administration and the orderly tapping of the trees. The whole plantation is crossed by a network of roads. Within the divisions are botanical research gardens, research and seed selection centres, rubber nurseries, sawmills, a brick factory, a club house, a hydro-electric power station, a soft drinks factory, a plant manufacturing rubber cups, sandals and soap, and a wireless transmitting station. The plantation is thus virtually self-contained.

The benefits to Liberia from such an economic enterprise may be summarised as follows:

Agricultural assistance: The company assists small-scale rubber growers, now numbering 4 200 compared with 150 in 1941, by supplying seeds and

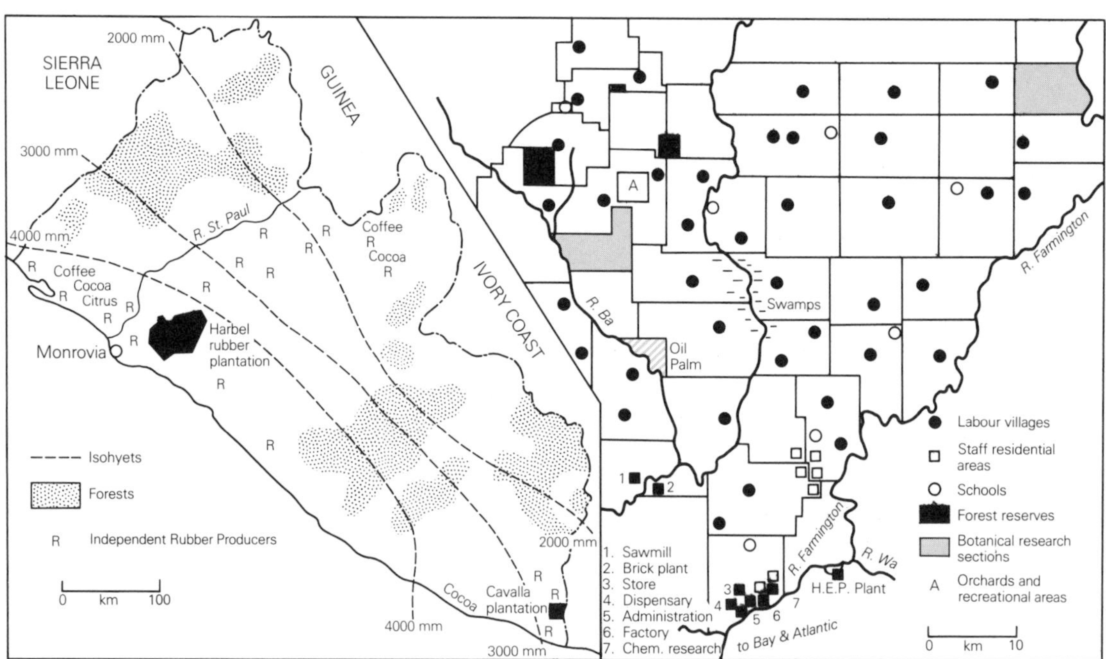

Fig. 5.4 Liberia – cash crop areas and the Firestone Harbel Rubber Plantation

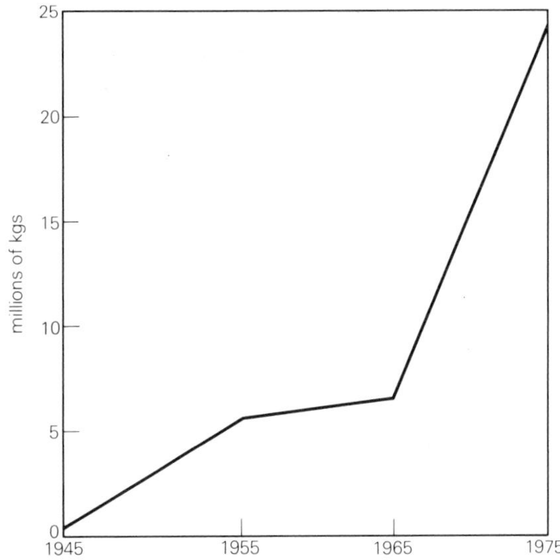

Fig. 5.5 Liberia – rubber production by independent growers

advice, and by buying their entire rubber production. In 1941 independent rubber farmers sold 0,23 million kilogrammes of rubber to Firestone, and in 1951 1,9 million kilogrammes. The current sales are now 24 million kilogrammes.

Crop research: The company also experiments with subsistence and cash crops suited to Liberia's soils and climate, which are considered excellent for coffee, cocoa, bananas, oil palm and rice. Experiments with livestock and poultry keeping, and with many fruits – mangoes, papayas, pineapples, bananas, avocados, oranges, and grapefruit – are promising.

Medical research: A company medical service provides two hospitals, dispensaries, pre-natal clinics and a child care service. Research into tropical diseases, medical research and expenditure on medical services amounts to more than US$2 million a year.

The Kenya Highlands – small and medium-sized estates and mixed farms

The soils and climate of the Kenya Highlands are suitable for a wide range of commercially profitable crops, such as coffee, tea, sisal, pyrethrum and pineapples. Sisal and pineapples are located on the drier eastern fringes which receive from 750 to about 1 020 mm of rainfall annually; coffee is grown north of Nairobi on the Aberdare dip-slopes (1 020 to 1 520 mm); tea is found on the wetter plateau around Kericho (1 270 mm and over); while pyrethrum

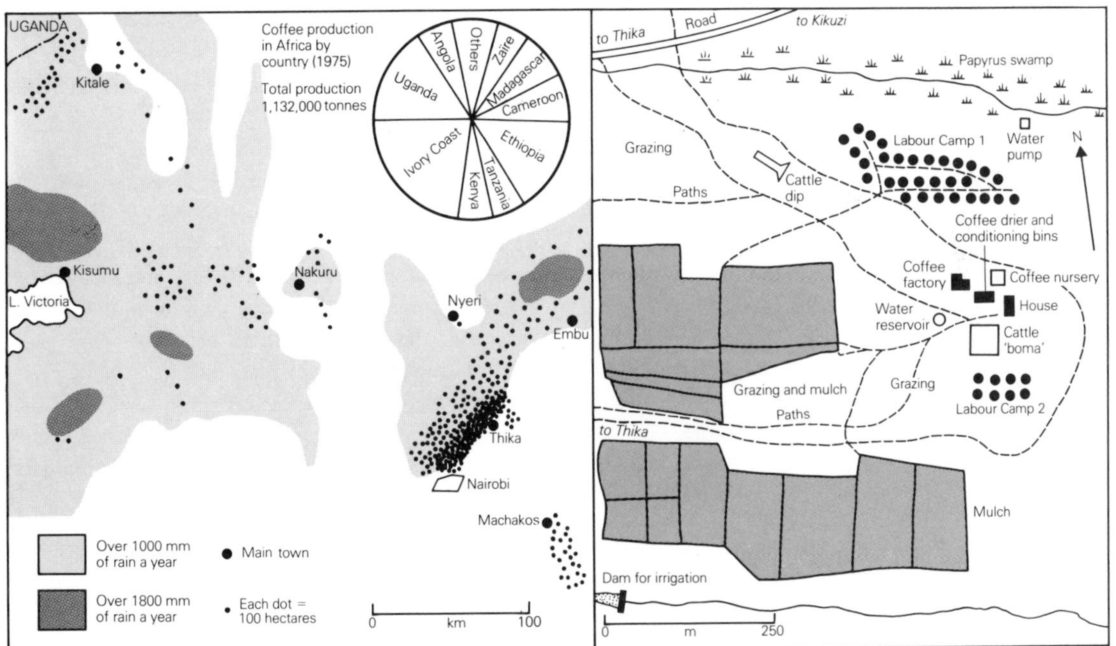

Fig. 5.6 Kenya – coffee production in the Kenya Highlands, and a coffee estate near Thika

needs the strong sunlight and coolness of the highlands for a good flowering head. These cash crops are mainly grown on large company estates although an increasing amount is being grown on small African *shambas*.

The moderate rainfalls, cool temperatures at 1 800 to 2 300 m, and rolling green pastures and shady woodlands are also ideal for herds of imported dairy cattle – Guernseys, Jerseys, Friesians and Ayrshires – and the Highlands are probably the foremost dairying region in tropical Africa, comparable with subtropical Natal and the temperate south-west Cape Province.

The Highlands of Kenya thus form an economic heartland, and original forest, savanna and bush have been converted during 70 years of European settlement into an agricultural concentration of stud farms, cattle ranches and plantations and estates covering 21 000 square kilometres. Many of these farms have been broken up into smaller units, as we have seen, and are being farmed by African cultivators. Thus, whereas in 1960 large estates produced 80 per cent of the coffee, they now produce less than 70 per cent. Again, African farmers cultivate 5 000 ha of tea on small quarter-hectare plots compared with approximately 10 500 ha on large estates. However, company estates and farms still figure largely in the economy.

A coffee estate

Coffee is the most important export crop in Kenya, with 47 per cent of production from estates, the rest from smallholdings. It is also the first export crop of Uganda and the third export of Tanzania. The main plantation zone is a broad belt 25 km wide and 60 km long, extending north-east of Nairobi where there are several large estates. West of this area many small African *shambas* include coffee as a cash crop, producing nearly 40 000 t a year. Other coffee growing areas are found on the volcanic soils of Mount Elgon near the Kenya–Uganda border, on the Cherangani slopes in the Rift Valley, and in the Mua hills near Machakos.

Zaïre: Rows of coffee bushes, Eastern Highland region.

The coffee estate shown in Fig. 5.6 lies 50 km north-east of Nairobi, and covers 200 ha of which 90 ha are under coffee. In this region, which is marginal for coffee growing, the farmer keeps a modest sized herd of Ayrshire cattle and a smaller one of sheep, and is experimenting with cotton. The landscape here is undulating, cut into broad flat ridges by dip-slope rivers of the Aberdares. Average temperatures are modified by altitude (1 450 m, 10°C) while rainfalls are moderate and fairly reliable (Table 7).

Work on the estate: Before planting, the coffee seeds are dried in ash, then planted in a primary nursery when ten centimetres tall; later they are transplanted to a second nursery and left for two years. They are then transferred to prepared fields, and shaded by grass coverings which are later used for mulch. After two years the plants begin to bear fruit, and they reach maturity when ten years old.

Green oval beans appear on the bushes after the whitish, sweet-smelling flower has germinated and died. The beans develop in bunches and gradually

Table 7 Kenya: Rainfall figures for Sassa coffee estate

Month	*Jan.*	*Feb.*	*Mar.*	*April*	*May*	*June*	*July*	*Aug.*	*Sept.*	*Oct.*	*Nov.*	*Dec.*	*Year*
Rainfall (mm)	43,2	27,9	106,7	231,1	88,9	5,1	7,6	20,3	38,1	137,2	241,3	160,0	1076,9

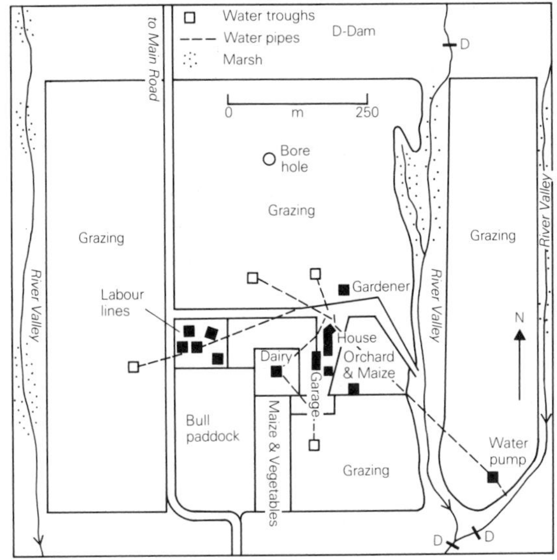

Fig. 5.7 Kenya – a dairy farm in the Highlands

turn a reddish brown. They are then hand-picked, taken to the plantation factory by lorry or in baskets, and pulped to remove the skins and fleshy parts which are used as fertiliser. The beans ferment overnight, and are then washed and covered with polythene sheets to prevent excessive drying by the sun. After further washing and browning in the sun, they are stored in conditioning bins prior to despatch to the roasting mills in Nairobi. These methods are exactly the same as those on small coffee farms in Kenya, where individual small-scale farmers belong to a central co-operative which collects, processes and markets their produce.

A coffee estate is thus a concern unsuitable for a farmer in a hurry. Constant vigilance is needed against insects and plant diseases, bushes are sprayed regularly, weeding continuously carried on, and moisture retained in the soils by mulching. Production at the estate varies considerably with rainfall amount, from 60 t in a poor year to 150 t in a good year.

A dairy farm

Dairy farming began in Kenya in 1911 and butter and cheese were first exported to London in 1921. By 1930 exports had increased thirty-fold and today dairy products are worth US$12 million a year.

Table 8 Kenya: Sample farms in the Kenya Highlands

Location	*Area in hectares*	*Altitude in metres*	*Av. ann. rainfall mm*	*Soils*	*Stock and crops (Figs in brackets indicate hectarage)*	*Work force*
1 Nr. Kitale, Trans-Nzoia Plateau	370	2 000	1 041 (28 Apr. to Aug.)	Red loams and Black Cotton	Coffee, oranges, rye, maize, sunflowers, wheat, tomatoes	40
2 Nr. Kitale, Trans-Nzoia Plateau	230	1 900	1 041	Poor sandy types needing much fertiliser	Maize (57), sun-flowers, seed grass, apples, oranges. 150 pedigree Guernsey dairy cows	25
3 Tana River region, south of Mt. Kenya	18 200	1 600	711 very variable	Black Cotton, sandy and red clays	Coffee (80), maize (80), pineapples, and lucerne. 3 500 Boran beef cattle	60
4 Northern Highlands, north of Mt. Kenya near Nanyuki	3 600	1 920	635 very variable from 305 to 1 090	Black Cotton and red loams	1 000 Sahiwal and Ayrshire cattle, 60 sheep, 150 pigs, 300 laying hens	40
5 Thika District, 47·5 km north-east of Nairobi	410	1 500	813 variable	Red sandy and clayey types	Coffee, sisal, pine-apples, apples, plums, cherries, vegetables	40
6 Rift Valley, near Njoro, 32,5 km west of Nakuru	305	2 220	1 067	Dark-brown loams	57 Friesland and Jerseys, 25 pigs, 300 Hampshire Down, Cheviot and Romney sheep, 150 beef cattle. Maize (1,6), potatoes (4), wheat (100)	50

About one-third of production is exported to Ethiopia, the Middle East, Uganda, Tanzania and Malaŵi.

The sample dairy farm north-west of Nairobi (Fig. 5.7) is fairly typical of the smaller estate in Africa. It covers 53 ha on the higher part of a broad ridge from which most of the forest has been cleared, except for shade trees. Although a few subsistence crops are grown, practically the whole area is used to graze sixty Ayrshire cows and two bulls. The farm was originally used for coffee and pyrethrum and this mined the soils of minerals, but the use of fertiliser and inferior stock to clear the rank grass and provide manure helped the soils to recuperate. Many of the original cattle were lost through diseases such as East Coast Fever, but once the land was cleared better grades of cattle were introduced. Since dairy farming in Kenya suffers from droughts from November to March, farms must be near water supplies. On this farm a spring and small stream supply 10 000 litres per day in normal periods and double that during droughts. The milk yield, usually 850 litres a day, goes to Nairobi.

There are many other types of small estates and mixed farms in the Kenya Highlands and Table 8 indicates the wide variety, sizes and uses of these farms. It is very noticeable how the types of crops grown and the breeds of animals vary with location, and with rainfall amount and reliability.

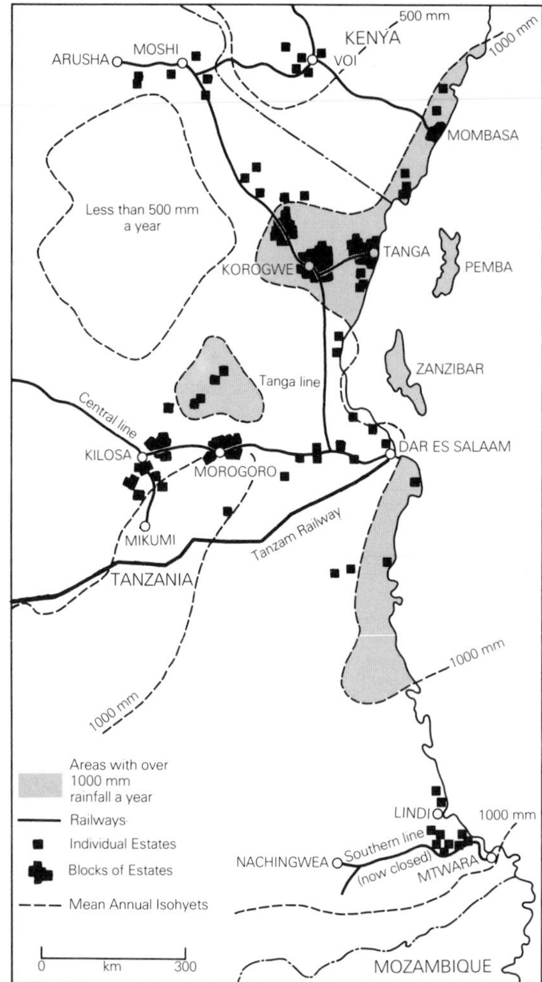

Fig. 5.8 Tanzania – distribution of sisal estates in relation to annual rainfall

Sisal in East Africa

Sisal is found in the drier eastern fringes of the Kenya Highlands, in the coastal zone near Mombasa and in Tanzania, and along the main railways. There is a correlation between sisal distribution and the 1 000 m isohyet (Fig. 5.8). The plant will grow on a wide variety of soils, but red earths and those derived from coral limestone, the latter typical of East Africa's coastal plains, are best. The richer the soil, the better the fibre yields in quality and quantity, for sisal takes a heavy toll of soil minerals. High temperatures, plentiful sunshine and rainfalls between 680 and 1 200 mm, are well suited to sisal.

Sisal was first introduced into Tanganyika in 1892 by Dr. Richard Hindorf, who brought Mexican bulbils from Florida and planted them at Kikogwe near Pangani. The first exports were made in 1900 and had reached 20 000 t by 1913, but production fell during the First World War, and in 1920 only 8 000 t were exported. However, since the 1920s sisal has figured large in Tanzania's exports, at one time averaging about 25 per cent, and reaching a record of 60 per cent in 1951 with its use in the Korean War. It now forms about 3 per cent of exports (cotton 14 per cent, coffee 15 per cent). About US $70 million is invested in Tanzania's sisal, a crop grown on plantations seldom less than 1 200 ha in size. It has allowed areas unsuitable for most crops to be used fully.

In Kenya sisal makes a smaller but significant contribution to the economy, employing 25 000 men

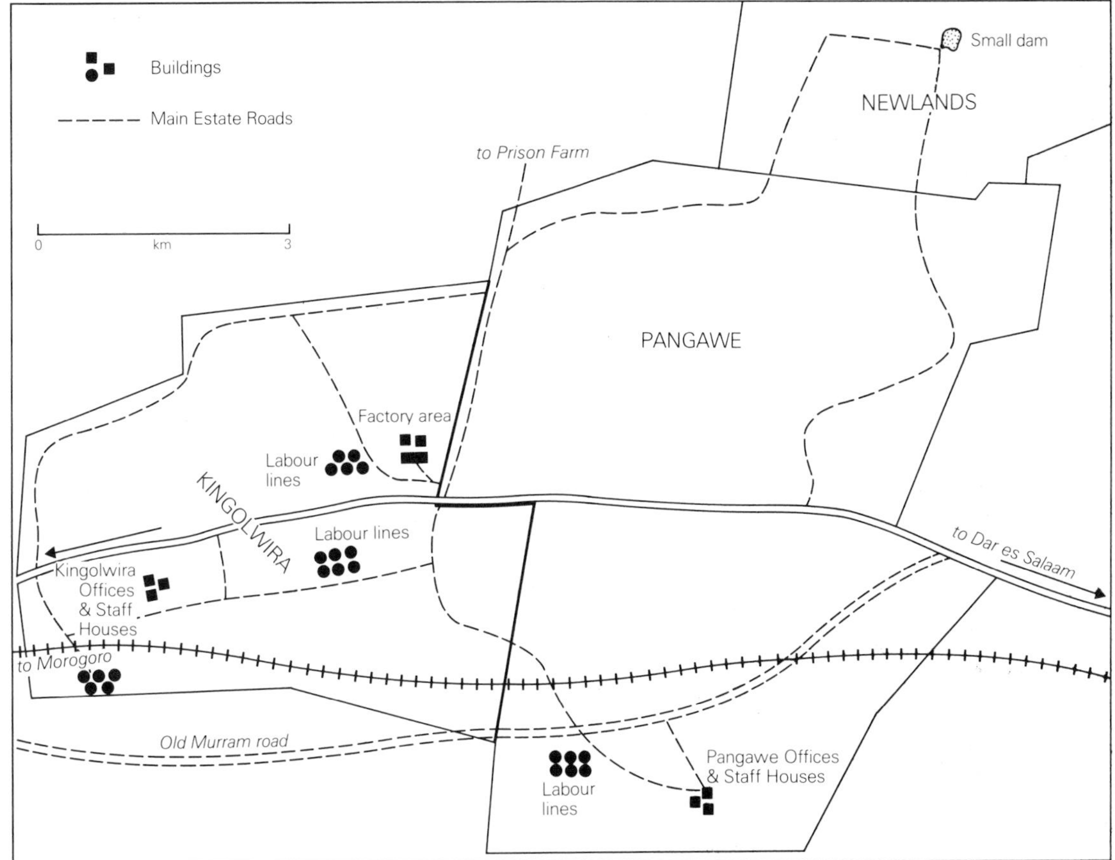

Fig. 5.9 Tanzania – Morogoro sisal estates

and representing 10 per cent of national income. It was introduced in 1907 when 400 ha were planted in the Thika District; in 1913 there were 2 800 ha and 1 000 t were exported. The hectarage rose to 2 400 in the mid-1920s and to 81 000 in the 1940s. Sisal exports are worth about US $3 million a year.

A sisal estate

Sisal cultivation, once largely in the hands of large companies due to the considerable expense incurred in transport and specialised processing machinery, is now a government-controlled operation. The Morogoro Sisal estate (Fig. 5.9) is one of a group and lies 13 km east of Morogoro. Here the land is flat or undulating, with shallow valleys of intermittent streams, and soils ranging from reddish-brown types to Black Cotton. Much of the original bush and scattered trees have been cleared. The rainfall is very unreliable and confined to a sharply defined season from December to April. Annual rainfalls have varied between a low of 565 mm and a high of 1 075, with an average of about 840 (Table 9). The weather is unpleasantly hot and humid during the rains with day temperatures about 28° to 30°C, but August to September is a pleasantly dry period with clear, cloudless skies.

Table 9 Tanzania: Average monthly rainfall totals, Morogoro sisal estate

Month	*Jan.*	*Feb.*	*Mar.*	*April*	*May*	*June*	*July*	*Aug.*	*Sept.*	*Oct.*	*Nov.*	*Dec.*	*Year*
Rainfall (mm)	125,9	113,0	111,5	123,7	61,9	25,4	18,0	23,1	21,8	46,9	82,8	87,5	838,2

The whole estate covers 7 200 ha and the land is used as shown in Table 10. About 2 000 men are employed. There are ten supervisors, three clerks, and the rest are truck drivers, mechanics, sisal cutters, and weeders. The estate is divided into sections, each planted at staggered intervals so that the sisal is ready in stages. The sections furthest from the processing centre are cut during the dry season to reduce carting over long distances during wet seasons. Each of the twelve sections is worked on a nine-year rotation scheme.

The workers once planted maize and beans between sisal rows to keep down weeds, but this was unsuccessful and a legume called *mbuki* was grown instead; this was an excellent cover crop providing nitrogen and shade, and prevented soils from baking hard.

The sisal plants are well spaced out in rows to allow easy cutting and there are between 800 to 1 000 plants per hectare. Each plant has a life span of from 8 to 14 years. The plant produces leaves for cutting when about three years old, and yields up to 200 leaves during its lifetime. The leaves, like broad-bladed swords, grow 1,5 or 2 m outwards from the bowl and are quite heavy, about 10 t being obtained from one hectare. Before it dies the plant sends up a 'pole' topped by a cluster of flowers and fresh bulbils from which seeds are obtained.

While the plants are growing, regular weeding, insecticide spraying and soil fertilisation is needed. On some estates sisal has been grown for fifty years with satisfactory yields, but there is now evidence of soil decline and fertilisers are applied liberally every five years. The slashing of long grass to prevent shade, and leaf-cutting, are year-round occupations, each mature plant being cut once a year. The cut leaves are bundled, sent by lorry or locomotive to the processing factory, and there stripped of their fibre before the plant juices become sticky. The leaves are scraped, washed, and brushed, and then fed into a decorticator at a rate of 600 a minute to remove, in running water, the softer tissues from the fibres. Waste fibre is recovered, dried, and made into 'flume tow' for padding. The main fibres are hung over wires to dry in the sun, brushed in machines, graded, baled and weighed. From Morogoro they are shipped to Dar es Salaam for export. The fibre is used to make rope, twine, sackcloth, bags, matting and other articles requiring a strong fibre.

Tea plantations

While sisal can be grown on most soils, tea is more selective and needs deep, well-aerated soils which are permeable and well drained. Tea requires at least 1 500 mm of rain in tropical regions, well distributed throughout the year, and can flourish where temperatures fall as low as 13°C. Such conditions are found in the western Kenya Highlands, the Paré, Usambara, Udzungwa and Ufipa Highlands of Tanzania, and the Mlanje Highlands of Malaŵi.

The first country to grow tea in Africa was Nyasaland, now Malaŵi, where it was first planted near Blantyre in 1888. It spread to the coffee estates around Mlanje and soon ousted coffee as a commercial crop. In 1908, more tea estates were begun at Cholo and later in the Nkata Bay area.

Kenya

In Kenya the main tea area lies around Kericho, between 1 800 and 2 100 m. Introduced in the early 1900s from Asia, it is Kenya's second agricultural export by value and now covers about 10 000 ha in the Kericho area, with smaller acreages at Nandi, Sotik, Limuru, Kitale and Molo. Kenyans have taken an increasing interest in this crop since independence and it is not entirely grown on large estates. In fact,

Table 10 Tanzania: Land use on the Morogoro sisal estate

	Mature	*Immature*	*Nurseries*	*Fallow*	*Waste*	*Roads, buildings*
Pangawe	27%	4%	0,5%	2%	6,5%	2%
Kingolwira	34%	12%	0,5%	1%	7,5%	3%

about 16 000 t, or nearly 30 per cent of total output, are produced annually by smallholders. There are now 93 000 Kenyan smallholders growing tea and 20 processing factories, with 52 planned. Kenya is now the largest producer and exporter of tea in Africa, one-half of its exports going to Britain.

Tea is also the third most important agricultural export of Uganda, where estate yields per hectare are said to be higher than those of India and Sri Lanka. The Uganda Government has recently acquired several large estates from former European owners and has set up a training programme for African farmers.

Other areas in Africa where tea is becoming an important commercial crop are in Mozambique with nearly 20 000 ha now producing, the Eastern Highland of Zimbabwe with about 2 000 ha, and there are lesser producing areas in Rwanda and Burundi, and eastern Zaïre.

A tea plantation

The following account of the organisation and work on a tea plantation would apply to practically any medium-sized estate in Africa. As on the sisal plantation, growth must be regulated so that there is constant production; the most economical size for this is about 400 ha, which would need a workforce of about 600 women, who are usually defter at the work than men, and 70 general workers. The workforce is housed on the estate or travels to the estate each day. The usual facilities, such as a school, canteens and dispensaries, are provided by the management.

The best land for tea is heavily forested land with slightly acid soils which are well drained. The larger trees are cut down and the stumps removed since they would attract termites. Grass cover and herbaceous growth are also removed, and the slopes are then terraced to prevent excessive soil erosion in these heavy rainfall areas.

After about two and a half years, the young seedlings are transferred from their nursery beds into prepared holes on the terraces, with a metre between each plant. During growth the bushes are constantly pruned so that they develop many short branches. After two or three years they begin to bear suitable leaves, and picking is increased gradually until the mature bush can be picked every fortnight. Every four or five years the bush is pruned. Yields vary; in Malaŵi the average production of picked leaf per hectare ranges from 140 to 160 kg, while in Kenya it is slightly higher. A four-hundred hectare estate would produce about 1,6 million kilogrammes of green tea annually.

The plucked leaves are taken by the pickers in baskets slung on their backs to a collecting point, where they are loaded onto lorries and speeded to the processing factory. Here they are weighed, spread on racks and dried in warm air currents. The dried leaf is passed through rollers, which crush it and free the natural juices; this helps in the next stage of fermentation. After the leaves have fermented for four hours they pass into the drying rooms, and are then allowed to cool off before grading and packing in foil-lined chests.

Sugar plantations

Sugar cane has a much wider distribution in Africa than either sisal, tea or oil palm. Its lower temperature limit is 20°C which is easily attained in all lowland areas in tropical Africa, but cane cannot be grown at high elevations without a considerable increase in the length of the growing season. Much sugar cane is grown by African farmers for their own use. In Nigeria, especially on the 'fadamas' (the riverine flats of the north) nearly 610 000 t are produced each year and this is almost wholly consumed locally; large sugar estates in Nigeria are located at Bacita and Numon. Most of the sugar cane which enters commerce is grown on large plantations on the Natal coast of South Africa, the Kilombero Valley and coastal lowlands of Tanzania, the shores of Lake Victoria in Kenya and Uganda, and on the islands of Madagascar, Mauritius, Fernando Po and São Thomé. Sugar cane is also produced in the Sudan, Ethiopia, Egypt, Swaziland, Ghana and Zimbabwe. Africa produces about 6 per cent of the total world production.

Natal

It is, however, in the coastal lowlands of Natal and Mozambique that plantation sugar cane is most important. In the Natal region it covers over 200 000 ha. Here sugar cane can be grown as far south as latitude 30° due to the climatic effect of the warm Mozambique Current. But the rainfall is rather marginal, for sugar cane requires 1 800 to 2 500 mm a year, although it will grow in regions with rainfall as low as 1 000 mm. In the Natal coastal belt the south receives on average about 1 000 mm, increasing northwards to about 1 500 mm, with 70 per cent falling in the summer half of the year from October to April. The low rainfalls and their irregularity are compensated in many areas by the high water table levels. Since sugar cane cannot withstand frost, it is confined to a rather narrow belt extending rarely more than 15 km inland from the coast, where cool season temperatures are moderated.

The soils within this belt are very variable. The best are the alluviums of the river valleys, but space for cane is limited here since these are regions of intensive agriculture. The granitic soils of the south and some of the sandier soils are fairly good, but they need liberal doses of fertiliser. Many planters grow legumes for short periods between sugar plantings (once every nine years), and this returns some nitrogen. The keeping of livestock and the growing of other crops in rotation have been suggested to help maintain soil fertility but, like tea and sisal estates, the mills must be supplied with cane throughout the year if their running is to be economic.

Sugar cane was first brought to the Natal coast in the mid-nineteenth century and after 1860 expansion was rapid. Indentured labour was brought from India and many of these early plantation workers settled in Natal on completion of their indentured service. There are now few Asians working in the plantations, and most of the cutting is done by Black labour.

Sugar cane is planted at staggered intervals so that production never ceases. The freshly planted cane takes from 18 to 20 months before it is ready for cutting, and then another 18 months elapse before it is ready again. Cutting goes on for nine years, and then the soil lies fallow for nine months under a legume. The cut cane is taken by lorry or rail to the factory and there weighed, chopped and crushed. Giant presses extract the juice and this is chemically treated, heated, clarified, brought to boiling point and then cooled, when the crystals separate from the brown molasses. The sugar is allowed to dry, and is then graded and bagged.

South Africa is now the fifth largest sugar producer in the world and annual production is approximately 1,5 million tonnes from 2,2 million tonnes of cane. Altogether there are 21 sugar mills – 7 in northern Natal, 4 in southern Natal, 5 in Zululand, 2 in the Natal midlands, and 3 in eastern Transvaal.

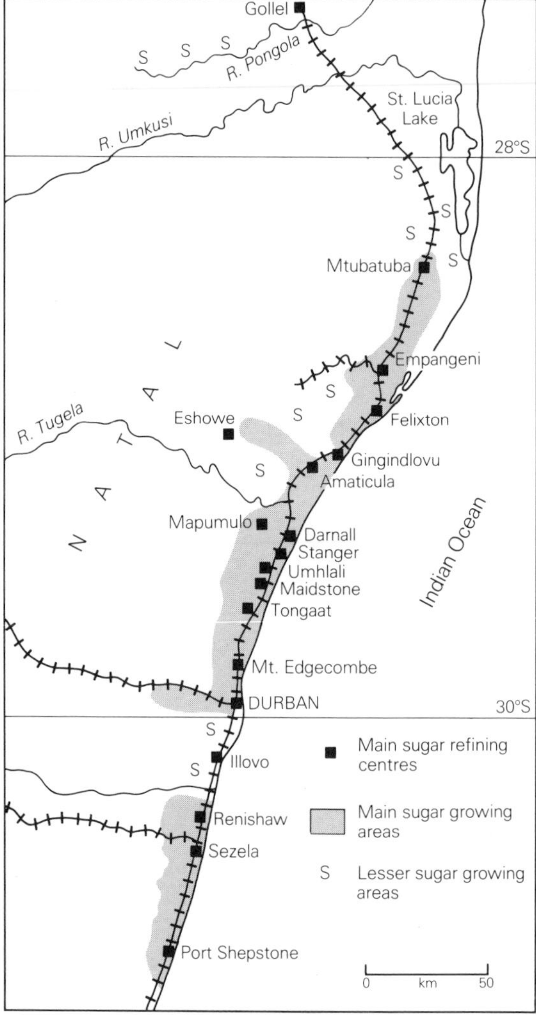

Fig. 5.10 Natal, South Africa – sugar growing regions

Most of South Africa's sugar is produced in Natal, and the output of about 1,5 million tonnes a year is more than South Africa consumes internally. Considerable amounts are exported to the United States, Japan, Canada and the United Kingdom.

Tobacco in Zimbabwe

The amount of tobacco produced in Africa is only a

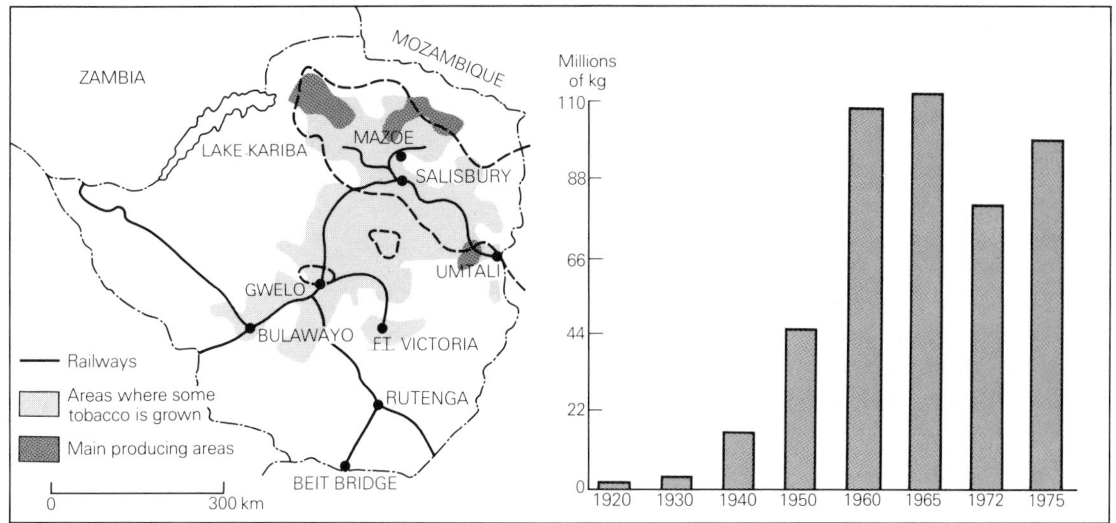

Fig. 5.11 Zimbabwe – area of tobacco cultivation and tobacco production

fraction of world output, just over 5 per cent. Over a quarter of this is grown in Zimbabwe which ranks seventh in world production, a position reached in a comparatively short period. In the 1945–6 season, Rhodesia produced 20 million kilogrammes of tobacco and in 1950, some 47 million kilogrammes. In the 1960s, annual production reached nearly 230 million kilogrammes, but after the unilateral declaration of independence in 1965 and the imposition of sanctions, production was cut back, and in the 1970s it had dropped to 130 million kilogrammes a year. Prior to 1965, the United Kingdom took the bulk of Rhodesia's tobacco exports, but the main market now in South Africa. The production and export of flue-cured tobacco was the most important industry of Rhodesia and Zimbabwe's economy still relies heavily on it. Tobacco represented over a third of the country's total exports in pre-sanction days, and brought in more revenue than any other commodity.

Tobacco cultivation began in Southern Rhodesia in 1893 when a small amount was grown near Umtali, but it was not until 1911 that large-scale cultivation began at Marandellas, 80 km east of Salisbury. The failure of cotton helped tobacco to establish itself in the north-eastern parts of the country a year later. In these early years the tobacco growers were assisted by the British South Africa Company which experimented with tobacco seeds, gave advice and generally encouraged tobacco growing. Following a short depression period, high-grade tobacco production was greatly increased when the Imperial Tobacco Company of Great Britain began to buy regular and large amounts, and an export packing factory was opened at Masasa in 1927. There followed a series of legislative acts which led to Southern Rhodesia's pre-eminence in the then Central African Federation in the production of flue-cured tobacco.

Today the crop is grown over a wide area especially in the north and east of Zimbabwe near Salisbury, Marandellas, Makoni, Hartley and Lomagundi, with lesser areas at Mazoe, Umtali, Mrewa and Urungwe. In these areas climate and soils are almost ideal for tobacco. The plant needs a constant and even annual rainfall of about 640 mm at least, with no droughts or heavy rainy periods, while optimum temperatures lie between 20° and 30°C. Deep, well-drained and aerated sandy soils with rich organic content are best. These conditions are fulfilled in Zimbabwe where, during the growing season from October to March, temperatures are between 20° and 30°C with a small range of 2°C, humidities rarely fall below 60 per cent, and there is plenty of sunshine. The lighter, sandy veld soils are well drained and very suitable for tobacco, although the plant is also grown in regions with poorer and more varied soils.

In the early days land was freely available and farmers could afford to crop their fields with tobacco for two years, then the land reverted to fallow or natural grass for periods of up to twenty years. As land became scarcer with the influx of settlers, and tobacco demands increased, the fallow period was reduced to ten years. This caused serious soil deterioration and erosion, but a liberal use of fertiliser, the ploughing in of green crops, and soil conservation methods checked this. A rotation system evolved with two out of every three fields kept constantly under crops. Later, a less exhaustive system was used involving the grazing of cattle on improved pastures and the growing of alternative crops such as maize and nitrogen-rich legumes. The following official account, slightly abridged, gives a clear picture of the methods of growing tobacco in Zimbabwe and the special problems with which the tobacco farmer has to contend.

> . . . tobacco is not a planter's crop, but a farm crop which fits into a definite rotation – one year of tobacco followed by three or four years of improved grass ley and back to tobacco for one year only. It is the most expensive and risky crop on the farm, the most difficult and tiresome one to produce, which requires constant attention for eleven months in the year. The farmer must prepare his seed beds, probably over a hectare on the average tobacco farm, and fumigate them against eelworm; if he has any irrigated tobacco he will begin sowing his beds in the first week in July and then has to protect them against sunburn and water them twice daily, and they must also be sprayed regularly against a variety of possible diseases. Sowing goes on for two months, and transplanting the seedlings to the fields takes place two to three months later. Before any land can be planted it must be ridged up and fertilised with phosphates and potash.
>
> Planting is done by hand, and a mixed fertiliser, predominantly nitrogenous will be added. The land will need to be cleaned twice; plants which have failed will be replaced; a top dressing of nitrogen may be required if there has been excessive rainfall. Suckering of the plants is the next task – the picking off of little shoots which grow off the stem. After that topping must be carried out so that the plant does not run to flower. Reaping will begin about two months after the land has been planted up, the bottom leaves first and so on up the plant until each plant has been re-visited and repeated at least six times in all over a period of some two months. Reaping will continue into April.
>
> With each reaping the tobacco is carried into the barns for curing and one barn is needed for every 2 to 3 ha of tobacco grown. Curing takes about a week, and the crop can easily be ruined by lack of attention to temperature control. After curing the tobacco is taken into the bulking shed and stacked, and after a while it is graded by the farm labour into colours and sizes, probably at least twelve different grades in all. Finally it is packed into special waterproof paper and hessian and the bales are transported to the auction floors in Salisbury.

The profits from tobacco farming in former Rhodesia have gone a long way in forming the base on which the whole of agricultural production in the country rests. Rhodesia's unilateral declaration of independence in 1965 meant, however, that traditional markets for tobacco, especially the United Kingdom, were denied to the country for political reasons. About 1 000 farmers decided to cease growing tobacco and today there are about 1 600 active growers. The government gradually reduced the quota of tobacco which it subsidised with guaranteed payments and the weight of tobacco sold has dropped from 230 million kilogrammes in the early 1960s to approximately 130 million kilogrammes in the mid-1970s. About half the land used for tobacco before 1965 is now given over to other crops.

The decline of tobacco has stimulated other crops which had an assured market despite sanctions. Maize production has increased in recent years and beef production has received new interest with the introduction of Charollais and Brahman breeding-stock. The area devoted to beef farming has increased in Mashonaland, Zimbabwe's northern province, due to a decline in tobacco area. Here, European farmers are adopting intensive farming techniques and increasing the number of cattle.

Beef, maize and tobacco have always been the mainstay of Zimbabwe's farming economy. But farmers are also anxious to diversify into new crops to spread the risk of not being able to market their crops. Cotton, which had never been a popular crop before UDI, is now a major crop. Dry-land cotton is produced on a large scale in most parts of northern and western Mashonaland and ginneries are located at Gatooma, near Shamva, and at Banket. In south-eastern Zimbabwe cotton is grown under irrigation on the Triangle Estate. This region of the south-eastern lowveld is also the main area for the growth of irrigated winter wheat which has also expanded since 1965. Other crops which European farmers have turned to, and which have an assured local market, are tea and coffee in the Eastern Highlands, sugar cane and paddy rice in the irrigated south-eastern lowveld, and pine and wattle plantations in the Inyanga, Melsetter and Vumba regions of the Eastern Highlands.

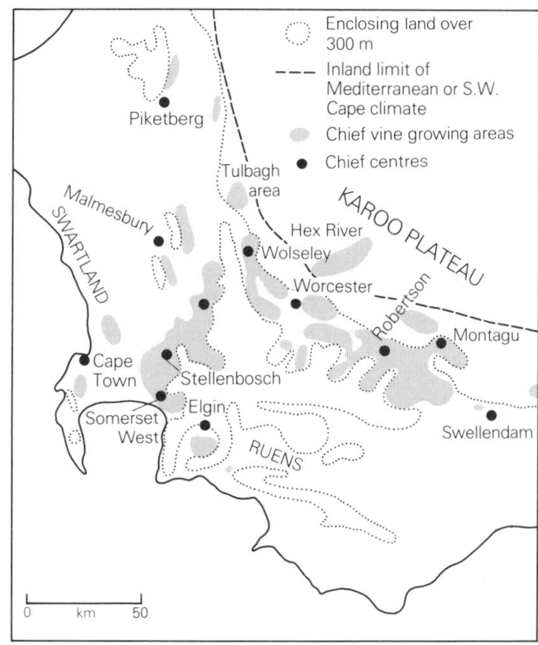

Fig. 5.12 Cape Province, South Africa – chief vine growing regions

Viticulture and fruit farming in the south-west Cape

While dairy and mixed farming are important in the Kenya Highlands, citrus fruits (oranges, lemons, grapefruit and tangerines or naartjes) have never been significant crops there. Citrus fruits suffer from the reduced temperatures at these altitudes, and from frequent cold spells experienced in June and July, while deciduous fruits grow continuously throughout the winterless year and are generally of poor quality.

In contrast, cereals and fruit cultivation are two important occupations of the white farmers of the south-western Cape Province of South Africa. Here, in the broad valleys and flat coastal plains in the Cape Town hinterland, stretches a broad arc 320 km long and from 30 to 130 km wide of small farms varying from 20 to 120 ha in size.

Stock rearing is of minor importance and cattle are often kept merely for manuring the soils, but fruit farming here is one of the most intensive uses of the soil to be found in Africa. In the valleys to the east of Cape Town, viticulture – the growing of grapes for wines – is most important, with small areas of citrus especially along the Breede River Valley. On the cooler, higher plateau of the interior, deciduous fruits – peaches, apricots, apples, table grapes, pears, plums and prunes – are the main fruits grown. Wheat is also important in the south-west Cape and is grown in two broad regions stretching from Paarl to Het Kruis north of Cape Town (the Swartland wheat belt), and south of a line from Caledon to Swellendam (the Ruens wheat belt).

The importance of fruit to the South African economy may be judged from the fact that citrus fruits make up about 10 per cent of total exports and, together with deciduous fruit and wine exports, these three items make up about one-fifth of all exports. There are nearly ten million citrus trees throughout the Republic with 4 200 growers, many of whom belong to the 45 citrus co-operatives in the country. Not all citrus and deciduous fruit is grown in the Cape, however, for there are large plantations in the northern and eastern Transvaal and in Natal. On a percentage basis the Cape produces about one-fifth to one-quarter of total production and the Transvaal about two-thirds, while much of the remainder comes from Natal Province. Britain is one of South Africa's best customers for fruit and regularly takes about a third of all the Republic's exports. Other markets include Scandinavia, France, West Germany, the Netherlands and Belgium.

The cultivation of fruit is probably the oldest agricultural activity in South Africa, originating to supply citrus to passing ships of the Dutch East India Company to prevent scurvy among the crews. But interest soon shifted to grapes which grew better in the Mediterranean-type climate and which, converted to wine, withstood long sea journeys; citrus fruits were grown mainly for local markets. When the Boer farmers trekked from the Cape to the Transvaal, they took with them citrus fruit seeds and, with the opening of the Rand goldfields in the late nineteenth century, demands for fruit increased. Farmers in the Cape were also able to supply the mines when trunk railways were completed. The export trade in fruit increased in the early twentieth century with the establishment of regular sailings of refrigerated vessels. This trade was mainly with Britain and Western Europe, where winter supplies of fruit are limited during the summer harvest seasons at the Cape. The trade was curtailed during the Second World War but after 1945 new plantings were carried out which have led to the present huge ouput.

Viticulture

The main vineyards of the south-west Cape lie within a radius of approximately 160 km of Cape Town, where nearly 24 000 ha are planted with 90 million vine plants. This region produces on average some 380 million litres of wine each year, but exports have suffered in recent years with the reduction of the British market, now bound by EEC regulations, and over-production has resulted in a quota system limiting farm output.

The vine does best in the winter rainfall area in the south-west Cape, and the chief centres are at Stellenbosch, Paarl, Worcester, Tulbagh and Robertson. The slight climatic variations result in different types of wine; the cooler, higher slopes with lower temperatures (18° to 24°C) are best for dry wines, while in the valleys with summer temperatures over 27°C, heavier, sweeter wines are produced. The summers must be dry since the vine is very subject to fungoid diseases, and rainfall from January to April should not exceed 65 mm. The annual amount of rainfall needed is about 640 mm and this is received in the western coastal zone and in the Tulbagh and Ceres Valleys. But east of Worcester in the Breede and Hex Valleys, the annual totals often fall below 500 mm and vineyards must be irrigated; about half of the

Table 11 South Africa: Sample vineyards, south-west Cape Province

Location	*Area in hectares*	*Alt. in metres*	*Av. ann. rainfall*	*Soils*	*Types of fruit with hectarages in brackets where available*
1 Nr. Paarl	20	148	610 mm	Fertile granitic	Table grapes (9), wine grapes (1, 6), apricots, peaches. Irrigated only during severe droughts.
2 Nr. Stellenbosch	68	122	610 mm	Sandy with clay loam	Wine grapes (6), deciduous fruits (14) – plums, prunes, pears.
3 Nr. Tulbagh	30	145	533 mm	Grey sandy soils	Wine grapes (12), deciduous fruits (8) – prunes with small acreages of apricots, peaches and plums; partly irrigated. Wheat important.
4 Hex River Region	30	450	279 mm	Sandy	Table grapes (16), wine grapes (0,2). Wholly irrigated.

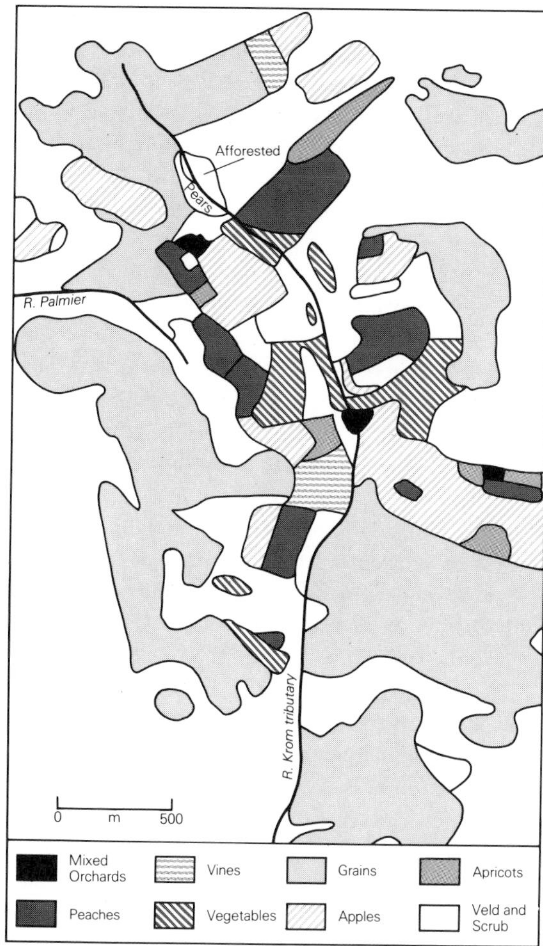

Fig. 5.13 Cape Province, South Africa – land use in the Elgin Basin

annual crop comes from irrigated vineyards. The best sites for vineyards are on the eastward-facing slopes of the highlands where soils are deep, well drained, and fairly fertile sandy loams, with better types weathered from granite rocks. For variations in size of farms and the crops grown with vines, see Table 11.

Conclusion – some comparisons

We are now in a position to draw some comparisons between the various methods of farming in Africa. As we have seen, introduced cultivation on an intensive scale tends to be concentrated in certain regions on the continent – coastal Algeria, the Kenya Highlands, the Zimbabwe highveld, the south-west Cape and Natal. The soils and climate of these regions are ideally suited to the introduction of cultivation techniques and farming systems direct from Europe – strict crop rotations, liberal use of fertiliser, enclosed pastures, high-class dairy and beef herds, electrification and mechanisation. In particular, in areas such as the Kenya Highlands, some 60 years of European adjustment and experimentation had laid a firm economic base for the country and provided an excellent basis for the future development of African farming. It must be noted, however, that the very existence of European settlers in Kenya for a long time hindered the development of cash crop farming by the African.

Most estate-type farming tends to produce cash crops for the overseas markets and is thus of an extractive nature, while crops grown for African subsistence cover a relatively small proportion of land on such farms. On the African farm the reverse is usually true, a considerable proportion of the land being devoted to subsistence crops and usually less than one-third given over to cash crops.

Estates and plantations have nearly always had the advantage of capital backing both from private or from government sources as in Zimbabwe, whereas one of the greatest limitations which has hindered the African farmer has been the lack of capital. With such capital backing the European could afford to experiment, while it was more difficult for the African farmers to change from their proved traditional cultivation methods to new and probably risky ideas. Nevertheless, the African cultivator has frequently adopted the European techniques within his own cultivation system, especially in relation to cash crops such as coffee, tea, pyrethrum and tobacco.

Estates and plantations in Africa, unlike those generally to be found in Europe, tend to be on a large scale in contrast to the small size of traditional African farms. Such estates, as we have seen, support a much lower population density than those of the African and, although producing large amounts of cash crops for export, tend to produce little that is immediately useful in supporting African populations. Some of the settlement schemes in East, Central and North Africa are designed to break down such large estates into more viable units suited to the African's needs, to support a larger population per hectare, but also to maintain cash crop production for export by more intensive cultivation of the soil.

From the point of view of quality it is often assumed that plantations and estates produce a higher quality crop, but this is not always the case. Where the African farmer produces a cash crop for sale to local factories or estate processing plants, the quality often surpasses that of the plantation, since the farmer cannot afford to lose money on crops which he has carefully tended for several years on land which could have been devoted to subsistence crops for his family. In Kenya, for example, it is in the new tea areas opened up by African cultivators that the better quality tea is produced.

The cultivation of the smallholding is the more natural form of agriculture for the African farmer. The retention of such smallholdings within the framework of a co-operative, the intensification of research into cultivation methods, the granting of increased credit facilities by both national and international bodies to deserving cases, and the aim to produce an economic balance between cash crop and subsistence crops production, seem to be the major trends in African agriculture today.

Questions

1 Compare and contrast the methods of production of any *two* cash crops grown in Africa (*a*) on plantations; (*b*) on small peasant-owned farms.

2 What are the main advantages and disadvantages of small-scale cultivation in Africa? Illustrate your answer with reference to examples familiar to you.

3 The nomadic herdsman makes the best possible use of the desert and semi-desert regions of Africa. Discuss this statement with reference to specific peoples.

4 It is rainfall, and not temperature, soils and relief, which exerts the greatest influence on the distribution and range of crops grown in Africa. Discuss this statement with reference to particular crops.

5 What proposals would you suggest to improve small-scale cultivation in Africa generally? Answer this question with reference to any improvements being made in your own country or in an area familiar to you.

6 The cash crop is of vital importance to the economy of many African countries. Select a country where this statement is valid, and prove the statement by showing how cash crops form a large proportion of the exports and dominate the general economy of the country.

7 Compare and contrast two areas of plantation type cultivation in Africa.

8 What is meant by shifting cultivation? What is the basic difference between shifting cultivation and bush fallowing? Illustrate your answer with specific references to particular peoples in Africa.

9 How is land fragmentation caused? Describe, with specific reference to particular schemes, how land fragmentation can be solved.

10 Describe any land re-settlement scheme known to you. Explain the advantages and disadvantages of such schemes for the local farmer, and for the economy of the country in general.

11 Discuss, with reference to West Africa, the role of the small farm and the large plantation in the production of (i) palm oil, and (ii) cocoa.

12 Where and under what conditions is *one* of the following commodities produced in Africa: cocoa, palm oil, tobacco, sisal, cotton, tea?

13 Review the types of farming to be found in *either* East Africa *or* Zambia, Malaŵi and Zimbabwe, and comment on their distribution in the area you have chosen.

14 Where and under what conditions is transhumance practised in Africa?

15 With reference to specific examples, discuss the decline of nomadism in and around the Sahara.

Discussion topics

The following is a list of topics which would provide a basis for group discussion, essays or additional notes:

1 Shifting agriculture as practised by one tribal group other than the ones described in Chapter Four.

2 The agricultural system of any one region.

3 The relationship of farming practices to climatic regimes, e.g. sheep, cattle and maize in South Africa, the agricultural zones of Nigeria, the

importance of groundnut cultivation in the drier parts of West Africa.

Practical work

A typical question on practical work in the agricultural field of geography might be:

Describe the farming methods and the relationship of agriculture to relief, climate and soil in any one small area with which you are familiar.

The following topics are suggested as vacation work:

1 A geographical description of an African- or European-owned farm, plantation or estate. The account should include: *a* a location map; *b* large-scale map of the farm; *c* climatic statistics; *d* soil profiles; *e* history of the farm's development; *f* a list of crops grown and their suitability for that particular area; *g* methods of cultivation; *h* processing of crops; *i* marketing.

2 A selection of a particular crop of the country and the plotting of its distribution from the latest data obtainable from agricultural departments. Dots or shading may be used to show the crop's distribution on a map, and isohyets may be drawn to show any significant climatic relationships. Details of the crop's requirements, methods of production and marketing might also be collected, and graphs prepared to show the increases (or decreases) in production.

CHAPTER SIX

Agriculture 3 – Problems and solutions

In Chapters Four and Five, the various methods used to produce food in Africa were discussed. In this chapter we look at the problems which the African farmer has to face and examine the ways in which African governments are attempting to solve these problems.

Problems of food supply

The major question now being asked is whether agricultural production in Africa is sufficient to feed, and continue to feed, a population growing at rates of up to 3,7 per cent a year. Countries such as Mauritania, Libya and Liberia, which have relatively small populations and receive large amounts of foreign exchange for their exports of oil and iron ore, are easily able to afford imported foodstuffs. But even these countries are faced with future food problems as their mineral reserves decline and they have to compete with such nations as the Soviet Union, which at present is taking nearly 20 per cent of the 150 million tonnes of grain entering world trade. Other countries are facing immediate problems: the Food and Agricultural Organisation (FAO) reported recently that 16 countries of Africa had per capita agricultural production figures below the 1961–5 average.

Despite massive injections of aid from Europe and the United States over the past 25 years, Africa is now facing increasing deficiences in food supplies. In the rain forests, the Sahel and the semi-deserts of the continent bush fallowing is still the basis of a semi-subsistence agricultural system which provides few or no reserves of food. In these regions food production is declining as more people leave the land to seek better paid and less arduous employment in the cities and towns. Urban populations swell and money is diverted to pay a growing army of civil servants and industrial workers. Thus an increasing number of people depend on a farming community whose average age is increasing, but whose production is increasing only marginally and, in some cases, actually declining. As a result, food prices increase, people eat less or buy cheaper foods, and malnutrition spreads.

There are growing signs that African governments are beginning to realise the enormity of the problems facing agriculture and are now making serious efforts to increase food production through national schemes. With the aid of international bodies such as the FAO, agricultural ministries are investigating land use and mis-use, problems of soil deficiency, farm planning, more efficient mechanisation, the use of fertilisers and improved seeds, and livestock management. In this chapter, the methods used to tackle the problem by several countries in tropical Africa are examined. Nigeria is considered in some detail since, with its large and rapidly growing population, and its ecological zones of tropical rain forest, savanna, semi-desert and desert, the country illustrates many of the problems which Africa itself faces.

Nigeria – 'Operation Feed the Nation'

Nigeria is the most populous state in Africa: based on 1963 census figures and an annual growth rate of 2,7 per cent, the population estimate for 1978 stands at 83 million people. Each year, at present growth rates, 2,24 million children are added to Nigeria's population, which is expected to double within the

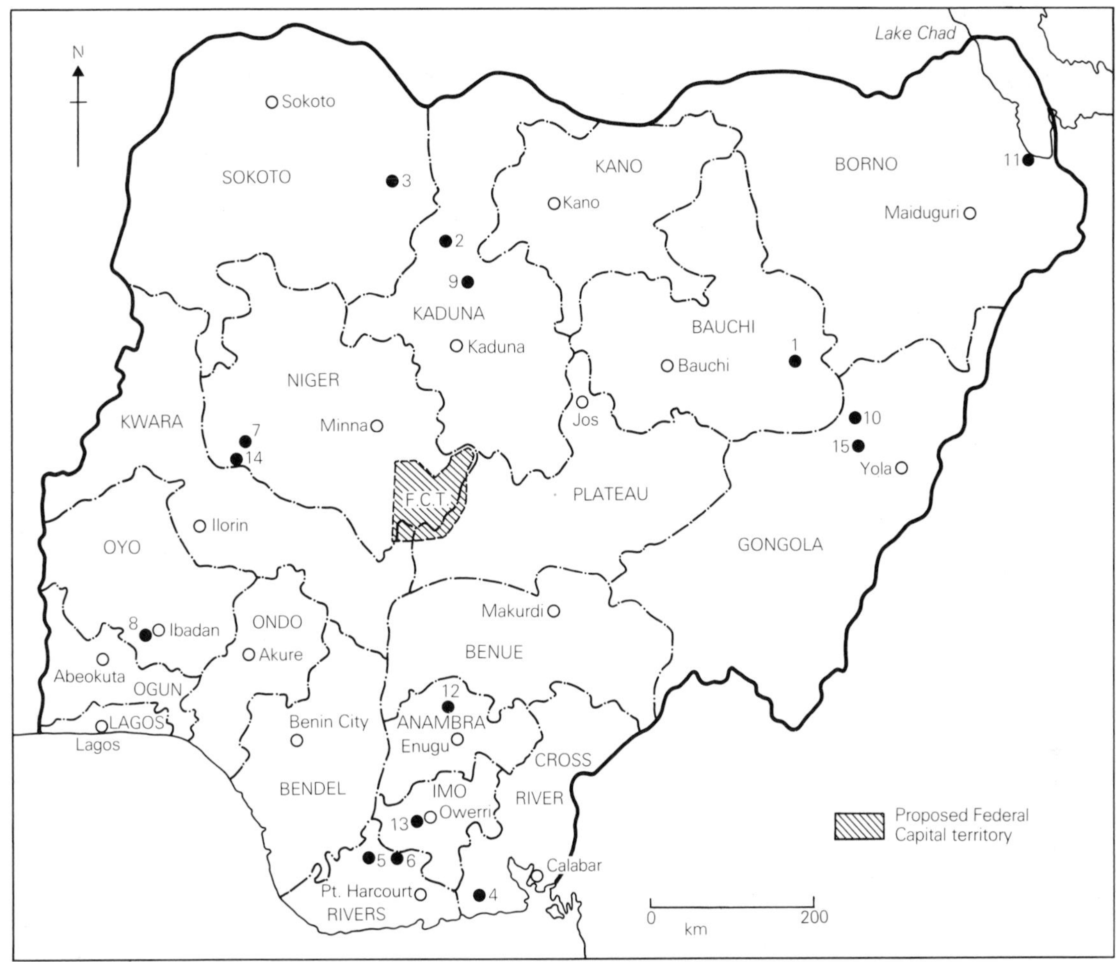

Fig. 6.1 The 19 states of Nigeria. Kano State is the most populous, with about six million people, while Rivers State is the least populous, with about 1,6 million. The map shows the location of the proposed new capital territory of Nigeria, and some of the economic projects mentioned in the text.

1 Gombe	4 Abak	7 Mokwa	10 Kiri	13 Owerri
2 Funtua	5 Ohaji	8 Ibadan	11 Ngala Plain	14 Sunti
3 Gusau	6 Ulonna	9 Samaru	12 Nsukka	15 Numan

next 25 years. About 80 per cent of the population lives in rural areas and 70 per cent of the labour force is engaged in agriculture. A wide range of staple foods is produced – cassava, yams, rice, millet, groundnuts, kola, palm products, meat and fish – yet the present average daily food intake of each Nigerian is approximately 8,4 kilojoules. Since a man performing an average amount of work per day uses up about 12,6 kj (3 000 calories) and a woman 10,5 kj (2 500 calories) it is clear that the majority of Nigerians are not getting enough to eat. Moreover, even when people have enough food to eat and are not hungry, the diet may contain insufficient protein and Vitamin C foods which provide energy and help resistance to disease. In a recent survey of Uboma village in the rain forest of the northern Niger Delta, an Ibadan University research team found that the average villager received 10 kj (2 400 calories) a day, but protein foods such as milk, meat and eggs made up only 7 per cent of the kilojoules, while starchy foods such as yams and cassava made up 62,5 per cent.

There are other indications that Nigerian agriculture is unable to meet the demand for foodstuffs. Between 1974 and 1975 the prices of basic staple foods such as maize, *garri* (pounded cassava), plantains and rice had risen by over 55 per cent, while the prices of chickens and fresh vegetables had risen in one year by between 200 and 400 per cent. Again, Nigeria is having to import more and more food and the cost is soaring: in 1960 food imports cost US $39,7 million, in 1972 the figure was US$73,0 million, and in 1975 it rose to US $385,1 million. The aggregate index of Nigerian agricultural production kept by the Nigerian Central Bank was 100 in 1960 and 105 in 1971, but dropped to 71 in 1974. In 1966–7 groundnut production was over a million tonnes but it fell to 150 000 t in the late 1970s; the highest cocoa harvest was in 1964–5 when it reached 300 000 t, but now it averages 235 000 t. Throughout the country, supply is clearly not meeting demand for, while agricultural production (including the production of non-edible crops such as cotton and rubber) is increasing at approximately 2 per cent per annum, demand for all crops is increasing at 4,5 per cent per annum. Some experts are predicting that famines will become a frequent occurrence in Nigeria by the 1980s if drastic action is not taken now. The reasons for this situation in one of Africa's largest countries are numerous and complex.

They include:

The peasant farming system: The Nigerian farmer is essentially an individual who belongs to a village, but cultivates a small plot almost in isolation. The land tenure system does not encourage co-operation, and sub-division of land produces fragmented holdings. The average peasant farmer lacks the money and credit to purchase improved seed, fertiliser and equipment, and his knowledge of modern farming principles is scant. He is often illiterate, fails to appreciate the importance of new methods and machinery, and is quite content to cling to his familiar methods of subsistence cultivation. Until recently, he received no guaranteed price for his crops, and thus lacked the incentive to produce more and better foodstuffs. His yields are low: according to the FAO, the correct use of fertiliser and pesticides would produce 12 t of yams per hectare, but the Nigerian farmer's average yield is a meagre 1,5 t per hectare.

The poor infrastructure: The majority of peasant holdings are situated in remote, often inaccessible areas, with few good feeder roads linking with markets. Only one-third of all marketed foodstuffs in Nigeria is transported by lorry, while over half is still transported by head, bicycle and cart. Storage and marketing facilities are either poor or non-existent and advisory services are infrequent, with a national average of one extension worker per 3 000 farmers, and one per 20 000 in the worst areas. In some villages, 30 per cent of harvested food is lost due to inadequate storage.

Labour supply: This is an acute problem. The active and strongest members of village communities – the young people – are attracted by the higher wages and less strict way of life to be found in the urban areas. The average earnings per annum in the agricultural sector are about US $330, while double this amount could be earned in a factory. The seasonal daily rate in the cocoa plantations is US $5, while it is over US $10 in the construction industry where the work is not seasonal. In Rivers State a job in the oil mining industry is often easier to obtain than a job in the palm oil industry.

Land use: At present only one-quarter, or about 230 000 square kilometres, of the total area of Nigeria is under cultivation, and a large proportion of this area is devoted to non-edible cash crops such as rubber and cotton. Including this area, the amount of cultivable land is 690 000 square kilometres or three-quarters of Nigeria's total area, and three times the present area cultivated. However, much of this unused cultivable land is remote from major markets, and to bring it into production would entail a huge programme involving mass population movements and resettlement, as well as the construction of a vast network of feeder roads.

The range of crops: Nigeria still grows a large amount of non-edible food crops, largely for export, and exports a large proportion of her edible food production. This is a legacy from colonial times when Nigerian agriculture was geared to the production of cash crops such as rubber, oil palm products, cotton, cocoa and groundnuts for overseas markets at the expense of subsistence crops for internal consumption.

Soils: Nigeria's soils are generally of low quality. More than two-thirds of the country, chiefly in the centre and north, have lateritic or sandy soils with only small areas, e.g. around Katsina and Kano (fine sandy loams), and around Zaria (loess and loam), which can be described as really fertile. The fertility of the lateritic soils in the guinea savanna vegetation zone is reduced even further by the clearing of virgin woodland, which exposes the soil to the harsh drying rays of the sun. In the southern belt of forest soils, the vegetation protects and supplies much humus, but leaching is heavy and reduces the amount of natural plant food. To improve Nigeria's soils, massive doses of fertiliser would be needed; at present the average peasant farmer uses the meagre amount of only 2 kg of artificial fertiliser per hectare per year on his fields, and only 1,25 t of chemical aids are used each year per square kilometre of cultivated land.

Climate: Fluctuating rainfall totals and unexpected drought in Nigeria can reduce crop output drastically. For example, the 1974 droughts in the northern part of the country reduced the groundnut crop from a previous average of 500 000 t a year to a mere 42 000 t. This resulted in a sharply increased cereal import bill from US $51 million in 1972 to US $116 million in 1974. This same drought reduced the cattle herds of the Fulani by some two million head.

The rise of oil: A considerable amount of government time and money has been devoted to the oil industry, especially in the early stages of the industry's establishment. This led to an overall neglect of the agricultural sector and to the usurping by oil of agriculture's place in the Nigerian economy. Before the Civil War (1967–70) agriculture accounted for more than half of the gross domestic product, employed 85 per cent of the workforce, and produced 80 per cent of Nigeria's exports. In 1975, however, crude petroleum exports earned the country US $6 400 million or 90 per cent of all export earnings; agricultural exports earned only US $436 million or just over 6 per cent. Exports of palm oil from Nigeria are now almost non-existent, while the Ivory Coast, with its economy based almost entirely on agriculture, is now the world's largest exporter.

Having defined the shortcomings evident in the Nigerian agricultural sector, the remedies can be seen more clearly: the introduction of a less rigid land

Nigeria: Traditional cultivation methods. Simple tools – panga, spade and hoe – are used to clear the vegetation and prepare the ground.

Nigeria: Modern cultivation methods. Tractor and mechanical hoes preparing the ground on a farm in Bendel State.

tenure system; injections of capital (largely derived from oil wealth) into the agricultural sector to make farming a more profitable venture, and to stem the drift of young people to the urban centres; the provision of improved farming equipment and storage facilities, better seed, credit and advisory services; an extension of the area under cultivation; the improvement of the feeder road network; investment in dams and irrigation projects in regions of recurring drought; the creation of larger units of production where mechanisation can be adopted easily; the encouragement of new agricultural ventures such as the production of fresh vegetables for export; finally, a national campaign to make all sectors of the population aware of the problems and to encourage them to assist in their solution.

'Operation Feed the Nation'

The Federal Government of Nigeria is well aware of the problems and has recently embarked on a vigorous campaign to stimulate food production. A national programme under the name 'Operation Feed the Nation' has been introduced as part of the Third National Development Plan begun in 1975. Over US \$3,6 million are to be allocated to agriculture, of which 75 per cent will be spent on crop production, 15 per cent on the livestock industry, and the rest on forestry and fisheries. In 1976 nine river basin authorities were set up to integrate the development of agriculture within their regions and harness the rivers for crop production. The following are some of the ways in which the Nigerian government intends to increase the production of food crops, reduce reliance on costly food imports, and eventually place the country once more in the position of a major exporter of food:

1 *Encouragement* is being given to every adult Nigerian to grow some food in his own garden and to avoid wasting food. Schools, colleges, universities and army units are all urged to participate in the national campaign.
2 *Prices* paid to the farmer for selected food crops – maize, rice, *garri*, beans, guinea corn and yams –

are to be guaranteed to encourage production of these staple foodstuffs.

3 *Agricultural services* are being improved. For example, in Kaduna State there are 78 planned service centres situated so as to allow farmers easier access to their requirements. These centres have been stocked with cotton sprayers, improved seeds, ploughs, fertilisers, insecticides and carts. In regions which are acutely depressed, improvement in all services is designed to stimulate production and increase the farmer's income. The Gombe, Funtua and Gusau regions (see map, Fig. 6.1) have been singled out for special treatment. Here the average income of the peasant farmer is only US $40 a year, yet these farmers support some 2 million people from 17 000 square kilometres of land. Here the government aims to increase production of maize, cowpeas, groundnuts, sorghum and cotton, funds being invested to provide 200 tractors, 20 000 ox carts and 10 000 t of improved seed, and for the construction of 3 500 km of new roads and 200 small dams.

4 *The creation of larger farming units* is to be encouraged. Over US $26 million have been allocated for the resettlement of Nigerian refugees from Equatorial Guinea, because these farmers have considerable experience in plantation methods and would form the nucleus of a skilled workforce on government co-operative farms. Farm Settlement Schemes have already been introduced to encourage co-operative methods. Three of these schemes are situated at Abak, Ohaji and Ulonna in the coastal region. The settlements are on a community basis and involve the growing of cash crops (oil palm, cocoa, rubber and citrus fruits) together with subsistence crops for the farmers themselves. The settlements are on newly-cleared land and vary in size from 1 200 to 5 000 ha and each year receive between 100 and 120 student farmers, until a maximum of 720 is reached on the bigger schemes. The students are housed in specially laid-out villages each with its own administration block, medical centre, shops and schools. Each student is granted one hectare of land for subsistence and, until his tree cash crops are producing, approximately US $8 a month. The student farmers are supervised by expert agricultural officers who advise on seeds, fertilisation, cultivation and harvesting.

Other large-scale agricultural ventures are the state-run farms such as the 8 000-ha rice scheme at Epe near Lagos and a 3 000-ha rice farm at Tada in the Pategi region.

5 *Research projects* are to receive more money. The maize breeding research stations at Mokwa, Ibadan and Samaru are investigating the local suitability of improved plant varieties, fertilisers, and problems of weed control. The International Institute of Tropical Agriculture at Ibadan is carrying out research on the growing of the yam in the west and north of the country, and on cheap but secure methods of storing maize crops. Other funds have been allocated for research into the most suitable machinery for Nigerian farms; the University of Ife's engineering department has already produced a wide range of implements and machines suited to Nigerian conditions – a cassava planter and peeler, a grain winnower and a special type of grain store.

6 *The area under irrigation* is to be extended by over half a million hectares. In Sokoto State, work has begun on irrigation works which will provide some 6 000 ha devoted to wheat, rice, sugar, and tomatoes. In Gongola State a large sugar growing project irrigated by waters from a dam near Kiri on the Gongola River is under way, while in Bornu State lies the South Chad Irrigation Pilot Project, in which 67 000 ha on the Ngala Plain are to be irrigated from Lake Chad to produce crops of wheat, rice, cotton, and sugar cane on a large scale. At Nsukka north of Enugu in Anambra State, an all-season irrigation project will have some 1 000 ha under rice.

7 *Production of cash crops* for export is to be increased to halt the decline in this sector of agriculture. One project is the revival of the oil palm industry, and a company has been created to encourage the establishment of new estates in Bendel State. A 10 000 ha estate near Owerri has been laid out, and the government hopes that Nigeria will once again become a huge estate producer of this crop. Massive investments are also being made in the cocoa industry with an eventual target of 117 000 ha, while the area under rubber plantations is to be increased to 55 000 ha. Moreover, to lessen the food import bill, money is to be

invested to make Nigeria self-sufficient in certain crops. Sugar is one example, with imports varying between 100 000 and 130 000 t a year. A large sugar estate and refinery is being established at Sunti on the northern bank of the River Niger in Niger State at a cost of US $90 million. An even larger project is the Savanna Sugar Company's estate at Numan in the north east which, when completed, will cost US $250 million and will produce 100 000 t of sugar annually by 1982.

8 *The production of protein-rich foods* is to receive more attention. In northern Oyo State the World Bank is investing in the establishment of a state cattle industry and is financing the nucleus of five ranches designed to accommodate 19 000 head of cattle, after bush clearing has reduced the numbers of tsetse fly and other diseases. The growing of cowpeas as the most important source of vegetable protein in certain areas of Nigeria, e.g. around Ibadan, is now receiving attention.

Other fields of agricultural expansion now under consideration as part of 'Operation Feed the Nation' include the establishment of piggeries to reduce imports of bacon and pork; large-scale commercial production of chickens both for eggs and meat; the extension of market gardening areas adjoining large urban centres; and the growing of fresh fruits and vegetables for air transport to Europe during that continent's winter.

Only a few of the schemes operating in Nigeria have been mentioned in this section. By inaugurating 'Operation Feed the Nation', the Nigerian Government has recognised that land is Nigeria's greatest asset. To restore Nigeria's position as West Africa's leading agricultural producer and exporter is not impossible, despite the country's rapidly growing population, for Nigeria has the vast income from oil to finance its agricultural undertakings.

Nigeria's problems have been discussed in some detail since they help in the understanding of Africa's agricutural problems as a whole. It is now time to turn our attention to the methods used to increase the food supply in other countries in Africa, where it can be seen that, although the solutions are many and varied, the problem remains the same – that of providing sufficient food for rapidly increasing populations.

Ghana's farm settlements

In the post-independence period, Ghana experimented with many schemes such as state and brigade farming systems which had been adapted from models existing in Europe. None of these systems brought significant increases in food production. In 1975, however, a Farm Settlement project backed by West German finance was transferred to the government of Ghana. The settlement is at Peki, about 130 km north of Accra, and the project is to become a model for similar schemes throughout the country. At present the scheme has 100 settlers and covers 2 500 ha which are divided into palm plantations and fields for vegetables (yams, sweet potatoes, beans, etc.) and for tobacco. The settlement is almost self-contained with a water pump, an electric generator, an animal feed manufacturing plant, and a poultry section with 1 500 hens. Similar projects will concentrate on other crops such as sugar cane, bananas, ginger and apples. Families from the same traditional area are to be settled on such schemes, and the land will be owned by the village as a whole rather than by individuals. This will lead to more large-scale methods and the use of machinery.

Tanzania's ujamaa villages

A somewhat similar community scheme has been in operation for some years in Tanzania. Here the government is attempting to revolutionise agriculture and make the country self-sufficient in foodstuffs by resettling peasants from over-crowded regions into village communities, called *ujamaa* villages. The land belongs to the village community rather than to individuals. By 1975 the government had succeeded in resettling 3,5 million Tanzanians, or about one-third of the peasant population, in 7 500 *ujamaa* villages. The main aims of the *ujamaa* scheme are to increase agricultural production, organise the efforts of the people more effectively, and make the provision of public services such as medicine and education easier. About US $24 million were spent in 1974 on rural improvements, educational and literacy programmes and training in management and book keeping in *ujamaa* settlements. The villagers are engaged in such projects as reafforestation, dairying, the digging of small-scale irrigation projects, the construction of new wells, and the improvement of local roads as well as cultivation.

Mwenge village in the Lindi region is a good example of an *ujamaa* settlement. Begun in 1972 by five peasant farmers, the village now has 90 inhabitants. Land, tools, farming equipment and a small cash grant were donated by the government. Today the Menge settlement is self-sufficient in food, the main crops being maize, cassava, soya beans, rice, beans, potatoes, sweet potatoes, green vegetables and fruit. The villagers have also built a community hall, a dispensary and a small clinic. The Tanzanian government aims at having over 20 000 *ujamaa* villages throughout the country by 1980.

Malaŵi's young pioneers

In Malaŵi the problem is being tackled by opening up new areas for cultivation, and by planned large-scale resettlement involving the Young Pioneer Movement. One of the most important of the several major agricultural development schemes now in operation is the Shire Valley development project. Here farmers have been encouraged to convert their land to cotton as a cash crop; at Ngabu, for example, a crop of 1 125 kg per hectare has been produced from smallholdings whose average size is 1,4 ha. The Young Pioneer Movement runs a 10-month course for all youths, during which emphasis is laid on the theory and practice of agriculture. Training includes the production of cash crops such as tobacco or cotton and also subsistence crops such as maize. After training, Young Pioneers may return to their villages or may go to one of the 19 settlement schemes in the country where they can obtain a living as farmers with the assistance of government loans. The Pioneers are also entitled to demonstrate new methods of farming to local communities.

Commercial crops grown in Malaŵi such as maize, rice, fruit, vegetables, cotton and groundnuts are marketed by the Agricultural Development and Marketing Corporation which has 800 centres throughout Malaŵi. There is also a smallholders' tea authority which trains Malaŵi tea growers up to the tea estate standards. Each smallholder has slightly less than one hectare of land.

Gambia's rice schemes

In the Gambia farmers are taking advantage of government efforts to diversify the economy and reduce the reliance on groundnuts. The construction of access causeways into swamp and mangrove areas, tractor ploughing and discing, training programmes and demonstration plots have convinced the farmers of the value of rice cultivation. With the example of projects such as the Gambia Rice Farm at Sapu, between Georgetown and Kuntaur, and the rice station at Jenoi, a spectacular expansion of rice cultivation has taken place since the Second World War. Rice is now the principal food crop in most parts of the Gambia and is being grown as a secondary cash crop.

Zambia's peasant farm schemes

Zambia's agricultural problems are being tackled by a series of peasant farming schemes. These provide capital for simple farm planning, land clearing, implements and oxen, and enable subsistence cultivators to establish themselves as small-scale commercial farmers. More than 5 000 farmers cultivating some 42 000 ha are enrolled in such schemes. Livestock owners are encouraged by means of bonuses and subsidies to keep better stock, and controlled grazing schemes are expanding. Experiments with drainage and irrigation are being carried out with the object of making use of over half a million hectares of undeveloped flood plain in Zambia.

Cameroon's 'Green Revolution'

In the Cameroon Republic agriculture employs 85 per cent of the population and provides 70 per cent of the country's exports. To boost production the government has inaugurated the 'Green Revolution' and provided capital for tools and fertilisers for those farmers who belong to co-operatives. Food crop farms are being established around large cities and are somewhat like the market gardens of temperate regions. World Bank loans are being used to finance a cattle breeding scheme and for the eradication of the tsetse fly.

This chapter began with several somewhat gloomy predictions about Africa's agricultural production; it will end with a success story – the example of the Ivory Coast.

The Ivory Coast's success story

The Ivory Coast is a relatively small country with an area of 322 000 square kilometres (about one-third the size of Nigeria). Its population is just over 6 million, including over one million Voltaics and several hundred thousand Guineans, Senegalese and Ghanaians. There are also 45 000 French nationals. At independence in 1960, the country was a minor producer of tropical crops, but since then the gross domestic product has increased five times and exports have increased seven times. Today, the Ivory Coast is one of the world's largest producers and exporters of tropical produce. Excluding those African countries with vast oil and other mineral wealth, no nation in Africa has achieved as fast a growth rate. The Ivory Coast is now Africa's biggest coffee producer, third only in the world after Brazil and Colombia. It is also the world's largest producer of cocoa after Ghana, having overtaken Nigeria in 1974, and the country's palm oil production has increased seven-fold since 1960. Pineapple production has risen 12-fold in the same period while banana production has quadrupled, and the output of coconuts has quintupled. The country is now the second biggest producer of cotton in the Franc Zone after Chad, and home needs in rice, once a major import, are now satisfied. Sugar and avocado production have also been expanded greatly in recent years. These successes have been achieved by an agricultural sector highly dependent on the peasant farmer: 94 per cent of production comes from the small-scale African farmer, while the remaining 6 per cent is from large-scale producers.

With a gross national product per head of US $380, the Ivory Coast can be classed as one of Africa's wealthier countries. How has this been achieved in the short time since independence in 1960? Good planning, wise use of foreign financial assistance and technical aid, and sheer hard work by the farming community are the chief reasons:

Economic planning: In general, agricultural policy has been to encourage the growth of crops which are in constant demand on world markets, and to make the Ivory Coast self-sufficient in subsistence crops. For example, a massive oil palm plantation scheme involving thousands of square kilometres of land was begun after independence; the country now has 80 000 ha under oil palms and by 1980 expects to be the world's largest producer of palm oil. Another vital product – rubber – has received much attention. Production started in 1961 and 1 000 ha had been planted by 1963, increasing to 18 000 ha by 1975. A further 13 500 ha of rubber are now being laid out in the Dodo Valley near Grand Bereby, and other plantations at San Pedro, Grabo, Sassandra and Bongo are being expanded.

In the early 1970s a staple foodstuff, rice, was being imported in ever increasing quantities, imports having doubled from the 1960s total of 42 000 t to 97 000 t. A rice growing programme was

Table 12 The Ivory Coast: Balance of trade and major Exports, 1970–5 (US $M)

	1970	*1971*	*1972*	*1973*	*1974*	*1975*
Exports	520,8	506,0	558,0	763,2	1166,8	1018,4
Imports	430,8	443,2	457,2	630,0	929,2	965,6
Trade surplus	90,0	62,8	100,8	133,2	237,6	52,8
Major exports						
Green coffee	172,4	168,4	147,2	n.a.	255,2	246,8
Cocoa and cocoa products	127,6	105,2	108,8	n.a.	312,4	261,2
Timber	117,2	123,6	151,6	n.a.	206,0	139,2
Bananas	12,8	11,6	13,6	n.a.	14,4	12,0

immediately begun and by 1975 the Ivory Coast became a net exporter of rice with an annual production of 320 000 t. A state-owned rice organisation now prepares new paddy fields and runs a model farm in each rice-growing area. Rice plantations help farmers by providing expertise and access to the marketing system.

The government also recognised the importance of the demand for fresh fruit during the winter period in Europe and the area under bananas, pineapples and avocados was rapidly expanded. Exports of avocados have risen from 40 t in 1970 to 1 000 t in 1978; production, however, is to be increased to 5 000 t by 1980, and new markets are to be sought. In addition, there are now more than 90 small plantations producing high grade pineapples, and exports have reached 70 000 t a year.

So as to maintain food production for home consumption as the population grows at a rate of 2,9 per cent a year, staple foodstuffs such as maize and cassava are not neglected, and experiments with new crops, such as the soya bean, are being carried out to avoid protein deficiencies in diets. Agricultural spheres in which there is good potential are being investigated. For example, in the north of the country investment is being made in the livestock industry, with the enclosure of pastures, improvement of livestock quality, and the setting up of training centres to teach good husbandry. A huge ranch situated west of Mankono supplies peasant farmers with quality beasts. Another venture is the establishment of chicken processing plants to provide eggs and meat for the population. The sugar deficiency is now being tackled with the establishment of four sugar plantations.

Guaranteed food prices: The Caisse de Stabilisation or Marketing Board fixes farm prices according to market trends. The farmer is assured of a fair price for his produce, and this encourages him to ensure that the quality of his crop is acceptable by the Board. In the 1974–5 season, coffee payments were increased by 25 per cent over the previous year, cotton payments by 56 per cent, and cocoa payments by 60 per cent. The prices for high quality rice have quintupled over the last few years.

Investment in infrastructure: The swift movement of farm produce to markets and to processing factories has been assured by massive expenditure on road construction, so that the Ivory Coast now has the best tarmac road network of West Africa. Three new hydro-electric power schemes will help extend power supplies to country districts. The state shipping company has been granted US $120 million for the purchase of more refrigerated banana boats and palm oil tankers. Moreover, investment in industry is chiefly in those concerns which will process the products of the agricultural sector – rubber, textiles, fruit, sugar and timber.

Emergency programmes: Where the agricultural economy appears to be falling behind the national average, emergency measures have been taken to remedy the situation. The northern regions of the Ivory Coast lag behind the southern zone; here the average monthly income is only US $15,5 compared with the south-east's US $86. An emergency programme has been set up in addition to the normal development programme for the northern region: this includes direct financial assistance for cotton, rice and stock breeding ventures, expansion of the number of boreholes to provide water for irrigation and stock; and an improvement in the social amenities available in the villages.

Effective use of foreign aid: To finance its various programmes the Ivory Coast is borrowing heavily from industrialised countries. Between 1970 and 1975, for example, foreign loans increased from 35 per cent of invested money to 67 per cent. In 1974, US $56 million were borrowed from various sources, chiefly in western Europe, and in 1976 the amount borrowed had increased to US $88 million. The Ivory Coast now owes over US $800 million to various creditors, but the government believes that the strong economic base which has been created through the wise investment of foreign money is worth the present debt.

Questions

1 With reference to any *two* countries in tropical Africa, describe the problems facing the agricultural sector of their economies, and outline the measures being taken by the governments to combat these problems.

2 'Nigeria illustrates many of the problems which the continent of Africa itself faces.' Discuss this

statement with reference to population growth and food production.

3 'There are growing signs that African governments are beginning to realise the enormity of the problems facing agriculture.' With reference to particular examples, describe what measures are being taken to solve agricultural problems in Africa, and suggest what other measures could be taken.

Discussion topics

1 Foreign loans, even though they lead to heavy indebtedness, are justified if a strong economy is achieved by the borrowing nation.

2 Land is a nation's greatest asset.

3 The most important duty of any government is to see that its people are fed adequately.

Practical work

A visit to any scheme in your country which typifies the efforts being made by your government to increase food production. Write notes on the organisation of the scheme, supporting these with diagrams of production, and show how the scheme fits into the national plan.

CHAPTER SEVEN

Settlement – Villages, towns and cities in Africa

In Chapter Two we saw some of the great urban centres which developed in Africa as nuclei of industry and trade as long as 2 000 years ago. In this chapter we shall be concerned chiefly with more recent developments. Despite the phenomenal growth of towns and cities in Africa the village still retains an important position in the evolving pattern of settlement on the continent. Even though many people live and work in towns, most of them regard their villages as their true homes and look forward to retiring there later. Industrial workers try to save some money to build near their village, and keep up their contacts by frequent visits. Very often, however, they come to prefer the life of the towns and become townsmen.

Villages

Factors affecting the growth of villages

The presence of good soil is one of the chief considerations influencing the choice of site of a village. Others are nearness to water supply, proximity to routes to maintain contact with other people and to export products and, in troubled areas, the value of the site for defence.

But settlements will flourish only in response to political, social or economic influences. Villages may develop because they are the site of a chief, or because officials feel the site a good one for administration. Again, local mineral deposits will attract companies who use the village as a base and employ male workers. Commercially useful crops may help development as a marketing and collecting centre. Conversely, some villages decline because the menfolk go to work in towns, or the demand for the villagers' crops falls as new substitutes are found, or routeways are built which divert trade away from the settlement.

Factors affecting the site and settlement pattern of villages

It is not always easy to explain the pattern of village settlement or why one village has flourished and another declined. Villages tend to be nucleated and lie fairly close to each other to maintain mutual links; it is rare to find single scattered homesteads, except where people felt remote or strong enough to resist invasions. The major considerations affecting the settlement pattern of rural communities in Africa are:

a *Defence* – producing small nucleated hamlets on high vantage points.

b *Water supply* – especially important in savanna and semi-desert regions, where villages congregate near water sources in valleys. On extensive plateaux settlement is usually more scattered.

c *Good soils* – attract settlements, while poor soils or dry regions are neglected; pastoralism becomes more important on poorer soil zones, and villages are rare.

d *The tsetse fly* – a contributory cause to villages being centred in large clearings in bush country; here settlements are nucleated and often far apart.

e *Good communications* – essential in cash crop areas to speed crops to processing centres and export routes; villages will lie near to them. In tropical rain forests, villages usually stay close to routes along interfluves.

f Political and administrative considerations – a village may become the residence of a chief, or develop as the regional headquarters of the central government.

g Modern influences – the establishment of a mine or plantation will attract people, and villages and shanty towns may spring up. Later specially planned settlements develop.

Examples of village settlement

The following examples of village settlement in Africa show the variety of influences on choice of site and the settlement pattern. Often more than one of the above factors have had a combined influence.

Nigeria — the Jos Plateau

The Jos Plateau of central Nigeria was a favourite hunting ground of slave traders and the site of many battles between rival peoples. Villages were built in secluded spots hidden by rocky ridges, dense bushes and cacti thickets. Huts were clustered to help easy escape along narrow alleyways, and one hut would be built on higher rocks to warn of danger. Enclosed cultivated fields were nearby, enabling the villagers to return quickly to their homes. Thus villages on the Nigerian plateaux are often nucleated but well spaced from one another, although with more peaceful times isolated settlements are found in more open country.

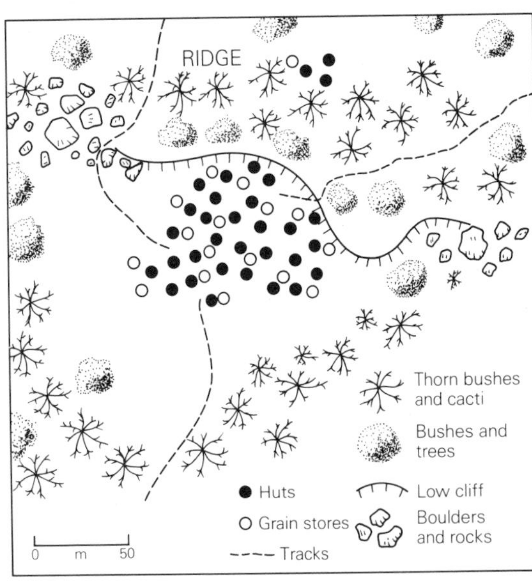

Fig. 7.1 A village settlement on the Bauchi Plateau

The Kenya Highlands

In the Kikuyu zone of the Kenya Highlands the effect of defensive measures is seen more recently. Kikuyu cultivation methods led to an open settlement pattern, the thick forests providing protection. As the population grew and more patches were settled this basic pattern remained, resulting in few villages but many scattered homesteads. During the emergency of 1952–60, the colonial authorities concentrated the Kikuyu in large villages surrounded by defensive walls. By 1956 almost the entire rural population of Kiambu, Murang'a and Nyeri Districts had been moved into villages. Over 170 000 new huts were built, each village averaging 1 500 huts. About 830 000 people were moved and land consolidation was made easier. Villages were generally placed on top of broad ridges (Fig. 7.2a).

Malaŵi

In Malaŵi villages tend to be small, about thirty huts occupied by related members of a family group, the numbers carefully limited so that field boundaries do not extend too far from the village. In parts of the Lilongwe Plain, early villages were near springs at the foot of valleys, while the more level plateau surfaces were used for grazing or shifting cultivation. Later, more war-like peoples set their villages on rocky outcrops for defence, but with the decline of warfare the earlier sites were re-occupied and today many villages are found near springs.

Zimbabwe – Mashonaland

Further south, in Mashonaland, live the Shona peoples of northern Zimbabwe. The land here lies between 600 and 1 400 m and has several level surfaces broken here and there by isolated granitic koppies and inselbergs. Little natural woodland is left except patches of forest, and the region displays the long dry season (May–October) and low rainfalls (500 to 760 mm) of the savanna areas of Zimbabwe. Springs are few and rivers empty during the dry season. In the rural areas, villages are small and cultivated fields lie close by, often abutting onto those of a neighbouring village. The settlements

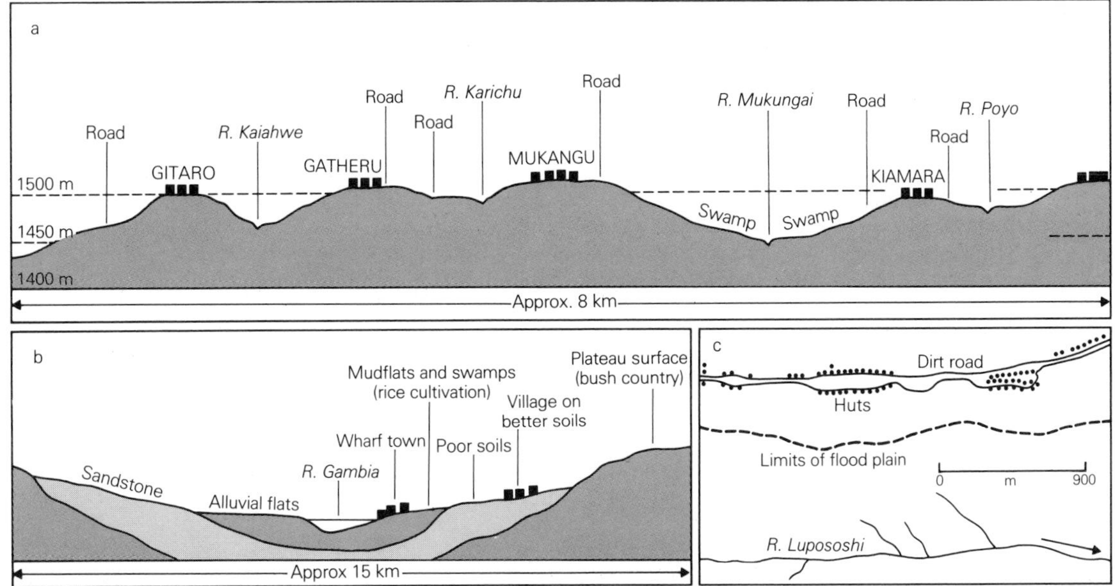

Fig. 7.2 Influences on village siting – *a* Kikuyu villages on interfluves, Murang'a District, Kenya; *b* village siting in Gambia; *c* linear settlement near Lupososhi River, Zambia

extend on both sides of a wide open space or dirt roadway, and the larger the village population the greater the village extent. The fields are usually separated from those of the neighbouring village by low thorn hedges. The form of village settlement is thus not nucleated but elongated and villages tend to be fairly close together. This pattern has been altered in the north-eastern borderlands of Zimbabwe by the creation of 'protected villages' similar to those built in Kenya between 1952 and 1960. As in Kenya, these new sites may become the focal points of future urban growth.

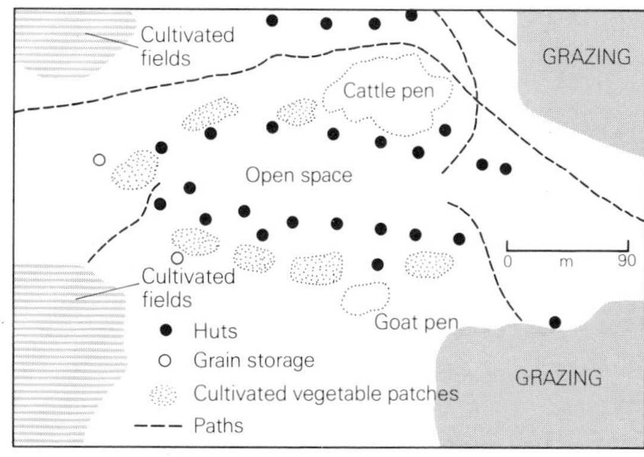

Fig. 7.3 Mashonaland – a Shona village layout

Pemba and Zanzibar

In Pemba and Zanzibar there is often a close relationship between relief, rock type and water availability (Fig. 7.4). Villages are situated at the foot of a central coral ridge with a thin soil cover. On the lower slopes are springs and deeper soil, and settlements here string out along a line. The central ridge is also avoided because it is deeply cut by streams and the soils are thin. Settlements avoid the flat coastal

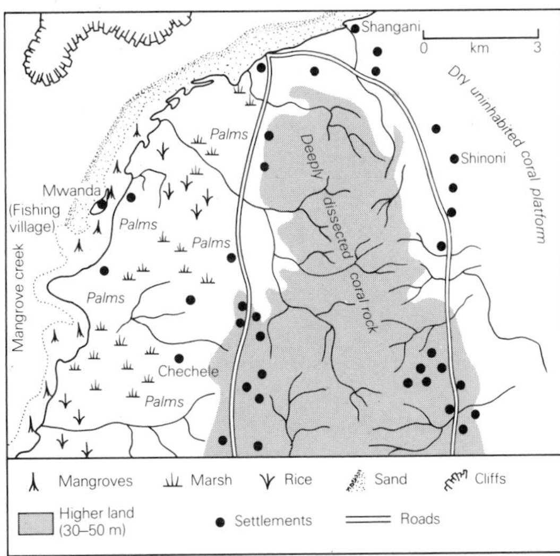

Fig. 7.4 The influence of relief on village siting, north-east coast of Zanzibar

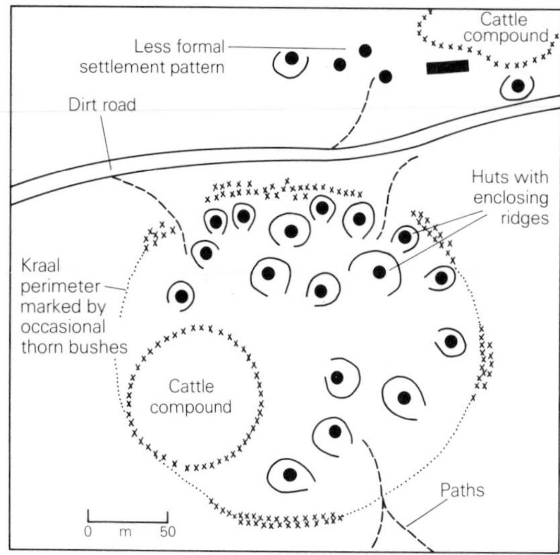

Fig. 7.5 Traditional defensive layout of Zulu kraal in northern Natal, South Africa

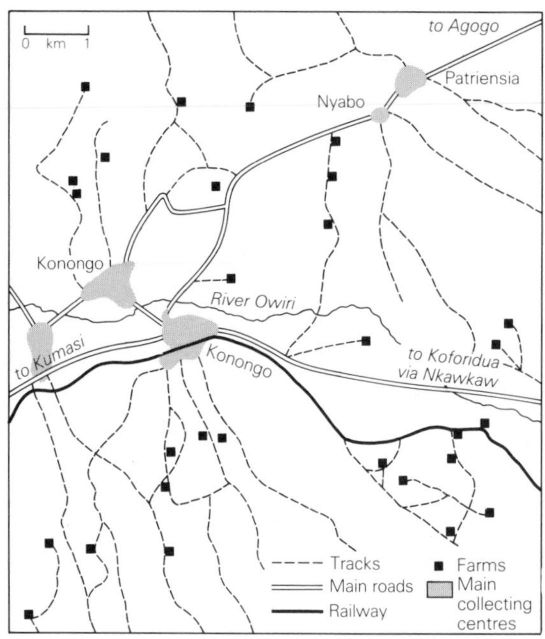

Fig. 7.6 Marketing centres in the cocoa regions of Ghana

marshes because of floods and insects, but there are isolated fishing hamlets. There is no settlement on the coral platform to the east. Natural conditions have thus produced an elongated village settlement pattern.

The Gambia

In the Gambia village sites are influenced by both physical features and commercial interests. In the upper river course, where the waters have deeply incised themselves into the soft sandstone, the valley is narrow and there is little swampland. The villages lie on the high plateau above the bluffs. In the middle course the Gambia River has a wider valley and is flanked by flat swampy lowlands (the *banto faros*), flooded during the rains and infested with insects. Here two types of settlement are found; on the plateau are the chief groundnut areas, in the *banto faros* the patches of swamp rice. To reach both sets of fields easily, villages extend along the middle slopes, each village surrounded by small patches of vegetables (Fig. 7.2b). Small hamlets have grown near the river's edge, where goods from downstream and groundnut exports are handled.

Ghana – Southern Ashanti

The Southern Ashanti District of Ghana illustrates clearly the effect of cash crop farming on settlement distribution, and the need for villages to be near communications. This region is densely populated with villages only a few kilometres from one another, and small townships have grown as collecting centres for cocoa and vegetables. These settlements string out along the main roads while outlying farms are connected to marketing centres by track (Fig. 7.6). Most farms and settlements south of Konongo have been established within the last thirty years. Konongo, once a gold mining centre, has grown from a small hamlet to an important market centre. Away from the main roads many villages are stagnating because of transport difficulties over the rugged terrain.

Towns

The growth of towns

If a village is particularly fortunate in its natural and economic advantages it may develop into an important township or city. Factors which may aid this growth include:

Defence: Peninsulas, islands and hills offer good

defence, and excellent examples are found in Lagos and Mombasa (islands), Tunis (isthmus), Kano and Kampala (hills).

Strategic considerations: Ports like Dakar, Freetown and Cape Town occupy strategic positions commanding ocean trade routes and have grown as important naval bases; Suez and Port Said command the approaches to the Suez Canal.

Routes: Where routes meet or cross, settlement tends to develop to handle the trade, and the site is often a good defensive one. Khartoum on the White and Blue Niles, Algiers on the Mediterranean sea lanes and coastal land routes, Bulawayo at the junction of major roads and railways, Tabora, Dodoma and Kilosa in Tanzania on former Arabic slave and modern routes, are good examples.

Administration: Some sites are chosen by officials as good places from which to govern. The marshy and insanitary site of Bathurst was an excellent spot from which to control the Gambia mouth; Nairobi's physically poor site was chosen for the central government; Addis Ababa's site, chosen towards the end of the nineteenth century, is virtually in the geographical heart of Ethiopia.

Industry: Towns grow rapidly with the establishment of industry, and industry usually lies close to power supplies. Jinja in Uganda, Tema in Ghana, and the Rand cities in South Africa have developed rapidly due to industrial establishment. Towns grow up on the sites of mineral deposits and flourish with continuous production and demand – the copper belt towns in Zambia and Shaba, Johannesburg and its neighbours, Enugu in Nigeria, and others owe their origins to mineral discoveries.

Stages in the growth of a town

A well chosen village site may form the base for the development of a town, but unless some important mineral is discovered nearby, the progression from village to township to town is a gradual one, perhaps speeded by industrial establishment. The following stages apply to many towns in Africa:

1 An African people selected a village site and the village grew as a market centre. A town would develop if the site was on major trading routes, as did many of the urban centres of West Africa.

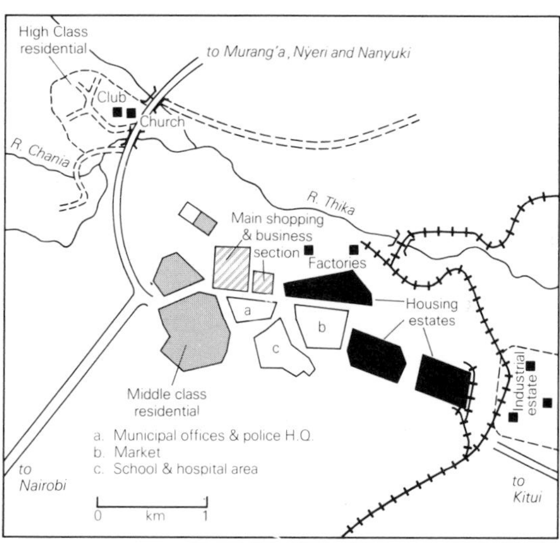

Fig. 7.7 The functional zones of Thika township, Kenya (*simplified*)

2 Sometimes colonial officials chose the site for administrative purposes. This often happened in East and Central Africa.

3 Traders, often Asians or Levantines, arrived to serve the basic needs of the Africans and Europeans.

4 Roads to the village were improved, schools and better houses built.

5 Industrialists may have seen the possibilities of establishing a factory, especially if the village had developed as a collecting centre for raw materials. A trained workforce often becomes a settled community with purchasing power to form a good market.

An example of town growth – Thika

The stages outlined above are well illustrated by the growth of Thika, a flourishing industrial and commercial centre 45 km north-east of Nairobi on the eastern edge of the Kenya Highlands. At the end of the nineteenth century Thika was a small African village, a resting place for travellers, and an administrative *boma* of the British colonial government. The local tribes – Kikuyu and Wakamba – traded here because it lay between their reserves, and a small market developed. Asian traders settled in the village and set up *dukas* (shops) to sell personal items to the Africans, while bigger stores catered for European farmers from the surrounding coffee, sisal and pineapple plantations. The African market flourished, and the sale and purchase of fruit and vegetables grew steadily.

A wattle extract factory was attracted in 1932, followed by a leather tanning factory in 1942. By 1945 Thika had 2 000 Africans, 2 000 Asians and 100 Europeans. The improvement of road conditions, the low land costs, the government's policy of decentralising industry, the good water supply in the nearby Thika River, and the large numbers of local Africans seeking work, helped attract more industry – a metal box factory (1952), a fruit and vegetable canning plant (1952), a paper mill (1958), and three textile factories (all after 1960). Many Africans came to work in Thika from the Kikuyu and Kamba reserves, and from the Luo regions near Lake Victoria. New housing estates were set up, training schools built, a walled market constructed, and the old village swept away for new improvements.

Today Thika (estimated population 25 000), has a workforce of 5 000, who are employed in the numerous Kenya, British, Japanese and Asian owned firms. With a population growth rate of approximately 12 per cent per annum, Thika may become part of the growing urban complex of Nairobi within the next 25 years. The map (Fig. 7.7) shows the present layout of this growing township.

Cities and ports

One of the most striking features of the growth of population in Africa is the rapid expansion of urban communities. The populations of cities and towns are now increasing at the annual rate of 3,5 to 4,5 per cent (8,7 per cent in the case of Lusaka). The annual growth of Yaoundé in the Cameroons, for example, has doubled within seven years, and that of the Guinean capital, Conakry, has quadrupled; the population of Dar es Salaam, Tanzania's capital, has more than doubled since 1956, and the population of the capital of Ghana, Accra, has more than trebled in twenty years. Africa's, and probably the world's, fastest growing city is now Lagos.

Urban development may take place in the most unlikely spot – Nairobi developed on a most unfavourable site, but unlikely physical conditions were overcome by later commercial and political advantages. Man is thus able to choose a spot for settlement for purely administrative and social reasons and, if other factors, especially economic, are favourable, the settlement will flourish. If these factors are absent the settlement may decline.

In the classification of towns we used earlier, the importance of defence and the situation on routeways was stressed, and these give a settlement an initial impetus. Later, considerations such as defence become less important and towns take on new functions as marketing centres, industrial nodes and regional capitals, many towns combining several of these spheres of activity.

Ports

Ports lie at the junction point of sea and land routes, and handle the produce of overseas territories and their own hinterlands. They are entrepôts – points through which exports and imports pass and which become large store houses for raw materials. Later they may acquire industries based on these raw materials, and become regional capitals or route nodes for the regions in which they stand. The following examples of ports in Africa are described with reference to the dominant influences which have most aided their development.

Two ports of North West Africa

The ports of North West Africa have been greatly influenced by their commercial and political ties with Europe. Many of their sites were chosen by the Romans as military outposts or collecting points for their Mediterranean empire. Later Arab occupation brought a new style of architecture in the narrow streets of the medina and the small market places. European colonisation encouraged extensive building development, industry and trade, and population, both European and Africa, grew. Casablanca developed from a small village in 1900 to a city with over one million inhabitants today, and the same is true of Algiers (2 million), and Tunis (800 000).

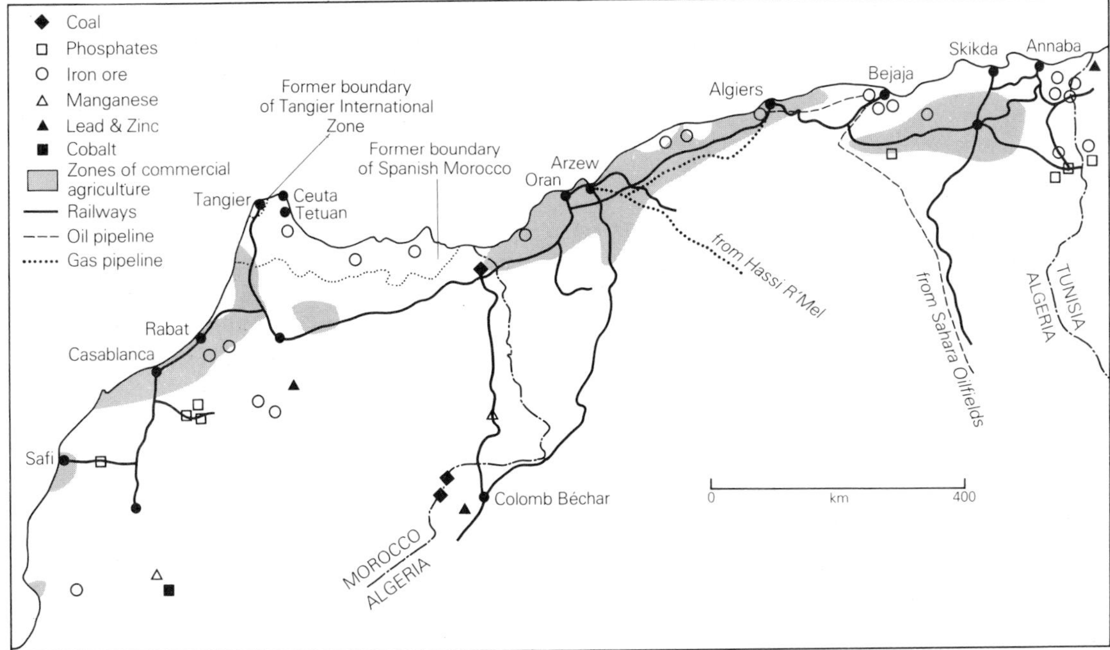

Fig. 7.8 The ports of the Maghreb and their hinterlands

A capital port with many functions — Algiers

Algiers is the capital and the largest administrative, commercial and industrial centre of Algeria, serving the whole of the Algerian coast and much of the country's hinterland. Its site was selected by the Romans for defence and it attracted the Arabs at a later date. Algiers was later occupied by the Spaniards, the Turks and the Barbary pirates, the latter finally succumbing to the French in 1830.

The port was then developed to serve both Algeria and France, and a long harbour was constructed enclosing four smaller harbours which have facilities for handling oil, grain, ore and coal. The port is well served by rail which brings the products of the Metidja and the hinterland for export – cereals, wine, olive oil, esparto grass, sheep, wool, iron ore, phosphates, gypsum and coal, most destined for France. The port handles large imports of coke, timber, manufactured goods, chemicals and foodstuffs and is the chief passenger port in the country.

Algiers has excellent road and rail connections with Oran, Constantine and Blida, and has become the largest collecting and industrial centre in Algeria. Most of the industries are concentrated in the south-east sector and include flour-milling, fish canning, engineering and cement, beer and soap manufacture. Other concerns produce wine barrels, tobacco and cigarettes, superphosphates, chemicals, bricks and tins, and there are railways workshops and ship repair yards.

The chief factors which have led to Algiers' growth may thus be summarised as:

a its early selection as a defensive site;
b its maritime connections with Europe and the development of routes by the French to tap the hinterland;
c its selection as an administrative capital;
d its growth as an industrial centre based on the bulky products which it handles.

The Maghreb's largest city — Casablanca

Casablanca is the largest city in Morocco and the most important port in North West Africa. Its fantastic growth is shown in the following population figures:

1900–20 000	1952–682 388
1926–106 608	1960–965 277
1946–500 000	today–over 1,25 million

The city's rise to importance is due to:

a Its strategic position in relation to Atlantic shipping routes.

b French government stimulation during their occupation of Morocco; the port was developed to serve the French sphere of control at the expense of Tangier, which was converted into an international port.

c The fairly deep harbour which does not suffer from riverine silting as do many of Morocco's ports.

d The tremendous flow of goods from the vast hinterland which includes virtually the whole of Morocco. Casablanca handles about 75 per cent of Morocco's trade, importing manufactured goods (cars, trucks, machinery) and exporting phosphates, manganese ores, grains, vegetables, fruits, fish and sugar. Trade has grown from 200 000 t in 1914 to 7 million tonnes in 1948, and today it is about 10 million tonnes.

e The development of the city at a natural focal point of routes. Electrified railways run south to Marrakesh and the phosphate deposits of Ben Guerir, with a branch line to the Wed Zem phosphate mines in the east, to Rabat and Kenifra on the coast to the north, and further north to the productive Fez-Meknes agricultural region.

f The growth of industries based on the bulky raw materials. Casablanca now has over half of Morocco's industrial concerns, many supplied with power from a huge electric power plant. Industries include flour milling, grain conditioning, oil milling, fish canning, soap, cement and superphosphate manufacture, and sugar refining.

Four ports of West Africa

The coast of West Africa is limited in the number of good natural harbours suitable for major port development. Dakar is an artificial construction, but it has the protection of a rocky promontory. However, south-eastwards from Dakar to Cape St. Ann, the coast is a drowned one providing many natural

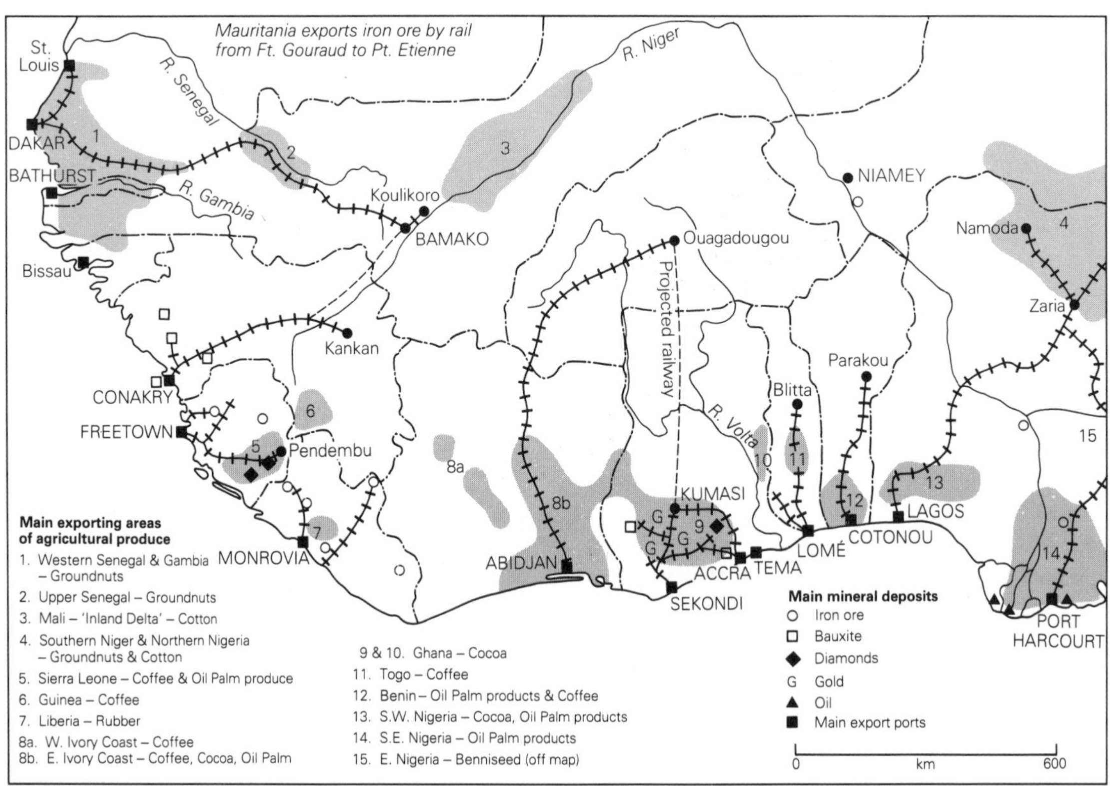

Fig. 7.9 The ports of West Africa and their hinterlands

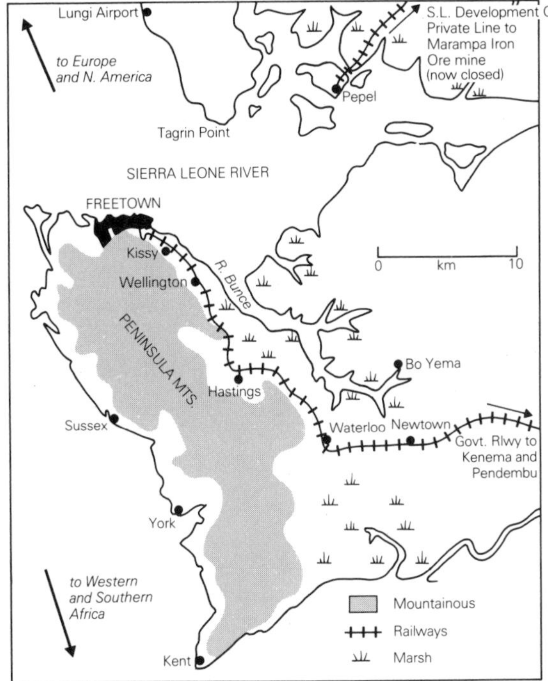

Fig. 7.10 The site of Freetown, Sierra Leone

inlets and good harbours. From Cape St. Ann eastwards to the Niger delta, the off-shore water is shallow with numerous sandbars backed by lagoons. There are one or two larger inlets as at Lagos, but many of the ports are artificial – Takoradi, Abidjan, Sekondi, Tema – and most harbours must be constantly dredged.

A natural and strategic port – Freetown

The Sierra Leone estuary provides a deep, well-sheltered and easily entered harbour for the largest of ocean-going vessels, the site easily recognised by the Peninsula Mountains which rise up steeply behind the port to over 760 m.

Freetown was founded in 1792 as a settlement for freed slaves and by 1800 had about 3 000 inhabitants. When the peninsula became a crown colony of Britain in 1808, the port was developed as a naval base because of its strategic importance in suppressing the slave trade and for the bigger role of policing the Atlantic approaches to West Africa. In 1899 Freetown was linked by railway to the interior as far as Songo and later as far as Pendembu, and this enabled the port to take over much of the trade of smaller ports such as Sulima and Bonthe. Freetown soon became the chief British settlement along the West African coast and temporarily took over administrative responsibility for other British-controlled territories. The population grew slowly to 64 576 in 1948; by 1960 this had risen to 90 000 and is about 200 000 today.

The harbour was greatly improved in 1953 by the completion of the Queen Elizabeth Quay which can accommodate large ocean-going vessels, for previously ships had to anchor off-shore. Freetown handles virtually all of Sierra Leone's products – diamonds, palm kernels and cocoa beans – and practically all the imports – sugar, rice, grain, flour, meat, fuel oils, chemicals, machinery, transport equipment, cement, clothing and footwear. Over 800 vessels call and half a million tonnes of goods are handled annually.

Freetown has few industries but they are growing in number – groundnut and rice mills, cigarette manufacture, brewing, liquor distilling, and paint, nails, cement, shoe and clothing manufacture. But its development has largely depended on its strategic position and its role as an entrepôt for Sierra Leone.

A modern industrial port – Tema

Tema is an ambitious attempt by Ghana to combine a modern port to serve the eastern regions of the country with the rapid growth of industry which the huge power potential of the Volta Scheme makes possible. Moreover, Tema has greatly reduced the strain on ports such as Takoradi which have found Ghana's increasing volume of exports difficult to handle.

The site of the new port is 30 km east of Accra. This was the home of the Ga people who had settled in this area in the sixteenth century or before, and some 4 000 of whom fished the waters where the new harbour was to be constructed; they were later settled into a new fishing village east of Tema. The site of the port was chosen because it was close to the Volta Project, with suitable building stone in the nearby Shai Hills, and comparatively deep off-shore water which would reduce the amount of dredging needed.

Tema had to be integrated with Ghana's major road and rail network and rail connections were built to Accra and Kumasi via Achimota and a link to major road routes by 20 km of new trunk roads. Tema harbour was built to accommodate one million

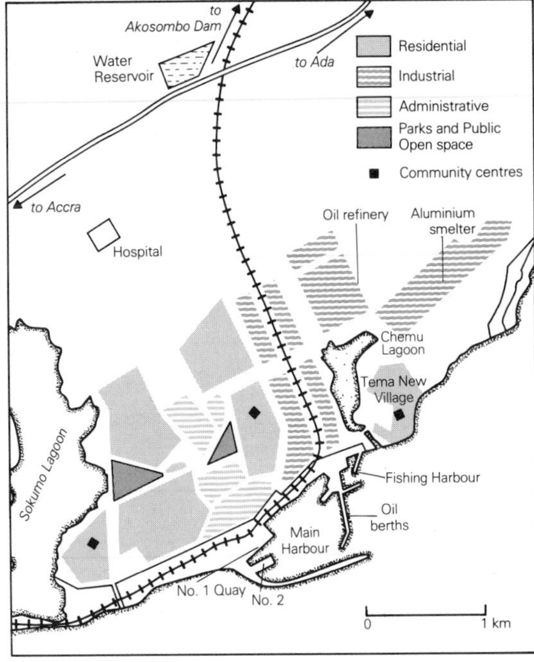

Fig. 7.11 The site of Tema, Ghana

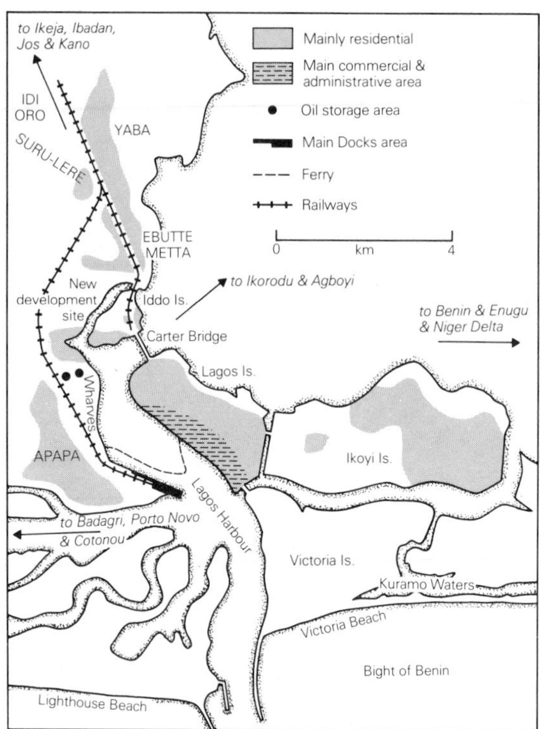

Fig. 7.12 The site of Lagos, Nigeria

tonnes of shipping and it covers 200 ha. Cocoa storage sheds, a modern railway station, a lighthouse, offices, a ship repair dockyard, and servicing and oil berths for 35 500 t tankers are the main features of the harbour installations.

Tema city consists of community estates containing 3 000 to 5 000 people. Each estate has its own shops, market, churches, and schools, and a group of four estate units has a clinic, secondary schools, nurseries and service industries. Tema's population is rapidly increasing, and plans envisage a population of 200 000 by 1985.

Tema is destined to become the foremost industrial centre of Ghana, using power from the Akosombo Dam. A well-planned estate of over 400 ha, with 1 000 ha reserved for expansion, has been laid out and has attracted many industries. The Valco Aluminium company's smelting plant went into production in 1967 with a capacity of 183 000 annually, and other industries established include oil refining, block and pre-cast concrete manufacture, lorry assembly and sheet metal, corrugated iron, suitcase, paint, cement and insecticide manufacture. Fish canning, fish cold storage, metal utensil manufacture, a mattress works, an angle steel plant, a radio and electronics concern, and a large chocolate factory are all well established. Two recent concerns are a large textile plant and a chemical factory.

Tema is thus a flourishing industrial centre and a modern port. Two factors have led to its success – the need by Ghana for a modern outlet for increasing exports, and the rapid growth of industry attendant on the Volta Power Scheme.

A trade focus and federal capital – Lagos

Lagos is the federal capital, largest city and best port of Nigeria; it is also a leading commercial, industrial, and culture centre. A trading focus from the earliest times, it was first settled as a defensive site by the Yoruba in the fifteenth century, and later became a flourishing trading centre for the Benin people and the Portuguese. Although badly drained and malaria-ridden, Lagos was used extensively by slave traders because of its easily defended position. Slaves were brought along the coastal lagoons up to 1861, when the British occupied the site and developed a less obnoxious trade. In 1867 there were 22 European traders and by 1898 there were 200 British residents, most of them concerned with shipping palm oil to Europe.

From 1900 the town developed rapidly. A canal was cut across Lagos Island to create Ikoyi Island in the east where a European settlement grew. In 1901 the railway to Ibadan was opened, in 1912 it was linked to Kano, and rail and road bridges were built to connect Lagos to the mainland. The narrow channel leading to the port was dredged in 1914 to admit ocean-going ships, and the port capacity was further increased by the completion of the Apapa wharves in 1926. Today the port provides sixteen berths with modern loading and discharging facilities and four more are to be added. Lagos now handles 60 per cent of Nigeria's exports – cocoa, groundnuts, cotton, palm kernels, rubber, hides, skins, beniseed, groundnut and palm oils. Imports include cars, electrical machinery, lorries, construction equipment, cotton goods, jute bags, tyres, constructional steel, fuel oils, salt, sugar and fish.

As an entrepôt for raw materials, Lagos has attracted the greatest concentration of industry in Nigeria, with nearly 600 factories of all sizes. The city's industries account for almost one-third of the value of industrial production in the whole country. In terms of national output value, Lagos produces half Nigeria's output in the metaliferous industries, 70 per cent in printing and publishing, and nearly 90 per cent in the beer and soft drinks industry. The city has attracted industries which depend on a large consumer market, such as clothing, baking and printing, those which require a large amount of imported raw materials, such as flour (wheat imports) and plastics (oil derivatives), and again, industries which require a skilled workforce and a supporting infrastructure, such as railway engineering and motor vehicle assembly. Industries which are most profitable through on-the-spot processing, e.g. saw-milling and vegetable oil milling, are few in number.

Apart from some very early factories such as the brick kilns (established in the early 1860s) and an oil mill (1865), the establishment of factory industries belongs to the post-Second World War period. The establishment of industry in Lagos was encouraged by income tax and import duty relief regulations established in the 1950s, which favoured the urban industrialist, and also by the creation of industrial estates with rail and road networks linking with the city communications system. There are eight industrial estates within the Greater Lagos area: at Ijora–Iganmu (light and commercial industries and a structural steel plant using imported steel); at Isolo (motor car assembly, batteries, textiles, air conditioners, gas); and at Yaba, Ikeja, Gbagada, Matori, Ilupeju, and Agidingbi. Besides those mentioned, industries housed on these estates produce the following range of goods: carbon dioxide, bitumen, soap, beer, metal containers, margarine, mineral waters, flour, furniture, printed packaging materials, plastic products, footwear, rubber products, tanned leathers, bricks and tiles, perfumes and cosmetics, boats, bicycles, pottery and glass, cement and concrete products, paints, and electrical machinery and appliances. Bulk palm oil, mineral oil depots and large railway workshops are located at Ebute Metta.

Lagos has probably reached the limits of its industrial expansion. Water and electric power supplies to factories are insufficient to support much further industrial growth, and the provision of housing and additional transport facilities present an expensive problem (see below). In future, priority will be given to those industries which require only a limited amount of land, and which are labour intensive.

Lagos is linked by air services to all major towns in Nigeria and to other West African countries. Eleven international airlines use Ikeja Airport, 20 km from the city centre. The city is also the seat of the federal legislature and the natural location for leading business and financial houses. The 1963 census showed Lagos to have a population of 1,44 million; this had risen to 2,47 million according to the 1973 census, but unofficial estimates suggest a figure of nearly four million for Lagos and its suburbs.

The role of Lagos as the federal capital of Nigeria is drawing to a close. Its coastal situation is a bad one from which to administer a country extending some 1 300 km from north to south, 725 km from east to west, and covering over 900 000 square kilometres. The city's early design and subsequent growth during colonial times did not fit it for the present booming economic development brought about largely by oil prosperity, nor to administer the needs of a population exceeding 80 million. Its greatest drawback is its lack of good communications with

Nigeria: One result of rapid urban growth – a traffic jam in Lagos.

the hinterland, despite road and rail improvements. The city's island site also imposes limitations on reorganisation, and future growth on the mainland must be channelled to the north and north-east towards Agege and Ikorodu because of the lagoon on the east and swamps and sandy ridges to the west. Housing problems are acute as the city administration tries to cater for an annual population growth of 200 000, many of whom are immigrants from rural areas. Nearly 60 000 new housing units are needed each year, in addition to 10 000 units required to replace old dwellings and slums.

Moreover, rapid population and industrial growth has resulted in traffic congestion. The port area on Lagos Island and at Apapa lie in the south of the city, while the major industrial estates at Ikeja and Ilupeju are in the north. A massive flow of traffic is generated between these zones, especially during early morning and late afternoon. Also, because of the huge hinterland which Lagos serves and the function of the city as an entrepôt for neighbouring countries such as Niger, Dahomey and Chad, the main arteries leading out of the city are often congested.

Because of these numerous problems, the Federal Government has decided that a new, more centrally situated capital is needed. The new site, almost in the geographical centre of the country, lies about 50 km south of the ancient town of Abuja and north of the confluence of the Niger and Benue rivers, where the four states of Kaduna, Niger, Plateau and Kwara meet (see map, Fig. 6.1 p. 113). A new Federal Capital Territory (FCT), somewhat on the lines of Australia's capital territory of Canberra, has been established, and covers an area of 8 000 square kilometres. A panel of experts chose this site because of its centrality, the pleasant climate, land availability, security and water supply, and because the area lies outside the control of any one major ethnic group in Nigeria. The countryside is thinly populated and land costs are relatively low, the railway passes nearby, road access is fairly easy, and nearby airfields could be extended. Work has already begun at the new site, but it will take between 10 and 15 years before the new capital is fully functioning.

A commercial centre and industrial port – Port Harcourt

The case of Port Harcourt illustrates the influence of good communications, a rich hinterland, nodality, and nearness to mineral resources, particularly oil, in stimulating urban development. The city is the second largest port and the eighth largest urban centre in Nigeria, and its growth has been extremely fast: in 1953 the population was a mere 72 000, by 1963 it had risen to 180 000, by 1971 it was 220 000, and today it exceeds a quarter of a million.

Port Harcourt is the capital of Rivers State and has long played the role of a gateway port to northern and eastern Nigeria. Situated on the Bonny River some 66 km upriver from the coast and at the terminus of the main eastern railway to the north, the city lies at the junction point of coastal marshes and interior lowlands. The port is the natural southern focus of the rail and road routes of the eastern and north-eastern parts of Nigeria. The railway linked the port to the coal fields at Enugu, the tin mines around Jos, and the beniseed and soya bean producing region around Makurdi. These commodities became early exports, in addition to the palm oil, rubber, palm kernels and cocoa of the southern forest zone, and the cotton and groundnuts of northern Nigeria. Port Harcourt also shared with Lagos the handling of Niger's imports and exports, while the eastern and north-eastern regions of Nigeria particularly depended on the port to handle the vast quantities of mixed imports required for their development.

To handle the increasing traffic and larger vessels, the Bonny River was dredged to increase its depth by a further six metres below low water-level, and the existing wharves were extended in the 1950s and mid-1960s. By this time, Port Harcourt had attracted a wide range of industries including bicycle assembly, tobacco processing, flour milling, and furniture making.

The rapid development of the oil fields immediately to the east of Port Harcourt during the 1960s provided a cheap source of energy for industry through the products of the refineries and from the

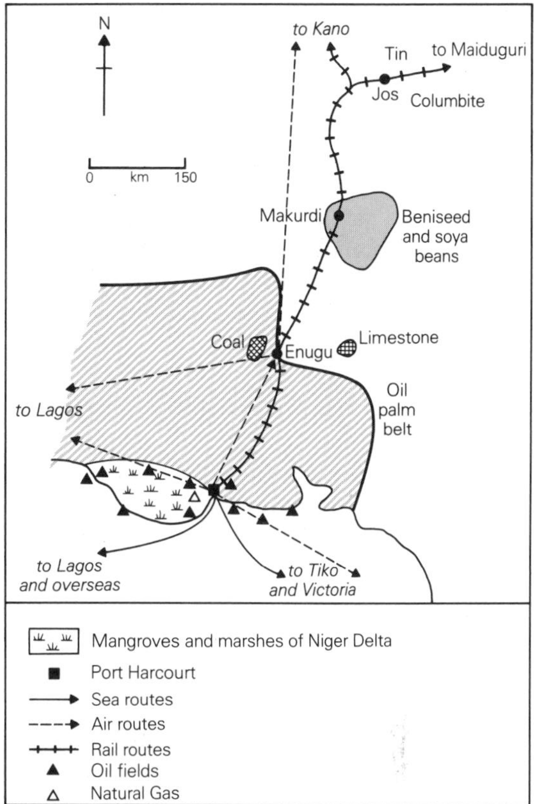

Fig. 7.13 Port Harcourt in relation to its hinterland

deposits of natural gas. The Elesa Eleme refinery began operating in November, 1965 with an initial capacity of 1,9 million tonnes per annum, enough to meet Nigeria's petroleum requirements at that time, and a liquefied petroleum gas plant with a capacity of 15 000 t a year was constructed in 1966. The natural gas from the Afam and Apara fields is piped to the industrial estate at trans-Amadi, which contains the huge Michelin tyre factory and a large glass plant.

The Civil War (1967–70) temporarily curtailed Port Harcourt's development, for the harbour was closed to shipping, and the refinery and other industrial plant were severely damaged. After the war the refinery was reconstructed and its capacity expanded to 2,75 million tonnes; it is planned to increase this by a further one million tonnes capacity. To handle increasing post-war tonnage, a new jetty has been constructed and more oil storage tanks have been built. An additional pipeline will link the refineries near Port Harcourt with eastern Nigeria as part of a national scheme to ease the flow of oil to remoter areas.

The development of Port Harcourt as Nigeria's most important port after Lagos can be ascribed to:

a Its site on a navigable and deepened river. Possible rival delta ports such as Warri, Burutu and Sapele have always suffered from obstructive sandbars.
b An immediate hinterland possessing a range of minerals, fuel supplies (coal), and agricultural products in demand overseas.
c A wider hinterland including eastern and northern Nigeria, and Niger.
d The advantage of early communications linking the port to these hinterlands. Port Harcourt's nearest rival, Calabar, although it has a natural deep-water ria, declined in relative importance because the railways linked the port with neighbouring Cameroon (served by Douala), and with Port Harcourt itself. No line was ever constructed to connect Calabar with the far interior.
e The opening up of the vast oilfields east of the port, and their subsequent development.

Port Harcourt has been chosen for the site of a new steel mill (see also p. 213). The city has a deepwater approach essential for iron ore vessels, Enugu coal is within easy reach (although it would have to be mixed with imported coking types), iron ore could be imported from Liberia in addition to local ores, Nigeria has the largest markets in terms of population and can also supply the largest amounts of scrap steel, and a wide range of chemical by-products are obtainable from the nearby petro-chemical industry.

Three ports of South Africa

South Africa does not possess any really good natural harbours and her major ports are largely artificial creations developed to serve the Republic's expanding economy. Cape Town was for a long time the only major port, administration centre, and entry port for settlers. Later, as the south-eastern parts were opened up and settled, Port Elizabeth, East London, and Durban grew to importance.

A strategic port – Cape Town

Cape Town dates from 1652 when Jan van Riebeeck established a victualling station to supply fresh produce to Dutch East India Company vessels on their way to the East. The harbour was ill-protected from gales (over 300 vessels have been wrecked to date) and cargo had to be lightered ashore. It was only in the 1870s that real protection was achieved with a long breakwater and the Albert Dock.

The strategic position of Cape Town between the Atlantic and Indian Oceans, the development of the fruit and grain trade, and the economic growth of South Africa, led to extensive improvements so that Cape Town's 150-ha harbour is now one of the best in the world. Pre-cooling sheds, a 30 000 t capacity grain elevator, coal and oil bunkers, ship repair yards, and modern cranage have been installed. The 10-ha Duncan Dock has made possible the reclamation of 120 ha of foreshore, where a new city section has been built.

Cape Town serves most of the Republic and also Zimbabwe, but its immediate hinterland is limited (Fig. 7.15). The chief exports include fruit, wine, wool, hides, skins, mineral ores, and general cargo. Cape Town is now an important oil and coal bunkering port and handles about 9 000 vessels annually. A new oil-tanker basin has just been completed and the restrictions on giant oil tankers using the Suez Canal has increased the use of Cape Town as a port-of-call for vessels carrying Middle East oil.

The city is the focus of road and rail routes. National highways give speedy access northwards to the Swartland, north-eastwards to Paarl and Worcester, and eastwards through the Elgin Basin to Swellendam. These national routes penetrate to the interior and east coast and are duplicated by major rail routes. The city is well served by the D. F. Malan Airport 20 km to the east.

Cape Town (1 064 602) has developed port industries and others based on hinterland produce – grain milling, fruit and jam canning, tobacco processing, tanning, textiles and woollen goods, general and electrical engineering, and the manufacture of footwear, paints and varnishes, and building materials.

The city thus owes its importance to:

a Its strategic position commanding ocean routes and the major feeder routes from the hinterland.
b Its growth as an entrepôt for both passengers and the produce and imports of the Republic.

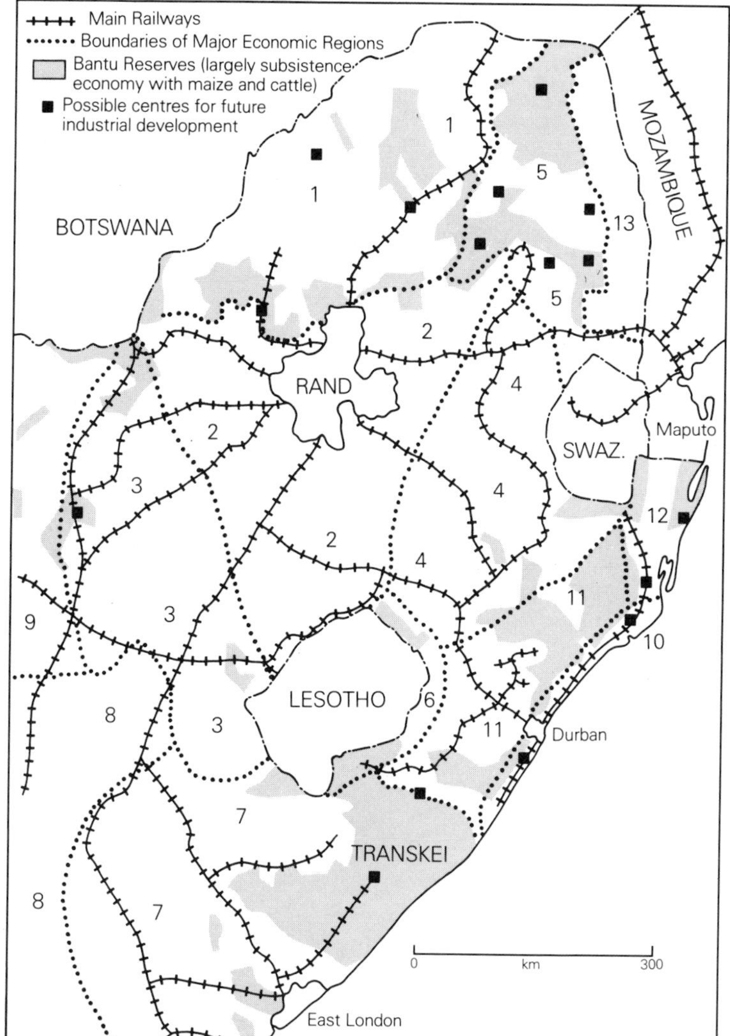

Fig. 7.14 Durban, East London and Maputo – their major hinterlands.

1. Northern Transvaal: Mainly cattle ranching.
2. Johannesburg-Northern Orange Free State-Southern Transvaal: Manufacturing, mining, sheep, cattle, dairying, maize.
3. Western Orange Free State: Sheep, cattle, dairying, maize.
4. Eastern Transvaal and North-Eastern Natal: Sheep, cattle, maize, dairying, timber, mining, some manufacturing.
5. North-Eastern Transvaal: Fruits, vegetables, timber, African cattle, maize and subsistence crops.
6. Lower slopes of Drakensberg: Sheep and cattle ranching.
7. Eastern Cape: subsistence and cattle in north; dairying, citrus fruits, sheep and cattle in south and south-west.
8. Cape Interior: Beginnings of large-scale pastoral economy based on sheep and goat rearing with some cattle.
9. Northern Cape: Cattle ranching on extensive scale.
10. Natal Coast: Sugar cane, sub-tropical fruits, timber.
11. Natal Interior: Mainly timber and dairying with some subsistence.
12. North-Eastern Zululand: Largely subsistence economy based on cattle and maize with some cotton, sugar and timber.

(Map based on material supplied by the State Information Office, Pretoria.)

Fig. 7.15 Site and functional zones of Cape Town
1 Dock area
2 Central commercial core
3 Industrial area
Routes:
a To Malmesbury
b National road to Paarl and North
c To Somerset West, Strand and Caledon

c Its later growth as a commercial, banking, administrative and industrial centre.

A regional capital and great entrepôt – Durban

In comparison, Durban did not achieve the early importance of Cape Town, but developed with the growth of agricultural and mineral production of Natal and the Transvaal. Established in 1824, its early development was hindered by hostile tribes and the rather dangerous entrance to the Bay of Natal. In the early days it served as an entry port for the growing colony of Natal but, with the discovery of Rand gold, it leaped to importance. Now covering 200 square kilometres the city has 550 000 inhabitants (220 000 Europeans).

The Transvaal and Natal hinterlands export a tremendous tonnage of coal and mineral ores (especially manganese), wool, sugar, dairy produce, citrus fruits, maize and tobacco. Oil, timber, and miscellaneous goods are the main imports, and Durban also acts as a coal bunkering port, although it has lost a lot of its oil bunkering trade to the more conveniently placed Cape Town. Due to the bulkiness of the cargoes handled, Durban deals with more tonnage than any other South African port. In a peak month, Durban handles 3 million tonnes and 550 ships (Cape Town 850 000 t, 450 ships; Port Elizabeth 855 000 t and 180; East London 300 000 t and 75 ships).

The harbour suffers from silt, almost entirely caused by the action of longshore drift along the coast, but the construction of breakwaters and constant dredging have minimised this. The harbour covers 12 square kilometres and has a floating dock, electrically operated coaling points, numerous oil fuelling and storage sites, a grain elevator, and pre-cooling and storage sheds. There is a whaling station and whale processing factories at the Bluff. Some 200 ha of dunes and swamps are being reclaimed for the establishment of a major shipbuilding industry.

Durban is an important industrial, commercial and holiday centre. The city has spread in a wide arc around the harbour between the Umlaas River in the south and the Umgeni in the north. The industrial zones contain factories making rope, paper, soap, matches, tyres, blankets, glass, plastics, clothing, enamelware, furniture, paint, chemical products, toilet articles, confectionary, jam and processed foodstuffs. There are also oil and sugar refineries, an important engineering works, and large railway workshops. Margarine, biscuits and fertilisers are also manufactured.

Durban undoubtedly owes its importance to:

a its comparatively good harbour which has been greatly improved artificially.

b its nearness to the Transvaal and the agricultural importance of its hinterland. Durban acts as a entrepôt for the whole of the south-east and much of the interior.

c its growth as a collecting centre which has led to its development as one of the foremost industrial areas of the Republic.

Growing congestion in Durban's harbour will be greatly relieved once the new port of Richard's Bay, 160 km to the north, is finally completed. This port will offer an alternative outlet for the Transvaal Industrial complex, and its harbour will be three and a half times the size of Durban's. There will be coal bunkering berths and oil terminals capable of handling the largest tankers afloat. Ships will approach the berths through a dredged channel, and a 16 km railway will link Richard's Bay with Empangeni and the national network. An electrified line, completed in 1976, connects with Pretoria via Ermelo. The Alusaf aluminium smelter, opened at Richard's Bay in 1971, uses 10 000 t of aluminium oxide a year in the manufacture of wire, die castings and other metal products. A bulk sugar terminal, an aluminium processing plant, and an air terminal are in operation.

An agricultural outlet and industrial port – Port Elizabeth

Port Elizabeth (400 000) stands on Algoa Bay, where Diaz landed in 1488. It was at first a garrison town, and by 1811 had facilities for beef exports and for whaling and fishing. By the end of the nineteenth century, Port Elizabeth had several industries processing local agricultural products – tanned leather, washed wool, soap, candles, harnesses, footwear, matches, cigarettes and also explosives. During the Anglo-Boer War, the port became the main supply centre for the British forces. The 1920s saw further industrial growth, with motor car assembly and concerns manufacturing tyres, cement, clothing, glass and electric batteries. The number of industrial undertakings has expanded from 200 in 1926 to nearly 800 today. These fall into several groups: leather goods (tanned leather, footwear, travel goods); clothing (knitwear, suits, workclothes, swimwear); textiles (combing and weaving of wool and cotton textiles); motor car assembly (Ford, Rover, General Motors, Citroën); allied industries to the motor industry (tyres, rubber materials, wheels, batteries); engineering and several miscellaneous industries (plastics, processed foods, chemicals and pharmaceutical goods, cement and glass); the electrical industry (electric cables, refrigerators, lamp bulbs and small generators).

Port Elizabeth is well placed between South Africa's east and south coasts and acts as a transit port for the Eastern Cape, the Orange Free State and, less importantly, for the Transvaal. The harbour was enclosed in 1934 and this gave protection from strong easterly winds. The harbour now has ore berths, a second inner quay, underground pre-cooling sheds for fruit exports and large ore-storage bins.

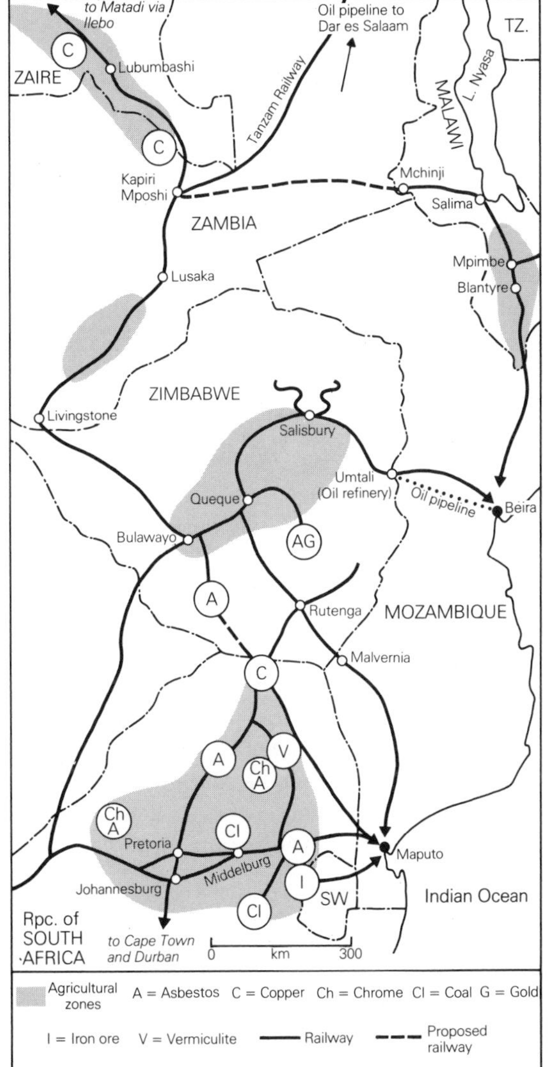

Fig. 7.16 The hinterlands of Beira and Maputo

Exports from Port Elizabeth reflect the agricultural hinterland – wool, mohair, hides and skins, citrus fruits and timber, and also manganese ores. Before the closure of Suez the port dealt with nearly five million tonnes a year, but this rose to nearly seven million tonnes after closure.

Port Elizabeth is also a noted holiday centre and an educational centre with a university, technical college and numerous schools.

The port is also an outlet for the products of Uitenhage (75 000) 25 km away, a growing industrial centre with wool washing, combing, railway workshops, motor car and truck assembly (Volkswagen), tyre, axles, motor components and lighting equipment. These two cities form a major industrial region of the Republic and produce 55 per cent of the country's vehicles.

Mozambique's capital and chief port – *Maputo*

Mozambique has plenty of small shallow harbours along her 2 700 km long coast but only three ports, Maputo, Beira and Nacala have harbours suitable for large-scale international trade. These ports are more important as outlets for inland territories than for Mozambique itself.

Maputo (185 000) owes its importance to the vast hinterland it serves – the Transvaal, Rhodesia (now Zimbabwe), and southern Mozambique. Delagoa Bay was first discovered in 1502 and forts were built in 1544 and 1787 to protect the slave and ivory trade, and to control the entrance to the Esperito Santo River. Once one of the most unhealthy sites in Africa, Maputo is now a pleasant city with broad, tree-lined avenues, spacious parks and modern buildings.

Although the capital since 1907, Maputo is badly situated in the south of Mozambique, with poor connections to the rest of the country, there being no good road connection to Beira until recently and no railway to northern Mozambique. Most services were run by the air and the shipping lines, and the railway system originally extended only as far as Rossano Garcia on the Transvaal border. With the linking of the port to Zimbabwe's system via the Incomati and Limpopo valleys to Malvernia, a vast new hinterland was opened up and both Zambia and the former Rhodesia used this line extensively.

The port thus handles Zambian copper, Swaziland iron ore along the rail extension to Bomvu, the ores, fruit and wool of the Transvaal, S. Africa minerals, and Mozambique cotton, sugar, cashew nuts and copra. The effect of economic sanctions against Rhodesia reduced or eliminated Zambian copper and Rhodesia's tobacco and minerals.

Maputo's bay is 40 km long and 35 km broad and protected by the Inhaca Peninsula. The port facilities have a shed storage capacity of a quarter of a million tonnes and the modern cranage can handle fifteen vessels at once. There are fruit pre-cooling sheds, fish-freezing plants, chrome, iron ore and timber wharves, while at Matola there is a modern bulk oil discharge quay. The harbour can deal with nine million tonnes annually; exports now amount to four million tonnes and imports to over five million tonnes annually. Constant dredging of the harbour is necessary, however, especially around the Matola dock, since ore vessels have deep draughts. Altogether 1 800 vessels call here yearly. Maputo has attracted a great number of industries, the chief being those making cement, furniture, cigarettes, pottery, beer, footwear, soap, oils, radios, railway wagons and river barges. There is an important oil refinery and a rubber processing plant.

But while Maputo is assured of a steady trade with the Transvaal and Swaziland, Beira's future is uncertain. Railway construction has diverted much trade away from Beira to the south. In the north, with the completion of the line from Mayuci in Malaŵi to Nacala, and with the reduction of traffic on the Umtali–Beira line, it would seem that Beira's trade is bound to decline.

Three ports of the East African coast

The ports of East Africa were founded by Oman and Hadramaut Arabs from Arabia, some as early as the first century A.D. They grew as embarkation points

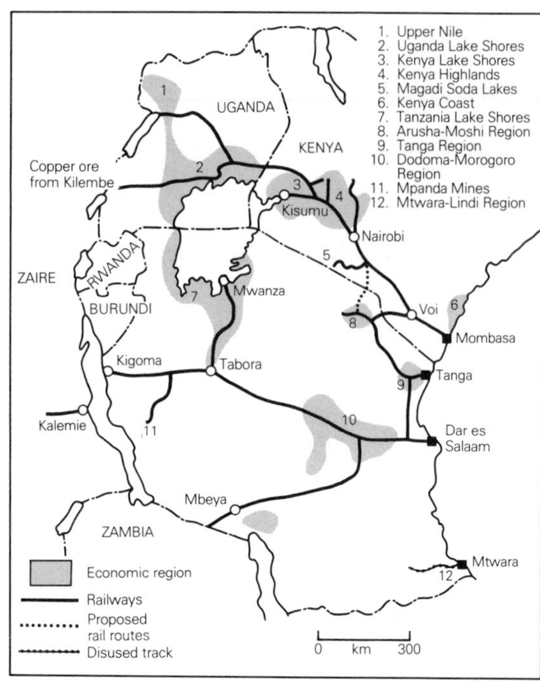

Fig. 7.17 East Africa – the hinterlands of the major ports

for slaves, defensive sites and marketing centres, and administrative headquarters. They handled cargoes from the Middle East, India and China. By the fourteenth century there were many flourishing centres – Kilwa with three hundred mosques; Malindi, a prosperous port-of-call; Mogadishu, Bagomoyo and Zanzibar, important slave centres. Many have lost their early importance and some, like Gedi, north of Mombasa, are now empty ruins.

With the development of the hinterland in the colonial era, port growth at the most favourable sites was accentuated – at Dar es Salaam, Mombasa and Tanga. These became termini for the railways and import points for the growing colonies. The map (Fig. 7.17) shows the way in which railways tap the economically important interior regions. It illustrates clearly how Mombasa has grown to preeminence.

A regional capital, international entrepôt and industrial port – Mombasa

Mombasa's early development was due to its deep, well-sheltered harbour and its excellent defensive position on an island. Founded in the tenth century, and occupied by the Portuguese in the sixteenth

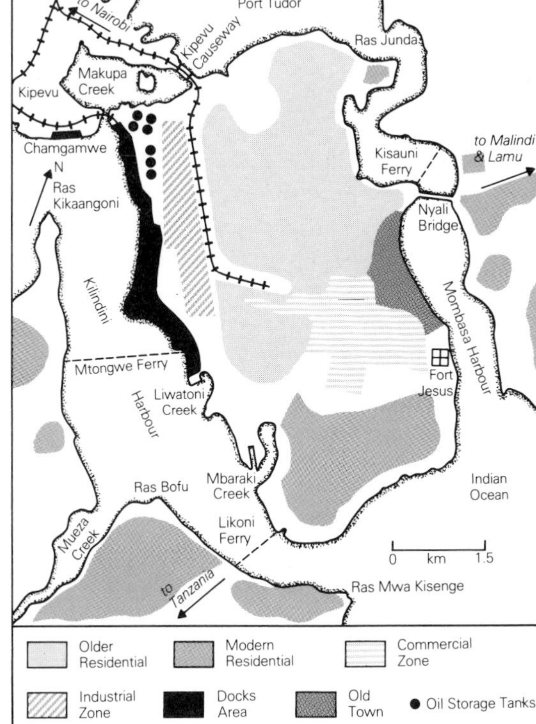

Fig. 7.18 The functional zones of Mombasa

century, it again became an Arab capital until 1832, when the court moved to Zanzibar. Mombasa's site was well chosen. The old city lies on an island four kilometres wide and five kilometres long, opposite a break in the off-shore coral reef. To the north lies Tudor Harbour approached by a narrow channel guarded by Portuguese-built Fort Jesus. The channel, Mombasa Harbour, is still used by Arab dhows, but is too shallow for bigger vessels. West and south-west of the island is the wider and deeper Kilindini Harbour which has undergone extensive improvements until it has become one of the finest of Africa's harbours, with fourteen deep-water berths, modern loading quays at Kipevu, and bulk petroleum wharves at Shimanzi and Changamwe.

Mombasa's hinterland includes Kenya, Uganda, northern Tanzania (from where much trade has been diverted from Tanga), Rwanda, Burundi, and parts of eastern Zaïre (although trade with the latter only amounts to about 25 000 t annually). The port handles Kenya's coffee, sisal, tea, pyrethrum, sodium carbonate, cement and meat; Tanzania's sisal, coffee and tea; and Uganda's copper, coffee, cotton and tea; as well as packaged oils, wattle extract, maize meal and cattle cake.

Mombasa handles 6,7 million tonnes of goods annually compared with Dar es Salaam's 3,2 million tonnes; petroleum fuel equals half of all imports, but coal imports have declined with the cessation of South African trade and the switch to oil fuels. There are many miscellaneous imports – cars, machinery, radios, machine tools and spare parts – the majority destined for Kenya's secondary industries. Vessels of 24 shipping lines use the port and over 90 000 passengers pass through each year. However, Mombasa handles less coastal trade than the Tanzanian ports. Coastal cargoes include mangrove poles, copra, cotton, cashew nuts, citrus fruits, sisal, cattle, skins, vegetables, ivory and fish. Arab dhows bring carpets, dates, dried figs, fish, firewood and pots from Arabia, returning with loads of cement, paraffin oil, coffee, tea, copra, coconuts and mangrove poles. This trade is a dying one for today only about 50 dhows ply along the East African coast, compared with 1 000 thirty years ago.

Despite the tendency for industries to concentrate up-country, Mombasa has many factories producing metal goods, soap, matches, furniture, glass, metal containers, bottles and light clothing. There are light engineering and railway workshops, and ship repair yards, while a modern oil refinery at Changamwe has a refining capacity of over nine million litres of crude oil annually.

The map (Fig. 7.18) shows the layout of the port. In the 1920s Mombasa contained only 20 000 people, but this had increased to 54 000 before the war; in 1948 it was 84 750 and according to a 1975 estimate it has now exceeded 250 000. Any future expansion must take place on the mainland, and a master plan has been drawn up to provide housing and facilities on land to the north, south and west of the island core.

A modern capital port – Dar es Salaam

Unlike Mombasa, Dar es Salaam was never fully developed under the Arabs and was largely overshadowed by Bagamoyo as a slaving port. Its development is therefore more recent. Its site lies near Mzinga Creek which, though well protected, could never accommodate as many vessels as Kilindini. The town itself has developed round a swampy lowland.

The Germans and British gave Dar es Salaam more attention than the Arabs, connecting it by road to the end of Lake Nyasa in the 1870s, and in 1891 the Germans transferred their headquarters from Bagamoyo to Dar es Salaam since it was a better anchorage. A railway, largely for administrative purposes, was built from Dar es Salaam directly westwards, reaching Kigoma on Lake Tanganyika in 1914, and a later British-built branch line was constructed to Mwanza on Lake Victoria.

Dar es Salaam handles only 22 per cent of East Africa's trade (Mombasa, 70 per cent) because of its more limited hinterland. On average, however, Dar es Salaam receives more trade from Zaïre, between 60 000 and 90 000 t a year. The railway brings sugar, cotton, sisal and diamonds from the Mwanza region, lead from Mpanda, and groundnuts, grains and sisal from points along the line. Machinery and transport material make up almost a third of all imports, and manufactured goods about 35 per cent. The port also handles a large coastal trade carried on by dhows carrying mangroves poles, copra and sisal.

But Dar es Salaam is not an international port like Mombasa. It is a port-of-call, a route focus, an administrative capital, a commercial, domestic marketing, and tourist centre. Like Mombasa, however, it is attracting a great deal of industry: meat processing, canning, grain and oil milling, brewing, paint manufacture, dyeing, soap making, textiles, printing, sisal spinning, cigarette making and furniture and shoe manufacture. Most industry is located on an estate in the south-west of the city. A large oil refinery was completed in 1966.

Dar es Salaam's present population is 280 000, a spectacular increase over the 5 000 of 80 years ago. Its growth has been partially overshadowed by Mombasa and competition from Tanga, Lindi and Mtwara (which together take about eight per cent of trade). Since the completion of the Tanzam line to Zambia's copper belt in October 1975, Dar es Salaam has been experiencing considerable congestion at its harbour.

The effect of competition – Tanga

Tanga (65 000) is the second largest urban area in Tanzania and again shows the importance of railway connections. The Germans built the railway from Tanga to Arusha-Moshi for administrative purposes, and to tap the sisal- and coffee-producing regions. The line, 350 km long, carries grain, timber, wattle, sisal, coffee and gypsum for export through Tanga. At one time Tanga's trade was greater than Dar's, but it has now been overshadowed by Mombasa and Dar. Tanga has a good though small harbour which can accommodate four ocean-going ships and several smaller vessels; about 700 vessels call each year. A soap factory and oil mills use power from Pangani Falls. But, sandwiched between Dar and Mombasa, Tanga is limited in its economic expansion.

Lake ports

Large natural lakes like Victoria and Malaŵi and the huge artificial lakes of Kariba, Volta and Nasser often act as contributors to the existing communications network and link areas differing widely in their economies. Around Lake Victoria several ports have developed to handle the produce of their hinterlands – *Bukatata* serves the north-western area and exports cotton and coffee; *Port Bell*, Kampala's outport, handles the sugar of the northern lowlands; *Mwanza* in the south-east is more important as a focal point of trade from both Uganda and Kenya and is the only large lake port in Tanzania. Mwanza has a considerable cross-trade in rice, groundnuts, cotton and sisal with Bukoba, and possesses several industries based on this trade – cotton seed oil milling, soap manufacture, cotton ginning, tanning, flour milling and ship repair.

Kisumu (26 000) has risen to pre-eminence among Africa's lake ports largely because it is a focal point for both rail, road and lake routes. In the late nineteenth century, Kisumu, then called Ogowe, was only a small African fishing village and a staging point on caravan routes. Later called Port Florence, it became a survey headquarters and a small garrison town. But its real importance dates from 1901 when the railway from the coast created it a railhead port, and it then grew as a collecting centre for cotton and other products of the lake shores.

Kisumu is now a flourishing port situated on the main road from Nairobi with regular steamship services across the lake. It is the administrative headquarters of Nyanza Province and a market centre

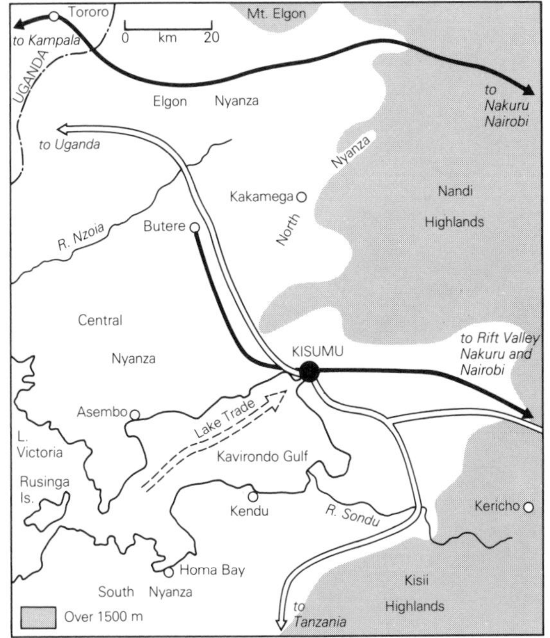

Fig. 7.19 The location of Kisumu, Kenya

for local agricultural produce. There is plenty of local labour to work in the large industrial estate, and power comes from Owen Falls. Kisumu's industries include the manufacture of soft drinks, textiles, footwear, cement, confectionery, soap and furniture, and there are saw mills, flour mills, fish-filleting and freezing plants, and a hides and skins preparation plant. Small vessels can be repaired in dry docks.

The port owes its importance to lake trade development and to its focal position for rail and road routes. Although Kisumu lost some of Uganda's trade when the northerly rail route was completed, the port has an assured growth as the regions bordering Lake Victoria develop and as more industry is attracted.

Towns and cities

While ports function as entrepôts for their hinterlands and their sites are largely dictated by natural features, the sites and functions of interior settlements are not always easy to explain. In the following examples the majority of the urban centres have developed complicated relationships with the regions which they serve.

A city at a focal point of river and land routes – Cairo

Cairo (4,5 million) is the largest city of Africa and the Arab world and is a superb example of a great religious and commercial capital which developed at a natural focal point of river and overland routes. Built in 969 A.D. at the site of a Roman fortress and an earlier Greek settlement, the city has spread along a low spur of the Mokotam Hills on the right bank of the Nile to cover nearly 20 square kilometres. The city was a centre of Moslem culture in the Middle Ages and, in the twelfth century during the religious crusades, it was a great citadel under Saladin. It became the national capital of Egypt in 1863.

Cairo grew rapidly as a trading centre; indeed, because of natural conditions it could hardly avoid becoming one. To the north of the city lies the great

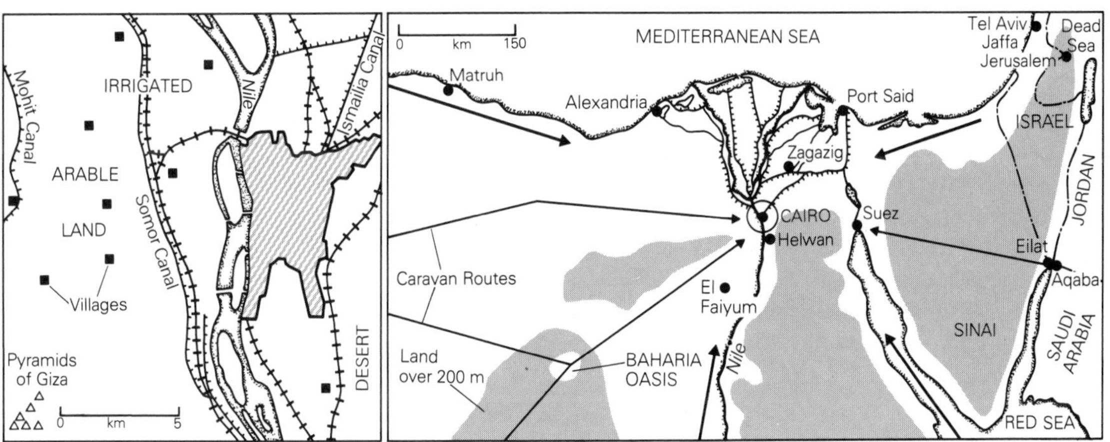

Fig. 7.20 The site and regional setting of Cairo, Egypt

triangular delta of the Nile, its many distributaries making it difficult to traverse by trade routes. From the south the Nile Valley forms a long corridor linking Upper and Lower Egypt. Thus the great trading routes from Tunis ran along the northern coast of Africa and, on reaching the delta, ran south-eastwards to skirt it. Here they met the great caravan routes running eastwards from Jerusalem and Asia Minor, and the natural artery of the Nile.

The ancient pattern of trading routes was accentuated during the railway age. Lines were constructed along the Nile corridor as far as Aswan, then on to Wadi Halfa and later to Er Roseires, 2 250 km from Cairo. Another line, now closed, runs north-eastwards through Israel to Turkey via Aleppo, and the western coastal route reaches the Libyan border. Other railways and modern motor roads link the major settlements of the delta – Suez, Port Said and Alexandria – with Cairo. Cairo airport stands at the junction of routes from Europe, the Middle East, India, Asia and the Soviet Union, and from all parts of Africa. A system of national air routes connects with Luxor, Port Said and Aswan.

Cairo is the administrative centre for Egypt and the great political centre of the Arab world. The modern section of the city lies in the west and near to the river where there are large blocks of commercial and government offices, European residences and public buildings. The eastern half of the city still retains its oriental character and contains the Mohammedan and Jewish quarters. Many parts of the city are congested and there is an absence of wide spacious planning found in other African cities. Cairo has also attracted several industries – grain milling, cotton and wool weaving and spinning, brewing and cement manufacture. It is also one of the world's foremost tourist centres.

A river confluence settlement – Khartoum

Rivers are often arteries of trade, goods being transported along the river or on roads and railways following the river valley. Where rivers join, a settlement often develops because the site is a natural node and easy to defend because of the water barriers. A good example is Khartoum, the capital of the Sudan Republic.

Khartoum (800 000) stands at the confluence of the White and Blue Niles, the two rivers joining and

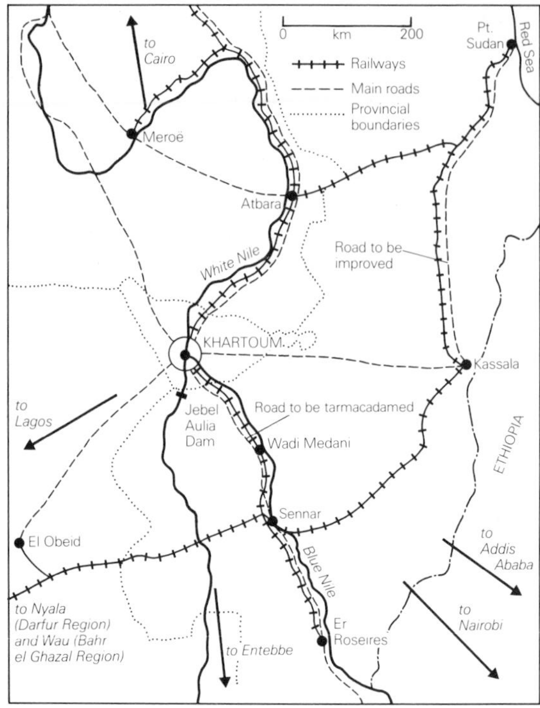

Fig. 7.21 The regional setting of Khartoum, Sudan Republic

flowing northwards as the main Nile River. It is not an ancient city, being founded in 1824 by the Egyptians who saw its defensive possibilities. By 1840 the population had grown to 15 000. The town was later destroyed by the Dervishes who were, in turn, defeated by the British who set about rebuilding the town.

Khartoum developed, however, as three separate townships, the Nile acting as a barrier to unified growth. On the left bank Omdurman remained as the old native city, while the more modern Khartoum developed to the south in the angle between the two Niles. On the north bank of the Blue Nile, Khartoum North grew as a separate settlement. The city was not unified until bridges were built across the rivers in 1909 and 1928.

The construction of railway lines strengthened Khartoum's role as a route focus. The line from Egypt via Wadi Halfa reached Khartoum in 1899 and a branch line to El Obeid was completed in 1912. Later, branch lines ran from Atbara to Port Sudan on the Red Sea coast, and the northern line was continued southwards in 1955 to Er Roseires. A line links Sennar to Port Sudan via Kassala, thus placing Khartoum on a circular rail route encompassing the Province of Butana.

Khartoum is now the capital, the seat of the central government, and the headquarters of foreign embassies, banks and commercial houses. It is a university city which is expanding, especially towards the south where new housing estates have been constructed. It is a market centre for livestock, cloth and spices, and many camels, goats and sheep are sold here and transported to Egypt. Omdurman has still retained its native Sudanese character, although many of its inhabitants work in other parts of the city. Many craft industries are found in Omdurman – the manufacture of furniture, beds, glassware, pottery and metalware. Modern industry is located in Khartoum North where there are ship repair facilities along the Nile, grain storage houses, light engineering concerns, the Mint, an ordnance factory, a large tannery and a brewery. The city's airport is situated on the main European air line routes serving Africa.

A commercial centre and trade focus – Kano

Kano (300 000) in northern Nigeria, owes its importance to several factors. It lies on the great trading routes which cross the Sahara and has become an important commercial centre, lying between West Africa and the Mediterranean North. The surrounding countryside supports one of the densest agricultural concentrations of populations in Africa, and Kano has thrived as a marketing centre.

Kano lies in the savanna zone of West Africa, roughly half way between the Sahara proper and the great southern forest belts. The site was first chosen because the rocky hills of Dalla and Goron Dutsi gave a commanding view over the surrounding plains, a small stream existed, and local ironstone attracted smelters. The settlement grew rapidly as a terminus of trans-Saharan trade routes (see Chapter Two). The huge walls, enclosing 36 square kilometres of houses and grazing land, were regarded as a refuge in troubled times.

The city entered a new phase of development when the British arrived in 1903. Headquarters were first set up outside the old city walls at Bompai to the east and later moved to Nasarawa near the emir's palace. In 1912 the railway arrived from the coast, commerce was stimulated and Kano became the head-

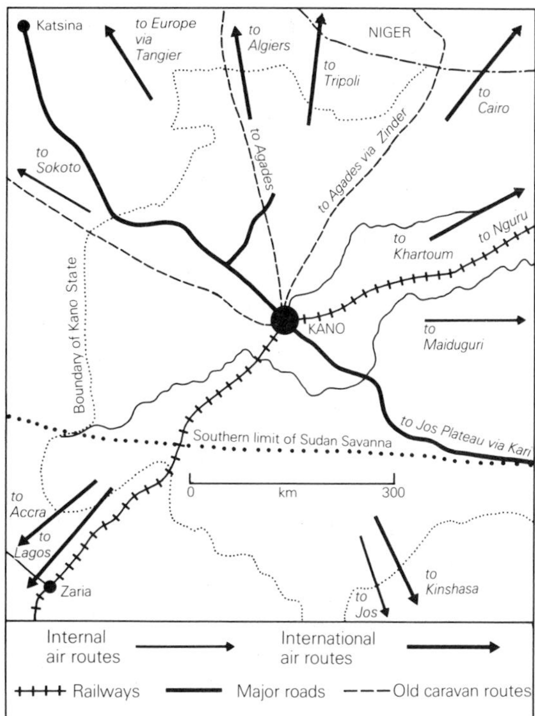

Fig. 7.22 The regional setting of Kano, Nigeria

quarters of the groundnut industry.

Today Kano is the third largest city in Nigeria and the capital of Kano State. The city is second after Lagos in industrial importance. Oilseed milling is traditional, the largest factory having a capacity of 200 000*t* a year. Local cotton seed is now milled here. There are some 150 other enterprises employing about 20 000 workers. The industrial estate at Bompai is now filled and a new industrial estate at Sharada is being expanded. Outside the city a vast area is being laid out for industry at Challawa.

The range of industry in Kano is wide and includes textiles, tanning, brewing, flour milling, and factories making shoes, cosmetics, metal goods, soap, pharmaceuticals, paints, etc. There are short-term plans for a glass industry and the manufacture of batteries and plastic pipes. Longer term projects will cover ceramics, animal fodder and brewing. Small scale industry is also encouraged – baking, blacksmithing, carpentry and textile printing. Kano also retains a tradition of ancient crafts – brass, silver and leather working, mat and rope making, cloth dyeing and tailoring.

Nigeria: Part of Kano city – sun baked mud houses in traditional style.

Kenya: Aerial view of Nairobi showing central business and commercial zones, with residential outskirts beyond.

The importance of the railway – Nairobi

Nairobi, Kenya's capital, illustrates clearly several factors influencing urban growth in Africa. Once occupying a site with no particular advantages, the city has become a regional centre for the whole of East Africa, an important collecting centre, and an industrial and communications node.

In 1899 the railway to Lake Victoria from Mombasa had passed through 480 km of dry bush to reach the flat Athi Plains, the approach to the fertile Kenya Highlands. It was a good place to halt before pushing on up to the steeper gradients towards the Rift Valley, and it formed a convenient storage point half way towards the proposed terminus at Port Florence (Kisumu). Railway headquarters were moved from Mombasa, workshops were set up, and government offices moved from Machakos. Nairobi became a natural resting place for travellers moving up-country. By 1902 the population was 4 300 and the settlement attracted many Africans thrown out of work by the railway's completion. An ugly shanty town developed and diseases were rife. But the settlement persisted and the development of the 'White Highlands' by European farmers and the flow of agricultural produce through Nairobi assured its

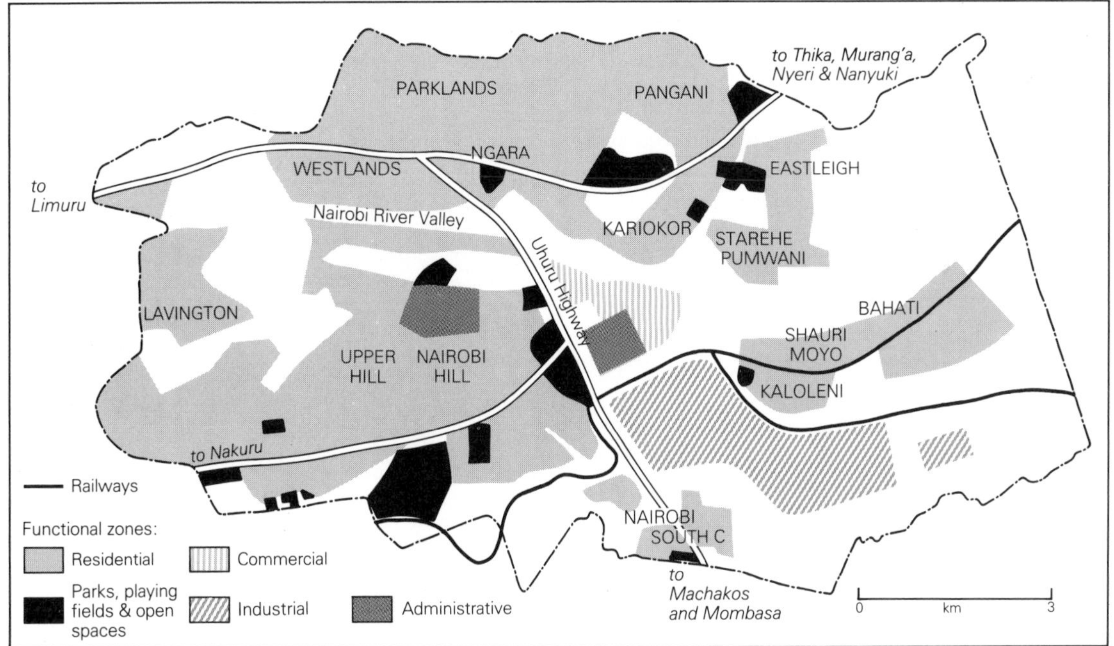

Fig. 7.23 The functional zones of Nairobi, Kenya

economic growth. The site was a good one for administration of the large Kamba, Kikuyu and Masai tribes. A branch railway was constructed northwards to Thika and later extended to Murang'a and Nanyuki.

From a collection of shacks at a temporary railhead, Nairobi has developed into a modern city with a population in 1976 of 530 000 within the administrative area. The controlled planning of the city, its pleasant climate at 1 700 m, and the spacious parks and gardens, make Nairobi one of the pleasantest capitals of Africa. Its layout is seen in the map (Fig. 7.23).

Nairobi has all the functions of a modern capital and, at one time, many aspects of administration of all three East African territories were carried on in the city. Many commercial firms have headquarters here and the city has become a cultural centre with several schools, colleges and theatres. It is an important tourist centre with several first-class hotels and safari organisations.

Nairobi has the heaviest concentration of industry in East Africa, the oldest connected with the railways, while others are mainly of the processing kind – coffee and flour milling, cigarettes and tobacco processing, tanning and hide preparation, timber cutting and furniture making, and the manufacture of boots, shoes, soft drinks, beer, bricks and tiles. Other concerns include general engineering, motor car servicing, paper bag manufacture, printing and tyre retreading.

Modern tarmac highways link Nairobi with important economic areas in the Highlands and railways lead to Uganda, Kisumu, Nanyuki and Mombasa. There are two small airports and a large modern international airport at Embakasi, 13 km to the south-east, designed to handle three million passengers a year.

Nairobi has benefited from judicious planning unhampered by major restrictions of site. The factors leading to its rapid growth over the last 60 years are:

a human persistence at a site which, although initially unfavourable, later received the full benefit of the economic development of the country as a whole;

b its early selection as an administrative centre and the widening of the administrative field to include Uganda and Tanganyika in colonial times;

c the position at the southern edge of the fertile

Highlands and the channelling of agricultural produce from there and Uganda through the city to the coast;

d the key communications position halfway from coast to lake with major routes into the Highlands and southward via Namanga to Tanzania;

e the early establishment of industry connected with the railway, and the suitability of the site for raw material collection and processing industries.

Agricultural collecting centres and market towns

A settlement in the middle of a rich agricultural region often becomes a natural collecting point for the agricultural produce which may either be processed in the town or sent to other centres. The following two examples, Nakuru in the Kenya Highlands and Kumasi in the Ashanti region of Ghana, lie in two contrasted agricultural zones – one greatly influenced by the European and one exclusively African.

Nakuru

Nakuru grew with the development of the former 'White Highlands', being little more than a Masai *manyatta* in the 1890s. It became a temporary railhead in 1900 when the railway from Nairobi reached it. As European settlers began to farm the surrounding highlands, tracks were constructed to link Nakuru with the farming districts of Eldoret and Kitale, Thomson's Falls and the Londiani–Lumbwa region. Goods needed by the farmers were railed from Mombasa through Nairobi or brought by bullock cart.

Nakuru became a centre where farmers met to buy goods, discuss business, and market their produce. By 1924 there were 24 firms connected with the purchase and export of agricultural produce. The continuation of the railway to Kisumu brought a steady flow of trade from the lake region, and the town became a rail junction with the completion of the line to Kampala. Local roads and the main highway were improved, and Nakuru became an important marketing centre, a headquarters of agricultural co-operatives, and a regional administrative centre.

Nakuru is now the third largest town in Kenya

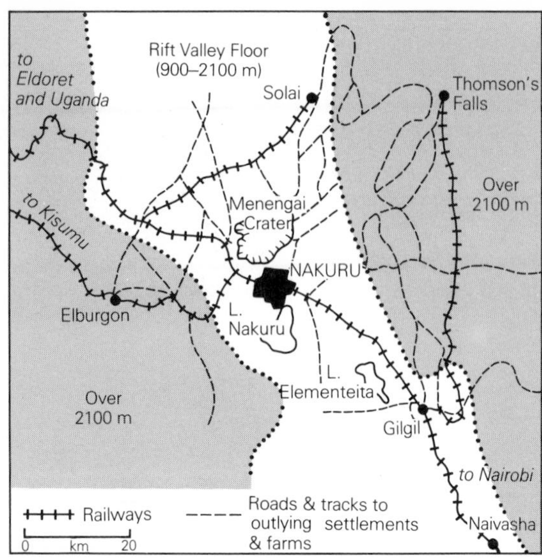

Fig. 7.24 The site of Nakuru, Kenya

and has experienced a rapid growth in post-war years – 1945 population, 11 032; 1952, 21 659; 1962, 38 181. Today, Nakuru's population is approaching 50 000. This increase is due to the growth of Nakuru's many industries based on local produce – the manufacture of animal foodstuffs, flour milling, a large creamery, a blanket factory, soap, leather goods, tobacco and vegetable canning concerns. The town has a modern marshalling yard to handle increasing rail traffic.

Kumasi

Kumasi is a much larger urban centre than Nakuru but shows a similar pattern of recent development. It is a regional collecting centre and market town, and a focus of roads linking with agricultural districts. Its good rail connections ensure the speedy export of goods. There the similarity ends, for Kumasi was first and foremost the seat of the rulers of the powerful states of Ashanti and has become a great cultural, political and commercial centre.

Kumasi is the rapidly growing capital of the Ashanti region of Ghana and has attracted a large number of people from the surrounding area. In 1900 its population was 3 000; by 1911, 18 850; in 1921, 23 700; in 1931, 35 800; in 1951, 80 000, while today it exceeds 340 000, second after Accra.

No more than a small town at the beginning of

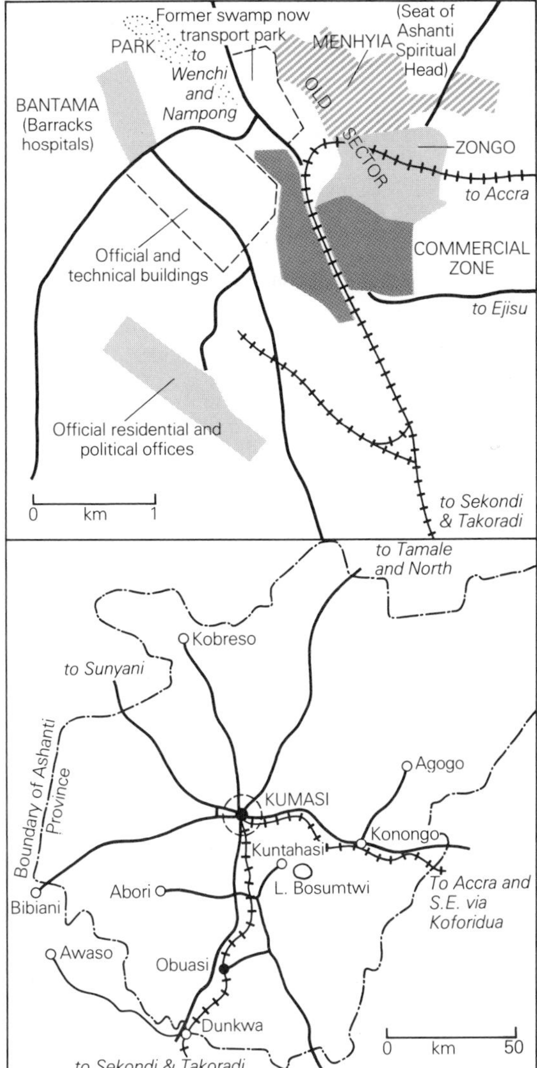

Fig. 7.25 The functional zones and regional setting of Kumasi, Ghana

this century, Kumasi experienced a rapid expansion with the arrival of the railways linking it to Sekondi on the coast (1903) and the capital, Accra (1923). A network of roads was constructed connecting the town with the surrounding cocoa-growing areas, with Takoradi and with the northern areas of Ghana. Thus its position as a collecting centre for cocoa and a redistribution point for imported goods was strengthened. Besides this, Kumasi is a great cultural, commercial and administrative centre, with a market for the shea butter, poultry, sheep and goats, yams and other products of the northern regions. The map (Fig. 7.25) shows the present layout of the town.

Administrative centres

The administrative capital of a country is not necessarily the largest city and its site, especially in the hot tropical regions of Africa, may have been chosen for its coolness rather than for its relation to economic resources. A central position and good communications are necessary if the centre is to fulfil its functions of administration. Examples of such capitals include Pretoria, Entebbe and Addis Ababa.

Entebbe

Entebbe (11 000) was the administrative capital of Uganda in colonial times but has since lost most of this function to Kampala. Climate played a large part in the selection of the site at the end of a peninsula jutting into Lake Victoria, for the cool lake breezes gave a pleasant relief to the high monotonous temperatures of Uganda. Founded in 1893 the town was almost wholly populated by civil servants and was situated in beautiful grassy parklands. It gained other importance in the 1920s and 1930s as a seaplane landing base on British Imperial air routes, and it is still a stopping point on air routes from Europe, although most of its traffic has been lost to Nairobi. The little town has not attracted any industry, but has become a residential centre for the President and the heads of government departments. It is connected to Kampala by a 35 km long road and to Kisumu by steamer service.

Addis Ababa

Addis Ababa (870 000), the capital of Ethiopia, is not an old city, for its site was selected by Menelik II in 1800. The site was an obvious one from which to govern the rugged and turbulent territory of Ethiopia, for it lies in the heart of the central province of Shoa and from here the emperor's rule was extended over the Harar and Ogaden Provinces. The city was difficult to attack because of its high elevation, 2 500 m on the Ethiopian Plateau.

In 1926 Addis Ababa was linked by rail to Djibouti, the chief outlet on the Red Sea and, during

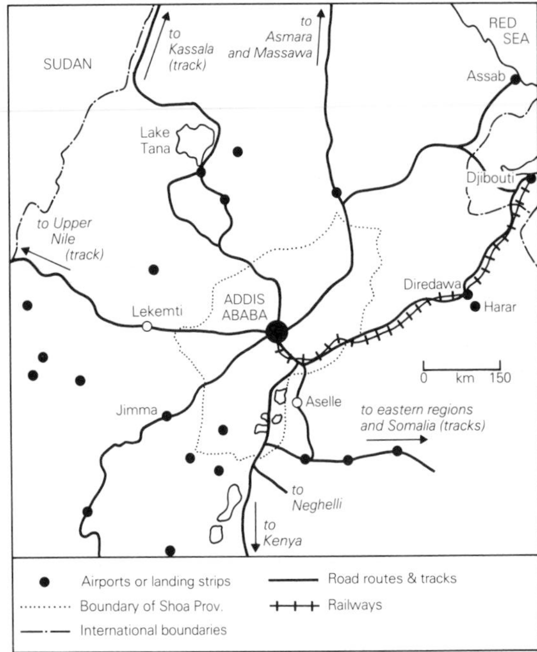

Fig. 7.26 The regional setting of Addis Ababa, Ethiopia

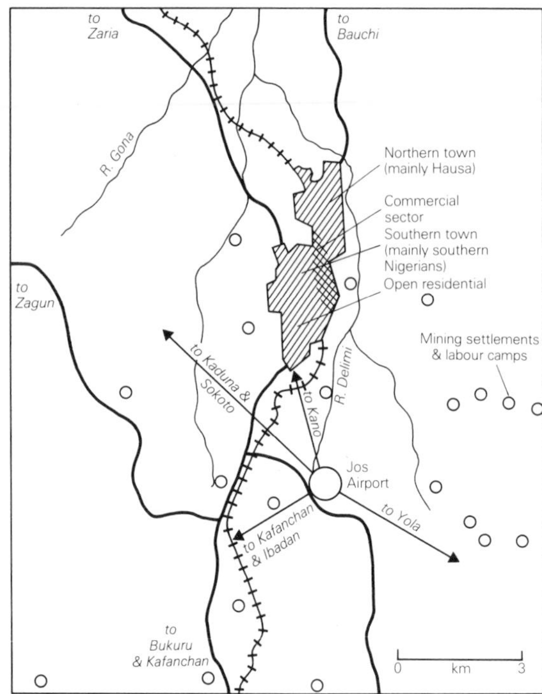

Fig. 7.27 The site of Jos, Nigeria

the Italian occupation (1936–41), its administrative role was enhanced by the construction of 6 900 km of tarmac and dirt roads leading to Asmara, Jimma, Dire Dawa and Neghelli (Fig. 7.26). The Italians made Addis Ababa their headquarters and the European population greatly increased.

The city has many fine modern buildings – the Ethiopia and Ghion hotels, the Stadium, Parliament House, the University, the Commercial Bank, and the new Africa Hall where the heads of African organisations meet. The broad boulevards contrast with narrow side streets and their tin-roofed houses.

There is little industry except for the processing of local produce and local crafts such as leather and gold working. The city's airport serves local and international flights, air connections being of vital importance in a country with so few good roads.

Mining towns

The presence of metalliferous ores, diamond deposits, and fuel supplies in large quantities will almost invariably lead to the growth of a mining settlement if communications are good and economic mining feasible. A mining town grows rapidly and just as quickly disappears with the exhaustion of the mineral. But where there are numerous minerals in a region, the mining settlement may grow into a township or a city such as Johannesburg, eventually merging with other settlements to form a conurbation of which only one exists in Africa at present – the Witwatersrand conurbation (p. 204). Mwadui in Tanzania (p. 195), Jos in the tin mining area of Nigeria, and Lubumbashi in the Copper Belt of Shaba are good examples of mining settlements.

Jos

Jos (50 000) grew with the development of the tin mining area on the Jos Plateau. Tin was first discovered in commercial quantities in 1895 but had been known to the local tribespeople much earlier than this. A deposit was discovered near the Delimi River to the east of Jos and a mining camp was set up. The mining progressed only slowly until the railway from Zaria to Bukuru 13 km to the south was completed and later extended to Jos in 1914. In 1927 facilities for tin export were improved by the completion of the line linking Bukuru and Jos to the main Eastern Line of Nigeria, and the cost of tin transport was greatly reduced. Coal supplies were railed from Enugu, although local hydro-electric power was already in use. Jos became the leading mining and administrative centre on the plateau, a regional headquarters, and an important route centre with roads leading north to Kaduna and Zaria, south to Makurdi and Enugu, and north-west towards Bauchi. Internal air services connect Jos with Zaria, Kaduna, Enugu, Kano, Sokoto, and other cities in Nigeria. Jos has become something of a tourist centre because of its pleasant climate and position.

Lubumbashi

Lubumbashi (formerly Elizabethville), with a population of 200 000, developed on much the same lines as Jos, beginning as a small copper mining settlement and then developing, with improved rail communications, as the administrative centre of the regional government of Shaba Province, formerly Katanga. It lies at approximately the same height as Jos (1 230 m) and first began as a collection of tents and shacks of the European mining community. The pleasant climate encouraged further European settlement.

The opening of the Star of the Congo Mine attracted African workers from Zaïre, Rwanda, Burundi and Zambia. Development was fairly rapid after the completion of the railway from Zimbabwe in 1910, the copper then being shipped south; after 1928 most ore went through Port Francqui, now Ilebo, to the north and some passed through Lubumbashi along the Benguela Line. The town was thus placed at an important rail junction and at the terminus of the Voie Nationale – the Zaïre River's own outlet.

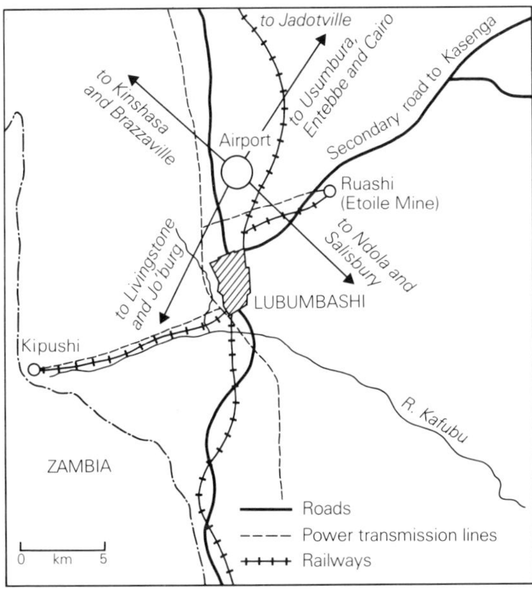

Fig. 7.28 The site of Lubumbashi, Shaba Province, Zaïre

New mining centres developed at Kolwezi, Jadotville and Kipushi, and Lubumbashi took on a new importance as a regional and commercial centre. Its role as a political centre was enhanced with political trends in the 1960s to form Katanga into a semi-autonomous state.

Lubumbashi has benefited from modern spacious planning and has broad avenues, hotels, large banks, parks, and a modern hospital. The airport lies 13 km north of the city and serves local, inter-territorial and international flights. The main industries at Lubumbashi are copper ore smelting, soap, cotton goods, cigarettes, beer and soft drinks manufacture.

A secondary industrial centre – *Jinja*

Jinja (50 000) is situated in eastern Uganda and is an excellent example of a rapidly developing industrial centre. The town lies at the head of Napoleon Gulf, an arm of Lake Victoria, and at a crossing point of the Victoria Nile. It has thus developed as an important transport node with routes converging from Kenya and from the Nile and western Uganda. Numerous minor roads also converge here, tapping the agricultural resources of the productive zone in which Jinja lies. Jinja is thus a route centre, a market town, a port, a collecting centre and a rapidly expanding industrial township.

Communications played an important part in Jinja's early development. The Busoga Railway was opened in 1912 to tap the cotton-growing areas of Busoga Province, and in 1928 Jinja was connected to the main Kenya railway which gave it an outlet through Mombasa; later in 1931 this line was continued westwards to Kampala and northwards to Tororo and Soroti. A recently completed extension also links Jinja with the White Nile region via Pakwach. Jinja's port also developed rapidly and now handles about 70 000 t of goods annually.

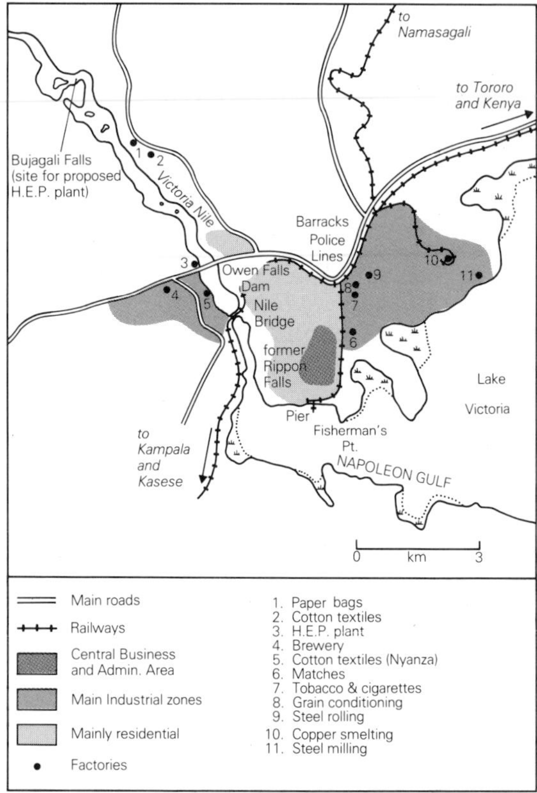

Fig. 7.29 The functional zones of Jinja, Uganda

But real growth only began with the completion of the Owen Falls Dam on the Victoria Nile in 1954; this led to a tremendous upsurge of commerce and industry. The biggest user of Owen Falls power is the large copper smelter completed in 1956 which now has an annual output of 17 000 t of blister copper extracted from ore railed from Uganda's western Kilembe Mine. The modern Nyanza Textiles concern produces nearly 30 billion bales of cloth every year.

The most noticeable aspect of Jinja's industries (see Fig. 7.29) is that they are not heavy industries but are largely of the processing kind using local raw materials – timber, cotton, tobacco, and minerals. This type of industry is typical of many urban industrial centres in Africa.

A communications node – *Bulawayo*

Bulawayo is perhaps the best example in Africa of the rapid growth of a town at a focal point of routes. From a small settlement in 1893, Bulawayo has grown into the second largest city after Salisbury, with a population of 284 000. In 1897 the railway from South Africa reached Bulawayo and extensions were built to Salisbury and Beira, to Wankie, Livingstone and Lusaka, to the Copper Belt and Elizabethville (Lubumbashi), thus placing Bulawayo at a strategic junction of major routes. A branch line runs from Heany junction east of the city southwards to West Nicholson, an important cattle rearing area and gold and asbestos mining region. At Somabula 130 km to the north-east another branch line runs to the asbestos and gold mines of Shabani, and 160 km north-eastwards lies Gwelo junction.

Major roads converge on Bulawayo from Beit Bridge on the South African border in the south-east, from the Salisbury region in the north-east (and indirectly from Umtali and Beira to the east), and from Lusaka and Livingstone in the north-west. Local air services link the city with Salisbury, Livingstone, Lusaka, and Johannesburg, with indirect services to Blantyre, Beira, Ndola and Lubumbashi.

The city is the logical headquarters of the country's railways and, because of the ease of assembling raw materials, it has developed metalliferous, engineering, electrical, and rubber tyre industries. There are factories making clothing, soft drinks, beer, agricultural implements, processed foods, tin, cement and asbestos goods.

Summary

The pattern and nature of urban settlements in Africa

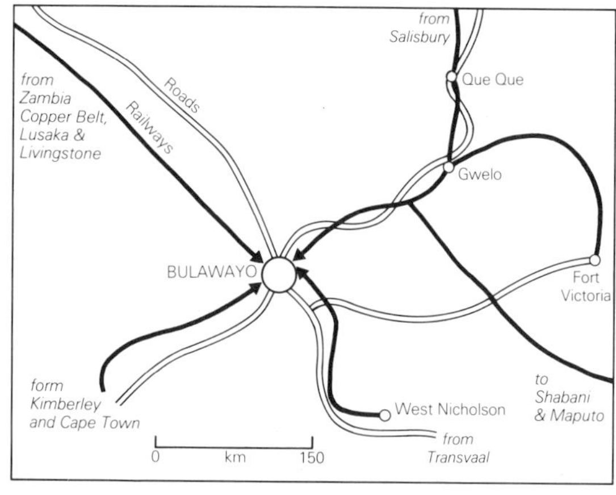

Fig. 7.30 A communications node – Bulawayo, Zimbabwe

is the result of many historical and economic factors which the foregoing sample studies have attempted to show. Although the urbanisation of African populations is proceeding at a rate faster than that of any other continent, it still remains true that, except for South Africa and Egypt, the rural populations of most countries in Africa are still in the vast majority, generally 70 per cent of the total. Even in Nigeria, where there has always been a relatively high concentration in urban areas, nearly 90 per cent of the population live in towns of under 30 000, a figure which would be considered small in Europe.

Approximately 40 per cent of urban populations in Africa live in the large ports while there are few countries which have really large cities inland. Exceptions to this are South Africa (the Rand region), Zimbabwe (Salisbury), Kenya (Nairobi), Nigeria (Kano and Ibadan), Sudan (Khartoum), Ethiopia (Addis Ababa), and Zaïre (Kinshasa and Lubumbashi). This is largely due to the early development of trade with Africa, which was confined to the coasts right up to the end of the nineteenth century. Arabs in East Africa, and Europeans elsewhere, built their trading stations on the coast and settlements tended to flourish there. Later the railways and, to a lesser extent the road routes, led directly from such early settlements inland, thus maintaining the trade flow towards the coasts. The political division of the continent between the various colonial powers, and the development of rival economies, hindered inter-territorial trade but fostered the growth of separate ports on the coast, even though these were often close to one another, e.g. Tanga and Mombasa (German and British), Lomé and Porto Novo (German and French).

The next stage of urban development began in the early twentieth century as minerals were discovered and exploited, and as suitable farming areas were developed by the Europeans. These areas became centres of attraction for African workers and for European and Asian immigrants; as commerce developed these interior regions became collecting centres for the transhipment of produce to the coast for export.

Other towns and cities have grown at the crossing or convergence points of routeways. These too became collecting centres or secondary industrial centres where raw materials could be assembled easily and cheaply. As we have seen, in some cases the climate had an influence in site selection, and many large cities have developed where the altitude reduces temperatures – Nairobi, Salisbury, Huambo, Bulawayo and Umtali were all early centres of European Settlement.

Some cities and towns have grown as transhipment points where natural routes along rivers have been broken by rapids and waterfalls; the best examples are Ilebo, Kinshasa, Brazzaville and Kisangani. Other large inland ports where products tend to gravitate for shipment to the coast are at N'Djamena, Bamako, Niamey, Bangui and Khartoum.

Once an urban centre is well established, amenities and services are improved and this in turn tends to attract more people. Such centres are attractive markets for industrialists and attract much secondary industry, much of it consumer-oriented. Again, as the centre grows even larger more and more governmental departments will be situated there. Thus the most likely trend in urban development in the future is for the already existing urban centres to grow even larger. It may be that future discoveries of minerals, the construction of hydroelectric power stations, or the improvement of agricultural regions will create the need for towns. But it is probable that the present pattern of urban settlement will persist and will be accentuated with further growth.

Problems and trends

Growth of urban centres is, in fact, one of the chief problems facing governments in Africa. At present, Africa has only one of the world's fifty giant cities – Cairo – which has an official population (1976) of 4,5 million but which, with outlying areas included, probably has 5,7 million inhabitants. Only one other city approaches this size in Africa – Lagos – whose present population of 2,5 million may reach four million by 1985 (some believe the city and its environs have already reached this total). Lagos is already experiencing the problems which beset many of the industrial cities of Europe and North America – overcrowded and slum conditions, inadequacy of the underground drainage system, traffic congestion and soaring land values. The Nigerian government estimates that approximately US$2 000 million will be needed to solve the problems. The new Central Federal Capital (see p. 134) is part of the plan to solve the problems of Lagos.

Except for Cairo and Casablanca, other major cities in Africa are nowhere near the size of Lagos and are small by world standards. But already cities such as Kampala, Nairobi, Kinshasa, Dakar, Dar es Salaam and Lusaka are experiencing growth problems. Kampala, for example, has grown rapidly since the 1939–45 war. In 1959 its population was nearly 47 000, double that of 1948. At present the population is about 350 000, a seven-fold increase in less than 20 years. The present area covered by the city is 96 square kilometres, but by the end of the century this will have expanded to 260 square kilometres at present growth rates. By 1980 the population of Kampala is expected to be over 400 000 and will have reached about 1,5 million by the year 2000.

The inadequacy of port facilities

The rising trade of African nations and political problems have dramatically underlined the inadequacy of port facilities. Congestion of shipping is a problem of all ports in West, East and southern Africa. The closure of the central Angola railway to Lobito due to civil war in 1975–6, placed a great strain on Dar es Salaam which had to handle more of Zambia's exports and imports via the Tanzam Railway and road routes. Before Lobito was closed, 45 per cent of Zambia's copper exports (25 000 t per month) and 40 per cent of its total imports (30 000 t) passed through Dar es Salaam. With Lobito closed, Dar es Salaam will have to handle 60 000 tonnes of imports destined for Zambia as well as non-Zambian traffic (480 000 t per month in 1975). In addition, the port will have to handle increased exports of minerals, especially kaolin and titanium ore from Tanzania, and including copper exports from Zaïre. Zambia's imports, which were over 80 000 t in 1975, are expected to increase, as the country's economy develops, to 1,25 million tonnes in 1990.

The problem is not confined to East Africa. In 1974 nearly all South Africa's ports were under great strain because of the need to export the biggest maize crop recorded in the country, and to take more traffic from Zimbabwe since Mozambique became independent in 1975. Increases in the gold price have meant that South Africa could afford to spend more on imports of machinery and raw materials since 1972. Imports rose by nearly 34 per cent in 1973–4 compared with 1972–3.

Solutions to such port problems include the introduction of more streamlined handling equipment, for example, the increased use of containerisation methods and the provision of alternative ports served by adequate rail and road facilities. Malaŵi, for example, has opened up a new rail route from the country's main line to Nacala on the north Mozambique coast, and is encouraging Zambia to construct a rail which would link with Malaŵi's newly created Salima-Michinje railway which ends at Zambia's eastern border. Mention has already been made of the construction of Richard's Bay port by South Africa to relieve congestion at Durban. The Republic has also completed the construction of a port at Saldanha Bay north of Cape Town. The harbour here covers 52 square kilometres and could contain all South Africa's present harbours. A railway line connects the harbour with the 4 000 million tonnes of iron ore reserves at Sishen in the northern Cape Province.

Questions

1 Discuss the factors which lead to the choice of site of village settlements in Africa. Confine your answer to specific examples.
2 With the aid of specific examples describe the main factors which lead to the development of towns in Africa.
3 Select a good example from urban settlements in Africa to explain the following urban definitions: *a* an entrepôt port; *b* a transport node; *c* an administrative centre; *d* a marketing centre; *e* a federal capital; *f* a railhead; *g* a river confluence town.
4 Discuss the importance of railways in the development of urban centres in Africa.
5 Describe and account for the growth of Casablanca as the largest port in Morocco.
6 Show how the relative growth and extent of Durban, Cape Town, Port Elizabeth and Swakopmund have been influenced by their position.
7 Describe the physical setting, foreign trade and

development of *a* Freetown; *b* Abidjan; *c* Dakar; *d* Lagos; *e* Takoradi; *f* Tema.

8 Write an account of the importance of site and communications in the growth of *a* Mombasa; *b* Dar es Salaam; *c* Tanga.

9 How far is it true to say that in each of the countries of West Africa communications and trade are dominated by one port?

10 Attempt to explain why *a* Johannesburg is the largest city in the Republic of South Africa, *b* Durban is the leading port for bulk commodities.

11 Suggest reasons for the relative sizes of the towns listed below:

City	*Approximate population*
Johannesburg	1 500 000
Cape Town	1 100 000
Durban	550 000
Pretoria	650 000
Port Elizabeth	410 000

12 Examine the situation and describe the importance of the following ports: *a* Beira; *b* Lobito; *c* Maputo; *d* Luanda.

13 Show how the location of mineral deposits has led to the growth of towns in Africa, illustrating your answer with examples from Zaïre, South Africa and any one country in either East or West Africa.

14 Discuss the factors influencing the growth of cities in East Africa (Kenya, Uganda and Tanzania).

15 Discuss the influence of trading routes, both ancient and modern, on the growth of *a* Kano; *b* Cairo; *c* Khartoum.

Discussion topics

The following list of topics provides a basis for group discussion, essays or additional notes.

1 The importance of Arab and European influence on the growth of towns in Africa.

2 The relative importance of *a* agricultural and *b* mineral production in the growth of ports in Africa.

3 The major influences which have led to the growth of those cities in Africa with over a million inhabitants.

4 The importance of road, rail and air communications in the growth of major cities in Africa.

5 Ports and their hinterlands in Africa.

6 Notes on the historical development and present functions of the following towns and ports: Alexandria, Oran, Dakar, Abidjan, Bathurst, Swakopmund, East London, Kinshasa, Salisbury, Walvis Bay, Ibadan, Port Said, Suez, Kampala.

Each account should be illustrated with a map showing the location of the port or town and the main factors which have helped its growth such as communications, mineral deposits, and agricultural production.

7 'The location and siting of towns can rarely be understood without reference to past conditions.' Discuss this statement with reference to the towns of any *one* country in Africa.

Practical work

Typical practical questions on urban geography might be:

1 Describe some particular piece of field-work you have carried out in connection with a study of village settlements.

2 In connection with any rural or urban survey in which you have taken part, outline *a* the aims, *b* the methods of procedure, and *c* the results.

3 Comment on the site, position and functions of any one town in Africa south of the Sahara of which you have first-hand knowledge.

The following topics are suggested as vacation work:

1 A geographical description of the town or city in which the student lives or one with which he is familiar, using the following plan:
a location map; *b* larger scale map to show functional zones of the settlement, e.g. residential areas, the industrial sector, the commercial area, etc.; *c* the site; *d* the historical growth; *e* communications, marketing and trade; *f* industries; *g* population growth; *h* future trends.

Sources of information may include town planning offices, factory and town tours, town council handbooks, local libraries.

2 The mapping of village layouts and the general settlement pattern in rural areas by visits and survey map consultation.

CHAPTER EIGHT

Water for power and irrigation

Africa's water supply and its distribution

Annual rainfall maps of Africa suggest that about half of the continent from latitude 14°N to 17°S receives a rainfall of over 500 mm a year, increasing to 1 000 mm in the core of this region and reaching a maximum of over 2 550 mm in Cameroon and Sierra Leone.

These totals would appear adequate for most types of farming but the seasonal rainfall maps quickly dispel this favourable impression. In January, the southward shift of the north-eastern trade wind belts brings dry parching conditions to most parts of West Africa, northern Zaïre and the southern Sudan. By April, with the sudden swing northwards of the rain belts, the southern third of the continent is beginning to experience drier weather, which reaches its maximum extent by July.

Only in a narrow equatorial belt is there continuous and reliable rainfall, and here the danger is rather from too much water than from too little. But outside this zone lie regions seriously affected by a seasonal lack of rain, by rainfall unreliability, or by a complete lack of rainfall for several years.

Thus one can recognise three general climatic divisions of Africa based on the amount and occurrence of annual rainfall:

a The humid tropics of equatorial Africa which experience no shortage of water supply.

b The semi-circular savanna region flanking the equatorial zone, with a season of irregular and deficient rainfall varying in length according to location. The Mediterranean regimes along the northern coast of Africa and in the extreme south-west Cape also experience short periods of rainfall deficiency.

c The desert regions with hardly any rainfall – the Sahara, the Kalahari and Namib and the semi-deserts of Somalia and Eritrea.

Unfortunately, many of Africa's major rivers – the Niger and the Zaïre particularly – flow away from those regions which need water most, and permanent rivers with an even volume of flow are practically non-existent outside the Zaïre Basin. The Nile and the Orange are the only major rivers which pass for much of their middle and lower courses through desert and semi-desert regions, while the Niger, the Volta and the Limpopo pass for only parts of their courses through dry regions. There are numerous medium- and small-sized rivers such as the Tana of Kenya which are also being developed, not only for irrigation, but also for hydro-electric power. However, all these rivers have one thing in common – they experience wide variations in their annual rate of flow, which makes the harnessing of their potentialities difficult. The new African nations realise that water is a vital key to economic development, and over the last score of years several major schemes have been planned and completed in an effort to make fuller use of this asset.

Africa's hydro-electric power potential

The rivers of Africa have a hydro-electric power potential greater than that of any other single continent in the world, except Asia. If fully developed, Africa's rivers could supply 23 per cent of potential world hydro-electric power, but at present Africa produces only about two per cent of the world's installed capacity. Although Africa is short of water, its rivers have a tremendous head of water essential

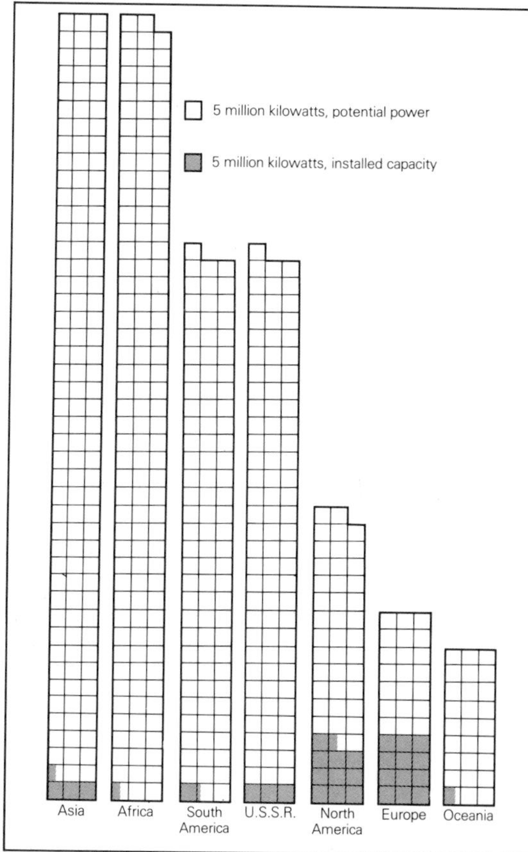

Fig. 8.1 Africa's installed and potential hydro-electric power compared with other countries

for power development – the Orange drops over 3 000 m from source to mouth, the Zaïre and its tributaries over 1 800 m, the Nile over 1 800 m from Lake Tana and nearly 1 200 m from Lake Victoria, the Niger over 900 m. But of these rivers the Zaïre is the only one which possesses a regular and continuous flow ideal for hydro-electric power development.

In contrast, the other rivers do not possess such a regular natural flow, but man-made dams are helping to adjust this. In the following sample studies of man's efforts to harness Africa's rivers, both larger schemes and smaller ones are discussed, and consideration is given to the use that is being made of them for both power production and irrigation.

Sudan – The Gezira Scheme

The Gezira Scheme, together with its western Mana-

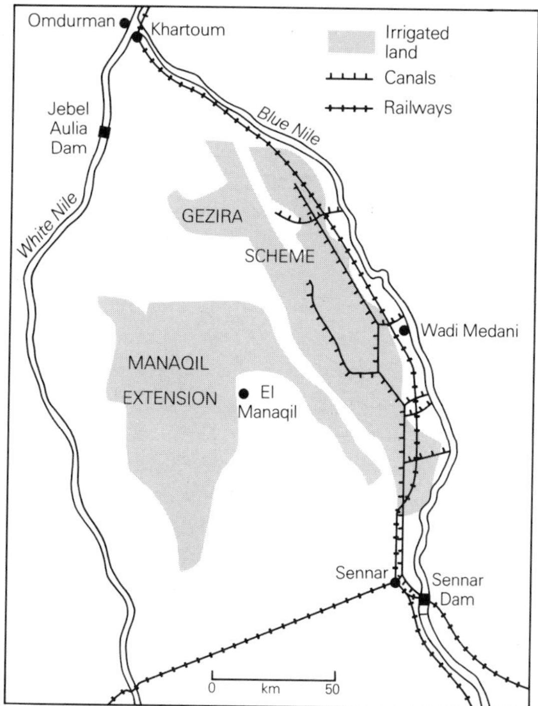

Fig. 8.2 The Sudan – the Gezira Scheme and Manaqil extension

qil extension, lies in the huge wedge of land between the Blue and White Niles. This is a region of flat or gently sloping land covered with dark-brown clayey soils, dusty and cracked in the dry seasons and sticky during the rains, and which formerly supported vast expanses of Sudan grass, scattered trees and, in the north, semi-desert bush and scrub. Rainfall varies from 460 mm a year at Sennar to 160 mm at Khartoum, mainly falling between May and October, while from November until April no rain falls over the parched plains. This region was once the home of people who cultivated poor cereals during the rainy season; if the rains failed they suffered extreme famine.

After the destruction caused by the wars between the Mahdi and the British, it was realised at the beginning of this century that if Anglo–Egyptian administration was to be successful the country's economy had to be revitalised. The soils, landscape and climate of the Gezira had been proved ideal for the cultivation of long staple cotton under irrigation from the Blue Nile, and work began in 1913 on the Sennar Dam. The Government formed a syndicate with the private Sudan Plantations Company to administer the scheme and took over complete control in 1950 through the Sudan Gezira Board.

Canal construction on the flat plains was fairly easy. The main irrigation canal was cut along the eastern edge of the region and from this water flowed along the westward dipping gradients of the branch canals, the flow controlled by the Sennar Dam. The first flood waters on the Blue Nile reach Sennar in June and the gates are closed to allow sufficient water to rise and flow into the main canal, while that not required passes through to the White Nile and Egypt. The reservoir reaches maximum capacity by late October, and this stored water is slowly released to the fields of the Gezira. In December the remainder is allowed to flow through to Egypt. Egypt's demands on Sudan's water, however, have been greatly reduced by the increased storage capacity afforded by the Aswan High Dam. Water from the Sennar reservoir is released once a fortnight into the subsidiary canals. The impervious clayey soils prevent loss by percolation, although during the rains this same imperviousness causes flooding.

The landscape of the Gezira is an extremely monotonous one – flat, with few trees, and cut into regular rectangles of cultivated land broken only by small villages and tenant houses. Each of the 10 000 tenants possesses between 10 and 20 ha subdivided into four fields, a large area by African standards. But there is still plenty of land in the Gezira and crop rotations include regular fallow periods every fourth year, unthinkable in the more crowded Nile lands of Egypt. The rotation system year by year is – cotton – fallow – millet, or sorghum – fallow – beans – fallow – cotton – fallow, and so on. Of the peasant's four fields two will be fallow, one will be growing cotton and one millet or beans at any one time of the year. Profits from cotton sales are divided between the Government (42 per cent), the tenant (42 per cent) and the Gezira Board and other departments (16 per cent) which run welfare schemes and supervise the whole operation. The tenant keeps the millet crop but he pays for seeds, tools and transport costs to the ginnery. In return for growing the cotton essential to Sudan's economy he obtains water, the use of large-scale machinery, expert advice and full ownership of up to 20 ha of land. The Gezira tenant is one of the richest of Africa's peasant farmers and, although many still prefer to live in traditional mud-brick houses, their profits are used to purchase a better education, radios, sewing machines, bicycles and cars.

The Gezira Scheme with the Manaqil extension completed in 1961 covers over 850 000 ha. The Manaqil region receives its waters from the new Roseires Dam; here the farms operate a three-year rotation of millet, beans and cotton on 5-ha farms. A further 0,5 million hectares are to be irrigated with Roseires Dam water in the Kenana Extension Scheme.

The Gezira Scheme and the Manaqil extension play a very important part in the Sudan's economy, its cotton crops providing nearly 50 per cent of the Sudan's total revenue, and the land supporting half-a-million people. But the Government has become alarmed by several factors – the fluctuations in cotton prices on world markets, the need to grow more subsistence crops for a rapidly growing population, and the low yields on the Gezira's rather poor soils despite fertilisation and regular fallowing. To attempt to solve these problems, the Government has embarked on a scheme of diversification in agriculture and the encouragement of secondary industries where possible.

To diversify crops in the Gezira the Sudan Government has recently introduced a new triple rotation scheme which has cut the amount of fallow land from 33 per cent to 13 per cent. Cotton, which normally covers a quarter of the Gezira cultivated land and a third in the Manaqil extension, is being replaced by wheat and groundnuts. Wheat area has increased from 65 000 ha in the 1972–3 season to 252 000 after 1975–6 while groundnuts have increased from 75 500 ha to 168 000 in the same period. In 1976, throughout the Sudan as a whole, the hectarage planted with wheat, groundnuts and sorghum rose from 735 000 to over one million hectares on mechanised schemes.

In addition, several new schemes are to be irrigated from the Nile and its tributaries, their planning based on the Gezira model. These schemes are the Rahad Project (120 000 ha), the Damazin Irrigated Ranch (200 000 ha), and the Kenana Sugar Plantation (30 000 ha). In these new schemes, the Government will seek to avoid the faults observed over the years in the Gezira–Manaqil areas. The major problem has been that the farms in the Gezira are too large for the farmers themselves to work efficiently, and each year over one million landless labourers and their families must help with the cotton and other harvests. About half these people are migrants, moving into the region for about four months in the year, from January to the end of April. Such a massive influx has posed tremendous social and economic problems in the Gezira region.

Zimbabwe–Zambia – The Kariba Dam

The post-war years saw in Central Africa a vast influx of people to the developing Copper Belt and to the mines and farms of Rhodesia. Secondary industry was expanding and the market for consumer goods was growing. Rhodesia's population leaped from 1,3 million in 1936 to nearly 2,5 million in 1956 – almost double in twenty years. This rapid growth placed a great strain on fuel resources and the existing rail network was unable to move the increasing amounts of coal from the Wankie field. Coal had to be imported from South Africa and the United States and local wood, three times as expensive as coal, was being removed from forests at an alarming rate. In the 1950s the annual demands of the Copper Belt (80 000 to 100 000 t) were unable to be met by Wankie, and factories had to limit production according to coal supply. Moreover the demand for energy was increasing (Fig. 8.5) and by 1955 the annual rate of increase of electricity consumption had reached 11 per cent.

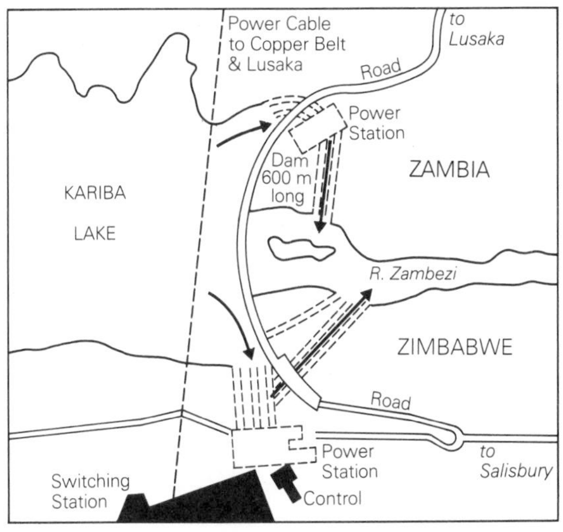

Fig. 8.3 Zimbabwe–Zambia – site of the Kariba Dam

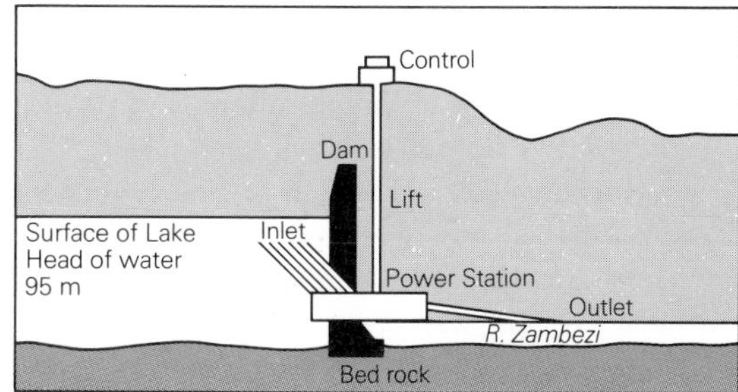

Fig. 8.4 Zimbabwe–Zambia – cross-section of the dam site at Kariba, south bank

Several alternative solutions were put forward to meet the increasing energy demands:

a The construction of an atomic power station similar to those being pioneered in Britain was not thought feasible because such stations were then in their infancy, and at that time their production costs were higher than the normal hydroelectric power station; fuel had to be imported, waste products disposed of, and highly specialised staff employed.

b An increase in the number of thermal power stations was suggested, but this would have cost as

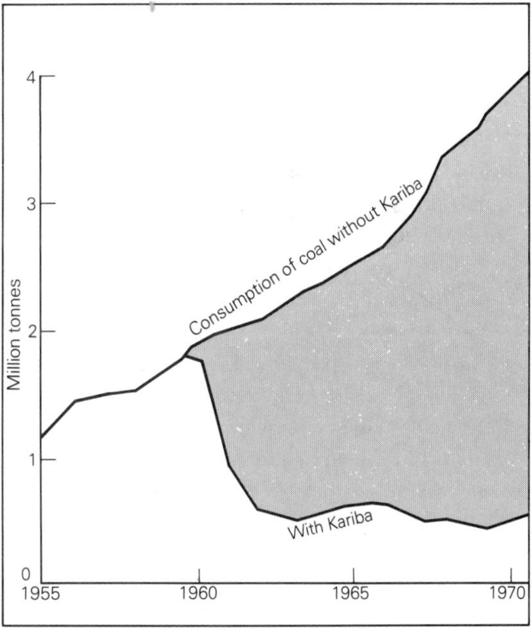

Fig. 8.5 The economic importance of Kariba

much as Kariba, and smaller stations might not have attracted overseas capital. The stations would have placed a big strain on railways and drained the country's coal reserves.

c An alternative site at Kafue in Northern Rhodesia (now Zambia) was suggested, but knowledge of that river was not as complete as Kariba. The Kafue Scheme was opened in 1977 and now contributes 600 megawatts to Zambia's power grids, lessening that country's dependence on Kariba.

A large hydro-electric power station and dam was the answer to central Africa's power problems. Water is not a wasting asset like coal, and its power is always on tap and can be regulated to the varying needs of industry.

The results

a Kariba was an economic necessity. This is shown in Fig. 8.5 which indicates the reduction that Kariba has produced in the price of energy over the years.

b The dam will provide plenty of power for any industrial expansion envisaged in central Africa. Mining, secondary industries and other users of electrical energy can expand in the knowledge that there is almost unlimited energy to be had.

c A great burden has been lifted from the railways. They no longer have to carry huge supplies of coal to industrial areas.

d Control of the Zambezi, a very turbulent river subject to heavy flooding (it twice overtopped the dam during construction), is assured. The lake now provides a safe method of communication and a small shipping service is in operation.

e The lake itself provides fish and is a substantial tourist attraction.

Kariba was the first of the big modern projects which have developed all over Africa. It was taken as a model by many African states and thus has indirectly stimulated and helped the greater control of Africa's rivers. Despite present political troubles, the water still flows through Kariba at the rate of 400 million litres a minute producing 600 000 kW of electricity, 49 per cent of which is used by Zimbabwe and the remaining 51 per cent by Zambia. At the end of 1976 the four generators at the newly completed Kariba North Bank power station went into operation and now supply extra power to Zambian industries and mines.

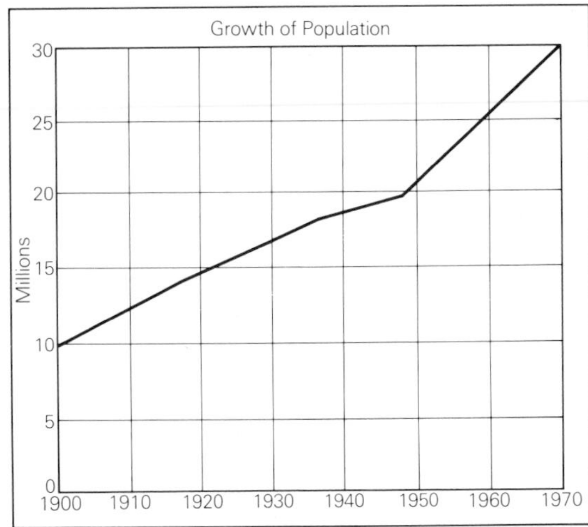

Fig. 8.6 Egypt – population growth

Egypt – The Aswan High Dam

Egypt's Sadd-el-Aali project – the construction of the Aswan High Dam with Soviet technical and financial aid – has been a tremendous achievement. The waters of the Nile are held back in a huge lake extending southwards from 8 km upstream from the old Aswan Dam to beyond Wadi Halfa, a distance of 502 km. This is the world's second largest man-made lake after Kariba, held by a 150 m high dam, the top of which carries a 4 km-long highway. A diversion tunnel on the east bank channels the Nile's waters through six spillway tunnels to a downstream hydro-electric power station housing twelve generators with a total capacity of 2,1 million kilowatts. Lake Nasser stores 106 000 million cubic metres of water for perennial irrigation and land reclamation. The first filling of water behind the dam was in 1964 and completely engulfed the border town of Wadi Halfa. The dam and its subsidiary works cost in the region of US$800 million.

The importance of the Nile to Egypt

The Nile, 6 530 km long, was a wonder of the ancient world, for its summer floods occurred when other rivers were at their lowest levels. This inundation is caused by the summer rains of the Ethiopian

Highlands swelling the Nile's tributaries – the Blue Nile, the Atbara and the Sobat.

These rivers vary greatly in their contributions to the Nile's volume and regularity. The Sobat is slow and sluggish because of the thick growths of sudd (masses of grass, reeds and weeds near the banks) which spread onto the water surface and break away to form floating islands. The river rises in May but its maximum floods are not felt in its lower reaches until November. These floods pond back the White Nile's waters in the Bahr el Ghazal swamps to the south-west, and this causes much loss by evaporation from the swamp surface. The Blue Nile flows throughout the year, fed from ice-blue Lake Tana. Its rise begins in June and goes on throughout July and August to reach a peak in September; again it causes ponding back of the White Nile above Khartoum. It subsides in November and December. The Blue Nile is the main cause of the Nile's summer floods, bringing irrigation water just when needed and thick layers of rich silt. The Atbara adds to the Blue Nile's waters in summer and early autumn but dwindles to a series of shallow water holes in the winter months.

Africa's greatest lake, Lake Victoria, provides little of the water which flows along the Nile's lower course and most is provided by the tributaries, whose flood waters reach their maximum at Khartoum by September and in the delta by October. By January the Blue Nile is almost exhausted, and the White Nile provides much of the volume until late May and June.

Life in Egypt was geared to this uneven flow and successful cultivation depends on the summer floods. Egypt faced an increasingly acute problem; her population had increased at an alarming rate, but the Nile's waters could not be controlled sufficiently to supply regular and increasing water supplies to enable irrigated areas and food production to be expanded. Thus, although Egypt covers one million square kilometres, only 36 000 square kilometres were fully cultivated. In the narrow strips flanking the Nile are crowded 40 million people, and in some parts densities reach 400 per square kilometre, rising to 600 per square kilometre in the delta.

Early attempts at solution

Before 1820, irrigation in Egypt depended on the annual floods; sowing started when the floods receded and harvesting began before the next flood. Only one crop a year could be obtained. When cotton and sugar cane were introduced in 1820, perennial irrigation was needed, and huge basins and a network of canals were constructed from Aswan to the sea. In 1861 two barrages were completed at the apex of the delta, which lifted the water level in the canals higher. By 1900 Egypt had 1,25 million hectares under perennial irrigation. The first Aswan Dam was completed in 1902 but, because water demands exceeded supplies, the dam water level was raised from 106 to 113 m in 1907 by raising the dam wall. Barrages were built at Nag Hammadi, Asyut and Esna to control the waters, and divert them to canals. The old Aswan Dam was again raised to 121 m in 1933 and, before the High Aswan Dam was constructed, 1,4 million hectares were perennially irrigated in Lower Egypt.

But problems were still present. Egypt's population had risen from three million in 1810 to 27 million in the early 1960s, and the agricultural yield could not keep pace with such increase. Long-term water supply was still not available because the various schemes could not control fluctuations; in low flood years the water supply has dropped to only 45 000 million cubic metres, and normal variations are between 65 000 million and 130 000 million cubic metres. A further problem was the accumulation of silt on the river bed behind the barrages, which steadily reduced the amount of water able to be stored. The sluice gates of the old Aswan Dam were partially closed in late November, when the Nile is comparatively free of silt and when lower Egypt has still plenty of water, and then reopened three months later for careful distribution to the cotton fields. Thus storage capacity was limited to when the Nile was falling and was seriously reduced when the Nile failed to produce its usual volume. The storage of sufficient water could thus never be guaranteed.

There were two solutions: the construction of a series of dams on the Nile and its tributaries to give greater control along the whole course, or one huge dam which would store all water needs from one year to the next, and make provision for silt accumulation. Egypt chose the second of these two alternatives.

The results

Undoubtedly the Aswan High Dam was a very expensive undertaking, an expense which was not thought worth the risk by the World Bank and Western Powers. But the benefits are great and Egypt claims the following results:

a An additional 690 000 ha of cultivated land; 280 000 ha able to be converted from basin to perennial irrigation, thus increasing Egypt's irrigated area by 25 per cent; guaranteed water has increased crop yields especially for a planned one million hectares of rice.

b Complete control of the Nile has reduced the risk of floods; money has been saved which was formerly spent on flood damage repair; labour involved has been diverted to food production.

c The lake has improved navigation since former dangerous bends and shoals are completely covered.

d A regular water flow for hydro-electric power production.It is hoped to double the present power capacity of the Old Aswan power plant and to establish several industries there.

e A guaranteed flow of water for the barrages on the lower Nile. Future HEP stations can be constructed should Egypt need them with no fear of irregular water flow. Egypt's future plans include the use of the Nile cataracts for HEP.

f The power from the dam has meant a five-fold increase in Egypt's power potential. The need for solid fuels in industry has been reduced by 2,5 million tonnes annually.

The Sudan is now expanding her agricultural schemes knowing that there will be an increased amount of water now available; water can be stored more freely and this means clearer water and less sediment in Sudan reservoirs; more water, formerly used for irrigation, can now be diverted to hydro-electric schemes.

But there were problems, especially the displacement of people who had lived in the area now covered by Lake Nasser. By July 1965, the population of the border town of Wadi Halfa and of 13 villages to the north – some 42 000 people with their livestock – had been evacuated 1300 km by rail across the Nubian Desert to Khasm El Girba, a small settlement 70 km from the Ethiopian border on the River

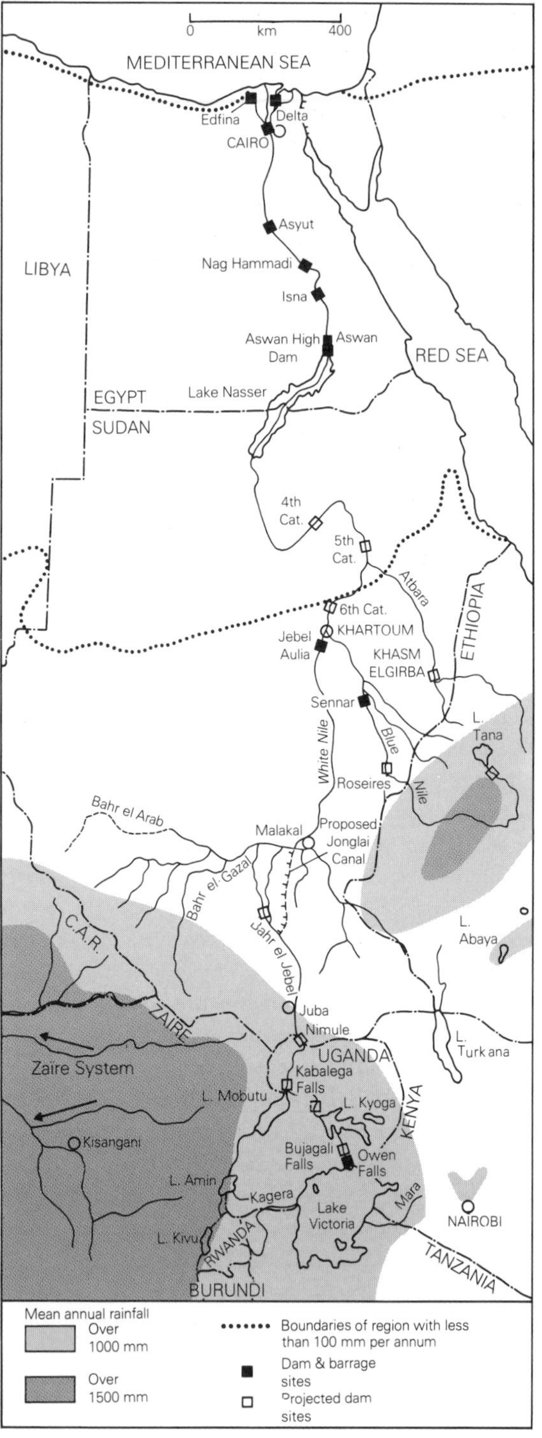

Fig. 8.7 The Nile – completed and projected schemes

Atbara. Here the peasants were given double their former hectarage and tenant cultivation rights on government-owned land in blocks of six hectares on which wheat, cotton and groundnuts are grown on a three-year rotation system. Khasm El Girba, a small administrative and market centre lying in a region where semi-nomadic tribesmen grazed their herds of cattle, camels and sheep, has had its population doubled to 6 000. Surrounding it are 26 new villages of 250 houses each. Irrigation and electric power come from a new dam.

In Egypt 75 new government townships have been built. Sixty-five kilometres north of the Aswan Dam the new township of Kom Ombo is flourishing, surrounded by 12 000 ha of new cropland divided into 2-ha plots.

Egypt has now embarked on several other irrigation schemes which were delayed by the Israeli–Arab war. Using water from the High Dam, underground supplies, and water from the joint Egypt-Sudan Jonglei Canal Scheme, the government plans to reclaim 1,8 million hectares before the end of the century in the Western and Eastern Deserts, the Sinai Peninsula, in Upper Egypt, and the northern delta. Plans include the extension of the sprinkler system now used over 60 000 ha, the introduction of drip irrigation, and the use of electric power from the High Dam to replace the 24 000 diesel pumps now in operation with electrically-driven pumps.

Such schemes are vital in a country where the population is increasing at almost a million a year. In the early 1950s there was 0,2 ha of cultivated land per head of population; in 1976 the amount had dropped to 0,08 ha per person. This will be even smaller by 2000 A.D. when the population will have reached 64 million at the present annual growth rate of 2,3 per cent. The total cultivated land in Egypt in 1976 was 2,5 million hectares, less than three per cent of the total area. In some cases, because of bad planning in the past, irrigated lands have shrunk to half their former size due to a drop in the water-table. In parts of the western delta region the land is deteriorating, e.g. the average grape yield, estimated to be 2,2 t per hectare at best, has dropped to less than one tonne per hectare. The rise in grain import costs from US$260 million in 1973 to US$500 million in 1974, completely absorbed the income of US$440 million from exports of cotton.

Ghana – The Volta River Project

Until 1962 the hydro-electric power and irrigation potential of Ghana's rivers had been little developed, despite the country's heavy annual rainfalls in the south-west and the numerous deep valleys suitable for dam sites. This lack of development was largely due to the extreme variations in the seasonal flow of Ghana's rivers.

Although Ghana has numerous short rivers in the well-watered south-west – the Tano, the Pra, the Ancobra and their tributaries – her major river systems, the Volta, the Black Volta, the White Volta and the Oti, derive their waters from savanna regions covering the northern two-thirds of the country. Here the long dry season from October to March is followed by heavy rains brought by south-westerly air currents.

During the dry season the rivers of northern Ghana dwindle to mere trickles, their courses marked by water holes. The Volta itself experiences a great reduction in its volume despite contributions by its more southern tributaries – the Puru and Afram. But in the rainy season the rivers become roaring torrents, frequently overflowing their banks and flooding large areas. Practically all the surface water of the northern half of Ghana is channelled into the Volta – during the Akosombo dam's construction record-breaking floods occurred unequalled over 50 years.

The reasons for the project

Why was this great project costing US$120 million embarked upon? Ghana possesses considerable reserves of bauxite, the aluminium ore, vital in the construction of modern aircraft, motor cars, railway engines and coaches, and household utensils. The large-scale production of hydro-electric power would make the cost of smelting the ore before export economically feasible, and refined aluminium would be less expensive to ship than the bulky ore. Aluminium exports would lessen the reliance on agricultural exports, particularly cocoa. The cheap power would also encourage the establishment of secondary industries and broaden Ghana's economy which relies too much on mineral extraction and a narrow range of export crops. Moreover, the Ghanaian Government had pushed on with the construction of the US$70 million port of Tema,

Ghana: Akosombo Dam and Lake Volta.

designed to handle the expected increases in exports and the inflow of constructional equipment. Tema is now the site of the Valco aluminium smelter, instead of Kpong near the dam site at Akosombo. This saved the cost of constructing a new settlement at Kpong. Ghana provided half the cost of the Volta project, with the remainder supplied by the United States, Britain and the World Bank.

The dam (*see Fig. 10.3, page 207*)

The building of the dam at Akosombo, although a more difficult site than the one originally proposed at Ajena, reduced construction time by four years and increased the potential amount of power that could be generated. The great lake, which covers three per cent of Ghana and stretches 320 km, covers 8 750 square kilometres and is the world's third largest man-made lake. A power-house, generating nearly 550 mW of hydro-electric power through its six turbines, distributes electricity over a 800 km-long transmission network. The dam rises 130 m above the river bed and its crest is 670 m long.

The results

While some critics have pointed out that it might have been wiser to invest the money in several smaller schemes on the many dam sites available in Ghana and thus spread the benefits of power and irrigation water over a wider area, there is no doubt that Ghana receives economic benefits from the Volta Project. These include:

a Large supplies of cheap power for Valco which takes 70 per cent of the power, and for the mining and secondary industries. This reduces Ghana's consumption of thermal power which has jumped over the last ten years from 40 million kilowatts to 200 million kilowatts. The grid supplies power from Sekondi in the west to Accra in the east.

b Foreign exchange earnings: power is sent to Togo and Benin, and the grid is to be linked with that of the Ivory Coast.

c Large benefits to agriculture. Irrigation experiments are being carried out on state farms north of the lake and on the Accra Plains, particularly with paddy and sugar cane. Downriver from the dam an area once devoted to shifting agriculture has been converted into small farms and state-owned plantations. Some 3 200 ha of sugar cane, 4 500 ha of rice, and 800 ha of groundnuts, maize, tobacco, vegetables and other crops have been laid out. The experimental area lies only 160 km east of the large Accra market and stretches for 80 km inland from the coast.

The lake itself yields some 25 000 t of fish a year, while the annual rise and fall of the lake surface along its 7 200 km long shores exposes much fertile grazing land.

d The economic development created by the dam has been felt throughout Ghana. The operations at Tema and Akosombo have created a skilled body of workers who are a valuable asset. The building of trunk and feeder roads to serve both the project and Tema is already stimulating economic activity in interior Ghana.

e The lake has become an inland waterway. New ports are planned and there is a lake service to transport goods and passengers. The lake provides an attraction for tourists.

As with the Aswan High Dam, the Volta Project has made a great change in many people's lives. Some 80 000 people were moved to 54 well-planned townships and have been introduced to modern co-operative methods of cultivation. Originally living in isolated villages and producing subsistence crops, they are now contributing to the national economy. The Volta River Authority (VRA) and the Ghanaian Ministry of Agriculture have resettled over 30 000 of the people as arable farmers. Some 7 000 families have been given 17 000 ha in plots of 2,5 ha; of these, 3 000 families concentrate on pineapple growing, others on vegetables, tree crops and pastoral farming. There are no plans to expand facilities at Akosombo. Instead, attention is being given to a new project at Kpong.

Nigeria – The Kainji Project

The Kainji Dam appears relatively small when compared with Lake Volta and with the vast area of Nigeria itself. Kainji's lake is 135 km long compared with Volta's 320 km and its area of 1 130 square

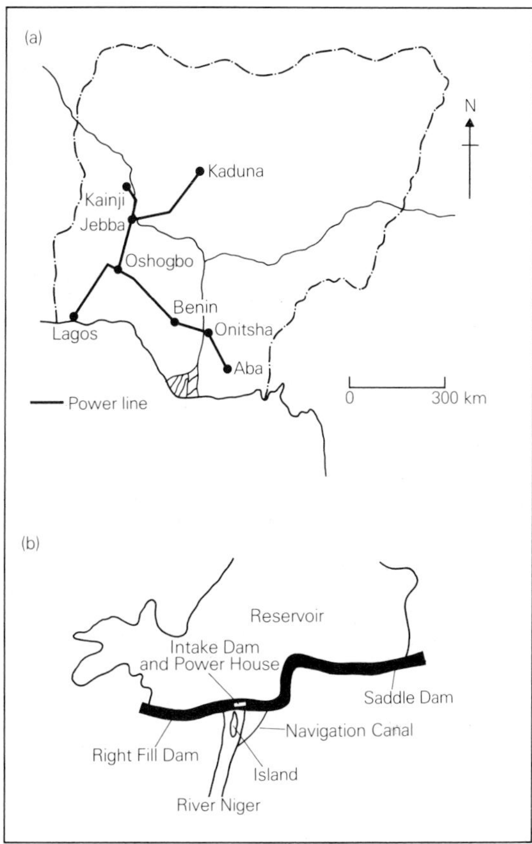

Fig. 8.8 The Kainji Dam; *a* relative position in Nigeria; *b* site and surrounding region

kilometres is only one-eighth that of Lake Volta. Nevertheless, the Kainji Dam is Nigeria's largest hydro-electric power project and is of major importance to the country's economy.

The dam is situated nearly 1 000 km from the Niger's mouth, and 65 km from Nigeria's western boundary with the Republic of Benin. The northerly aligned section of the boundary between the states of Sokoto, Niger and Kwara runs through the middle of the lake. This is a remote and rather sparsely populated region of Nigeria, but the site was considered as the most suitable for a hydro-electric power project. Although there is no narrow gorge here as at Cabora Bassa or Kariba, the flood plain narrows as the Niger flows through a low line of plateaux. The natural features of the area dictated the construction of a long narrow concrete wall over 4,5 km long and 65 m high at a point some 32 km south of the Bussa Rapids, which were subsequently drowned by the rising lake. The cost of this structure and the power turbines (US $150 million) was partly borne by the World Bank ($60 million), Italy ($15,5 million), Britain ($8,5 million), and the USA and the Netherlands (nearly $1,0 million each). The dam wall was completed in 1967.

In addition to the dam wall, a bridge was constructed across the Niger just below the dam, so that an alternative crossing point to the bridge at Jebba was available to traffic. The 4 000 people living in Bussa had to be moved to a new site on higher ground, now called New Bussa; the rising water also covered the village of Agwara and, in all, over 50 000 people had to be evacuated to new sites. The town of Yelwa, although not drowned by the lake, required protection from flood waters, and an 8 m high circular dyke wall was built to protect the settlement.

The Kainji Dam has brought several benefits to this north-western region of Nigeria. First, the creation of the lake and the increased depth of water in the Niger up-river from the lake, means that navigation is now possible at all seasons as far as Yelwa, and into the Niger and Benin republics during the rainy season. Transport has been further improved by the construction of a road along the top of the dam wall. Secondly, flood control and the regulation of water flow for irrigation purposes below the dam have been greatly improved; the former high fluctuation between high and low water of 6,5 m has now been reduced to 1,5 m. The third benefit is the provision of more food for the region; the lake itself is now a source of protein food in the form of fish, while below the dam irrigation schemes on the flood plain produce rice, sugar cane and vegetables.

But the most important benefit of the Kainji scheme is the provision of electric power for Nigeria as a whole. The present hydro-electric capacity of Kainji is now 760 mW, and it supplies over half of Nigeria's total generating capacity of 600 mW. The power is fed into a national grid of transmission cables which link Jebba, Ibadan, Lagos, Benin, Onitsha and Port Harcourt.

The Kainji Dam is the first phase in a three-stage scheme. The two other phases involve the construction of a second dam across the Kaduna River, the Niger's north-eastern tributary here, at the Shiroro Gorge about 75 km east of Kainji, and a dam at Jebba on the Niger, 70 km south of Kainji. The Shiroro Dam will provide additional power, while the Jebba Dam will raise the level of water and provide another navigable stretch. Like Kainji, the Jebba Dam wall will be fitted with lock gates to allow vessels to pass through. Thus, the Niger will be navigable as a lake for over 200 km. In addition, the Jebba Dam will provide flood control and irrigation water to a zone extending as far downriver as Lokoja, a distance of 250 km.

South Africa – The Orange River Project

The Republic of South Africa suffers from a very uneven distribution of its water resources. The main watershed of the country – the well-watered arc of the Drakensberg and Maluti mountain ranges of the south-east – lies only 160 km from the shores of the Indian Ocean but over 1 000 km from the South Atlantic. The map (Fig. 8.9) shows how this watershed divides the drainage system of South Africa. To the east and south, down the steep escarpment face and across the coastal plain, flow many short rivers – the Tugela, the Umkomaas, the Umzimvubu, the Great Kei, the Sundays and the Olifants. These rivers depend entirely on annual rainfalls falling on the Drakensberg and associated highlands. During the rainy periods in the early and late parts of the year, the rivers are rushing torrents; in the drier months they are sluggish and irregular, their levels dropping considerably.

Westwards from the Drakensberg flow the long rivers – the Orange and its tributaries the Hartz, the Vaal, the Modder and the Caledon. The Orange, flowing for 2 000 km to the desolate west coast near Alexander Bay, also suffers from seasonal rainfall variations, varying between a rushing, muddy torrent and a trickle. The South African Government has now succeeded in harnessing the vast power and irrigational potential of the Orange.

The Republic has several schemes, mainly for irrigation on the Sundays, the Great Fish and the Kei, and also on the main tributaries of the Orange. The biggest scheme is on the Vaal where the Vaaldam reservoir provides water for the densely settled mining and industrial complex of the Witwatersrand. This water is also used to feed many

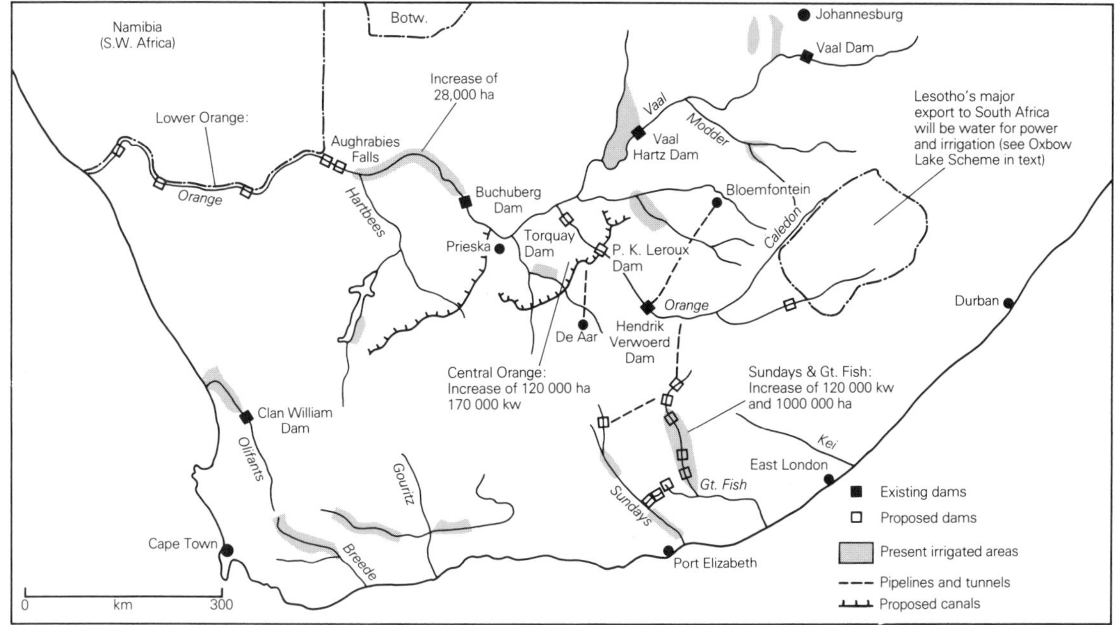

Fig. 8.9 South Africa – the Orange River Scheme

other towns and irrigation projects including the Vaal-Hartz irrigation settlement. Although the Vaal-dam's capacity was doubled in 1956, the ever-increasing demands of the Rand cities and mines has placed a severe strain on the river's resources. The Orange River irrigation and hydro-electric power scheme, which will take a further twenty years to complete, will greatly ease this burden.

The Orange River

The Orange is South Africa's largest river with a flow of water equal to all the other rivers combined. It drains 855 000 square kilometres of Lesotho, Botswana, Namibia (South West Africa) and the Republic. Its upper course lies in the well-watered (2 000 mm a year) Maluti mountain ranges where there are plans for several independent schemes, e.g. the Oxbow Project, which entails the joining of the numerous headwaters of the Orange by a series of tunnels and canals, and channelling the water through several power stations leading down to the Caledon River.

From the highland zone the Orange drops from 3 400 m, and crosses the flatter interior plateau between 1 200 and 1 500 m, forming the southern boundary of the Orange Free State; 700 km from its source it is joined by the Vaal. The Orange then flows south-westwards, skirts the southern highlands of Griqualand and then turns sharply northwards at Prieska, where annual rainfalls drop from about 640 to 250 mm and evaporation rates rise enormously. The 500 km stretch from the Caledon junction to Prieska is the vital section of the scheme, for it is here that the Orange receives over half of the total run-off of the whole drainage system.

Westwards from Prieska, the Orange drops steadily to 600 m in a 400 km-long stretch where rainfall totals fall to 130 mm in the west and evaporation rates rise to over 2 500 mm a year. The Orange has here formed wide plains of fertile soils which, with irrigation, support good crops. The river then topples through the Aughrabies Falls (145 m) and flows through rugged desert country for 500 km before reaching the Atlantic.

The scheme

The main aim of the Orange River Scheme is to make full use of the irrigation and hydro-electric power potential of the river, and provide a sound basis for agricultural and industrial development. The total cost will be US$900 million over the next twenty years. The scheme will enable a further 280 000 ha to be irrigated and will be carried out in six phases. The main control dam (70 m high) in the Ruigte Valley downstream from Bethulie will store 1 750 000 million litres; the P. K. LeRoux Dam downstream will provide more storage water for the interior plateau, and water will be pumped into irrigation canals leading to De Aar and the Riet, Brak, Ongers and Carnarvonleegte Valleys. A third dam at Torquay will provide irrigation water for land flanking the Orange as far as Prieska. All these dams will control the Orange River's water as far as its mouth, where there are great irrigation possibilities. An 80 km-long tunnel now leads from the Ruigte Valley through the southern mountains to the upper Great Fish River and thence by canal to the lower Sundays Valley; this improves existing irrigation and power facilities and helps expand the area devoted to sheep and fruit farming.

Work on the Hendrik Verwoerd Dam was completed in June 1971 and the lake is some 90 km-long and 15 km wide. The P. K. LeRoux Dam hydro-electric power station has an installed capacity of 220 mW.

The results

The Orange River Project will benefit South Africa in the following ways:

a The extra 2 800 ha of irrigated land will mean a crop increase of 25 per cent over the present crop value especially of fruits, vegetables, hay, stock-feed, maize, wheat, groundnuts and cotton. The dangers of severe droughts over a large area of the interior will be reduced and wool production will increase.

b A wide measure of flood control will reduce damage and stabilise water supplies for new and existing irrigation schemes.

c Existing irrigation and power schemes whose efficiency has been reduced by silting will be revitalised by fresh water supplies.

d In the long run, primary and secondary industries will be stimulated. Agricultural expansion will attract more fruit and vegetable canneries, wool scouring, washing and combing plants, textile and agricultural machinery factories. The cheap power will aid mining and communications development, and textile and chemical factories needing large supplies of water will benefit.

e By this scheme the Government plans to adjust the present economic imbalance in South Africa. South African industry is heavily concentrated in a few major regions – the Rand, Durban, Cape Town, Port Elizabeth and East London. New industry can now move away from these concentrations and stimulate the economy in less favoured regions. Existing water supplies, as at the Vaal reservoir, will be relieved. In general there will be a loosening up of the country's economic structure.

South Africa is also interested in the prospect of importing water and power from Lesotho. An industrial consortium is to construct a dam at Oxbow Lake which will produce 400 million kilowatt hours per annum; water for industry will be sold to South Africa. The plan will cost US$50 million and envisages the possibility of a 480 km-long pipeline to Vereeniging.

Mozambique – The Cabora Bassa Dam

The development of the hydro-electric and irrigation potential of the Zambezi at Quebrabassa Gorge 136 km north-west of Tete in Mozambique will provide a sounder base for the development of Mozambique's economy. The original agreement between the former Portuguese government and South Africa was for the latter to buy up to 80 per cent of the HEP in the initial phase. Work began on the dam wall construction in 1969 at a point where the river flowed through a narrow gorge and was completed in 1974. The wall is 155 m high (Kariba 140 m, Aswan High Dam 100 m) and cost US$120 million.

The first phase, now completed, has three generators with a capacity of 408 mW each, and two more were added by 1980. The power station is on the south bank, but a second power station of equal capacity is to be built on the north bank in the 1980s. Transmission lines have been completed and connect the power station with the South African grid system near Irene north-east of Pretoria. The lines are 1 370 km long with 864 km in Mozambique. The whole first phase has cost more than US$340 million to complete.

The power from the first stage is about the same as

that of Kariba now the latter's north bank station has been completed, but the completion of the second stage at Cabora Bassa will raise this to 2 000 mW, which will be double that of the Aswan High Dam.

Power is not the only consideration. The scheme will open up large tracts of land that are at present wild and inhospitable. Minerals known to exist in the region include a 19 km-long seam of coking coal, iron ore deposits, 35 million tonnes of titaniferous magnetite ore, and deposits of manganese, nickel, copper, fluorspar, chrome ore and asbestos. Approximately 1,6 million hectares could be irrigated for sugar cane, grains, citrus, vegetables, cotton and jute. The regulation of the Zambezi's waters will permit navigation far into the interior on the lake. If such plans came to fruition about one million people could be settled in the Cabora Bassa region. Even with the completion of the scheme there is still much further potential in the Zambezi and plans exist for the construction of another power dam and station at Mpanda-Uncua between Cabora Bassa and Tete.

Kenya – The Tana River Development Scheme

Although the Tana is a comparatively small river it is of great importance to Kenya's economy. Little more than a third of Kenya's 580 000 square kilometres – the coastal strip, the highlands above 1 500 m, and the Lake Victoria shores – have sufficiently reliable rainfalls to support good crops and healthy cattle. The remaining two-thirds is semi-desert, bush and scrub. With irrigation things could be different.

But Kenya is unfortunate in its rivers. The highlands, with annual rainfalls of 1000 to 1 800 mm acts as a watershed. Down their western slopes the Sondu, Nyanda and Nzoia Rivers flow only 80 km through well-watered country towards Lake Victoria. The rivers flowing eastwards to the Indian Ocean have more difficult courses. Hundreds of streams flow down the dip-slopes of the Aberdares and from Mount Kenya to join the Tana, Ewaso Ngiro and Athi (which later forms the Galana). Only two, the Tana and Athi-Galana, reach the sea across the 480 km-wide Nyika, for the Ewaso Ngiro drains into the Lorian Swamp.

Kenya is making great efforts to use these limited water resources to best advantage. With a rapidly growing population (5,4 million in 1948, now 15 million) it is vitally important to increase the area of productive land, and to develop power to expand

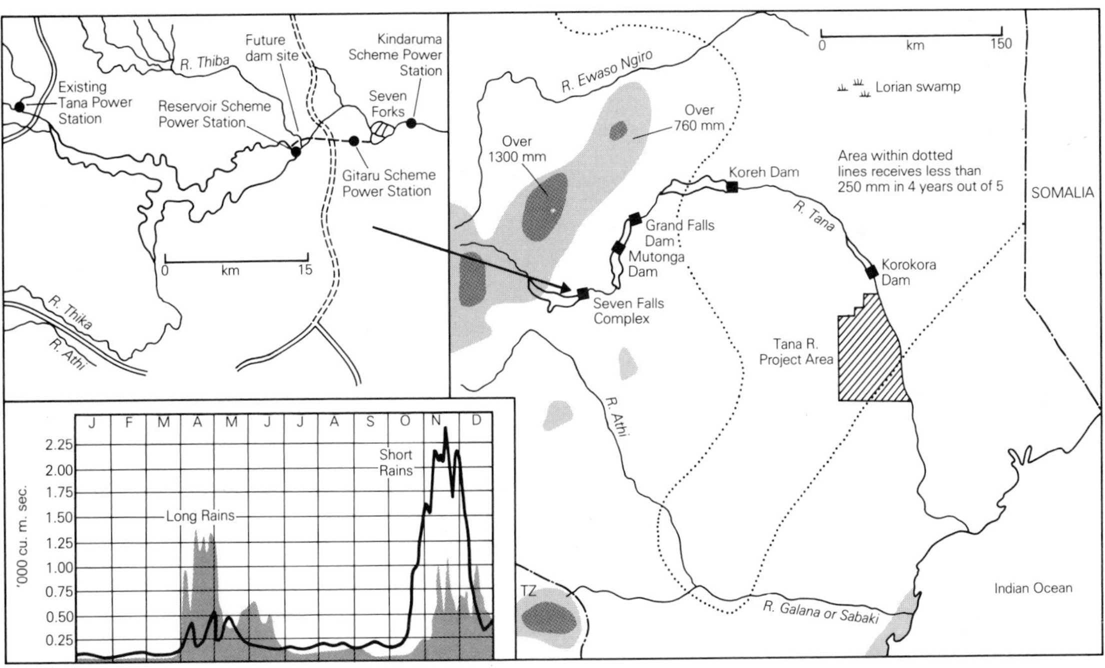

Fig. 8.10 Kenya – the Tana River Scheme. The graph shows the extreme variation in volume of the River Tana during Kenya's two rainy seasons between 1953 and 1965

existing industries and attract new ones. Apart from several small power plants there is no major power station in the country, and with no coal Kenya must rely on electric power from Owen Falls and fuel oils from overseas. Projects so far completed (for irrigation) – the Perkerra Scheme on Lake Baringo, the Yatta Furrow, and projects near Taveta – are all on a small scale. But the Tana offers good opportunities for the irrigation of large areas and the production of a substantial amount of hydro-electric power.

The Tana is approximately 650 km long and drains 100 000 square kilometres (equal to the area of Liberia). But rainfall over this catchment area is badly distributed with great variations from year to year and, except in the highlands, annual totals do not exceed 500 mm. Evaporation rates are high (Garissa – rainfall 200 mm, evaporation 3 000 mm). Moreover, the rain falls in two short seasons, October to December and March to April. The Tana thus experiences wide variations in its levels, but even so it is the only river which possesses a considerable potential. Already this potential is being tapped in the following schemes:

Irrigation schemes

a *The Mwea-Tebere Scheme:* The area of plateau land fringing the Aberdares and Mount Kenya and drained by the Tana and its tributaries is one of the richest agricultural areas in Kenya. Here, at about 1 300 km, there is enough water to serve the many coffee farms in the west, the new resettlement schemes, and to irrigate some 8 000 ha. The black, sticky impervious soils make the flatter parts ideal for rice cultivation, and on the Mwea-Tebere plains is Kenya's large rice scheme, irrigated by the Nyamindi and Thiba tributaries, which will eventually cover 5 000 ha. Some 10 000 people live on planned 1,5 ha farms in 19 new self-contained villages. Here annual rainfalls vary from 630 to 760 mm a year with long dry periods, so irrigation is essential. Sindana type rice gives high yields (16 bags per hectare) exceeded only by Australia and Ethiopia. The scheme reduces Kenya's reliance on imports by producing 12 200 t of rice annually.

b *The Galole Pilot Scheme:* Below the great bend of the Tana at Galole is an irrigation scheme which may be the forerunner of a much vaster operation. This is the dry (380 mm a year) country of the Pokomo who, unlike the neighbouring pastoral Somali and Galla, cultivate poor grains and root crops in the silt at falling flood times, often enduring famine when the rains fail. Here, on the right bank is an irrigation settlement covering 500 ha, to which water is pumped through an 18 km-long canal. Cotton, groundnuts, soya beans and rice are grown entirely by irrigation, and this small scheme has proved that good yields (180 to 270 kg per hectare) can be obtained from irrigated desert soils.

c *Future prospects – Plans for the Lower Tana Basin.* With the success of the Galole Scheme a large area flanking the Tana between Garissa and Garsen covering 1,2 million hectares has been aerially surveyed with the object of selecting 120 000 ha for irrigation. Such an area would be sufficient to settle 75 000 families or nearly a third of a million people. Its gross agricultural production would amount to US$40 million a year of which US$25 million would come from cotton. Extra employment would be created by cotton ginneries to be set up in the area.

Hydro-electric power

Five kilometres downstream from the Seven Forks Rapids is the Kindaruma power station with its dam lake some 50 km long and 13 km wide. Kindaruma was commissioned in 1968 to provide 40 mW of power. In 1976 the second phase of a scheme designed to harness the power potential of the Tana was completed at Kamburu where three generators produce 30 mW each. With increasing oil prices a third phase due for completion in 1978 was begun at Gitaru, sited between Kindaruma and Kamburu. Gitaru will have three generators each of 67 mW. Once this has been completed Kenya's electric power needs will be satisfied for several years but the country's rapid industrial expansion has prompted plans for further power sites lower down the Tana at Mutonga, Grand Falls, Koreh and Korokora.

The results

The development of the Tana River's potential, although small compared with the Volta, Zambezi and Orange schemes, will bring considerable economic benefits to Kenya, the most important being:

a Kenya's dependence on imported fuel and local wood will be greatly reduced. Increases in oil prices meant that Kenya's imported oil costs rose from US$30 million in 1973 to US$115 million in 1974, and to US$184 million in 1975. No oil reserves have been discovered in Kenya despite many years of exploration. Domestic production of electricity has risen from 557 mW in 1971 to 901 mW in 1975, while, during the same period, imported electricity has dropped from 293 mW to 260 mW.

b The industrial potential of the country will be increased by the great reserves of cheap power. More factories will be needed to process the products of the new irrigated areas.

c The irrigation schemes will eventually provide settlement for over a third of a million people who will support themselves, grow food crops for Kenya's growing population, and supply raw materials for industry.

Uganda – The Owen Falls Dam

In 1862, as a result of the journey of John Hanning Speke, the source of the Victoria Nile, the narrow outlet for the waters of Lake Victoria, became known

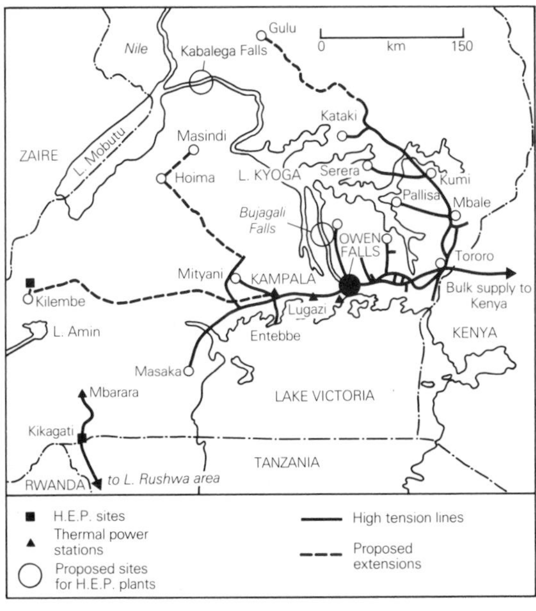

Fig. 8.11 Uganda – Owen Falls and the distribution of power

to the outside world. Here, the waters of the world's third largest lake poured over the Ripon Falls to enter marshy Lake Kyoga to the north, and eventually find their way via the northern tip of Lake Mobutu and the western arm of the Rift Valley to the main drainage system of the Nile. In 1907 Winston Churchill saw the huge possibilities of the tremendous volume of rushing water when he stated, 'It is possible that nowhere else in the world could so enormous a mass of water be held up by so little masonry.' But it was not until 1954, 92 years after Speke's journey, that the waters first produced hydro-electric power.

Unlike Kenya and Tanzania, Uganda is fortunate in her water supplies. Roughly one-seventh (35 000 square kilometres) of Uganda's total area (243 000 square kilometres) is covered by water. Rainfalls throughout most of the country are reliable and plentiful, and few regions receive less than 1 000 mm a year. With the warm humid atmosphere and the deep soils found over much of the country, the land supports a dense population and a wide variety of crops – cotton, sugar cane, tea, groundnuts, tobacco and tropical fruits.

But until 1954 the country had one major problem – the lack of power for industrial development. There are no coal deposits in Uganda and no major oil fields. Fuel imports, hauled 700 km from Mombasa, were expensive, and without cheap power a severe limit was set on industrial expansion. The government was anxious to develop industries for several reasons. The population was growing rapidly (3,5 million in 1931, 5 million in 1948) and large areas of agricultural land were already reaching their limits of production. New industries would help broaden the economy and provide alternative employment. Again, Uganda possessed other advantages – an increasing supply of raw materials for secondary industry (cotton, tea, sugar, coffee); a large supply of unskilled labour willing to be trained; several mineral deposits, especially the copper at Kilembe, and a good export outlet to Mombasa along the railway, which had been extended to Kilembe in 1931. Moreover, good roads linked most parts with Kampala, and lakes and rivers provided cheap water transport. All that was lacking was the power, and this was solved by the construction of the Owen Falls Dam across the Victoria Nile.

The dam

The dam was built across a narrow channel about 280 m wide, north of Owen Falls which, with the Ripon Falls, disappeared below the rising Nile waters. The dam is a low curving structure, 830 m long and 27 m high, containing six control sluices. By agreement with the Egyptian Government the dam was built one metre higher than was necessary for Uganda's needs. This allowed the level of Lake Victoria's water to rise nearly 300 mm higher and substantially increased the amount available for irrigation in the Sudan and Egypt. British, Danish and Dutch firms co-operated on the dam's construction.

The dam can accommodate ten turbo-alternator sets but, when opened in 1954, only six were installed until the demand for power increased. Today all ten are in operation producing a total of 150 000 kW – a sixteenth of Uganda's power potential. Today the Owen Falls Dam is the chief supplier of electricity in Uganda and much is exported via high-tension wires to Kisumu, Nakuru and Nairobi.

The results

The supplies of cheap power from the Owen Falls Dam benefit Uganda in the following ways:

a The overall planning of the national economy need no longer be restricted by fears of lack of energy. There is now ample power for Uganda's present and future needs, especially now that Kenya is developing its own power supplies.

b Industrial growth has been greatly stimulated. Jinja has become the industrial hub of the country, and using the power are cement and asbestos factories at Tororo and a whole range of industries in several towns – Kampala, Port Bell and Mbale.

c There has been an immense reduction of oil imports for the thermal power stations in Uganda. Only one of the turbo-alternators saves 4 000 t of oil a year.

Zaïre – The Inga Dam

The Zaïre or Congo is the only major river in Africa which flows with a constant high volume throughout the year. This is due to its huge catchment area, roughly half the size of Australia, parts of which will always receive some rain. The water channelled into the Zaïre's 4 800 km-long course passes through one of the narrowest and deepest sections at the Inga Rapids, 80 km upstream from Matadi and 190 km from Kinshasa. The potential power is increased because at this point the river drops 75 m over a distance of 24 km. This momentum produces a flow when the river is at low level of 22 700 cubic metres per second, and a flow of 60 900 cubic metres when the Zaïre is in flood. On average, 240 000 t of water pass this point each minute.

Under Belgian rule, Zaïre's economy had not developed sufficiently to warrant large scale development of hydro-electric power. Power dams were constructed to supply local pockets of industry at Bia and Francqui on the Lufira, and at Le Marinel and Delcommune on the Lualaba to serve the Shaba copper belt. With the expansion of the mining industry over the last two decades (mineral products are now worth US$500 million a year and represent 80 per cent of the national wealth) and the move to establish more processing and manufacturing industries throughout Zaïre, a major scheme became an economic necessity.

First studies of the Inga site were made in 1910, and a Belgian engineer, P. van Deuren, proposed a second plan in 1926. A detailed report made in the 1950s was shelved because of internal trouble, but a 1963 study was accepted and construction began in 1968 on the dam wall. The project will be completed in eleven stages and work will go on into the next century. When complete it will be the largest hydro-electric power scheme in the world, dwarfing Cabora Bassa and Kariba, and will have an ultimate generating capacity of 30 000 mW. The completed first phase producing 1 100 mW diverts the river through the Van Deuren valley which runs parallel to the Zaïre at Inga; this was completed in 1972. Phase two will bring capacity to 3 500 mW, and phase three will raise it to 28 850 mW. High tension cables now link Inga with the Kinshasa and Matadi industrial areas, and run through cleared rain forest for some 1 600 km to the mines of Shaba Province. In these centres a wide range of industries using Inga power have been established or are planned, and include iron and steel manufacture, aluminium smelting, vehicle assembly, fertilisers, cement, chemicals, tyres, wood products, electric lamps, and expansion of processing plant in palm oil and cocoa plantations.

The future

The location of hydro-electric power sites and layout of the existing grid system in Africa south of the equator would make the establishment of an international grid system for the whole of the southern continent a possibility. The Zaïre, Zambia and Zimbabwe grids are already linked, the Mozambique transmission lines from Cabora Bassa link with the South Africa grid, which in turn connects with the grid in South West Africa. The Cunene scheme has power lines running into southern Angola. New links needed would be Angola–Inga, Inga–Owen Falls, Kindaruma–Tanzania–Blantyre–Cabora Bassa and lines through Botswana linking the South West Africa–South Africa networks. Such a scheme would bring considerable benefit to remote regions, but it would mean that economic considerations would have to be given priority over political ideologies.

(See Chapter Thirteen, pages 248–253, for further discussion of Africa's energy and water resources.)

Questions

1 Examine the distribution of the major water resources of Africa south of the Sahara and discuss the attempts by man to harness them.
2 With the aid of well-chosen examples, discuss the factors which have generally hindered the use of rivers in Africa for power and irrigation purposes.
3 In what ways are rivers helping the economic development of nations in Africa? Confine your answer to specific projects.
4 Discuss the various factors which prompt governments of African nations to develop their river potential for power and irrigation purposes.
5 Consider the factors which affect the regimes of the rivers Zaïre, Niger, Zambezi, Tana, Volta and Nile.
6 With the aid of sketch-maps, describe in detail any one hydro-electric power scheme in Africa. Use the headings – *Reasons*, *Site*, *Benefits*, *Future*.

CHAPTER NINE

Industrial development in Africa 1 – The extractive industries

Africa is a late arrival in the field of industrial development. African landscapes are predominantly rural and, except for parts of South Africa, there are no smoke-blackened regions as in Europe or North America. The continent's industrial areas are spacious, well-planned, and usually located outside the major towns.

The basis for industry in Africa – fuel and raw materials

The growth and location of modern industry depends on several factors – large supplies of suitable coal, oil and hydro-electric power, a labour force with developed skills, large easily accessible markets with a high buying power, and an efficient transport network to serve markets and carry raw materials at economic rates. Few areas in Africa can claim these advantages. Except in the Transvaal there is no major combination of coal, iron ore and useful minerals to form the basis of heavy iron and steel industries, although Nigeria is now able to proceed with a national steel industry and Egypt has established steel plants by transporting raw materials over long distances.

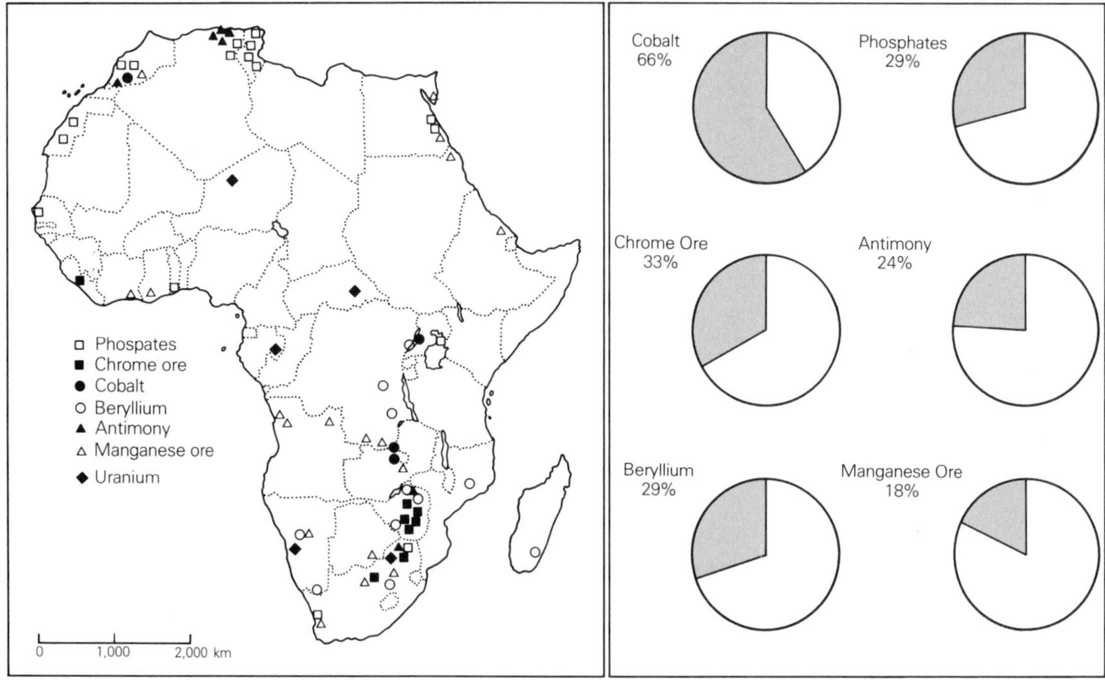

Fig. 9.1a Africa – location of some important minerals

Fig. 9.1b Africa – percentage of world production of some important minerals

Africa has thus played the role of a mineral supplier to the more industrialised nations. Mineral ore processing is still in its infancy, the continent producing only one per cent of the pig iron, one per cent of the crude steel, and only three per cent of the lead and zinc of the world. Africa is, however, the world's third largest producer of processed copper (25 per cent) after the USA and Chile, and possesses some rich deposits of minerals vital to the world's economy – diamonds (80 per cent world production), dobalt (66 per cent), gold (55 per cent), manganese (18 per cent) and chromite (33 per cent); her output of bauxite has increased from two per cent in 1950 to seven per cent today.

Except for the south, Africa is short of coal, her economy as yet too under-developed to make full use of the tremendous volume of oil her rocks are yielding, and her hydro-electric power potential has scarcely been touched. Coal lies in widely scattered deposits not all easy to get at. The chief producers are South Africa (annual production 65 million tonnes – compare Britain's 200 million tonnes), Zimbabwe (4,1 million tonnes), Nigeria (one million tonnes), Morocco (0,6 million tonnes) and Zaïre (0,5 million tonnes). While southern Africa has most of the known coal deposits, Africa north of the equator possesses almost all the oil, with Nigeria the foremost producer followed by Libya and Algeria. While production of hydro-electric power has taken great strides since 1945, Africa still produces only two per cent of the world's output although her power potential is 23 per cent of the world's.

It should be remembered, however, that Africa is one of the last continents to be fully explored geologically, and that the discovery of economically important minerals has been hampered in many places by the thick mask of sedimentary deposits which cover many parts of Africa's surface. New mineral deposits are coming to light with increasing frequency. The most dramatic example is that of Libya, where the discovery of oil transformed a country whose economy formerly rested almost entirely on the export of groundnuts, into one of the world's largest oil producers. Thus the economic position of any country in Africa may change overnight with the discovery of a vital mineral and the picture presented by today's statistics may be changed radically tomorrow. Figure 9.1 illustrates the more important mineral deposits in Africa.

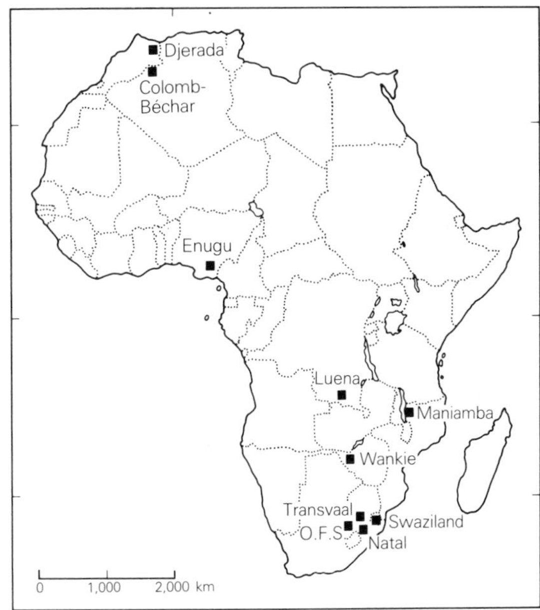

Fig. 9.2 Africa – location of important coal producing regions

Coal

Despite its size as the second largest continent, Africa is one of the poorest in coal reserves. Sizeable coal deposits are limited to isolated pockets, mainly in the southern half of the continent where luxuriant forest and fern growth flourished during the Permo-Carboniferous age – in South Africa and Zimbabwe. Lower grade coal is mined in Nigeria, Mozambique and Zaïre, and there are other deposits in Tanzania, Madagascar, Malaŵi and Zambia.

These deposits form only a fraction of the world's total coal reserves of nearly 9 000 000 million tonnes, of which the Soviet Union possesses 6 000 000 million tonnes, the United States 1 400 000 million tonnes, Europe 560 000 million tonnes and Africa a rather low 85 000 million tonnes.

South Africa – coal as the basis for heavy industry

The first coal mined at Molteno, Cape Province, in 1864 began the extraction of a mineral which was to

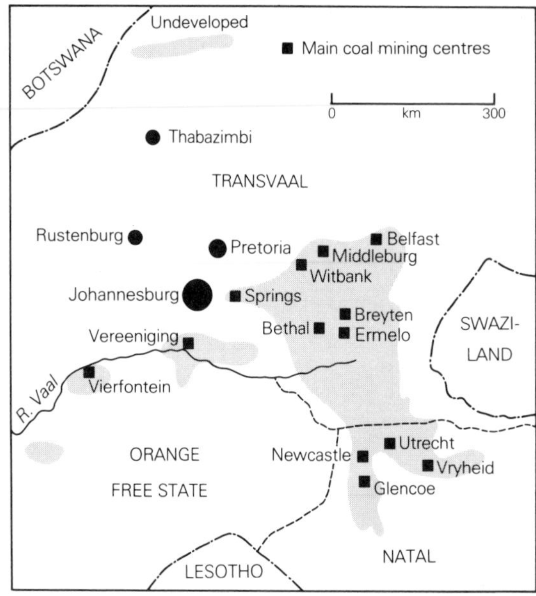

Fig. 9.3 South Africa – main coal producing areas

form a basis for South Africa's industrial expansion over the following 100 years. In 1879 the Vereeniging field was discovered and large-scale exploitation began. Helped by the discovery of gold, the general development of mining and secondary industry, and the needs of the railway and bunkering trade, South Africa soon became Africa's foremost coal producer. Increasing amounts were used for thermal electric power after 1900, and by the southern continents during the First World War.

The main producing fields are shown on the map (Fig. 9.3). Of the three producing states, the Transvaal is the largest (approximately 62 per cent of output), followed by the Orange Free State (23 per cent) and Natal (15 per cent). The Transvaal Witbank collieries are the heaviest producers and the coal is good steam coal, although rather unsuitable for coking. Its rapid exploitation is due to its closeness to the Rand (130 km) and to the ease of extraction. Seams average 20 m thick and lie close to the surface, while mining is safe, for the seams are stable and there is little gas. These factors and the low labour costs make the coal the cheapest in the world (US$2,60 per tonne at pit head). Other major mining centres in the Transvaal include Vereeniging, Bethal, Ermelo, Belfast and Boksburg. The Witbank field produces about 13 million tonnes a year, the Springs field 2 million and the Vereeniging 3 million tonnes.

In the Orange Free State coal mining is confined to the northern fringe centred around Vierfontein, with a small mining zone 27 km south-east of Vereeniging where the lower quality coal goes to the power station near Klerksdorp on the Vaal and to the Sasolburg oil-from-coal plant.

In Natal the chief centres are Vryheid (half the field's output), Utrecht, Dundee and Newcastle. Seams are thinner here and more faulted, but there is much high-grade coking and steam coal. South Africa's coal is vital to the nation's economy. Ten per cent of annual output is used on the railways and by the secondary industries. Urban centres take over a third, while the iron and steel industry uses 2,6 million tonnes annually of the higher-grade coking coals. The monthly internal consumption of coal in South Africa is greater than the annual production of Zimbabwe, Africa's second largest producer – 4,3 million tonnes of bituminous and 50 000 t of anthracite each month. A large proportion of Natal's output goes to Durban for bunkering, while 690 000 t of bituminous and 430 000 t of anthracite are exported annually.

What of the future? South Africa's coal reserves are estimated at a staggering 76 000 million tonnes with 90 per cent in the Transvaal, and at the present rate of consumption this will last South Africa for 1 500 years. Coal output is increasing rapidly – in 1970 the output was 55,5 million tonnes which had risen to 65 million tonnes by 1975, roughly equal to Australia's output and about one-seventh that of China. South Africa's exports of just over a million tonnes a year represent about 6 per cent of world sea coal trade and could be easily expanded, especially with increasing demands from power hungry Europe.

Central Africa – the strategic value of coal

Zimbabwe also possesses coal reserves of considerable size. In the Wankie area of the south-west there are 5 000 million tonnes of bituminous coal, much of high coking quality. At West Sabi there are 4 320 million tonnes of poorer grade non-coking coal with a rather high ash content in beds some 15 m thick.

The Wankie field is the only one to be exploited commercially in Zimbabwe, and, although produc-

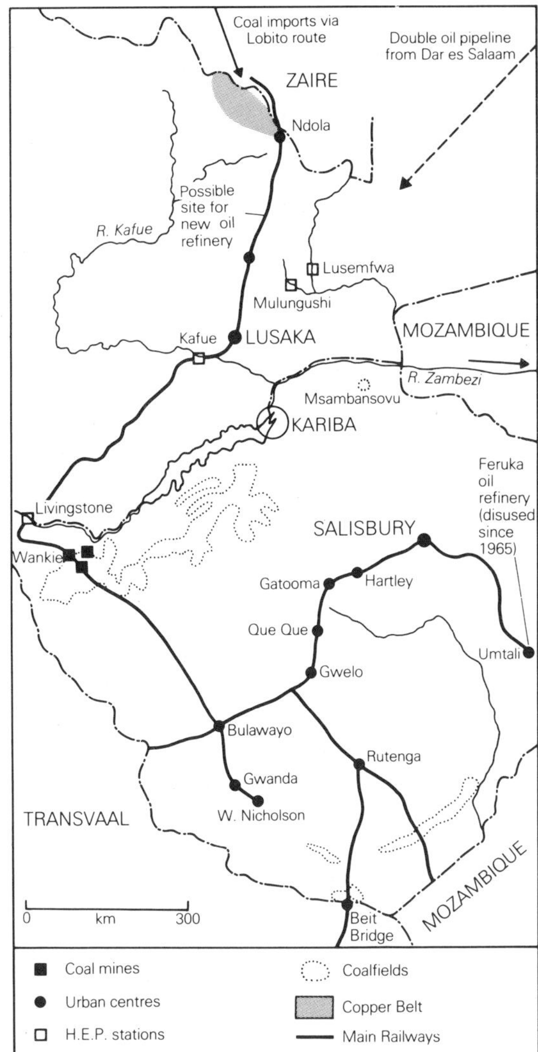

Fig. 9.4 Zimbabwe and Zambia – fuel and power resources

tion is but a tenth of South Africa's, the coal plays a vital role in the industrial economy of central Africa. The deposit lies close to the surface in seams 1 to 8 m thick and inclined shafts are used; the coal is amongst the world's cheapest (US$3 at the pit head and US$5 delivered price). Some 250 000 t of coke are produced annually for use in the iron and steel plants of Zimbabwe and in the Copper Belt. A special type of coke – char – is now being produced at Gwelo at the rate of 700 t a month for use in smelting ferro-chrome.

Coal production from Wankie began in 1903 and grew with the development of the Copper Belt and the railways. By 1927 over a million tonnes a year were being mined and with the post-war boom the three collieries at Wankie were able to produce six million tonnes. Although this amount was never needed by Rhodesia, Wankie could, like South Africa, be geared to a much greater export trade than at present.

The railways, on which depend the movement of Zimbabwe's many minerals, take over a quarter of production, the Wankie mines and associated industries take 10 per cent, and the rest goes to the Copper Belt and iron and steel plants. With the greater use of Kariba power there has been a lessening of demand from these consumers.

The coal was once more vital to Zambia's industrial structure than Zimbabwe's, for Wankie coal was one of the few imports Zambia could not replace from other sources. No less than 70 per cent of Zambia's fuel needs for her locomotives, thermal power stations and copper smelters came from Wankie. The Shaba–Zambia Copper Belt took 772 000 t of coal annually. Zambia has partly broken this economic dependence by using coal deposits within her own boundaries. But Nkandabwe coal mine, the first coal mine in Zambia and which once produced some 20 000 t each month, was closed down owing to flooding. The main mine in Zambia today is the Maamba colliery opened in 1965–66. The coal has to be transported down a 19 km-long aerial ropeway from the top of the Zambezi escarpment to Masuku, the railhead. Recently, the mine has produced an average of 4 000 t of coal per day, which is more than enough to supply the demand from all users in Zambia of 85 000 t a month. The main problem has been the inadequacy of the railways to move this amount. The coal is first washed to improve its quality before being sent to consumers. The chief users of coal are the ammonium nitrate plant at Kafue, the cement works at Chilanga, the rapidly growing brick industry and the power station at Chingola.

Tanzania – untapped reserves

Some 200 million tonnes of good quality coking coal also lie in the Ruhuhu River basin on the eastern side of Lake Malaŵi and in the Kivira-Songwe field near the north-western end of the lake in the Southern Province of Tanzania. Tanzania, with the aid of Chinese technicians, is already engaged on the construction of a link line from the railway to these mineral deposits. While only small, the reserves could be important in future industrial expansion in Tanzania.

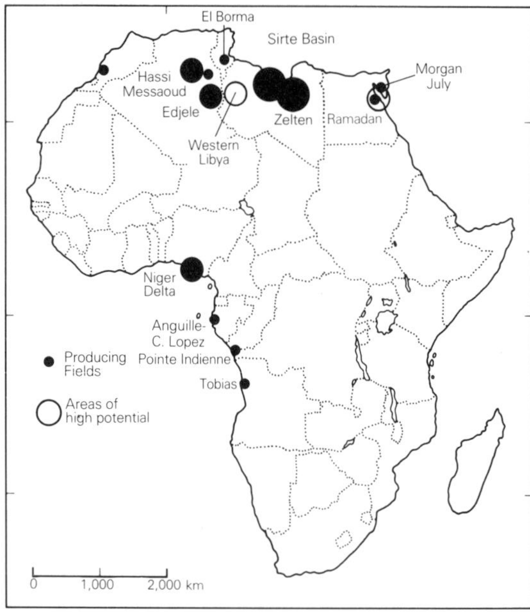

Fig. 9.5 Africa – main oil producing regions

Oil

While her coal output is negligible when compared with total world output, Africa is fast becoming one of the world's leaders in the production of mineral oil. In 1950 only Egypt was a significant producer (2,3 million tonnes) out of the world's 550 million tonnes; by 1960 Africa's output had leaped to 13,2 million tonnes (world 1 109 million tonnes), and in 1964 to 81 million tonnes (world 1 477 million tonnes). By the mid-1970s world production had risen to 2 600 million tonnes with Africa's share nearly 290 million tonnes or about 11 per cent. Proved reserves of petroleum are in the region of 100 000 million tonnes with probable reserves starting at about 250 million. Of the proved reserves, the Middle East has 53 per cent, the Soviet Union, eastern Europe and China have 15 per cent, Africa 15 per cent, the United States six per cent, and Latin America five per cent.

Nigeria, Libya and Algeria are now among the top fourteen world producers of oil. Nigeria and Algeria are also large producers of natural gas with exports to the United States, while Libya exports large quantities to Europe.

The oil-deficient south

While states south of the equator control Africa's coal, north African countries control the continent's oil. Except for Gabon, Congo and Angola there are no important fields in the south. Table 13 shows the production by country.

Africa south of the Sahara produces only nine per cent of the continent's oil with none from coal-rich South Africa and Zimbabwe. East Africa is also poor, no known commercially important deposits as yet discovered. In Kenya alone some millions of dollars have been spent in the seemingly fruitless search for oil. Countries in East Africa are forced to import vast quantities of oil. South Africa imported over US$100 million worth of crude petroleum, motor spirit and other oils in 1966, nearly 12,5 per cent of all her imports. To break the dependence on outside supplies the South African Government embarked on the Sasol Oil-From-Coal Project in 1952, some 27 km from Vereeniging, at a cost of US$100 million. The plant lies near 300 million tonnes of OFS coal and produces 260 million litres of petrol annually as well as gases, tars and 100 million litres of oils. The plant consumes each day 5 600 t of coal. A second plant is to be built in the eastern Transvaal and will have a capacity ten times that of the Sasolburg unit, and a new coal mine will be opened up to supply the plant, which is expected to be completed in 1981. The existing Sasolburg plant produces four per cent of South Africa's fuel needs, while the new plant is designed to produce 25 per cent of the country's needs by 1982, using 14 million tonnes of coal a year.

Zimbabwe

The recent political and economic disturbances in Central Africa have underlined the great dependence

Table 13 Africa crude oil production, 1975–1980 ('000 barrels daily)

OPEC members		*Non-OPEC members*			
	1975		*1975*	*1977*	*1980*
Nigeria	1 787	Egypt	230	450	530
Libya	1 510	Angola	166	175	225
Algeria	960	Tunisia	95	100	120
Gabon	200	Congo	38	35	45
		Zaïre	2	50	50

the central African States have on imported oil. Zimbabwe consumes over 400 000 t of crude oil annually, and oil accounts for 27 per cent of Zimbabwe's energy requirements; some is used in diesel locomotives and 40 per cent is used by motor vehicles. Before 1965 the oil was brought to Beira by tanker from the Middle East, then fed through pipelines to the Feruka oil refinery at Umtali. With sanctions, Beira was blockaded by the British Navy and Rhodesia imported oil by rail through Lourenço Marques (now Maputo). With Mozambique's independence this route has been replaced by routes from South Africa, particularly along the newly-built Rutenga rail route. This dependence on imported oil prompted Rhodesia to develop her coalfields and was a contributory factor to the construction of the Kariba Dam.

Zambia

Zambia also relied on the Mozambique pipeline, 92 per cent of its oil imports coming through Umtali and thence by lorry and rail; half of these imports are used as petrol. However, Zambia is less dependent on oil than Zimbabwe and it supplies only 14 per cent of Zambia's needs. Zambia uses about 320 000 t of oil a year.

The higher oil prices introduced during the 1970s have been detrimental to the economic growth of many developing nations in Africa. For example, eleven countries which have their own oil refineries in Africa paid US$530 million for oil in 1974 compared with US$155 million in 1973 (an increase of over 240 per cent), while the 22 African countries which import oil from refineries elsewhere paid US$360 million in 1974 compared with US$140 million in 1973 (a 157 per cent increase). Tanzania paid nearly US$100 million for oil imports in 1973, US$533 million for the same quantity of oil in 1974, and US$550 million in 1975.

The oil-rich north

While southern and central Africa import vast quantities of oil, the northern territories are among the world's largest exporters of crude petroleum, since their own industrial economies (except for Egypt) are insufficiently developed to absorb their huge production. Prior to 1957 only Egypt produced any oil of note, but since then several countries have leaped into prominence.

Egypt

Egypt has small oilfields west of the Suez Gulf and in the south-west of the Sinai Peninsula. Pre-war production averaged an annual 254 000 t, but with the development of secondary industries great efforts were made to increase oil production and cut imports. The late 1950s saw production rise to over three million tonnes and the 1975 oil production of nine million tonnes was about equal to consumption. Exploration in Egypt has proved the existence of 30 oil and gas fields, mostly small, with proved reserves of 450 million tonnes of oil and substantial natural gas reserves. The Morgan field in the Gulf of Suez area is the largest producer but is declining. It was largely responsible for Egypt's high production in 1971 of 16,4 million tonnes. The new July and Ramadan fields close to Morgan may repeat this record when fully exploited. A ten-year programme (1974–84) of exploration has been embarked on which has set a production target of 50 million tonnes a year by 1984 and requires the drilling of 400 exploratory wells. Egypt's crude oil production in 1976 was 18,4 million tonnes.

Algeria

Algeria's oil production began only in 1958. Oil was first discovered at Edjele in 1956 followed by several other finds, of which the most important was the Hassi Messaoud field. Algeria is now a major world producer: 1959 – 1,32 million tonnes, 1960 – 8,75 million tonnes, 1963 – 23,7 million tonnes, 1964 – 26,6 million tonnes, 1971 – 36,3 million tonnes, 1974 – 50 million tonnes. Present proved reserves in Algeria amount to about 1 000 million tonnes, 1,1 per cent of the world's and one-third Libya's. The world's largest natural gas field lies at Hassi R'Mel. Pipelines lead to coastal fuelling points – from Hassi Messaoud to Bougie (length 740 km, completed 1959) and from Edjele to La Skirra (800 km, opened June 1960), with a combined capacity of 25,4 million tonnes annually. A third pipeline (annual capacity 22,3 million tonnes) has been built from Haoud el Hamra to Arzew. In 1973 Algeria exported over US$1 000 million worth of oil which represented over 65 per cent of exports by value, while earnings in 1974 from oil trebled to US$3 200 million due to oil price increases. Of Algeria's total production, France takes 65 per cent; other important customers include West Germany, the United Kingdom, Italy, the Netherlands, Spain, Belgium and the United States.

While Algeria's oil production is small compared with the big Arab producers, her natural gas reserves are the third largest in the world. Large gas liquefaction plants are located at Skikda and Arzew and these have their counterparts (turning the liquid back to gas) on Canvey Island in Britain and in Le Havre, northern France.

Libya

Libya's rise as a world oil producer has been even more meteoric than Algeria's. Oil had been known to exist in 1900 and traces of oil and gas discovered before 1914. The Italians made extensive reconnaissances but the Second World War delayed efficient exploration, first concessions being granted to oil companies in 1959 and production beginning in 1961. By 1963 Libya was producing 22,3 million tonnes, over 40 million by 1964, and 51 million by 1965. In 1971 a peak of 126 million tonnes was reached but due to self-imposed restrictions this had dropped to 107 million tonnes in 1972. At the end of 1973 Libya was outstripped by Nigeria. Libya's proved reserves amount to 3,3 per cent of the world total and stand at over 3 000 million tonnes. British, United States, Italian, West German, Dutch and

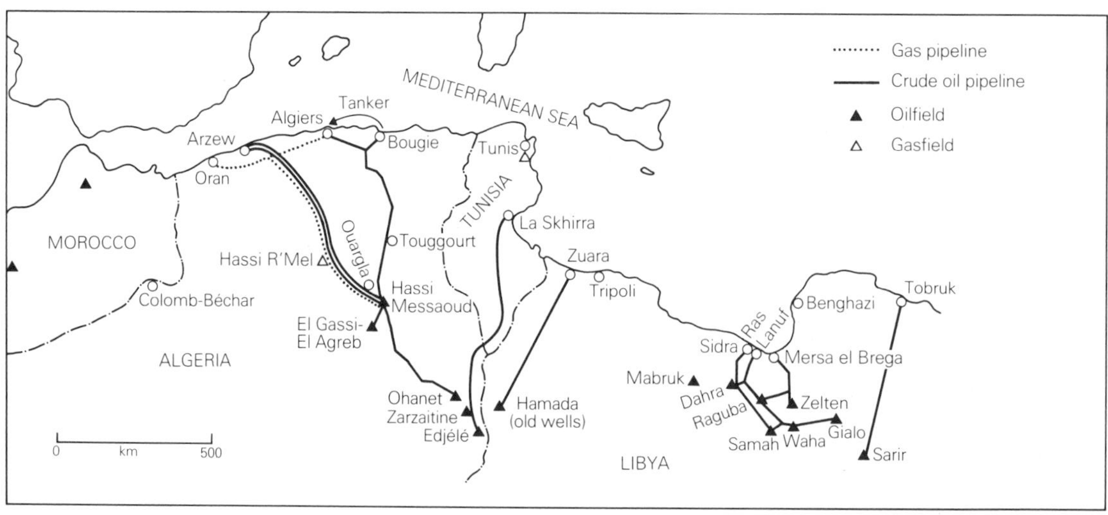

Fig. 9.6 North Africa – location of major oil fields

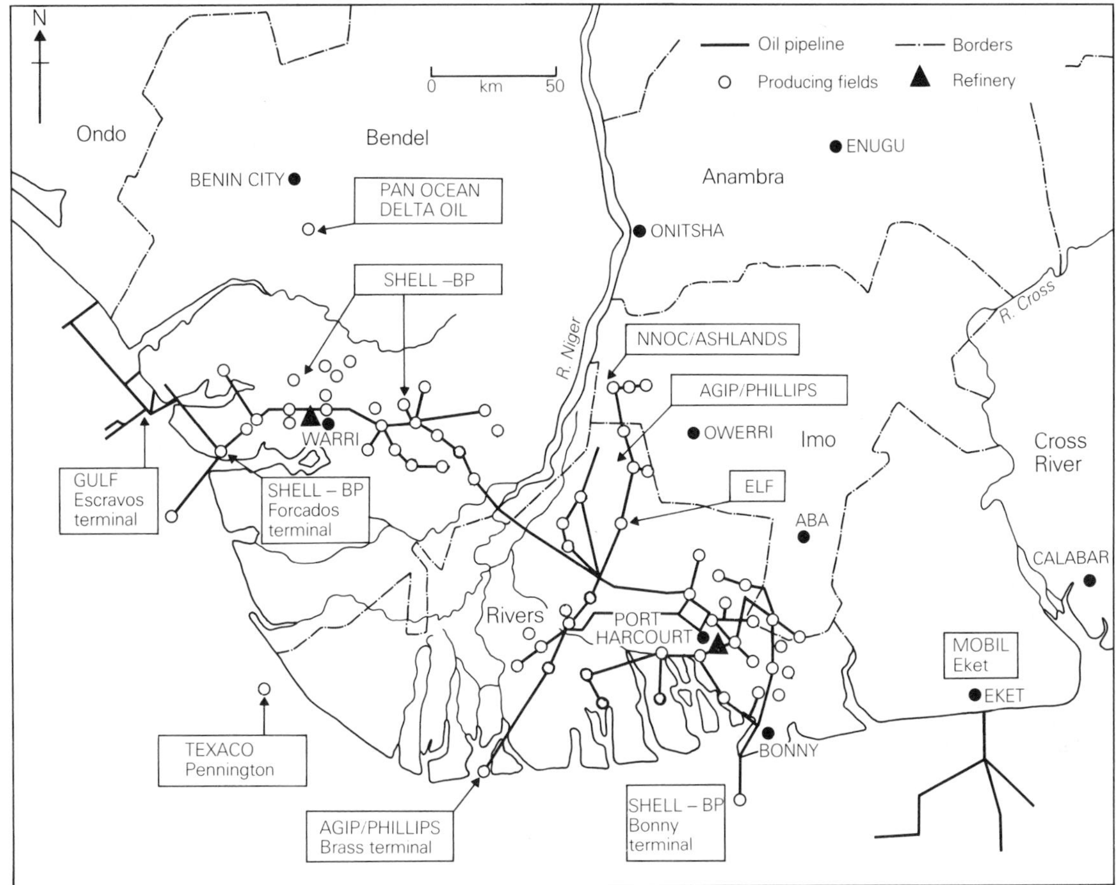

Fig. 9.7 Nigeria – the Niger Delta showing the development of the oil industry

Spanish firms are investing staggering sums of money. Today oil flows along four pipelines (Zelten and Raguba to Mersa el Brega, Dahra and Marbruk to Sidra, Gialo and Waha to Ras Lanuf, and Sarir to Tobruk).

The fact that crude oil is a wasting asset has been recognised by the Libyan Government which aims to diversify its economy and lessen dependence on oil. At present rates of production, Libya's proved oil reserves will last for about 40 years. National plans call for industrial development in the food processing, building and chemical and petro-chemical industries, and the establishment of a national iron and steel industry is under consideration. But it is in the agricultural sector, which employs 30 per cent of the labour force, where oil revenues are being invested, and where greatest expansion will take place. The aim is to make Libya self-sufficient in staple foods – wheat, barley and meat – by investment in agricultural research, experiments with irrigation methods, especially in the remote south of Libya, and in rangeland projects.

Nigeria

Nigeria, while short of high-grade coal (output about 51 000 t per year, mainly for the railways), is one of the fastest developing oil regions in the world and the Niger delta is one of the richest oil fields in Africa. Oil mining began in 1937, but it was not until 1956 that commercial deposits were discovered and production began in 1958 at the Oloibiri Field. Since 1958 production has increased from 257 000 t to 112,8 million tonnes (1974) although there was a 15 per cent reduction in output in 1975. During the period 1958–74, Nigeria's known crude oil reserves increased from 17 million tonnes to 4 800 million tonnes which, at present rates of production, would last Nigeria until the year 2020 A.D. New fields are being discovered frequently and probable reserves, estimated at 7 000 million tonnes, will be enough to last until 2040 A.D. In addition, Nigeria has huge reserves of natural gas, a cheap, clean industrial fuel.

There are also very good prospects of locating other oilfields within Nigeria, for about half of the country's total area consists of sedimentary basins in which oil-bearing strata are likely to occur. These basins cover approximately 450 000 square kilometres, occupying large areas inland from the delta and extending in two broad arms north-west along the Niger Valley through Sokoto State and into Niger, and north-east along the Benue valley towards the Chad Basin (see map, Fig. 1.12). Oil experts also believe that the continental shelf off Nigeria's coastline has yet to reveal its full oil potential.

Today, 19 companies, of which three are Nigerian, the rest being from the United States (11), Britain, France, West Germany, Italy and Japan, are engaged in Nigeria's oil industry. In 1975, oil exports earned Nigeria a staggering US$6 400 million and in 1977, a peak year, US$11 400 million (compare 1970 – US$845 million). Oil exports in 1977 represented 91,3 per cent by value of Nigeria's total exports. Nigerian oil sells at a higher price than most oils since it has a low sulphur content and is of a lighter specific gravity. Moreover, Nigeria is reasonably close to markets in Western Europe, South America and the United States. The country is now the United States' largest supplier, and satisfies about one-third of that country's requirements and about 15 per cent of Britain's needs. The United Kingdom, Italy and France take about half the output, the United States, a quarter. Nigeria is now the seventh ranking producer of oil in the world.

We must now examine in some detail how this new-found wealth has affected Nigeria's economy in the fields of energy supply, employment, foreign exchange position, and contribution to the country's gross domestic product:

1 *Energy supply:* Despite Nigeria's huge oil production, the country has suffered continuously from a shortage of petrol and petroleum products. This is due to the fact that the bulk of production is exported in crude form for refining overseas, and up to now there has been only one refinery, the Elesa Eleme refinery near Port Harcourt, to cater for Nigeria's needs. This refinery had an initial capacity of nearly 2,0 million tonnes of petroleum products but could not produce aviation fuels, lubricating oils and bitumen in the quantities needed. Production ceased during the Civil War but now the refinery is producing some 2,75 million tonnes per annum. This is to be expanded to 3,75 million tonnes and by 1980 two other refineries will be completed – one at Warri, and the other at Kaduna in the northern part of the country.

   Nigeria is also making use of the vast quantities of natural gas in industries associated with the oil centres, for thermal power generation, and as a fuel in the oil refining process itself.

2 *Employment:* A large number of employment opportunities were created during initial preparations at the oil sites on road and bridge building, site clearance, transport, and construction of housing facilities. Many Nigerians were trained in drilling techniques and as supervisors and managers. About 4 500 are employed in the industry, while a further 15 000 are engaged in concerns which are linked to the oil industry.

3 *Foreign exchange:* The oil sector of Nigeria's economy now accounts for most of the country's foreign exchange income. In 1963, Nigeria's total foreign exchange income was US$689 million, of which oil's contribution was 6,9 per cent; in 1970 the figures were US$527 million and 27,5 per cent; in 1974, US$9 983 and 86,3 per cent; in 1975, US$6 400 million and 90,3 per cent.

   Nigeria's oil refinery near Port Harcourt also saves the country much foreign exchange which she would otherwise have spent on imported oils. For example, in 1964 Nigeria spent nearly US$62 million on imported refined fuels and in 1965, US$54 million; during the first year, 1966, that the Elesa Eleme refinery was fully operating, the oil import bill dropped to US$8,8 million.

4 *The gross national product:* The oil industry's contribution to Nigeria's Gross National Product (GNP), that is, the value of output, less costs, of all sectors of the economy, is now 41 per cent. This is lower than may be expected because a substantial part of the payments received must be paid to outside companies who are financing

operations. In the future, oil contribution to the GNP is likely to fall to about 31 per cent as other sectors, e.g. agriculture and manufacturing industry develop and increase their own contributions.

5 *Other contributions:* The oil industry also helps Nigeria's economy by making direct payments to the government in the form of royalties, tax payments, rents, harbour dues, etc., and by injecting capital into society through wage payments, purchases of equipment and food, educational grants, employment of Nigerian contractors, and so on. About US$1 600 million is spent annually on goods and services and about US$1 130 million is paid each year to the government in royalties and rents.

Because of oil's contribution to the economy, Nigeria is one of the few developing countries which can go ahead with ambitious development programmes without having to rely on loans and grants from foreign sources. However, Nigeria faces vast problems, as mentioned elsewhere in this book. Most of the money derived from oil will be swallowed up in rural development, for there are many regions in Nigeria still untouched by the results of the oil boom. Looked at on a per capita basis, Nigeria falls far behind some of the Middle East states. For example, Saudi Arabia has a population of approximately 8 million and oil reserves of 24 000 million tonnes giving a per capita average of 3 000 million tonnes; comparative figures for Nigeria are 4 800 million tonnes and a population of about 80 million, giving 60 million tonnes per capita. However, Nigeria is assured of considerable development capital over the next 50 years. The oil wealth will obviously not last for ever, but, while it does, the government has the opportunity to build a solid foundation for the nation's economy in agriculture, secondary industry and the necessary infrastructure essential to these sectors.

The mineral ores

Copper – the Zambia–Shaba monopoly

Copper is one of the most sought after metals of the modern technical age. With its alloys, bronze and brass, it is used extensively in the manufacture of household utensils, food processing equipment, brewery vats and stills, machinery bearings, rust-resisting tubes, the wire of dynamo armatures and giant alternators, electronic equipment, coins, tele-

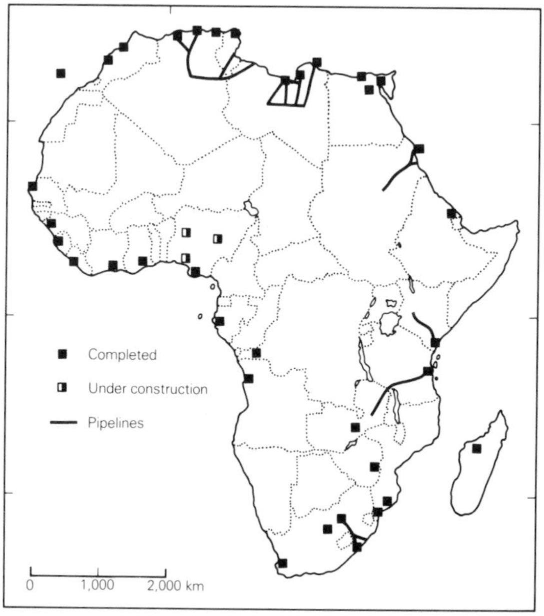

Fig. 9.8 Africa – location of oil refineries and pipelines

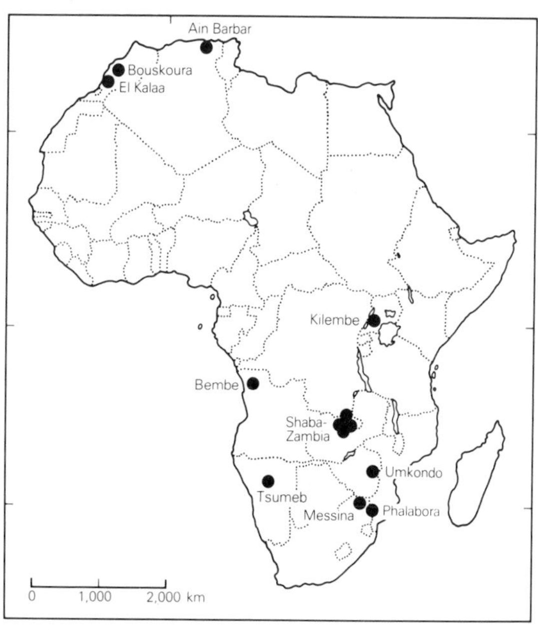

Fig. 9.9 Africa – major copper producing areas

vision screens, military weapons, and the world's network of submarine cables and high tension wires.

Copper is thus in great demand by the industrial nations and production has been increased to satisfy the demand. In 1865 world production was 100 000 t, in 1913 one million tonnes, in 1939 two million tonnes, in 1955 three million tonnes, in 1960 four million tonnes, in 1966 4,8 million tonnes and in 1975 7,6 million tonnes. Of this 87 per cent is taken by North America, Japan and Western Europe. World copper production at seven and a half million tonnes, is just sufficient for world demands.

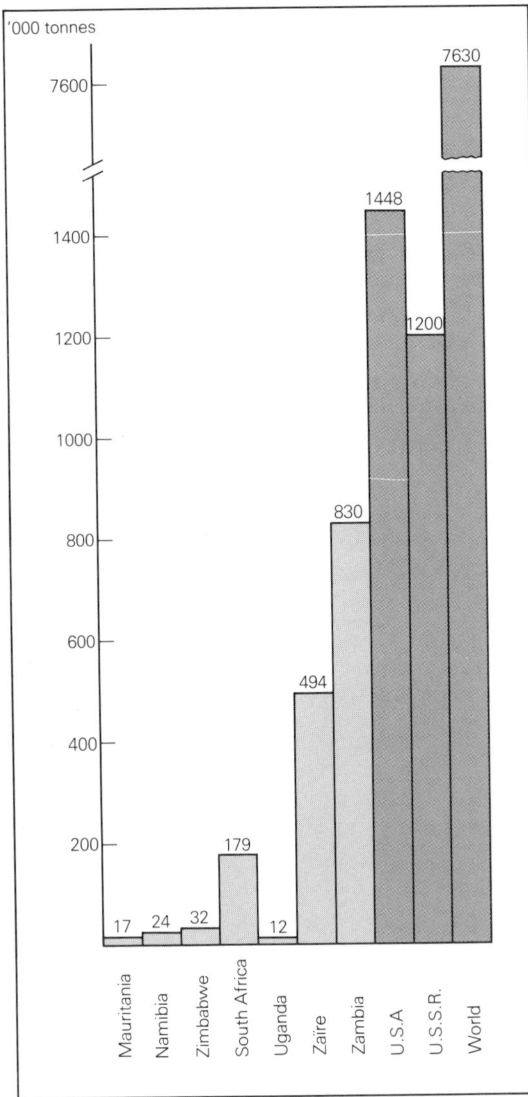

Fig. 9.10 World production of copper in 1975

Figure 9.10 shows the important position which Africa holds in the production of this vital mineral. Zambia ranks third after the United States and Shaba (Zaïre) lies fourth. Combined, the two form the Copper Belt of central Africa, a mining zone 450 km long by 260 km wide which produces 16 per cent of the world's copper and 66 per cent of its cobalt, a valuable heat-resisting alloy.

In 1867 Livingstone described the smelting of copper ore by the Katangans into large ingots weighing 20 to 50 kg, which were later used to make anklets and rings. At the end of the nineteenth century several British and Belgian prospectors discovered large copper ore deposits near the African diggings. A short-lived commercial partnership was struck between Belgian and British companies but with the establishment of the Union Minière du Haut Katanga in 1906 the Copper Belt was worked as two separate entities.

Zambia

Copper production in Zambia did not begin until the southern railway reached Kabwe in 1909.

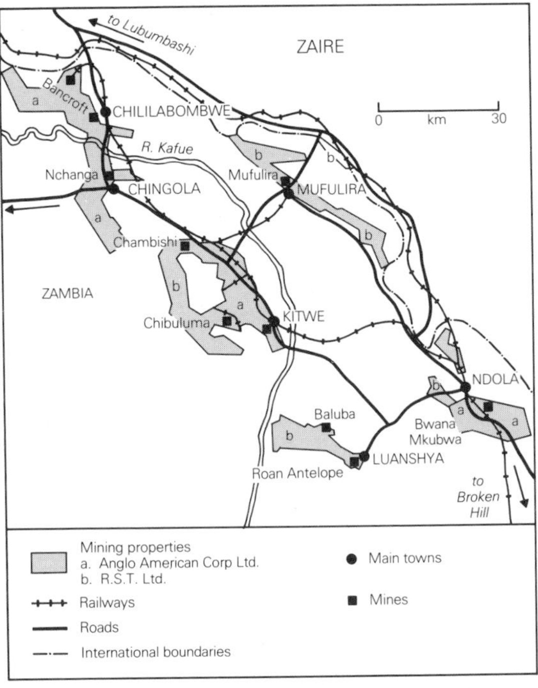

Fig. 9.11 Zambia – the Copper Belt towns and concession zones

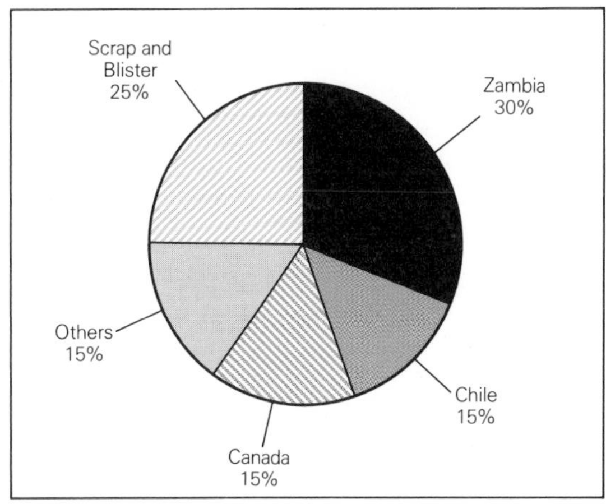

Fig. 9.12 The importance of Zambia's copper to Britain

Development was retarded by disease, inaccessibility and technical ignorance. The First World War caused further delay but by the 1920s large-scale development had begun, followed by the opening of several mines – Roan Antelope and Nkana (1931), Mufulira (1933) and Nchanga (1939). The Second World War stimulated production and the post-war years saw the opening of the Chibaluma (1955) and Bancroft (1957) Mines. The new Chambishi Mine became fully operational at the end of 1965 with the commissioning of the new concentrating plant there. The Anglo-American Corporation is now using improved recovery methods at a new mine near Nchanga – the Mimbula Fitula Mine where ore reserves estimated at 11,7 million tonnes with a 3,9 per cent copper content lie at a depth of only 150 m. This new mine cost about US$10 million and is of the open cast type. The Corporation is also developing the Bwana Mkubwa and Nampundwe Mines. Old mines such as the Allies Mine near Lusaka are to be opened up; this mine was abandoned in 1920 but it still contains some 170 000 t of ore.

Today the Zambian Copper Belt covers a zone 110 km long by 50 km wide and accounts for 10 per cent of total world production. The belt contains 25 per cent of the world's proved copper reserves. In 1970 Zambia received £366,6 million from copper out of a total mineral production valued at £384,2 million; in 1974 copper exports were valued at £654 million out of a total export value of £706 million. The mineral completely dominates the country's economy, the copper industry being the largest customer of the railways and the greatest consumer of power. The belt is a complex of mining towns with a total population exceeding a quarter of a million. Near each of the six major mines, townships have developed with shopping centres and commercial zones. The largest is Kitwe (250 000) near Nkana Mine, a commercial and industrial centre with electrolytic copper refineries. Ndola (230 000) lies north of the Bwana Mkubwa Mine (closed in 1931) and is the main junction for the Copper Belt and Shaba. It has copper, cobalt and sugar refineries and its regional airport serves Zambia.

Various other minerals are extracted in the Zambian belt – cobalt (Chibaluma and Nkaṇa), and gold and silver are removed during copper processing, while zinc, manganese and lead are mined in the Kabwe district. But copper is dominant and accounts for more than 97 per cent of Zambia's exports by value.

Like most countries which depend on one export commodity for their revenue, Zambia is at the mercy of overseas price fluctuations for copper. In 1971 the price per metric tonne reached £425 on the London market; this dropped to £400 in 1972, rose to £900 by the end of 1973 and by mid-1974 had risen to an all time high of £1 400 per tonne. In 1974 it had dropped to £600, further to £513 in 1975, and rose to £650 in 1977. Such fluctuations mean that a government is not able to plan very far ahead since it is unsure of the revenue it can expect from the mining companies.

Shaba, Zaïre

The Katanga Copper Belt was linked to the outside world when the Broken Hill line reached Lubumbashi, then Elizabethville, in September 1910, and the first copper exports reached Antwerp, Belgium, in 1912 via the southern rail routes. The completion of other outlet routes (see below) resulted in the Union Minière becoming the world's largest producer of copper and cobalt in the early 1930s, a place later yielded to Zambia.

The Shaba, or Katanga, Belt extends 320 km from Lubumbashi north-westwards to Kolwezi, and is a concentration of deep and open-cast mines, refineries, concentration plants and hydro-electric power stations. The main deposits lie close to the surface and are open-cast at Kolwezi, Ruwe and

Zaïre: Opencast mining of copper at Kolwezi.

Musonoi-Kamato. The ore, which contains six to eight per cent copper, is sent to the Shituri plant near Likasi and to the Luili refinery at Kolwezi. Poorer ores (four per cent copper) are mined at Kipushi, where shafts go down to 440 m. The belt produces between 410 000 and 460 000 t annually.

Besides copper, there are 150 various other mineral deposits including cobalt, radium and uranium (at Chinolobwe), lime, manganese, tin, zinc, coal and iron ore. Copper represents about 30 per cent of all Zaïre's exports. The chief city of Shaba Province is Lubumbashi, with Likasi as a secondary regional centre.

Problems

Two major problems have faced the Copper Belt throughout its development – the great fuel needs for copper refining processes and the need for commercial outlets for the refined copper. The Shaba Belt used rather poor coal from Luena but when this was exhausted expensive imports had to be railed from Rhodesia's Wankie field. Several hydro-electric stations were built, e.g. at Le Marinel on the Lualaba and at Mwadingushi on the Lufira, and before Kariba these supplied power to the Rhodesia Belt. The Rhodesia section was able to supply power by importing HEP, coal and oil, and by using local coal and wood. Today the Kariba Dam will be able to fulfil the Copper Belt's major power requirements for many years to come.

The construction of outlets for the refined copper from the land-locked Copper Belt illustrates how political considerations override economic ones. The routes which have been or are used for exporting are:

a The Cape route, briefly used during the early twentieth century.

b The Benguela route (1 500 km) begun by the British with Belgian and Portuguese consent in 1900 and completed 1933; the line was extended to Lobito since Benguela became unsuitable for large ore vessels; in normal times approximately

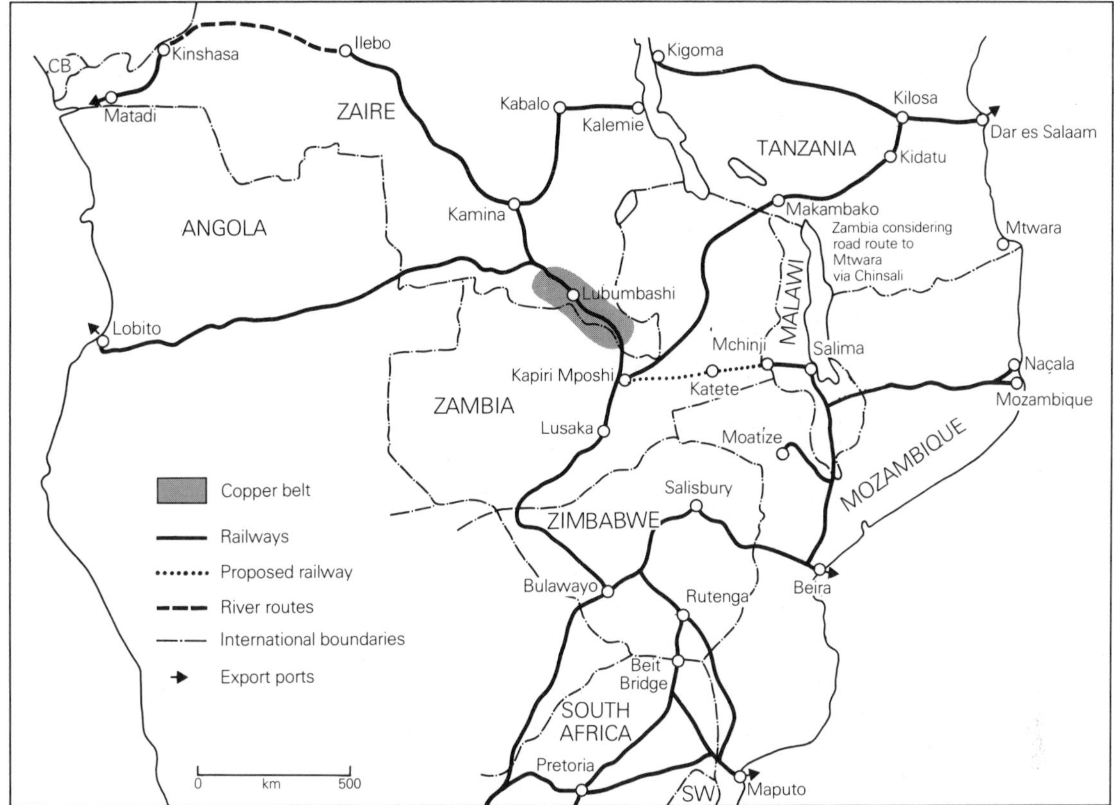

Fig. 9.13 The Copper Belt – main outlet routes

25 000 t or 45 per cent of Zambian copper ore were sent by this route.

c The Voie Nationale, conceived by King Leopold to break Katanga's dependence on foreign export routes. The railway runs north from Lubumbashi to Ilebo where the ore is unloaded onto river barges which take it down the Kasai River to Kinshasa; it then travels by rail to Matadi to be loaded onto sea-going ore vessels. A railway to link Ilebo with Kinshasa is now planned.

d The Kamina–Kalemie–Kigoma–Dar-es-Salaam route is now little used but is being considered as an alternative route by Zambia.

e The more direct railway route via Umtali, Zimbabwe and Beira, Mozambique. This was much used but Beira suffered congestion during the post-war boom period in the Rhodesias.

f A subsidiary rail route to Maputo via Bulawayo. This round-about route was replaced in 1957 by the Limpopo line via Bannockburn and this route took increasing amounts of copper concentrate until recent disturbances.

The new Tanzam (Tazara or Uhuru) Railway completed in 1975 provides a new outlet from Kapiri Mposhi through Makambako and thence to Dar-es-Salaam, a distance of 1 677 km. This is also paralleled by a road. This route has not been as successful as had been hoped largely due to the congestion at Dar-es-Salaam, and only about 45 000 t travelled this way each month in 1975. This still leaves a further 20 000 t a month to be transported and about 10 per cent of this goes by rail and road to Mombasa. An alternative route which could take a maximum of 10 000 t is by lorry on the road from Lusaka via Katete to Mchinji in Malaŵi, where it can be loaded on to rail trucks for railing via Salima to either Beira or Nacala in Mozambique.

The easiest route would be via Livingstone, across the Victoria Falls Bridge and via Bulawayo to either

Beira via Salisbury and Umtali or to Maputo. The border between Zimbabwe and Zambia has been opened. In 1975 and 1976 the more direct but longer route of the Benguela line was closed due to the civil war in Angola. Prior to Angola's independence from Portuguese rule it had been planned to double the capacity of this route by constructing a second line called the Cubal variant.

Southern Africa

Other important copper deposits known to exist in Southern Africa but not yet exploited commercially are the 33,5 million tonnes proven by the Roan Selection Trust in Botswana, and the rich reserves discovered in 1968 in Vendaland, in the northern Transvaal, South Africa; the latter, located near Sabasa, are believed to be twice as rich as the deposits in South West Africa and may have enough copper to support five or six mines.

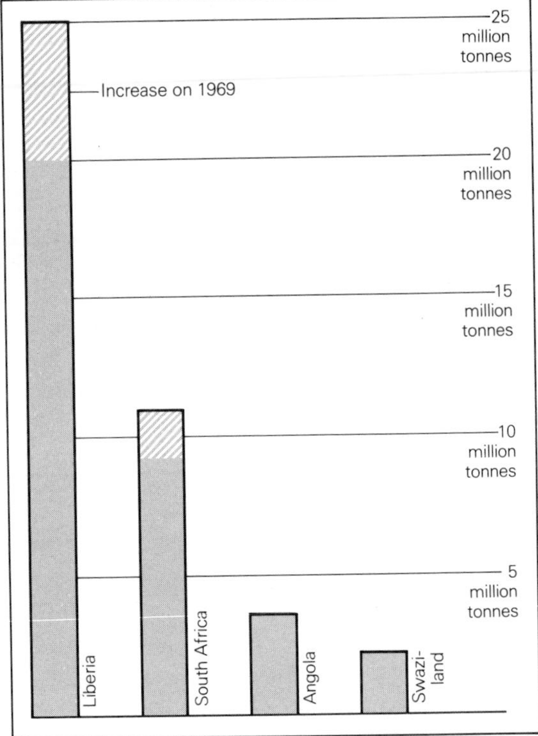

Fig. 9.14 Africa south of the Sahara – iron ore production, 1969 and 1974

Iron ore – its effects on the economy of African states

Iron ore is one of the basic minerals for heavy industrial development. While Africa produces only 4 per cent of the world's iron ore several important recent finds indicate that the continent could be a major producer (Fig. 9.15). The deposits so far exploited for large-scale steel production lie in South Africa and Zimbabwe near to limestone and coal. Elsewhere iron ore is mined by large foreign companies for export. Like oil, the discovery of iron ore has broadened the economy of several nations, e.g. Liberia, Swaziland and Mauritania, and has attracted tremendous international interest and investment.

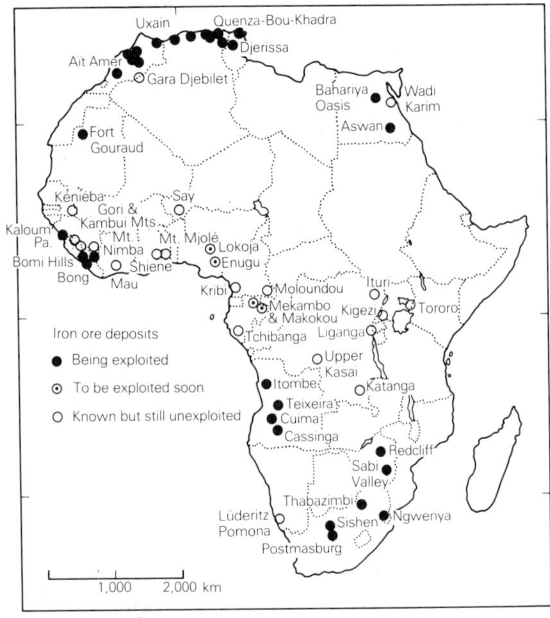

Fig. 9.15 Africa – location of iron ore deposits

Swaziland

In Swaziland, where the population is traditionally engaged in cultivation, minerals are helping to broaden the economy and already form 25 per cent of export earnings. The territory is rich in mineral deposits, particularly asbestos and iron ore, the latter being by far the most important discovery in recent years. Nearly 50 million tonnes of high-grade haematite were discovered at Bomvu Ridge (Ngwenya) in 1954, and this is now being mined by the Anglo-American Corporation and a British firm. The mine has an assured market in Japan until 1980. The exploitation of the deposit depended on the railway built from Ngwenya through Sipofabeni to the Mozambique border near Goba (completed September 1964) to link with the line to Maputo. This will make further exploitation of other Swazi minerals feasible, particularly her coal deposits.

Revenue from ore mining in Swaziland has risen steadily: in 1964 the value of iron ore production was nearly US$6 million which rose to US$11 million in 1965; by 1970 the output was valued at US$14 million which represented 23 per cent of exports by value; in 1974, the value of iron ore output was US$16 million which was about 10 per cent of export values. This lower proportion reflects the growing value of other exports from Swaziland which had more than doubled between 1970 and 1974. The country's iron ore deposits will be exhausted by 1990 and her asbestos by about the same year. The high grade deposits of iron ore at the Ngwenya mine will be worked out by 1980, as the medium grade ores were in 1978. Fortunately, Swaziland has large reserves of both bituminous and coking coal (180 million tonnes), which is being exported to Kenya and Mozambique.

Liberia

Liberia's economy has been broadened by the exploitation of her iron ore deposits. In an effort to diversify exports and break the dependence on rubber, the government granted concessions to Liberian, Swedish, United States and German firms to mine iron ore. A special railway was completed in 1951 to link Monrovia with the Bomi Hills deposits 70 km away; these deposits of very rich haematite (68 per cent iron content) are now almost exhausted. Iron ore accounted for two-thirds of exports by value in 1964 (US$80 million out of US$130 million) and nearly 73 per cent in 1975 (US$295 million out of US$406 million). Production rose from 14,7 million tonnes in 1965 to 25,6 million tonnes in 1974. In 1975 production dropped to 18,1 million tonnes. Two new deposits are to be opened up in 1981 – the Wologosi Mountain Range in western Liberia and the Bie Mountain Range in north-eastern Liberia. The Wologosi deposit has reserves of 1 000 million tonnes, of which 600 million are haematite and the average ferrous content is 40 per cent. The Bie ores occur in layers with 72 million tonnes of 43 per cent iron on top, 41 million tonnes with 40 per cent iron content below this, and a third layer of 1 000 million tonnes of 37 per cent iron.

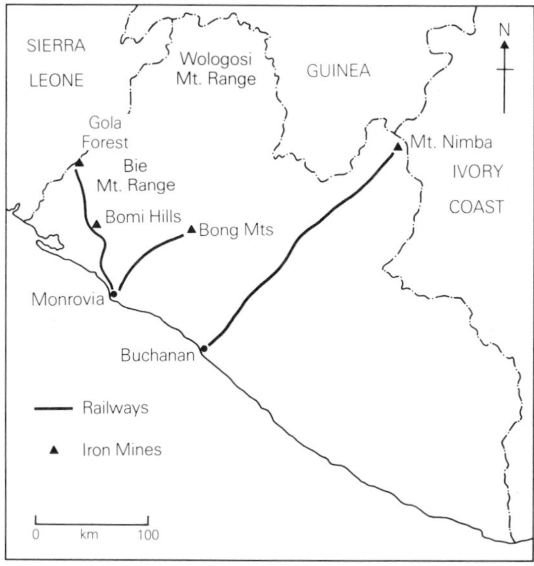

Fig. 9.16 Liberia – location of iron ore mines and deposits

The Bong iron ore mining area, situated about 80 km north-east of the Liberian capital of Monrovia, is representative of many of the large, self-contained mining settlements in Africa. Here, at a height of about 400 m lies a 35 km long range of ore with a 38 per cent iron content and estimated to contain 305 million tonnes of iron ore. First discovered in 1936, the field was prospected in 1958 by a German company working under an agreement with the Liberian Government, which now takes five per cent of all profits. Construction of the mine began in 1962 and it now has a potential production of 3 million tonnes of concentrated ore a year, which the company hopes to increase to 5 million tonnes a year in the future. Some 1 500 Liberians and 300 Europeans, mostly Germans, are engaged on the project.

The mining of the ore is done by open-cast methods, benches about 10 to 15 m high being cut into the mountain face; then the ore is drilled out and loaded by a huge grab crane into massive dumper trucks which transfer it to the crushing mill where it is mixed with water and the waste separated from the concentrate. From this mill the concentrate is sent along an 80 km-long railway to the Bong Mining

Company's pier loading terminal in Monrovia port. Here it is stockpiled until it can be loaded into ore vessels by a special grab. The mining site itself is now a self-contained settlement with its own workshops, warehouses, vehicle service station, schools, 60-bed hospital, shops, police station, club, laundry, stores and houses.

The Bong mine exports about 5 million tonnes of iron ore a year, or nearly 30 per cent of Liberia's iron ore exports. The most important buyers of Liberia's iron ore are the Federal Republic of Germany, Italy, the United States, the Netherlands, France and Belgium.

Liberia and Swaziland together with Mauritania and Angola are all exporters of iron ore to the industrialised nations of western Europe and North America – they have no iron and steel industry of their own. Lack of capital and skilled labour, the absence of suitable coal and limestone deposits, and the small local markets, have made the export of the ore an easier alternative.

In contrast, in countries where most of the requirements are available, iron and steel industries have been established. Algeria has established a steel complex at El-Hadjar near Constantine (capacity 12 million tonnes). Egypt's iron and steel plant at Helwan, 50 km south of Cairo, produces 2 million tonnes annually and is to be further expanded by bringing in new sources of iron ore from the Bahariya Oasis. Zimbabwe has an established iron and steel plant at Redcliffe near Gwelo, using local ores and limestones; this ore is high grade haematite and that with a higher content than 63 per cent iron is exported. The annual production of iron ore in Zimbabwe is about 1,5 million tonnes.

South Africa
It is in South Africa, however, that the exploitation of iron ore deposits has led to the establishment of an iron and steel industry comparable with those in industrialised nations. The country exploits only those ores with more than 50 per cent iron content at a rate of 10 million tonnes a year, and exports only about three to four million tonnes annually. At present rates of consumption in South Africa the iron ore deposits are almost inexhaustible. The main deposits are found in the Northwestern Cape (over 60 per cent iron, 5 000 million tonnes of reserves), Northwestern Cape–Transvaal borders (25–40 per cent iron, 2 000 000 million tonnes), the Bushveld Igneous Complex of the Transvaal (52–60 per cent iron, 2 000 million tonnes and 20 per cent iron, 2 000 million tonnes), Phalaborwa Igneous Complex, eastern Transvaal (60 per cent iron, 100 million tonnes), and several other smaller deposits in the Northwestern Cape Province.

Much of the production of iron ore from these mines is absorbed in the large government ISCOR (Iron and Steel Corporation) plants at Pretoria and Vanderbijlpark which produce over four million tonnes of steel a year, enough to meet three-quarters of the country's requirements. By 1980, ISCOR will be producing between 9 and 10 million tonnes of steel per annum.

With such large deposits of iron ore at its disposal, South Africa has decided to increase its exports considerably. The Sishen mine of the Northwest Cape has been expanded and a railway has been completed linking the mine to Saldhana Bay. Here a special harbour has been constructed, designed specifically for handling iron ore. A large iron ore processing plant is under construction at the harbour, which eventually will produce about five million tonnes of cast iron and semi-processed steel for export a year. By 1980, some 30 million tonnes of ore worth about US$170 million will be exported annually.

Gold – the basis of international finance and commerce

Gold is not the most valuable metal but it has been the foundation of the world's monetary system and modern commerce. The ore is found in quartz veins, metamorphic rocks or in redistributed sediments; usually it cannot be seen with the naked eye and it often takes the processing of one tonne of rock to obtain about 3 gm of gold.

Africa produces nearly 55 per cent of the world's gold. South Africa is the world's largest producer and in 1975 produced 52 per cent of the world total output of 1 454 metric tons. In 1974 South Africa produced 28,2 million ounces, about four times the 7,4 million ounces produced by the second

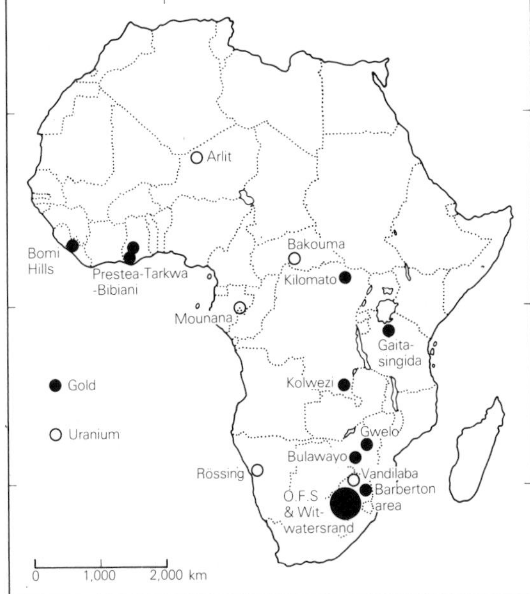

Fig. 9.17 Africa – location of major gold and uranium producing areas

world producer – the Soviet Union. In Africa, only Ghana (0,7 million ounces in 1974) and Zimbabwe (0,5 million ounces in 1974) are other significant producers. South Africa's output has, however, been steadily declining in the early 1970s, but the increased gold prices may counteract this tendency. The gold price increase of the late 1970s may also prompt other African producers to open up abandoned mines. Zaïre, with about one-fifth Ghana's production, could increase her output and Tanzania may open up two mines which were closed owing to rising costs. Kenya and Uganda also have small gold deposits which could prove profitable.

The goldfields of South Africa

Gold was first discovered near the Olifants River, Transvaal, in 1868 but it was only in September 1886, when the Witwatersrand Goldfields were proclaimed public diggings, that true expansion began. Since then over US$9 000 million worth of gold has been mined and expansion is still continuing – in January 1976, the first shaft of Anglo American Corporation's new gold mine at Elandsrand near Carltonville was begun; the mine will cost US$100 million and will begin producing in 1981. It is expected to have a life of 34 years and to produce 800 t of gold. Some old goldmines were also

Table 14 Africa – gold production (tonnes)

	1973	*1974*	*1975*
South Africa	855,6	759,5	758,5
Ghana	22,7	19,1	21,4
Zimbabwe	15,5	15,0	18,6
Zaïre	4,2	4,0	4,4
World total	1 138,0	1 028,0	1 454,0

reopened because of higher gold prices in the late 1970s.

However, about a third of the gold output is from old mines and costs are increasing as lodes become poorer and old machinery has to be replaced. The relative importance of the Rand as a gold producer is shown in Table 14.

Gold is not only an important earner of currency for South Africa but forms a broad base for other industrial operations. An important mineral mined with gold is uranium, the source of atomic energy, and South Africa's reserves are estimated to be 275 000 t, second only to Canada's. This is about 25 per cent of the world's known reserves, of which Africa possesses 40 per cent with five other African countries already producing – Niger, Gabon, the Central African Republic, Zaïre and Namibia. At Vandilaba, outside Pretoria, the ore is enriched by a special process; enriched ores need a smaller reactor core, making power station construction costs cheaper.

Gold and uranium are found together in the mines. The ores are ground to fine pieces and mixed with water to produce slimes which are passed through a cyanide solution. The cyanide dissolves the gold but not the uranium; the gold-bearing solution is drawn off to leave filter cake which contains uranium. The filter cake is fed into sulphuric acid tanks which dissolve the uranium and this liquid is filtered and purified with chemicals.

South Africa's largest goldfield — The Orange Free State

The Orange Free State Goldfield is the youngest of all the fields; today it stretches 50 km from north to south from Allanridge to Virginia and is about 11 km wide (Fig. 9.18). At present twelve mines are in full operation. Gold reefs were known to exist here in 1904 but it was not until 1946 that the Basal Reef

Republic of South Africa: Spoil heaps from the Rand gold mines near Johannesburg.

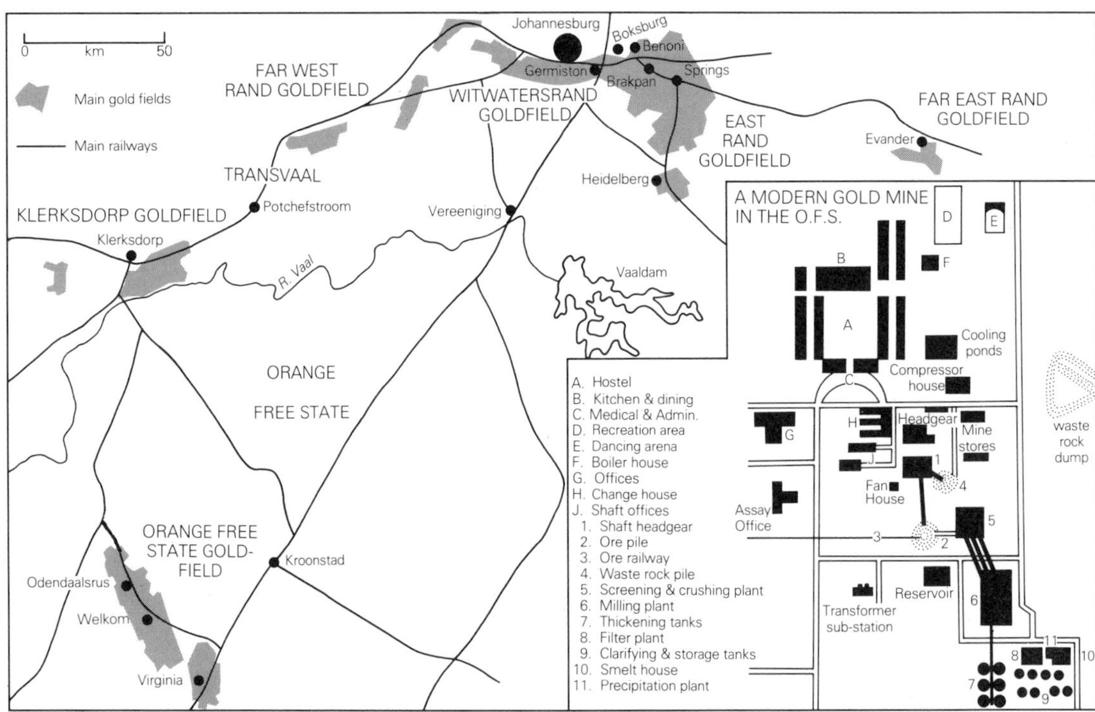

Fig. 9.18 South Africa – distribution of main gold mining areas in the Transvaal and Orange Free State. The inset diagram shows the layout of one of the Anglo-American Corporation's goldmines in the OFS goldfield. There are seven major goldfields and forty major goldmines which form an arc stretching 500 km.

was discovered by the Anglo–American Corporation. The first shaft was sunk on 1 January 1947 in the St. Helena section, and then leases were granted to several other companies. These companies mainly work the Basal Reef, a 190 mm thick stratum of steeply dipping gold-bearing ore found at an average depth of 1 200 m.

The opening of a new goldfield requires tremendous capital investment for the construction of towns, communications and mines. A huge power station was built at Vierfontein at a cost of US$40 million, more power is brought from the Taibos and Highveld stations, and water from Balkfontein 70 km away. Railway connecting lines were constructed and air services financed by the mining companies.

Welkom, a small hamlet with 100 Whites in 1947, was selected and designed as the chief centre. Its population now exceeds 200 000. The town has benefited from modern planning and has well-laid out shopping, entertainment, industrial and residential zones with pleasant parks and gardens. Many secondary industries have been attracted – flour milling, concrete pipe manufacture, panel beating, soft drinks and food processing.

Figure 9.18 shows the layout of one of the OFS mines of the Anglo–American Corporation. The labour of such a mine is largely local Bantu but many come from Malaŵi, Zimbabwe, Tanzania and Botswana. The unmarried men's hostels can accommodate 4 500 men and the mines are self-contained units with facilities for eating, shopping, recreation and welfare. The new Vaal Reefs South mine, for example, employs 9 000 Bantu and 900 Whites.

The gold industry in South Africa is facing several problems. One of these is the rising cost of production which has rocketed in recent years. This has been offset by recent gold price increases (once fixed at US$35 an ounce; 1978–US$220) which may give a new impetus to the industry, although since 1970 output has been declining. The major problem in the mining industry is, however, labour unrest. In 1974 only a quarter of the gold mine labour force of 400 000 came from within South Africa; the remainder came from Malaŵi (20 per cent), Mozambique (28 per cent), Lesotho (21 per cent), Botswana and Swaziland (6 per cent). In 1974 about 50 000 Malaŵians left the mines to return home and about 9 000 Basothos returned to Lesotho.

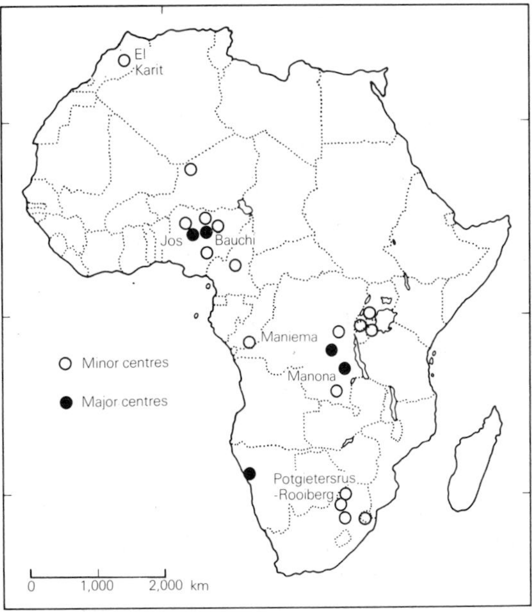

Fig. 9.19 Africa – main tin producing areas

Tin mining in Nigeria

Over half the world's tin output is used for coating steel, used in the manufacture of 'tin' cans, while the remainder is used in type metal, bearing alloys, bronze manufacture and solder. The brownish-black tin ore – cassiterite or tin oxide – contains almost 80 per cent tin and is found in fibrous masses, crusts or veins. Most tin comes from Malaysia (35 per cent world output), Indonesia (19 per cent) or Bolivia (17 per cent) but Africa is a growing producer with just over two per cent from Zaïre and three per cent from Nigeria. Nigeria produces about one-third of Africa's total tin output.

Nigeria ranks fifth in world tin production. Tin and columbite (a by-product used in heat-resisting steels) form the principal metalliferous minerals exported from Nigeria; in 1950 exports amounted to 8 530 t of tin concentrate and rose to 9 950 t in 1957 before production was limited by international agreement. Restrictions were lifted in 1960 on tin production. Production now is about 5 000 t a year. Today, practically all tin ore is smelted locally at Jos and exported as tin metal worth about US$12 million annually.

Tin has been mined from alluvial deposits on the

Jos Plateau since 1903 and until 1961 tin ore was exported for smelting. Now most tin is exported as ingots from two smelting plants opened at Jos. The United Kingdom takes the bulk of exports.

Practically all the tin produced in Nigeria is obtained by opencast methods from alluvial deposits associated with younger granites found on the Nigerian plateau of Bauchi, Benue, Kano and Kaduna States. The various methods used are:

a *Hand paddocking:* where labourers cut steps with spades in the overburden down to the cassiterite.

b *Ground sluicing:* where the area is covered by a network of drainage channels and water fed into the highest point of the network. Cassiterite is shovelled into the running water and the heavier tin ore sinks to the channel bed. Methods *a* and *b* are mainly used by private operators.

c *Gravel pumping:* the breaking up of the ground by water jets and the sludge trapped in sluice boxes. This method is termed *hydraulicing* when the sludge is lifted into sluice boxes by hydraulic elevators.

d *Mechanical mining:* by dragline and excavator, used for deep deposits. The spoil is dumped onto the surface from the pit and washed down with a monitor.

e *Lotoing:* used where the alluvial deposits lie more than 6 m below the surface; pits are dug into the overburden and tunnels connect each pit.

These methods produce a rough concentrate containing a mixture of cassiterite, columbite, quartz sand, zircon (a gem stone) and a variety of iron minerals. These are separated in the dressing mills.

Diamonds – Africa's monopoly of world production

Diamonds are pure carbon crystals formed by intense heat and are the hardest known substance. Imperfectly shaped and coloured stones are used in industry in lathe and dressing tools for the hardest steels, and in high speed drills and glass cutters. Diamonds are associated with volcanic pipes and are found in a matrix called kimberlite or Blue Ground. Erosion of these pipes has caused the resistant diamonds to be washed into rivers and later deposited on river banks lower downstream. There are thus two methods of

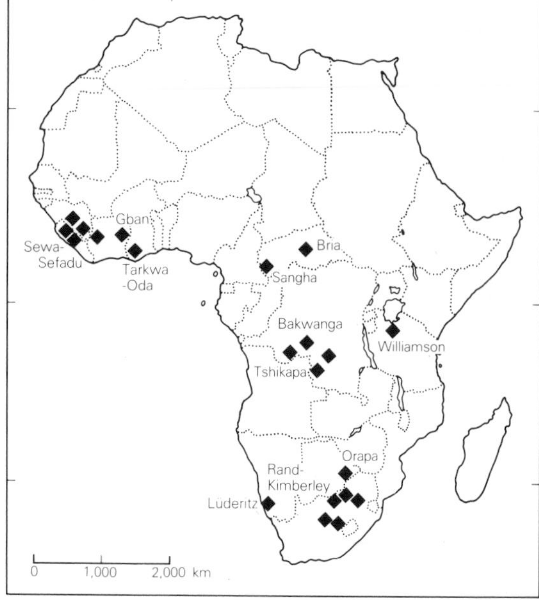

Fig. 9.20 Africa – main diamond producing areas

recovering the stones – by sifting the silts of rivers or by crushing the matrix rock from the pipe.

Africa produces about 80 per cent of the world's diamonds, Zaïre producing 30 per cent, South Africa about 17 per cent, and Ghana six per cent. Sierra Leone is seventh with just under four per cent, although this figure does not take into account the large number of illicit diamonds produced.

Botswana has become an important diamond producer during the 1970s. A diamond pipe was discovered in 1967 at Letlhakane, due west of Francistown, followed by one of the world's largest diamond pipes at Orapa nearby. The Orapa pipe produced 2,4 million carats in 1974 and this will be increased to 4,5 million carats by 1979. At the end of 1976, a new mine was commissioned 40 km south-east of Orapa which has an annual production of 0,4 million carats. (A carat equals 0,2 gm and there are approximately 450 gm to the pound.)

Prior to independence in 1975, Angola was also a large producer and supplied about 10 per cent of the world's gem diamonds. Diamonds earned Angola US$70 million a year and, after oil and coffee, they were the third export by value.

Diamonds are also an important export commodity from Liberia although production has fallen slightly in recent years. Usually diamonds form about 10 to 12 per cent of Liberia's exports by value and in 1973 reached a peak of 15,2 per cent, dropping to 7,5 per cent in 1974, and six per cent in 1975. Diamonds are mined in and around Genne, north of the Bomi Hills in western Liberia, near Gban in the north-east and at Graie, south of Gban.

Two countries illustrate the two different mining methods – Tanzania, where the rock is crushed by modern machinery, and Sierra Leone, where river panning by Africans and foreign companies is more important.

Mining a kimberlite pipe in Tanzania

At Mwadui (1 200 m) in the Shinyanga District of Tanzania, lies the Williamson Diamond Mine. It is close to the Mwanza–Tabora road and is linked by a private rail to the Mwanza–Dar-es-Salaam railway. Here, several million years ago, a volcanic explosion created a 1,6 km-wide crater several hundred metres deep which became filled with volcanic debris of kimberlite and granite breccia. Later eruptions infused this breccia with diamond bearing material, and subsequent erosion reduced the crater to a level gravel surface rich in diamonds, mostly clear, colourless gem stones.

The diamond-rich plug was discovered by Dr. J. T. Williamson in 1940, and a company was formed which now operates one of the most modern diamond plants in Africa. Since 1942 nearly one tonne of diamonds has been recovered from 15 million tonnes of treated rock. Mechanical shovels and draglines load the kimberlite into dump trucks or onto a conveyor belt at the opencast site. The material then goes into the treatment plant where it is crushed and washed, passed through filtering screens, and then through a special solution which separates the diamonds and heavier material from the lighter waste. For every 400 t entering the plant only one tonne remains as diamond-bearing concentrate. This concentrate is fed onto greased belts where the diamonds with their water-repellent surfaces stick to the belt and the waste rolls off the grease. An electrostatic separator removes the finer waste from the stones. Finally the diamonds are hand sorted. Figure 9.21 shows the lay-out of the plant and the Mwadui Township which is virtually self-contained.

The Williamson Diamond Mine earns valuable capital for Tanzania by its exports and pays approximately US$3 million a year to the government in taxes, royalties and dividends. Diamond production by the mine represents nearly 75 per cent of Tanzania's mineral production by value and is worth US$8 million a year. Diamond exports equal one-thirteenth of all exports by value.

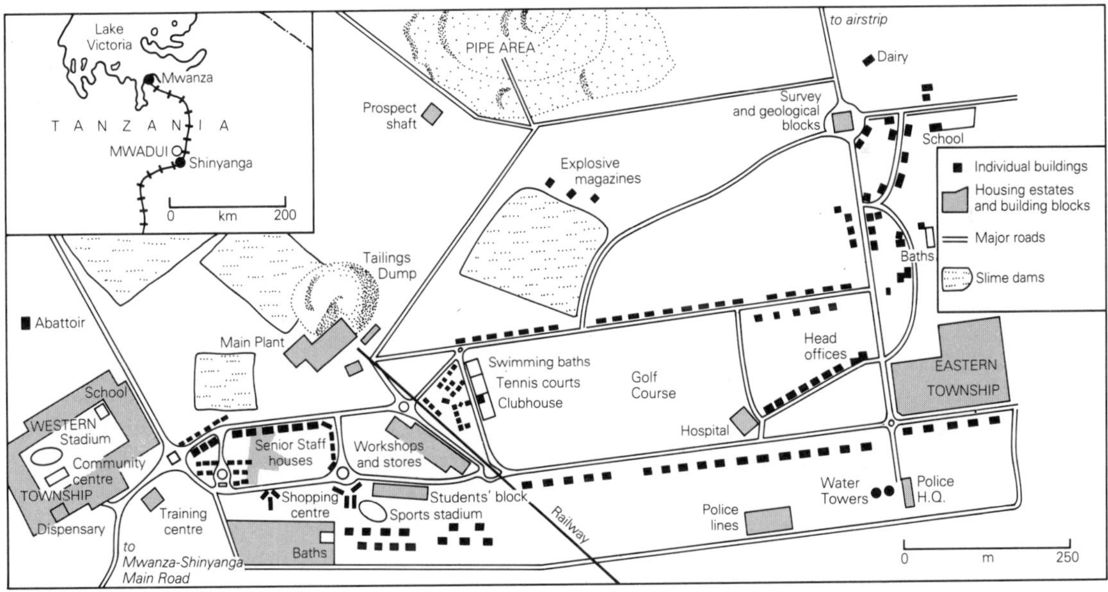

Fig. 9.21 Tanzania – the layout of Mwadui township (Williamson Diamond Mine), Shinyanga

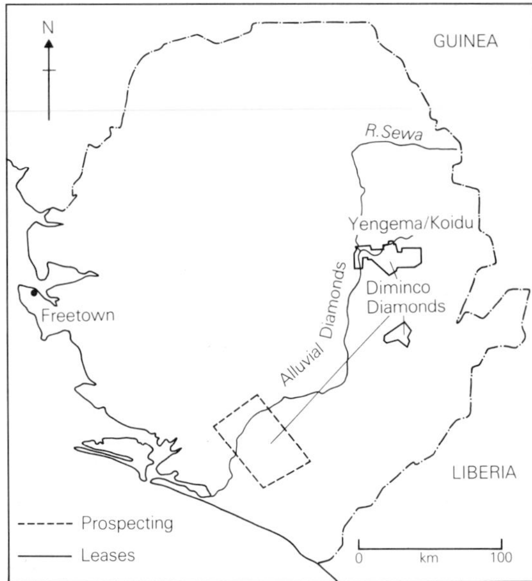

Fig. 9.22 Sierra Leone – mining concessions

Gravel diamond production in Sierra Leone

Diamonds form a very large proportion of the exports of Sierra Leone, and never less than half of export values. Diamonds were first discovered in 1930 in the Kono District and the National Diamond Mining Company of Sierra Leone was formed to prospect, produce and market the stones. But so great was the traffic in illicit mining that the Trust's territory was limited to 1 300 developed square kilometres and licences granted to private individuals. These private operators, working in partnership or employing workmen, obtain the diamonds by two main methods – river mining, and swamp and terrace mining.

River mining involves several simple methods. In early days divers crawled down underwater sticks to scoop the gravel from the river bed onto an anchored raft, but the divers now use aqualungs. Dams may be constructed to seal off and drain an arm of the river and the bed is then sifted. A more efficient method is to extract the gravel from the bed by suction through a tube and to dump it for sorting on the river bank.

In swamp and terrace mining the overburden is removed by pick and shovel, the gravel washed, sieved and sorted. Most of this activity is by private individuals or groups and takes place mainly along the Sewa River and its tributaries.

The National Diamond Mining Company operates on more large-scale lines in its 1 300 square kilometre tract around Yengema and Panguma. The overburden is stripped by dragline and the waste dumped into railway trucks or dumper trucks to be taken to the pan plant. Here the material is sluiced and fed onto a greased belt where the diamonds separate. There are several pan plants operating in various sections of the concession; each employs an average of 45 workers at the mine and 33 at the plant.

The diamonds are then sent to the Government office at Kenema for sorting and grading and are checked again at Freetown before export. The Government Diamond Office buys about US$7 million worth of diamonds a month, while the diamond polishing factory at Freetown takes a small amount. Licenced private buyers take the remainder. The importance of diamonds to Sierra Leone's economy is shown in Table 15. The figures for production would be much higher but for the activities of illicit diamond smugglers which the Sierra Leone authorities find extremely difficult to check. This is a problem which faces most diamond producing countries in Africa.

Another extractive industry – forestry

The Equatorial Forests represent a great natural asset in Africa. The exploitation of this asset has, however, been greatly retarded by several factors – the absence of pure stands of trees of one type, which means that particular types must be searched for; once found the tree must be hauled through the forest to waterways; the local market for wood is often very small and to be economical the wood must be exported; the wood is bulky and difficult to transport without special facilities. Thus the timber industry in Africa has become a specialised operation involving the selection of only expensive woods which can command high prices in overseas markets. The export of expensive timbers is an important aspect of the trade of Ghana, Nigeria, the Ivory Coast and Zaïre where wood represents nearly 80 per cent of exports by tonnage and 55 per cent by value. But in no other African country does the exploitation and export of timber assist the economy as in Gabon.

Table 15 Sierra Leone: Value of major exports 1971–1976 (US$ million)

	1971	*1972*	*1973*	*1974*	*1975*	*1976*
Diamonds	43,0	48,7	68,4	63,6	58,1	48,4
Iron ore	9,8	8,7	9,4	10,6	11,3	Nil
Bauxite	2,1	2,8	2,8	3,5	3,2	4,0
Palm kernels	5,0	3,3	4,4	6,6	3,6	4,3
Cocoa	2,3	2,7	4,6	6,3	7,5	6,9
Coffee	2,9	7,5	8,5	2,4	6,1	7,0

Gabon – an economy based on the forests

Gabon is a land of dense tropical rain forests which cover practically all the country except in the south-east and south. These forests contain the valuable okoumé (used for plywood) and are traversed by a convenient river system focusing on the Ogowe River (Fig. 9.24). Besides having a virtual monopoly of the world's supplies of okoumé, Gabon also has valuable reserves of ebony and mahogany. About 750 000 t of wood are exported annually, worth nearly US$17 million.

Production is mainly by large timber companies, although family production now represents about 15 per cent of total output. The companies are granted concessions in the forest and work these systematically. The forest concession is divided into rectangles and each of these rectangles is subdivided; teams of men under a supervisor move through these sections marking trees for cutting. The selected trees are then cut, trimmed and hauled by tractor and by hand through the forest to a base collecting point, usually situated near a river. Here the logs are rolled into the water and lashed together in huge rafts which are either rowed or pulled by tugboats downstream to one of the 17 plywood and timber dressing mills along the lower Ogowe. The largest mill and one of the biggest exporters of plywood in the world lies at

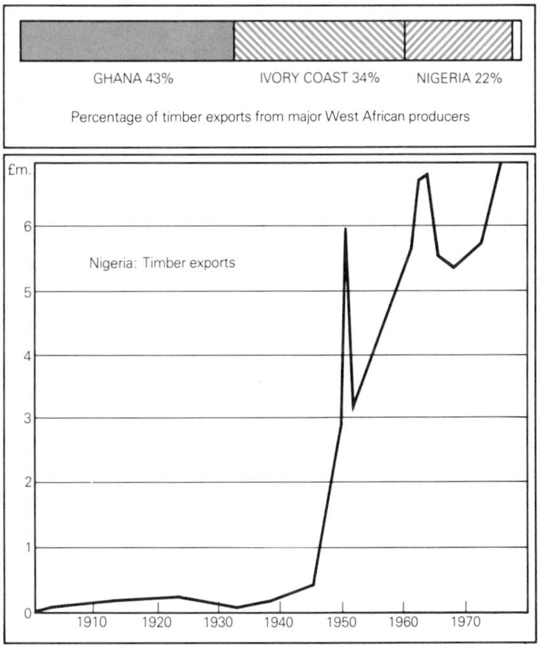

Fig. 9.23 West Africa – timber production

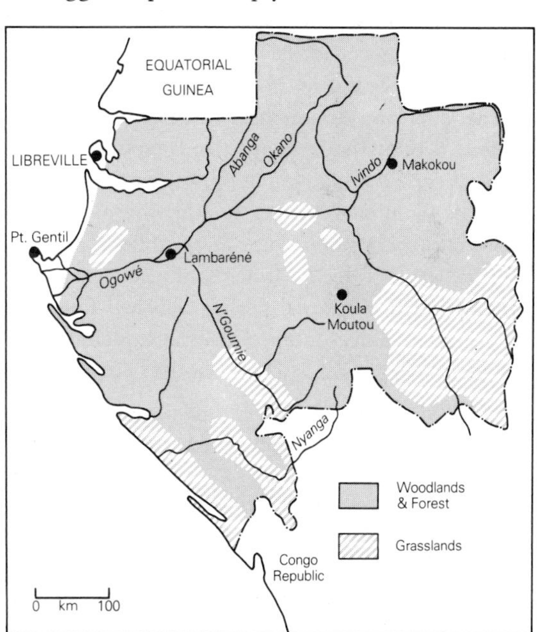

Fig. 9.24 Gabon – timber areas

Port Gentil. Here the African Co-operative Agency of Equatorial Woods handles all exports, which go largely to countries of the European Economic Community, of which Gabon is an associate member. The remainder is purchased by the United States and other West European countries.

Gabon's forests provide sufficient revenue to give the country a very favourable balance of trade but there have been several problems. The coastal areas, worked since 1902, have become exhausted of their timber through mismanagement, and conservation measures have had to be undertaken which will result in the saving of 1,8 million tonnes of okoumé over the next 30 years. Moreover, the economy was precariously dependent on timber, and agriculture had been largely undeveloped. The government has introduced cash crops – cocoa, coffee, groundnuts and rice. Recent valuable mineral finds will also help to diversify the economy – oil near Port Gentil, manganese, iron ore (254 million tonnes), uranium and potassium. However, timber and timber products still represent well over a half of Gabon's exports, and will continue in importance in Gabon's economy. Oil production, now at about 11 million tonnes a year, will level off and decline, unless new discoveries are made. The government is therefore investing in the timber industry; the new giant sawmill at Kango will enable over half of Gabon's timber to be processed within the country, compared with about one-fifth in 1976.

The chief problem facing the exploiters of these mineral deposits is the rugged and forested relief of the country. Over 320 km of railway are being built by large foreign companies to link the manganese deposit to the Pointe Noire line, while a 700 km-long railway is to be built across the country to Me Kambo to tap iron ore deposits. Gabon is fortunate in her geographical location for the exploitation of these minerals, for all parts are less than 800 km from the major port.

Ghana

Timber is also Ghana's second foreign exchange earner after cocoa and there is a great demand in Western Europe for logs, lumber and plywood made from Ghana's Wawa, Utile, Makore and Kokrodua woods. There are about 340 timber firms at present operating in Ghana, although most of these are small and only six account for 80 per cent of output. There are seven large veneer and plywood mills in Ghana and 74 sawmills. A large depot established for the sale of wood to the wood-deficient countries to the north has been set up at Bolgatanga near the upper Volta border, while exports for overseas are routed mainly through Takoradi. The United Kingdom takes over three-quarters of Ghana's output of sawn timber and 90 per cent of the veneer and plywoods.

Forest conservation is strictly carried out in Ghana and the Forestry Department controls the felling of trees on a rotation basis. The trees felled must be able to be replaced by fully grown trees within 25 years.

Ivory Coast

In the Ivory Coast a stage has been reached where readily accessible forest has been used up and the timber companies must now go further afield to the western Man mountains or to the south-west districts around San Pedro to find good timber. Between 1956 and 1973, dense forests in the Ivory Coast were depleted by 44 per cent. In the first quarter of 1973 the country exported over 30 000 t of timber and this was increased to over 60000 t in the same period of 1974. The government aims to produce some 250 000 t of wood pulp a year and has set aside a 250 000-ha area of virgin forest for this. In addition, a 110 000-ha pine plantation is being laid out. The pulp plant is likely to be situated in the west of the country near the timber export port of San Pedro.

Liberia

Logs are third in export value from Liberia. The country has a third of its area under tropical rainforest (about 4 million hectares) and a further 0,6 million hectares under open forest. The government has encouraged the export of sawn timbers rather than logs because these command a higher value, and log exports have been banned entirely since 1977. This measure has encouraged the growth of secondary processing industries in the country.

The future

There is no doubt that Africa is playing a major role as a world energy and mineral supplier. For example, in 1960 the continent supplied less than one per cent of the world's petroleum; at present this is 11 per cent, and already Europe draws 30 per cent of her petroleum requirements from Africa. Africa's reserves of 1,53 per cent of the world total is equal to that of the Soviet Union, eastern Europe and China combined. Moreover, the low sulphur content of Africa's oils make them more attractive than those of the Middle East.

The continent is also gaining importance as a natural gas supplier. Algeria is the most important producer and it is expected that gas will soon exceed oil as a foreign currency earner. The export of natural gas in liquified form mainly to the United States and Europe from Africa represents eight per cent of all gas entering international trade.

Although only one per cent of the world's coal reserves are located in Africa, it is the cheapest in the world and the huge reserves cannot possibly be used up by the economies of the countries in which the deposits lie. Coal could become an important export from Africa.

From the nuclear power point of view, South Africa possesses the world's second largest reserve of uranium and this will be sufficient to meet one-third of the world's demands by 1985 (see page 252).

(For Questions, Discussion Topics and Practical Work see the end of Chapter Ten, page 218.)

CHAPTER TEN

Industrial development in Africa 2 – The secondary industries

Secondary industrial growth

The comparatively recent knowledge of the full extent of Africa's minerals and their export to industrial nations reduced the pace of the continent's secondary industrial growth. Many colonial powers preferred to ship the raw materials to processing factories in their own countries rather than invest money in factories in the colonies. The world economic depression of the early 1930s, followed by the Second World War, also reduced the effectiveness of industrialisation policies for the colonies.

Secondary industrial development is therefore, except for South Africa, Zimbabwe and Egypt, largely the outcome of several influences which developed mainly in the post-war years:

a The war of 1939–45 caused import restrictions and stimulated home industry in South Africa and Zimbabwe with their large European markets.

b The occupation of Europe during the war caused many firms to move to the colonies and set up their factories there.

c War demands for tough fibres (sisal), lubricating oils (palm and seed oils), copper ore and other ores encouraged processing industries.

d The purchasing power of an emerging money-earning African labour force created a steadily increasing market for manufactured articles.

e European firms found it cheaper to process raw materials in Africa than to transport them to Europe for processing. Firms, attracted by the spacious building sites and cheaper labour, set up subsidiary factories in many African countries.

f The post-war years saw the granting of independence to many African nations. The new governments, anxious to broaden their countries' economies, encourage economic experts to evaluate the possibilities of industrial development and often act on this advice. With growing populations and many landless people, African governments are seeing the need to provide alternative employment in industry.

g While colonial powers ran their territories on limited budgets and discouraged investment by other nations, countries such as West Germany, the United States, Japan, the Soviet Union and China are now free to invest capital in the newly independent nations. Financial aid, greater foreign investment and the advice of skilled technicians have boosted industrial development in recent years.

Investment in secondary industry figures largely in the annual budgets and development plans of African nations. With growing populations even the smallest nations see secondary industrial expansion as an important solution to unemployment problems. Liberia, for example, with a population of only 1,7 million and a strong economic base of rubber, iron ore, timber and palm oil has a vigorous industrialisation plan. The value of Liberian manufacturing industries has risen from US$21 million in 1970 to over US$100 million in 1975. Major industries include the manufacture of cement, cigarettes, matches, biscuits, flour and sawmilling, printing and publishing, distilling and furniture making. There are plans to expand this range to include citrus fruit juice canning, salt refining, glass manufacture and cocoa butter processing. Tyres, rubber goods and a steel plant are also potential areas of expansion.

Algeria (population over 17 million) is another example of Africa's drive to economic independence in the industrial sphere. The Algerian 1974–7 second economic plan contained investments totalling US$19 000 million with about 45 per cent of this devoted to secondary industries. New refineries and gas liquification plants, a new steel mill at Oran, a machine tool plant, three cement factories, a car and lorry plant near Algiers, a tractor plant near Constantine, paper mills and textile mills are either completed or already under construction.

Stages in the growth of industry

Industrial enterprises are not new to Africa. The processing of dyes, the manufacture of gold, silver and ivory ornaments, the treating of hides and skins flourished along the coast of East Africa as long ago as the tenth century; West Africa was famed for its iron, gold and tin smelting, weaving and dyeing, basket making and wood carving; the Maghreb was noted for its blue pottery, carpets, leather goods and brassware. These specialised industries have survived through the centuries (see Chapter Two).

Today the modern African states have reached various stages of industrial development. South Africa is the most industrially advanced; Zimbabwe, Egypt, Morocco and Shaba Province have attained some industrial variety; Kenya, Tanzania, Ghana and Mozambique have yet to see great industrial expansion. The various levels of industrial attainment have generally been reached through certain recognisable stages:

a African countries were at first mainly suppliers of raw materials to external nations, usually the colonising power – Algeria produced grains, fruit, vegetables, hides and meat for France; West Africa and Zaïre exported palm oil, cocoa beans, rubber, timber and tropical fruit to France, Belgium and Britain; East Africa exported cotton, coffee, sisal and tea; South Africa shipped wool, gold and diamonds.

b Processing plants were then set up – cotton ginneries in the Sudan, Nigeria and Uganda; coffee mills in Kenya; oil mills in the palm belt, and groundnut-oil crushing mills in Senegal and Nigeria.

c The new factories needed labour, spare parts, improved transport facilities. Ancillary services developed – vehicle maintenance, the manufacture of containers for export produce, electrical and mechanical engineering, coach building, machine tool maintenance and tyre retreading.

d The growing urban labour force needed housing, offices and administrative buildings which led to the development of the construction industry – the manufacture of bricks, corrugated iron sheets, pipes, wire, paints and constructional timber.

e The growing wage-earning workforce needed consumer goods, and factories were set up to supply canned foods, beer, cigarettes, household utensils, light clothing, soap and polishes.

Most African countries have reached these last stages of industrial development. But there is one limiting factor – low purchasing power. In Africa the annual monthly wage of most manual workers lies somewhere between US$35 and US$70 – not a great deal with which to support a family and buy a suit of clothes or a modern radio. In the Nile delta, for example, a peasant farmer with a one-hectare piece of land is lucky to earn US$350 a year while many of the landless farmers of Egypt earn only US$170 a year. Many people still rely on food grown on their small plots of land, while money is spent on basic necessities such as razor blades, soap and household utensils. But purchasing power is growing as many Africans enter jobs formerly held by Europeans, and many are obtaining good cash returns from agriculture. The growth of this huge middle-class market is a great attraction for industry.

In the following samples South Africa represents the most heavily industrialised nation in Africa; Egypt illustrates a country where industrialisation has progressed steadily despite several natural disadvantages; Ghana exemplifies a nation where there has been massive industrial development and foreign investment; Nigeria shows us a country where internal revenue is being used to establish a modern industrial base; and finally Kenya is representative of a developing country with few natural resources.

The Republic of South Africa – Africa's most industrialised nation

Before the 1930s South Africa played the traditional

role of a raw materials supplier and a market for manufactured articles. As late as 1938 South Africa was importing far more than she was exporting by value, since a large proportion of the imports were manufactured articles. But the post-war period saw a rapid expansion of secondary industries, and of South Africa's total exports, approximately one-third consists of manufactured articles; this is the measure of secondary industrial expansion in South Africa.

Today, South Africa has a developing manufacturing industry and a highly developed transport and communication infrastructure comparable to those of Western Europe. Agriculture, once the mainstay of the South African economy, has been surpassed by the manufacturing sector which is growing at a faster rate than any other sector of the economy. South Africa is today involved in the nuclear power industry, in the construction of computers and jet aircraft, in the manufacture and export of motor vehicle components and has a highly developed oil-from-coal industry. Although only occupying about four per cent of Africa's total area, South Africa produces about half the total electric power generated on the continent from thermal and hydro-electric plants. Moreover, the highly developed infra-structure in South Africa is undergoing rapid expansion with the world's largest entirely new port being built at Richard's Bay on the Indian Ocean, and the huge Saldanha harbour project on the Atlantic coast. About a quarter of Africa's total railway track lies within South Africa, with about 22 000 km of single track of which about a third is electrified. Some 52 million tonnes of cargo are handled by South Africa's four main ports each year.

The reasons for industrial expansion

The rapid expansion of South Africa's secondary industries is due to:

a *The solid base provided by coal and gold.* Lacking fuel oil South Africa's secondary industries would hardly have developed but for the colossal reserves of coal. The gold mining industry provided a tremendous market for secondary industries and purchases annually nearly US$350 million worth of goods and stores from local industries, particularly benefiting engineering, footwear, electrical and construction concerns.

b *The range of minerals.* Besides coal and gold South Africa also produces substantial quantities of iron ore, tin, lead, manganese, silver, tungsten, vanadium, vermiculite, salt, fluorspar, limestone, phosphates, clay and antimony and other minerals (Table 16).

c *Agricultural raw materials* have given rise to many secondary industries – wool for scouring mills and knitting plants; fruits for jam, canning and bottling factories; sugar for confectionery, syrups and refineries; fish for canning, freezing, fish meal and fertiliser plants; grapes for wine producers; tobacco for pipe and cigarette factories, and hides and skins for the production of 20 million boots and shoes a year. South Africa's industries use 65 per cent of raw materials from home sources.

d *Foreign investors* find South Africa attractive with its low-wage labour, large European market, unrestricted sites and cheap coal and raw materials. The Government actively encourages foreign investment to reduce exports of raw materials and to process them within South Africa. Examples of

Table 16 South African mineral production, 1939–75 ('000 tonnes)

Mineral	*1939*	*1969*	*1975*
Gold	400	970	713
Asbestos	21	250	375
Chrome	171	1 120	2 075
Copper	11	124	179
Manganese	421	2 770	5 881
Coal	19 600	51 300	69 440
Fluorspar	10	118	203
Iron ore	490	8 760	12 298

foreign investment appear in the motor industry (Ford, Leyland, General Motors), rubber (Dunlop), and electrical goods (Hoechst of Germany and English Electric).

e *Government policy* encourages home production by restricting certain imports and financing large basic industries – iron and steel, electricity supply, the Sasol oil-from-coal plant, phosphate, and cellulose production. Individual projects are also sponsored – the phosphate and copper plants at Phalaborwa, the paper plant at Tugela River in Natal, a wood and rayon factory at Umkomaas, a textile factory at Kingwilliamstown. The Government is also spending US$45 million a year on improving and extending the communications system.

These powerful influences have caused a rapid development in the field of secondary industry. Manufacturing industries are now the biggest single contributor to South Africa's national income. Despite this growth, however, the country still relies on overseas sources for more complicated machinery and electrical goods, and approximately two-thirds of her imports are classed as manufactured articles.

An indicator of South Africa's position as an industrialised nation is the per capita Gross National Product. This is obtained by dividing the value of output of the country – derived from manufacturing, mineral and agricultural production – by the total population. In 1977, South Africa's per capita GNP was estimated to be US$1 320, a low figure compared with the average for the countries of Western Europe (United Kingdom US$4 020, West Germany US$7 380) the United States' US$7 890 and Scandinavia's US$4 910, but it is the third highest in Africa after Libya US$5 080 and Gabon US$2 240. In the latter two countries oil and mineral exports and low populations boost the per capita GNP. Gabon's population is barely above 500 000 and Libya's is 2,7 million, while South Africa's population is more than 26 million. The per capita GNP for other countries in Africa for comparisons are listed in Appendix 1.

The range of South Africa's industries

The food and processing industry is the biggest industrial sector and has doubled its production since 1939. It exports 90 per cent of its output chiefly to the United Kingdom. Metal working and engineering are second in importance and have progressed rapidly with the demands of the mining and iron and steel industries. There are over 700 electrical machinery and equipment factories in South Africa, 226 clothing and textile plants and 100 leather goods and shoe factories. The chemical industry has been encouraged by the gold and uranium mine demands; SASOL and FOSKOR, the oil refinery at Wentworth, Natal and the Moddersfontein explosives plant near Johannesburg produce a wide range of chemical by-products. Pulp and paper manufacturing is very dependent on imports; the Umkomaas plant in Natal uses over 180 000 t of eucalyptus trees a year and produces 45 000 t of rayon pulp. Other important industries in South Africa include motor car assembly, tyres and rubber goods manufacture, the making of glass, pottery, cement, aluminium and hollow ware, brushware, plastic goods, beer, soft drinks and confectionery. The heavier iron and steel and metallurgical industries are concentrated in the Rand.

The distribution of South Africa's industries

Two-thirds of South Africa's gross national output is derived from four major industrial concentrations – the Rand, the Western Cape centred on Cape Town, the Eastern Cape centred on Port Elizabeth and East London, and the Durban–Pinestown region of Natal. Secondary industries have tended to concentrate at markets and in the major ports, and in each of these centres there is a duplicated range of industries catering for the local market. Some industries such as dairying, leather working, fruit and vegetable canning are more widely distributed, and lie nearer their raw materials.

The Rand is the only true industrial conurbation in Africa. Extending 100 km from Randfontein to Springs on the level veld, its location and growth is due to the gold fields, the local coal and iron ore, the Vaal's water, the ease of communication construction on the veld, the cheap labour supplies, and numerous local minerals – fluorspar, fireclay, dolomite, chromite and magnesite (Fig. 10.1).

The Rand has 35 per cent of all industrial establishments in South Africa and employs 43 per cent of all industrial workers. Johannesburg (1 225 000) is a

Republic of South Africa: Docks and commercial zone of Port Elizabeth.

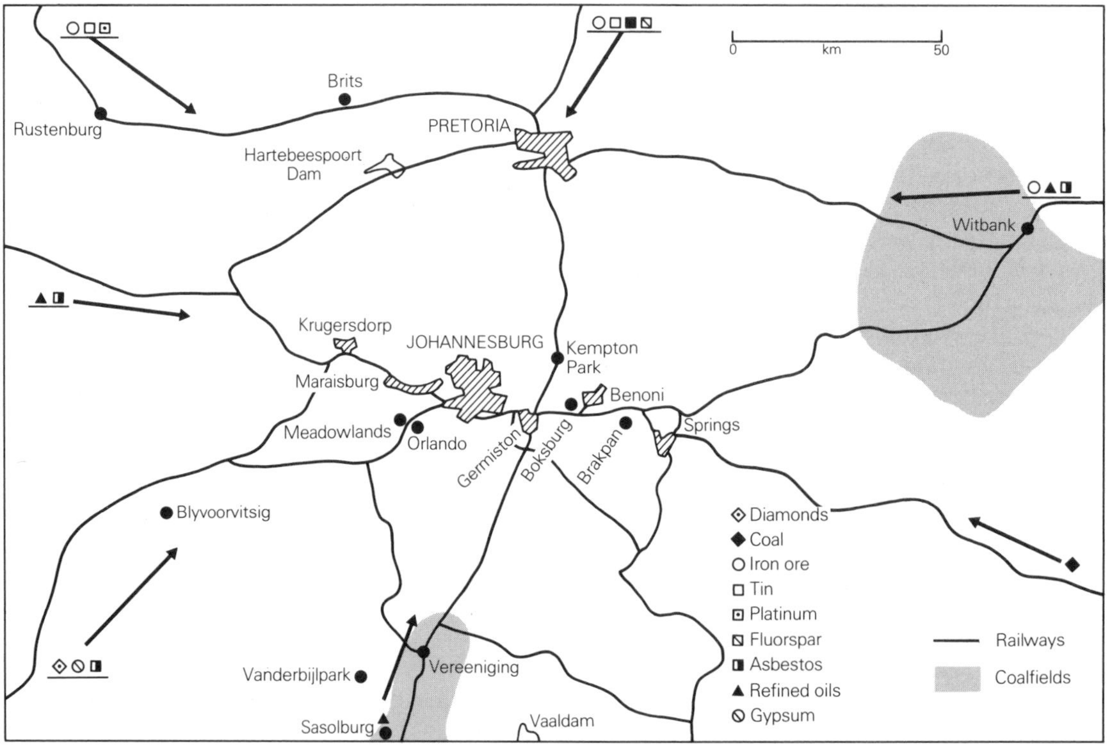

0 km 50

Brits

Rustenburg

PRETORIA

Hartebeespoort Dam

Witbank

Krugersdorp

JOHANNESBURG

Kempton Park

Maraisburg

Benoni

Meadowlands

Orlando

Germiston

Boksburg

Brakpan

Springs

Blyvoorvitsig

Vanderbijlpark

Vereeniging

Sasolburg

Vaaldam

◇ Diamonds
◆ Coal
○ Iron ore
□ Tin
⊡ Platinum
⧄ Fluorspar
◧ Asbestos
▲ Refined oils
⊘ Gypsum

— Railways

Coalfields

Fig. 10.1 South Africa – the Rand

gold mining, banking and commercial centre with numerous secondary industries – metal working, engineering, textiles manufacture, diamond cutting, paper and printing, chemicals, tobacco and food processing, canning, electrical equipment, jewelry manufacture, saw milling and furniture making. Springs (150 000) is a coal and gold mining centre with factories manufacturing mining machinery, electrical goods, printing machinery, sheet glass, paper, alloy steels, cycles and canned foods. Germiston (220 000) has gold refineries and explosive plants, Krugersdorp (90 000) has gold and manganese mines. Pretoria (430 000), the capital, has railway workshops and plants making glass, sheet metal, cement and matches. The nearby ISCOR steel works and the Vanderbijl Park plants near Vereeniging produce 76 per cent of South Africa's steel; steel ingot production was 1,5 million tonnes in 1956, 1,8 million tonnes in 1960, 3,7 million tonnes in 1969, and in 1975 exceeded four million tonnes. Most of the production is from ISCOR's three steel plants at Vereeniging, Pretoria and Newcastle, and this total will be increased with the completion of the fourth ISCOR steelworks at Saldanha Bay north of Cape Town.

Three major factors will affect the future distribution of industry in South Africa. The Rand region is prohibited to new industries with heavy water demands since the Vaal is already overburdened. The Government's official policy is committed to the segregation of the Black population into 'bantustans' and many future industries will be established along the edges of these regions; over 100 000 workers are now employed in border industries, which include a large hosiery factory at Rustenburg, a cotton mill at Harrismith, a jersey factory at Roodepoort, and a Siemens plant producing telecommuncations products at Rosslyn. Moreover, although secondary industrial development will be greatest in the populous south and east, the Orange River Scheme will certainly exert an attraction for industry in more western areas of South Africa.

The development of secondary industry in Egypt

Egypt, like South Africa, has experienced a rapid growth in her secondary industries since 1938, and her industrial output is now increasing by about 10 per cent per annum. But the country's basis for industry – raw materials, markets both internal and external, fuel supplies and communications net-work – have never become fully integrated like those of South Africa, and this has been a limiting factor for industrial expansion.

Thus, although Egypt possesses several industrially useful minerals, they do not occur in sufficiently large quantities. The most important minerals produced include mineral oil, manganese, feldspar, and iron ore which is sent to the Helwan iron and steel plant near Cairo (annual output half a million tonnes). There is also a small range of other materials

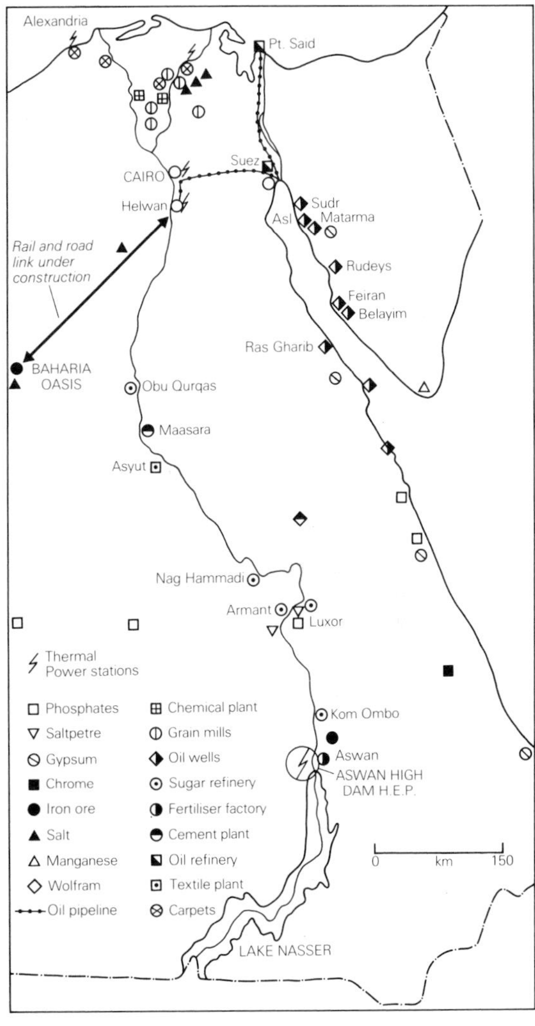

Fig. 10.2 Egypt – location of minerals and manufacturing centres

– lead, zinc, gypsum, copper, gold, phosphates and chrome ore. Several new mineral deposits have been found in recent years, e.g. the iron ore deposit at Bahariya Oasis, but exploitation has been restricted up to now by the inadequacy of the transport network and the lack of water facilities in desert locations. Iron ore imported from Europe was actually cheaper by the time it reached Helwan than Egyptian ore from the deposits near Aswan. Many of Egypt's secondary industries rely heavily on imported raw materials such as tobacco, rubber latex, and chemicals, and on imports of specialised modern machinery.

The pace of Egypt's industrial expansion has also been hampered by lack of fuel. Egypt has few coal deposits, her first coal mine being opened in the Sinai Peninsula only in 1964, and although her oil production has been increased since the pre-Second World War years, it is still small and the reserves are low. The country produces about 80 per cent of her needs in oil but over one million tonnes still have to be imported; about 60 per cent of her output comes from the Belayim field in western Sinai, where the new fields of July and Ramadan have helped increase production. The return of the Sinai Peninsula oil-fields in 1975 by the Israelis has also increased the output of oil to 18 million tonnes in 1978. Egypt's present ten-year development programme calls for an output of 50 million tonnes of oil by 1983. Important strikes have already been made in the Western Desert, notably at Qattara and El Alamein, which have a potential annual output of 2,5 million tonnes. In the Nile delta large reserves of natural gas have been discovered which are estimated to be sufficient for 25 years supply.

Egypt also lacks the large highly sophisticated market which South Africa possesses. Although many richer Egyptians demand more manufactured goods of a high quality, the general mass of the people buys little – only about one-fifth of all purchases made in Egypt consist of manufactured articles. This means that there is only a limited opportunity for a few firms to sell their manufactured goods, and there is not the industrial competition that one finds in western industrialised states. Moreover, most of the production of processed articles is in the hands of a few cartels who exclude competitors by dominating the market. The average Egyptian is a farmer at heart and his profits from the small plots are usually so low that he never acquires enough capital to invest in industrial enterprises. Most of the big concerns are in government hands.

As a result there are few large firms and many small concerns running on limited capital; about 80 per cent of all industrial units in Egypt employ less than 50 workers, and about one-fifth have between 50 and 500. The smaller concerns are mainly handicraft establishments making carpets, shoes, textiles, leather goods and ceramic ware. The government is actively encouraging this type of industry and the development of cottage and village industries – the weaving of rugs and carpets, the home spinning of cotton and fruit bottling. The bigger firms are concerned with petroleum refining, paper making and textile manufacture. Typical of the bigger concern is the Aswan fertiliser factory constructed with the help of German and French engineers. The plant uses power from the old Aswan dam, but will make use of that from the new dam further upstream, and has a capacity of 500 000 tonnes of calcium nitrate per annum; the plant employs 2 000 Egyptian staff and workers. Another large nitrogen fertiliser plant is located at Suez.

The greatest growth since the pre-war years has been in the textile industries (today five times the 1938 output), seed oil production (twice 1938) and cement production (six times 1938). New factories erected since the war include iron and steel, oil refining and motor car assembly plants. About half of the industrial concerns are located in Cairo and Alexandria (Fig. 10.2), although the Aswan region is becoming a focal point for new industry, and more industries will be established along the Nile Valley as electric power becomes more readily available. Egypt suffers somewhat from the rather elongated shape of the country, accentuated by the narrowness of the fertile strip flanking the Nile. Transport lines are thus stretched out and this makes the hauling of raw materials more expensive. For this reason industry has been attracted mainly to the delta region with its easy access to markets in Europe, its convenience for imports, its well-developed transport network, and its dense local market and skilled workforce. Most of the foreign capital invested in Egyptian industry tends to gravitate here.

Egypt's industrialisation programme is thus hampered by over-concentration of industry in certain locations, by an expensive transport network and raw materials, and lack of capital for greater internal investment by Egyptians themselves. Too great a proportion of the country's rapidly growing population is devoted to producing enough to eat to be spared for industrial work. Moreover, hostilities with Israel and the loss of Canal royalties, now restored, placed a great strain on the economy; for example, the destruction of the refinery installations at Suez in October 1967 removed the source of 80 per cent of the country's domestic fuel supply.

Despite these drawbacks, the Egyptian government has embarked on plans to increase power supplies and foreign investment. Among the most notable industrial undertakings planned or under construction are a petro-chemical plant at Alexandria to produce insecticide, chemicals, drugs, plastic, rubber, nylon, animal fodder and chemical cleaning fluids; a heavy oil, coking and petro-chemical plant at Suez using local oil; a factory at Mex near Alexandria to extract 70 000 t of rutile (titanium ore) and 70 000 t of iron oxides from black sand deposits; four plants for atmospheric and vacuum oil distillation in Alexandria and Suez, and an aluminium factory and coal station in Alexandria. Many of these projects fell into abeyance because of the drain on the economy caused by hostilities with Israel.

In 1975–6, following peace agreements with Israel, Egypt embarked on a massive reconstruction and development plan. The main region of development will be in the Suez Canal and western Sinai peninsula region. Three giant road and rail tunnels will be constructed under the Suez Canal to link the Sinai more closely with Egypt. The tunnels will be located at El-Shatt, Kantara, Deversoir, Ismailia and Port Said. Port Said, Ismailia and Suez will be linked with a new four-lane highway, and these three centres will be the main beneficiaries of industrial expansion. At Ismailia the existing gypsum factory is to be expanded and several factories for canning fruit and vegetables, and for vegetable oil processing are to be established. At Port Said the shipbuilding industry is to be restored and expanded, the textile factory will be reconstructed, and a new flour mill will be built. The oil refinery and fertiliser plant at Suez are to be reconstructed and new factories manufacturing cement, lime and flour are to be built.

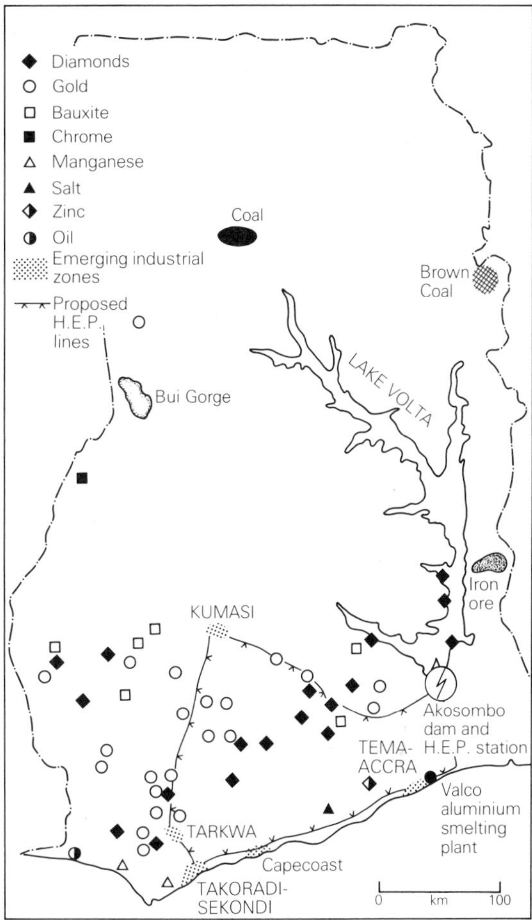

Fig. 10.3 Ghana – location of minerals and industrial zones

Secondary industry in Ghana

In contrast, Ghana is not a heavily industrialised country and her economy relies heavily on the returns from exports of agricultural produce and minerals. As we have seen (Chapter Four), the cultivation of cocoa and the products of the forests together make up half of Ghana's gross domestic product and dominate Ghana's exports.

In the industrial field development has been concentrated until recently on the mining sector. Over 22 000 Ghanaians are employed in the gold mines and a further 6 000 on the diamond diggings, while nearly 40 000 are classed as miners of some sort. While gold and diamonds are important earners of foreign currency for Ghana, minerals useful to secondary industry and which occur in sufficiently large quantities are few. Manganese is mined at Nsuta and there are several other scattered deposits. At present most of this is exported, Ghana being the world's largest exporter of manganese; the United States takes just under two-thirds, Britain a quarter and Norway the remainder. Besides gold, diamonds and manganese, Ghana possesses some large reserves of bauxite, the mineral ore of aluminium, about 200 million tonnes. Deposits are worked at Kanayerebo near Awaso in the Western Region and some 70 km north-west of Dunkwa. Other deposits are at Yenahin, 60 km west of Kumasi and, although these are the largest, they are untapped since no transport facilities are available at present. Another large deposit lies near Kibi, not far from Tema, and this is likely to be used in the Valco smelter. Other minerals include beryllium (a strengthener of alloyed metals) and small depsits of copper. An iron ore deposit (270 million tonnes) lying near Shiene in the Northern Region now lies close enough to Lake Volta to be exploited (Fig. 10.3), while a second deposit of 150 million tonnes (45–50 per cent iron) was discovered in 1968 in the Opon–Mansi Forest about 110 km north of Takoradi.

But minerals vital to secondary industries are absent. Ghana lacks fuel although some oil has been discovered off-shore; all coal is imported for use on the railways (about 40 000 t per year) and timber is the major source of fuel outside the larger towns (annual consumption 5 million cubic metres mainly from the natural forests). A large oil refinery at Tema supplies Ghana's present needs but all the crude oil is imported. The lack of fuel was one of the major reasons for embarking on the Volta River Scheme. Another hindrance which has retarded the development of secondary industries has been the lack of capital due to the diversion of much of it into the larger schemes, while most of the foreign capital invested in the past has gone to the mining and agricultural sectors of the economy. Again, Ghana has lacked the skilled manpower necessary for running highly specialised industries, since where there is little secondary industry there can be little scope for training.

The successive governments of Ghana, both colonial and independent, have realised the need to broaden the country's economy by encouraging secondary industrialisation. In 1947 the Industrial Development Corporation, now a government body, was set up with the purpose of investigating and promoting industrial undertakings. The Development Corporation plans to increase the pace of industrialisation by certain measures – the replacing of imported goods with those which could be manufactured locally, the processing within the country wherever possible of those minerals and agricultural products which were being exported in their raw form, the expansion of the building and construction industry, and the development of fields of industry hitherto neglected and which would be necessary to larger-scale industries – machine tools and electrical industries.

Although secondary industries still make only a small contribution to Ghana's total domestic output it is a rapidly growing sector. However, many industrial concerns are small, some only employing five or six people, and many 'factories' employ relatives who are unpaid.

Most of these small firms tend to concentrate in the urban centres and are largely 'consumer' industries catering for the needs of the local market, their range of goods including cloth, woven articles, soap, silver and gold ornaments, simple metal instruments and tools, furniture, coconut oil, lime juice, bricks, tiles, pottery, bread, confectionery, baskets and so on. These local industries continue to multiply, however, and over the last ten years or so there has been an increasing proportion of comparatively large establishments. There has certainly been an emergence of secondary industrial complexes on a small scale in the Accra and Tema industrial areas, and at Takoradi-Sekondi, Cape Coast, Kumasi, Nsawam, Tarkwa and Tamale.

The greatest possibilities for development lie in the aluminium industry. Aluminium is in increasingly great demand by all industrial nations for it is a strong, rustless, and lightweight metal extensively used in the aircraft and motor car industries. The processing of bauxite to produce aluminium requires vast quantities of electric power which Ghana now possesses in the Volta Scheme. Since it requires 10 t of bauxite to produce one tonne of aluminium, and aluminium is worth about seven times as much as the same weight of bauxite, the development of this industry will greatly benefit Ghana and earn her

Ghana: Part of the industrial estate at Tema. The well-ventilated, low-profile buildings, planned transport facilities, spacious layout and lack of pollution are typical of industrial estates in Africa.

considerable foreign exchange. Almost all of the present output of 315 000 t is exported, chiefly to the United Kingdom, but the Valco smelting plant at Tema produces about 4 000 t of refined aluminium from imported alumina for export which commands a much higher price. The Ghana government, in conjunction with Japanese and US firms, is to develop further bauxite mining at Kibi in Eastern Ghana and will construct another aluminium plant with an annual capacity to produce 600 000 t of aluminium. Half of the metal will be used in Ghana.

One of the main aims of Ghana's government is to make the country self-sufficient in industrial raw materials and to make fuller use of minerals and agricultural products within Ghana. The production of local industrial raw materials such as cotton, palm oil, livestock, cereals and shea butter is encouraged. Recent investments have been in a new ceramics factory at Saltpond using local clays, a food processing factory concentrating on baby foods, instant coffee and milk products, a meat processing plant, and a battery factory. At Tema a major food processing complex with several separate factories has developed, with a flour mill, animal feed plant, a fish meal factory, a fish cannery, a vegetable oil mill and a margarine factory. The government has also reactivated many old factories which have fallen into disuse, for example, the prefabricated panel board factory built with Soviet aid and closed in 1966 is now in production again.

Probably the most important recent development in the industrial field, however, is the decision by the government to proceed with the construction of an iron and steel plant at Sekondi. The West German firm of Krupp will plan and build the factory which is expected to be completed by 1980 at a cost of US$1 000 million. Iron ore will be extracted by opencast methods at a site in the Opong Valley and railed to Sekondi, limestone will come from the Nauli deposits, and caustic soda will be supplied by a new factory located at Cape Hope.

Despite these achievements, Ghana's industrialisation is as yet insufficient to reduce reliance on imported manufactured goods; machinery, transport equipment, manufactured consumer goods, processed foods and vehicles are still increasing in exchange for Ghana's cocoa, gold, bauxite, timber and diamonds.

Industrial development in Nigeria

The part played by the manufacturing sector in Nigeria's economy is exceedingly small, especially when one considers the huge market and labour force represented by over 80 million people. Secondary industry's contribution to the Gross Domestic Product is still a mere eight per cent (compared with five per cent in 1960), and industry earns only two per cent of Nigeria's foreign exchange. The average workforce size of industrial establishments is small, about 140, while the whole manufacturing sector employs a mere 150 000 workers, representing about 17 per cent of the total national workforce.

The industrial sector of Nigeria's economic structure has three major weaknesses:

1 *Dominance of light industry:* Nigeria's industrial base lacks diversity and is dominated by light industries designed to produce goods as substitutes for consumer imports. Food, beverage and tobacco processing account for about 34 per cent of production values in manufacturing, while clothing and textile industries account for a further 17 per cent. The engineering industry is almost non-existent, and there is an urgent need for basic industries, producing heavy machinery, chemicals, machine tools, and agricultural, electrical and engineering equipment. These industries depend, to a large extent, on the existence of an

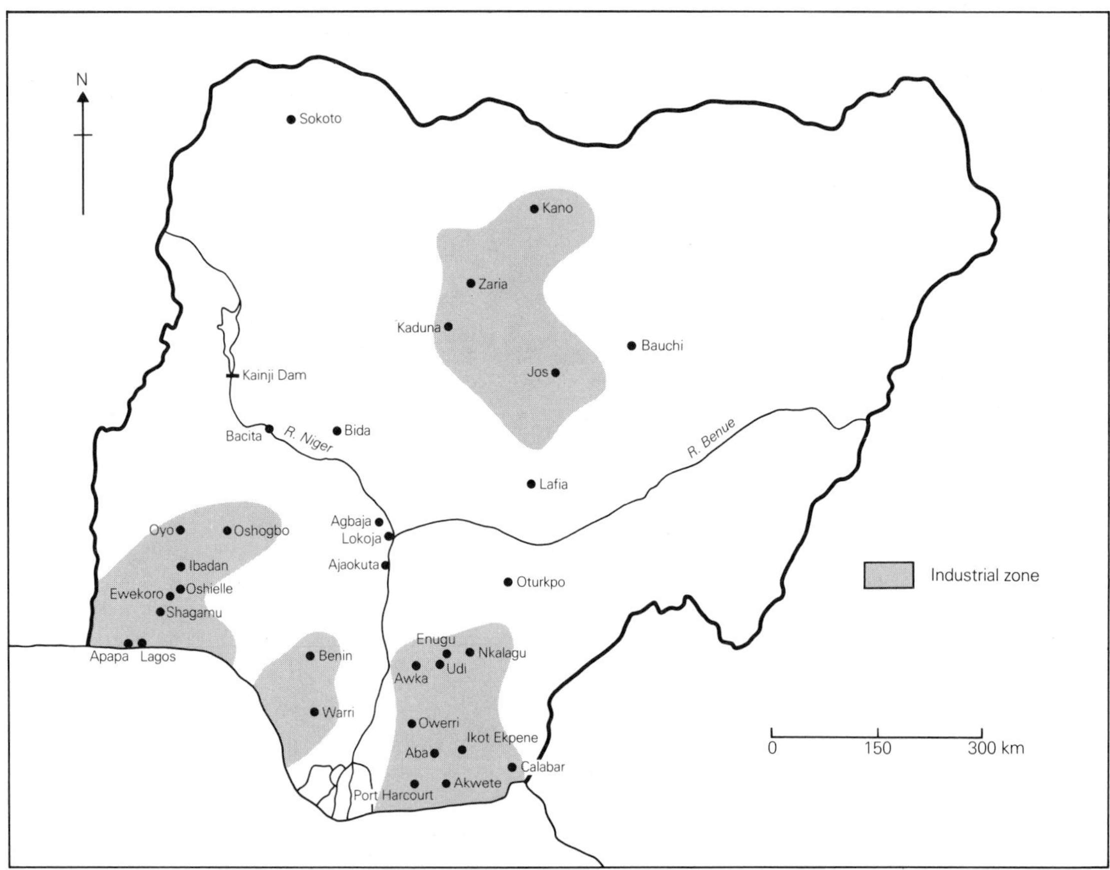

Fig. 10.4 Nigeria – industrial areas and locations mentioned in the text

indigenous iron and steel industry which Nigeria at present does not possess. Many industries of the processing kind – palm oil extraction, cotton ginning, timber processing, cigarette manufacture, brewing and soft drinks – are the legacies of a colonial past.

2 *Foreign control:* France, Japan, Britain and West Germany have major interests in the secondary industrial field in Nigeria and, in fact, 70 per cent of capital invested in manufacturing industries comes from private foreign sources. Although there are considerable benefits to be derived from foreign investment, there are two major drawbacks. First, foreign capital concentrates on industrial projects which are consumer oriented, but which require only simple training programmes, for example, the textile industry. The workforce which develops is of the artisan type and is not highly skilled. Secondly, foreign investors require their profits to be paid abroad so that a great deal of capital in the form of interest, dividends and payments to overseas contractors leaves Nigeria.

3 *Inadequate infrastructure:* Secondary industry must be served with an efficient network of communications, modern handling facilities, and an uninterrupted power supply if it is to develop effectively. Lagos and Port Harcourt are the country's major entry points but, since the greater part of Nigeria's industry and commerce is situated in the Lagos area, ships often prefer to wait here to offload rather than use the other ports. Although handling is efficient, a backlog of shipping builds up, usually about 100 vessels at once, causing delays. At present Lagos is handling 500 000 t of cargo a month, several times the amount for which the facilities were designed. Moreover, the railway system, little changed from the colonial network laid in 1898, is unable to move the stockpiles of goods from Lagos, so that 80 per cent has to be sent by road. Port Harcourt is equally poorly served, while Calabar serves a limited hinterland, and has inadequate handling facilities. Much of the interior traffic is carried by the roads, but only about a quarter of these are tarmaced and they are now showing signs of damage due to increasing traffic volume. Besides these problems, industry is also faced with water shortages and recurring power cuts.

Although Nigeria's manufacturing sector is underdeveloped relative to the size and general development of the economy as a whole, there is tremendous potential for future growth. We will now consider the present structure of Nigerian industry and government plans for the expansion of this sector.

Nigeria has a long tradition of local craft industries – the leather and dyeing industry around Kano, cotton weaving and dyeing at Kano, Bida and Benin, wood carving at Awka, Benin and Ikot Ekpene. In addition to these craft industries, the colonial power established processing industries geared to her own needs – palm oil milling in the palm belt, cotton ginning and groundnut oil milling in the Kano and Zaria areas, rubber and timber processing in the forests of the delta and south-western region, and tin smelting on the Jos Plateau. Market-orientated consumer industries also developed, using local raw materials – textiles at Kaduna and Lagos, cigarette manufacture at Ibadan and Zaria, brewing at Apapa, and soft drinks factories in Lagos, Ibadan and Kano. Engineering was confined to railway workshops in Lagos, Zaria and Enugu, to bicycle assembly at Zaria and Port Harcourt, and to small boat and ship repair concerns in the ports. The chemical industry was represented by soap manufacture in Apapa, Kano and Aba, the metal industry by the container and door frames produced in Lagos and Port Harcourt, and 'heavy industry' by the steel-from-scrap plant at Enugu and the cement plants at Ewekoro and Nkalagu. These generally light industries of the import-substitution type still form the base of Nigeria's manufacturing sector.

The 1960s saw a considerable industrial expansion. While the gross domestic product rose by about five per cent per annum, the manufacturing sector's production increased by 10 per cent each year. After the Civil War, industrial output rose rapidly: in 1971 by 35 per cent, by 17 per cent in 1972, and by 10 per cent in 1974, with an annual average rate of increase between 1971 and 1975 of 9,5 per cent. The main fields of advance have been in:

a *The textile industry:* This is the most important industry in the manufacturing sector employing more than 50 000 workers. There are 60 mills now producing in Nigeria and another 46 are planned

Nigeria: Interior of a textile factory, Kaduna.

or under construction. Nearly half of these are located in Kaduna State near to the raw material and Kaduna city itself has six large mills owned by Japanese, British and other foreign companies. Even with a production figure of 500 million metres of cloth in 1975, Nigeria's textile industry is still unable to satisfy the domestic market.

b *Car assembly:* This is a comparatively new industry in Nigeria, with the French firm of Peugeot establishing an assembly plant in Kaduna in 1974, and West Germany's Volkswagen a plant on the Badagry road near Lagos. British Leyland also began to assemble lorries in 1975 in partnership with the government. The Peugeot plant produces 80 cars a day and the Volkswagen factory 60 cars daily but this will hardly satisfy the Nigerian market (the country imported 60 000 vehicles in 1977).

c *The cement industry:* There are cement factories situated at Nkalagu, Ewekoro and Sokoto, but their output is totally insufficient to satisfy home demand. Port congestion became crucial at Lagos in 1975 because the harbour was choked with some 400 cement vessels waiting to unload cement imports. By the end of 1976, the Nkalagu plant had increased its production from 500 000 to 750 000 bags by expanding its facilities. A new plant at Shagamu was opened in 1977. Even with these increases, the local industry is only able to supply 60 per cent of Nigeria's needs.

Third National Development Plan (1975—1980)

Although there is a reasonably wide range of industries in Nigeria, the engineering industry is still very small, the chemical industry is in its infancy with a very small production of fertilisers and pesticides, and there is no iron and steel industry. These deficiencies in Nigeria's industrial structure have been recognised by the government as indicated by current efforts at industrialisation through the Third Development Plan.

The Third National Development Plan for the period 1975–80 is the most ambitious and far-reaching plan yet to be devised by any nation in Africa. It is significant that finance for the plan is to come almost wholly from Nigerian sources, largely oil revenues, with little or no contribution from foreign sources. The establishment of a strong industrial base is the main theme of the Plan, with priorities given to the establishment of a long-discussed iron and steel industry, diversification of the petroleum industry, the encouragement of the growth and wider distribution of light and heavier industry, and the establishment of a comprehensive electric power network.

Work on a fundamental part of the plan – the iron and steel complex at Ajaokuta – has already begun. Since this will be West Africa's major steel plant (Ghana has a smaller scheme), the geographical and economic reasons for its establishment will be examined in some detail.

Interest in an iron and steel plant for Nigeria began in 1958 when various deposits of iron ore were discovered at Udi, Agbaja and elsewhere. The availability of coal at Enugu and the completion of the Kainji hydro-electric dam meant that power was available for the scheme, while new processes in steel production made the use of high-grade coking coal unnecessary. In 1965 the United Nigerian Iron and Steel Company (UNISCO) was formed and experiments were held in Canada using electric smelting methods and Nigerian iron ore. Nigerian ore was found to be of too poor quality and too full of impurities to warrant large-scale steel production.

This failure was followed in 1970 by an intensive search programme for higher grade iron ore over an area covering 200 000 square kilometres of south-west Nigeria. In 1971 a Nigerian Steel Development Authority was established to co-ordinate research and planning. In 1973 drillings at Itakpe in Kwara State near Lokoja revealed a deposit estimated at between 86 and 105 million tonnes of high-grade iron ores.

A search was then conducted to find higher quality coals of the coking type than those already being mined. The main area of investigation has been at Lafia just south of the Jos Plateau. Low quality coking coals have been found at depths of 32 m and good quality coking coal at about 100 m. Refractory clay suitable for the manufacture of heat-resistant bricks used in steel manufacture is located at Onibode and Oshielle, dolomite is obtainable from Burum, and limestone from Jakura. The best site in relation to these deposits was at Ajaokuta.

Initial infrastructure here will include a rail link from Oturkpo to transport coal, an electricity grid, roads, and a housing estate. In addition to the Ajaokuta plant, two steel reduction plants are to be built at Warri and Port Harcourt, and will use natural gas fuel.

The quality of the iron ore at Itakpe is not exceptional, and higher grade iron ore will have to be imported from Liberia and Guinea. These imports will continue to supplement Nigeria's iron ore output for some considerable time.

With full output at Ajaokuta, Warri, Port Harcourt, and the newly repaired steel rolling mill at Enugu, Nigeria's steel output will be over two million tonnes a year, and this will be increased to five million tonnes when three other planned mills come into production as part of a long-term plan for steel.

The next major industrial project under the Plan is the construction of a US$430 million natural gas-based petro-chemical complex, probably sited near Port Harcourt. This will include installations producing chlorine, ethylene, vynil chloride, and polythene. By 1980, Nigeria's petro-chemical industry will be supplying raw material to the growing plastics industry as well as providing petro-chemicals for neighbouring states. In addition, two refineries are to be built at Warri and Kaduna for internal markets, and two refineries for the export of refined products.

Other fields of expansion are in the fields of motor car assembly, cement production, and sugar refining. Besides the recently established vehicle assembly plants of Peugeot, Volkswagen and Leyland, an Austrian motor company is to set up a factory at Bauchi, and a third lorry plant is to be established. The extensions to existing cement plants already mentioned will increase Nigeria's output to 3,5 million tonnes per annum by 1980 and save much foreign exchange. A large sugar refining complex is being built at Benin, and the existing refinery at Bacita is to increase its production with newly installed plant. Longer term projects include the liquifying of natural gas, the large scale carbonisation of coal, the development of the fishing industry and the expansion of pulp and paper industries.

The government's policy is to spread these new industries as widely as possible in modern industrial estates, beginning in the state capitals, and already estates have been completed at Owerri and Oshogbo.

Such an imaginative and massive scheme as Nigeria's Third National Plan is bound to attract foreign interest and investment. In 1971, however, the government announced its indigenisation programme which reserved a range of industries, including radio assembly and electrical equipment manufacture, for Nigerian investment only, while large-scale industries requiring massive capital investments had to have a 40 per cent Nigerian investment. This latter group included the chemical, textile, soap and leather industries. These measures effectively cut down foreign influence, without totally discouraging foreign investment. A second Indigenisation Decree has advanced the indigenisation process yet further, with many firms now being required to have a 60 per cent Nigerian investment.

The eventual aim of the government is to make Nigeria an exporter of industrial products. In addition to petroleum and petro-chemicals, possibilities for exports are seen in machine tools, cooling systems, agricultural machinery, automobile parts, and pumping equipment. An export council will promote these products in neighbouring countries.

Industrial development in Kenya

Kenya's economy is largely based on the production of agricultural raw materials for export – coffee, tea, pyrethrum, sisal, canned fruits, hides and skins. There are no fuels except wood, no useful minerals in commercial quantities except sodium carbonate, and at present the rather small hydro-electric power potential of the country is in its first stages of development. Coal, oil and hydro-electricity have to be imported and, despite intensive searches, no major oil deposits have been found.

Kenya is therefore heavily dependent on imports of manufactured articles, especially machinery, motor vehicles, rubber products, metal goods, fertilisers, fabrics and paper products.

The country thus displays an economy typical of a developing nation – a high percentage of workers engaged in agriculture, a high unemployment rate, few opportunities for jobs outside the agricultural sphere, a small income per capita, and thus a low buying power in internal markets. But the country has certain assets – a large volume of agricultural raw materials, an emerging African middle class, and stability of government. Of the three East African territories the rate of secondary industrial expansion has been greatest in Kenya. The pattern of growth and the present industrial structure is fairly typical of the developing territories of Africa. This pattern has been reached through certain stages and is largely a post-war development.

Before the Second World War Kenya possessed few industries except those processing local raw materials – coffee, wheat, sugar and tea. There was a small increase during the war in industrial production due to shortages but it was only at the beginning of the 1950s that industrial expansion really began. Table 17 illustrates the industrial structure of Kenya.

There is thus no heavy industry although there is a large oil refinery at Mombasa and a small steel mill using scrap metal at Nairobi. The map (Fig. 10.5) shows the location of Kenya's major centres and natural resources.

Kenya: A section of the industrial estate, Nairobi.

Table 17 Kenya: the present structure of industry

Industrial sector	*Range of goods produced*	*Major locations*
Food processing	Flour, beer, canned fruits, hams and vegetables, dairy products, coffee, tea, sugar, canned and fresh meat, tobacco and cigarettes, edible oils, soft drinks	Nairobi, Mombasa, Nakuru, Thika, Limuru, Nyeri, Miwani, Machakos
Material manufacture	Matting, rope, sacks, coarse fabric, cordage, soap, tannin, wooden products, knitted goods, paper, shoes, tyres, polishes	Nairobi, Mombasa, Limuru, Thika
Ancillary services	Motor vehicle repair, motor engineering, rolling stock and locomotive engineering, ship construction and repair	Nairobi, Mombasa, Kisumu

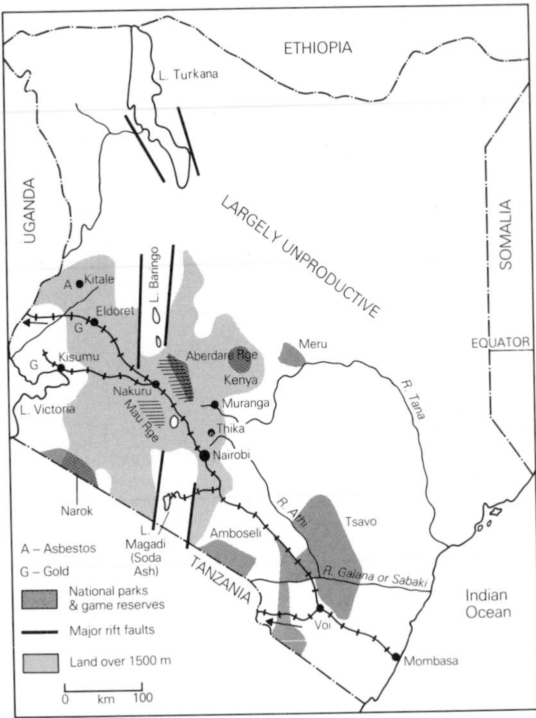

Fig. 10.5 Kenya – the Highlands, game areas and communications

Most of the factories are small in size – just over 70 per cent have workforces of less than 20. Most major concerns are located in urban areas in specially designed estates with railway and road access, and which are close to markets and to export routes. A few factories lie outside the major urban areas, close to labour supplies and to raw materials, and these are usually self-contained units with accommodation, eating and entertainment facilities for their employees. The Bata Shoe factory at Limuru is typical of this enterprise, employing over 900 workers and producing footwear, cycle tyres, and inner tubes. Local materials are used – chalk, salt, soda, wattle extract, hides and skins – but rubber, chemicals and fuels are imported.

In 1940 there were 40 companies with factories in Kenya, most of them subsidiaries of British firms. Today there are nearly 4 000 representing a wide range of foreign investors – Japan, West Germany, the United States, India, France and Italy. These companies can afford to construct factories and market the products efficiently. Up to the present the lack of capital on a large scale has prevented the African from entering this section of the economy. However, with government loans, numerous small manufacturing concerns and businesses have been established. In 1973–4 Kenya received over US$250 million of investments from overseas sources and the government plans to invest some US$265 million over the next few years in various projects. Just over US$80 million will be invested in industrial and commercial development, that is, about 30 per cent of total expenditure. Major industrial investment will be in Nairobi (biscuit, pharmaceutical and metal box factories), Thika (yarn and car assembly plants), Nanyuki (textile mill and an industrial estate), Kisumu (industrial estate, cotton mills, brewery), the expansion of the cement factory at Bamburi near Mombasa, and the establishment of a further 22 new tea factories throughout the country.

Kenya, however, possesses one source of wealth which she is now developing to the full – her national parks, game reserves, magnificent scenery and sunny climate. Nairobi is the centre for tourism in East Africa and serves as the base for visits to Tanzanian and Kenya parks. Tourism is Kenya's biggest currency earner, exceeding coffee. In 1972 revenue from tourism was US$32 million; in 1975 half a million tourists spent US$51 million. West Germany and Japan are particularly interested in promoting holiday facilities along the coast, and the Kenya government has opened tourist offices in London, Frankfurt, New York, and Tokyo.

Because of its unfavourable trade balances Kenya is making every effort to use this asset to the full. The parks and reserves are being made more accessible by the provision of tarmac roads, new game lodges are being set up, and increased hotel facilities are being provided in Nairobi. However, continuing activity by poachers threatens the existence of the large game animals in East Africa. Recently both the Kenyan and Tanzanian governments have decided to ban the issue of game licences for hunting.

Conclusions

Secondary industrialisation in Africa depends on a variety of factors – the appropriate infrastructure, the availability of skilled labour, qualified technicians and engineers, wide markets, and increasing investment. Outside South Africa, Zimbabwe, and, to a lesser extent Egypt – most manufacturing is concerned with the processing of primary produce such as coffee milling, palm oil extraction, timber preparation, fish canning and so on. In most tropical African countries there has been a big increase in food processing factories – Benin, the Ivory Coast, Senegal and Cameroon are steadily increasing their output of palm oil, Zaïre and Malagasy their refined sugar production, while flour mills are increasing in number in many countries as the market demands more white flour products.

By granting concessions to home and overseas investors, African countries are encouraging the establishment of textile and clothing industries, constructional concerns, metal and rubber industries. But most of these establishments tend to be small or medium sized; exceptions are ore smelting plants, wood processing and veneer mills, and some large textile concerns.

Questions

1 Comment on the prospects for the further development of mining and manufacturing industries in *one* of the following countries: Ghana, Nigeria, Guinea, Tanzania, Egypt.

2 Locate by sketch-map *a* the Rand, *b* the Shaba mining areas, and describe the exploitation of minerals and the industrial activity associated with each.

3 Locate and assess the importance of deposits of coal, iron ore, diamonds and copper in Africa south of the Sahara.

4 Illustrate from specific examples the contribution made by Africa to the industrial needs of Western Europe.

5 Give a reasoned account of the distribution and character of manufacturing industry in South Africa.

6 Examine the importance of mining to the economy of any one country in Africa.

7 Outline and comment on the distribution and problems of manufacturing industry in Zambia and Zimbabwe.

8 Discuss the relative distribution of fuel resources in Africa and comment on their relative use for industrial purposes *within* the continent.

9 *a* What are the factors which are indicative of developing countries in Africa? *b* Discuss the ways in which secondary industry can aid development. Confine your answer to one country with which you are familiar.

10 Briefly compare the industrial development of South Africa *or* Egypt with one less developed country in Africa.

11 Trace the factors which led to the establishment of secondary industries in African states. In what ways does this secondary industrial development benefit the country in which it is established?

12 Discuss Africa's role as a raw mineral ore supplier to industrialised nations.

Discussion topics

1 Your country as a market and raw materials supplier.

2 In what ways can African states make a fuller use of their raw materials?

3 What are the chief methods of promoting industrial expansion in African states?

4 What are the difficulties in establishing a major iron and steel plant in East or West Africa?

Practical work

Typical practical questions on industry might be:

1 Select any mining centre of which you have first-hand knowledge and discuss the effects of mining upon the growth of settlements and communications within its immediate area.

2 Discuss the reasons for the establishment of secondary industries in any region familiar to you.

3 In what ways could secondary industrial development be stimulated in *either* your home district *or* in a region in your country with which you are familiar.

The following topics are suggested as vacation work:

1 A visit to a local mine and the writing of an account of the mine using the following headings: *a* Location (with map); *b* General facts – labour force and, if possible, their origins; annual and monthly production figures; *c* Further processing,

and mining techniques; *d* Markets, present and prospective; *e* Importance of the mine's products to the general economy of the country.

2 The mapping of the location of secondary industries in the country, especially large concerns, in relation to the raw materials they use. Local newspaper cuttings giving news of new factories should be collected and the information inserted on the map in note form.

3 A visit to a local factory and the writing of an account. Particularly important in the account should be the marketing, the use of local or imported raw materials, and the factory's importance to the economy of the country as a whole. The students should not dwell too much on processing, welfare schemes and similar topics.

CHAPTER ELEVEN

Transport and communications

Although work on the first railway in Africa was begun at Cape Town in 1859, it was not until the late ninteenth century that the spate of railway building began to open up the continent. Until then the chief form of transport, in tropical regions at least, was by human porterage, an exceedingly slow and laborious method. Here, except in the tsetse-free highlands, transport animals were virtually unknown. In the Maghreb the donkey and the horse were the chief methods of transport, in the Sahara the camel was superbly adapted to its environment, and on the high level veld the ox-wagon was the chief wheeled vehicle.

The rivers

From what has been said on Africa's rivers in Chapter Eight it will be obvious that they are severely limited in their usefulness for transporting passengers and goods. The tremendous seasonal variation in volume, the dangerous shoals and sandbanks, the numerous falls and rapids, and the floating masses of vegetation are all physical obstacles to smooth transport. But despite these handicaps the rivers are used for carrying passengers and goods along parts of their courses at least. The Zaïre is navigable up to 140 km inland, then its course is broken by a series of rapids and falls up to Stanley Pool; from here to Stanley Falls is a navigable stretch of 1 600 km. The upper Niger and its tributary the Benue are also navigable, the Benue as far as Garoua in the Cameroon, 170 km from its confluence with the Niger, during the rains; the Niger, 4 200 km long, is navigable in its upper course between Kouroussa and Bamako, but between Bamako and Koulikoro is interrupted by rapids, and again between Ansongo and the Labbezenga rapids near the Mali–Niger border. The completion of the Kainji Dam in 1968 has improved the navigability and the Niger is now fully navigable between August and April from Gaya on the Nigeria–Benin border to its delta mouths. The Niger River and Steam Transport Company operates twelve barges, three tug boats and two cutters on the river. During the dry season the company can only operate from within the Nigerian border to western delta ports such as Burutu, negotiating the dam wall at Kainji via a lock.

Other rivers in West Africa which can be used for navigation mainly during the wet season include the Senegal (as far as Kayes, 900 km) and the Gambia (as far as Georgetown, 280 km, for light vessels). Mention should also be made of the lagoons along the coast which provide safe water courses for small vessels.

The River Nile is navigable from Lake Mobutu to Nimule on the Sudan border with Uganda but the steamer service has now been discontinued. At Nimule the papyrus reeds close in and navigation is impossible until Juba is reached. The river is then navigable for all seasons to Khartoum (about 1 300 km) but is then interrupted by a series of cataracts until Lake Nasser.

Most of the other rivers of Africa – Orange, Vaal, Limpopo, Zambezi – are virtually useless for navigation over long stretches because of seasonal variations in level. The Zambezi may have considerable potential as a transport artery with the completion of the Cabora Bassa dam. The river is navigable at present for only 160 km from its mouth. To open it up as a waterway to the Cabora Bassa lake, smaller dams and ramps would be needed at Lake Lupata, Tete and Mpanda Unca. Similar works would be required between Lakes Cabora Bassa and Kariba.

The lakes

The lakes of Africa are extremely useful for commercial shipping. Lake Victoria provides an important inter-territorial communications network for Tanzania, Kenya and Uganda. A train ferry service operates with terminals at Kisumu, Jinja, Mwanza and Musoma. Large cargoes of coffee, cotton, oil seeds, sugar cane, and many passengers are transported annually.

Considerable amounts of tung oil, groundnuts and rice are transported on Lake Malaŵi between Kota Kota, Karonga, Nkata Bay and Chipoka. The Malaŵi lake service has been operating since 1935 when the railhead was completed to Salima. Following Malaŵi's economic expansion after independence, much improved facilities were needed on the lake. For example, Malaŵi's new rice-growing scheme at Karonga needed larger boats to carry exports. New harbours are to be built at Chipoka and Chinteche to cater for the products from the northern Vipya pulp and paper mills.

The railways

The arrival of the colonial powers and the final agreement on their political spheres of control led to the rapid development of railways, the fastest means of gaining access to the interior and establishing strategic control. No attempt was made to coordinate the various lines, which were often of different gauges. Railways usually ran directly inland for strategic rather than economic reasons, although economic development usually followed the line – Mombasa to Lake Victoria (1896–1900), Lourenço Marques and Cape Town to Johannesburg and Pretoria (1895), from Tanga inland (from 1891), from Djibouti to Addis Ababa (in 1917), and from Matadi to Kinshasa (1898) to by-pass the Stanley Pool.

The pioneer railway builders faced innumerable difficulties. Although Africa consists of broad, flat plateaux, the construction of communications was still difficult. The plateaux often lie at between 900 and 1 500 m and may be reached only by traversing several steep escarpments and deep river valleys. The grain of the land often runs parallel to the coasts, erosion levels rising by steep steps into the interior, and deep *dongas* and rivers present continuous obstacles. The tremendous variations in relief along railway routes is shown in Fig. 11.1.

Physical features are not the only problems which railway builders and maintenance teams have to contend with – disease, dense vegetation, and the problem of fuel supplies have to be overcome. Frequent tropical thunderstorms may wash away vital sections of line, sandstorms cover the railway to great depths, and landslides destroy bridges. Such storms can be quite serious; at times most of Kenya and Uganda are completely cut off from the coast because rains may wash away vital bridges and make the roads impassable. Railway lines in the Congo were completed only after the removal of dense masses of tropical forest.

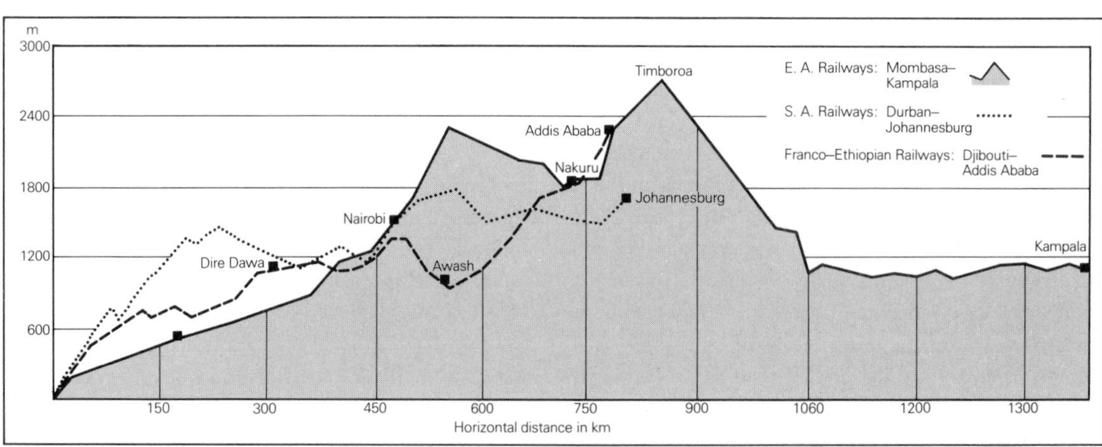

Fig. 11.1 Variations of relief along three railway routes

Once the railway has been built it has to be supplied with fuel, easy in coal-rich Zimbabwe and South Africa, but a great problem in East Africa and all West African states except Nigeria. Angola still uses vast quantities of timber as a fuel for engines on its railways. Another great difficulty is the vast unproductive distances over which track must be maintained.

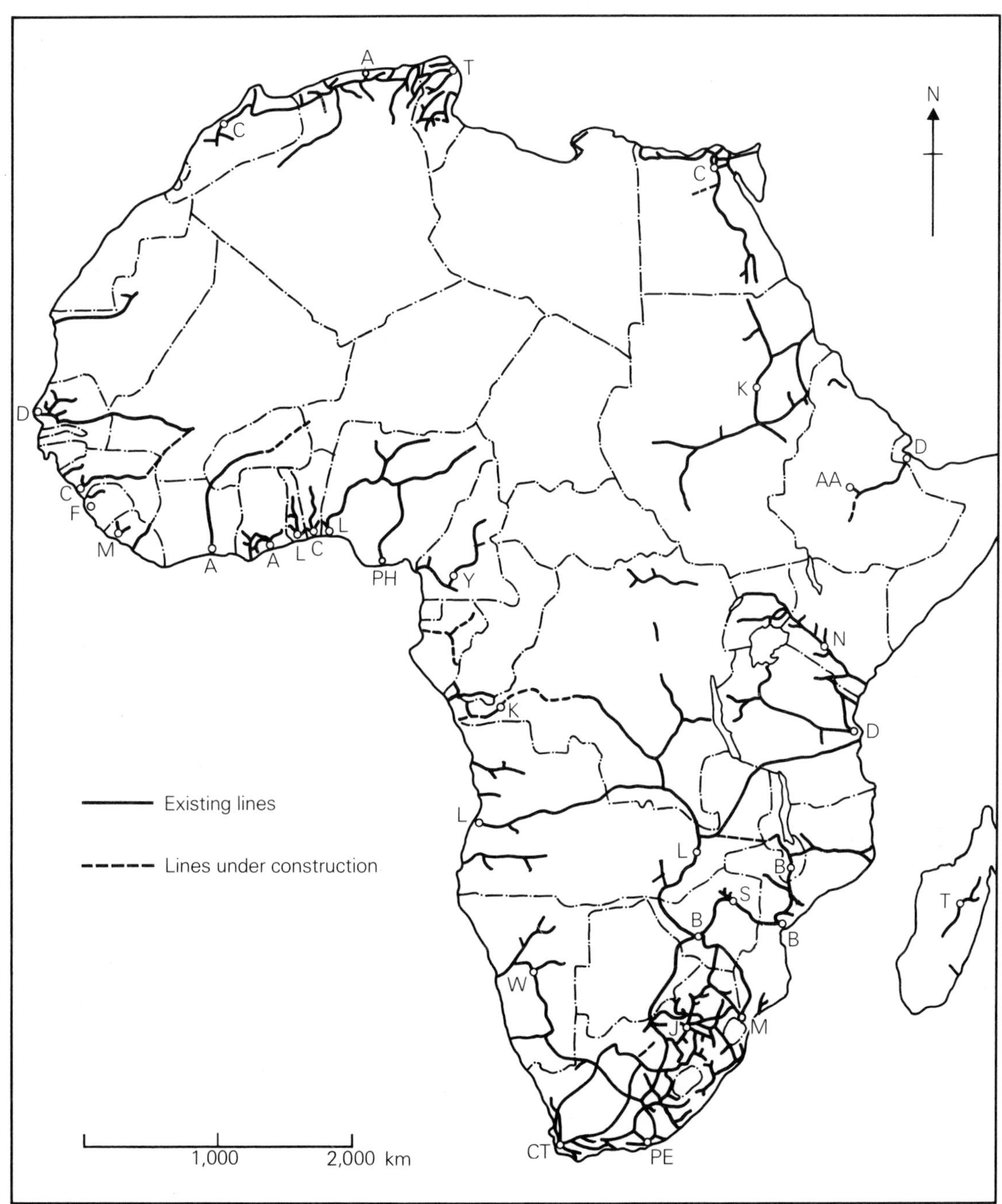

Fig. 11.2 The railways of Africa

The railway network

The legacy of colonial separatism in railway construction is reflected in today's map of railway communications in Africa (Fig. 11.2). Only in South Africa is there a true network directly comparable with those in Europe or North America; northwards, railways become long straggling lines running to the interior with vast areas where railways do not exist at all. Moreover, large areas such as the Chad Basin (covering over a million square kilometres, equal to an eighth of Europe) were too poor economically to warrant railway lines, although one is now being constructed through Cameroon. Even today political factions prevent the economic and sensible planning of railway networks. The excessive restrictions imposed by the Spanish Saharan authorities on a passage through their territory, forced the Mauritanian Government to construct a US$5 million tunnel for their Kedia d'Idjil line; again, the railway running between Mali and Senegal was severed when these two territories broke politically and alternative routes had to be used through the Ivory Coast. In early colonial days, the denial of the Gambia River as an outlet for the French in Senegal in part resulted in their constructing the 246 km long railway between St. Louis and Dakar in 1885. Again, the Sierra Leone and French Guinea lines were deliberately built on different gauges to prevent joining, the Guinean line being built across the Futa Jalon Plateau to forestall British penetration in that area. This line has now been realigned in parts.

But there are signs of more rational planning of railway routes within the framework of Africa's economic communities – the Trans-Cameroon Railway within the framework of the Central African Economic and Customs Union (Fig. 11.3) is a good example, as is the construction of the connecting line between the Uganda–Kenya railways and the Tanzanian lines (the Mruazi–Ruvu connection). The latter, with the southerly extension of the Central Tanzanian Line from Kilosa to Kidatu and beyond, are the first signs of the beginnings of a true railway network for East Africa. The Tanzam (Tazara or Uhuru) Railway built with Chinese finance, links Tanzania via Makambako to Kapiri Mposhi in Zambia, a distance of 1 023 km. The line was completed in 1975 and became fully operational in 1976. It is a magnificent engineering feat and passes through some of Africa's most rugged country in the mountainous Mlimba and Makambako sections. Designed to provide Zambia with an alternative import–export route and to open up remote parts of Tanzania, it is also a major link in an evolving Cape to Cairo railway network.

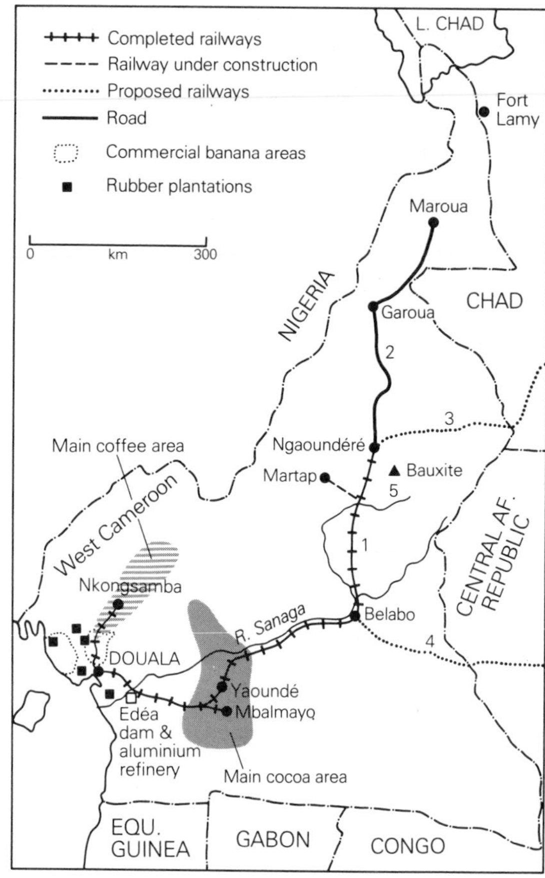

Fig. 11.3 The Trans-Cameroon Railway. If agreement is reached on all parts of the plan this will be one of the first planned integrated railway networks in Africa. Work is now completed on the 710 km-long line from Yaoundé to Ngaoundéré (1). This now connects with a modern tarmac road to Maroua and thus unites the economically different north to the south. The railway was finished in 1968 and it is planned to construct a 560 km branch line (3) which will run to the important cotton growing region around Sarh (Fort Archamboult) in southern Chad. Another branch line of 560 km (4) may then be built from Belabo to Banqui, the CAR capital, to promote the external trade of that country. The Trans-Cameroon Railway should certainly stimulate economic growth of the Cameroon Republic, particularly the port of Douala and the development of the bauxite site south-east of Ngaoundéré (5).

The inadequacy of the railways

The railways of Africa are, however, beginning to

Tanzania: Part of the Tan-Zam railway.

feel the strain of the tremendous economic developments taking place on the continent. African countries now produce 60 per cent more cultivated crops than they did in the 1930s, exports of groundnuts doubled in the last twenty years, coffee production is five times higher than in the 1930s, cocoa production has increased 30 per cent since 1946, and the output of cotton is 30 per cent higher than the 1930s average annual total. Mineral production too has increased at a colossal rate – Africa produces twice as much copper, iron ore and manganese, four times as much cobalt, six times as much asbestos, and a third as much again of tin concentrates as were produced in 1938. Imports of heavy machinery and transport equipment now form between 20 and 35 per cent of the imports of most countries, and bulky imports of fuel oils represent between 6 and 12 per cent of imports. The rapid post-war development of secondary industries has accentuated this growth.

The increasing volume of imports and exports has not been accompanied by a similar increase in the rate of development of the transport system of Africa. While the volume of freight carried on Africa's railways is now three-and-a-quarter times what it was in 1938, the length of railways has remained virtually stable, and in some parts of Africa has even decreased, e.g. the southern Tanzania line has been removed between Mtwara and Nachingwea because of lack of trade. Africa today possesses little more than five per cent of the world's total length of railway track. The periodic congestion of shipping in Mombasa, Beira, Maputo and other major ports testifies to the inability of the railways to cope with the increasing flow of goods.

Nigeria's railway system is a prime example of a network whose adequacy has been outstripped by national economic development. The basic pattern of the present system was virtually completed between the years 1898 and 1930: Lagos to Minna (1898–1912), Baro to Kano (1910–1912), Port Harcourt to Enugu to Jos (1915–1916–1927), Zaria to Kaura Namoda, and Kano to Nguru (1929–1930). The longest extension in recent years was the Kano to Maiduguri line (1958–1964). These lines were constructed during the colonial period to tap Nigeria's crops and minerals and channel them to Lagos and Port Harcourt for export.

Thus, Nigeria's rail network comprises 3 505 km of single-track lines which have altered little since they were first laid. The track is light weight and narrow gauge (3′ 6″), there are long curved stretches, and bridges which were not designed to carry today's heavy trains. Consequently speeds must be kept low and traffic congestion is common. Because attention has been focused on road construction, railways have lost a lot of custom: in the financial year 1958–59 the railways carried 850 000 t of agricultural produce, but by the early 1970s this had dropped to 350 000 t. Total tonnages of all commodities have decreased from 2,6 million tonnes in 1954–55 and 3 million tonnes in 1961–62 to less than 2 million tonnes in 1973–74. In addition, fewer people use the railways as roads are extended and more cars come on the market: in 1961–62, over 11 million passengers used the railways, while in 1973–74 the figure had dropped to under five million. The railway network was hopelessly inadequate to cope with the massive increase in imports after the Civil War, imports which rose from 200 000 t a month in 1974 to 300 000 t a month in 1975.

Plans to change this intolerable state of affairs have been put into operation by the Nigerian Government under the Third National Development Plan. Over 1 000 km of standard gauge track has been constructed to run parallel with the old narrow gauge single track, avoiding major curves and gradients. The old track will be improved and altered to standard gauge, more rolling stock will be provided, bridges strengthened, and major railway workshops constructed in Lagos, Enugu, Zaria and Kafanchan. Once the present railway system has been improved the government will be in a position to extend the existing lines so that an east–west line will link with the rail systems of Nigeria's neighbours, and eventually with all members of the Economic Community of West African states.

The roads

The present slow rate of railway expansion in Africa can be explained partly by the vast increase in the number of roads being built on the continent. This is the fastest growing medium of transport in Africa. Within the last twenty years Algeria and Zimbabwe have doubled their existing road network, Ghana has increased hers by 2½ times and Kenya by a half. Thus some of the extra burden created by developing economies has been taken away from the railways, but not all, for the railway is especially adapted to the cheaper transport of bulky goods – ores, mineral oils, and coal. Moreover roads vary tremendously in Africa; they may be simply bulldozed tracks of *murram* or red earth, hard, corrugated and flinty during the dry season, slippery and impassable during the rains, and kept reasonably level from time to time by a grading machine. From this there are many intermediate stages – some countries have in many places single tarmac strips the width of one car, while the 2 000 km long Cape Town–Beit Bridge road is one of the finest super highways in the world. Many African nations are devoting large amounts of capital to the construction of all-weather roads, realising that an efficient transport system usually stimulates economic growth. Algeria and Kenya now have over four times as many kilometres of hard-surface road as they did in 1948, and Egypt, Ghana, Nigeria and Zambia two-and-a-half to three times as much.

But it is only recently that true road networks have begun to evolve. Before the 1950s the road transport system of most African countries was based on the railways which linked the main commercial zones with the major ports, and these were often several hundred kilometres apart, especially in eastern and southern Africa. The post-war expansion of agricultural production led to the development of feeder roads in the main agricultural areas, linking them directly to the railheads. Thus the main flow of traffic remains in most cases mainly from the interior to the coast rather than between individual countries. For example, in eastern and central Africa international trade is negligible, except between Kenya, Uganda and Tanzania, and outside this region most goods are transported by other means than roads. The Sudan, except for its trade with Egypt, has very

Nigeria: A dirt road during the rainy season; such roads are often impassable for ordinary vehicles.

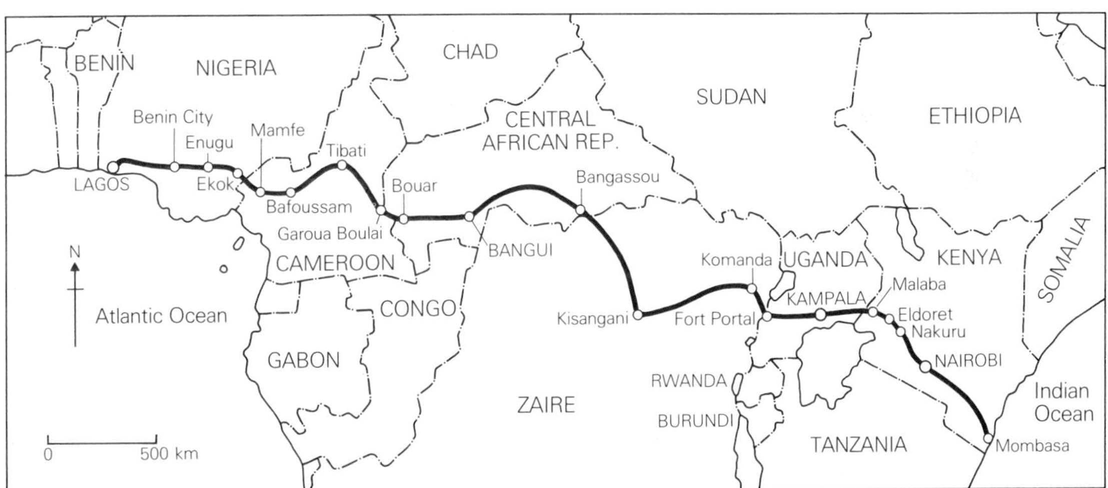

Fig. 11.4 The Trans-African Highway. This 6 500 km long highway was due for completion in 1978 and runs through Kenya, Uganda, Zaïre, Central African Republic and Nigeria, thus linking the east and west coasts of Africa from Mombasa to Lagos. The road was built with aid from Western Europe, the USA and the World Bank, and cost over US$500 million. Most tarmac work was done on the stretch through Zaïre. Trade and contacts between West and East Africa will now be greatly stimulated

restricted trade connections with its southern neighbours – coffee, tea, dairy produce and fresh vegetables come either via the Nile or on sea routes, while her grain exports to countries abroad go entirely by sea. Ethiopia uses her own rail routes and then sea to import metal boxes, butter, soda and aluminium sheeting from East Africa. Malaŵi sends only tea to the Nairobi auctions and imports butter in exchange, while Zambia exports mainly zinc and metal products to East Africa. The principal commodities moving between Kenya and Uganda and Zaïre – petroleum, machinery, vehicles, fish, tea and palm oil – go largely by rail via Kigoma, Kalemie and Bujumbura.

Thus cross-frontier transport by road in these regions is confined to specific areas – between Kenya, Uganda and Tanzania; between Zambia, Malaŵi and Tanzania, and between Rwanda, Zaïre and Uganda. Of these only the Tanzania–Zambia–Malaŵi routes can be classed as long-distance traffic; commodities, mainly petroleum and some copper ore, at present move between Kapiri Mposhi and Mikumi, the present terminus of the branch railway from Tanzania's Central Line. Malaŵi's trade with Kenya travels along the Iringa–Dodoma–Arusha route, while a considerable amount of Tanzania's exports from her southern regions uses this road northwards to Kenya. Many of the roads in East Africa carry a growing amount of tourist traffic, especially in Kenya, where there are good road links to all the major game parks, an important aspect in promoting the tourist industry.

It is clear that there is a great need to improve the linking roads between countries to promote international trade within Africa. The main basis for such a road network is the so-called Great North Road which, if fully developed, could form a major trans-Africa highway running from Cairo through to Cape Town. This road is shown in diagrammatic form in Fig. 11.5. The main sections which greatly need improvement are between Iringa (Tanzania) and Kapiri Mposhi (Zambia), since the political trend in Zambia is towards greater trade orientation towards the Dar-es-Salaam outlet. However, the Kapiri Mposhi–Mikumi route does not pass through the Iringa region which Tanzania wishes to develop. A development programme for a Zambia–Tanzania–Nairobi trunk road has been advocated since 1957 but it has been hindered by lack of capital. Another weak link lies between the Sudan and Ethiopia.

The Great North Road is crossed at three points by east–west highways – the Mombasa, Uganda, Kivu Province route to Kisangani and Matadi; the Port Sudan–Geneina route; and the Beira–Lobito route. Of these three the Mombasa to Lagos route has the most potential from the point of view of international trade. The road from Mombasa to the western Uganda border is tarmacadamed throughout, while the road to Kisangani has always been well maintained. This east–west route is joined by the second major north–south route (Cape Town–Lubumbashi–Likasi–Kalemie–Uvura) at Bukavu.

In the western region of Africa one of the greatest needs is for the improvement of the trans-Sahara routes. The Sahara is already being crossed by specially designed vehicles but it is still a hazardous journey and methods are too uneconomic for truly large-scale movement of goods. Already tarmac cover runs for 800 km to Insalah, but there are then 1 600 km of rough tracks. Eight West African states (Egypt, Mali, Chad, Niger, Tunisia, Mauritania, Algeria and Morocco) together with assistance from oil companies, have planned a route from Hassi Messaoud to Tamanrasset in the Ahaggar and then branch routes to Gao and Agades. The project is to be completed by 1980 and will cut freight costs by 50 per cent. A British company is already using the Sahara route, driving giant trucks and their contents for sale in Kano and Lagos.

It is in Nigeria that tremendous improvements in the road system have been accomplished in recent years. The basic trunk road system linking major administrative centres was begun in 1925 under British supervision but as the economy developed this system soon became inadequate. Even as late as 1950 Nigeria had only 1 800 km of bituminous roads, a ridiculously low figure for a country covering 924 000 square kilometres. A major road improvement and expansion plan was begun, and between 1951 and 1972 the length of bituminous roads was increased ten-fold to over 18 000 km; during the same period, the whole national network, including dirt and gravel roads, more than doubled from nearly 45 0000 km to over 95 000 km. The administration in Lagos was responsible for trunk 'A' roads, mainly

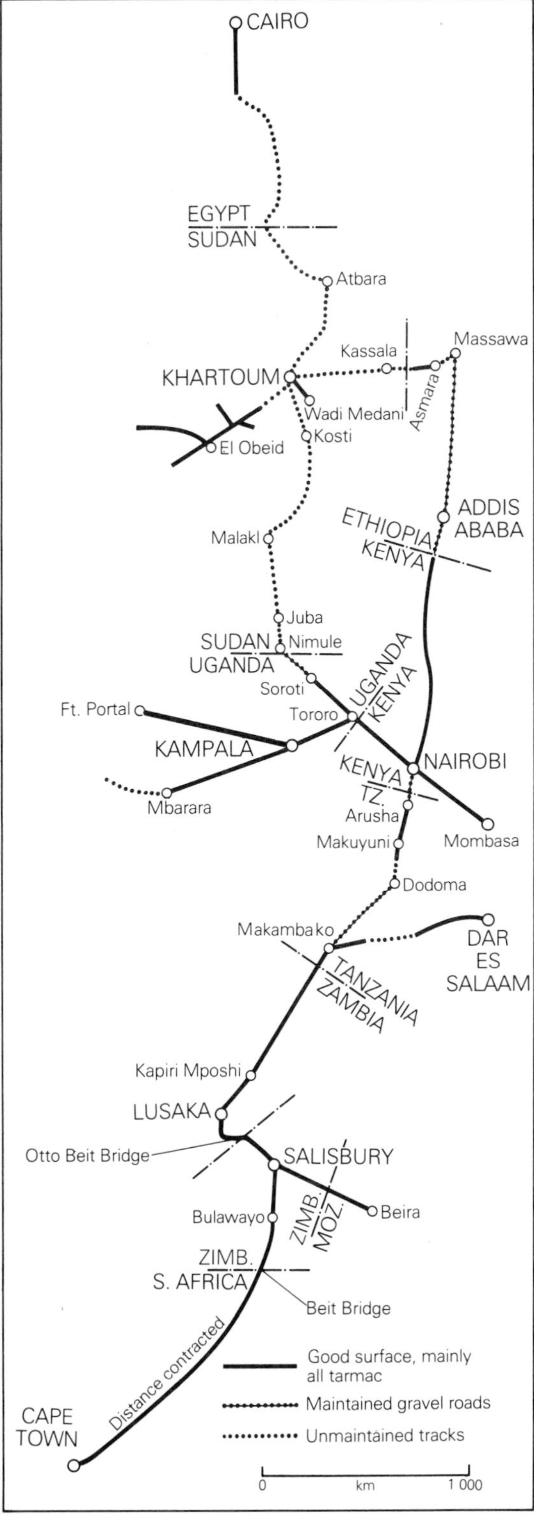

north–south feeder routes linking the port with important agricultural zones, while the individual states were allocated responsibility for the trunk 'B' or secondary roads.

Even this extended road network was unable to cope with the boom in traffic following the Civil War and by the mid-1970s road surfaces in Nigeria were deteriorating under the strain, and traffic jams were frequent, especially in urban centres. Under the Third National Development Plan the government allocated massive funds for road development. The money is being spent on the tarmacing of 3 000 km of gravel roads, the building of flyovers and by-passes to relieve traffic congestion in most major urban centres, the construction of 4 000 km of new roads with strengthened bridges such as the Lagos–Ibadan motorway costing US$150 million, and the conversion of a further 4 000 km of earth and single-lane roads to hard-surface dual carriageways.

Fig. 11.5 Africa – the Great North Road probably carries more international traffic in Africa than any other route but, as the diagrammatic illustration here shows, it will need much improvement before it becomes a true highway of trade. In the Sudan all-weather roads exist only in the southern part, while the northern parts have mere desert tracks which are several kilometres wide in parts and cross numerous rocky outcrops. With the longer rains further south, these roads become impassable for long periods. The Khartoum–Nimule stretch is a poorly maintained gravel track but a longer, better maintained alternative route goes from El Obeid to Wau and from Wau to Nimule.

In Ethiopia it is only around Addis Ababa and Asmara that there is a true road network; the Kassala–Asmara road is better maintained on the Ethiopian side, where it has a tarmac surface over a quarter of its length. Road connections with Kenya have been greatly improved by a tarmac highway from Nairobi to the Ethiopian border.

Uganda has one of the best road systems to be found in East Africa, with large stretches of tarmac connecting to Kenya and the border regions with Zaïre. Together with the roads in Kenya this forms the main east-west highway leading to Zaïre and West Africa. In Zaïre it links with an alternative route to the north (Cape Town–Lubumbashi–Uvira). In Kenya the main trunk road is nearly all tarmac and there is a good network of tarmac roads in the highlands and well-maintained roads to game parks and outlying regions. A gravel road links with Tanzania whose government has tarmaced the stretch from the border at Namanga to just beyond Makuyuni in the Lake Manyara region (about 130 km). But from there to Makambako the roads are very bad and long stretches are being improved in view of possibilities of increasing trade with Zambia. In Zambia the stretch to Kapiri Mposhi is now a tarmac road now taking considerable traffic, particularly loads of oil and copper ore. From there to Chirundu on Zambia's southern border the road is tarmaced, and through Zimbabwe and South Africa the Great North Road has tarmac surfaces all the way to Cape Town. Malaŵi is completely by-passed by the road, but road connections with Zambia have been improved.

Chad Republic: Overloading of public transport causes rapid deterioration of vehicles and road surfaces.

Roads therefore are receiving great attention in Africa and most of this attention has been concentrated into the last fifteen years. But roads are costly to build and their maintenance is often more expensive than that of railways. Many of Africa's poorer nations are therefore content to realign and tarmac the existing roads, while new road building is undertaken on a 'feeder' basis from important economic regions.

Air transport

Air transport has undergone an even more rapid expansion than roadways in Africa since the Second World War. In the 1930s British Imperial Airways made only one flight each week through Cairo, Entebbe, Nairobi, and Salisbury to Cape Town and return. Today there are several flights daily to all these places, not only by British airlines but by the national airlines of Kenya, Ethiopia and Egypt, and regular flights to London from Johannesburg and Cape Town by South African Airways. Less frequent services are provided by many other international airlines to Europe, to the Far East and India, and to North America. The Second World War hostilities in the Mediterranean and North Africa meant that alternative routes had to be found and West Africa in particular benefited by the great improvement programmes to many of its local airstrips and by the construction of new airfields. Today Africa is less than a day's journey from any one of the major continents of the world.

Nigeria has recognised the importance of an efficient air service in a developing economy and is expanding both its internal and external air services. As per capita incomes increase, more Nigerians are using the airlines in preference to the slower road and rail routes. In 1968, 64 000 passengers used air transport, 100 000 in 1969, and more than 300 000 in 1974. To cater for the increased air traffic, the Third National Development Plan allocated US$654 million for expenditure on the re-development of 16 airports, the construction of three new international airports at Port Harcourt, Ilorin and Maiduguri, the expansion of Lagos Airport to handle Concorde jets and of Kano Airport to handle Beoing 747s, and the purchase of several new aircraft. Nigeria also wishes to partly finance a West African airline system which would link all the members of the Economic Community of West African States.

Kenya's new US$35 million airport, opened in 1978, can handle three million passengers annually and is served by 30 international airlines. Kenya provided 55 per cent of the cost, the World Bank the remainder.

In addition to transporting passengers and goods, the use of air transport for shipping exports abroad, especially those of a perishable nature, and of moving food supplies from one region to another is increasing. Fresh fruits are flown from Nairobi to London and dairy produce to Aden, fresh vegetables from agricultural areas to mining districts, meat supplies are air freighted from Somalia to the Middle East.

Loads of exports carried by air are increasing in volume. Exports from Africa have traditionally been shipped by sea because of the low value and heavy weight. Because of this, north-bound transport aircraft, once having delivered their loads in African countries, returned almost empty to Europe. Airlines have now reduced tariffs for freight on return flights from Africa to Europe, with the result that the farmer in Kenya or Senegal can obtain a satisfactory profit on exports. This has meant, however, that the quality and packaging of produce must be rigidly controlled. Kenya now operates grading stations throughout the country to which small-scale farmers can bring their produce for export. Other countries which make use of these cheap flights are Zambia (tobacco), Rwanda and Burundi (tea), and Malaŵi (vegetables and fruit). Other land-locked countries which are planning to take advantage of such flights are Uganda, Niger, Botswana and the Central African Republic.

Aircraft are now widely used in geological and cartographical surveying, especially in relation to the planning of land resettlement schemes and new cultivation zones. The aeroplane is invaluable for the policing and administration of remote districts in Ethiopia, northern Kenya and the Sudan. The ease with which security forces can be moved from one trouble spot to another is an important factor in maintaining political stability.

The Suez Canal

The Suez Canal was completed in 1869 and is 166 km long. The Canal was closed due to Israeli–Egyptian hostilities in 1967 but was reopened again in 1975. At present the Canal has a width of 60 m and a draught of 12 m and can take vessels of 70 000 t deadweight. Before closure in 1967, over 20 000 vessels passed through the Canal each year, nearly one-third of them being oil tankers. Nearly 85 per cent of north-bound traffic consisted of oil (160 million tonnes) while approximately 15 per cent consisted of soya beans, minerals, textiles, fibres, rubber and oil seeds. South-bound cargoes consisted of machinery, metal goods, cement, cereals, pulp, timber and paper. Egypt received approximately US$170 million annually from tolls just before closure.

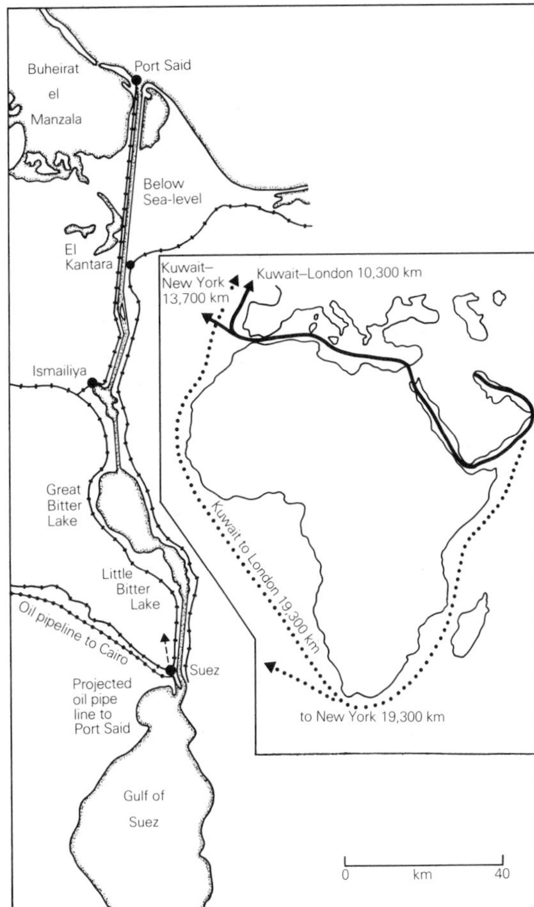

Fig. 11.6 Egypt – The Suez Canal

The closure of the Canal had the effect of stimulating trade round the Cape sea route, although tankers operating from the Persian Gulf had to take 63 days on the journey to Europe instead of the 39 days through Suez. The round trip was 7 600 km longer than via Suez. The second effect was to boost the production of giant oil tankers of up to half-a-million tonnes capacity to make the per unit cost of oil transport round the Cape cheaper.

With the re-opening of the Canal, the Egyptian government has put into operation a widening and deepening programme to almost double the draught and to enable vessels of 250 000 t deadweight to pass through. However, many of the larger tankers will still use the Cape route. By the end of 1975 about 40 vessels a day were passing through the Canal compared with 62 a day before closure. The Egyptian government has increased tariffs in order to give Egypt about US$400 million a year and has completed an oil pipeline linking Suez with Port Said. The giant tankers will be able to pump oil in at the Suez end and have it pumped onboard waiting tankers at Port Said. The Israelis have also completed another pipeline from Eilat on the Gulf of Aqaba across the Negev Desert to the Mediterranean coast near Askkalon; tankers of 152 000 t can berth at Eilat.

Questions

1 Discuss the relative merits and demerits of rail and road transport in fostering the economy of African states.
2 In what ways have political considerations overridden economic ones in the construction of railways in Africa?
3 Compare the part played by rivers, railways and roads in the internal communications of *either* East Africa *or* West Africa.
4 Which factors have hampered and which stimulated railway construction in Africa?
5 You are to plan two new railways to supplement those already existing in Africa. With the aid of a sketch-map justify your proposals.
6 Where and why is inland water transport important in Africa south of the Sahara?
7 With the aid of a sketch-map illustrate the main proposals you would make to improve the communications system in your own country in relation to the available resources.
8 Describe the communications system of any one country in Africa and show how it is related to the economic resources of the country.

CHAPTER TWELVE

Trade, aid and development programmes

Trade

The newly independent territories of Africa rely heavily on the export of primary produce and partially processed minerals for their foreign earnings. All are making great efforts to diversify the range and increase the exports of their produce, and to find new markets. The revenue obtained in this way is preferable to that obtained by loans from abroad, since no interest has to be paid on a nation's own efforts. The main difficulties facing most African states, which are currently passing through a stage of economic transition, are the lack of capital and trained labour.

The dominance of traditional markets

Africa is still oriented in its trade to traditional markets, usually those of the former colonial powers who developed the economy to supply their home industries with raw materials. Trade was restricted with other countries and, although many African countries have widened their range of markets, this dominance still persists. The former French states of West Africa and the Maghreb, for example, are strongly tied to France commercially. Algeria (regarded as part of France from 1870 until 1962) sends about a quarter of her exports to France and nearly half of her imports are French; the Ivory Coast obtains about half of its imports from France and sends about two-fifths of its exports there.

Similarly, the Commonwealth countries formerly had strong trading relations with Britain, membership of the Commonwealth ensuring them certain trade preferences over non-members. These trade preferences have now fallen away since Britain became a member of the European Economic Community and came under that organisation's rulings covering trade.

South Africa, a former Commonwealth member, has always had traditional markets in Britain, especially for her fruits and wines, and she still relies heavily on Britain for specialised machinery and electrical goods. Britain supplies South Africa with about one-fifth of her imports annually and takes about one-third of her exports. The United States forms South Africa's second biggest market and supplier, providing about one-sixth of South Africa's imports and taking one-tenth annually of her exports; South Africa is an important supplier of strategic minerals to the USA. Uranium oxide,

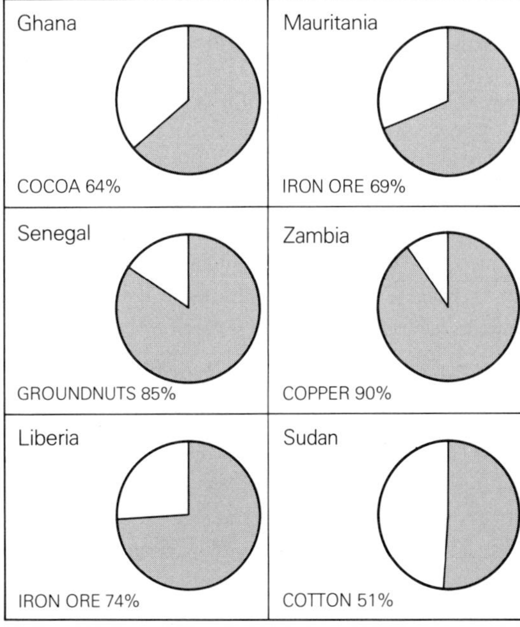

Fig. 12.1 The dominance of single products in exports of selected African states

diamonds, wool, copper metal and sugar molasses are the main exports, machinery, motor vehicles and agricultural equipment the main imports.

New trading partners

Since the granting of independence to African countries, the United States, West Germany and Japan have become increasingly important suppliers and markets. West Germany now takes more imports, mainly natural gas and oil, from Algeria than does France, once Algeria's foremost trading partner. Nearly 15 per cent of Zambia's copper exports go to West Germany, Zambia's third largest customer, and eight per cent of Zambia's imports are from West Germany. West Germany is also one of the biggest European buyers of Libyan and Nigerian oil, and Liberian iron ore.

Japan has deeply penetrated African markets in the last decade and now has trade relations with every country on the continent. Japan's main export markets in order are South Africa, Nigeria, Libya, Algeria, Zambia, Kenya, Tanzania and Zaïre. To these countries she exports heavy industrial products, machinery, instruments and transport machinery. Japan's main suppliers of raw materials in Africa are, in order, South Africa, Nigeria, Libya, Zambia and Egypt who provide oil, iron ore, manganese, chromium ore, copper, palm oil, tin, cotton and foodstuffs. Strong trade relations exist between Japan and Kenya, Ethiopia, Morocco and Sudan, but with these countries and many others there are large trade imbalances. In 1975 only Nigeria, Libya, Zambia, Mauritania, Chad, Angola, Swaziland, Mozambique and Senegal had favourable trade balances with Japan. For example, Japan supplied the three East African territories of Tanzania, Uganda and Kenya with a tremendous volume of expensive high precision articles – cameras, transistor radios, cars, binoculars and other optical instruments – while taking only nominal quantities of agricultural produce in exchange. Many of Japan's other articles are also in direct competition with African industries – textiles for instance. Tanzania, for example, imported four times the value of her exports to Japan in 1974 and Kenya was in a similar position. To check this unfavourable trade the East African territories were forced temporarily to ban all Japanese goods except spare parts.

Another significant feature of the trend to find new markets is the increasing trade with Communist bloc territories. Thus the first exports of soda ash left Kenya for the Soviet Union in 1966; Tanzania now supplies East Germany with coffee and has signed trade agreements with Hungary and Poland; Nigeria exports to Czechoslovakia; Sierra Leone exchanges agricultural produce for Soviet agricultural machinery; Morocco has trade agreements with the Soviet Union and China; Ghana exports about eight per cent of her goods to communist countries and these supply five per cent of her imports. These trading partners have, to a large extent, replaced South Africa as a supplier and a market, since most African-governed nations refuse to trade with that country on account of its internal policies. After her unilateral declaration of independence, nearly all African states severed trade relations with former Rhodesia.

The composition of exports

Since the development of secondary industry is only in its initial stages in most countries in Africa, exports from the continent still consist largely of raw or semi-processed agricultural and mineral products. In many cases exports are dangerously dominated by one product. For example, countries who rely heavily on one export commodity include Kenya (coffee, one-quarter of exports), Tanzania (cotton, one-sixth), Uganda (coffee, one-third), Liberia (iron ore, nearly three-quarters), Gabon (timber, over one-half), Benin (oil seeds, 80 per cent), Senegal (groundnuts, 85 per cent), Egypt (cotton, nearly one-half), Sudan (cotton, over 50 per cent). Such one-product-dominance is a weakness in a country's economy: restrictions by world agreement have caused a cutting back of production of coffee in Kenya, the extreme fluctuations in cocoa prices have caused considerable unease in Ghana, the manufacture of man-made fibres is always a danger to sisal in Tanzania. Moreover, minerals such as oil and iron ore are a wasting asset; although recent mineral finds are tremendous, the rate of exploitation by giant companies may soon exahust them (see Chapter Thirteen).

For these reasons, African nations are attempting to make a fuller use of their raw materials by developing secondary industry and producing more manufactured and processed articles themselves. However, the high percentage of imported manufactured goods, particularly machinery and vehicles, reflect the underdeveloped nature of secondary industry in Africa.

The balance of trade

Among the most important factors affecting a country's balance of trade are the amount of productive land within the territory's boundaries, the degree of industrialisation, and the amount of expensive manufactured articles and food needed by the growing population. In the mid-1970s the increased cost of oil considerably upset the balance of trade in many countries of Africa and has caused severe cutbacks in economic expansion and development plans.

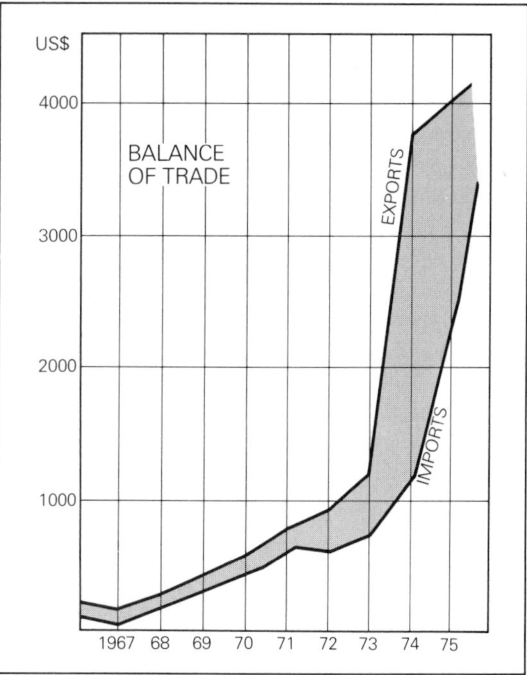

Fig. 12.2 Nigeria – Balance of Trade, 1967–1975. The drop in the rate of export values after 1973 is due to cut-backs in oil production and the effects of droughts

Kenya

Kenya will serve as a good example to illustrate the factors influencing trade balances in Africa. Of the three East African territories Kenya has always had an unfavourable trade balance. In 1959, for example, four years before independence, Kenya exported US$76 million worth of goods and imported US$148 million worth – a trade deficit of US$72 million. At that time Kenya had a fairly large European (66 000) and Asian (170 000) population and consequently a high demand for imported expensive consumer goods such as cars, refrigerators and radios. Railway rolling stock, farm machinery, commercial vehicles and factory equipment were also high on the list of imports. Again, Kenya's main exports were largely agricultural – coffee, pyrethrum, tea – and these were subject to price fluctuations on the London market.

Since independence, Kenya's trade gap has widened even further: 1964 – exports US$128 million worth, imports US$183 million; 1967 – exports US$144 million, imports US$270 million; 1970 – exports US$177 million, imports US$326 million; 1974 – exports US$390 million, imports US$812 million. Between 1970 and 1974 Kenya's trade deficit rose from US$150 million to US$403 million. Although Kenya doubled the value of her export value in that period, her trade deficit trebled. (In 1976 the deficit was lowered to US$152 m, in 1977 to 72 m.)

The reasons for this unfortunate trend, common to many of the developing countries of Africa without large mineral resources are:

a *Population increase:* In 1965 Kenya's population was about 9,5 million; in 1975 it was 13,5 million – an increase of 4 million in ten years. Money which should pay for imports now has to be diverted to educational, medical facilities and social schemes for these extra four million. More land has to be devoted to food crops at the expense of land formerly under export cash crops. Food imports cost Kenya some US$58 million a year.

b *Nature of exports:* Kenya's exports are traditionally agricultural – coffee, tea, pyrethrum, meat products, hides and skins, etc. Prices for such commodities fluctuate with demand while the prices of imported manufactured goods continue to rise. In 1974, for example, Kenya's major imports were petroleum (price increase in 1974 over 1968–73 average – 280 per cent), fertilisers (up 250 per cent), motor vehicles (up 90 per cent), iron and steel products (87 per cent) and paper and board (72 per cent increase). This gives an average increase of 160 per cent in import prices.

c *Lack of mineral resources:* Kenya's major mineral export for many years has been soda ash, over 90 per cent of which is exported to the Far East, where it is used in the manufacture of glass, soap, cleaners and chemical reagents. There are no large iron ore deposits like those in Swaziland, no chrome deposits like those of Zimbabwe, no copper deposits like those of Zambia. The position, however, is improving with the exploitation of recent mineral discoveries – fluorspar in the Kerio Valley (used in steel making), wollastonite (used for insulation) in the Rift Valley, lead and silver ores at Kinangoni north of Mombasa, and chrome and nickel at West Pokot. Kenya has already secured markets for these minerals.

d *Lack of fuels:* Kenya has no coal and, despite intensive searches over the last twenty years, no oil has been discovered. Imports of oil are becoming increasingly expensive due to the oil price rise – Kenya paid US$38 million for oil imports in 1973, US$147 million in 1974, and US$217 million in 1975. The transport of this oil also means the import of costly pipes and tankers; the newly completed oil pipeline from Mombasa to Nairobi cost US$68 million to build. Costly equipment must also be imported for other energy projects – the Kindaruma and Kamburu hydro-electric power schemes on the Tana and the geo-thermal plants now being established in the Rift Valley.

Kenya is making strong efforts to reduce the trade gap. Although tea, coffee, and sisal still dominate exports, refined petroleum is now exported, cement exports have been doubled and new exports such as fresh fruits and vegetable oils have been introduced. To some extent the receipts from the tourist industry (US$52 million in 1975) offset losses through trade, but the impact of this is reduced because of the large amount of money which has to be constantly invested in tourism.

In general, therefore, countries which rely on large exports of agricultural produce in return for heavy imports of expensive manufactured articles show an adverse trade balance. The sudden discovery of an economically important mineral could, however, change the position drastically. Nigeria's oil exports, for example, have produced an increasingly favourable trade balance. In 1970, Nigeria's exports were valued at US$1 380 million of which oil accounted for US$803 million; in 1973 exports were valued at US$3 418 million with oil at US$2 900 million. Nigeria's trade surplus rose from US$230 million in 1970 to US$1 430 million in 1973. In 1977 Nigeria's exports were valued at US$12 500 million, of which oil accounted for US$11 400 million; the trade deficit was only US$120 million, the first deficit in many years. These facts have all the greater significance when one realises that in 1965 Nigeria had a trade deficit of about US$1 350 million.

Common Markets in Africa

The concept of the common market, that is, the removal of trade barriers and customs duties between the former territories of neighbouring states to promote trade and widen markets, has met with varying degrees of success in Africa.

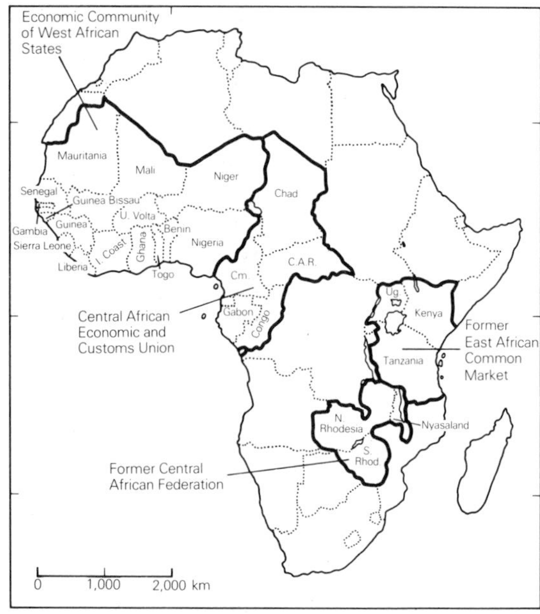

Fig. 12.3 Africa – common markets referred to in the text

The Central African Federation

The Central African Federation (between Northern Rhodesia, Nyasaland and Southern Rhodesia) was formed in 1953 but from the start it had little chance of success. The Federal Government took over responsibility for external affairs, posts and telegraphs, communications, agriculture and trade. At first there were visible economic benefits from the free movement of goods between the territories. But the countries differed vastly in their historical evolution, Southern Rhodesia – now Zimbabwe – being a zone of European settlement (population then 3,7 million Africans, 240 000 Europeans), contrasting with Northern Rhodesia – now Zambia (Africans 2,7 millions, Europeans 80 000) and Nyasaland – now Malaŵi (four million Africans, 9 000 Europeans). Moreover, Northern Rhodesia produced little that was needed in Southern Rhodesia except copper and her former partners in the Federation formed small markets; Southern Rhodesia's imports were US$17 million and Nyasaland's US$1,25 in 1964. With imports of US$77 million out of a total of US$195 million from Southern Rhodesia, Northern Rhodesia had a very unfavourable trade balance with that country. For these and political reasons the Federation was dissolved, in 1963. In later years Zambia and Rhodesia drifted even further apart and economic trade barriers increased rather than eased.

The East African Common Market

Until quite recently the idea of a common market in East Africa (Kenya, Uganda and Tanzania) was strong. It had everything to recommend it. The three had been governed by Britain, who had imposed similar systems of local government and education, and had run essential services such as railways and harbours, posts and telegraphs, defence, currency distribution and trade through the East African High Commission formed in 1948. Except for certain goods, there were no customs duties between the territories. Kenya found valuable markets for her manufactured articles and high quality produce; Uganda found a large demand for her sugar, cottonseed oil and raw tobacco and exported electricity to Kenya; Tanzania's chief inter-territorial exports were raw tobacco, coconut oil and pulses.

In recent years, economic and political trends have led to the break-up of the common market in East Africa. Protective trade tarrifs were placed on certain inter-territorial imports by all three territories to foster their own industries, and each territory now has its own banking and monetary system. The fundamental cause underlying the beginnings of the trend to break up the East African Common Market is the feeling (as in the Central African Federation) that the profits of the market may not be equally shared. In the past Kenya has attracted the secondary industrial development, especially at Nairobi and Mombasa, and the value of her exports (mainly processed or manufactured articles) to the other two territories has steadily increased without a corresponding increase in imports. Two solutions have been put forward – the sharing of profits and costs fairly among the three territories, and the establishment of industries in underdeveloped regions by giving incentives to investors.

The break-up of the East African Common Market may be detrimental to the economy. Industrialists are attracted by large markets and, as a customs-free market, East Africa has a population of about 45 million potential buyers. Divided, it becomes three separate smaller markets of about 17 million (Tanzania), 15 million (Kenya) and 12,5 million (Uganda). Again, with agreement among the three territories, industries could be located in the most favourable spots; with each territory pursuing its own industrialisation programme there is bound to be duplication of certain industries as, for example, the oil refineries at Mombasa and Dar-es-Salaam. Planned industrialisation has been successfully carried out in the Central African Economic and Customs Union (see below).

The Central African Economic and Customs Union (UDEAC)

The Central African Federation and the East African Common Markets are concepts formed under colonial governments which have proved unacceptable to the independent African states. The Central African Economic and Customs Union (the UDEAC) formed on 1 January 1966 between Gabon, Congo, Chad, the Central African Republic and Cameroon is an organisation which has stemmed from the desire of the African governments themselves. The UDEAC countries cover 2,5 million square kilometres and have a population of 15 million people. The main economic products of the region include cocoa, coffee, cotton, manganese, uranium, diamonds, petroleum, bauxite and tropical timber.

The five states as separate entities have several problems. Gabon (population 0,5 million) and Congo (1,4 million) are amongst the smallest nations in Africa, the resources of all territories are underdeveloped, and the CAR and Chad have no access to the sea. But the states, all former French possessions, have a common language and similar institutions, and had been integrated from 1910 to 1959 in the Federation of French Equatorial Africa. The most significant measure of co-operation is the system of duties and taxes aimed at encouraging trade and industry. The more populous interior states, who are seriously handicapped by their position in setting up industries and exporting materials, are compensated for loss of customs duty if they purchase goods from within the union from the new industries in countries near the coast. A single tax replaces a whole series of taxes and dues levied on imports and exports and manufactured items, the tax divisible between the territories annually.

Within the Union, trade and industrial growth have been logically planned. Chad, for example, forgoes establishing a cement plant but buys from a new factory in North Cameroon; in exchange Chad obtains certain advantages in the textile industry and trade. Again, the five states reached agreement on the setting up of the oil refinery at Port Gentil, feeling that this was the best geographical location. The ideologies of the member countries of the UDEAC, however, are somewhat contrasted, and this caused Chad and the CAR to withdraw from the union in 1968. But economic considerations drew the CAR once more into the union, and Chad returned in 1975 with observer status.

The Economic Organisation of West African States (ECOWAS)

Nigeria has been a leading advocate for a closer union among West African states. The country played a leading role in the formulation of the Lomé Convention, an economic agreement between 46 African, Pacific and Caribbean nations and the European Common Market. The success of this venture in transcending political, economic and language difficulties, encouraged Nigeria (and Togo) to attempt to reconcile West African differences in an economic union. The result was a treaty, signed in Lagos in 1975, joining the 15 nations of West Africa (see map, Fig. 12.4) into the Economic Organisation of West African States (ECOWAS). The aims of ECOWAS are to develop a complete customs union by 1990, to increase trade between the member states, to improve communications, to finance dam projects and mineral extraction, and eventually to establish a common currency.

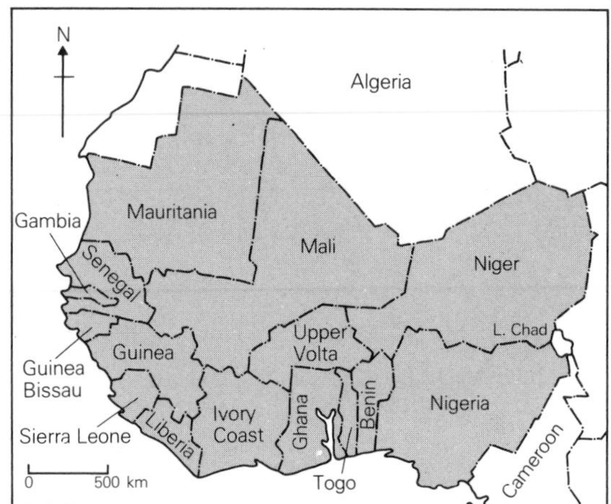

Fig. 12.4 The fifteen members of the Economic Community of West African States (ECOWAS)

ECOWAS is a bold idea but the organisation contains weaknesses and faces several problems. The union includes some very poor countries which naturally look to the richest members, especially Nigeria, for support. Again, border disputes between Benin and Togo and between Mali and Upper Volta still continue. Moreover, Nigeria cannot supply the member countries with cheap oil as they expected, since she is a member country of OPEC (the oil producing and exporting countries) and must agree to its ruling on oil prices. In the long run, Nigeria must play a dominating role in any such economic union and, indeed, has been a leader in signing trade and co-operation treaties with her neighbours – for sugar and cement schemes in Benin, to exchange oil for Togo's phosphates, and to assist in iron ore extraction in Guinea. An indication of what might be achieved by ECOWAS is seen in the *Mano River Union*, an economic union between Liberia and Sierra Leone. These two states have established a common external tariff (as from 1 April 1977), and allow completely free movement of trade, goods, capital, and labour within the new Union boundaries.

Southern Africa

In southern Africa also there appears to be the emergence of a common market; the smaller countries here – Lesotho, Swaziland and Botswana – have very close economic ties with South Africa and are entirely dependent on South Africa's infrastructure. They have a common currency and a large proportion of their working population finds employment in the Republic. The three countries became part of a customs union with South Africa in 1910 and this now accounts for 50 per cent of the income of all three countries. The present Customs Union Agreement was signed in 1969 and replaces the 1910 one. This new agreement forbids any member from entering into negotiations for a trade agreement with other countries without the agreement of the other members. South Africa, of course, dominates such a union and the smaller territories receive considerable benefits. Recently, however, Lesotho and Swaziland have been accepted as associate members of the European Common Market.

The significance and success of logical planning of economic resources on a regional basis which goes beyond political boundaries has been demonstrated by ECOWAS to some extent. The community has gained some success because it stemmed from a genuine desire of its member states to improve their common economic status and is not a system devised by foreign governments. The economic success of a union between politically separate states could be one of the first stages in the growth of such ideas on the continent of Africa; it is an essential prerequisite for the sound economic development of the continent's resources.

Fig. 12.5 Africa – members of the Commonwealth

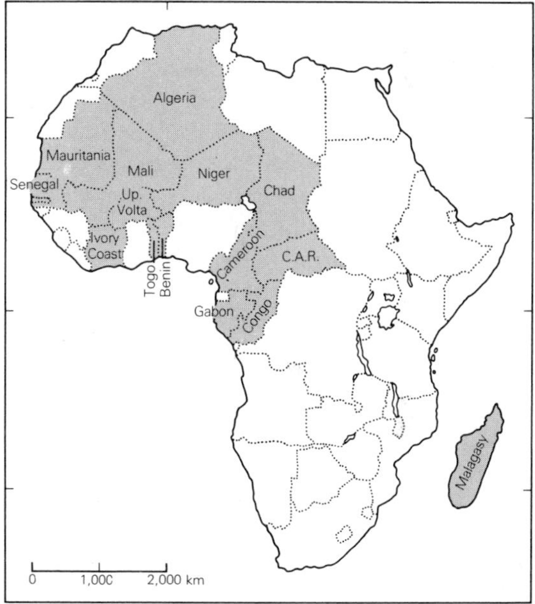

Fig. 12.6 Africa – members of the Franco–African Community

Aid and development programmes

The new African nations are in the first stages of independent economic development after sixty years of colonial rule. It is clear that they will not be in a position to develop their economies and their administrative and social systems entirely on their own. Those systems of social government, welfare and administration, introduced during the colonial era, are beneficial but entirely non-productive, and African nations at their present stage of development cannot be expected to find the funds to support these systems and at the same time to expand their economies.

Economic expansion in the new African nations

depends on several factors. Most important is the encouragement of the efforts of the African peoples themselves by introducing programmes of development, self-help, new secondary industries and agricultural projects. But these programmes cost money, and, at present, some of this must be obtained from external sources. This overseas aid must be regulated so that it tends to encourage greater efforts within the recipient country, and the amount must be related to the ability of the country to meet the recurrent costs of new projects. Moreover, most countries in Africa desire to be independent of foreign aid as soon as possible and they do not wish to have their development programmes too heavily dependent on overseas capital.

Aid may come from two main sources apart from that generated in the country itself. It may be private aid in which a company makes a direct investment and sets up a subsidiary organisation in the country concerned. This is very advantageous because the country gets the benefit of technical experts, direct financial investment, a continuing flow of capital from the re-investment of profits, and the employment of local staff. A less useful form of investment is where a loan is raised in an overseas money market for investment in some enterprise in an African country. This is termed an 'indirect loan', but it means that money flows out of the country concerned in the form of dividends to shareholders abroad.

The second type of loan is that provided by government bodies, in Africa or overseas. Such money can be obtained from various organisations:

a Large international organisations such as the International Bank for Reconstruction and Development (the IBRD), the World Bank, the United Nations Fund, the African Development Bank based in Abidjan, or the Arab Bank for Economic Development in Africa.

b Economic Communities such as the European Economic Community (the EEC) or the Special Commonwealth Africa Assistance Plan.

c Single governments, e.g. a direct loan from West Germany to Togo. This is termed bilateral aid.

This aid may be in the form of straight loans, 'soft' loans, or direct grants. A straight or ordinary loan may have an interest rate of between six and eight per cent and be repayable immediately over a term of from 15 to 20 years. This is not very useful to a developing country for it finds it has to start repaying the money with interest immediately, and over the long term of the loan, interest charges alone amount to 25 per cent and more. Moreover, such loans take a very high proportion of the country's income from its sales of exports just when it needs ready cash the most. Thus the value of such loans is greatly reduced. A 'soft' loan however has a lower interest rate – usually about three per cent, the first payments need only be made after about ten years, and the term of repayment is stretched over a longer period. This gives the recipient chance to develop its economy before repayment begins. In recent years, many outstanding loans have been cancelled by the donor governments.

There is always the tendency among receiving nations to view aid from single countries or continental associations with some reserve and to fear interference in the recipient country's internal affairs. Yet it is not unnatural for the donor countries to expect evidence of the wise use of the money which they loan or grant. The European Economic Community has trade relations with several African states who provide markets and raw materials, while customs duties are so arranged as to give them trade preferences over non-members. Some African nations see such a community as a genuine attempt at closer co-operation, others regard it as merely another form of exploitation which will benefit Europe more than Africa. However, the Lomé Agreement with the EEC, mentioned earlier, has done much to provide large soft loans, beneficial trade preferences, technical aid, and stabilised export prices for African countries. Britain also provides trade preferences, technical, economic and educational aid to African Commonwealth members. The Franco–African Community (La Communauté) formed in 1958 was also an association of states, all formerly French administered. The original French conception of internal self-governing members within an economic framework was unacceptable to African governments; Guinea refused to join and the others obtained full independence but retained the framework of the Community for their own economic plans. Customs unions were formed and the aims of the Community were to foster agricultural production, improve public health, education, transport, mining and energy production.

The development of such organisations, while a step in the right direction, has not resulted in the fostering of really strong and trusting bonds of trade and economic association between Africa and the western European nations. The hard-won independence of the African states is still recent and the new nations are slightly suspicious of any aid originating from former colonial rulers. They prefer instead the aid and assistance provided by non-political bodies such as the United Nations Economic Commission for Africa (UNECA). It is appropriate here to note the aims of this body which was founded on 29 April 1958. These are:

> To promote and facilitate concerted action for the economic development of Africa, including its social aspects, with a view to raising the level of economic activity and the level of living in Africa and for maintaining and strengthening the economic relations of countries and territories of Africa, both among themselves and with other countries of the world.

The Commission sponsors research, studies problems of economic and technological development, formulates development policies and provides advisory services for its member states in Africa.

Communist countries are also providing increasing amounts of development aid to African countries. Between 1959 and 1975 the Soviet Union has given nearly US$1 000 million and Communist China about US$2 000 million. This compares with the World Bank's grants of US$1 100 million and the US$2 500 million donated by Western nations during the same period. China spent over US$300 million on the construction of the Tanzam Railway in Tanzania and Zambia, gave aid worth nearly US$100 million to Zaïre in 1974 and has granted a US$50 million loan to Mozambique for agricultural developments and large-scale irrigation projects.

The Arab oil-producing countries have also set up an Arab Loan Fund for Africa with a capital of US$200 million. The chief recipients in 1975 were Zambia, Zaïre, Tanzania and Uganda. Unfortunately, the increased price of oil in recent years has negated the value of such monetary aid; between 1973 and 1974, for example, the cost of oil imports to OAU members rose from US$350 million to US$950 million.

The use of development aid

How do development programmes work and how is the foreign aid used? One can only answer these questions by examining their application in selected countries at varying stages of development. It must be remembered that such aid is supplementary to that generated in the country itself. Let us consider one of the poorest countries in Africa first – the Republic of Benin (Dahomey).

The Republic of Benin

With a population of three million and a comparatively high density of 20 per square kilometre, a persistent trade deficit and a lack of important raw materials, the Benin Republic's economy is one of the poorest in West Africa. Her overall trading position has deteriorated and the value of her main export, oil palm produce, has fallen by over 70 per cent and groundnut sales have fallen by 35 per cent. Benin depends very largely on France to buy her produce, although she also exports to neighbouring West African countries. Benin's high level of imports comprises vehicles, foodstuffs, machinery, clothes and petroleum products.

Benin is thus a poor country and has to rely almost entirely on outside aid to cover her budget deficit and to finance the development of industry and social services. Considerable assistance has been received from France and the EEC and the United States (which has helped to construct a new harbour at Cotonou). Various schemes are under way to improve cotton, palm oil, coffee and tobacco industries. Benin has few mineral resources of any kind, but a Canadian firm built an aluminium rolling mill which came into production in 1967. The government is concentrating on rural and agricultural development; about 75 per cent of the money for this will have to come from overseas sources and the Benin Republic will obviously have to rely on foreign aid for many years to come.

Mali

Mali is another West African country which requires substantial aid to support its economy. A landlocked country, Mali is ranked as one of the world's poorest 25 nations by the United Nations, and is a victim of recurrent droughts, e.g. in 1974. The 1974 droughts were followed by the heaviest rainfalls in over 30 years, which flooded the capital Bamako and cut communications between Bamako and Senegal. The cost of food and relief operations in this one year alone were US$430 million and 750 000 t of food were donated. A new recovery and rehabilitation plan has been inaugurated and the United States has been foremost in promoting medium and long-term projects. These include the improvement of river navigation and a livestock industry. The Soviet Union is also engaged on expanding the cement plant at Diamou, helping the development of the future gold mining industry at Kalana, and supporting agricultural schemes started by the French. The Chinese have constructed shoe, match and cigarette factories and intend to enlarge the textile mill at Segou, since exports of textiles to neighbouring countries brings considerable foreign exchange. France, once the former colonial power, is an important donor and is subsidising industrial, agricultural and energy programmes, and plans to finance the construction of a dam at Selinque.

Senegal

Senegal is a good example of a country which has realised the need to diversify its economy since it relies almost entirely on the production of groundnuts (75 per cent of exports). To embark on a programme of diversification Senegal will need plenty of capital. Senegal is expanding production of rice along the Senegal river banks to reduce imports, developing sugar and cotton plantations and giving attention to increasing production of bananas, tomatoes, strawberries (for the Paris market), pineapples, fishing and cattle raising. The government is also developing a ship repair industry and a free port and industrial zone at Dakar. Foreign aid to finance these programmes is being provided largely by France, the EEC and the United States.

Liberia

Some countries depend on one foreign power to supply them with the necessary finance for their development. Liberia has long looked to the United States for assistance, but there are signs that this monopoly is decreasing. Nevertheless, Liberia still relies for the bulk of her foreign capital inflow from USA sources. USA suppliers have instigated plans for the expansion of the hydro-electric plant at Mount Coffee and a water supply programme, and American companies have also made investigations in the pharmaceutical, soluble coffee, and distilling industries. An agricultural programme has been planned with aid from the Food and Agricultural Organisation (the FAO) and a loan is to be provided by the IBRD for two roads to farming and rubber producing areas. A Five-Year Plan is now being prepared to co-ordinate these projects.

Mauritania

Gabon and Mauritania are two African countries whose economy is being transformed by overseas investment. In the case of Mauritania there has been a tremendous increase in foreign investment in the iron ore mining industry. In addition, Mauritania possesses several other minerals vital to modern industry and these have attracted aid and finance from all over the world. One of the larger of recent mineral discoveries is a 30 million tonne deposit of copper at Akjoujt, initially developed by a French consortium which constructed the installations at Akjoujt. They were replaced by an international group consisting of British, American, Canadian and French concerns; several leading Japanese firms are also interested in the project, while numerous other foreign firms are engaged in prospecting for oil, gypsum, manganese and titanium. As is usually the case, once the spotlight has been thrown on a country, it attracts attention from other organisations. The EEC, for example, is partly financing the present Four-Year Plan, which entails the improvement of transport and communications and urban development. Further funds are being made available for the development of Nouadhibou, formerly Port Etienne.

Gabon

Gabon, encouraged by the discovery of large deposits of important minerals, has embarked on a new development plan, which gives priority to the expansion of mineral production, the further development of timber processing, and the encouragement of secondary industrial undertakings. Industrial projects under the Plan include the building of an oil refinery, a brewery, a battery plant, a cement factory, and a glass works. It is hoped that foreign private investment will provide 60 per cent of the total finance. Investment in other ventures include the exploitation of Gabon's high-grade iron ore deposits with the construction of a 570 km-long railway to a new deep-water port by a consortium including the World Bank, the expansion by Shell-Gabon of oil production from newly discovered fields, and the financing of geological research, mineral prospecting and rural development by the French Government.

Botswana

Other countries in Africa are not as fortunate as Gabon and Mauritania, for they do not possess large deposits of minerals and their economies are precariously based on one product. At one time Botswana obtained 95 per cent of its export revenue from the sales of livestock and livestock products. On several occasions severe droughts badly damaged the country's economy and 400 000 cattle, about 25 per cent of the total, were lost. It is hoped that copper deposits will be found in workable quantities in the Matsitamma area and that production of sodium carbonate from the Makarikari salt pans will provide additional revenue. There are also some deposits of low- and medium-grade coal which could be used to provide future power. In 1967 a group of Kimberlite pipes was discovered in the Letlhakane area, the largest being the Orapa pipe. A diamond mine was opened here in 1971. In 1972, a mine was opened to develop the rich nickel-copper deposits in the Selebi–Pikwe area. These finds have already lessened dependence on foreign aid.

Lesotho

Lesotho is in an even more difficult economic position than Botswana, although recent diamond finds have helped the economy. In view of their landlocked geographical position and the fact that a high proportion of their male workers are dependent on the Rand Mines for their incomes, it seems likely that these two countries will be economically dependent on South Africa for some considerable time and will require much foreign investment and aid.

Conclusion – the need for co-operation

Africa is the continent of the future, for in no other continent is there such a huge potential for development. But the overriding problem which faces an Africa emerged from colonial rule is the hindrance to economic growth of individual countries caused by the artificial division of the continent into 48 separate states, a division stemming from the political ambitions of European states of some 75 years ago. That these political divisions bear little relation to the distribution of population and the economic needs of Africa can be gathered from the facts that nearly one-third of Africa's total population is contained in three countries (Egypt, Ethiopia and Nigeria), a further third in eight other countries, and the rest among some 38 states which, although several times larger than many European countries, have populations no greater than some European cities.

Are the smaller African states doomed to only gradual economic growth, their revenues too small to provide for ambitious programmes of development, or must they continue to supplement their finances with overseas loans for development, when it is their desire to be economically independent from outside help at the earliest possible opportunity? The real answer to economic viability is economic integration with other African nations on a regional basis. On their own, such countries are economically unbalanced, but seen within a regional framework within Africa they would be able to plan their economies and avoid unnecessary waste and duplication of effort and investment.

The world today displays a general pattern of co-operation which is evolving in many regions. While the idea of a global union among all nations is still remote, there is the definite emergence of regional groupings among nations. Throughout history people have grouped together for defence or for economic advancement – the Greek City States, the Hanseatic League, the Customs Union of nineteenth-century German states. The most successful alliances have not been those formed for political reasons, but those which have been based on economic activities, e.g. the European Common Market has stimulated the economy of Western Europe and formed a strong balancing power between Russia and the United States; in Asia regional groupings have been formed to remove trade barriers and promote economic growth; in the Americas the

Central American Common Market has increased commercial activity within its sphere considerably since its formation in 1961.

Thus, while political co-operation is often vague and based on 'a gentlemen's agreement', economic co-operation with its abolition of customs duties and high degree of legislative agreement, results in a large measure of practical action and integration between participating countries. But religious and political ideals and differences often form barriers or at least strong obstacles to economic integration, as, for example, between the Maghreb Arab states and Egypt, or between the strongly Islam-orientated north African states and the African states south of the Sahara. The membership of both English-speaking and French-speaking African countries in the EEC is an outward-looking tendency, whereas the national pride of newly emergent countries is yet another factor reacting against regional economic integration.

The Organisation of African Unity (OAU)

The record of several economic unions has already been discussed. On a continental scale, perhaps the Organisation of African Unity formed in Addis Ababa in May 1963 has been the most successful so far in attracting the attention of all African states, although its aims are largely political. All independent states in Africa (except South Africa and former Rhodesia) joined this organisation. It could be a possible framework on which to build a wider economic organisation designed to include all African-governed states.

Questions

1 What economic advantages are to be gained by the co-operation of African states within the framework of common markets? Discuss this question with reference to specific examples.

2 With reference to specific examples, discuss the trade problems which face the newly independent states of Africa.

3 Discuss the reasons which lead to an unfavourable balance of trade and suggest ways in which African nations can reverse these tendencies.

4 With reference to particular examples discuss the causes which lead to the breakdown and growth of common market concepts in Africa.

5 In what ways are African nations attempting to diversify their exports and their range of markets?

6 Illustrate the relative importance of the United Kingdom, the United States, West Germany, Japan and the Communist bloc nations in the external trade of the African continent.

7 Select any country in Africa with whose trade figures you are familiar. With reference to these figures show to what degree that country's trade is representative of African states as a whole.

8 'Foreign aid is essential for the assured growth of African economies at their present stage of development.' Discuss this statement with reference to particular nations in Africa, and show how foreign aid is being used in your country.

CHAPTER THIRTEEN

The natural resources of Africa – Their use, abuse and conservation

In Chapter Three on Population the term 'exponential growth' was explained. We saw how the population of Africa, after a stage of slow growth, began increasing at an ever accelerating rate. The effects of this steep exponential growth rate of Africa's population are being increasingly reflected in the accelerating use of the continent's natural resources: the exponential growth principle is now applicable to the use of Africa's natural resources such as oil, coal, metal ores, and natural gas; to the destruction of vegetation cover; to the erosion of the soil; to the growth of urban areas; to the expansion of industry; to the demand for food. But the resources of Africa, like those of the world in general, are finite and are either non-renewable, or renewable only with great difficulty by re-cycling; they cannot be exploited indefinitely in order to support an unlimited number of people increasing at an accelerating rate.

In this final chapter we will bring together some of the themes already outlined in this book and discuss the manner in which some of the natural resources of Africa – land, energy resources, water, the seas and wildlife – are in grave danger because of increasing exploitation.

The land

Land is Africa's most important resource. Approximately 78 per cent of the continent's population live in rural areas and derive their livelihood directly from the land, while about one-third of Africa's area can be classified as agricultural land (land under permanent cultivation plus grazing). Table 18, based on FAO statistics, compares Africa's land resources and protein output with five major regions of the world.

Several conclusions can be drawn from this table; the most important one is that, although Africa has more than three times the arable land per person than Asia, twice that of Europe, and half as much again as Latin America, consumption of protein per day per head of population is the least of all the regions. The

Table 18 The world: population, agricultural land and protein supply by regions

Region	*Total population 1977 in millions*	*% of world population*	*% rural population*	*Agricultural land as % of total land area*	*Arable hectares (acres per person)*	*Average per capita grammes of protein per day*	*Kilojoul (calory) intake per person per day*
Africa	423	10	78,2	33	0,68(1,67)	59	9,2(2 200)
Asia	2 325	57	74,6	33	0,22(0,54)	61	8,8(2 100)
Latin America	336	8	45,6	33	0,42(1,05)	63	10,5(2 500)
Europe	478	12	37,0	50	0,33(0,82)	97	13,0(3 100)
USSR	259	6	37,7	25	0,94(2,32)	101	13,4(3 200)
North America	240	6	24,9	25	0,94(2,33)	104	13,8(3 300)

A child awaits emergency relief rations, a common sight in the poorer nations of Africa.

average energy food intake per person in Africa is 9,2 kj (2 200 calories) per day, only higher than the figure for Asia. Dieticians estimate that in societies eating largely plant protein the daily allowance needed is 65 g, while a man doing moderate work requires about 11,7 to 12,6 kj (2 800 to 3 000 calories) per day. Since the figure for Africa is an average one, the conclusion is that a considerable proportion of the continent's population is living at or near starvation levels – the land is not producing sufficient foods, nor foods with a high enough protein content. The land carrying capacity has thus been exceeded and a state of overpopulation exists over wide areas of Africa.

How does this state of affairs develop? A fixed area of land can only support a limited number of people continuously and, when that number is exceeded without an increase in food supplies through improved cultivation methods, the land begins to deteriorate and its productivity is eventually destroyed. Food and other commodities become scarce and, in the absence of imported aid, famine ensues. In the rural areas of Africa, this sequence of events leading to the destruction of the land follows a set pattern. Initially, an increase in population causes an increase in cultivated land and livestock numbers. As land becomes scarcer, the prolonged use of the existing cultivated land and a reduction in the length of the fallow period causes a drop in soil fertility and a lowering of crop yields, until the land is barely feeding the people. The cultivated land is extended to meet the demand for food, pressure on grazing land increases, and overstocking results; the deterioration of the grazing area is the first sign that the land is becoming overpopulated in human terms. Other signs are the reduction in numbers and finally the elimination of wild game, and the increasing scarcity of wood for fuel and construction purposes. The cattle herds are slowly replaced by the hardier goat (for meat) and the donkey (for draught purposes). At this stage the land carrying capacity has been exceeded, there is a drastic drop in the living standards of the people, and famines result in deaths and a mass exodus.

Niger Republic: Bags of imported sorghum being loaded for despatch to drought stricken areas in the Sahel zone.

Many parts of Africa lying on the desert fringes have reached this final stage of land deterioration. The desert is extending partly because of recurring cycles of drought, but also because man, in his increasing numbers, is indulging in deforestation, over-cultivation and over-grazing. Each year nearly 100 000 ha of arable land are lost to the desert in north Africa alone, while over the last 50 years the Sahara has advanced to cover over one million square kilometres of pasture and arable land, an area equal to that of Egypt or Mali, nearly twice that of Kenya, and more than the area of Nigeria or Tanzania.

Mali

The Sahelian states, stretching in a broad arc across Africa from Senegal in the west to Chad in the east, are particularly vulnerable to land loss by desertification. Mali, covering a vast area of 1,24 million square kilometres, provides an almost classic example of how an increasing population can exhaust the land carrying capacity and produce famine conditions. The southern region of Mali, the Sudanese zone covering 600 000 square kilometres, is the most fertile and densely settled, and where most food is grown – millet, sorghum and groundnuts. North of the Sudanese zone lies the Sahelian region covering 400 000 square kilometres, where normal annual rainfalls (100 to 400 mm) are insufficient to allow cultivation but permit the grazing of livestock. North of the Sahel lies the desert.

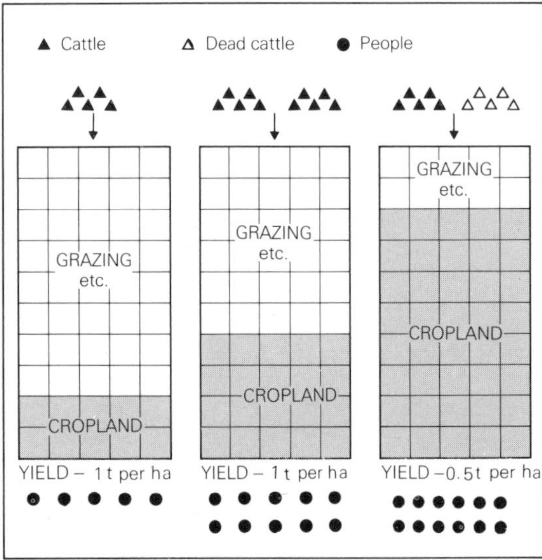

Fig. 13.1 Diagrammatic representation of the effects of population growth on land use in rural areas of Africa

At the time of its independence in 1960, Mali was almost self-sufficient in staple foodstuffs and, indeed, there was some export of grain, cattle and fish to neighbouring states. Between 1953 and 1962, during a period of exceptionally high rains, Mali herdsmen allowed their cattle to multiply. At the same time, the cultivated lands of the southern Sudanese zone were extended northwards by slash and burn methods with the inevitable loss of vegetation cover and soil deterioration. By 1968, Mali's cattle population (over five million each of cattle, sheep and goats) was greater than that of any other Sahelian state. In that year, and for the next five years, Mali suffered drought, and a process of desertification, aided by man's abuse of the land, swallowed up thousands of square kilometres of grazing and arable land. Between 1968 and 1974, Mali lost nearly a third of its cattle and a quarter of its sheep and goats. Grain crops failed, and in 1973 Mali experienced a grain deficit of over 350 000 t. Famine was only averted by massive imports of food supplies.

There are several reasons why Mali was converted from an exporter of foodstuffs to an importer: government mismanagement, poor communications, inadequate water supplies for stock and crops, recurring drought, and mismanagement of land resources. However, the high growth rate of Mali's population (it rose from 4,7 million in 1970 to 5,8 million in 1976) was a major contributory factor to the abuse of land resources. The case of Mali shows that, at its present stage of development, a state of overpopulation exists and the land carrying capacity has been exceeded.

Somalia and the Sudan

The loss of land through desertification is not only confined to the Sahelian states of Mali, Niger, Upper Volta, Senegal, Mauritania and Chad. It is also seen in East Africa – in the Kenya–Ethiopian borderlands, in parts of Tanzania, in Somalia and the Sudan. In Somalia, population pressure (growth 2,6 per cent per annum) and climatic change are causing overgrazing and land deterioration. The severe drought of 1974–5 reduced the carrying capacity of rangelands resulting in the deaths of over one million cattle and the migration of 175 000 nomads. In the coastal zone south of Mogadishu there are 51 000 ha of sand dunes which are slowly encroaching on valuable irrigated land, houses and roads. In Sudan, deserts have advanced 100 km in 17 years and the present rate of advance is about 6 km a year. In Kordofan Province a farmer now needs five times the land he used in 1961 to produce the same tonnage of groundnuts. Since the early 1960s cereal production per hectare in the province has declined steadily: sorghum has dropped from 1 047 kg per hectare to 472 kg per hectare, maize from 810 kg per hectare to 380 kg per hectare, and millet from 1 340 kg per hectare to 175 kg per hectare. Former shrub woodlands are now barren deserts supporting only poor grass during the rains, and woodcutters now have to travel 100 km instead of 10 km from Khartoum to obtain acacia cuttings for charcoal.

The desertification process caused by human and animal population pressures on a fixed land area in the Kordofan Province of Sudan is classically illustrated in the following description by a member of an international environment information unit stationed there:

> The Acacia-grassland ecosystem is the climax vegetation in this area, with the trees forming an open canopy. As in a tropical rainforest, the soil is extremely poor and the nutrients and moisture are held overwhelmingly in the vegetation rather than in the soil. As the trees die, their prickly fallen branches shelter from grazing some taller grasses and herbs. In the dry season this growth is liable to catch fire, allowing open grassland to appear until Acacia seedlings once again establish themselves.
>
> In Kordofan, traditional agriculture is an adaptation of this natural fire-fed scrub-grassland-scrub cycle. First, the acacia scrub is cleared by burning, and sesame, millet, sorghum, maize and other crops are grown in the sandy soil for four to 10 years; the Sudanese are a hoe people, and do not plough with livestock. The soil is by now exhausted, and the fields are abandoned to fallow. Weeds, grass and eventually acacia seedlings invade the land, and after about eight years the young *hashabs* are ready for tapping. After another six to 10 years, the thorn trees start to die; they are felled, burned, and the land cleared once again.
>
> Each farmer has some gum orchards for a cash crop, and some arable fields for his subsistence crops. Several crops are usually grown in close proximity, either in small separate patches or intercropped in adjacent rows. This mosaic offers the best insurance against the unpredictable rainfall, as well as protection against pests: Kordofan seems rarely to suffer the depredations of weaver birds (*Quelea*) which are such a plague in the monocultures of Sudan.
>
> This ecologically-balanced cycle of gum gardens, fire, grain crops, and fallow is now breaking down, the 1968–73 drought having in many areas given it the *coup de grace*. Under pressure of a growing population, the cultivation period is extended by several years, and the soil becomes too impoverished to recover. Overgrazing in the fallow period prevents the establishment of seedlings. Gum trees are lopped for firewood. More and more widely, *Acacia senegal* no longer returns after the fallow, but is replaced by non-gum-producing scrub: the thorns *Acacia tortilis* and *A. raddiana*, and the broom-like shrub *Leptadaenia pyrotechnica*. And without the gum to harvest for cash, the farmers must repeatedly replant their subsistence crops until the land becomes useless sand.
>
> Not far from El Beshiri, 15 km or so south of Mazroub, is an area that was once gum gardens. Today, 90 per cent of the *Acacia senegal* trees lie dead on the ground, killed in the past year or two of the 1968–73 drought. But if lack of water was the proximate factor in their deaths, the ultimate factors were the degeneration of the soil through over-cultivation, the deterioration and destruction of the grass cover by overgrazing, and direct browsing of the trees by animals unable to find more palatable food. Come drought, neither grass nor soil retained enough moisture for the trees to survive.
>
> There are, of course, many other aspects to the desertification process, even in this same gum arabic belt, than the destruction of the gum groves. Improved veterinary care and the digging of pumped wells and *hafirs* or surface reservoirs are the two main causes of the livestock explosion. For a kilometre around the Mazroub watering area, for

example, there is not a blade of grass to be seen, only a few scattered tree stumps and the odd surviving thorn tree. Even after 5 km, ground vegetation is only established under the thorny protection of dead trees. From the air, each village with a watering point can be seen to create an irregular area of sand around it, extending in some directions for 10 km or more, even for 40 km for several hundred metres to either side of the tracks leading from the nomads' waterholes.

The energy crisis makes its own contribution to desertification, by increasing the demand for wood and charcoal. Around the larger towns, the charcoal burners and woodcutters scour the countryside for 40 km and more, often chopping wood even from living gum arabic trees.'[1]

Solutions

What measures are being taken to check desertification and reclaim lost land? In Nigeria the fast growing *neem* tree has been planted to provide shelter belts from dessicating winds in the northern states. Experiments with trees planted on several types of soil with different water levels are being carried out. Irrigated plantations are being laid out in Mali, in the Niger's inland delta region, and in the northern Sudan. Besides protecting arable land, the windbreaks also provide shade for livestock and wood for fuel. The Forestry Department in Somalia is experimenting with acacia, casuarina pine, cactus, commiphora, tamarisk and the date palm in an effort to anchor moving dunes. Some 650 000 seedlings are grown annually at the tree nursery at Afgoi near the dune areas to be planted on the dunes during the rainy season. The Sudan has embarked on an ambitious scheme to combat the dune encroachment, including afforestation, crop legume rotation in place of non-cropping, prevention of cropping in areas subject to wind erosion, the establishment of grazing co-operatives, a range-management scheme, and soil and water conservation measures.

It will, however, take more than the planting of protective trees to recover lost land assets. In the Sahelian states no real progress can be made without the creation of a vital infrastructure of communications, the tapping of the vast underground reservoirs of water, and a family planning programme to reduce population growth rate. All of this will need vast amounts of money.

[1] J. Tinker, 'Sudan Challenges the Sand-Dragon,' *New Scientist* 24 February 1977, p. 449.

Water

In Chapter Eight we discussed how man has harnessed the rivers of Africa for irrigation and power supplies. In this section we examine water deposits as a natural resource rather than as an artificially created one, first in the form of subterranean deposits and secondly in the form of natural surface lakes.

Natural subterranean water resources

The Sahara

The Sahara is the world's largest desert, covering nearly 8,03 million square kilometres. This vast, barren region could support a considerably higher population than at present if its subterranean water supplies were used more fully. Geologists have only recently realised the full extent of these underground aquifers, much of the information coming to light with extensive explorations for oil. As the map (Fig. 13.2) shows, the Sahara's underground water supplies are mainly contained in seven large basins. These basins and their estimated storage capacities in millions of cubic metres are: 1) Great Western Erg (1 500 000); 2) Great Eastern Erg (1 700 000); 3) Tanezrouft (400 000); 4) Niger (1 800 000); 5) Fezzan (400 000); 6) Western Egyptian Desert (600 000); 7) Chad (3 500 000).

Most of the water in these aquifers was laid down in past millenniums during pluvial periods when the Sahara experienced far more rain than it does today. They are constantly being recharged by rainwater falling along the wetter fringes of the desert and soaking along porous beds.

Some of the problems which will have to be solved before these water resources can be fully used are the improvement of the present wasteful systems of

Lesotho: Unchecked gulley erosion is common throughout this country.

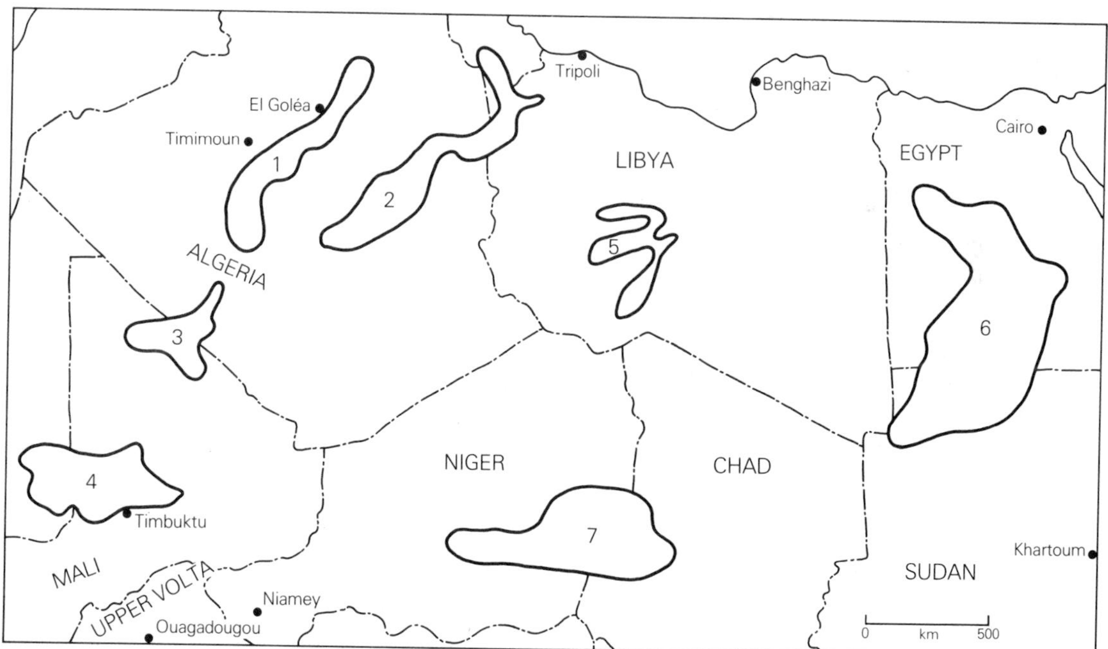

Fig. 13.2 The underground water reserves of the Sahara

irrigation practised by many oasis Arabs; the prevention of salt concentration in the soil due to the high rates of evaporation; the maintenance of the balance between water use and re-charging rates; and solving of political difficulties which may develop since most of the basins lie across international boundaries.

Capital in large amounts will also be needed before a serious beginning can be made in harnessing these subterranean water resources. But capital and technological capacity are in short supply in the Sahelian states. Mali, for example, possesses an underground aquifer system holding water reserves of several hundred billion cubic metres. Yet, in a country covering 1 240 000 square kilometres (an area double that of France), there are only 610 square kilometres of irrigated land and only 1 000 wells when 8 000 wells would be barely adequate. The country can only afford to establish 100 wells a year on average, so that it would take about 60 or 70 years to establish a further 7 000, by which time the population, human and animal, will have tripled.

The creation of more wells, however, is not the real answer to the water problems of the Sahelian states. Wells soon become concentration points for large numbers of cattle, goats, donkeys and camels and this leads to local deterioration of the environment through destruction of vegetation cover, soil compaction and subsequent soil erosion. A much wider programme involving all the Sahelian states is required which would involve the introduction of water control policies (e.g. the closing of certain water holes for rest periods), a programme of cattle disease prevention and livestock control, the introduction of integrated livestock breeding with cultivation, and general range management. That such co-operation is possible is evidenced by agreement on river schemes, for example, the Organisation for the Improvement of the Senegal River Valley, in which the heads of state of Gambia, Upper Volta, Mali, Chad, Senegal, Niger and Mauritania have overcome political differences and capital problems to coordinate their efforts for the development of this vital river artery. The value of international cooperation in resource management cannot be overstressed, since natural disasters do not recognise national boundaries.

Natural surface water resources

Evidence of regional co-operation between neighbouring states is seen in the management of natural surface water supplies, for example, in the Chad Basin. Lake Chad covers some 22 000 square kilometres at its maximum extent and about 13 000 square kilometres during drought periods, and it is part-owned by the states of Niger, Chad, Nigeria and Cameroon. Co-operation on the use of the waters of this natural ecological unit was urged by the United Nations as early as 1953 and by 1964 the four states had established a commission to work out policies not only on hydrological problems but also on economic development in general, and how this would affect flora and wildlife. Under the terms of an international agreement, each state must consult the others before embarking on any scheme which would alter the flow of surface or subterranean water in the basin. Other matters which must be jointly agreed on are rules for navigation and transport, methods of using water efficiently, and the land use of areas surrounding the lake. The high degree of co-operation which has evolved has attracted finance and expertise from outside Africa in the form of French support for a tsetse eradication programme, a US$3 million investment by the United Nations for water resource conservation, and an animal husbandry scheme supported by several international organisations. In fact, the co-operative development of the water resources of the Chad basin has provided much information for other states, for example Botswana (Okavango Basin – see below) and Kenya (Lake Turkana Basin), in the study of their own water problems.

The Seas

In this section we will discuss the value of Africa's coastal waters as a food source and as a future source of vital minerals.

The ecology of the sea

In Chapter Four we saw how African nations were

developing their fishing fleets and increasing their catches of protein-rich fish. Governments are giving more attention to the sea as populations increase and protein supplies of terrestrial origin decline. But, as on land, the ecology of the sea coasts is a delicately balanced one, easily upset by man's land-based activities. These detrimental activities may be listed as follows:

1 *Excessive exploitations of marine life* reduces fish numbers, cuts down breeding capacity, and frequently causes replacement by other species. For example, excessive fishing in waters off the South African coast almost eradicated the Cape pilchard which was replaced with the anchovy. The rock lobster population of the Vermna Seamount, discovered in 1964, was nearly wiped out within three years through intensive fishing by an international fishing fleet.
2 *Damage to nearshore marine environment* can be caused by pollution, e.g. industrial waste entering the sea, as at Lagos or Mombasa, or pollution from industrial activities, e.g. in the oil drilling regions of the Niger Delta. There is also the constant danger of tanker disaster, especially along the southern coasts of Africa where the shipping lanes narrow. Bad farming in river catchment areas increases soil erosion and increased siltation in coastal waters.
3 *Beach erosion* results from diversion of currents by groynes and sea walls, e.g. at Lagos, Tema and Durban. Deposition of normal silt loads is interrupted by dam construction, e.g. Cabora Bassa and the Aswan Dam. The nutrients contained in the silt of the Nile before the Aswan Dam was built fed plankton in the Mediterranean, which in turn supported large shoals of fish – in 1964 the fish catch of sardines was 34 000 t, but today hardly any sardines are caught.

Fortunately, Africa does not suffer the same degree of coastal pollution and degradation as do the industrialised nations of Europe, the United States and Japan. But it is not too early, in view of the rapid growth of Africa's population and the increasing pace of her industrialisation, to research methods of controlling man's effects on the marine environment, in order that past mistakes are not repeated.

Mineral wealth

The seas also possess mineral riches whose exploitation could be turned to Africa's benefit. It is estimated that the oceans as a whole possess some US$3 000 billion worth of copper, manganese, nickel, cobalt and other minerals. In addition there are vast oilfields (offshore oil accounts for 25 per cent of present world production), and gas fields on the continental shelves. The bed of the Red Sea alone is estimated to have nodule deposits of lead, silver, zinc and copper worth some US$4 billion. In a recent Law of the Sea conference, it was agreed that nations have national sovereignity over a 12-mile zone from their coasts and broad rights over fish and mineral resources within a 200-mile limit.

The new limits give rights only to those nations which have a sea coast, while land-locked states – Zambia, Chad, Uganda, Swaziland, Malaŵi and others – receive no benefits. Moreover, many coastal African nations do not possess the technology to exploit their sea resources; they will have to depend on foreign companies and be content with receiving royalties. Moreover, as seabed minerals are exploited elsewhere in the world, the dependence of industrialised nations on Africa's land-based minerals could decline.

Energy

Power from fuels

Population growth and steady economic development will mean an ever increasing demand for energy in Africa. Only Nigeria, Gabon, Libya and Algeria with their oil reserves can be said to be in a favourable position. Commercially exploitable wells are also located in Chad and Ghana, and reserves are known to exist in Benin, Cameroon, Mozambique and Senegal. Proven reserves of oil in Africa total approximately 14 000 million tonnes. Despite this, in the rural areas of most African countries, wood, charcoal and animal waste still provide the major energy sources.

These energy sources are being used up at such an

alarming rate that even the oil-rich countries may have to consider alternative sources of energy. During the early 1970s Africa's production of crude petroleum averaged about 270 million tonnes a year; at this rate the proven reserves would only last 52 years. Libya has already restricted its output of oil and Nigeria is considering doing so. In the Sahelian states alone nearly three tonnes of wood are consumed each year per family which means a total of 50 million tonnes extracted annually.

Africa has vast reserves of coal, mostly in the southern part of the continent (see p. 175). Total African production is about 65 million tonnes per annum and at this rate reserves would last 1 400 years. Outside Zimbabwe and South Africa, deposits are generally of low grade, seams thin and faulted, and costs are high in relation to output. Unless oil prices rise further, coal will not be an economic substitute, at least in the developing countries of Africa.

Oil shales provide an alternative energy source but extraction is expensive and would only be justified by higher oil prices. Oil shales have been located in quantity in Uganda, Somalia, Zaïre, Niger, Morocco, Mali, Gabon and Egypt.

Geothermal power

Considerable interest has been aroused in the possibilities of geothermal power – energy from the earth's interior store of heat. The greatest potential lies in areas where there is volcanic activity with associated geysers, hot springs and fumaroles. The Rift Valley area of East Africa, south-eastern Nigeria, Madagascar and parts of the Niger valley are likely areas for geothermal power production. Kenya is already conducting experiments near Lakes Hannington and Naivasha in the Rift Valley.

Hydro-electric power

Africa possesses considerable potential in the hydro-electric power field and estimates lie between 27 and 40 per cent of the world's total HEP potential. Zaïre possesses approximately 10 per cent of world HEP potential and the generating capacity of the Inga rapids alone is equivalent to 40 per cent of Britain's installed capacity. Despite many large schemes and numerous smaller ones Africa's developed HEP capacity is only about two per cent of the world total and many African nations have been accused of neglecting the potential of HEP resources. There are however, several explanations for this – markets for electricity are often dispersed and solid fuel plants are often a more economical proposition; most large schemes are more suited to specific industrial enterprises or mining needs; the variability of flow of Africa's rivers often makes the big scheme with high dam wall more economical than widespread smaller schemes and, because of this, initial capital investments can be very high. Moreover, the best HEP sites are often great distances from market areas with a consequent loss of power in the transmission lines: Inga is 1 725 km from the copper industries of Shaba Province, while Cabora Bassa is 1 400 km from the Rand industrial zone; over such distances power losses can be in the region of 15 per cent. There is also the high cost of installing a distribution network of power lines and sub-stations. Even a modest scheme is often as expensive a job as the actual construction of the dam and installations. However, hydro-electric power is probably the best answer in the short and medium term to the excessive exploitation of Africa's other finite energy reserves.

Nuclear power

Africa possesses nearly a third of the world's small reserves of uranium and this is seen by some nations as an important source of future energy on the continent. Reserves, however, are very unevenly distributed with South Africa having 25 per cent of the world's reserves (202 000 t). This compares with Namibia (100 000 t), Niger (40 000 t), Gabon (20 000 t), the Central African Republic (8 000 t) and Zaïre (1 800 t). Only South Africa has been able to harness its ores for energy supply, with an experimental nuclear reactor near Johannesburg and two power plants due to produce two million kilowatts of electric energy in 1982 and 1983 at Koeberg north of Cape Town. Nuclear power plants are costly (South Africa's will cost US$1 billion) and have a relatively short life compared with other plants (about 25 years on average), and these aspects make it unlikely that nuclear power will be a feasible energy proposition for less developed countries in Africa.

Solar energy

In recent years a great deal of attention has been given to solar energy in Africa and this appears to be an area where a small investment would bring considerable benefits. Solar energy units are best adapted to small projects such as the provision of heating and power for rural factories and hospitals, or for water pumps in drainage and irrigation schemes. There would be a large saving on liquid fuel and electricity costs and also a reduction in the amount of wood used as fuel; estimates show that the Sahel states could save some 25 million tonnes of wood fuel per annum if solar cookers were used instead of wood and charcoal fires.

Wildlife

The threat of extinction

Africa is unique among the continents in the richness and variety of its wildlife, but this resource is now under extreme pressure from man. Before man populated Africa in significant numbers, a natural but delicate balance had been attained in the animal kingdom between herbivorous and carnivorous species. But this balance was upset by man's increasing need for land and food, and by his greed. Wholesale slaughterings of animals began, sometimes leading to the extinction of certain species: the unique Dodo bird of Mauritius was exterminated by the early eighteenth century; the last Quagga, a zebra-like animal which once roamed the veld of southern Africa in thousands, was killed on 18 August, 1883; the White Rhino was eliminated in

Upper Volta: A hide and skin preparation factory at Ouagadougou. Such businesses, while earning foreign currency, deplete the continent's wildlife reserves.

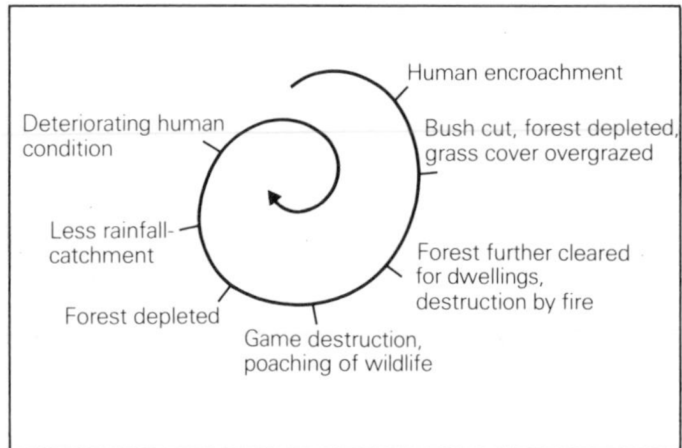

Fig. 13.3 Stages in the deterioration of the environment due to population pressure on land use in times of drought

Central Africa in 1895; the last Black-maned Lion was shot in the Atlas Mountains in 1923; more recently, the Giant Sable has disappeared from the scene in Angola. Of the 711 animal species in the world which are now in danger of extinction, 31 are in Africa and include the Roan Antelope, the Black Rhinocerus, the Cheetah, the Leopard, the African Wild Dog, and the Brown Hyena.

Many of the larger mammals and certain species of birds have been decimated and eliminated in certain areas where vegetation has been cleared and the land converted for cultivation. Increasingly, the wildlife of Africa is being concentrated into isolated sanctuaries, often adjacent to heavily populated cultivated land or expanding urban settlements. Even in these sanctuaries, the animals are not safe from hunters and poachers. For example, it is estimated that Kenya's present elephant population of approximately 120 000 is being reduced by 10 000 a year by illegal poaching. In the Marsabit area of northern Kenya, elephants have to share their age-old habitat increasingly with growing cattle herds of the Samburu and Rendille peoples who have been forced, because of drought, to take over many of the water holes once exclusively used by the elephants. The manner in which the delicate ecological balance existing between man, animals and the environment can so easily be disturbed has been recorded in the Marsabit region during the prolonged droughts of 1972–4 in Kenya:

> The main Marsabit forest is above 1 500 m in altitude, although the forest line varies with the shape of the mountain. Its efficiency at catching rain clouds is considerable. The vegetation is an unusually dense evergreen woodland of croton, strychnos, and open juniper. It is termed a 'moist forest' in that rainfall alone does not account for the quantity of moisture. Trees are often shrouded in cloud which causes moisture to run down the leaves and bark and adds to moisture caused by ordinary rainfall. As water catchment areas the forests are absolutely essential. Below the woodland lies a belt of thick grassland ringing the mountain like a collar as much as three kilometres wide. The soil is deep and humiferous and normally produces a crop of tall, perennial grass. . . . For about 15 years cultivation has been encouraged around the mountain and a few very good farms have developed. Many Boran have taken up part-time farming and some have left herding altogether. . . .
>
> The dry conditions . . . caused increased destruction of the forest by game animals, particularly elephant, buffalo, and baboon. As all wildlife became more desperate for water, many dry land browsers such as bushbuck, giraffe, dik-dik, and zebra moved up into the mountain in search of water and better grazing. Elephant and buffalo, competing for the dwindling food supply, damaged trees, bark, leaves, roots and seed pods. Such conditions made poaching easy. Taking advantage of the weakened state of the animals and their large concentrations, the incidence of illegal killings rose at an astonishing rate. While the animal population was decimated, the entire ecological system was disrupted. . . . In the resulting competition among pastoralists and the new horde of poachers, both the wildlife and the mountain terrain fared very badly.[2]

Economic value of wildlife

Many African governments, however, have realised the economic value of wildlife and this is a guarantee that realistic conservation policies will be followed. By judicious investment over the years, the Kenya

[2] 'Journey in a Forgotten Land.' Part 1: *Food and Drought in the Ethiopia—Kenya Border Lands* by Norman N. Miller; Fieldstaff Reports, American Universities Field Staff Inc. Vol. XIX No. 4, p. 7, 8.

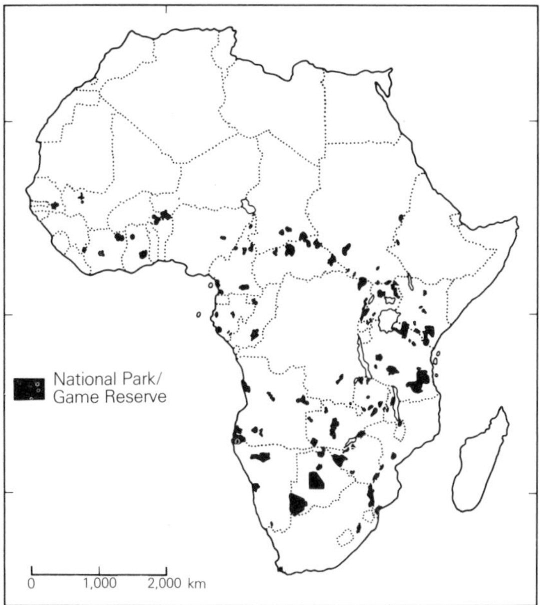

Fig. 13.4 Africa – Creation of National Parks and Games Reserves

Government has developed her game parks and wildlife reserves for the benefit of tourists; in 1975 the tourist industry netted Kenya over US$51 million compared with US$22 million in 1963. Unfortunately the concentration of animals in reserves can be detrimental to the environment: in the 1971 drought thousands of elephants in the Tsavo East National Park died, but not before they had destroyed hundreds of square kilometres of vegetation. Similar conditions were experienced in the Ghonarezou National Park in Zimbabwe's south-eastern lowveld, and thousands of elephants had to be culled by game wardens to preserve the habitat. The parks had simply become over-populated and had begun to deteriorate rapidly.

A possible solution to the over-concentration of animals in restricted game areas has been evolved by the Kenya Government in collaboration with the FAO and World Bank experts. Financial incentives are to be given to pastoralists to allow game animals to use their grazing lands for the benefit of the tourist industry. Although the money returns may be lower than by using the land exclusively for cattle, the scheme is being supported by loans of US$18 million from the World Bank, with US$12 million being invested by the Kenya Government. A similar scheme is in operation in Zimbabwe.

The Okavango Delta, Botswana

In several areas of Africa there are, as yet, virtually untouched natural wildlife sanctuaries which could be destroyed by man's encroachment if rational planning is not undertaken. Such an area is the Okavango Delta of north-eastern Botswana where a balance has been achieved between man and nature unparalleled anywhere else in Africa. The range of wildlife here is extensive – elephant, buffalo, waterbuck, cheetah, leopard, giraffe, zebra, lion and hippopotamous, as well as some 200 species of birds including cranes, spoonbills, herons, fish eagles and kingfishers. During the dry season, as the waters of the Okavango Delta recede, the animals move slowly over the area following the water's edges and, by so doing, the grasslands are never overgrazed. Occasionally, the animals are hunted but losses are small, while the tourist industry, still in its infancy, has as yet had little impact on the region.

Unfortunately, the Okavango Delta is the only permanent water body in northern Botswana, and is therefore attractive to both the farmer for irrigation and to the industrialist. The major water schemes envisaged by these two groups would slowly change the present environment and destroy the balance already achieved between man and nature. The Botswana Government is well aware of the problems and is to plan the long-term development of the Okavango region so that the needs of industry and agriculture can be accommodated without destroying the value of wildlife and the developing tourist industry. This solution by compromise between industrialists, agriculturalists and conservationists could be a model for other similar areas in Africa.

Resources and population growth

All resource problems are directly related to human population increase, to man's apparent infinite capacity to overbreed. Rapid rates of population increase sustained over a number of years can seriously retard the economic development of any nation and frustrate ambitious national development plans. African nations lacking major mineral resources, and faced

Nigeria: End of the school day. Large and growing numbers of young people place a great strain on national budgets.

Table 19 Average land available per person in hectares, 1976–2000

Country	*1976*		*1980*		*1990*		*2000*			
							Optimistic		*Pessimistic*	
	a	*b*	*a*	*b*	*a*	*b*	*a*	*b*	*a*	*b*
Nigeria	82,7	1,17	91,7	1,00	116,6	0,79	148,8	0,62	150,0	0,61
Ghana	10,1	2,37	11,2	2,13	14,2	1,68	18,1	1,32	21,2	1,12
Ivory Coast	6,8	4,73	7,5	4,30	9,3	3,47	11,6	2,77	13,1	2,46
Kenya	13,8	4,22	15,7	3,72	20,7	2,81	27,3	2,13	31,3	1,86
Tanzania	15,6	6,03	19,8	4,75	25,2	3,74	32,0	2,94	33,4	2,82
Zambia	5,1	14,76	5,7	13,14	7,5	9,96	9,8	7,65	11,3	6,66
Malaŵi	5,1	2,3	5,6	2,1	6,9	1,70	8,6	1,37	9,7	1,22
Botswana	0,7	85,71	0,7	78,47	0,9	63,80	1,2	51,43	1,4	42,85

a – Estimated total population in millions
b – Hectares of land per person

with rising energy costs, are particularly vulnerable. Nor does the situation for Africa appear to be improving for, in a recent UN report,[3] it was found that, although the pace of population growth had slackened in most regions of the world, it had actually increased in Africa and Asia. How will this increasing population growth rate affect the economies of countries in Africa?

Table 19 shows how land, Africa's most important resource, will be affected by population growth at present rates – the amount per person will decrease steadily. The 'optimistic' column is based on a slight levelling out of increase rates in the latter part of the century, while the 'pessimistic' column reflects no levelling out.

These figures refer only to the *total* land area available per person within each country and not to cultivated or cultivable land, which is considerably less. Thus, to take an extreme example, Botswana covers an area of about 600 000 square kilometres, and in 1976 its population was 700 000 people, giving an average of 85,7 ha per person. However, only three per cent or about 18 000 square kilometres of the country is cultivable, and only 0,45 per cent of 2 700 square kilometres is actually cultivated at present. This gives an average of only 0,385 ha per person of cultivated land – a clear example that land space is not as valuable as it may seem. Botswana will have approximately half this amount of land per person at the end of the century, if present population growth rates are maintained.

The goal of every national government is basically to ensure, as far as its resources will allow, a healthy and educated population which in itself becomes a valuable resource. In addition to providing enough of the correct foodstuffs, education and medical facilities must be at least adequate. Rapid population growth, however, can retard or even reverse such schemes because of the sheer costs of providing facilities. For example, at the present annual growth rate of 3,1 per cent, the number of children in Zambia's primary schools, now about 700 000, will have increased to 1,3 million by 2000 A.D. If the rate of population increase was reduced from 3,1 to 2 per cent, however, there would be 300 000 less pupils to cater for. There would also be a considerable saving of capital because 30 000 fewer teachers would need to be trained and employed and, at present construction costs of schools, US$100 million would be saved on classroom building.

With her wealth from oil exports, Nigeria is in a more favourable position than Zambia to undertake an ambitious educational expansion programme. The problems are, nevertheless, enormous. In 1976 there were over 6 million pupils and about 160 000 teachers in Nigerian primary schools. Under the Third National Development Plan primary education was made compulsory, so that by 1981 some 18 million children will attend primary school and will need about 600 000 teachers. At the present population growth rate of 2,7 per cent a year, there will be about 30 million children requiring primary school education by 2000 A.D. and nearly one million teachers will be required in the schools. The capital costs will be enormous, for in 1976 alone the Nigerian government spent US$430 million on classroom construction and books. In addition to education, Nigeria is to spend vast sums in the medical field. In a recent study, the World Health Organisation estimated that, to cater for Nigeria's urban and rural population, a sum of US$3 320 million would have to be spent on hospitals, clinics, staff training and equipment.

One method of assessing the wealth of a nation, like that of an individual, is to calculate the money earned by the population. The per capita income is the total value of materials, goods, etc. produced by a country in one year, divided by the total population. Nigeria's per capita income is relatively high, about US$200 per person in 1976, due to her oil earnings, while Botswana's US$100 per person reflects her poorer economic base. Despite rapid economic growth since independence, Kenya's per capita income has risen only slowly from US$112 to US$140 during the ten years 1967–77. However, this is a considerable achievement when one realises that the population has risen in the same period from about 10 million to nearly 15 million. Since independence, Kenya's economy has been growing at about 5,3 per cent a year, but, with the population growing at the rate of 3,4 per cent a year, per capita income has been increasing at only 1,9 per cent per annum. At this rate it will take about 35 years for the

[3] *A Concise Guide to World Population, 1970—75 and its Long-range Implications.*

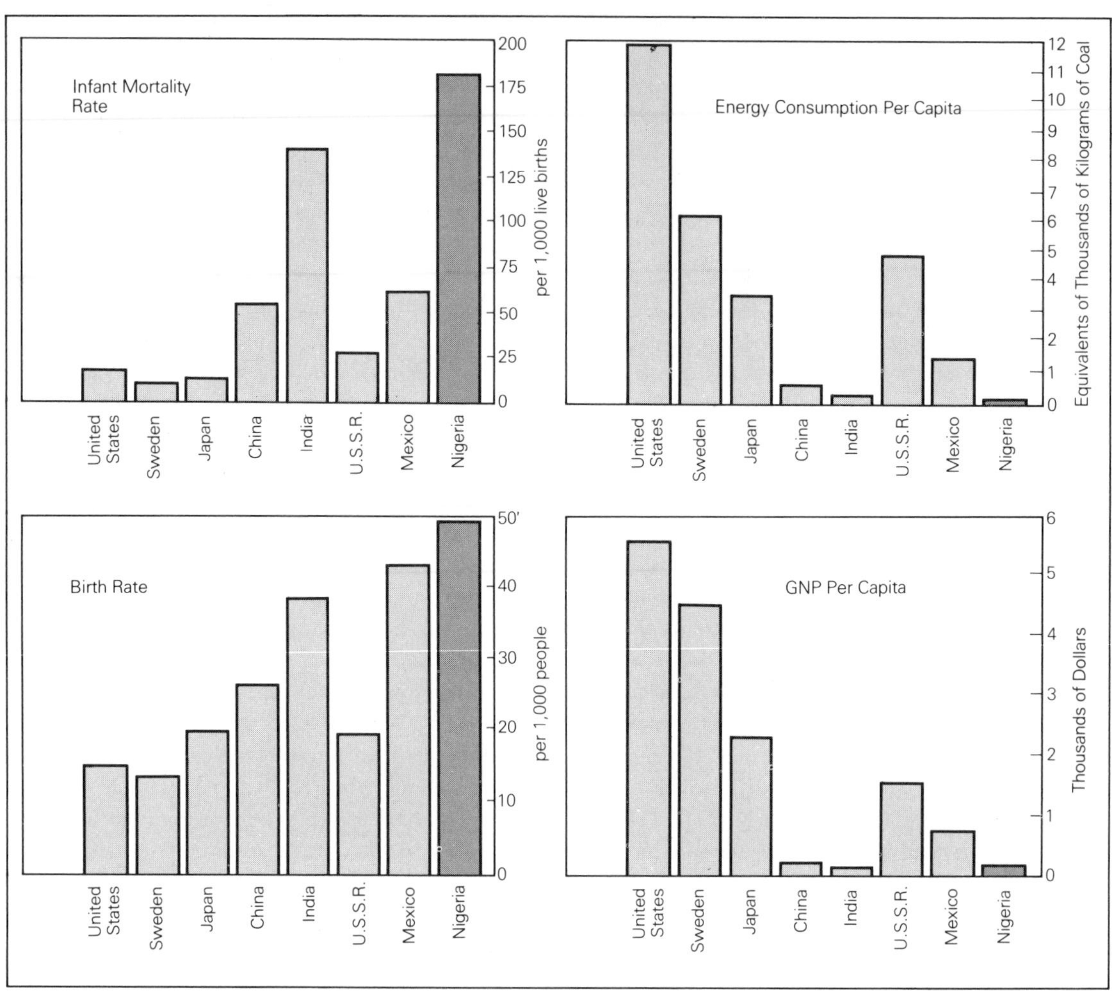

Fig. 13.5 The development gap. Nigeria, the most populous state in Africa, is here compared with other countries on the bases of infant mortality rate, energy consumption per capita, birth rate and Gross National Product per capita.

Table 20 Productive and dependent sectors of African populations

Country	*Working population 15–54 as percentage of total population*	*Dependent population as percentage of total population*		*Total dependent population as percentage of total population*
		0–14	*55 years and over*	
Kenya	44	48	8	56
Tanzania	46	44	10	54
Zambia	47	45	8	53
Nigeria	53	43	4	47
Sierra Leone	53	37	10	47

per capita income to be doubled, but if the population growth rate was reduced to about two per cent a year, per capita income would double in about 23 years. There would be fewer people to share the national wealth.

The national wealth is created largely by the working sector of the population, usually taken in Africa to mean those people between the ages of 15 and 54 inclusive. The working sector must also support the non-productive sector – pupils at school and the non-working old age group of 55 and over. In many nations of Africa the non-productive sector is often larger than the productive one as Table 20 shows.

This means that, for example, in Nigeria every 100 workers are supporting 89 dependents, while in Kenya 100 workers support 127 dependents; for comparison, in Sweden 100 adults support 84 non-working dependents. Not only do these dependents produce nothing to help the economy but capital spent on this sector cannot be spent in other spheres – communications, agriculture, industries, and the creation of new jobs. Lower birth rates would ease this situation for the benefit of all.

Unemployment in urban centres, partly due to rural-urban migration and the high birth rates, is now a grave problem in many African countries. Annual urban population growth rates are now as high as 10 per cent. In just over the thirty years Dakar has grown from 130 000 to nearly one million and Abidjan from 6 000 to half a million. Urban unemployment rates have risen to 20 per cent in the Ivory Coast and Morocco and to between 15 and 17 per cent in Nigeria and Kenya. Botswana is attempting to solve this problem (Gaborone increased from 5 000 to 40 000 in ten years) by offering incentives to encourage people to stay on the land – the introduction of rural-based industry, the granting of credit, and the supply of equipment. Other countries are experiencing mass migration to neighbouring states by people seeking employment; Upper Volta loses some 75 000 people every year, chiefly to Ghana and the Ivory Coast, and 600 000 take up seasonal employment outside the country. In southern Africa unemployed males from Swaziland, Lesotho, Botswana and Mozambique migrate to the industrial centres of South Africa, 200 000 from Lesotho alone.

By the year 2000 Africa's population will have almost doubled if present growth rates are maintained, and unbearable pressure will be put on the environment with increasingly rapid exploitation of existing irreplaceable resources. Present populous areas may be converted to the over-grazed, eroded scrubland and desert zones which have been created in the Sahelian states unless a conscious and planned effort is made to stabilise the growth of Africa's population.

Questions

1 'Land is Africa's most important resource.' Discuss this statement with reference to Africa in general and to any one country in Africa.
2 Explain the term 'desertification' in relation to Africa's land resources, illustrating your answer with references to specific countries.
3 By the end of the century, unless major discoveries are made, Africa's oil reserves will have dwindled. Briefly review Africa's present oil position and outline the alternative energy sources available on the continent.
4 'The economic problems of the Sahelian states can only be overcome by regional co-operation.' Discuss, with reference to examples of such co-operation.
5 Compromise is necessary between conversationists, industrialists and agriculturalists if Africa's wildlife is to be preserved. Discuss this statement with reference to areas where the ecological balance of nature is threatened.
6 What are the advantages and disadvantages of the tourist industry to the economies of African states?
7 'All resource problems are related to human population increase.' Discuss this statement, with reference to the use of Africa's resources by man.
8 'The goal of every national government is basically to ensure, as far as its resources will allow, a healthy and educated population.' Expand on this statement by referring to the work being done in Africa and particularly in your own country, to ensure adequate and correct diets and basic education.

APPENDIX 1

The modern states of Africa: population statistics (1977)[1]

Region or country	Population estimate mid-1977 (millions)	Birth rate	Death rate	Rate of natural increase (annual, percent)	Number of years to double population	Population projection to 2000 (millions)	Infant mortality rate	Population under 15 years (percent)	Population over 64 years (percent)	Life expectancy at birth (years)	Urban population (percent)	Per capita gross national product (US$)
World	4 083	30	12	1,8	38	6 182	103	36	6	59	38	1 530
Africa	423	45	19	2,6	27	811	154	44	3	46	24	400
Northern Africa	100	42	14	2,8	25	185	130	44	3	53	39	570
Algeria	17,8	48	15	3,2	22	36,5	142	48	3	53	52	780
Egypt	38,9	36	12	2,3	30	63,9	116	41	3	52	45	310
Libya	2,7	48	9	3,9	18	5,2	130	49	4	55	30	5 080
Morocco	18,3	48	16	3,2	22	35,5	130	46	2	53	38	470
Sudan	16,3	48	18	3	23	32,7	141	45	3	51	13	290
Tunisia	6	34	11	2,3	30	10,8	125	45	4	55	47	760
Western Africa	125	49	23	2,6	27	243	175	45	3	42	19	300
Benin (Dahomey)	3,3	50	23	2,7	26	6	185	46	4	41	14	140
Cape Verde	0,3	29	9	2	35	0,4	79	48	5	50	8	470
Gambia	0,6	42	21	2,1	33	0,9	165	41	2	44	14	190
Ghana	10,4	47	20	2,7	26	21,1	156	47	4	48	31	460
Guinea	4,7	47	23	2,4	29	8,5	175	43	3	41	20	130
Guinea-Bissau	0,5	40	25	1,5	46	0,8	208	37	4	38	23	390
Ivory Coast	7	46	21	2,5	28	13,2	164	43	3	44	20	500
Liberia	1,7	50	21	2,9	24	3	159	42	3	45	28	410
Mali	5,9	50	26	2,4	29	11	188	49	2	38	13	90
Mauritania	1,4	45	25	2	35	2,4	187	42	6	38	23	310
Niger	4,9	52	26	2,7	26	9,6	200	43	3	38	9	130
Nigeria	83,5	49	23	2,7	26	134,9	180	45	2	41	18	310
Senegal	5,3	46	21	2,5	28	9,3	159	43	3	44	32	370
Sierra Leone	3,2	45	21	2,4	29	5,8	136	43	3	44	15	200
Togo	2,3	51	23	2,7	26	4,6	127	46	3	41	15	270
Upper Volta	6,4	48	26	2,3	30	11	182	43	3	38	4	90
Eastern Africa	120	46	19	2,7	26	239	151	44	3	45	12	220
Burundi	3,9	41	20	2,1	33	7,2	150	44	2	40	2	100

Region or country	Population estimate mid-1977 (millions)	Birth rate	Death rate	Rate of natural increase (annual, percent)	Number of years to double population	Population projection to 2000 (millions)	Infant mortality rate	Population under 15 years (percent)	Population over 64 years (percent)	Life expectancy at birth (years)	Urban population (percent)	Per capita gross national product (US$)
Comoros	0,3	45	20	2,5	28	0,5	160	43	3	46	10	260
Ethiopia	29,4	43	18	2,5	28	53,8	181	44	3	42	12	100
Kenya	14,4	49	16	3,3	21	31,5	119	46	3	50	10	220
Madagascar	7,9	50	21	2,9	24	16,4	102	35	3	44	14	200
Malaŵi	5,3	48	24	2,4	29	9,9	142	35	3	43	10	150
Mauritius	0,9	25	8	1,7	41	1,2	46	41	4	63	44	580
Mozambique	9,5	43	20	2,3	30	17,4	165	43	3	44	6	310
Reunion	0,5	28	7	2,1	33	0,7	47	43	4	63	51	1 550
Rwanda	4,5	51	22	2,9	24	8,7	133	44	3	41	3	90
Seychelles	0,1	33	9	2,4	29	0,1	39	43	6	65	26	520
Somalia	3,4	47	22	2,6	27	6,5	177	45	2	41	28	100
Tanzania	16	47	22	2,5	28	33,1	162	47	2	44	7	170
Uganda	12,4	43	16	2,7	26	24,7	160	44	3	50	7	250
Zambia	5,2	50	19	3,1	22	11,3	160	46	3	46	36	540
Zimbabwe	6,8	48	14	3,4	20	15,2	122	48	2	52	20	540
Middle Africa	**48**	44	22	2,3	**30**	**88**	165	43	3	42	24	270
Angola	6,3	47	24	2,3	30	11,7	203	42	3	38	18	680
Cameroon	6,7	40	22	1,8	38	11,6	137	40	3	41	20	270
Central African Rep.	1,9	43	22	2,1	33	3,3	190	42	3	41	36	230
Chad	4,2	44	24	2	35	6,9	160	40	3	38	14	120
Congo Rep.	1,4	45	21	2,4	29	2,7	180	42	3	44	40	500
Equatorial Guinea	0,3	37	20	1,7	41	0,5	165	37	3	44	45	320
Gabon	0,5	32	22	1	69	0,7	178	32	4	41	32	2 240
Sâo Thomé/Principe	0,1	45	11	3,4	20	0,1	64	—	—	53	16	570
Zaire	26,3	45	20	2,5	28	50,5	160	44	3	44	26	150
Southern Africa	**30**	40	16	2,5	**28**	57	119	41	4	51	44	1 220
Botswana	0,7	46	23	2,3	30	1,4	97	48	6	56	12	330
Lesotho	1,1	39	20	1,9	36	1,8	114	40	4	46	3	180
Namibia	0,9	44	23	2,1	33	1,7	177	41	4	41	32	800
South Africa	26,1	40	15	2,5	28	51,2	117	41	4	52	48	1 320
Swaziland	0,5	49	22	2,7	26	1	149	48	3	44	8	470

[1] Reference: *Population Reference Bureau Inc.*

Statistical section

The statistics in this section are intended to supplement information in the general text and to provide material for the compilation of graphs and charts in practical exercises. Population statistics for separate countries are included in Appendix 1. The tables are quoted in national currencies. The following rates may be used for conversion:

Country	*Currency*	*Value of £ sterling*	*Value of US dollar*
Nigeria	Naira	1,4	0,6
Ghana	Cedi	2,7	1,1
Franc Zone	CFA franc	488,0	211,0
Angola	Escudo	58,0	25,0
Sudan	S. pound	0,8	0,3
Swaziland	Emalangeni	1,6	0,6
Liberia	L. dollar	2,4	1,0
Zambia	Z. kwacha	1,5	0,6
Egypt	E. pound	0,9	0,4
Kenya	K. shilling	16,7	7,1
Tanzania	T. shilling	16,7	7,1
South Africa	Rand	1,6	0,6
Sierra Leone	Leone	2,0	0,8

Agricultural statistics

Ghana: Cocoa production 1973–6 (tonnes)

1973	*1974*	*1975*	*1976*
343 000	381 600	396 200	349 500

Africa: Coffee production 1975–1977 ('000 bags at 60 kilos)

Country	*1975*	*1976*	*1977*
Angola	1 160	1 200	1 400
Benin	19	50	15
Burundi	279	359	363
Cameroon	1 480	1 438	1 583
CAR	150	208	221
Congo	28	22	28
Ethiopia	2 913	3 333	3 166
Gabon	1	10	10
Ghana	46	111	60
Ivory Coast	5 217	4 703	4 200
Kenya	1 220	1 270	1 250
Liberia	68	150	120
Madagascar	1 066	900	917
Nigeria	59	67	80
Rwanda	377	580	400
Sierra Leone	57	170	192
Tanzania	938	850	1 000
Togo	151	200	200
Uganda	2 214	2 700	2 780
Zaïre	1 100	1 350	1 400

Africa: Tea production in tonnes, 1974 and 1975

Country	*1974*	*1975*
Kenya	53 440	56 256
Uganda	21 688	18 409
Tanzania	12 974	13 733
Malaŵi	23 318	26 237
Mozambique	17 639	13 143
Rhodesia	23 318	–
Zaïre	6 329	–
Burundi	3 433	–
Mauritius	3 971	–

Liberia: Rubber production in 1975

Source	*Planted area (acres)*	*Area in tapping (acres)*	*Concession production (lb.)*	*Total purchased from farmers (lb.)*	*Total plus stocks (lb.)*	*Exports (lb.)*	*Yield (lb./acre)*
The Liberia Co.	5 831	4 643	5 618 929	–	6 085 287	5 049 450	1 210
Firestone	90 024	52 602	73 483 895	39 038 261	126 707 911	113 101 038	1 397
Alan L. Grant	–	–	–	12 637 754	16 755 874	14 102 950	–
African Fruit Co.	5 700	5 412	6 088 827	–	7 602 170	6 511 586	1 125
B. F. Goodrich	14 416	13 000	16 142 374	1 383 265	20 296 129	18 588 438	1 242
Salala Rubber Corp.	5 133	5 133	7 266 869	–	9 187 230	6 135 402	1 416
Liberian Agric. Co. (Uniroyal)	19 186	18 164	19 507 403	383 383	21 096 686	18 963 686	1 074
Total	140 290	98 954	128 108 297	53 441 653	207 731 278	182 452 550	

Nigeria: Groundnut production 1966–74 (tonnes '000)

Year	*Production*	*Exports*
1966	978	573
1967	1 026	520
1968	684	648
1969	764	525
1970	634	291
1971	281	136
1972	302	107
1973	546	195
1974	100	–

Aid statistics

Investment in Kenya: 1975–6: Estimates

	Loans and grants £'000
World Bank/IDA	2 479
United Nations	26 308
European Economic Commission	1 279
Britain	3 211
West Germany	1 313
Sweden	6 634
Canada	569
United States of America	4 588
Japan	1 042
Denmark	1 035
Switzerland	3
Norway	1 671
Netherlands	1 565
Finland	200
African Development Bank	548
Other	9 918
Total	62 314

Energy statistics

Egypt: Petroleum production

	Estimates in million tonnes		
	1974	*1975*	*1976*
Crude oil	7,4	11,7	18,4
Refining capacity	6,9	8,7	10,1
Domestic consumption	6,8	7,5	8,3
Value of exports (million £E)	73,0	121,0	255,0
Value of imports	165,0	151,0	120,0

Mineral statistics

Liberia: Production of iron ore 1970–4 (million long tons)

1970	*1971*	*1972*	*1973*	*1974*
23,4	22,9	24,7	25,1	25,3

Liberia: Quantity and value of diamond exports 1970–4

Year	*Millions of carats*	*Value (US$ millions)*
1970	0,8	27,9
1971	0,7	28,2
1972	0,9	31,7
1973	0,8	49,3
1974	0,6	29,9

Africa: Gold production 1975 (tonnes)

South Africa	758,5
Ghana	21,4
Zimbabwe	18,6
Zaïre	4,4
Total world	1 454,0

Africa: Crude oil imports of selected countries, 1974 (thousands of barrels per day)

Kenya	56	Ghana	14
Senegal/Ivory Coast	32	Malagasy	14
Tanzania	17	Zaïre	11
Zambia	17	Ethiopia	10
Sudan	15	Liberia	9
Mozambique	15	Sierra Leone	4

Africa: Crude oil production, 1975–80 (thousands of barrels per day)

OPEC members		*Non-OPEC members*			
	1975		*1975*	*1977**	*1980**
Nigeria	1787	Egypt	230	450	530
Libya	1510	Angola	166	175	225
Algeria	960	Tunisia	95	100	120
Gabon	200	Congo	38	35	45
		Zaïre	2	50	50
		Morocco	1	n.a.	n.a.

*Expected production.

Africa: Refinery capacity of selected countries, 1975 (thousands of barrels per day)

Nigeria	60
Kenya	48
Ivory Coast	43
Angola	36
Ghana	28
Zambia	25
Sudan	22
Gabon	17
Mozambique	17
Tanzania	16
Zaïre	16
Malagasy	15
Senegal	15
Ethiopia	14
Liberia	11

Angola: Crude oil exports 1968–73 ('000 tons)

1968	17	1971	4 747
1969	1 502	1972	6 829
1970	4 269	1973	7 323

Libya: Oil production, 1961–75

Year	*Output '000 barrels per day*	*Percentage change over previous year*	*Year*	*Output '000 barrels per day*	*Percentage change over previous year*
1961	20	–	1969	3 110	+19,4
1962	185	+825,0	1970	3 320	+ 6,8
1963	465	+151,4	1971	2 765	−16,7
1964	860	+ 84,9	1972	2 240	−18,9
1965	1 220	+ 41,9	1973	2 180	− 2,8
1966	1 505	+ 23,4	1974	1 525	−19,9
1967	1 745	+ 15,9	1975	1 120	−40,6
1968	2 605	+ 49,3			

Note. 1975 figures are for first half year only. Comparison is with first six months of 1974.

Nigeria: Petroleum production and exports 1958–74

Year	*Crude oil production*		*Crude oil exports*		*Natural gas production*
	Thousand barrels	*Thousand tonnes*	*Thousand barrels*	*Thousand tonnes*	*Million cubic feet*
1958	1 876	257	1 695	230	1 609
1959	4 096	561	4 065	552	4 939
1960	6 367	872	6 244	849	5 095
1961	16 802	2 283	16 506	2 243	10 943
1962	24 624	3 346	24 680	3 421	17 179
1963	27 913	3 793	27 701	3 754	22 106
1964	43 997	5 978	43 432	5 878	36 333
1965	99 853	13 567	96 985	13 234	79 438
1966	152 428	20 710	140 118	19 333	103 820
1967	116 525	15 832	109 057	15 011	93 950
1968	51 907	7 053	52 847	7 180	51 628
1969	197 204	26 794	197 246	26 984	145 714
1970	395 905	53 791	383 455	52 100	285 512
1971	558 828	75 928	542 545	73 984	458 973
1972	665 286	90 392	650 980	88 431	604 642
1973	750 609	101 985	723 314	99 688	772 777
1974	823 349	112 788	795 710	109 662	959 524

Population statistics

Nigeria: Population census 1973

State	*Total population in millions*
East-Central	8,06
Mid-Western	3,24
South Eastern	3,46
Lagos	2,47
Western	8,92
Rivers	2,24
Benue Plateau	5,17
Kwara	4,46
North Central	6,79
North Eastern	15,38
Kano	10,90
North Western	8,50
Total	79,76

Port statistics

South and South West Africa: Tonnage and ships handled

Port	*November 1974*	*April 1975*	*November 1974*	*April 1975*
	Number of ships		*Cargo in tonnes*	
Durban	468	545	2 595 931	2 949 549
Cape Town	438	450	900 270	834 200
Port Elizabeth	191	177	857 503	855 703
East London	98	74	348 408	303695
Walvis Bay	92	84	169 047	179 046
Mossel Bay	24	36	3 931	30 697
Lüderitz	12	11	5 073	3 525

East Africa: Main import and export commodities handled by major ports, 1972–3 (in tons)

Mombasa

Exports

	1972	*1973*
Coffee	329 643	379 931
Maize	714	173 964
Tea	86 849	81 842
Oil seed cakes	56 753	58 781
Sisal	29 728	37 321
Cotton	80 444	77 166
Timber	2 580	7 724
Soda ash	126 974	189 286
Cement	24 235	5 811
Miscellaneous	278 922	335 778
Other	15 212	7 948
Total exports	1 032 054	1 355 552

Imports

	1972	*1973*
Wheat	69 326	50 218
Rice	5 995	63
Sugar	115 157	92 575
Fertilizer and salt	203 748	177 835
Coal and bitumen	58 594	66 128
Cement clinker	73 354	16 470
Iron products	155 367	171 140
Sleepers and rails	3 892	10 084
Vehicles	24 215	18 444
General cargo	509 362	554 288
All other cargo	1 237 137	1 174 602
Oil imports	2 564 459	2 998 349
Miscellaneous	17 900	17 342
Total imports	5 038 506	5 347 548

Dar-es-Salaam

Exports

	1972	*1973*
Sisal	38 059	26 996
Cotton	63 894	63 521
Oil seed cake	52 998	32 216
Castor oil seed	9 070	998
Cashew nuts	25 800	28 608
Coffee	26 058	21 025
Hides and skins	7 130	6 166
Tea	9 777	10 346
Canned and frozen meat	1 963	839
Sunflower seed	9 070	998
Wattle and bark extract	10 622	8 281
Maize flour	8 460	5 029
Tobacco	4 700	5 426
Copper from Zaïre	79 853	73 737
Copper from Zambia	205 965	265 707
Sisal rope	11 585	12 365
Miscellaneous	49 619	89 477
Total exports	614 629	651 737

Imports

	1972	*1973*
Bulk cement	114 339	56 206
Vehicles	27 376	32 682
General cargo	411 371	396 982
Railway equipment	39 016	58 538
Maize	93 790	234
Sugar	41 879	46 223
Wheat	34 556	4 145
Fertilizer	19 091	55 214
Bitumen	7 724	6 565
Salt	4 521	2 743
Paper and paper bags	11 773	16 052
Other	145 280	121 518
Total imports	950 716	797 102

Tanga

Exports

	1972	*1973*
Sisal	105 713	82 461
Timber	2 731	5 509
Maize and maize meal	100	1 233
Tea	4 258	4 286
Wattle bark and extract	103	146
Sisal ropes	10 983	18 046
Coffee	7 991	8 004
Pulses	6 281	6 463
Other	7 745	5 443
Total exports	145 909	131 591

Imports

	1972	*1973*
Vehicles	192	207
Cement	23 798	11 884
Fertilizer	3 796	4 994
Iron and steel	3 800	5 000
Coffee	1 475	217
Salt	378	633
Milk	341	21
General cargo	41 735	58 314
Other (chiefly bulk oils)	15 123	29 692
Total imports	90 638	110 960

Mtwara

Exports

	1972	*1973*
Cashew nuts	90 235	83 047
Cassava	16 602	4 065
Sisal	6 853	4 735
Pulses	337	331
Timber	1 666	447
Coffee	2 361	1 386
Tobacco	1 098	1 071
Sesame	7 312	4 143
General cargo	3 426	9 021
Other (chiefly groundnuts)	69	127
Total exports	129 959	108 373

Imports

	1972	*1973*
Bulk oils	1 155	n.a.
Bulk cement	2 321	41
Bagged cement	1 813	1 401
Maize flour	1 787	115
Tinned milk	0	14
Rice	729	71
Sugar	1 661	10
Fertilizers	2 900	6 775
General cargo	20 575	35 704
Other (chiefly bulk oils)	3 203	500
Total imports	36 144	44 631

Tourist statistics

Tanzania: Tourist arrivals 1965–74

1965	21 500	1970	79 000
1966	28 359	1971	88 400
1967	34 619	1972	89 945
1968	49 105	1973	101 900
1969	55 884	1974	85 000

Gambia: Tourists on charter 1968–74

Season	*Charter tourists*	*% increase*
1968–69	1 000	–
1969–70	1 450	45
1970–71	2 703	82
1971–72	8 031	209
1972–73	15 584	94
1973–74	20 383	31

Kenya: Origins of tourists 1975

Europe	172 600
Africa	131 100
North America	52 800
Asia	21 900
Others	7 400
Total	385 800

Trade statistics

Egypt: Trade balance and exports and imports (millions of Egyptian pounds)

	1970	*1973*	*1974*
Imports	310,9	325,0	835,6
Exports	331,2	444,2	593,3
Trade balance	+20,3	+119,2	−242,3
Major exports			
Cotton (raw)	119,9	161,2	274,0
Rice	51,6	37,6	39,7
Cotton yarn	36,2	33,3	–
Woven cotton	16,0	18,7	–
Oil	9,4	14,1	72,8

Kenya: Trade balance, 1971–5 (K£M)

	1971	*1972*	*1973*	*1974*	*1975*
Imports	184	178	206	353	337
Export	78	95	129	170	176
Trade balance	−106	−83	−77	−183	−161

Ivory Coast: Trade balance and major exports, 1971–6

	1971	*1972*	*1973*	*1976*
Exports	126,5	139,5	190,9	392,5
Imports	110,8	114,3	157,5	311,5
Trade balance	+15,7	+25,2	+33,3	+81,0
Main exports				
Coffee	42,1	36,8	43,9	n.a.
Cocoa and products	26,3	27,2	33,4	n.a.
Timber	30,9	37,9	56,2	n.a.

Kenya: New markets for exports, 1972–4 (K£M)

	1972	*1973*	*1974*
West Germany	9,46	13,56	17,58
Zambia	3,88	6,21	8,52
Belgium	0,78	3,17	8,09
Japan	2,09	5,01	5,36
Singapore	0,25	1,04	5,28
Greece	0,23	1,20	1,92
Egypt	0,27	0,23	1,92
Yugoslavia	0,24	0,99	1,05
Total	17,29	31,41	50,00

Liberia: Trade balance and major exports (millions of US dollars)

	1964	*1971*	*1972*	*1973*	*1974*	*1975*
Exports	125,7	247,0	270,0	318,0	400,3	405,8
Imports	111,2	162,0	179,0	190,0	288,4	311,2
Trade balance	+14,5	+85,0	+91,0	+128,0	+111,9	+74,6
Major exports						
Iron ore	80,6	160,6	182,1	196,7	262,0	295,0
Rubber	29,7	32,3	29,0	42,8	64,5	46,2
Logs	0,0	8,0	8,2	16,6	17,6	11,4
Diamonds	–	28,2	31,7	49,3	29,9	18,4
Coffee	6,0	4,0	4,6	5,0	4,0	n.a.
Palm kernels	0,8	2,2	0,5	–	–	–
Cocoa	0,6	1,1	1,5	2,0	4,3	n.a.

Nigeria: Rise in food imports 1965–1975

Commodity	*1965*		*1975*	
	Quantity in tonnes	*Value '000 nairas*	*Quantity in tonnes*	*Value '000 nairas*
Fresh fish	2 585	435	4 130	1 640
Stock fish	27 001	13 346	13 160	24 313
Canned sardines	1 078	362	12 965	7 985
Other canned fish	2 899	417	9 622	4 462
Fresh meat	624	371	3 710	3 245
Canned meat	78	15	1 261	1 252

Nigeria: External trade (million nairas)

Nigeria	*1970*	*1971*	*1972*	*1973*	*1974*	*1975*	*1976*
Exports	877,1	1 280,8	1 399,1	2 278,0	5 762,0	5 246,0	6 622,0
Imports	756,4	1 078,9	995,0	1 224,0	1 715,0	3 629	5 140,0
Trade balance	+128,9	+214,5	+417,1	+1 054,0	+4 047,0	+1 617,0	+1482,0
Main exports							
	1970	*1971*	*1972*	*1973*	*1974*	*1975*	*1976*
Crude petroleum	509,8	953,0	1 157,0	1 849,3	5 317,0	3 856,0	6 196,0
Cocoa beans	133,1	143,1	101,1	112,0	149,0	230,0	217,8
Cocoa products	15,4	10,4	12,2	16,0	0,8	14,0	
Groundnuts	43,5	25,0	19,1	44,0	6,6	–	–
Groundnut oil and cake	34,2	19,6	16,8	23,0	9,8	0,4	3,4
Palm kernels	21,7	25,9	15,7	18,0	42,9	10,8	25,8
Palm kernel oil	8,4	6,2	5,6	10,0	n.a.	n.a.	–
Palm oil	1,1	3,4	0,2	–	–	–	–
Rubber	17,6	12,4	7,4	20,0	37,6	7,8	14,0
Cotton	13,1	11,1	0,6	5,0	–	–	–
Timber and plywood	8,0	7,0	8,0	14,0	11,5	4,8	1,4
Tin metal	33,2	24,8	19,1	15,0	23,1	18,2	14,6
Total exports	756,4	1 078,9	995,0	2 278,0	5 672,0	4 270,0	6 622,0
Main imports							
	1970	*1971*	*1972*	*1973*	*1974*	*1975*	*1976*
Food and live animals	57,7	87,9	95,1	126,0	155,2	232,0	441,8
Drink and tobacco	4,0	4,5	4,4	4,0	9,1	19,6	63,7
Crude materials	16,7	20,5	20,7	21,0	63,4	67,0	79,3
Mineral fuels, etc.	22,1	9,0	10,3	13,0	50,9	92,0	181,2
Oils and fats	0,8	0,7	1,1	1,0	3,6	6,8	24,7
Chemicals	88,5	122,0	102,6	133,0	188,7	284,0	398,4
Manufactured goods	226,1	319,4	267,9	324,0	512,1	888,0	1 135,7
Machinery and transport equipment	282,6	428,9	392,6	496,0	608,3	1 306,0	2 447,4
Misc. manufactures	39,5	70,8	83,1	99,0	113,4	208,0	351,4
Other	18,5	15,4	8,8	8,0	10,7	8,2	8,5
Total imports	756,4	1 078,9	986,7	1 224,0	1 715,0	3 112,0	5 140,0

Sierra Leone: Trade balance and exports (millions of Leones)

	1973	*1974*	*1975*	*1976*
Exports	106,5	122,2	116,7	111,0
Imports	127,0	188,8	167,9	177,0
Trade balance	−20,5	−66,6	−51,2	−66,0
Main exports				
Diamonds	79,6	74,0	67,6	56,3
Iron ore	10,9	12,4	13,2	0,0
Bauxite	3,3	4,1	3,7	4,7
Cocoa	5,4	7,3	8,8	8,0
Coffee	9,9	2,8	7,1	8,2

South Africa: Exports to Africa 1955–72 (millions of Rand)

Year	*Total exports*	*Exports to Africa*	*Africa exports as % of total exports*
1955	660,8	128,1	19,28
1960	797,2	140,4	17,61
1965	1 056,3	146,1	13,92
1970	1 542,9	263,9	17,10
1971	1 568,8	292,4	18,64
1972	2 044,1	305,6	14,96

Sudan: Trade balance and major exports 1973–6 (S£M)

	1973	*1974*	*1975*	*1976*
Imports	130,2	207,0	284,4	238,2
Exports	157,7	139,0	146,3	208,7
Trade balance	+27,5	−68,0	−138,1	−29,5
Main exports				
Cotton	84,3	43,3	70,2	97,8
Gum arabic	7,4	14,3	7,5	11,2
Groundnuts	13,0	18,6	34,4	39,0

Tanzania: Trade balance and exports and imports (T£M)

	1971	*1972*	*1973*	*1974*
Exports	99,4	113,8	129,0	149,0
Imports	136,2	146,4	174,0	264,0
Trade balance	−21,1	−32,6	−45,0	−115,0
Main exports				
Coffee	11,3	19,1	24,7	18,7
Cotton	12,2	16,8	16,6	23,6
Sisal	6,6	7,2	11,0	13,2
Main imports				
Machinery	48,7	43,9	n.a.	n.a.
Manufactures	42,2	53,2		

Zambia: Trade balance and exports and imports (Millions of Kwacha)

	1970	*1971*	*1972*	*1973*	*1974*
Exports	714,8	484,9	541,7	744,0	904,0
Imports	358,5	395,2	403,8	349,0	503,0
Trade balance	+356,3	+89,7	+137,9	+349,0	+401,0
Main exports					
Copper	681,1	450,3	490,9	699,0	838,0
Tobacco	2,9	3,5	2,7	4,7	6,2
Maize	–	0,2	0,1	0,6	7,3
Zinc	10,9	11,5	16,3	16,7	25,2
Cobalt	6,3	4,1	8,5	4,9	7,9

Direction of trade
Exports 1974: Japan 176,0; Britain 195,0; West Germany 114,7; USA 5,3
Imports 1974: Britain 100,0; S. Africa 39,0; Japan 48,6; USA 39,5; West Germany 41,0; East Africa 13,1

Swaziland: Trade balance and exports (millions of Emalengeni)

	1970	*1971*	*1972*	*1973*	*1974*
Exports	50,8	56,6	61,7	72,8	122,6
Imports	42,7	47,8	53,3	66,6	79,6
Trade balance	+8,1	+7,5	+8,4	+6,2	+43,0
Main exports					
Iron ore	11,03	12,11	9,33	7,92	12,28
Asbestos	5,24	5,90	4,55	6,67	5,55
Meat and products	1,69	1,82	2,15	3,67	3,01
Citrus fruit	3,58	4,33	3,49	3,94	4,00
Sugar	11,83	12,50	19,21	18,28	44,11
Woodpulp	9,55	9,56	11,06	15,32	31,32

Transport statistics

Nigeria: Railway transport of passengers and freight, 1954–74

Years	*Goods traffic*		*Passenger traffic*	
	Tonnages (000)	*Ton-miles (m.)*	*Passengers (000)*	*Pass.-miles (m.)*
1954–55	2 602	1 079	5 451	349
1959–60	2 803	1 250	7 881	358
1961–62	3 003	1 412	11 061	481
1967–68	1 868	986	6 916	247
1969–70	1 553	950	8 370	453
1970–71	1 604	982	8 942	611
1971–72	1 406	750	6 151	597
1972–73	1 670	344	5 819	640
1973–74	1 978	958	4 670	473

Zambia: Transport routes July 1974

Copper exports in tonnes		
Dar-es-Salaam	25 000	45%
Lobito (closed August)	25 000	45%
Other routes	5 000	10%
Total	50 000	100%

Cargo imports in tonnes		
Dar-es-Salaam	30 000	40%
Lobito	35 000	47%
Other routes	10 000	13%
Total	75 000	100%

APPENDIX 3

The major cash and subsistence crops of Africa

Cash crops (*=also used substantially as subsistence crops)

Crop	*Climatic needs*	*Soils*	*Major producers*
Banana/ Plantain	Hot, moist tropical climate; average temperature 20°C; minimum temperature is 15°C; total annual water requirement, 1 400 to 2 500 mm with at least 200 mm a month; high humidity, warm moist nights, heavy dews are beneficial; dislikes strong winds	Heavy, deep, well-drained soils, organically rich; heavy clays or very sandy soils unsuitable; alluvial river deposits best	Cameroon, Guinea, most tropical African countries produce plantain for subsistence
Cocoa	24 to 28°C; found only in lowlands and at moderate elevations, upper limit, 750 m; annual average rainfall 1 800 mm uniformly distributed; likes shade and high humidity but too high humidity encourages fungus growth	Loams developed on granite with low quartz content are best; sandy soils rich in quartz unsuitable; soils must retain water, be deep and permeable; best areas are those previously under primary or secondary forest; humus content must be high	Ghana, southwestern Nigeria, Ivory Coast, Cameroon, Fernando Po, Equatorial Guinea
Coffee	Average annual temperature, 20°C; optimum for Arabica, 17° to 22°C; for Robusta, 20° to 25°C; altitude ranges from 450 to 1 700 m; likes alternate wet and dry seasons; Arabica lowest annual rainfall, between 1 000 and 1 500 mm; Robusta, 2 000 mm; shading and shelter trees needed	Deep, freshly cleared virgin forest soils with high organic content best; permeable and moisture retaining although not subject to waterlogging	Ivory Coast, Angola, Ethiopia, Kenya, Uganda, Rwanda, Burundi, Tanzania, Malagasy
Copra (coconut palm)	Uniform warmth; minimum temperature, 20°C; average annual temperature, 25° to 30°C; rainfall, 1 500 to 2 000 mm uniformly distributed; smaller rainfalls tolerated where water-table is high	Deep, sandy loams, rich in humus derived from coral, limestone and volcanic rocks; withstands brackish or salty water	Coasts of Mozambique, Zanzibar
Cotton	Minimum temperature, lies between 15° and 16°C; optimum, 18° and 30°C; temperatures should lie between 77°F (15,5°C) during growing period; regions with 60 per cent cloudiness are unsuitable; water needs are low, often less than 500 mm; distribution of rain very important; dislikes high humidities	Except for extreme sandy or clayey soils all soils are suitable; well drained with low water-table	Egypt, the Sudan, Northern Nigeria, Uganda, Tanzania, Zaïre, Zimbabwe, Mozambique
Groundnut*	Between 14° and 19°C needed during growing season (3½ to 4 months); sensitive to night frost; higher temperatures produce higher oil content; needs plenty of sunshine; rainfall between 500 and 600 mm; dry weather during harvesting	Light permeable, sandy soils best with no special humus requirements	Senegal, Gambia, Northern Nigeria

Crop	*Climatic needs*	*Soils*	*Major producers*
Oil palm	Average annual temperature, 24° to 28°C; will not grow at high altitudes (up to 700 m in the Cameroons); temperatures must be fairly constant throughout the year; rainfall, 2 000 to 3 000 mm per annum, minimum 150 mm with high soil moisture content; optimum humidity conditions, 50 to 70 per cent at mid-day	Best yields on deep, permeable soils rich in humus; deep roots may tap better sub-surface soils	Throughout tropical rain forest belt at low altitudes about 8° north and south of the Equator, heaviest producers Nigeria and Zaïre Basin
Olive	Average annual temperature, 12° to 15,5°C; 250 to 760 mm of winter rainfall; in areas with low rainfall trees may be grown but must be more widely spaced	Well-drained calcareous, clayey, sandy or gravelly soils will suffice; can grow in thin soils if well spaced	Tunisia, Libya, Algeria, Morocco
Pineapple	Average annual temperature, 15° to 32°C; optimum, 24° to 29°C; about 760 mm of rain should be available in hot season for growth but can exist on much less than this; over 2 540 mm a year is detrimental	Dislikes waterlogged ground; drainage must be good; medium to heavy loams best with slightly acid reaction; soils must be well aerated, rich in nutrients; some heavy black cotton soils found very suitable	In most tropical coastal regions especially Mozambique, Tanzania and Kenya; Kenya Highlands produce large amounts
Rubber	Average annual temperature, 24° to 30°C with a mean of 27°C; minimum rainfall, 1 520 mm with even distribution; will grow up to nearly 600 m in equatorial regions	Deep, not too heavy soil at least 5 feet (1,5 m) deep because of tap roots; shallow soils may result in wind damage; high water table injurious to growth	Hot, wet tropical rain forest regions; Liberia, Southern Nigeria, Zaïre
Sisal	Average annual temperature, 20° to 28°C, plenty of sunshine; minimum rainfall, about 400 mm; maximum about 1 200 mm per annum; can withstand dry season of up to 3 months duration	Deep sandy soils and loams are most suitable although sisal will flourish on poorer types; Red Earths and coral derived soils best; heavy, moist soils generally unsuitable although Black Cottons are used	Tanzania, Kenya, Mozambique
Sugar cane*	Lowest temperature, 20°C; optimum, between 25° and 28°C; found in tropical lowlands mainly but can be grown at up to 1 100 m; can be grown at much higher altitudes but is less profitable and requires longer growing season (up to two years); cannot stand frost or very long periods; needs 1 780 to 2 540-mm of rain per annum or irrigation (in Egypt the cane is watered up to twenty-six times during the growing period); long sunny days are best	Deep and well-drained soil needed; volcanic, sandy, weathered limestone, alluvial, and laterite soils can be used. Must be well aerated and moist heavy sticky soils unsuitable due to bad aeration	In practically all lowland areas of tropical Africa and along Natal coast, South Africa and Nile Valley of Egypt under irrigation
Tea	Optimum temperature, 18° to 25°C; some varieties can grow at low temperature of 13°C and withstand short frost periods; but warm, moist climate is best with high air humidity; evenly distributed rainfall of about 1 900 to 3 300 mm; protection from drying winds necessary; shade trees are grown on estates but is now believed that their value is not important to growth	Deep, well-aerated, permeable soil is best; good humus content with good drainage needed; moist soils suitable; former forested land often best	Kenya Highlands, Malaŵi, Zimbabwe, Mozambique, Rwanda, Burundi, Cameroon

Crop	*Climatic needs*	*Soils*	*Major producers*
Tobacco	Optimum temperature for germination of 31°C; minimum temperature for growth is 10°C; optimum, 35°C; needs 100 to 120 frost-free days; about 400 to 610 mm of rain needed with humid air during harvesting; plenty of sunshine needed	Deep, well-drained, aerated soil best; sandy or loamy types suitable with permeable sub-soils which retain some moisture	Zimbabwe, Malaŵi, Zambia, Natal coast, Lower Nile Valley on commercial scale and in many smaller areas throughout tropics
Vines	Temperature limits, between 9° to 21°C annual average temperature; sensitive to frost and high temperatures; growing period, 180 to 250 days; withstands long dry period due to deep root penetration; about 500 to 660 mm of rain needed annually without irrigation; heavy showers during ripening unfavourable; dislikes high humidity which causes fungoid diseases	Best grown in medium fertile, loamy types which are well-drained and easy to cultivate	Algeria, Tunisia, South Africa

Subsistence crops

Crop	*Climatic needs*	*Soils*	*Major producers*
Barley	Minimum temperature for germination, 3° to 4°C; optimum growth at 20°C; can grow at high altitudes and needs little water, 460 to 560 mm	Friable loams best, loess and black earths also suitable; some types adapted to heavier soils	Throughout North Africa and desert oases and Ethiopia
Cassava or Manioc	Nine-month frost-free period; mean annual temperature, 10°C during growing season; heavy and well-distributed rainfall, but will grow in dry regions if sub-soil soaked; high humidity, sunshine and wind protection are beneficial	Deep, well-drained soils most suitable, sandy, loose permeable soils best; waterlogging very bad	Very important in Zaïre Basin and fringe regions, East African Coast, Southern Tanzania and Malagasy
Maize	Demands much warmth and no frost; below 1°C not tolerated. Minimum germination temperature, 8°C; optimum temperatures, 30° to 32°C; tolerates wide rainfall range from 250 to 5 080 mm; short showers with sunny intervals most suitable for growth	Deep, well-drained, humus-rich loams best; sandy or peaty soils in better-watered warm regions	Coastal belts of North West Africa, Lower Nile, in most lowland and areas up to 1 800 m in Africa south of latitude 10°
Millet	Fairly high temperatures during day with high diurnal range; can grow in most regions requiring under 710 mm but generally in regions with 270 to 400 mm annually; dislikes humidity and needs sunny weather	Light loamy or sandy soils with little humus	Main cereal in all drier areas of tropical Africa
Rice	Minimum temperature, 20°C during main growing period; upland rice requires minimum temperature of 18°C; temperature for optimum growth, 28° to 32°C; growing period, 50 to 100 days; very high water requirement (in Egypt 1,9 to 3,5 million litres per hectare); with no irrigation rice requires 350 to 760 mm a month during growing season	Alluvial swamp soils, loess are best; topsoil should have high water capacity and clays and loams are very suitable; in Africa, Black Cotton soils have proved successful	Very important in Malagasy, river basins and coastal lowlands of Tanzania, Sierra Leone, Liberia, Northern Zaïre Basin

Crop	*Climatic needs*	*Soils*	*Major producers*
Wheat	Minimum temperature for germination, 3° to 4°C; optimum, 25°C; winter wheat withstands temperatures well below freezing point; minimum annual rainfall for most varieties is 480 mm with 250 mm distributed over four growing months	Sandy or peaty soils generally unsuitable, black earths and loess soils are best and clays suitable; low permeability is unsuitable but can be offset by good drainage	Throughout North Africa and in desert oases, Ethiopia, Kenya Highlands, South Africa
Yams	A tropical plant needing high temperatures although some rainfalls varying between 500 and over 10 000 mm per annum in Africa; can withstand dry periods well if soil is fairly moist	Permeable loams and sandy soils give good yields with high humus content required; grown on hills to avoid waterlogged soils if irrigation is used; makes large demands on soil nutrients	Equatorial areas of Africa, especially lowland area and in Malagasy

Index

Figures in bold refer to diagrams or maps and are preceded by the number of the chapter in which the diagram appears. Figures in italic indicate the page numbers of illustrations.